D0651859

PART III

PART III

The Christian Testament since the Bible

FIRETHORN PRESS

First published in Great Britain in 1985 by
Waterstone & Co. Limited
49 Hay's Mews
London W1X 7RT

FIRETHORN PRESS is an imprint of Waterstone & Co. Limited

First published in the United States of America in 1985 by
Harper & Row, Publishers, Inc.
10 East 53rd Street
New York, NY 10022
as THE LIVING TESTAMENT

Distributed by Sidgwick & Jackson Limited
1 Tavistock Chambers
Bloomsbury Way
London WC1A 2SG

Typeset by Unicus Graphics Ltd,
Horsham, Sussex.
Printed and bound by Garden City Press Ltd,
Letchworth, Herts.

CONTENTS

EDITORIAL BOARD

ACKNOWLEDGEMENTS

The publishers wish to thank the following for their kind permission to reprint copyright material.

Extract from Origen's *De Principiis*, trans. by G W Butterworth (1936). Reproduced by permission of SPCK.

The Sayings of Anthony the Great from *The Sayings of The Desert Fathers*, trans. by Benedicta Ward, SLG (1975). Reproduced by permission of A R Mowbray & Co Ltd.

Letter of St Jerome to Heliodorus from *The Letters of St Jerome, vol. 1*, trans. by Charles Christopher Mierow, from *The Ancient Christian Writers* series (1963). Reproduced by permission of Paulist Press.

The Pastoral Prayer from *Aelred of Rievaulx: Treatises and the Pastoral Prayer*, trans. by Sister Penelope Lawson, CSMV (1971, 1982). Reproduced by permission of Cistercian Publications.

Extracts from *The Book of Common Prayer* 1662, which is Crown Copyright in the United Kingdom. Reproduced by permission of Eyre & Spottiswoode, Her Majesty's Printers, London.

Extract from *A Selection from the Journals of Søren Kierkegaard*, trans. and ed. by A Dru (1938). Reproduced by permission of Oxford University Press.

Extract from *Autobiography of a Saint: St Thérèse de Lisieux*, trans. by Ronald Knox (1958). Reproduced by permission of William Collins, Sons & Co Ltd and Fount Paperbacks.

Part I from *The Way of a Pilgrim* and *The Pilgrim Continues His Way*, trans. by R M French (1930). Reproduced by permission of The Seabury Press, Minneapolis, Minnesota in the United States of America and dependencies, the Philippines, Mexico and Central America (©Mrs Eleanor French). Reproduced by permission of SPCK in the rest of the world.

"Saved by Grace" from *Deliverance to The Captives* by Karl Barth. © 1961 by SCM Press Ltd. Reproduced by permission of Harper & Row, Publishers, Inc.

"The Weight of Glory" from *Screwtape Proposes a Toast* by C S Lewis (1965). Reproduced by permission of William Collins, Sons & Co Ltd and Fount Paperbacks.

The speech "I've Been to the Mountain Top" by Martin Luther King, Jr. ©1968 by the Estate of Martin Luther King, Jr. Reproduced by permission of Joan Daves.

Extract from *In The Silence of The Heart: Meditations by Mother Teresa of Calcutta and her Co-workers*, ed. by Kathryn Spink (1983). Reproduced by permission of SPCK.

Extract from pamphlet *Billy Graham Speaks on Issues of Life and Death* (1982). Reproduced by permission of Billy Graham Evangelistic Association, 27 Camden Road, London NW1 9LN.

FOREWORD

Ever since the earthly ministry of Jesus Christ, there have been those who wanted to erect in His memory a fixed, formalised religion of the kind He most consistently abominated. But Christianity is not, like some other religions of the world, an institution. It is a way of being free. It is the recognition that all men are able to call God *Father*. Those who follow "this Way" (as it was called at first in New Testament times) have often excited the agonised disapproval of moralists and systematic theologians. St Paul describes how he escaped his deadening devotion to the Jewish Law and found a glorious freedom in the gospel. The gospel of John speaks of our new found ability to "worship in spirit and in truth". And in the other gospels we read of Jesus quarrelling with the formal religious teaching of the scribes and Pharisees, and prophesying the destruction of formal religion as embodied in the Temple. He said that He himself would pull the Temple down and build it again in three days.

St Peter, or whoever wrote the first epistle which bears his name, was perhaps thinking of these sayings of Jesus when he applied to his master the old saying in the Psalm: "The stone which the builders rejected has become the chief cornerstone". This stone, Peter says, is *a living stone*. The token of the truth of Jesus is the life of Jesus, His resurrection from the dead. This Jesus, whom God raised up, did not immediately found a new religion in the sense that the Pharisees had a religion. On the contrary, that living cornerstone of the new Temple brings into life a living organism, "a people set apart to sing the praises of God" (I Peter 2:8).

When that letter was written, the numbers who followed "this Way" were tiny. Since then, they have increased and multiplied, so that they have absorbed all sorts and races of men and women, beggars and kings, saints and sinners. "This Way" is the foundation of our civilisation.

But in spite of all the temptations to institutionalise Christianity, and to make of it something which, of its essence, it can never be, it has remained an organic, living thing. Its life derives from the origin of life itself, from God; from the Lord of Life whom the cross and the tomb could neither crush nor contain; to the giver of life who "enlightens every man coming into the world". It is this life, the life of Christ, which lives in His followers and which we can see in the great treasury of Christian utterance which this book represents. For the Christian revelation does not stop when the New Testament ends; in fact, the New Testament is only the beginning of the Christian relevation.

It has been said that we live in a post-Christian age. But Christ has come, and if that is true, there can be no post-Christian age. Nevertheless, because of our collective and individual loss of faith in the western world, there are many otherwise intelligent people today who are quite ignorant of what Christianity is.

Jesus Christ wrote no book, and the written word is not necessarily the best method of catching the flavour of "this Way". For myself, I have learnt as much about Christianity by looking at Christian architecture and listening to Christian music as I have by reading Christian books. And more than any word, or building, or sound, the eloquence of other Christian lives has touched me, lives which embody so many of those baffling phrases in the New Testament, and thus make sense of them: "your life is hid with Christ in God"; "let this mind be in you which was also in Christ Jesus"; "if any man is in Christ, he is a new creature". Words mean very little without being made flesh, but the mystery of the Incarnation is a perpetually unfolding one. Christ, who came down to share our life of flesh, can take us up to share His life in the spirit. This collection of words by some of the wisest men and women in Christian history, from its origins until the present day, will give some inkling to the enquirer of that life which is Christ. Believers and half-believers, likewise, will find refreshment in these magnificent expressions of faith, reminders of something which, for millions of people throughout the world, is as real an experience today as it was for the first believers in the garden of the Resurrection.

A. N. Wilson
Oxford

INTRODUCTION

ONE TO ONE

Many men have argued against the divinity of Jesus, and indeed it may be that we need the eye of faith to see it. But no reasonable man can deny that Jesus's ministry marked a decisive change in human behaviour that has had no parallel anywhere any time.

For from the time of Jesus came the idea of the one universal God, and as a natural counterpart to this idea, the notion that one human being is of inestimable worth, not just as part of a people but in him or herself, that he or she has a personal destiny, the fulfilment of which is of inestimable importance to the history of the universe. The relationship between immortal and mortal that Jesus proclaimed was one of iconoclastic intimacy and revolutionary delicacy. With Jesus people began to feel that individual human lives were valuable in a way that they would not have understood earlier. Sensitivity, sympathy and intelligence of the heart blossomed with unprecedented sweetness. People became kind, gentle, thoughtful and loving. They began to care for one another in a manner which we take for granted now, but which was new then.

Perhaps Jesus's most original idea was his conception of grace, which he used to describe the One to one relationship between God and human being: grace being, in his interpretation, the free and spontaneous giving of love beyond people's deserts. God became the best and most influential role-model in history. If I am gracious as God is to me, I will not give others bad for bad and good for good, but I will return good for bad and better for good. I will discard the morality of an eye for an eye and a tooth for a tooth, and I will give my enemies love in return for their hatred, and I will give my friends a greater love than they give me. Martin Luther preaches on this theme in a passage that will lift the heart of a Christian of any denomination:

> Lo! my God, without merit on my part, of His pure and free mercy, has given to me, an unworthy, condemned, and contemptible creature, all the riches of justification and salvation in Christ. For such a Father who has overwhelmed me with these inestimable riches of His, why should I not freely, cheerfully, and with my whole heart, and from voluntary zeal, do all that I know will be pleasing to Him and acceptable in His sight?
>
> Thus from faith flow forth love and joy in the Lord, and from love a cheerful, willing, free spirit, disposed to serve our neighbour voluntarily, without taking any account of gratitude or ingratitude, praise or blame, gain or loss. Its object is not to lay men under obligations, nor does it distinguish between friends and enemies, or look to gratitude or ingratitude, but most freely and willingly spends itself and its goods, whether it loses them through ingratitude, or gains goodwill.

The Invention of the Interior Life

Jesus's third innovation (with individualism and grace) was the idea of interior life. As individualism is the natural counterpart of monotheism, so the interior life is the natural counterpart of grace. People found that if they did go beyond merely satisfying their social obligations to act graciously they discovered a new sort of satisfaction that declared itself as being above all others. A greater capacity for happiness was revealed, and hitherto overlooked areas of their minds became illumined. The individual discovered that in order to feel good, he or she did not only have to get relationships right with others, but also with him or herself. In effect Jesus showed the many different ways there are of achieving this inner peace. He taught that apart from the physical laws of nature and the laws of state there are other, deeper laws of the human condition, and that the only way people can be really happy is by living in accord with these laws. As Pascal writes: "There is no one as happy as a true Christian, or so reasonable, virtuous and lovable."

Some sceptics have tried to pervert the Christian message into a promise of consolation after death for misery in life. In fact, the good news was that for the first time man could be wholly happy on earth, not just as a foretaste of heaven, but as a step towards the realisation of the Kingdom of God in history. Before Jesus, people did not really know what happiness was. They had at best a premonition of it. Martin Luther argues that the only happiness worth having is the sort Jesus shows us:

> . . . the soul can do without everything except the word of God, without which none at all of its wants are provided for. But, having the word, it is rich and wants for nothing, since that is the word of life, of truth, of light, of peace, of justification, of salvation, of joy, of liberty, of wisdom, of virtue, of grace, of glory and of every good thing.

The Secret Laws of Human Happiness

Jesus's good news was not well received. People were slow to see the advantages of the new happiness. Most then, as now, were timid and lazy, afraid to let go of their old habits, and preferring to opt for the more or less cheap thrills that the world offers, rather than attempt anything more difficult. As C. S. Lewis says: "We are far too easily pleased." Moreover, what Jesus was saying was too new for the majority of people to grasp.

After the death of Jesus, though, the most inspired Christians, the few who did understand, set about the biggest intellectual enterprise in history: to apply the teachings of Jesus to all areas of human experience, and so to uncover the secret laws of human happiness. What could be more important?

It is this monolithic enterprise that the present book represents. Because we live in such an irreligious age and see history through a secular lens, we easily forget that it is the task on which most of the greatest minds in the civilised world have been working for most of the past two thousand years. It amounts to the submerged nine-tenths of the Western intellectual tradition, far surpassing in scope and sophistication and utility the achievements of the secular arts and sciences. No system of philosophy matches its insight into the human condition.

Moreover clarity of perception in this book is matched by beauty of style. For example, the *Gloria in Excelsis*, some parts of *The Pilgrim's Progress* and some of the hymns, are so familiar that we tend to forget to think of them as beautiful. Others have become lost in recesses of old libraries, frequented only by scholars. Unjustly so, for they were intended to spread the word to as many people as possible, and indeed these treasures of the Christian literary tradition are as fresh, as clear and as sublimely beautiful today as on the first day they were written, spoken or sung. For immediacy, urgency and the power to move, they equal anything in the secular tradition. Compare Montaigne, Shakespeare, Pope, Keats and Nietzsche with St John Chrysostom, St Augustine, St Bernard of Clairvaux, Cranmer and Pascal, and it is not at all apparent where the superiority lies. Can we find prose more noble, more glorious than in this description by St John Chrysostom (literally "The golden mouthed") of what the world would be like if everyone learned how to love?

> Yea, and if this were duly observed by all, there would be neither slave nor free, neither ruler nor ruled, neither rich nor poor, neither small nor great; nor would any devil ever have been known: I say not Satan only, but whatever such spirit there may be, nay, rather were there a hundred or ten thousand such, they would have no power while love existed. For sooner would grass endure the application of fire than the Devil the flame of love. She is stronger than any wall, she is firmer than any adamant; or if you can name any material stronger than this, the firmness of love transcends them all. Her, neither wealth nor poverty overcome: nay, rather there would be no poverty, no unbounded wealth, if there were such love, but the good parts only from each situation. For from the one we should reap its abundance, and from the other its freedom from care; and we should neither have to undergo the anxieties of riches, nor the dread of poverty. For tell me not of this ordinary sort, the vulgar and low-minded and really a sort of disease rather than love, but of that which Paul seeks after, which considers the profit of them that are loved, and you shall see that no fathers are so affectionate as persons of this stamp. And even as they that love money cannot endure to spend it, but would rather live uncomfortably than see their wealth diminishing; so too, he that is kindly affected towards everyone would choose to suffer ten thousand evils than see his beloved one injured.

Do the works of Shakespeare contain writing more dramatic than this description by St Bernard of Clairvaux of the Virgin Mary as she hesitates on the brink of accepting her divine destiny?

> You have heard, O Virgin, the announcement of that which is about to take place; and the manner in which it will take place; in each there is

> matter for wonder and rejoicing. Rejoice then, daughter of Zion, daughter of Jerusalem. And since you have heard news of gladness and joy, let us too hear from you the glad response for which we wait, so that the bones which have been humbled by sorrow may leap for joy. You have heard, I say, the fact and have believed, believe also in the manner in which it shall be accomplished. By the operation of the Holy Spirit, not of a man, you shall conceive and bear a Son; and the angel waits only for the reply, to return to God who sent him. We too, O Lady, we who are weighed down by the sentence of condemnation, wait for the word of pity. The price of our salvation is offered to you: soon shall we be freed, if you consent to give yourself to the Divine plan. Alas! we, who all are the creatures of the eternal word of God, are perishing; we are to be restored by your brief response, and recalled to life. Unhappy Adam with his miserable progeny exiled from Paradise, Abraham also and David, entreat this, O pious Virgin, of you. Others joins in the entreaty, holy fathers and ancestors of your own, who also dwell in the valley of the shadow of death. The whole world, prostrate at your knees, waits for your consent; and not without reason; since upon your lips hangs the consolation of the unhappy, the redemption of the captives, the freedom of the condemned; in short, the safety of the children of Adam, of the whole human race. Reply quickly, O Virgin: give the word which the earth, hell and the heavens themselves wait for.

Or what secular piece of prose sinks more deeply into the human heart than this Collect from the Sacramentary of Gelasius prayed by millions of Christians all over the world every Sunday?

> O God, from whom all holy desires, all good counsels, and all just works do proceed; give to Your servants that peace which the world cannot give; that both our hearts may be set to obey Your commandments, and also that by You we being defended from the fear of our enemies may pass our time in rest and quietness; through the merits of Jesus Christ our Saviour. Amen.

To most people, Christian spiritual wisdom is a closed book. St Jerome, St Francis, John Calvin and George Fox, though their names are known, go unread. The intention here is to open that book, to make accessible the vast body of Christian writings by concentrating its best, most readable works in one volume.

The Abysses of Nothingness

In order to point the way to happiness, Jesus showed man that he was much more unhappy than he thought he was, that he was desperately lacking in happiness. Christianity has been misrepresented by sceptics as something sentimental and superficially comforting, but in fact no world view exhibits a deeper and more searching appreciation of the nature of evil, and of people's defencelessness in the face of danger.

After the three persons of the Trinity, the being most often mentioned in this book is the Devil. He appears, as among other things, Satan, the enemy, the tempter, the deceiver, the prince of this world, the adversary and the evil one. We read also of legions of demons. What these figures represent is the knowledge that humankind is in the grip of evil which it is not in its power to resist, and which can only be eradicated by supernatural powers for the good. Christians are soldiers struggling to expel the forces of evil from a world God has made for them, but they cannot do so without divine aid. *St Patrick's Breastplate* is both a war cry and a plea for protection

> Against every cruel, merciless power
> Which may come against my body and my soul,
> Against incantations of false prophets,
> Against black laws of heathenry,
> Against false laws of heretics,
> Against craft of idolatry,
> Against spells of women and smiths and druids,
> Against every knowledge that defiles men's souls.

Where evil threatens to prevail, divine help sometimes comes in the form of miracles. The martyr Polycarp proves invulnerable to fire, and when he is stabbed a dove flies out of the wound; Polycarp dies, glorifying God. *The Passion of Perpetua and Felicity* relates how St Saturus, on the eve of his martyrdom, is granted a vision of Heaven that has filled the imagination of Christians ever since:

> [We were gone forth from the flesh,] and we were beginning to be borne by four angels into the east; and their hands touched us not. And we floated as if ascending a gentle slope. Being set free, we at length saw the first boundless light; and I said, "Perpetua" (for she was at my side), "this is what the Lord promised to us; we have received the promise." And while we were borne by those same four angels, there appeared to us a vast space which was like a pleasure-garden, having rose-trees and every kind of flower. And the height of the trees was after the measure of a cypress, and their leaves were falling incessantly. Moreover, there in the pleasure-garden four other angels appeared, brighter than the previous ones, who, when they saw us, gave us honour, and said to the rest of the angels, "Here they are! Here they are!" with admiration. And those four angels who bore us, being greatly afraid, put us down; and we passed over on foot the space of a furlong in a broad path. "And we came near to a place, the walls of which were such as if they were built of light; and before the gate of that place stood four angels, who clothed those who entered with white robes. And being clothed, we entered and saw the boundless light, and heard the united voice of some who said without ceasing, "Holy! Holy! Holy!" And in the midst of that place we saw as it were a hoary man sitting, having snow-white hair, and with a youthful countenance. And on His right hand and on His left were four-and-twenty elders, and behind them a great many others were standing. We entered with great wonder, and stood before the throne; and the four angels raised us up, and we kissed Him, and He passed His hand over our face.

St Teresa of Avila is worried by doubts when a vision of Jesus convinces her:

> . . . how trifling is the power of all devils in comparison with Yours, and how he who is pleasing to You can trample upon all the hosts of Hell. Here we see with what reason the devils trembled when You descended into Hades: well might they have longed for a thousand deeper hells in order to flee from such great majesty!

The miraculous healing ministry of St Sebastian continued Jesus's fight with the forces of evil in this sphere, and St Francis (the "Second Christ") received the stigmata, the wounds of Jesus on the cross, as special marks of favour.

Without the miracle of divine intervention man is too weak to overcome the temptations of evil. Pascal said he was amazed that people were not amazed at their own weakness. Perhaps if we forget to share his amazement, it is because sinning has become second nature to us. Again, the superficial view is the popular one with humanists today that wrongdoing or sin can be overcome by an act of will, that it is something negative, a mere absence of good. The Christian view is represented by the seventeenth century puritan Richard Baxter. "Sin is alive", he asserts, and if we think we have it under control, we delude ourelves:

> Oh, what sad discoveries are made in the hour of temptation! What swarms of vice break out in some, like vermin, that lay hid in the cold of winter, and crawl about when they feel the summer's heat! What horrid corruptions which we never observed in ourselves before, do show themselves in the hour of temptation!

Baxter's *Warning to the Born Again* gives us one of the most clever analyses ever of the different way that sin outwits us.

As true happiness is a foretaste of Heaven, the misery of our present sinful condition foreshadows Hell. The sermon *Sinners in the Hands of an Angry God*, by Jonathan Edwards, is a tremendous example of nineteenth-century American bombast:

> Sin is the ruin and misery of the soul; it is destructive in its nature; and if God should leave it without restraint there would need nothing else to make the soul perfectly miserable. The corruption of the heart of man is immoderate and boundless in its fury . . .
>
> . . . . The manifold and continual experience of the world in all ages, shows this is no evidence, that a man is not on the very brink of eternity, and that the next step will not be into another world. The unseen, unthought of ways and means of persons going suddenly out of the world are innumerable and inconceivable. Unconverted men walk over the pit of Hell on a rotten covering, and there are innumerable places in this covering so weak that they will not bear their weight, and these places are not seen. The arrows of death fly unseen at noon-day; the sharpest sight cannot discern them.

The modern Protestant theologian Karl Barth makes the same point:

> All of us, the people without and you within, are prisoners of our own obstinacy, of our many greeds, of our various anxieties, of our mistrust and in the last analysis of our unbelief. We are all sufferers. Most of all we suffer from ourselves. We each make life difficult for ourselves and in so doing for our fellow men. We suffer from life's lack of meaning. We suffer in the shadow of death and of eternal judgment toward which we are moving. We spend our life in the midst of a whole world of sin and captivity and suffering.

Pascal is succinct: "Apart from Christ there is only vice, wretchedness, error, darkness, death and despair."

When, as is often the case today, people find the promises of the gospel insipid, and do not care whether they are true or not, when people shun Christianity as boring and the product of neurosis, it is because they lack a realistic understanding of evil or sin; they do not appreciate how unhappy they are and how much more happy they are capable of being. They do not see their soul trembling in the balance.

The Good Side of Evil

This soft view of life, prevalent now, was not available to the early Christians, for danger was then only too apparent. Jesus left them in a hostile world that threatened them with extinction. But awareness of great unhappiness made them want all the more what Jesus had promised. We must admire, for example, the courage of the saint and martyr Ignatius, writing days from a terrible death:

> Let there come to me fire, and cross, and struggles with wild beasts, cutting, and tearing asunder, rackings of bones, mangling of limbs, crushing of my whole body, cruel tortures of the devil, may I but attain to Jesus Christ!

In modern times Christians are still martyred. In the speech he made, poignantly enough, the day before he was shot, Martin Luther King also showed sublime courage in the face of mortal danger

> . . . I don't know what will happen now. We've got some difficult days ahead. But it doesn't matter with me now, because I've been to the mountain top. And I don't mind. Like anybody, I would like to live a long life; longevity has its place. But I'm not concerned about that now. I just want to do God's will. And He's allowed me to go up to the mountain. And I've looked over. And I've seen the promised land. I may not get there with you. But I want you to know tonight, that we, as a people, will get to the promised land. And I'm happy tonight, I'm not worried about anything. I'm not fearing any man. Mine eyes have seen the glory of the coming of the Lord.

Martyrdoms are less frequent now than in early times. It may be that you or I will not be called to such "sensational acts of piety", that our cross, like that of the nineteenth-century French saint, Thérèse of Lisieux, is to be fashioned from an accumulation of smaller sacrifices:

> It is not for me to preach the gospel, or to shed my blood as a martyr, but I see now that all that doesn't matter; even a little child can scatter flowers, to scent the throne-room with their fragrance; even a little child can sing, in its shrill treble, the great canticle of Love. That shall be my life, to scatter flowers – to miss no single opportunity of making some small sacrifice, here by a smiling look, there by a kindly word, always doing the tiniest things right, and doing it for love.

But one thing is certain, that every Christian will be tested in a way that is peculiarly painful to him or her; and whether we are tried by torture and persecution or by indifference and sarcasm, we can surely take a lead from St Polycarp's frank avowal of faith in the face of adversity: "Listen plainly, I am a Christian, and if you wish to learn the doctrine of Christianity fix a day and listen."

THE SURVIVAL OF CHRISTIANITY

The Teaching of the Twelve Apostles to the Heathen is a manual of church practice formerly ascribed to the Apostles and which is, at lest, old enough for them to have contributed to it. It offers a fascinating glimpse of how the first Christians lived years, perhaps even days, after Jesus had ceased to be with them in body. We get the impression of a small, tight-knit community of outsiders who have a strong conviction against all the evidence that history will prove them right; that, as it had been prophesied, a great period of calamity was coming when the Devil, "the Deceiver of the World", would present himself as a son of God, mankind would be subjected to a "fiery trial", and then Jesus would return, "coming on the clouds of Heaven". This doctrine has not always been equally emphasised, and has been given more attention by some denominations than others. But we find it for example in the *Christian Sibylline* Oracles, reminiscent of the Old Testament prophets in the zeal with which they preach doom on the unrighteous, (and incidentally Michelangelo's inspiration for his painting of the Sistine Chapel):

> The faithful and the faithless shall see God
> Exalted with the saints at the end of time.
> The souls of fleshly men upon his throne
> He will judge, when the whole world is laid waste
> And thorns spring up. And men will cast away
> Their idols and all wealth. And searching fire
> Will burn the land, the Heaven and the sea.

We also attest to this belief when we sing Charles Wesley's magnificent hymn:

> Lo! He comes with clouds descending,
> Once for favour'd sinners slain;
> Thousand thousand saints attending
> Swell the triumph of His train.

The Discipline of Worship

To survive, the early Christians needed to be very strict with one another. *The Teaching of the Twelve Apostles* shows how strangers were regarded with extreme suspicion, and how those who wanted to join the community were severely tested. Everyone must choose between the Way of Life and the Way of Death. People had been promised that God would inhabit their praise of Him, and, huddled together, they disciplined themselves in worship in order to ward off harm. Creed, baptism, confession, eucharist and thanksgiving were the earliest and most closely Biblical forms of worship, from which over the centuries grew rich traditions in ritual, prayer and, later, hymn-singing. Thomas Aquinas for example was to give the eucharist its fullest meaning that, whilst their outward appearance remains the same, the substance of the bread and wine is changed into the substance of Christ's body and blood. His doctrines are illustrated in this volume by his eucharistic hymns. The most heart-rending form of the confessional prayer was perhaps to be Thomas Cranmer's for the English *Book of Common Prayer*, and the most exuberant prayer of thanksgiving that written by Edward Reynolds for the same book. Early prayers were often adaptations of Old Testament passages: for example, *The Sanctus* is derived from the book of *Isaiah,* while the recently discovered *Odes of Solomon*, expressing the beliefs of first and second early Syriac Christians, may remind us of the *Psalms* in their spirit of exalted mystery:

> Behold! the Lord is our mirror.
> Open your eyes and see them in Him.
> And learn the manner of your face,
> And sing out praises to His spirit.
> And wipe off the filth from your face,
> And love His holiness,
> And clothe yourselves with it.
> And you will be blameless at all times before Him.
> Hallelujah.

Early Christians had an unquestioning belief in the power of prayer, especially group prayer. Ignatius, for example, on the way to martyrdom asked the Church at Rome to pray to God to give him the strength to go through with it. Prayer is here the means of hearing God's voice, allowing it to enter, guide and energise: to arm one for the struggle. Inspired individuals have continued to make very personal contributions to the history of Christian prayer, making themselves an opening for the Holy Spirit to flood into the world. Francis of Assisi is perhaps the best-loved Christian ever. His *Canticle of the Sun* expresses all the simple-hearted adoration of God and creation that has made him so popular:

> Bless You, Lord, for this gift of all Your creatures and especially for our brother sun, by whom the day is enlightened. He is radiant and bright, of great splendour, bearing witness to You, O my God.

> Blessed be You, my Lord, for our sisters, the moon and the stars; You have formed them in heavens, fair and clear.
>
> Bless You, my Lord, for my brother the wind, for the air, for cloud and calm, for every kind of weather, for by them You sustain all creatures.

Some three hundred years after the *Teaching of the Twelve Apostles*, St Ambrose, Bishop of Milan, and the man who was to baptise Augustine, instituted congregational hymn-singing in the western Church. Hymns have since played a key part in making Christianity attractive. *Let All Mortal Flesh Keep Silent,* for example, one of the poetic gems of Christian hymnody, is an incomparable expression of the mystery of the eucharist. The hymn-writing genius of Charles Wesley helped spread the word among the English working-classes and later, in missionary work, to Africans and Asians. Inspiriting Victorian hymns, such as Cardinal Newman's *Lead Kindly Light amid the Encircling Gloom* or H. F. Lyte's *Abide with Me, Fast Falls the Eventide* take us back to the terrible predicament of Christians in the first century AD.

The Discipline of Daily Life

Discipline also grew in the organisation of the Church. Ignatius in his letter to the Ephesians, written at the end of the first century, shows the church hierarchy of bishop, deacon and presbyter in embryonic form.

The notion of Christian leadership is difficult and some would say paradoxical: how can it make sense for others to interfere in what is essentially a One to one relationship? We have to wait until Gregory the Great to find a meaning ascribed to this idea which extends beyond mere expediency. Among the many illuminating comparisons that he makes is that between the Christian leader and the good Samaritan:

> For whosoever superintends the healing of wounds must needs administer in wine the smart of pain and in oil the softness of loving kindness, to the end that through wine what is festering may be purged, and through oil what is curable may be soothed. Gentleness, then, is to be mingled with severity; a sort of compound is to be made of both; so that subjects be neither paralysed by too much asperity, nor relaxed by too great kindness.

Symbolism also grew up around the institution of the priesthood, and Gregory the Great offers a fascinating explanation of the colours of priestly robes:

> Thus in the priest's robe before all things gold glitters, to show that he should shine forth principally in the understanding of wisdom. And with it blue, which is resplendent with aerial colour, is conjoined, to show that through all that he penetrates with his understanding he should rise above earthly favours to the love of celestial things; lest, while caught unawares by his own praises, he is emptied of his very understanding of the truth. With gold and blue, purple also is

> mingled: which means that the priest's heart, while hoping for the high things which he preaches, should repress in itself even the suggestions of vice, and, as it were by virtue of a royal power rebut them.

The good-heartedness of Gregory's examination of the responsibilities and pitfalls of leadership is echoed in Aelred of Rievaulx's charming *Pastoral Prayer*, which includes the disarming declaration: "My God, You know what a fool I am."

The day and the year came to be structured in Christian terms. *The Teaching of the Twelve Apostles* instructs Christians to say the Lord's Prayer three times a day. By the time of St Ambrose, as we see from his *Hymns of the Little Hours,* worship is presented hourly. The Christian year was organised according to the main events in the life of Jesus: Advent, Christmas, Lent, Easter, Ascension. By the time of St John Chrysostom's *The Joys of Christmas* (fourth century), the schematic cycle had largely acquired the form it still has today. This sermon may be some 1,600 years old, but you are unlikely to hear a sermon today that is as fresh or as reinvigorating in the way it re-exposes you to the surprise, wonder and awe of the miracle that is celebrated here:

> I behold a new and wondrous mystery. My ears resound to the shepherd's song, piping no soft melody, but chanting full forth a heavenly hymn. The angels sing. The archangels blend their voice in harmony. The cherubim hymn their joyful praise. The seraphim exalt His glory. All join to praise this holy feast, beholding the Godhead here on earth, and man in Heaven. He who is above, now for our redemption dwells here below; and he that was lowly is by divine mercy raised.

Preserving the Word

Bodily harm, laxity in worship and moral indiscipline were all threats to the early church. But the danger it feared most was none of these, but heresy. Both Clement, the second bishop of Rome after St Peter, and Ignatius warn of the horrors of schism. People were always trying to make Jesus's message less difficult, less challenging and therefore less rewarding than it actually was. Vital Christian beliefs remained to be formulated. Christian theoreticians therefore set about protecting the word, and the period of the third, fourth and fifth centuries became the great age of theologising.

The idea that they were writing scripture would have been foreign to the authors of the New Testament. Origen showed why their writings should be regarded as such, and described, further, how in the very act of reading inspired writings, the divine breath strikes the mind of the reader him or herself. Working out the implications of Jesus's being the Son of God, Athanasius gave a clear and concise account of the Incarnation. Basil the Great described in intellectual terms his experience of the wholly otherness of God, and the attempt yielded most of the theoretical terms we use to describe Him today: immutable, indivisible, omnipresent, impassive and co-eternal. Of the Spirit, he writes: "just as when a sunbeam falls on bright and transparent bodies they themselves become brilliant too, and shed forth a fresh brightness from themselves, so souls wherein the spirit dwells, illuminated by the Spirit, themselves become spiritual, and send forth their grace to others".

The Church fathers were concerned to see the immediate practical application of their theology. Gregory of Nazianzus put intellectualising back into the mode of worship, by illustrating the enrichment of praise that the concept of Trinity should inspire. The New Testament clearly teaches that there is life after death, but it is alluded to rather than exhaustively elaborated, so Gregory of Nyssa addressed himself two questions: How can it make sense to think of the person existing in a disembodied state? and What is it like after death? He offers a vivid account of Purgatory and Resurrection which culminates in a sweeping description of God's plan for the universe. Because we can only find true fulfilment when we know what we are for, that is, what function we have been created to fulfil, Jesus came to remind us of the higher and holier end for which we have been made. Gregory here places the life and death of the individual within the context of God's purging from the universe everything inimical to Him, so that when "the completed universe no longer admits of further increase, when the complete whole of our race shall have been perfected from the first man to the last – some having at once been in this life cleansed from evil, others having afterwards in the necessary period been healed by the fire", we will all be offered "participation in the blessings which are in Him which the scripture tells us 'eye has not seen nor ear heard', nor thought ever reached". Through all his dizzying speculation St Gregory maintains a fitting sense of the mystery of these things:

> and then there will be no more need of phrases to explain the things which we now hope for. Just as many questions might be started for debate amongst people sitting up at night as to the kind of thing that sunshine is, and then the simple appearing of it in all its beauty would render any verbal description superfluous.

The Definition of Chalcedon of 451 summarises the advances in understanding that had taken place during this age of theology.

ILLUMINING THE INTERIOR LIFE

In the meantime many different ways of being a Christian had been emerging. *The Sayings of Anthony the Great*, for example, give us the teaching of the hermit who is famous in folklore and in painting as a strange Elijah-like figure, battling against the forces of evil. He teaches us how to gain spiritual strength from solitude:

> He said also: "Just as fish die if they stay too long out of water, so the monks who loiter outside their cells or pass their time with men of the

world lose the intensity of inner peace. So like a fish going towards the sea, we must hurry to reach our cell, for fear that if we delay outside we will lose our inner watchfulness."

The person who follows the teaching of Anthony is promised great powers:

He also said: Obedience with abstinence gives men power over wild beasts.

If Anthony seems a slightly strange and distant figure, the Jerome of the *Epistle to Heliodorus* is endearingly tender and close. He speaks directly to the agony of an old friend, who, rejecting the call to the life of a monk, has left the life of the desert and succumbed to the pressures of city life. Jerome pleads with Heliodorus to return, urging him to remember the holy freedom of life in the wild:

O desert of Christ, burgeoning with flowers! O solitude in which those stones are produced of which in the Apocalypse the city of the great king is constructed! O wilderness that rejoices in intimacy with God! What are you doing in the world, brother, you who are greater than the world? How long will the shadows of houses oppress you? How long will the smoky prison of these cities close you in? Believe me, I behold a little more light. It is a delight to cast aside the burden of the flesh and to fly to the sheer glory of the ether.

Not everyone is called to the sort of solitary life recommended by Anthony and Jerome, but the joys of solitude are an essential part of the higher happiness, the inner peace which Jesus revealed. It is necessary for all Christians to withdraw sometimes:

We shall never find God anywhere so perfectly, so fruitfully and so truly as in retirement and in the wilderness; like the blessed mother of God, St John the Baptist and Mary Magdalene, and other saints and patriarchs. They all fled from the world, from society, and all the cares and anxieties of the creature, and went into the forests and into the desert, or wherever they could find the greatest solitude. Oh! truly, much intercourse and society, and much outward conversation and necessary business lead up to an evil old age, and drive out God, however good our intentions may have been. For, when we fill our hearts with the creature, and with strange useless images, God must of necessity remain outside, neither does He desire to enter there.

(John Tauler)

Thomas à Kempis talks of being alone in a room with God:

In silence and in stillness a religous soul advantageth herself, and learneth the mysteries of Holy Scriptures. There she findeth rivers of tears, wherein she may every night wash and cleanse herself; that she may be so much the more familiar with her creator, by how much the farther off she liveth from all wordly disquiet. Whoso therefore withdraweth

> himself from his acquaintance and friends, God will draw near unto him with His holy angels.

The way of the mystic is as old as Christianity itself. There are fewer finer mystical passages in Christian literature than Ignatius's description of the mystery of the nativity:

> And the virginity of Mary, and her giving birth were hidden from the Prince of this world, as was also the death of the Lord. Three trumpet-tongued secrets which were wrought in the stillness of God. How then was he manifested to the world? A star shone in heaven beyond all the stars, and its light was unspeakable, and its newness caused astonishment, and all the other stars, with the sun and moon, gathered in chorus round this star, and it far exceeded them all in its light; and there was perplexity, whence came this new thing, so unlike them.
>
> By this all magic was dissolved and every bond of wickedness vanished away, ignorance was removed, and the old kingdom was destroyed, for God was manifest as man for the "newness" of eternal life, and that which had been prepared by God received its beginning. Hence all things were disturbed, because the abolition of death was being planned.

Dionysius the Areopagite was the first Christian to attempt systematic instruction in mysticism:

> Most exalted Trinity, divinity above all knowledge, whose goodness passes understanding, who guides Christians to divine wisdom; direct our way to the summit of Your mystical oracles, most incomprehensible, most lucid and most exalted, where the simple and pure and unchangeable mysteries of theology are revealed in the darkness, clearer than light; a darkness that shines brighter than light, that invisibly and intangibly illuminates with splendours of inconceivable beauty the soul that sees not. Let this be my prayer. But give yourself diligently to mystical contemplation, leave the senses, and the operations of the intellect, and all things sensible and intelligible, and things verifiable, that you may rise by ways above knowledge to union with Him who is above all knowledge and all being; that in freedom and abandonment of all, you may be carried through pure, entire and absolute abstraction of yourself from all things, into the supernatural radiance of the divine darkness.

Great Christians such as Pascal have always realised that real religion is beyond mere logic: "The last step of reason is to recognise that there is an infinite number of things which are beyond reason."

The most influential writer on the monastic way was St Benedict. Life lived according to his rules adds to the joys of solitude and silence those of humility and obedience. Humility is the means by which we approach joy:

> If we wish to arrive at the highest point of humility, and speedily to reach that heavenly exaltation to which we can only ascend by the

> humility of this present life, we must by our ever-ascending actions erect such a ladder as that which Jacob saw in his dream, by which the angels appeared to him descending and ascending. This descent and ascent signifies nothing else than that we descend by self-exaltation and ascend by humility.

George Fox was to take up this theme in his *Epistle to the New World*: "He that inhabits eternity, dwells with the humble heart." Particularly moving is Benedict's instruction to his monks to see Jesus in all visitors: "Let all guests be received like Christ Himself, so He will say 'I was a stranger and you took me in'." At the arrival and departure of the guest, monks are told to prostrate themselves before him. In *The Weight of Glory* C. S. Lewis writes in the spirit of St Benedict:

> There are no ordinary people. You have never talked to a mere mortal. Nations, cultures, arts, civilisations – these are mortal, and their life is to ours as the life of a gnat. But it is immortals whom we joke with, work with, marry, snub, and exploit – immortal horrors or everlasting splendours.

Mother Teresa too, asks us to pray for those people we might be most tempted not to serve:

> The "shut-in", the unwanted, the unloved, the alcoholics, the dying destitutes, the abandoned and the lonely, the outcast and the untouchables, the leprosy sufferers – all those who are a burden to human society – who have lost all hope and faith in life – who have forgotten how to smile – who have lost the sensibility of the warm hand-touch of love and friendship – they look to us for comfort. If we turn our back on them, we turn it on Christ, and at the hour of our death we shall be judged if we have recognised Christ in them, and on what we have done for and to them. There will only be two ways, "come" or "go".

Martin Luther was one of the men to have best understood the joys of service:

> This is the truly Christian life, here is faith really working by love, when a man applies himself with joy and love to the works of that freest servitude in which he serves others voluntarily and for nothing, satisfied in the fullness and riches of his own faith.

Luther is also illuminating on the way of the preacher. He says that to preach Christ is to feed the soul, and if we love our neighbour, what greater gift can we give Him?

> For if the touch of Christ was healing, how much more does that most tender spiritual touch, that is the absorption of the word, communicate to the soul all that belongs to the word!

One of the most endearing qualities of the Quakers is their egalitarianism. George Fox encourages everyone to spread the good news whatever his or her situation in life:

> Come, tradesmen, tent-makers, physicians and custom-men, what can

> you say for God. Do you not read that your fellow tradesmen in ages past could say much for God? Do not degenerate from their spirit. Do you not remember the accusations of the wise and learned Grecians, when the apostles preached Christ among them, that they were called poor tradesmen and fishermen? Therefore be faithful. The preachers of Jesus Christ now, are the same to the wise of the world as then.

The Psychology of the Christian Individual

The masterpieces of the greatest Christians are crammed with help and advice on how to achieve peace of mind. These are addressed to all Christians, whether they are martyrs, priests, hermits, mystics, monks, preachers or people who serve in their place of work or at home. Their insights represent the spirit of Jesus applying itself to areas of life not specifically mentioned in His ministry as recorded in the Gospel. *The Teaching of the Twelve Apostles*, for example, instructs that no two people who have quarrelled may take the eucharist together until they have been reconciled, and similarly St Benedict instructs all monks who have quarrelled to make up before sundown. St Anselm's moving *Prayer to Christ for My Enemies* guides us through the becalming thoughts we ought to try to have if we find ourselves hating someone.

Those who, taking Anselm's advice, treat their neighbour well, may as Thomas à Kempis writes, enjoy the happiness of a good conscience:

> No man rejoiceth securely, unless he hath within him the testimony of a good conscience . . . Have a good conscience and thou shalt ever have joy. A good conscience is able to bear very much and is very cheerful in adversities. Thou shalt rest sweetly, if thy heart does not reprehend thee.

Avoid one-upmanship, and we will do away with much discord, both in our relationships with others and in ourselves:

> the man who wishes to prove himself always in the right, in everything that he does, sees, hears and discusses, and who will not give way and be silenced, will never be at peace with himself, and will have a barren, sullen and wandering mind; he will prey upon himself, even if he is left in peace by all, and is tried by no outward pressure.
>
> (John Tauler)

Above all we will find happiness in loving one another. Love illumines all our faculties, Thomas à Kempis believes: "Oh he that hath but one spark of true charity would certainly discern that all things be full of vanity." In one of his most brilliant passages St John Chrysostom explains how acting out our love brings innumerable joys:

> Consider how great a blessing it is to exercise love. What cheerfulness it produces! With what great grace it fills the soul! For the other parts of virtue have each their troubled guilt yoked to them. As he that gives up his possessions is often puffed up on this account; the eloquent is affected with a wild passion for glory: the humbled-minded, on this

very ground, not seldom thinks highly of himself. But love along with its benefits has great pleasure too and no trouble: and like an industrious bee, gathering the sweets from every flower, it desposits it in the soul of him who loves. Though anyone be a slave, it renders slavery sweeter than liberty. For he who loves rejoices not so much in commanding as in being commanded; although to command is sweet. Love changes the nature of things, and presents herself with all blessings in her hands, gentler than any mother, wealthier than any queen, and makes difficulties light and easy, showing virtue to be easy, but vice to be bitter. Imagine one single person loved and loving genuinely, as he ought to love. Why, he will so live on earth as if it were Heaven, everywhere enjoying calm and weaving for himself innumberable crowns. For both from envy, and wrath, and jealousy, and pride, and vainglory, and lust and every profane love such a man will keep his soul pure. Yea, even as no-one would do himself an injury, so neither would this man his neighbours. And being such, he will stand with Gabriel himself even while he walks on earth.

The happiness of reconciliation with fellow human beings is, of course, an echo of the much greater happiness of reconciliation with God. When God has offered this happiness through the vibrant words of Billy Graham, countless sinners have repented:

No matter what sin you have committed, or how black, dirty, shameful or terrible it may be, God loves you. You may be at the very gate of Hell itself, but God loves you with eternal love.

When Jesus shows us the full extent of the sin inside us he also reveals how to assuage our misery by thc happiness that comes from being forgiven:

And though I come to a present rising, a present deliverance from the power of all sin, uet if I can feel the dcw of Thy tears upon me, if I can discern the eye of compassion bent towards me, I have comfort all the way, and that comfort will flow into an infallibility in the end.

(John Donne)

Once we have accepted God's forgiveness and the happiness of forgiving ourselves that accompanies it, we will see the world in a new way. In Clement's phrase: "The eye of the heart will be opened", our perceptions will be refreshed, and our minds will be impressed by the beauty and order of the Creation:

1 The heavens moving at His appointment are subject to Him in peace;

2 Day and night follow the course allotted by him without hindering each other.

3 Sun and moon and the companies of the stars roll on, according to His direction, in harmony, in their appointed courses, and swerve not from them at all.

4 The earth teems according to His will at its proper seasons, and puts forth food in full abundance for men and beasts and all the living things that are on it, with no dissension, and changing none of His decrees.

5 The unsearchable places of the abysses and the unfathomable realms of the lower world are controlled by the same ordinances.

6 The hollow of the boundless sea is gathered by His working into its allotted places, and does not pass the barriers placed around it, but does even as He enjoined on it;

7 For He said "Thus far shalt thou come, and thy waves shall be broken within thee."

8 The ocean, which men cannot pass, and the worlds beyond it, are ruled by the same injunctions of the Master.

9 The seasons of spring, summer, autumn, and winter give place to one another in peace.

10 The stations of the winds fulfil their service without hindrance at the proper time. The everlasting springs, created for enjoyment and health, supply sustenance for the life of man without fail; and the smallest of animals meet together in concord and peace.

11 All these things did the great Creator and Master of the universe ordain to be in peace and concord, and to all things does he do good, and more especially to us who have fled for refuge to his mercies through our Lord Jesus Christ,

12 To whom be the glory and the majesty for ever and ever, Amen.

A man who is at one with his Creator and is in accord with his role in the universe becomes at one with himself, and this integrity, this sincerity, brings with it great gifts:

> The more a man is united within himself and becometh inwardly simple and pure, so much the more and higher things doth he understand without labour; for that he receiveth intellectual light from above.

It is startling claims like these that have made *The Imitation of Christ* by Thomas à Kempis the most read Christian book after the Bible. Similarly:

> If thy heart were sincere and upright, then every creature would be unto thee a looking glass of life and a book of holy doctrine.

Reconciled to God and himself and accepting God's forgiveness and his own, a man becomes assured that there is a goodness at the heart of the universe, an intimation of which may come to him particularly at what Kierkegaard called "blessed moments".

> As I stood there one quiet evening as the sea struck up its song with a deep and calm solemnity, whilst my eye met not a single sail on the vast expanse of water, and the sea set bounds to the heavens, and the heavens to the sea; whilst on the other side the busy noise of life subsided and the birds sang their evening prayer – the few that are dear to me came forth from their graves, or rather it seemed to me as though they had not died. I felt so content in their midst, I rested in their embrace, and it was as though I were out of the body, wafted with them into the ether above.

The person who is deeply convinced of these things will find happiness even in suffering:

> Were God to deal with us according to our deserts, would he not have just cause to chastise us daily in a thousand ways? Nay more, a hundred thousand deaths would not suffice for a small portion of our misdeeds! Now, if in his infinite goodness he puts all our faults under his foot and abolishes them, and instead of punishing us according to our demerit, devises an admirable means to convert our afflictions into honour and a special privilege, inasmuch as through them we are taken into partnership with his Son, must it not be said, when we disdain such a happy state, that we have indeed made little progress in Christian doctrine?
>
> (John Calvin)

If we begin to falter in our fortitude, we must turn to the consolations of prayer:

> When the bitter cold pierces me, I begin to say my prayer more earnestly and I quickly get warm all over. When hunger begins to overcome me, I call more often on the name of Jesus, and I forget my wish for food. When I fall ill and get rheumatism in my back and legs, I fix my thoughts on the prayer and do not notice the pain. If anyone harms me I have only to think, "How sweet is the prayer of Jesus!" and the injury and the anger alike pass away and I forget it all. The fussy business of the world I would not give a glance to. The one thing I wish for is to be alone, and all by myself to pray, to pray without ceasing; and doing this, I am filled with joy.
>
> (The Way of the Pilgrim)

Man is never happier than when praising and thanking God. The language of Christian literature is at its most exalted in, for example, St Anselm's *Prayer of Praise and Thanksgiving to God*, Charles Wesley's carol *Hark, the Herald Angels Sing* or this *Ode* of *Solomon*:

> As the honey distils from the comb of the bees,
> And the milk flows from the woman that loves her children,
> So also is my hope on Thee, my God.
> As the fountain gushes out its water,
> So my heart gushes out the praise of the Lord.

The Fulfilment of the Individual

We have looked at some broad categories into which Christians have fallen and generalised about their insights into happiness. But individual destinies must, by definition, be different in every case. So what must a person do to find out exactly how God wants him to fulfil himself? Great Christians reply as in a chorus:

> If you keep watch over your heart, and listen for the voice of God and

learn of Him, in one short hour you can learn more of Him than you could learn from man in a thousand years. (John Tauler)

Be humble feeble reason! Realise that man infinitely transcends man . . . Listen to God. (Blaise Pascal)

Dwell in the Living Spirit, and quench not the motions of it in yourselves. (George Fox)

. . . saving faith is the heart's trust in Christ. (Charles Finney)

As for the instruction I get, our Lord bestows that on me in some hidden way, without ever making His voice heard. (Thérèse of Lisieux)

We cannot read anywhere what God wants from us, nor can we work it out, but if we ask to know in our prayers, God's message will diffuse itself into our hearts. As Karl Barth says: "No human being has ever asked for this in vain".

The bad news is that simply to know what God wants us to do does not enable us to do it. The evil, sinful part of our nature will try to distort God's message to discourage us, and to tempt us to do other things. St Augustine's account of his conversion is almost excruciating in its intimacy. There is no more personal account of a man's discovery of his divine destiny: ". . . You have created us for Yourself", he confesses, "and our hearts can find no peace till they rest in You". Augustine takes us step by step through what he had to suffer before he obtained that peace, describing all the twists and turns of a soul that tries to evade God's call. There can be few people who will not identify with the man who was to become the greatest Christian since St Paul, as he struggles on the brink of commitment, but is still held back by that part of him that wants to continue to enjoy sin:

Sick and tormented, I reproached myself more bitterly than ever, rolling and writhing in my chain so that it almost snapped, but still it held me fast. And You, O Lord, were urgent in my inmost heart, applying with austere mercy the scourges of fear and shame, to prevent me failing once more, and the remnant of my worn and slender fetter, instead of breaking, growing strong again, and bind me harder than ever. For I kept saying to myself, "O let it be now, let it be now;" and as I spoke I was on the verge of resolution. I was on the point of action, but did not act; but I did not slip back into my former indifference. I tried again, and came a little nearer and still nearer, I could all but touch and reach the goal, yet I did not quite reach or touch it, because I still shrank from dying to death and coming alive to life, and the worse, which was ingrained, was stronger in me than the better, which was untrained.

We learn from Augustine's experience that no man is strong enough to overcome the evil inside him. Some people need alcohol to enable them to conquer shyness and so come into their own at a party, but all people need the help of a supernatural power to overcome their timid, lazy, sinful nature and so fulfil themselves. In the words of John Wesley, whoever invites the power of Jesus to enter him or herself: "'purifies the heart' from pride, anger, desire 'from all unrighteousness' from all filthiness of flesh and spirit", and replaces it "with love stronger than death, both to God and all mankind." Thus, Wesley asserts, a man who accepts the Holy Spirit will be able to answer "yes" to the following questions:

> Can you cry out: "My God, and my all!"? Do you desire nothing but him? Are you happy in God? Is he your glory, your delight, your crown of rejoicing? And is this commandment written in your heart: "That he who loveth God love his brother also?" Do you then love your neighbour as yourself? Do you love every man, even your enemies, even the enemies of God, as your own soul? As Christ loved you?

If we will let it, the love of God will cascade through us to our fellow human beings. The pleasures of the world (that "irksome and unprofitable maze") will become sour to us, and we will want to align our wills to that of our Creator:

> The scripture says God has made all for His own glory, so surely His Creatures ought to conform, as much as they can, to His will? In Him should all our affections centre, so that in all things we should seek only to do His will, not to please ourselves. And real happiness will come, not in gratifying our desires, or in gaining transient pleasures, but in accomplishing God's will for us; even as we pray every day: "Your will be done in earth, as it is in Heaven." O chaste and holy love! O sweet and gracious affection! O pure and cleansed purpose, thoroughly washed and purged from any mixture of selfishness, and sweetened by contact with the divine will! To reach this state is to become god-like.
>
> (Bernard of Clairvaux)

The Everyday Miracle

It is a cause of some scepticism that the sort of miracles ascribed to St Anthony or St Francis or St Sebastian seem not to happen these days. But the true miracle, the one by which the whole Christian enterprise stands or falls, is the everyday miracle of the Holy Spirit guiding, energising and enabling people to live a life of goodness and happiness that is qualitatively different from the one they would otherwise have been able to achieve. What follows is a collection of deeply sincere, authentic testimonies to the truth of this miracle. Perhaps, as Pascal would suggest: "There is enough light for those who desire only to see, and enough darkness for those of a contrary disposition."

Mark Booth

The APOSTLES' Creed

I believe in God the Father Almighty, Maker of Heaven and earth, and in Jesus Christ, His only Son, our Lord, Who was conceived by the Holy Ghost, born of the Virgin Mary, suffered under Pontius Pilate, was crucified, died, and was buried. He descended into Hell: the third day He rose again from the dead. He ascended into Heaven, And sitteth on the right hand of God the Father Almighty: from thence He shall come to judge the quick and the dead.

I believe in the Holy Ghost, the holy Catholic Church, the Communion of saints, the forgiveness of sins, the resurrection of the body, and the life everlasting.

The Teaching of the Twelve APOSTLES to the Heathen

The Lord's teaching to the heathen by the twelve apostles.

I

1 There are two Ways, one of Life and one of Death, and there is a great difference between the two Ways.

2 The Way of Life is this: "First, thou shalt love the God who made thee, secondly, thy neighbour as thyself; and whatsoever thou wouldst not have done to thyself, do not thou to another."

3 Now, the teaching of these words is this: "Bless those that curse you, and pray for your enemies, and fast for those that persecute you. For what credit is it to you if you love those that love you? Do not even the heathen do the same?" But, for your part, "love those that hate you," and you will have no enemy.

4 "Abstain from carnal" and bodily "lusts". "If any man smite thee on the right cheek, turn to him the other cheek also," and thou wilt be perfect. "If any man impress thee to go with him one mile, go with him two. If any man take thy coat, give him thy shirt also. If any man will take from thee what is thine, refuse it not"; not even if thou canst.

5 Give to everyone that asks thee, and do not refuse, for the Father's will is that we give to all from the gifts we have received. Blessed is he that gives according to the mandate; for he is innocent. Woe to him who receives; for if any man receive alms under pressure of need he is innocent; but he who receives it without need shall be tried as to why he took and for what, and being in prison he shall be examined as to his deeds, and "he shall not come out thence until he pay the last farthing".

6 But concerning this it was also said: "Let thine alms sweat into thine hands until thou knowest to whom thou art giving."

II

1 But the second commandment of the teaching is this:

2 "Thou shalt not do murder; thou shalt not commit adultery"; thou shalt not commit sodomy; thou shalt not commit fornication; thou shalt not steal; thou shalt not use magic; thou shalt not use philtres; thou shalt not procure abortion, nor commit infanticide; "thou shalt not covet thy neighbour's goods".

3 Thou shalt not commit perjury; "thou shalt not bear false witness"; thou shalt not speak evil; thou shalt not bear malice.

4 Thou shalt not be double-minded nor double-tongued, for to be double-tongued is the snare of death.

5 Thy speech shall not be false nor vain, but completed in action.

6 Thou shalt not be covetous nor extortionate, nor a hypocrite, nor malignant, nor proud; thou shalt make no evil plan against thy neighbour.

7 Thou shalt hate no man; but some thou shalt reprove and for some shalt thou pray, and some thou shalt love more than thine own life.

III

1 My child, flee from every evil man and from all like him.

2 Be not proud, for pride leads to murder, nor jealous, nor contentious, nor passionate, for from all these murders are engendered.

3 My child, be not lustful, for lust leads to fornication, nor a speaker of base words,

nor a lifter up of the eyes, for from all these is adultery engendered.

4 My child, regard not omens, for this leads to idolatry; neither be an enchanter, nor an astrologer, nor a magician, neither wish to see these things, for from them all is idolatry engendered.

5 My child, be not a liar, for lying leads to theft, nor a lover of money, nor vainglorious, for from all these things are thefts engendered.

6 My child, be not a grumbler, for this leads to blasphemy, nor stubborn, nor a thinker of evil, for from all these are blasphemies engendered.

7 But be thou "meek, for the meek shall inherit the earth".

8 Be thou long-suffering, and merciful and guileless, and quiet and good, and ever fearing the words which thou hast heard.

9 Thou shalt not exalt thyself, nor let thy soul be presumptuous. Thy soul shall not consort with the lofty, but thou shalt walk with righteous and humble men.

10 Receive the accidents that befall thee as good, knowing that nothing happens without God.

IV

1 My child, thou shalt remember, day and night, him who speaks the word of God to thee, and thou shalt honour him as the Lord, for where the Lord's nature is spoken of, there is He present.

2 And thou shalt seek daily the presence of the saints, that thou mayest find rest in their words.

3 Thou shalt not desire a schism, but shalt reconcile those that strive. Thou shalt give righteous judgment; thou shalt favour no man's person in reproving transgression.

4 Thou shalt not be of two minds whether it shall be or not.

5 Be not one who stretches out his hands to receive, but shuts them when it comes to giving.

6 Of whatsoever thou hast gained by thy hands thou shalt give a ransom for thy sins.

7 Thou shalt not hesitate to give, nor shalt thou grumble when thou givest, for thou shalt know who is the good Paymaster of the reward.

8 Thou shalt not turn away the needy, but shalt share everything with thy brother, and shalt not say that it is thine own, for if you are sharers in the imperishable, how much more in the things which perish?

9 Thou shalt not withhold thine hand from thy son or from thy daughter, but thou shalt teach them the fear of God from their youth up.

10 Thou shalt not command in thy bitterness thy slave or thine handmaid, who hope in the same God, lest they cease to fear the God who is over you both; for he comes not to call men with respect of persons, but those whom the Spirit has prepared.

11 But do you who are slaves be subject to your master, as to God's representative, in reverence and fear.

12 Thou shalt hate all hypocrisy, and everything that is not pleasing to the Lord.

13 Thou shalt not forsake the commandments of the Lord, but thou shalt keep what thou didst receive, "adding nothing to it and taking nothing away".

14 In the congregation thou shalt confess thy transgressions, and thou shalt not betake thyself to prayer with an evil conscience. This is the Way of Life.

V

1 But the Way of Death is this: First of all, it is wicked and full of cursing, murders, adulteries, lusts, fornications, thefts, idolatries, witchcrafts, charms, robberies, false witness, hypocrisies, a double heart, fraud, pride, malice, stubbornness, covetousness, foul speech, jealousy, impudence, haughtiness, boastfulness.

2 Persecutors of the good, haters of truth, lovers of lies, knowing not the reward of righteousness, not cleaving to the good nor to righteous judgment, spending wakeful nights not for good but for wickedness, from whom meekness and patience is far, lovers of vanity, following after reward, unmerciful to the poor, not working for him who is oppressed with toil, without knowledge of Him who made them, murderers of children, corrupters of God's creatures, turning away the needy, oppressing the distressed, advocates of the rich, unjust judges of the poor, altogether sinful; may ye be delivered, my children, from all these.

VI

1 See "that no one make thee to err" from this Way of the teaching, for he teaches thee without God.

2 For if thou canst bear the whole yoke of the Lord, thou wilt be perfect, but if thou canst not, do what thou canst.

VII

1 Concerning baptism, baptise thus: having first rehearsed all these things, "baptise, in the Name of the Father and of the Son and of the Holy Spirit," in running water.

2 But if thou hast no running water, baptise in other water.

3 And before the baptism let the baptiser and him who is to be baptised fast, and any others who are able. And thou shalt bid him who is to be baptised to fast one or two days before.

VIII

1 Do not pray as the hypocrites, but as the Lord commanded in His Gospel, pray thus: "Our Father, who art in Heaven, hallowed by Thy Name, Thy Kingdom come, Thy will be done, as in Heaven so also upon earth; give us today our daily bread, and forgive us our debt as we forgive our debtors, and lead us not into trial, but deliver us from the Evil One, for Thine is the power and the glory for ever." Pray thus three times a day.

IX

1 And concerning the Eucharist, hold Eucharist thus.

2 First concerning the Cup: "We give thanks to Thee, our Father, for the Holy Vine of David Thy child, which Thou didst make known to us through Jesus Thy Child; to Thee be glory for ever."

3 And concerning the broken Bread: "We give Thee thanks, our Father, for the life and knowledge which Thou didst make known to us through Jesus Thy Child. To Thee be glory for ever.

4 As this broken bread was scattered upon the mountains, but was brought together and became one, so let Thy Church be gathered together from the ends of the earth into Thy Kingdom, for Thine is the glory and the power through Jesus Christ for ever."

5 But let none eat or drink of your Eucharist except those who have been baptised in the Lord's Name. For concerning this also did the Lord say: "Give not that which is holy to the dogs."

X

1 But after you are satisfied with food, thus give thanks:

2 "We give thanks to Thee, O Holy Father, for Thy Holy Name which Thou didst make to tabernacle in our hearts, and for the knowledge and faith and immortality which Thou didst make known to us through Jesus Thy Child. To Thee be glory for ever.

3 Thou, Lord Almighty, didst create all things for Thy Name's sake, and didst give food and drink to men for their enjoyment, that they might give thanks to Thee, but us hast Thou blessed with spiritual food and drink and eternal light through Thy Child.

4 Above all we give thanks to Thee for that Thou art mighty. To Thee be glory for ever.

5 Remember, Lord, Thy Church, to deliver it from all evil and make it perfect in Thy love, and gather it together in its holiness from the four winds to Thy Kingdom which Thou hast prepared for it. For Thine is the power and the glory for ever.

6 Let grace come and let this world pass away. Hosannah to the God of David. If any man be holy, let him come! If any man be not, let him repent: Our Lord! Come! Amen."

7 But suffer the prophets to hold Eucharist as they will.

XI

1 Whosoever then comes and teaches you all these things aforesaid, receive him.

2 But if the teacher himself be perverted and teach another doctrine to destroy these things, do not listen to him, but if his teaching be for the increase of righteousness and knowledge of the Lord, receive him as the Lord.

XII

1 On the Day of the Lord come together, break bread and hold Eucharist, after confessing your transgressions that your offering may be pure.

2 But let none who has a quarrel with his fellow join in your meeting until they be reconciled, that your sacrifice be not defiled.

3 For this is that which was spoken by the Lord, "In every place and time offer me a pure sacrifice, for I am a great king", saith the Lord, "and my name is wonderful among the heathen".

XIII

1 "Watch" over your life: "let your lamps" be not quenched "and your loins" be not ungirded, but be "ready", for ye know not "the hour in which our Lord cometh".

2 But be frequently gathered together seeking the things which are profitable for your souls, for the whole time of your faith shall not profit you except ye be found perfect at the last time.

3 For in the last days the false prophets and the corrupters shall be multiplied, and the sheep shall be turned into wolves, and love shall change to hate.

4 For as lawlessness increaseth they shall hate one another and persecute and betray, and then shall appear the deceiver of the world as a Son of God, and shall do signs and wonders and the earth shall be given over into his hands and he shall commit iniquities which have never been since the world began.

5 Then shall the creation of mankind come to the fiery trial and "many shall be offended" and be lost, but "they who endure" in their faith "shall be saved" by the curse itself.

6 And "then shall appear the signs" of the truth. First the sign spread out in Heaven, then the sign of the sound of the trumpet, and thirdly the resurrection of the dead.

7 "The Lord shall come and all his saints with him."

8 Then shall the world "see the Lord coming on the clouds of Heaven".

The Epistle of Saint CLEMENT to the Corinthians

The Church of God in Rome to the Church of God in Corinth, to those who are called and sanctified by the will of God through our Lord Jesus Christ. Grace and peace from God Almighty be multiplied to you through Jesus Christ.

I

1 Owing to the sudden and repeated misfortunes and calamities which have befallen us, we consider that our attention has been somewhat delayed in turning to the questions disputed among you, beloved, and especially the abominable and unholy sedition, alien and foreign to the elect of God, which a few rash and self-willed persons have made blaze up to such a frenzy that your name, venerable and famous, and worthy as it is of all men's love, has been much slandered.

2 For who has stayed with you without making proof of the virtue and steadfastness of your faith? Who has not admired the sobriety and Christian gentleness of your piety? Who has not reported your character so magnificent in its hospitality? And who has not blessed your perfect and secure knowledge?

3 For you did all things without respect of persons, and walked in the laws of God, obedient to your rulers, and paying all fitting honour to the older among you. On the young, too, you enjoined temperate and seemly thoughts, and to the women you gave instruction that they should do all things with a blameless and seemly and pure conscience, yielding a dutiful affection to their husbands. And you taught them to remain in the rule of obedience and to manage their households with seemliness, in all circumspection.

II

1 And you were all humble-minded and in no wise arrogant, yielding subjection rather than demanding it, "giving more gladly than receiving", satisfied with the provision of Christ, and paying attention to His words you stored them up carefully in your hearts, and kept His sufferings before your eyes.

2 Thus a profound and rich peace was given to all, you had an insatiable desire to do good, and the Holy Spirit was poured out in abundance on you all.

3 You were full of holy plans, and with pious confidence you stretched out your hands to Almighty God in a passion of goodness, beseeching Him to be merciful towards any unwitting sin.

4 Day and night you strove on behalf of the whole brotherhood that the number of His elect should be saved with mercy and compassion.

5 You were sincere and innocent, and bore no malice to one another.

6 All sedition and all schism was abominable to you. You mourned over the transgressions of your neighbours; you judged their shortcomings as your own.

7 You were without regret in every act of kindness, "ready unto every good work".

8 You were adorned by your virtuous and honourable citizenship and did all things in the fear of God. The commandments and ordinances of the Lord were "written on the tables of your heart".

III

1 All glory and enlargement was given to you, and that which was written was fulfilled: "My beloved ate and drank, and he was enlarged and waxed fat and kicked".

2 From this arose jealousy and envy, strife and sedition, persecution and disorder, war and captivity.

3 Thus "the worthless" rose up "against those who were in honour", those of no reputation against the renowned, the foolish against the prudent, the "young against the old".

4 For this cause righteousness and peace are far removed, while each deserts the fear of God and the eye of faith in Him has grown dim, and men walk neither in the ordinances of His commandments nor use their citizenship worthily of Christ, but each goes according to the lusts of his wicked heart, and has revived the unrighteousness and impious envy, by which also "death came into the world".

IV

1 For it is written thus: "And it came to pass after certain days that Cain offered to God a sacrifice of the fruits of the earth, and Abel himself also offered of the firstborn of the sheep and of their fat.

2 And God looked on Abel and his gifts, but he had no respect to Cain and his sacrifices.

3 And Cain was greatly grieved and his countenance fell.

4 And God said to Cain: 'Why art thou grieved, and why is thy countenance fallen? If thou offeredst rightly, but didst not divide rightly, didst thou not sin?

5 Be still: he shall turn to thee, and thou shalt rule over him.'

6 And Cain said to Abel his brother: 'Let us go unto the plain.' And it came to pass that, while they were in the plain, Cain rose up against Abel his brother and slew him."

7 You see, brethren, jealousy and envy wrought fratricide.

8 Through jealousy our father Jacob ran from the face of Esau his brother.

9 Jealousy made Joseph to be persecuted to the death, and come into slavery.

10 Jealousy forced Moses to fly from the face of Pharaoh, King of Egypt, when his fellow countryman said to him: "Who made thee a judge or a ruler over us? Wouldst thou slay me as thou didst slay the Egyptian yesterday?"

11 Through jealousy Aaron and Miriam were lodged outside the camp.

12 Jealousy brought down Dathan and Abiram alive into Hades, because they rebelled against Moses the servant of God.

13 Through jealousy David incurred envy not only from strangers, but suffered persecution even from Saul, King of Israel.

V

1 But, to cease from the examples of old time, let us come to those who contended in the days nearest to us; let us take the noble examples of our own generation.

2 Through jealousy and envy the greatest and most righteous pillars of the Church were persecuted and contended unto death.

3 Let us set before our eyes the good apostles:

4 Peter, who because of unrighteous jealousy suffered not one or two but many trials, and having thus given his testimony went to the glorious place which was his due.

5 Through jealousy and strife Paul showed the way to the prize of endurance.

6 Seven times he was in bonds, he was exiled, he was stoned, he was a herald both in the East and in the West, he gained the noble fame of his faith,

7 He taught righteousness to all the world, and when he had reached the limits of the West he gave his testimony before the rulers, and thus passed from the world and was taken up into the holy place, the greatest example of endurance.

VI

1 To these men with their holy lives was gathered a great multitude of the chosen, who were the victims of jealousy and offered among us the fairest example in their endurance under many indignities and tortures.

2 Through jealousy women were persecuted, suffering terrible and unholy indignities; they steadfastly finished the course of faith, and received a noble reward, weak in the body though they were.

3 Jealousy has estranged wives from husbands, and made of no effect the saying of our father Adam: "This is now bone of my bone and flesh of my flesh."

4 Jealousy and strife have overthrown great cities, and rooted up mighty nations.

VII

1 We are not only writing these things to you, beloved, for your admonition, but also to remind ourselves; for we are in the same arena, and the same struggle is before us.

2 Wherefore let us put aside empty and vain cares, and let us come to the glorious and venerable rule of our tradition.

3 And let us see what is good and pleasing and acceptable in the sight of our Maker.

4 Let us fix our gaze on the blood of Christ, and let us know that it is precious to His Father, because it was poured out for our salvation, and brought the grace of repentance to all the world.

5 Let us review all the generations, and let us learn that in generation after generation the Master has given a place of repentance to those who will turn to Him.

6 Noah preached repentance and those who obeyed were saved.

7 Jonah foretold destruction to the men of Nineveh, but when they repented they received forgiveness of their sins from God in answer to their prayer, and gained salvation, though they were aliens to God.

VIII

1 The ministers of the grace of God spoke through the Holy Spirit concerning repentance,

2 And even the Master of the universe Himself spoke with an oath concerning repentance: "For as I live, said the Lord, I do not desire the death of the sinner so much as his repentance," and He added a gracious declaration:

3 "Repent, O house of Israel, from your iniquity. Say to the sons of my people, if your sins reach from the earth to Heaven, and if they be redder than scarlet, and blacker than sackcloth, and ye turn to me with all your hearts and say 'Father', I will listen to you as a holy people."

4 And in another place He speaks thus: "Wash you and make you clean, put away your wickedness from your souls before my eyes, cease from your wickedness, learn to do good, seek out judgment, rescue the wronged, give judgment for the orphan, do justice to the widow, and come and let us reason together, saith the Lord; and if your sins be as crimson, I will make them white as snow, and if they be as scarlet, I will make them white as wool, and if ye be willing and hearken to me, ye shall eat the good things of the land, but if ye be not willing, and hearken not to me, a sword shall devour you, for the mouth of the Lord has spoken these things."

5 Thus desiring to give to all His beloved a share in repentance, He established it by His Almighty will.

IX

1 Wherefore let us obey His excellent and glorious will; let us fall before Him as suppliants of His mercy and goodness; let us turn to His pity, and abandon the vain toil and strife and jealousy which leads to death.

2 Let us fix our gaze on those who have rendered perfect service to His excellent glory.

3 Let us take Enoch, who was found righteous in obedience, and was translated, and death did not befall him.

4 Noah was found faithful in his service, in foretelling a new beginning to the world, and through him the Master saved the liv-

ing creatures which entered in concord into the Ark.

X

1 Abraham, who was called "the Friend", was found faithful in his obedience to the words of God.

2 He in obedience went forth from his country and from his kindred and from his father's house, that by leaving behind a little country and a feeble kindred and a small house he might inherit the promises of God. For God said to him:

3 "Depart from thy land and from thy kindred and from thy father's house to the land which I shall show thee, and I will make thee a great nation, and I will bless thee, and I will magnify thy name, and thou shalt be blessed; and I will bless those that bless thee, and I will curse those that curse thee, and all the tribes of the earth shall be blessed in thee."

4 And again, when he was separated from Lot, God said to him: "Lift up thine eyes and look from the place where thou art now, to the north and to the south and to the east and to the west; for all the land which thou seest, to thee will I give it and to thy seed for ever.

5 And I will make thy seed as the dust of the earth. If a man can number the dust of the earth thy seed shall also be numbered."

6 And again he said: "God led forth Abraham, and said to him, 'Look up to the Heaven and number the stars, if thou canst number them; so shall thy seed be.' And Abraham believed God, and it was counted unto him for righteousness."

7 Because of his faith and hospitality a son was given him in his old age, and in his obedience he offered him as a sacrifice to God on the mountain which He showed him.

XI

1 For his hospitality and piety Lot was saved out of Sodom when the whole countryside was judged by fire and brimstone, and the Master made clear that He does not forsake those who hope in Him, but delivers to punishment and torture those who turn aside to others.

2 For of this a sign was given when his wife went with him, but changed her mind and did not remain in agreement with him, so that she became a pillar of salt unto this day, to make known to all that those who are double-minded and have doubts concerning the power of God incur judgment and become a warning to all generations.

XII

1 For her faith and hospitality Rahab the harlot was saved.

2 For when the spies were sent to Jericho by Joshua the son of Nun, the King of the land knew that they had come to spy out his country, and sent men to take them, that they might be captured and put to death.

3 So the hospitable Rahab took them in, and hid them in the upper room under the stalks of flax.

4 And when the king's men came and said, "The spies of our land came unto thee, bring them out, for the king orders thus," she answered, "The men whom ye seek did come to me, but they went away forthwith, and are proceeding on their journey," and pointed in the wrong direction.

5 And she said to the men: "I know assuredly that the Lord God is delivering to you this land; for the fear and dread of you has fallen on those who dwell in it. When therefore it shall come to pass, that ye take it, save me and my father's house."

6 And they said to her: "It shall be as thou hast spoken to us; when therefore thou knowest that we are at hand, thou shalt gather all thy folk under thy roof and they shall be safe; for as many as shall be found outside the house shall perish."

7 And they proceeded to give her a sign that she should hang out a scarlet thread from her house, foreshowing that all who believe and hope in God shall have redemption through the blood of the Lord.

8 You see, beloved, that the woman is an instance not only of faith but also of prophecy.

XIII

1 Let us, therefore, be humble-minded, brethren, putting aside all arrogance and conceit and foolishness and wrath, and let us do that which is written, for the Holy Spirit says, "Let not the wise man boast himself in his wisdom, nor the strong man in his strength, nor the rich man in his riches, but he that boasteth let him boast in the Lord, to seek Him out and to do judg-

ment and righteousness," especially remembering the words of the Lord Jesus which He spoke when He was teaching gentleness and long suffering.

2 For He spoke thus: "Be merciful, that ye may obtain mercy. Forgive, that ye may be forgiven. As ye do, so shall it be done unto you. As ye give, so shall it be given unto you. As ye judge, so shall ye be judged. As ye are kind, so shall kindness be shown you. With what measure ye mete, it shall be measured to you."

3 With this commandment and with these injunctions let us strengthen ourselves to walk in obedience to His hallowed words and let us be humble-minded, for the Holy Word says:

4 "On whom shall I look, but on the meek and gentle and him who trembles at my oracles."

XIV

1 Therefore it is right and holy, my brethren, for us to obey God rather than to follow those who in pride and unruliness are the instigators of an abominable jealousy.

2 For we shall incur no common harm but great danger if we rashly yield ourselves to the purposes of men who rush into strife and sedition, to estrange us from what is right.

3 Let us be kind to one another, according to the compassion and sweetness of our Maker.

4 For it is written: "The kind shall inhabit the land, and the guiltless shall be left on it, but they who transgress shall be destroyed from off it."

5 And again He says: "I saw the ungodly lifted high and exalted as the cedars of Lebanon. And I went by, and behold He was not; and I sought His place, and I found it not. Keep innocence, and look on uprightness; for there is a remnant for a peaceable man."

XV

1 Moreover let us cleave to those whose peacefulness is based on piety and not to those whose wish for peace is hypocrisy.

2 For it says in one place: "This people honoureth me with their lips, but their heart is far from me."

3 And again: "They blessed with their mouth, but cursed in their hearts."

4 And again it says: "They loved him with their mouth, and they lied upon Him with their tongue, and their heart was not right with Him, nor were they faithful in His covenant."

5 Therefore "Let the deceitful lips be dumb which speak iniquity against the righteous." And again: "May the Lord destroy all the deceitful lips, a tongue that speaketh great things, those who say, 'Let us magnify our tongue, our lips are our own, who is lord over us?'

6 For the misery of the poor and groaning of the needy, now will I arise, saith the Lord, I will place him in safety, I will deal boldly with him."

XVI

1 For Christ is of those who are humble-minded, not of those who exalt themselves over His flock.

2 The sceptre of the greatness of God, the Lord Jesus Christ, came not with the pomp of pride or of arrogance, for all His power, but was humble-minded, as the Holy Spirit spoke concerning Him. For it says:

3 "Lord, who has believed our report, and to whom was the arm of the Lord revealed? We declared him before the Lord as a child, as a root in thirsty ground; there is no form in him, nor glory, and we saw him, and he had neither form nor beauty, but his form was without honour, less than the form of man, a man living among stripes and toil, and acquainted with the endurance of weakness; for his face was turned away, he was dishonoured, and not esteemed.

4 He it is who beareth our sins, and is pained for us, and we regarded him as subject to pain, and stripes and affliction.

5 But he was wounded for our sins and he has suffered for our iniquities. The chastisement of our peace was upon him; with his bruises were we healed.

6 All we like sheep went astray, each man went astray in his path.

7 And the Lord delivered him up for our sins, and he openeth not his mouth because of his affliction. As a sheep he was brought to the slaughter, and as a lamb dumb before its shearer, so he openeth not his mouth. In humiliation his judgment was taken away.

8 Who shall declare his generation? For his life is taken away from the earth.

9 For the iniquities of my people is he come to death.

10 And I will give the wicked for his burial, and the rich for his death; for he wrought no iniquity, nor was guile found in his mouth. And the Lord's will is to purify him from stripes.

11 If ye make an offering for sin, your soul shall see a long-lived seed.

12And the Lord's will is to take of the toil of his soul, to show him light and to form him with understanding, to justify a righteous man who serveth many well. And he himself shall bear their sins.

13 For this reason shall he inherit many, and he shall share the spoils of the strong; because his soul was delivered to death, and he was reckoned among the transgressors.

14 And he bore the sins of many, and for their sins was he delivered up."

15 And again he says himself: "But I am a worm and no man, a reproach of men, and despised of the people.

16 All they who saw me mocked me, they spoke with their lips, they shook their heads. He hoped on the Lord, let Him deliver him, let Him save him, for He hath pleasure in him."

17 You see, beloved, what is the example which is given to us; for if the Lord was thus humble-minded, what shall we do, who through Him have come under the yoke of His grace?

XVII

1 Let us also be imitators of those who went about "in the skins of goats and sheep", heralding the coming of Christ; we mean Elijah and Elisha, and moreover Ezekiel, the prophets and, in addition to them, the famous men of old.

2 Great fame was given to Abraham, and he was called the Friend of God, and he, fixing his gaze in humility on the glory of God, said: "But I am dust and ashes."

3 Moreover it is also written thus concerning Job: "Now Job was righteous and blameless, true, a worshipper of God, and kept himself from all evil."

4 But he accuses himself, saying: "No man is clean from defilement, not even if his life be but for a single day."

5 Moses was called "faithful with all his house", and through his ministry God judged Eygpt with their scourges and torments; but he, though he was given great glory, did not use great words but when an oracle was given to him from the bush said: "Who am I that Thou sendest me? Nay, I am a man of feeble speech, and a slow tongue."

6 And again he said: "But I am as smoke from a pot."

XVIII

1 But what shall we say of the famous David? Of him God said: "I have found a man after my own heart, David the son of Jesse, I have anointed him with eternal mercy."

2 But he too said to God: "Have mercy upon me, O God, according to Thy great mercy, and according to the multitude of Thy compassion, blot out my transgression.

3 Wash me yet more from mine iniquity, and cleanse me from my sin; for I know my iniquity, and my sin is ever before me.

4 Against Thee only did I sin, and did evil before Thee, that Thou mightest be justified in Thy words, and mightest overcome when Thou art judged.

5 For, lo, I was conceived in iniquity, and in sin did my mother bear me.

6 For, behold, Thou has loved truth, thou didst make plain to me the secret and hidden things of Thy wisdom.

7 Thou shalt sprinkle me with hyssop, and I shall be cleansed; Thou shalt wash me, and I shall be whiter than snow.

8 Thou shalt make me hear joy and gladness; the bones which have been humbled shall rejoice.

9 Turn thy face from my sins, and blot out all mine iniquities.

10 Create a clean heart in me, O God, and renew a right spirit in my inmost parts.

11 Cast me not away from Thy presence, and take not Thy Holy Spirit from me.

12 Give me back the gladness of Thy salvation, strengthen me with Thy governing spirit.

13 I will teach the wicked Thy ways, and the ungodly shall be converted unto Thee.

14 Deliver me from blood-guiltiness, O God, the God of my salvation.

15 My tongue shall rejoice in Thy righteousness. O Lord, Thou shalt open my mouth, and my lips shall tell of Thy praise.

16 For if Thou hadst desired sacrifice, I would have given it; in whole burnt offerings Thou wilt not delight.

17 The sacrifice unto God is a broken spirit, a broken and a humbled heart God shall not despise."

XIX

1 The humility and obedient submission of so many men of such great fame have rendered better not only us, but also the generations before us, who received His oracles in fear and truth.

2 Seeing then that we have received a share in many great and glorious deeds, let us hasten on to the goal of peace, which was given us from the beginning, and let us fix our gaze on the Father and Creator of the whole world and cleave to His splendid and excellent gifts of peace, and to His good deeds to us.

3 Let us contemplate Him with our mind, let us gaze with the eyes of our soul on His long-suffering purpose, let us consider how free from wrath He is towards all His creatures.

XX

1 The heavens moving at His appointment are subject to Him in peace.

2 Day and night follow the course allotted by Him without hindering each other.

3 Sun and moon and the companies of the stars roll on, according to His direction, in harmony, in their appointed courses, and swerve not from them at all.

4 The earth teems according to His will at its proper seasons, and puts forth food in full abundance for men and beasts and all the living things that are on it, with no dissension, and changing none of His decrees.

5 The unsearchable places of the abysses and the unfathomable realms of the lower world are controlled by the same ordinances.

6 The hollow of the boundless sea is gathered by His working into its allotted places, and does not pass the barriers placed around it, but does even as He enjoined on it.

7 For He said: "Thus far shalt thou come, and thy waves shall be broken within thee."

8 The ocean, which men cannot pass, and the worlds beyond it, are ruled by the same injunctions of the Master.

9 The seasons of spring, summer, autumn and winter give place to one another in peace.

10 The stations of the winds fulfil their service without hindrance at the proper time. The everlasting springs, created for enjoyment and health, supply sustenance for the life of man without fail; and the smallest of animals meet together in concord and peace.

11 All these things did the great Creator and Master of the universe ordain to be in peace and concord, and to all things does He do good, and more especially to us who have fled for refuge to His mercies through our Lord Jesus Christ.

12 To whom be the glory and the majesty for ever and ever, Amen.

XXI

1 Take heed, beloved, lest His many good works towards us become a judgment on us, if we do not good and virtuous deeds before Him in concord, and be citizens worthy of him.

2 For He says in one place: "The Spirit of the Lord is a lamp searching the inward parts."

3 Let us observe how near He is, and that nothing escapes Him of our thoughts nor of the devices which we make.

4 It is right, therefore, that we should not be deserters from His will.

5 Let us offend foolish and thoughtless men, who are exalted and boast in the pride of their words, rather than God.

6 Let us reverence the Lord Jesus Christ, whose blood was given for us, let us respect those who rule us, let us honour the aged, let us instruct the young in the fear of God, let us lead our wives to that which is good.

7 Let them exhibit the lovely habit of purity, let them show forth the innocent will of meekness, let them make the gentleness of their tongue manifest by their silence, let them not give their affection by factious preference, but in holiness to all equally who fear God.

8 Let our children share in the instruction which is in Christ, let them learn the strength of humility before God, the power of pure love before God, how beautiful and

great is His fear and how it gives salvation to all who live holily in it with a pure mind.

9 For He is a searcher of thoughts and desires; His breath is in us, and when He will He shall take it away.

XXII

1 Now the faith which is in Christ confirms all these things, for He himself through His Holy Spirit calls us thus: "Come, children, hearken to me, I will teach you the fear of the Lord.

2 Who is the man that desireth life, that loveth to see good days?

3 Make thy tongue cease from evil, and thy lips that they speak no guile.

4 Depart from evil, and do good.

5 Seek peace, and pursue it.

6 The eyes of the Lord are upon the righteous, and His ears are open to their petition; but the face of the Lord is against those that do evil, to destroy the memory of them from the earth.

7 The righteous cried, and the Lord heard him, and delivered him out of all his afflictions.

8 Many are the scourges of the sinner, but mercy shall encompass those that hope on the Lord."

XXIII

1 The all-merciful and beneficent Father has compassion on those that fear Him, and kindly and lovingly bestows His favours on those that draw near to Him with a simple mind.

2 Wherefore let us not be double-minded, nor let our soul be fanciful concerning His excellent and glorious gifts.

3 Let this Scripture be far from us in which He says: "Wretched are the double-minded, who doubt in their soul and say, 'We have heard these things even in the days of our fathers, and behold we have grown old, and none of these things has happened to us.'

4 Oh, foolish men, compare yourself to a tree: take a vine, first it sheds its leaves, then there comes a bud, then a leaf, then a flower, and after this the unripe grape, then the full bunch." See how in a little time the fruit of the tree comes to ripeness.

5 Truly His will shall be quickly and suddenly accomplished, as the Scripture also bears witness that "He shall come quickly and shall not tarry; and the Lord shall suddenly come to His temple, and the Holy One for whom ye look."

XXIV

1 Let us consider, beloved, how the Master continually proves to us that there will be a future resurrection, of which He has made the first fruits, by raising the Lord Jesus Christ from the dead.

2 Let us look, beloved, at the resurrection which is taking place at its proper season.

3 Day and night show us a resurrection. The night sleeps, the day arises: the day departs, night comes on.

4 Let us take the crops: how and in what way does the sowing take place?

5 "The sower went forth" and cast each of the seeds into the ground, and they fall on to the ground, parched and bare, and suffer decay; then from their decay the greatness of the providence of the Master raises them up, and from one grain more grow and bring forth fruit.

XXV

1 Let us consider the strange sign which takes place in the east, that is in the districts near Arabia.

2 There is a bird which is called the phoenix. This is the only one of its kind, and it lives five hundred years; and when the time of its dissolution in death is at hand, it makes itself a sepulchre of frankincense. and myrrh and other spices, and when the time is fulfilled it enters into it and dies.

3 Now, from the corruption of its flesh there springs a worm, which is nourished by the juices of the dead bird, and puts forth wings. Then, when it has become strong, it takes up that sepulchre, in which are the bones of its predecessor, and carries them from the country of Arabia as far as Egypt until it reaches the city called Heliopolis.

4 And in the daylight in the sight of all it flies to the altar of the sun, places them there, and starts back to its former home.

5 Then the priests inspect the registers of dates, and they find that it has come at the fulfilment of the five hundredth year.

XXVI

1 Do we then consider it a great and wonderful thing that the creator of the universe will bring about the resurrection of

those who served Him in holiness, in the confidence of a good faith, when He shows us the greatness of His promise even through a bird?

2 For he says in one place, "And Thou shalt raise me up, and I will praise Thee," and "I laid me down and slept, I rose up, for Thou art with me."

3 And again Job says: "And Thou shalt raise up this my flesh which has endured all these things."

XXVII

1 In this hope then let our souls be bound to Him who is faithful in His promises and righteous in His judgments.

2 He who has commanded not to lie shall much more not be a liar Himself; for nothing is impossible with God save to lie.

3 Let therefore faith in Him be kindled again in us, and let us consider that all things are near Him.

4 By the word of His majesty did He establish all things, and by His word can He destroy them.

5 "Who shall say to Him what hast Thou done, or who shall resist the might of His strength?" When He will, and as He will, He will do all things, and none of His decrees shall pass away.

6 All is in His sight and nothing has escaped from His counsel.

7 Since "The heavens declare the glory of God and the firmament telleth His handiwork, day uttereth speech unto day, and night telleth knowledge to night. And there are neither words nor speeches, and their voices are not heard."

XXVIII

1 Since then all things are seen and heard by Him, let us fear Him, and leave off from foul desires of evil deeds, that we may be sheltered by His mercy from the judgments to come.

2 For whither can any of us fly from His mighty hand? and what world shall receive those who seek to desert from Him?

3 For the writing says in one place: "Where shall I go and where shall I hide from Thy presence? If I ascend into Heaven Thou art there, if I depart to the ends of the earth there is Thy right hand; if I make my bed in the abyss there is Thy Spirit."

4 Whither then shall a man depart or where shall He escape from Him who embraces all things?

XXIX

1 Let us then approach Him in holiness of soul, raising pure and undefiled hands to Him, loving our gracious and merciful Father, who has made us the portion of His choice for Himself.

2 For thus it is written: "When the Most High divided the nations, when He scattered the sons of Adam, He established the bounds of the nations according to the number of the angels of God. His people Jacob became the portion of the Lord, Israel was the lot of his inheritance."

3 And in another place He says: "Behold the Lord taketh to Himself a nation from the midst of nations, as a man taketh the first fruit of his threshing-floor, and the Holy of Holies shall come forth from that nation."

XXX

1 Seeing then that we are the portion of one who is holy, let us do all the deeds of sanctification, fleeing from evil speaking, and abominable and impure embraces, drunkenness and youthful lusts, and abominable passion, detestable adultery, and abominable pride.

2 "For God", He says, "resisteth the proud but giveth grace to the humble."

3 Let us then join ourselves to those to whom is given grace from God; let us put on concord in meekness of spirit and continence, keeping ourselves far from all gossip and evil speaking, and be justified by deeds, not by words.

4 For He says: "He that speaketh much shall also hear much; or doth he that is a good speaker think that he is righteous?

5 Blessed is he that is born of woman and hath a short life. Be not profuse in speech."

6 Let our praise be with God, and not from ourselves, for God hates those who praise themselves.

7 Let testimony to our good deeds be given by others, as it was given to our fathers, the righteous.

8 Forwardness and arrogance and boldness belong to those that are accursed by God, gentleness and humility and meekness are with those who are blessed by God.

XXXI

1 Let us cleave, then, to His blessing and let us consider what are the paths of blessing. Let us unfold the deeds of old.

2 Why was our father Abraham blessed? Was it not because he wrought righteousness and truth through faith?

3 Isaac in confident knowledge of the future was gladly led as a sacrifice.

4 Jacob departed from his country in meekness because of his brother, and went to Laban and served him, and to him was given the sceptre of the twelve tribes of Israel.

XXXII

1 And if anyone will candidly consider this in detail, he will recognise the greatness of the gifts given by Him.

2 For from Him come the priests and all the Levites, who serve the altar of God, from Him comes the Lord Jesus according to the flesh, from Him come the kings and rulers and governors in the succession of Judah, and the other sceptres of his tribes are in no small renown seeing that God promised that, "thy seed shall be as the stars of heaven."

3 All of them therefore were renowned and magnified, not through themselves or their own works or the righteous actions which they had wrought, but through His will.

4 And therefore we who by His will have been called in Christ Jesus, are not made righteous by ourselves, or by our wisdom or understanding or piety or the deeds which we have wrought in holiness of heart, but through faith, by which Almighty God has justified all men from the beginning of the world; to Him be glory for ever and ever. Amen.

XXXIII

1 What shall we do then brethren? Shall we be slothful in well-doing and cease from love? May the Master forbid that this should happen, at least to us, but let us be zealous to accomplish every good deed with energy and readiness.

2 For the Creator and Master of the universe Himself rejoices in His works.

3 For by His infinitely great might did He establish the heavens, and by His incomprehensible understanding did He order them; and He separated the earth from the water that surrounds it, and fixed it upon the secure foundation of His own will; and the animals that move in it did He command to exist by His own decree; the sea and the living things in it did He make ready, and enclosed by His own power.

4 Above all, man, the most excellent and from his intellect the greatest of His creatures, did He form in the likeness of His own image by His sacred and faultless hands.

5 For God spake thus: "Let us make man according to our image and likeness; and God made man, male and female made He them."

6 So when He had finished all these things He praised them and blessed them and said: "Increase and multiply."

7 Let us observe that all the righteous have been adorned with good works; and the Lord Himself adorned Himself with good works and rejoiced.

8 Having therefore this pattern let us follow His will without delay, let us work the work of righteousness with all our strength.

XXXIV

1 The good workman receives the bread of his labour with boldness; the lazy and careless cannot look his employer in the face.

2 Therefore we must be prompt in well-doing: for all things are from Him.

3 For He warns us: "Behold the Lord cometh, and his reward is before His face, to pay to each according to his work."

4 He exhorts us therefore if we believe in Him with our whole heart not to be lazy or careless "in every good work".

5 Let our glorying and confidence be in Him; let us be subject to His will; let us consider the whole multitude of His angels, how they stand ready and minister to His will.

6 For the Scripture says: "Ten thousand times ten thousand stood by Him, and a thousand thousands ministered to Him, and they cried, Holy, Holy, Holy is the Lord of Sabaoth, the whole creation is full of His glory."

7 Therefore, we too must gather together with concord in our conscience and cry earnestly to Him, as it were with one mouth, that we may share in His great and glorious promises.

8 For He says: "Eye hath not seen, and ear hath not heard, and it hath not entered into the heart of man, what things the Lord hath prepared for them that wait for Him."

XXXV

1 How blessed and wonderful, beloved, are the gifts of God!

2 Life in immortality, splendour in righteousness, truth in boldness, faith in confidence, continence in holiness; and all these things are submitted to our understanding.

3 What, then, are the things which are being prepared for those who wait for Him? The Creator and Father of the ages, the All Holy One Himself knows their greatness and beauty.

4 Let us then strive to be found among the number of those that wait, that we may receive a share of the promised gifts.

5 But how shall this be, beloved? If our understanding be fixed faithfully on God; if we seek the things which are well-pleasing and acceptable to Him; if we fulfil the things which are in harmony with His faultless will, and follow the way of truth, casting away from ourselves all iniquity and wickedness, covetousness, strife, malice and fraud, gossiping and evil speaking, hatred of God, pride and arrogance, vainglory and inhospitality.

6 For those who do these things are hateful to God, and "not only those who do them, but also those who take pleasure in them".

7 For the Scripture says: "But to the sinner said God, Wherefore dost thou declare my ordinances, and takest my covenant in thy mouth?

8 Thou hast hated instruction, and cast my words behind thee. If thou sawest a thief thou didst run with him, and thou didst make thy portion with the adulterers. Thy mouth hath multiplied iniquity, and thy tongue did weave deceit. Thou didst sit to speak evil against thy brother, and thou didst lay a stumbling block in the way of thy mother's son.

9 Thou hast done these things and I kept silent; thou didst suppose, O wicked one, that I shall be like unto thee.

10 I will reprove thee and set thyself before thy face.

11 Understand then these things, ye who forget God, lest He seize you as doth a lion, and there be none to deliver.

12 The sacrifice of praise shall glorify me, and therein is a way in which I will show to him the Salvation of God."

XXXVI

1 This is the way, beloved, in which we found our salvation, Jesus Christ, the high priest of our offerings, the defender and helper of our weakness.

2 Through Him we fix our gaze on the heights of Heaven, through Him we see the reflection of His faultless and lofty countenance, through Him the eyes of our hearts were opened, through Him our foolish and darkened understanding blossoms towards the light, through Him the Master willed that we should taste the immortal knowledge, "who, being the brightness of His majesty is by so much greater than angels as He hath inherited a more excellent name".

3 For it is written thus, "who maketh His angels spirits, and His ministers a flame of fire".

4 But of His Son the Master said thus: "Thou art my son: today have I begotten thee. Ask of me, and I will give thee the heathen for thine inheritance, and the ends of the earth for thy possession."

5 And again He says to Him: "Sit thou on my right hand until I make thine enemies a footstool of thy feet."

6 Who then are the enemies? Those who are wicked and oppose His will.

XXXVII

1 Let us then serve in our army, brethren, with all earnestness, following His faultless commands.

2 Let us consider those who serve our generals, with what good order, habitual readiness, and submissiveness they perform their commands.

3 Not all are prefects, nor tribunes, nor centurions, nor in charge of fifty men, or the like, but each carries out in his own rank the commands of the emperor and of the generals.

4 The great cannot exist without the small, nor the small without the great; there is a certain mixture among all, and herein lies the advantage.

5 Let us take our body; the head is nothing without the feet, likewise the feet are nothing without the head; the smallest members of our body are necessary and valuable to the whole body, but all work together and are united in a common subjection to preserve the whole body.

XXXVIII

1 Let, therefore, our whole body be preserved in Christ Jesus, and let each be subject to his neighbour, according to the position granted to him.

2 Let the strong care for the weak and let the weak reverence the strong. Let the rich man bestow help on the poor and let the poor give thanks to God, that He gave him one to supply his needs; let the wise manifest His wisdom not in words but in good deeds; let him who is humble-minded not testify to his own humility, but let him leave it to others to bear him witness; let not him who is pure in the flesh be boastful, knowing that it is another who bestows on him his continence.

3 Let us consider then brethren, of what matter we were formed, who we are, and with what nature we came into the world, and how He who formed and created us brought us into His world from the darkness of a grave, and prepared His benefits for us before we were born.

4 Since therefore we have everything from Him we ought in everything to give Him thanks, to whom be glory for ever and ever. Amen.

XXXIX

1 Foolish, imprudent, silly and uninstructed men mock and deride us, wishing to exalt themselves in their own conceits.

2 For what can mortal man do, or what is the strength of him who is a child of earth?

3 For it is written: "There was no shape before mine eyes, but I heard a sound and a voice."

4 What then? Shall a mortal be pure before the Lord? Or shall a man be blameless in his deeds, seeing that he believeth not in His servants, and hath noted perversity in His angels?

5 Yea, the heaven is not pure before him. Away then, ye who inhabit houses of clay, of which, even of the same clay, we ourselves were made. He smote them as a moth, and from morning until evening they do not endure; they perished without being able to help themselves.

6 He breathed on them and they died because they had no wisdom.

7 But call now, if any shall answer thee, or if thou shalt see any of the holy angels; for wrath destroyeth the foolish, and envy putteth to death him that is in error.

8 I have seen the foolish taking root but their habitation was presently consumed.

9 "Let their sons be far from safety; let them be mocked in the gates of those less than they with none to deliver; for what was prepared for them the righteous shall eat, and they themselves shall not be delivered from evil."

XL

1 Since then these things are manifest to us, and we have looked into the depths of the divine knowledge, we ought to do in order all things which the Master commanded us to perform at appointed times.

2 He commanded us to celebrate sacrifices and services, and that it should not be thoughtlessly or disorderly, but at fixed times and hours.

3 He has Himself fixed by His supreme will the places and persons whom He desires for these celebrations, in order that all things may be done piously according to His good pleasure, and be acceptable to His will.

4 So then those who offer their oblations at the appointed seasons are acceptable and blessed, for they follow the laws of the Master and do no sin.

5 For to the high priest his proper ministrations are allotted, and to the priests the proper place has been appointed, and on Levites their proper services have been imposed. The layman is bound by the ordinances for the laity.

XLI

1 The apostles received the Gospel for us from the Lord Jesus Christ, Jesus the Christ was sent from God.

2 The Christ therefore is from God and the apostles from the Christ. In both ways then, they were in accordance with the appointed order of God's will.

3 Having therefore received their commands, and being fully assured by the

resurrection of our Lord Jesus Christ, and with faith confirmed by the word of God, they went forth in the assurance of the Holy Spirit preaching the good news that the Kingdom of God is coming.

4 They preached from district to district, and from city to city, and they appointed their first converts, testing them by the Spirit, to be bishops and deacons of the future believers.

5 And this was no new method, for many years before had bishops and deacons been written of; for the Scripture says thus in one place: "I will establish their bishops in righteousness, and their deacons in faith."

XLII

1 Let him who has love in Christ perform the commandments of Christ.

2 Who is able to explain the bond of the love of God?

3 Who is sufficient to tell the greatness of its beauty?

4 The height to which love lifts us is not to be expressed.

5 Love unites us to God. "Love covereth a multitude of sins." Love beareth all things, is long-suffering in all things. There is nothing base, nothing haughty in love; love admits no schism, love makes no sedition, love does all things in concord. In love were all the elect of God made perfect. Without love is nothing well pleasing to God.

6 In love did the Master receive us; for the sake of the love which He had towards us did Jesus Christ our Lord give His blood by the will of God for us, and His flesh for our flesh, and His soul for our souls."

XLIII

1 See, beloved, how great and wonderful is love, and that of its perfection there is no expression.

2 Who is able to be found in it save those to whom God grants it? Let us then beg and pray of His mercy that we may be found in love, without human partisanship, free from blame.

3 All the generations from Adam until this day have passed away; but those who were perfected in love by the grace of God have a place among the pious who shall be made manifest at the visitation of the Kingdom of Christ.

4 For it is written: "Enter into thy chambers for a very little while, until my wrath and fury pass away, and I will remember a good day, and will raise you up out of your graves."

5 Blessed are we, beloved, if we perform the commandments of God in the concord of love, that through love our sins may be forgiven.

6 For it is written: "Blessed are they whose iniquities are forgiven, and whose sins are covered; blessed is the man whose sin the Lord will not reckon, and in whose mouth is no guile."

7 This blessing was given to those who have been chosen by God through Jesus Christ our Lord, to whom be the glory for ever and ever. Amen.

XLIV

1 Let us then pray that for our transgressions, and for what we have done through any attacks of the adversary, forgiveness may be granted to us. And those also who were the leaders of sedition and disagreement are bound to consider the common hope.

2 For those who live in fear and love are willing to suffer torture themselves rather than their neighbours, and they suffer the blame of themselves, rather than that of our tradition of noble and righteous harmony.

3 For it is better for man to confess his transgressions than to harden his heart, even as the heart of those was hardened who rebelled against God's servant Moses, and their condemnation was made manifest.

4 For "they went down into Hades alive" and "death shall be their shepherd".

5 Pharaoh and his army and all the rulers of Egypt, "the chariots and their riders", were sunk in the Red Sea, and perished for no other cause than that their foolish hearts were hardened, after signs and wonders had been wrought in the land of Egypt by God's servant Moses.

XLV

1 The Master, brethren, is in need of nothing: He asks nothing of anyone, save that confession be made to Him.

2 For David the chosen says: "I will confess to the Lord, and it shall please Him

more than a young calf that groweth horns and hoofs: let the poor see it and be glad."

3 And again he says: "Sacrifice to God a sacrifice of praise, and pay to the Highest thy vows; and call upon me in the day of thy affliction, and I will deliver thee and thou shalt glorify me.

4 For the sacrifice of God is a broken spirit."

XLVI

1 For you have understanding, you have a good understanding of the sacred Scriptures, beloved, and you have studied the oracles of God. Therefore we write these things to remind you.

2 For when Moses went up into the mountain, and passed forty days and forty nights in fasting and humiliation, God said to him: "Go down hence quickly, for thy people, whom thou didst bring out of the land of Egypt, have committed iniquity; they have quickly gone aside out of the way which thou didst command them; they have made themselves molten images."

3 And the Lord said to him: "I have spoken to thee once and twice, saying, I have seen this people, and behold it is stiff-necked; suffer me to destroy them, and I will wipe out their name from under heaven, and thee will I make into a nation great and wonderful and much more than this."

4 And Moses said: "Not so, Lord; pardon the sin of this people, or blot me also out of the book of the living."

5 O great love! O unsurpassable perfection! The servant is bold with the Lord, he asks forgiveness for the people, or begs that he himself may be blotted out together with them.

XLVII

1 Who then among you is noble, who is compassionate, who is filled with love?

2 Let him cry: "If sedition and strife and divisions have arisen on my account, I will depart, I will go away whithersoever you will, and I will obey the commands of the people; only let the flock of Christ have peace with the presbyters set over it."

3 He who does this will win for himself great glory in Christ, and every place will receive him, for "the earth is the Lord's, and the fullness of it".

4 This has been in the past, and will be in the future, the conduct of those who live without regrets as citizens in the city of God.

XLVIII

1 Let then us also intercede for those who have fallen into any transgression, that meekness and humility be given to them, that they may submit, not to us, but to the will of God; for so will they have fruitful and perfect remembrance before God and the saints, and find compassion.

2 Let us receive correction, which none should take amiss, beloved. The admonition which we make one to another is good and beyond measure helpful, for it unites us to the will of God.

3 For the Holy Word says thus: "With chastisement did the Lord chastise me, and He delivered me not over unto death.

4 For whom the Lord loveth He chasteneth, and scourgeth every son whom He receiveth."

5 "For", he says, "the righteous shall chasten me with mercy, and reprove me, but let not the oil of sinners anoint my head."

6 And again he says: "Blessed is the man whom the Lord did reprove; and reject not thou the admonition of the Almighty, for He maketh to suffer pain and again He restoreth.

7 He wounded, and His hands healed.

8 Six times shall He deliver thee from troubles, and the seventh time evil shall not touch thee.

9 In famine He shall rescue thee from death, and in war He shall free thee from the hand of the sword.

10 And He shall hide thee from the scourge of the tongue, and thou shalt not fear when evils approach.

11 Thou shalt laugh at the unrighteous and wicked, and thou shalt not be afraid of wild beasts.

12 For wild beasts shall be at peace with thee.

13 Then thou shalt know that thy house shall have peace, and the habitation of thy tabernacle shall not fail.

14 And thou shalt know that thy seed shall be many and thy children like the herb of the field.

15 And thou shalt come to the grave like ripened corn that is harvested in its due

season, or like a heap on the threshing-floor which is gathered together at the appointed time."

16 You see, beloved, how great is the protection given to those that are chastened by the Master, for he is a good father and chastens us that we may obtain mercy through His holy chastisement.

XLIX

1 You therefore, who laid the foundation of the sedition, submit to the presbyters, and receive the correction of repentance, bending the knees of your hearts.

2 Learn to be submissive, putting aside the boastful and the haughty self-confidence of your tongue, for it is better for you to be found small but honourable in the flock of Christ, than to be pre-eminent in repute but to be cast out from His hope.

3 For "the excellent wisdom" says thus: "Behold I will bring forth to you the words of my spirit.

4 And I will teach you my speech, since I called and ye did not obey, and I put forth my words and ye did not attend, but made my counsels of no effect, and disobeyed my reproofs; therefore will I also laugh at your ruin, and I will rejoice when destruction cometh upon you, and when sudden confusion overtaketh you and catastrophe cometh as a storm, or when persecution or siege commeth upon you.

5 For it shall come to pass when ye call upon me, I will not hear you. The evil shall seek me and they shall not find me. For they hated wisdom and they chose not the fear of the Lord, neither would they attend to my counsels but mocked my reproofs.

6 Therefore shall they eat the fruits of their own way, and shall be filled with their own wickedness.

7 For because they wronged the innocent they shall be put to death, and inquisition shall destroy the wicked. But he who heareth me shall tabernacle with confidence in his hope, and shall be in rest with no fear of any evil."

L

1 Let us then be obedient to His most holy and glorious name, and escape the threats which have been spoken by wisdom aforetime to the disobedient, that we may tabernacle in confidence on the most sacred name of His majesty.

2 Receive our counsel, and there shall be nothing for you to regret, for as God lives and as the Lord Jesus Christ lives and the Holy Spirit, the faith and hope of the elect, he who with lowliness of mind and eager gentleness has without backsliding performed the decrees and commandments given by God shall be enrolled and chosen in the number of those who are saved through Jesus Christ, through whom is to Him the glory for ever and ever. Amen.

LI

1 But if some be disobedient to the words which have been spoken by Him through us, let them know that they will entangle themselves in transgression and no little danger.

2 But we shall be innocent of this sin, and will pray with eager entreaty and supplication that the Creator of the Universe may guard unhurt the number of His elect that has been numbered in all the world through His beloved Child, Jesus Christ, through whom He called us from darkness to light, from ignorance to the full knowledge of the glory of His name.

3 Grant us to hope on Thy name, the source of all creation, open the eyes of our heart to know Thee, that Thou alone art the highest in the highest and remainest holy among the holy. Thou dost humble the pride of the haughty, Thou dost destroy the imaginings of nations, Thou dost raise up the humble and abase the lofty, Thou makest rich and makest poor, Thou dost slay and make alive, Thou alone art the finder of spirits and art God of all flesh, Thou dost look on the abysses, Thou seest into the works of man, Thou art the helper of those in danger, the saviour of those in despair, the creator and watcher over every spirit; Thou dost multiply nations upon earth and hast chosen out from them all those that love Thee through Jesus Christ Thy beloved Child, and through Him has Thou taught us, made us holy, and brought us to honour.

4 We beseech Thee, Master, to be our "help and succour". Save those of us who are in affliction, have mercy on the lowly, raise the fallen, show Thyself to those in need, heal the sick, turn again the wanderers of Thy people, feed the hungry, ransom our prisoners, raise up the weak, com-

fort the faint-hearted; let all "nations know Thee, that Thou art God alone", and that Jesus Christ is thy Child, and that "we are Thy people and the sheep of Thy pasture."

LII

1 For Thou through Thy operations didst make manifest the eternal fabric of the world; Thou, Lord, didst create the earth. Thou that art faithful in all generations, righteous in judgment, wonderful in strength and majesty, wise in Thy creation, and prudent in establishing Thy works, good in the things which are seen, and gracious among those that trust in Thee, O "merciful and compassionate", forgive us our iniquities and unrighteousness, and transgressions, and shortcomings.

2 Reckon not every sin of Thy servants and handmaids, but cleanse us with the cleansing of Thy truth, and "guide our steps to walk in holiness of heart, to do the things which are good and pleasing before Thee" and before our rulers.

3 Yea, Lord, "make Thy face to shine upon us" in peace "for our good" that we may be sheltered by Thy mighty hand, and delivered from all sin by "Thy uplifted arm", and deliver us from them that hate us wrongfully.

4 Give concord and peace to us and to all that dwell on the earth, as Thou didst give to our fathers who called on Thee in holiness with faith and truth, and grant that we may be obedient to Thy almighty and glorious name, and to our rulers and governors upon the earth.

LIII

1 Thou, Master, hast given the power of sovereignty to them through Thy excellent and inexpressible might, that we may know the glory and honour given to them by Thee, and be subject to them, in nothing resisting Thy will. And to them, Lord, grant health, peace, concord, firmness that they may administer the government which Thou has given them without offence.

2 For Thou, heavenly Master, king of eternity, hast given to the sons of men glory and honour and power over the things which are on the earth; do Thou, O Lord, direct their counsels according to that which is "good and pleasing" before Thee, that they may administer with piety in peace and gentleness the power given to them by Thee, and may find mercy in Thine eyes.

3 O Thou who alone art able to do these things and far better things for us, we praise Thee through Jesus Christ, the high priest and guardian of our souls, through whom be glory and majesty to Thee, both now and for all generations and for ever and ever. Amen.

LIV

1 You will give us joy and gladness, if you are obedient to the things which we have written through the Holy Spirit.

2 And we have sent faithful and prudent men, who have lived among us without blame from youth to old age, and they shall be witnesses between you and us.

3 We have done this that you may know that our whole care has been and is directed to your speedy attainment of peace.

LV

1 Now may God, the all-seeing, and the master of spirits, and the Lord of all flesh, who chose the Lord Jesus Christ, and us through Him for "a peculiar people", give unto every soul that is called after His glorious and holy name, faith, fear, peace, patience and long suffering, self-control, purity, sobriety, that they may be well-pleasing to His name through our high priest and guardian, Jesus Christ, through whom be to Him glory and majesty, might and honour, both now and to all eternity. Amen.

LVI

1 Send back quickly to us our messengers Claudius Ephebus and Valerius Vito and Fortunatus, in peace with gladness, in order that they may report the sooner the peace and concord which we pray for and desire, that we also may the more speedily rejoice in your good order.

2 The grace of our Lord Jesus Christ be with you and with all, in every place, who have been called by God through Him, through whom be to Him glory, honour, power and greatness and eternal dominion, from eternity to eternity. Amen.

The Epistle of Saint IGNATIUS to the Ephesians

Ignatius, who is also called Theophorus, to the Church, worthy of all felicitation, which is at Ephesus in Asia, blessed with greatness by the fullness of God the Father, predestined from eternity for abiding and unchangeable glory, united and chosen through true suffering by the will of the Father and Jesus Christ our God, abundant greeting in Jesus Christ and in blameless joy.

I

1 I became acquainted through God with your much beloved name, which you have obtained by your righteous nature, according to faith and love in Christ Jesus our Saviour. You are imitators of God, and, having kindled your brotherly task by the blood of God, you completed it perfectly.

2 For when you heard that I had been sent a prisoner from Syria for the sake of our common name and hope, in the hope of obtaining by your prayers the privilege of fighting with beasts at Rome, that by so doing I might be enabled to be a true disciple, you hastened to see me.

3 Seeing then that I received in the name of God your whole congregation in the person of Onesimus, a man of inexpressible love and your bishop, I beseech you by Jesus Christ to love him, and all who resemble him. For blessed is He who granted you to be worthy to obtain such a bishop.

II

1 Now concerning my fellow servant, Burrhus, your deacon by the will of God, who is blessed in all things, I beg that he may stay longer, for your honour and for that of the bishop. And Crocus also, who is worthy of God and of you, whom I received as an example of your love, has relieved me in every way, may the Father of Jesus Christ refresh him in like manner, together with Onesimus and Burrhus and Euplus and Fronto, in whose persons I have seen you all in love.

2 May I ever have joy of you, if I be but worthy. It is therefore seemly in every way to glorify Jesus Christ, who has glorified you, that you may be joined together in one subjection, subject to the bishop and to the presbytery, and may in all things be sanctified.

III

1 I do not give you commands as if I were someone great, for though I am a prisoner for the Name, I am not yet perfect in Jesus Christ; for now I do but begin to be a disciple, and I speak to you as to my fellow learners. For I needed to be prepared by you in faith, exhortation, endurance, long suffering.

2 But since love does not suffer me to be silent concerning you, for this reason I have taken it upon me to exhort you that you live in harmony with the will of God. For Jesus Christ, our inseparable life, is the will of the Father, even as the bishops, who have been appointed throughout the world, are the will of Jesus Christ.

IV

1 Therefore it is fitting that you should live in harmony with the will of the bishop, as indeed you do. For your justly famous presbytery, worthy of God, is attuned to the bishop as the strings to a harp. Therefore by your concord and harmonious love Jesus Christ is being sung.

2 Now do each of you join in this choir, that being harmoniously in concord you may receive the key of God in unison, and sing with one voice through Jesus Christ to the Father, that He may both hear you and may recognise, through your good works, that you are members of His Son. It is therefore profitable for you to be in blameless unity, in order that you may always commune with God.

V

1 For if I in a short time gained such fellowship with your bishop as was not human but spiritual, how much more do I count you blessed who are so united with him as the Church is with Jesus Christ, and as Jesus Christ is with the Father, that all things may sound together in unison!

2 Let no man be deceived: unless a man be within the sanctuary he lacks the bread of God, for if the prayer of one or two has such might, how much more has that of the bishop and of the whole Church?

3 So then he who does not join in the common assembly, is already haughty, and has separated himself. For it is written "God resisteth the proud": let us then be

careful not to oppose the bishop, that we may be subject to God.

VI

1 And the more anyone sees that the bishop is silent, the more let him fear him. For every one whom the master of the house sends to do his business ought we to receive as him who sent him. Therefore it is clear that we must regard the bishop as the Lord himself.

2 Indeed Onesimus himself gives great praise to your good order in God, for you all live according to truth, and no heresy dwells among you; nay, you do not even listen to any unless he speak concerning Jesus Christ in truth.

VII

1 For there are some heretical preachers who make a practice of carrying about the Name with wicked guile, and do certain other things unworthy of God; these you must shun as wild beasts, for they are ravening dogs, who bite secretly, and you must be upon your guard against them, for they are scarcely to be cured.

2 There is one Physician, who is both flesh and spirit, born and yet not born, who is God in man, true life in death, both of Mary and of God, first passible and then impassible, Jesus Christ our Lord.

VIII

1 Let none therefore deceive you, and indeed you have not been deceived, but belong wholly to God. For since no strife is fixed among you which might torture you, you do indeed live according to God. I am dedicated and devoted to you Ephesians, and your Church, which is famous to eternity.

2 They who are carnal cannot do spiritual things, neither can they who are spiritual do carnal things, just as faith is incapable of the deeds of infidelity, and infidelity of the deeds of faith. But even what you do according to the flesh is spiritual, for you do all things in Jesus Christ.

IX

1 I have learnt, however, that some from elsewhere have stayed with you, who have evil doctrine; but you did not suffer them to sow it among you, and stopped your ears, so that you might not receive what they sow, seeing that you are as stones of the temple of the Father, made ready for the building of God our Father, carried up to the heights by the engine of Jesus Christ, that is the cross, and using as a rope the Holy Spirit. And your faith is your windlass and love is the road which leads up to God.

2 You are then all fellow travellers, and carry with you God, and the Temple, and Christ, and holiness, and are in all ways adorned by commandments of Jesus Christ. And I share in this joy, for it has been granted to me to speak to you through my writing, and to rejoice with you, that you love nothing, according to human life, but God alone.

X

1 Now for other men "pray unceasingly", for there is in them a hope of repentance, that they may find God. Suffer them therefore to become your disciples, at least through your deeds.

2 Be yourselves gentle in answer to their wrath; be humble-minded in answer to their proud speaking; offer prayer for their blasphemy; be steadfast in the faith for their error; be gentle for their cruelty, and do not seek to retaliate.

3 Let us be proved their brothers by our gentleness and let us be imitators of the Lord, and seek who may suffer the more wrong, be the more destitute, the more despised; that no plant of the devil be found in you but that you may remain in all purity and sobriety in Jesus Christ, both in the flesh and in the Spirit.

XI

1 These are the last times. Therefore let us be modest, let us fear the long suffering of God, that it may not become our judgment. For let us either fear the wrath to come, or love the grace which is present, one of the two, only let us be found in Christ Jesus unto true life.

2 Without Him let nothing seem comely to you, for in Him I carry about my chains, the spiritual pearls in which may it be granted me to rise again through your prayers, which I beg that I may ever share, that I be found in the lot of the Christians of Ephesus, who also were ever of one

mind with the Apostles in the power of Jesus Christ.

XII

1 I know who I am and to whom I write. I am condemned, you have obtained mercy; I am in danger, you are established in safety.

2 You are the passage for those who are being slain for the sake of God, fellow-initiates with Paul, who was sanctified, who gained a good report, who was right blessed, in whose footsteps may I be found when I shall attain to God, who in every Epistle makes mention of you in Christ Jesus.

XIII

1 Seek, then, to come together more frequently to give thanks and glory to God. For when you gather together frequently the powers of Satan are destroyed, and his mischief is brought to nothing, by the concord of your faith.

2 There is nothing better than peace, by which every war in Heaven and on earth is abolished.

XIV

1 None of these things is unknown to you if you possess perfect faith towards Jesus Christ and love, which are the beginning and end of life; for the beginning is faith and the end is love, and when the two are joined together in unity it is God, and all other noble things follow after them.

2 No man who professes faith sins, nor does he hate who has obtained love. "The tree is known by its fruits": so they who profess to be of Christ shall be seen by their deeds. For the "deed" is not in present profession, but is shown by the power of faith, if a man continue to the end.

XV

1 It is better to be silent and be real, than to talk and to be unreal. Teaching is good, if the teacher does what he says. There is then one teacher who "spoke and it came to pass", and what He has done even in silence is worthy of the Father.

2 He who has the word of Jesus for a true possession can also hear His silence, that he may be perfect, that he may act through his speech, and be understood through his silence.

3 Nothing is hid from the Lord, but even our secret things are near Him. Let us therefore do all things as though He were dwelling in us, that we may be His temples, and that He may be our God in us. This indeed is so, and will appear clearly before our face by the love which we justly have for Him.

XVI

1 Do not err, my brethren; they who corrupt families shall not inherit the Kingdom of God.

2 If then those who do this according to the flesh suffer death, how much more if a man corrupt by false teaching the faith of God for the sake of which Jesus Christ was crucified? Such a one shall go in his foulness to the unquenchable fire, as also shall he who listens to him.

XVII

1 For this end did the Lord receive ointment on his head that he might breathe immortality on the Church. Be not anointed with the evil odour of the doctrine of the prince of this world, lest he lead you away captive from the life which is set before you.

2 But why are we not all prudent seeing that we have received knowledge of God, that is, Jesus Christ? Why are we perishing in our folly, ignoring the gift which the Lord has truly sent?

XVIII

1 My spirit is devoted to the cross, which is an offence to unbelievers, but to us salvation and eternal life. "Where is the wise? Where is the disputer?" Where is the boasting of those who are called prudent?

2 For our God, Jesus the Christ, was conceived by Mary by the dispensation of God, "as well of the seed of David" as of the Holy Spirit: he was born, and was baptised, that by himself submitting he might purify the water.

XIX

1 And the virginity of Mary, and her giving birth, were hidden from the prince of this world, as was also the death of the Lord. Three trumpet-tongued secrets which were wrought in the stillness of God.

2 How then was He manifested to the world? A star shone in Heaven beyond all

the stars, and its light was unspeakable, and its newness caused astonishment, and all the other stars, with the sun and moon gathered in chorus round this star, and it far exceeded them all in its light; and there was perplexity, whence came this new thing, so unlike them.

3 By this all magic was dissolved and every bond of wickedness vanished away, ignorance was removed, and the old kingdom was destroyed, for God was manifest as man for the "newness" of eternal life, and that which had been prepared by God received its beginning. Hence all things were disturbed, because the abolition of death was being planned.

XX

1 If Jesus Christ permit me through your prayers, and it be His will, in the second book, which I propose to write to you, I will show you concerning the dispensation of the new man Jesus Christ, which I have begun to discuss, dealing with His faith and His love, His suffering and His resurrection.

2 Especially if the Lord reveal to me that you all severally join in the common meeting in grace from His name, in one faith and in Jesus Christ, "who was of the family of David according to the flesh", the Son of Man and the Son of God, so that you obey the bishop and the presbytery with an undisturbed mind, breaking one bread, which is the medicine of immortality, the antidote that we should not die, but live for ever in Jesus Christ.

XXI

1 May my soul be given for yours, and for them whom you sent in the honour of God to Smyrna, whence I also write to you, thanking the Lord and loving Polycarp as I do also you. Remember me as Jesus Christ also remembers you.

2 Pray for the Church in Syria, whence I am led a prisoner to Rome, being the least of the faithful who are there, even as I was thought worthy to show the honour of God. Farewell in God our Father and in Jesus Christ, our common hope.

The Epistle of Saint IGNATIUS to the Romans

Ignatius, who is also called Theophorus, to her who has obtained mercy in the greatness of the Most High Father, and of Jesus Christ His only Son; to the Church beloved and enlightened by the will of Him who has willed all things which are, according to the love of Jesus Christ, our God, which also has the presidency in the country of the land of the Romans, worthy of God, worthy of honour, worthy of blessing, worthy of praise, worthy of success, worthy in its holiness, and pre-eminent in love, named after Christ, named after the Father, which also I greet in the name of Jesus Christ, the Son of the Father; to those who are united in flesh and spirit in every one of His commandments, filled with the grace of God without wavering, and filtered clear from every foreign stain, abundant greeting in Jesus Christ, our God, in blamelessness.

I

1 For as much as I have gained my prayer to God to see your godly faces, so that I have obtained more than I asked, for in bondage in Christ Jesus I hope to greet you if it be His will that I be found worthy to the end.

2 For the beginning has been well ordered, if I may obtain grace to come unhindered to my lot. For I am afraid of your love, lest even that do me wrong. For it is easy for you to do what you will, but it is difficult for me to attain to God, if you do not spare me.

II

1 For I would not have you "men-pleasers" but "God-pleasers", even as you do indeed please Him. For neither shall I ever have such an opportunity of attaining to God, nor can you, if you be but silent, have any better deed ascribed to you. For if you are silent concerning me, I am a word of God; but if you love my flesh, I shall again be only a cry.

2 Grant me nothing more than that I be poured out to God, while an altar is still ready, that forming yourselves into a

chorus of love you may sing to the Father in Christ Jesus, that God has vouchsafed that the bishop of Syria shall be found at the setting of the sun, having fetched him from the sun's rising. It is good to set the world towards God, that I may rise to Him.

III

1 You never have envied anyone, you taught others. But I desire that those things may stand fast which you enjoin in your instructions.

2 Only pray for me for strength, both inward and outward, that I may not merely speak, but also have the will, that I may not only be called a Christian, but may also be found to be one. For if I be found to be one, I can also be called one, and then be deemed faithful when I no longer am visible in the world.

3 Nothing visible is good, for our God, Jesus Christ, being now in the Father, is the more plainly visible. Christianity is not the work of persuasiveness, but of greatness, when it is hated by the world.

IV

1 I am writing to all the churches, and I give injunctions to all men, that I am dying willingly for God's sake, if you do not hinder it. I beseech you, be not "an unseasonable kindness" to me. Suffer me to be eaten by the beasts, through whom I can attain to God. I am God's wheat, and I am ground by the teeth of wild beasts that I may be found pure bread of Christ.

2 Rather entice the wild beasts that they may become my tomb, and leave no trace of my body, that when I fall asleep I be not burdensome to any. Then shall I be truly a disciple of Jesus Christ, when the world shall not even see my body. Beseech Christ on my behalf, that I may be found a sacrifice through these instruments.

3 I do not order you as did Peter and Paul; they were Apostles I am a convict; they were free, I am even until now a slave. But if I suffer I shall be Jesus Christ's freedman, and in Him I shall rise free. Now I am learning in my bonds to give up all desires.

V

1 From Syria to Rome I am fighting with wild beasts, by land and sea, by night and day, bound to ten "leopards" (that is, a company of soldiers), and they become worse for kind treatment. Now I become the more a disciple for their ill deeds, "but not by this am I justified".

2 I long for the beasts that are prepared for me; and I pray that they may be found prompt for me; I will even entice them to devour me promptly; not as has happened to some whom they have not touched from fear; even if they be unwilling of themselves, I will force them to it.

3 Grant me this favour. I know what is expedient for me; now I am beginning to be a disciple. May nothing of things seen or unseen envy me my attaining to Jesus Christ. Let there come on me fire, and cross, and struggles with wild beasts, cutting, and tearing asunder, rackings of bones, mangling of limbs, crushing of my whole body, cruel tortures of the devil, may I but attain to Jesus Christ!

VI

1 The ends of the earth and the kingdoms of this world shall profit me nothing. It is better for me to die in Christ Jesus than to be king over the ends of the earth. I seek Him who died for our sake. I desire Him who rose for us. The pains of birth are upon me.

2 Suffer me, my brethren; hinder me not from living, do not wish me to die. Do not give to the world one who desires to belong to God, nor deceive him with material things. Suffer me to receive the pure light; when I have come thither I shall become a man.

3 Suffer me to follow the example of the passion of my God. If any man have Him within himself, let him understand what I wish, and let him sympathise with me, knowing the things which constrain me.

VII

1 The prince of this world wishes to tear me in pieces, and to corrupt my mind towards God. Let none of you who are present help him. Be rather on my side, that is on God's. Do not speak of Jesus Christ, and yet desire the world.

2 Let no envy dwell among you. Even though when I come I beseech you myself, do not be persuaded by me, but rather obey this, which I write to you: for in the midst of life I write to you desiring death. My lust has been crucified, and there is in me no fire of love for material things; but

only water living and speaking in me, and saying to me from within: "Come to the Father."

3 I have no pleasure in the food of corruption or in the delights of this life. I desire the "bread of God", which is the flesh of Jesus Christ, who was "of the seed of David", and for drink I desire His blood, which is incorruptible love.

VIII

1 I no longer desire to live after the manner of men, and this shall be, if you desire it. Desire it, in order that you also may be desired.

2 I beg you by this short letter, believe me. And Jesus Christ shall make this plain to you, that I am speaking the truth. He is the mouth which cannot lie, by which the Father has spoken truly.

3 Pray for me that I may attain. I write to you not according to the flesh, but according to the mind of God. If I suffer, it was your favour; if I be rejected, it was your hatred.

IX

1 Remember in your prayers the Church in Syria which has God for its Shepherd in my room. Its bishop shall be Jesus Christ alone, and your love.

2 But for myself I am ashamed to be called one of them, for I am not worthy; for I am the least of them, and "born out of time"; but I have obtained mercy to be someone, if I may attain to God.

3 My spirit greets you, and the love of the Churches which have received me in the Name of Jesus Christ, not as a mere passer-by, for even those which did not lie on my road according to the flesh went before me from city to city.

X

1 Now I am writing these things to you from Smyrna by the blessed Ephesians, and Crocus, a name very dear to me, is also with me, and many others.

2 Concerning those who have preceded me from Syria to Rome to the glory of God, I believe that you have received information; tell them that I am close at hand; for they are all worthy of God and of you, and it is right for you to refresh them in every way.

3 I write this to you on the 24th of August. Farewell unto the end, in the endurance of Jesus Christ.

The Martyrdom of Saint POLYCARP, Bishop of Smyrna

The Church of God in Smyrna, to the Church of God in Philomelium, and to the Holy Catholic Church in every place. "Mercy, peace and love" of God the Father and our Lord Jesus Christ be multiplied.

I

1 We write to you, brethren, the story of the martyrs and of the blessed Polycarp, who put an end to the persecution by his martyrdom as though adding the seal. For one might almost say that all that had gone before happened in order that the Lord might show to us from above a martyrdom in accordance with the Gospel.

2 For he waited to be betrayed as also the Lord had done, that we too might become his imitators, "not thinking of ourselves alone, but also of our neighbours". For it is the mark of true and steadfast love, not to wish that oneself may be saved alone, but all the brethren also.

II

1 Blessed then and noble are all the martyrdoms which took place according to the will of God, for we must be very careful to assign the power over all to God.

2 For who would not admire their nobility and patience and love of their Master? For some were torn by scourging until the mechanism of their flesh was seen even to the lower veins and arteries, and they endured so that even the bystanders pitied them and mourned. And some even reached such a pitch of nobility that they neither groaned nor wailed, showing to all of us that at that hour of their torture the noble martyrs of Christ were absent from the flesh, or rather that the Lord was standing by and talking with them.

3 And paying heed to the grace of Christ they despised wordly tortures, by a single hour purchasing everlasting life.

And the fire of their cruel torturers had no heat for them. For they set before their eyes an escape from the fire which is everlasting and is never quenched. And with the eyes of their heart they looked up to the good things which are preserved for those who have endured, "which neither ear hath heard nor hath eye seen, nor hath it entered into the heart of man", but it was shown by the Lord to them who were no longer men but already angels.

4 And in the same way also those who were condemned to the beasts endured terrible torments, being stretched on sharp shells and buffeted with other kinds of terrible torments, that if it were possible the tyrant might bring them to a denial by continuous torture. For the devil used many wiles against them.

III

1 But thanks be to God, for he had no power over any. For the most noble Germanicus encouraged their fears by the endurance which was in him, and he fought gloriously with the wild beasts. For when the pro-consul wished to persuade him and bade him have pity on his youth, he violently dragged the beast towards himself, wishing to be released more quickly from their unrighteous and lawless life.

2 So after this all the crowd, wondering at the nobility of the God-loving and God-fearing people of the Christians, cried out: "Away with the atheists; let Polycarp be searched for."

IV

1 But one, named Quintus, a Phyrgian lately come from Phrygia, when he saw the wild beasts played the coward. Now it was he who had forced himself and some others to come forward of their own accord. Him the pro-consul persuaded with many entreaties to take the oath and offer sacrifice. For this reason, therefore, brethren, we do not commend those who give themselves up, since the gospel does not give this teaching.

V

1 But the most wonderful Polycarp, when he first heard it, was not disturbed, but wished to remain in the city; but the majority persuaded him to go away quietly, and he went out quietly to a farm, not far distant from the city, and stayed with a few friends, doing nothing but pray night and day for all, and for the churches throughout the world, as was his custom.

2 And while he was praying he fell into a trance three days before he was arrested, and saw the pillow under his head burning with fire, and he turned and said to those who were with him: "I must be burnt alive."

VI

1 And when the searching for him persisted he went to another farm; and those who were searching for him came up at once, and when they did not find him, they arrested young slaves, and one of them confessed under torture.

2 For it was indeed impossible for him to remain hidden, since those who betrayed him were of his own house, and the police captain who had been allotted the very name, being called Herod, hastened to bring him to the arena that he might fulfil his appointed lot by becoming a partaker of Christ, while they who betrayed him should undergo the same punishment as Judas.

VII

1 Taking the slave then police and cavalry went out on Friday about supper-time, with their usual arms, as if they were advancing against a robber. And late in the evening they came up together against him and found him lying in an upper room. And he might have departed to another place, but would not, saying: "The will of God be done."

2 So when he heard that they had arrived he went down and talked with them, while those who were present wondered at his age and courage, and whether there was so much haste for the arrest of an old man of such a kind. Therefore he ordered food and drink to be set before them at that hour, whatever they should wish, and he asked them to give him an hour to pray without hindrance.

3 To this they assented, and he stood and prayed, thus filled with the grace of God, so that for two hours he could not be silent, and those who listened wre astounded, and many repented that they had come against such a venerable old man.

VIII

1 Now when he had at last finished his prayer, after remembering all who had ever come his way, both small and great, high and low, and the whole Catholic Church throughout the world, the hour came for departure, and they set him on an ass, and led him into the city, on a "great Sabbath day".

2 And the police captain Herod and his father Niketas met him and removed him into their carriage, and sat by his side trying to persuade him and saying: "But what harm is it to say 'Lord Caesar' and to offer sacrifice, and so forth, and to be saved?" But he at first did not answer them, but when they continued he said: "I am not going to do what you counsel me."

3 And they gave up the attempt to persuade him, and began to speak fiercely to him, and turned him out in such a hurry that in getting down from the carriage he scraped his shin; and without turning round, as though he had suffered nothing, he walked on promptly and quickly, and was taken to the arena, while the uproar in the arena was so great that no one could even be heard.

IX

1 Now when Polycarp entered into the arena there came a voice from Heaven: "Be strong, Polycarp, and play the man." And no one saw the speaker, but our friends who were there heard the voice. And next he was brought forward, and there was a great uproar of those who heard that Polycarp had been arrested.

2 Therefore when he was brought forward the pro-consul asked him if he were Polycarp, and when he admitted it he tried to persuade him to deny, saying, "respect your age", and so forth, as they are accustomed to say: "Swear by the genius of Caesar, repent, say 'Away with the atheists'." But Polycarp, with a stern countenance, looked on all the crowd of lawless heathen in the arena, and waving his hand at them, he groaned and looked up to Heaven and said: "Away with the atheists."

3 But when the pro-consul pressed him and said, "Take the oath and I let you go, revile Christ", Polycard said, "For eighty and six years have I been His servant, and He has done me no wrong, and how can I blaspheme my King who saved me?"

X

1 But when he persisted again, and said, "Swear by the genius of Caesar", he answered him, "If you vainly suppose that I will swear by the genius of Caesar, as you say, and pretend that you are ignorant who I am, listen plainly: I am a Christian. And if you wish to learn the doctrine of Christianity fix a day and listen."

2 The pro-consul said: "Persuade the people." And Polycarp said: "You I should have held worthy of discussion, for we have been taught to render honour, as is meet, if it hurt us not, to princes and authorities appointed by God. But as for those, I do not count them worthy that a defence should be made to them."

XI

1 And the pro-consul said: "I have wild beasts. I will deliver you to them, unless you repent." And he said: "Call for them, for repentance from better to worse is not allowed us; but it is good to change from evil to righteousness."

2 And he said again to him: "I will cause you to be consumed by fire, if you despise the beasts, unless you repent." But Polycarp said: "You threaten with the fire that burns for a time and is quickly quenched, for you do not know the fire which awaits the wicked in the judgment to come and in everlasting punishment. But why are you waiting? Come, do what you will."

XII

1 And with these and many other words he was filled with courage and joy, and his face was full of grace so that it not only did not fall with trouble at the things said to him, but the pro-consul, on the other hand, was astounded and sent his herald into the midst of the arena to announce three times: "Polycarp has confessed that he is a Christian."

2 When this had been said by the herald, all the multitude of heathen and Jews living in Smyrna cried out with uncontrollable wrath and a loud shout: "This is the teacher of Asia, the father of the Christians, the destroyer of our gods, who teaches many neither to offer sacrifice

nor to worship." And when they said this, they cried out and asked Philip the Asiarch to let loose a lion on Polycarp. But he said he could not legally do this, since he had closed the sports.

3 Then they found it good to cry out with one mind that he should burn Polycarp alive, for the vision which had appeared to him on his pillow must be fulfilled, when he saw it burning while he was praying, and he turned and said prophetically to those of the faithful who were with him, "I must be burnt alive."

XIII

1 These things then happened with great speed, quicker than it takes to tell, and the crowd came together immediately, and prepared wood and faggots from the workshops and baths and the Jews were extremely zealous, as is their custom, in assisting at this.

2 Now when the fire was ready he put off all his clothes, and loosened his girdle and tried also to take off his shoes, though he did not do this before, because each of the faithful was always zealous which of them might the more quickly touch his flesh. For he had been treated with all respect because of his noble life, even before his martyrdom.

3 Immediately, therefore, he was fastened to the instruments which had been prepared for the fire, but when they were going to nail him as well he said: "Leave me thus, for He who gives me power to endure the fire will grant me to remain in the flames unmoved even without the security you will give by the nails."

XIV

1 So they did not nail him but bound him, and he put his hands behind him and he was bound, as a noble ram out of a great flock, for an oblation; a whole burnt offering made ready and acceptable to God. And he looked up to Heaven and said: "O Lord God Almighty, Father of Thy beloved and blessed Child, Jesus Christ, through whom we have received full knowledge of Thee, the God of angels and powers, and of all creation and of the whole family of the righteous who live before Thee!

2 I bless Thee, that Thou hast granted me this day and hour that I may share, among the number of the martyrs, in the cup of Thy Christ, for the resurrection to everlasting life both of soul and body in the immortality of the Holy Spirit. And may I today be received among them before Thee as a rich and acceptable sacrifice, as Thou, the God who lies not and is truth, hast prepared beforehand, and shown forth, and fulfilled.

3 For this reason I also praise Thee for all things. I bless Thee. I glorify Thee through the everlasting and heavenly high priest, Jesus Christ, Thy beloved Child, through whom be glory to Thee with Him and the Holy Spirit, both now and for the ages that are to come. Amen."

XV

1 Now when he had uttered his Amen and finished his prayer, the men in charge of the fire lit it, and a great flame blazed up and we, to whom it was given to see, saw a marvel. And we have been preserved to report to others what befell.

2 For the fire made the likeness of a room, like the sail of a vessel filled with wind, and surrounded the body of the martyr as with a wall, and he was within it not as burning flesh, but as bread that is being baked or as gold and silver being refined in a furnace. And we perceived such a fragrant smell as the scent of incense or other costly spices.

XVI

1 At length the lawless men, seeing that his body could not be consumed by the fire, commanded an executioner to go up and stab him with a dagger. When he did this, there came out a dove, and much blood, so that the fire was quenched and all the crowd marvelled that there was such a difference between the unbelievers and the elect.

2 And of the elect was he indeed one, the wonderful martyr Polycarp who in our days was an apostolic and prophetic teacher, bishop of the Catholic Church in Smyrna. For every word which he uttered from his mouth both was fulfilled and will be fulfilled.

XVII

1 But the jealous and envious evil one who resists the family of the righteous, when he saw the greatness of his martyr-

dom and his blameless career from the beginning, and that he was crowned with the crown of immortality and had carried off the unspeakable prize, took care that not even his poor body should be taken away by us, though many desired to do so, and to have fellowship with his holy flesh.

2 Therefore he put forward Niketas, the father of Herod and the brother of Alce, to ask the Governor not to give his body, "Lest", he said, "they leave the crucified one and begin to worship this man." And they said this owing to the suggestions and pressure of the Jews, who also watched when we were going to take it from the fire. For they do not know that we shall not ever be able either to abandon Christ, who suffered for the salvation of those who are being saved in the whole world, the innocent for sinners; or to worship any other.

3 For him we worship as the Son of God, but the martyrs we love as disciples and imitators of the Lord; and rightly, because of their unsurpassable affection toward their own king and teacher. God grant that we too may be their companions and fellow-disciples.

XVIII

1 When therefore the centurion saw the contentiousness caused by the Jews, he put the body in the midst and burnt it.

2 Thus we, at last, took up his bones, more precious than precious stones and finer than gold, and put them where it was meet.

3 There the Lord will permit us to come together according to our power in gladness and joy and celebrate the birthday of his martyrdom, both in memory of those who have already contested and for the practice and training of those whose fate it shall be.

XIX

1 Such was the lot of the blessed Polycarp who though he was, together with those from Philadelphia, the twelfth martyr in Smyrna, is alone especially remembered by all so that he is spoken of in every place, even by the heathen. He was not only a famous teacher, but also a notable martyr, whose martyrdom all desire to imitate, for it followed the gospel of Christ.

2 By his endurance he overcame the unrighteous ruler, and thus gained the crown of immortality. He is glorifying God and the Almighty Father, rejoicing with the apostles and all the righteous, and he is blessing our Lord Jesus Christ, the Saviour of our souls and Governor of our bodies, and the Shepherd of the Catholic Church throughout the world.

XX

To Him who is able to bring us all in His grace and bounty to His heavenly kingdom, by His only begotten Child, Jesus Christ, be glory, honour, might and majesty for ever. Greet all the saints. Those who are with us, and Evarestus who wrote the letter, with his whole house, greet you.

The Passion of Saints PERPETUA and Felicity

If ancient examples of faith which both testify to God's grace and tend to man's edification are collected in writing, so that by the perusal of them, as if by the reproduction of the facts, God may be honoured and man may be strengthened, why should not new instances be also collected, that shall be equally suitable for both purposes, if only on the ground that these modern examples will one day become ancient and available for posterity?

But some things of later date must be esteemed of more account, as being nearer to the very last times, in accordance with the exuberance of grace manifested to the final periods determined for the world. For "in the last days, saith the Lord, I will pour out my Spirit upon all flesh; and their sons and their daughters shall prophesy. And upon my servants and my handmaidens will I pour my Spirit; and your young men shall see visions, and your old men shall dream dreams."

I

1 The young catechumens Revocatus and his fellow-servant Felicity, Saturninus and Secundulus were apprehended. Among them also was Vivia Perpetua, respectably born, liberally educated, a mar-

ried matron, having a father and mother and two brothers, one of whom like herself was a catechumen, and an infant son at the breast. She herself was about twenty-two years of age. From this point onward she shall herself narrate the whole course of her martyrdom, as she left it described by her own hand and with her own mind.

2 "While", says she, "we were still with the persecutors, and my father, for the sake of his affection for me, was persisting in seeking to turn me away and to cast me down from the faith, 'Father', said I, 'do you see, let us say, this vessel lying here to be a little pitcher, or something else?' And he said, 'I see it to be so.' And I replied to him, 'Can it be called by any other name than what it is?' And he said 'No.' 'Neither can I call myself anything else than what I am, a Christian.' Then my father, provoked at this saying, threw himself upon me as if he would tear my eyes out. But he only distressed me, and went away overcome by the devil's arguments.

"Then, becaue I was without my father for a few days, I gave thanks to the Lord; and his absence became a source of consolation to me. In that same interval we were baptised, and the Spirit told me in the water of baptism nothing else was to be prayed for than bodily endurance. After a few days we were taken into the dungeon, and I was very much afraid because I had never felt such darkness. O terrible day! O the fierce heat because of the pressing of the crowds! I was very unusually distressed by my anxiety for my infant. There were present there Tertius and Pomponius, the blessed deacons who ministered to us and had arranged by means of a gratuity that we might be refreshed by being sent out for a few hours into a pleasanter part of the prison. Then going out of the dungeon, I suckled my child, which was now enfeebled with hunger.

"In my anxiety for it, I addressed my mother and comforted my brother, and commended to their care my son. I was languishing because I had seen them languishing on my account. Such solicitude I suffered for many days, and I obtained leave for my infant to remain in the dungeon with me. Forthwith I grew strong, and was relieved from distress and anxiety about my infant; and the dungeon became to me as it were a palace, so that I preferred being there to being elsewhere.

3 "Then my brother said to me, 'My dear sister, you are already in a position of great dignity, and are such that you may ask for a vision and that it may be made known to you whether this trial is to result in a passion or an escape.' And I, who knew that I was privileged to converse with the Lord, whose kindnesses I had found to be so great, boldly promised him, and said, 'Tomorrow I will tell you.' And I asked, and this was what was shown me.

"I saw a golden ladder of marvellous height, reaching up even to Heaven, and very narrow, so that persons could only ascend it one by one; and on the sides of the ladder was fixed every kind of iron weapon. There were swords, lances, hooks, daggers; so that if any one went up carelessly, or not looking upwards, he would be torn to pieces and his flesh would cleave to the iron weapons. And under the ladder itself was crouching a dragon of wonderful size, who lay in wait for those who ascended and frightened them from the ascent. And Saturus went up first, who had subsequently delivered himself up freely on our account, not having been present at the time that we were taken prisoner. He attained the top of the ladder and turned towards me, and said, 'Perpetua, I am waiting for you; but be careful that the dragon does not bite you.' And I said, 'In the name of the Lord Jesus Christ, he shall not hurt me.' And from under the ladder itself, as if in fear of me, he slowly lifted up his head; and as I trod upon the first step, I trod upon his head.

"I went up, and I saw an immense extent of garden, and in the midst of the garden a white-haired man sitting in the dress of a shepherd of large stature milking sheep; and standing around were many thousand white-robed ones. And he raised his head and looked upon me and said to me, 'Thou art welcome, daughter.' And he called me and from the cheese as he was milking he gave me as it were a little cake, and I received it with folded hands, and I ate it, and all who stood around said Amen. And at the sound of their voices I was awakened, still tasting a sweetness which I cannot describe. I immediately related this to my brother, and we understood that it was to be a passion, and we ceased henceforth to have any hope in this world.

II

1 "After a few days there came a report that we should be tried. Then my father came to me from the city, worn out with anxiety. He came up to me that he might cast me down, saying, 'Have pity, my daughter, on my grey hairs. Have pity on your father, if I am worthy to be called a father by you. If with these hands I have brought you up to this flower of your age, if I have preferred you to all your brothers, do not deliver me up to the scorn of men. Have regard to your brothers, have regard to your mother and your aunt, have regard to your son, who will not be able to live after you. Lay aside your courage, and do not bring us all to destruction; for none of us will speak in freedom if you should suffer anything.' These things said my father in his affection, kissing my hands and throwing himself at my feet; and with tears he called me not daughter, but lady. And I grieved over the grey hairs of my father, that he alone of all my family would not rejoice over my passion. I comforted him, saying, 'On that scaffold whatever God wills shall happen. For know that we are not placed in our power, but in that of God.' And he departed from me in sorrow.

2 "Another day, while we were at dinner, we were suddenly taken away to be heard, and we arrived at the town hall. At once the rumour spread through the neighbourhood of the public place, and an immense number of people were gathered together. We mounted the platform. The rest were interrogated and confessed. Then they came to me and my father immediately appeared with my boy, and withdrew me from the step, and said in a supplicating tone, 'Have pity on your babe.' Hilarianus the procurator, who had just received the power of life and death in the place of the pro-consul Minucius Timinianus said, 'Spare the grey hairs of your father, spare the infancy of your boy, offer sacrifice for the well-being of the emperors.' And I replied, 'I will not do so.' Hilarianus said, 'Are you a Christian?' And I replied, 'I am a Christian.' And as my father stood there to cast me down from the faith, he was ordered by Hilarianus to be seized and was beaten with rods. My father's misfortune grieved me as if I myself had been beaten, I so grieved for his wretched old age. The procurator then delivered judgment on all of us and condemned us to the wild beasts, and we went down cheerfully to the dungeon. Then, because my child had been used to receive suck from me and to stay with me in the prison, I sent Pomponius the deacon to my father to ask for the infant, but my father would not give it him. And even as God willed it, the child no longer desired the breast, lest I should be tormented by care for my babe.

3 "After a few days whilst we were all praying, on a sudden, in the middle of our prayer, I called out a word and named Dinocrates; and I was amazed that that name had never come into my mind until then, and I was grieved as I remembered his fate. And immediately I knew myself to be worthy, and to be called on to pray on his behalf. For him I began earnestly to make supplication, and to cry with groaning to the Lord. Without delay on that very night this was shown to me in a vision. I saw Dinocrates going out from a gloomy place, where also there were several others, and he was parched and very thirsty, with a filthy countenance and pallid colour, and the wound on his face which he had when he died. (This Dinocrates had been my brother, who, seven years of age, died miserably with disease, his face being so eaten out with cancer that his death caused repugnance to all men.) For him I had made my prayer, and between him and me there was a large chasm, so that neither of us could approach the other. Moreover, in the same place where Dinocrates was there was a pool full of water, having its brink higher than was the stature of the boy, and Dinocrates raised himself up as if to drink. I was grieved that although that pool held water still, on account of the height of its brink, he could not drink. I awoke and knew that my brother was in suffering, but I trusted that my prayer would bring help to his suffering; and I prayed for him every day until we passed over into the prison of the camp, for we were to fight in the camp-show. Then I made my prayer for my brother day and night, groaning and weeping that he might be helped.

4 "Then on the day before the fight this was shown to me: I saw that that place

which I had formerly observed to be in gloom was now bright; and Dinocrates, with a clean body well clad, was finding refreshment. And where there had been a wound, I saw a scar; and that pool which I had before seen, I saw now with its margin lowered even to the boy's navel and upon its brink was a goblet filled with water; and Dinocrates drew near and began to drink from it. When he was satisfied, he went away from the water to play joyously after the manner of children, and I awoke. Then I understood that he was translated from the place of punishment.

III

1 "Again, after a few days, Pudens, a soldier, an assistant overseer of the prison, who began to regard us in great esteem, perceiving that the great power of God was in us, admitted many brethren to see us, so that both we and they might be mutually refreshed. When the day of the exhibition drew near my father, worn out with suffering, came in to me and began to tear out his beard and to throw himself on the earth and to cast himself down on his face, and reproach his years, and to utter such words as might move all creation. I grieved for his unhappy old age.

2 "The day before that on which we were to fight I saw in a vision that Pomponius the deacon came hither to the gate of the prison and knocked vehemently. I went out to him, and opened the gate for him; he was clothed in a richly ornamented white robe. And he said to me, 'Perpetua, we are waiting for you, come!' And he held his hand out to me, and we began to go through rough and winding places. At last we arrived breathless at the amphitheatre, where he led me into the middle of the arena, and said to me, 'Do not fear, I am here with you, and I am labouring with you', and he departed. I gazed upon an immense assembly in astonishment, because I knew that I was to be given to the wild beasts, I marvelled that the wild beasts were not let loose upon me. Then there came forth against me a certain Egyptian, horrible in appearance, with his helpers to fight with me. And there came to me, as my helpers and encouragers, handsome youths; and I was stripped and became a man. Then my helpers began to rub me with oil, as is the custom for contest, and I beheld that Egyptian on the other hand rolling in the dust. And a certain man came forth, of wondrous height, so that he even overtopped the top of the amphitheatre. He wore a loose tunic and a purple robe between two bands over the middle of the breast, and he carried a rod as if he were a trainer of gladiators, and a green branch upon which were apples of gold. He called for silence and said, 'This Egyptian if he should overcome this woman shall kill her with the sword; and if she shall conquer him, she shall receive this branch.' Then he departed. And we drew near to one another, and began to deal out blows. He sought to lay hold of my feet, while I struck at his face with my heels; and I was lifted up in the air, and began thus to kick at him as if spurning the earth. But when I saw that there was some delay, I joined my hands so as to twine my fingers with one another, and I took hold upon his head, and he fell on his face, and I trod upon his head. And the people began to shout, and my backers to exult. And I drew near to the trainer and took the branch; and he kissed me, and said to me, 'Daughter, peace be with you,' and I began to go gloriously to the Gate of Life. Then I awoke and perceived that I was not to fight with beasts, but against the devil. Still I knew that the victory was awaiting me. This, so far, I have completed several days before the exhibition but what passed at the exhibition itself let who will write."

IV

1 Moreover, also, the blessed Saturus related this his vision, which he himself committed to writing: "We had suffered," said he, "and we were beginning to be borne by four angels into the east; and their hands touched us not. And we floated as if ascending a gentle slope. Being set free, we at length saw the first boundless light; and I said, 'Perpetua' (for she was at my side), 'this is what the Lord promised to us; we have received the promise.' And while we were borne by those same four angels, there appeared to us a vast space which was like a pleasure garden, having rose trees and every kind of flower. And the height of the trees was after the measure of a cypress, and their leaves were falling incessantly. Moreover, there in the pleasure garden four other angels appeared,

brighter than the previous ones, who, when they saw us, gave us honour, and said to the rest of the angels, 'Here they are! Here they are!' with admiration. And those four angels who bore us, being greatly afraid, put us down; and there we found Jocundus, Saturninus and Artaxius who, having suffered the same persecution, were burnt alive; and Quintus who, himself a martyr, had departed this life in the prison. And we asked of them where the rest were. And the angels said to us, 'Come first, enter and greet your Lord.'

2 "And we came near to a place, the walls of which were such as if they were built of light; and before the gate of that place stood four angels, who clothed those who entered with white robes. And being clothed, we entered and saw the boundless light, and heard the united voice of some who said without ceasing, 'Holy! Holy! Holy!' And in the midst of that place we saw as it were a hoary man sitting, having snow-white hair and with a youthful countenance. And on his right hand and on his left were four-and-twenty elders, and behind them a great many others were standing. We entered with great wonder, and stood before the throne; and the four angels raised us up, and we kissed Him, and He passed His hand over our face. And the rest of the elders said to us, 'Let us stand,' and we stood and made peace. And the elders said to us, 'Go and play.' And I said, 'Perpetua, you have what you wish.' And she said to me, 'Thanks be to God, that joyous as I was in the flesh, I am now more joyous here.'

3 "And we went forth, and saw before the entrance Optatus the bishop at the right hand, and Aspasius the presbyter, a teacher, at the left hand, separate and sad. They cast themselves at our feet and said to us, 'Restore peace between us, because you have gone forth and have left us thus.' And we said to them, 'Art not thou our father, and thou our presbyter, that you should cast yourselves at our feet?' And we prostrated ourselves, and we embraced them. Perpetua began to speak with them, and we drew them apart in the pleasure garden under a rose tree. And while we were speaking with them the angels said unto them, 'Let them alone, that they may refresh themselves; and if you have any dissensions between you, forgive one another,' and they drove them away. And in that place we began to recognise many brethren and moreover martyrs. We were all nourished with an indescribable odour which satisfied us. Then I joyously awoke."

V

1 The above were the more eminent visions of the blessed martyrs Saturus and Perpetua themselves, which they themselves committed to writing.

2 But respecting Felicity: when she had already gone eight months with child (for she had been pregnant when she was apprehended), as the day of the exhibition was drawing near she was in great grief lest on account of her pregnancy she should be delayed, because pregnant women are not allowed to be publicly punished, and lest she should shed her sacred and guiltless blood among some who had been wicked subsequently. Moreover, also, her fellow-martyrs were painfully saddened lest they should leave alone so excellent a friend, and as it were companion, in the path of the same hope. Therefore, joining together their united cry, they poured forth their prayer to the Lord three days before the exhibition. Immediately after their prayer her pains came upon her; and when, with the difficulty natural to an eight months' delivery, in the labour of bringing forth she was sorrowing, one of the prison servants said to her, "You who are in such suffering now, what will you do when you are thrown to the beasts, which you despised when you refused to sacrifice to the gods?" And she replied: "Now it is I that suffer what I suffer; but then there will be another in me, who will suffer for me, because I also am about to suffer for Him." Thus she brought forth a little girl, which a certain sister brought up as her daughter.

3 Since then the Holy Spirit permitted, and by permitting willed, that the order of the games should be committed to writing, although we are unworthy to complete the description of so great a glory; yet we obey as it were the command of the most blessed Perpetua, nay, her sacred trust, and add one more testimony concerning her constancy and her loftiness of mind. When they were being treated with more severity by the tribune because, from the slanders of certain deceitful men, he feared lest they

should be withdrawn from the prison by some sort of magic incantations, Perpetua answered to his face and said, "Why do you not at least permit us to be refreshed, being as we are objectionable to the most noble Caesar, and having to fight on his birthday? Or is it not to your glory if we are brought forward fatter on that occasion?" The tribune shuddered and blushed, and commanded that they should be kept with more humanity, so that permission was given to their brethren and others to go in and be refreshed with them.

4 Moreover, on the day before, when in that last meal which they call the free meal they were partaking as far as they could, not of a free supper, but of the love supper; with the same firmness they were uttering such words as these to the prison warders, bearing witness to the felicity of their passion; while Saturus said, "To-morrow is not enough for you, for you to behold with pleasure that which you hate. Friends to-day, enemies to-morrow. Yet note our faces diligently, that you may recognise them on that day of judgment." Thus all departed thence astonished, and from these things many believed.

VI

1 The day of their victory shone forth, and they proceeded from the prison into the amphitheatre as if to an assembly, joyous and of brilliant countenances; if perchance shrinking it was with joy, and not with fear. Perpetua followed with placid look, and with step and gait as a matron of Christ, beloved of God, casting down the lustre of her eyes from the gaze of all. Moreover, Felicity was there, rejoicing that she had safely given birth, so that she might fight with the wild beasts; from the blood of the midwife to the blood of the gladiator, to wash after childbirth with a second baptism. And when they were brought to the gate, and were being constrained to put on the clothing, the men that of the priests of Saturn and the women that of those who were consecrated to Ceres, that noble-minded woman resisted even to the end with constancy. For she said, "We have come thus far of our own accord that our liberty might not be restrained. For this reason we have yielded our minds, that we might not do any such thing as this; we have agreed on this with you." Injustice acknowledged the justice; the tribune yielded to their being brought as simply as they were. Perpetua sang psalms, already treading under foot the head of the Egyptian; Revocatus, Saturninus and Saturus uttered threatenings against the gazing people. When they came within sight of Hilarianus, by gesture and nod, they began to say to Hilarianus, "Thou judgest us but God will judge thee." At this the people, exasperated, demanded that they should be tormented with scourges as they passed along the rank of the gladiators. And they indeed rejoiced that they should have experienced something of their Lord's passion.

2 But He who had said, "Ask, and ye shall receive", gave to them when they asked that death which each one had wished for. For when at any time they had been discoursing among themselves about their wish in respect of their martyrdom, Saturninus indeed had professed that he wished that he might be thrown to all the beasts; doubtless that he might wear a more glorious crown. Therefore in the beginning of the exhibition, he and Revocatus confronted the leopard and later they were harassed by the bear. When a wild boar was supplied, it was the huntsman who had supplied the boar who was gored by that same beast and died the day after the shows. Saturus was bound on the floor near to a bear but the bear would not come forth from his den. And so Saturus for the second time was recalled unhurt.

3 Moreover, for the young women the devil prepared a very fierce cow, mocking their sex in that of the beasts. And so, stripped and clothed with nets, they were led forth. The populace shuddered as they saw one young woman of delicate frame and another with breasts still dropping from her recent childbirth. So, being recalled, they were unbound. Perpetua was first led in. She was tossed and fell on her loins; when she saw her tunic torn from her side, she drew it over her as a veil for her middle, rather mindful of her modesty than her suffering. Then she was called for again and bound up her dishevelled hair; for it was not becoming for a martyr to suffer with dishevelled hair lest she should appear to be mourning in her glory. So she rose up and when she saw Felicity crushed, she approached and gave her her

hand and lifted her up. And both of them stood together; and the brutality of the populace being appeased, they were recalled to the Sanavivarian gate.

Then Perpetua was received by a certain one who was still a catechumen, Rusticus by name, who kept close to her; and she, as if aroused from sleep, so deeply had she been in the Spirit and in an ecstasy, began to look round her and to say to the amazement of all, "When are we to be led out to that cow?" And when she had heard what had already happened she did not believe it until she had perceived certain signs of injury in her body and in her dress. Afterwards, causing that catechumen and her brother to approach, she addressed them, saying, "Stand fast in the faith, and love one another, all of you, and be not offended at my sufferings."

4 The same Saturus at the other entrance exhorted the soldier Pudens, saying, "Assuredly here I am, as I have promised and foretold, for up to this moment I have been wounded by no beast. And now believe with your whole heart. Lo, I am going forth to that beast, and I shall be destroyed with one bite of the leopard." And immediately at the conclusion of the exhibition he was thrown to the leopard and with one bite he was bathed with such a quantity of blood that the people shouted out to him in mockery as he was returning the testimony of his second baptism, "Saved and washed, saved and washed." Manifestly he was assuredly saved who had been glorified in such a spectacle. Then to the soldier Pudens he said, "Farewell, and be mindful of my faith; and let not these things disturb, but confirm you." And at the same time he asked for a little ring from his finger, and returned it to him bathed in his wound, leaving to him an inherited token and the memory of his blood. And then lifeless he was cast down with the rest, to be slaughtered in the usual place. And when the populace called for them to be led back into the middle of the arena, that as the sword penetrated into their body they might make their eyes partners in the murder, they rose up of their own accord and transferred themselves whither the people wished; but they first kissed one another, that they might consummate their martyrdom with the kiss of peace. The rest indeed, immoveable and in silence, received the sword-thrust; much more Saturus, who also had first ascended the ladder and first gave up his spirit, for he also was waiting for Perpetua. But Perpetua, that she might taste some pain being pierced between the ribs, cried out loudly, and she herself placed the wavering right hand of the youthful gladiator to her throat. Possibly such a woman could not have been slain unless she herself had willed it, because she was feared by the impure spirit.

O most brave and blessed martyrs! O truly called and chosen unto the glory of our Lord Jesus Christ! Whom whoever magnifies, and honours, and adores, assuredly ought to read these examples for the edification of the Church, not less than the ancient ones, so that new virtues also may testify that one and the same Holy Spirit is always operating even until now, and God the Father Omnipotent, and His Son Jesus Christ our Lord, whose is the glory and infinite power for ever and ever. Amen.

The SANCTUS

Holy, holy, holy, Lord God of hosts,
Heaven and earth are full of Thy glory:
Glory be to Thee, O Lord most High.
Amen.

The Odes of SOLOMON

I

Behold! the Lord is our mirror.
Open the eyes and see them in Him.
And learn the manner of your face,
And sing out praises to His spirit.
And wipe off the filth from your face,
And love His holiness,
And clothe yourselves with it.
And you will be blameless at all times
before Him.
Hallelujah.

II

A cup of milk was offered to me,
And I drank it in the sweetness of the delight of the Lord.
The Son is the cup,
And He who was milked is the Father.
And the Holy Spirit milked Him,
Because His breasts were full.
And it was necessary for Him that
His milk should be released.
And the Holy Spirit opened His bosom
And mingled the milk from the two breasts of the Father.
And gave the mixture to the world without their knowing.
And they who receive in its fullness are the ones on the right hand.
The Spirit opened the womb of the Virgin and she received
conception and brought forth;
And the Virgin became a Mother with many mercies.
And she travailed and brought forth a Son, without incurring pain.
And she brought Him forth openly,
And acquired Him with great dignity,
And loved Him in His swaddling clothes,
And guarded Him kindly,
And showed Him in majesty.
Hallelujah.

III

As the honey distils from the comb of the bees,
And the milk flows from the woman that loves her children;
So also is my hope on Thee, my God.
As the fountain gushes out its water,
So my heart gushes out the praise of the Lord
And my lips utter praise to Him,
And my tongue His psalms.
And my face exults with His gladness
And my spirit exults in His love,
And my soul shines in Him.
And I trust in Him.
And redemption in Him stands assured,
And His abundance is immortal life,
And those who receive it are incorrupt.
Hallelujah.

The Prophecies of the CHRISTIAN SIBYLLINE

I

The Immortal's mighty Son, renowned in song,
Proclaim I from the heart, to whom a throne
The most high Father gave for a possession
Ere He was born; and then He was raised up,
In flesh given Him, and washed in Jordan's stream,
Which bears with gleaming foot the waves away.
He having fled from fire first shall behold
The blessed Spirit of God descending down
With white wings of a dove. And He shall bloom
A blossom pure, and all things shall burst forth.
And He will show to men the ways, will show
The heavenly paths, and with wise words teach all.
And He will lead to righteousness, and win
The hostile people, boasting a descent
From a celestial Father. He will tread
The billows, and men's maladies destroy.
He will raise up the dead, and many woes
Drive far away; and from one root shall come
Enough of bread for men, when David's house
A scion shall bring forth, and in His hands
Shall be the whole world, land and heaven and sea.
He will flash lightning on the earth, as once
The two born from each other's sides beheld
The light appear. And this shall come to pass
When earth rejoices in hope of a son. But for thee only, Sodomitic land,
Are miseries in store, for with fell mind
Thou didst not give attention to thy God,
Who laughs at mortal schemes, but out of thorns
Didst plait for Him a crown, and fearful gall
In wanton insolence of spirit didst mix.
This shall bring on thee bitter miseries.
O wood most blessed, on which God was stretched,

Earth shall not hold thee, but a heavenly house
Shalt thou behold, when the new form of God
Shall flash forth as the lightning into view.

II

Earth will sweat when the judgment sign appears,
And the eternal King will come from Heaven
In person to judge all flesh and all the world.
The faithful and the faithless shall see God
Exalted with the saints at the end of time.
The souls of fleshly men upon His throne
He will judge, when the whole world is laid waste,
And thorns spring up. And men will cast away
Their idols and all wealth. And searching fire
Will burn the land, the heaven and the sea;
And burn the gates of Hades' prison-house.
Then to the free light of the saints shall come
All the flesh of the dead, but lawless ones
The fire will try forever. Every thing
One did in secret will He then declare,
For dark breasts God will open to the light.
Wailing will come from all, and gnashing of teeth;
The brightness of the sun will be eclipsed,
And the dances of the stars; the heaven shall whirl.
And the moon's beaming lustre be destroyed.
He will exalt the valleys and destroy
The heights of hills, and no more shall appear
A gloomy height among men. With the plains
The mountains will be level, and no more
Will there be any sailing on the sea.
For earth with springs shall be by thunder parched,
And dashing streams shall fail. The trump from heaven
Shall send a woeful sound, and bellow forth
Approaching pest and sorrows of the world.
And then the widely yawning earth will show
Tartarean chaos, and all kings shall come
Unto God's judgment seat. From Heaven shall flow
A stream of fire and brimstone. But the wood
Shall then be to all mortals for a sign,
Among the faithful a distinguished seal,
The longed-for horn, the life of pious men,
But the world's stumbling block, bestowing light
On the elect by water in twelve streams.
And then the shepherd rod of iron shall rule.
This one now in acrostics written down
Is our God, Saviour, and immortal King,
Even the One who suffered for our sake.

III

The Self-begotten, Undefiled, Eternal,
Dwelling in Heaven and measuring with His power
The fiery blast, who also holdeth fast
The clashing sceptre with ferocious fire,
And calms the rolling thunder's crashing noise,
He shakes the earth and holds the rusing winds,
And blunts the lightning's whip of fiery flame,
The vast outpour of storms, and vernal hail,
And chilling stroke of clouds, and winter's shock.
For these were every one marked out in thought,
As many as seemed good to Thee Thyself,
And to whose movements Thou didst nod assent;
Who, ere yet any creature had been formed
Was with Thy Son as bosom counsellor,
Former of mortal men, and judge of life.
Him with the first sweet utterance of mouth
Thou didst address and say: "Let us make man
According to our likeness and our form,
And give him vital breath to whom, though mortal
All worldly things shall be subordinate,
And to whom, dust-formed, we subject all things."
Thus spakest Thou to the Word, and by Thy mind
All things occurred, and all the elements
At once obeyed Thy order, and a creature
Eternal was in mortal image formed;

Heaven also, air, fire, earth, and the sea's wave,
Sun, moon, chorus of stars, mountains and day,
Night, sleep, awaking, spirit and emotion,
Soul and intelligence, art, voice and strength,
And the wild tribes of living things, of fish,
And birds, land animals, amphibia,
And also creeping things, and double natures;
For He Himself arranged all things for Thee,
Under Thy rule. But in the latest times
The earth has changed itself, and there has come
A humble one, from the Virgin Mary's womb;
A new light rose, and coming from the heavens
He entered mortal form. And therefore first
Did Gabriel show his strong and holy frame,
And second to the virgin he by voice
Spoke, being himself a messenger, and said:
"Virgin, receive God in thy holy breast."
So speaking, God breathed grace. But as for her,
Always a virgin, terror and surprise
Seized her at once as she heard, and she stood
In trembling, and her mind was filled with fear,
Her heart leapt at the messages unknown.
But she again was gladdened, and her heart
Was by the voice cheered, and the maiden laughed,
And her young cheek blushed, merry with the joy;
And she was spellbound in her heart by awe.
But confidence came to her, and the Word
Flew in her womb, and became flesh in time,
Was gendered and was made a human form,
And came to be a youth, of virgin born,
This was a mighty wonder to mankind,
But it was nothing greatly wonderful
To God the Father, and to God the Son.
And the glad earth received the new born babe,
The heavenly throne laughed, and the world exulted.
The new appearing and prophetic star
Was honoured by the wise men, and the babe
Was shown to those obedient unto God.
And of the Word was Bethlehem fatherland
Called by the keepers of herds, goats and sheep.

IV

To be of lowly mind, to hate base plans,
Wholly to love one's neighbour as oneself,
And from the soul to love God and to serve Him.
Therefore we, from the holy heavenly race
Of Christ sprung, shall be called of common blood,
And in our service have a sense of joy,
Following the paths of piety and truth.
Let us not venture in the inmost shrine
Of temples, nor to graven images
Pour out libations, nor revere with prayers,
Nor with the pleasant perfume of the flowers,
Nor light of lamps, nor yet with votive gifts
Adore them, nor with smoke of frankincense
Upon the altar sending forth its flame,
Nor with the sacrifice of bulls to send
The cruel gory slaughtering of sheep,
Those mysteries of recompense on earth,
Nor with the smoke of flesh-consuming fire
And odours foul pollute the light of Heaven;
But, joyful with pure minds and cheerful soul,
With love abounding, and with generous hands,
With soothing psalms, and songs that honour God,
We are commanded to sing praise to Thee,
Imperishable and without deceit,
All Father God, of understanding mind.

ORIGEN: The Scriptures are Divinely Inspired

1 So that the Scriptures may have certain and undoubted credibility it is necessary to show that they are divine Scriptures, that is that they are inspired by the

Spirit of God. Therefore we shall mark out as briefly as possible the passages from those sacred Scriptures that especially move us to this opinion; passages, that is, first from Moses, the lawgiver of the Hebrew nation, and then from the words of Jesus Christ, the author and head of the Christian religion and teaching.

Although a great many lawgivers were eminent among Greeks and barbarians, as well as numberless teachers or philosophers who promised they were declaring the truth, we remember no lawgiver so influential that he was able to inspire the minds of other nations with zeal either to adopt his laws willingly or to defend them with the entire effort of their minds. Therefore no one was able to introduce and to implant what seemed to him the truth even in one nation, to say nothing of many other foreign nations, in such a way that his knowledge or his belief should reach everyone.

Moreover it cannot be doubted both that the lawgivers wanted all men to observe their laws if possible and that the teachers wanted everyone to know what seemed to them the truth. But since they knew that they were entirely incapable of this, and that they did not have such great power as to rouse even foreign nations to observe their laws or doctrines, they did not even dare to undertake such a project at all, lest what had been begun but could not be finished should mark them out as men without foresight. Nevertheless in every part of the world, in all of Greece and in every foreign nation, there are numberless throngs of people who have left their ancestral laws and those they supposed gods and who have dedicated themselves to the observance of Moses' Law and to the discipleship and worship of Christ. And they have done this not without finding an immense hatred stirred up against them from those who worship idols, with the result that they are often afflicted with tortures by these people and sometimes are led away to death. Nevertheless they embrace and guard fast the word of Christ's teaching with all their desire.

2 Anyone can see in how short a time this religion has grown, making progress by the penalties and deaths exacted of its adherents, still more by the plundering of their possessions and by every kind of suffering endured by them. And it is all the more amazing that while their teachers are neither very capable nor very many, nevertheless this word is preached throughout the whole world (Matthew 24:14) so that Greeks and barbarians, wise and foolish (Romans 1:14) uphold the religion of Christ's teaching. Because of this it cannot be doubted that it is not because of human powers or abilities that the word of Christ Jesus grows strong with all authority and persuasion in the minds and souls of all.

Moreover, these very things were predicted by Him and confirmed by Him with divine oracles. This is evident when He says, "you will be dragged before governors and judges for my sake, to bear testimony before them and the Gentiles" (Matthew 10:18; Mark 13:9). And again, "This Gospel will be preached to all nations" (Mark 13:10; Matthew 24:14). And again, "On that day many will say to me, 'Lord, Lord, did we not eat and drink in Your name, and cast out demons in Your name?' And I shall say to them, 'Depart from me, you evildoers, I never knew you'" (Matthew 7:22; Luke 13:26). If these things had been said by Him and yet had not come to pass as they had been predicted, perhaps they would seem to fall short of the truth and to have no authority. But as it is, since the things that had been predicted by Him have in fact come to pass even though they were predicted with such great power and authority, then it is made evident with the greatest clarity that it is truly God who was made man and delivered saving teachings to men.

3 Indeed, what need is there to say that the prophets before Him predicted in regard to Him that "princes shall not depart from Judah nor leaders from his loins, until the one comes for whom it (that is, the kingdom) is kept safe, and until the expectation of the Gentiles comes" (Genesis 49:10)? For it is perfectly clear from the narrative itself and from what can be examined at the present day that from the time of Christ no further kings arose among the Jews. Moreover, all those Jewish pomps in which they used to boast as much as possible and in which they used to exult, that is the beauty of the temple, the magnificent altars, and all those priestly ornaments and garments of the high priests, all

of them have been destroyed together. For the prophecy has been fulfilled that said, "The children of Israel shall dwell many days without king or prince. There will be neither sacrifice nor altar, nor priesthood nor oracle" (Hosea 3:4).

And so, we use these witnesses against those who apparently maintain the verses spoken in Genesis by Jacob that refer to Judah, but who say that a prince from the tribe of Judah does remain to this day, namely the one who is head of their nation and whom they call the patriarch. And they say that there cannot fail those of his seed to remain until the coming of that Christ whom they represent for themselves. But suppose what the prophets say is true, that "the children of Israel shall dwell many days without king or prince. There will be neither sacrifice nor altar nor priesthood" (Hosea 3:4). And note that the temple has been overthrown and that no sacrifices are offered, no altar may be found, no priesthood is established. It most certainly follows that "princes" have departed "from Judah and a leader from his loins, until the one comes for whom it is kept safe," as it was written (Genesis 49:10). Thus it is clear that the one for whom it was kept safe has come, in whom is also "the expectation of the Gentiles". And this is seen obviously fulfilled by the multitude of those from different nations who have believed in God through Christ.

4 Moreover, in the song of Deuteronomy (32:21) the election of a foolish nation because of the sins of the former people is prophetically described for the future, and that election is no other than the one that has taken place through Christ. For this is what it says: "They have stirred me to jealousy with their idols; so I will stir them to jealousy; I will provoke them with a foolish nation".

It is then quite plain to understand how the Hebrews, who are said to have stirred God to jealousy by those that are not gods and to have provoked Him with their idols, have been themselves provoked to jealousy by "a foolish nation", which God chose through the coming of Christ Jesus and His disciples. For the apostle says, "For consider your call, brethren; not many of you were wise according to worldly standards, not many were powerful, not many were of noble birth; but God chose what is foolish in the world . . . even things that are not to bring to nothing things that are," so that Israel according to the flesh (for so it is named by the apostle (I Corinthians 10:18) "might not boast in the presence of God" (I Corinthians 1:26–29).

5 And what need is there to mention what is prophesied of Christ in the Psalms, especially in the one with the title, "A song for the beloved", where it is reported that His tongue is "the pen of a scribe who writes quickly", that He is "beautiful in appearance beyond the sons of men" because "grace is poured upon His lips" (Psalms 45:1–2). Moreover, the proof of the "grace poured upon His lips" is that although He accomplished His teaching in a short time (for He taught only a year and a few months), nevertheless the whole world has been filled with His teaching and with faith in His religion. For "in His days righteousness sprang up and an abundance of peace" enduring to the end, which is called "the taking away of the moon". "And He has dominion from sea to sea, and from the river to the ends of the earth!" (Psalms 72:7–8). Moreover, a sign was given to the house of David, for "a virgin" had conceived and borne "Emmanuel", which is interpreted "God with us" (Isaiah 7:13–14; Matthew 1:23). And what the same prophet said has been fulfilled. "God is with us. Know this, O nations, and be conquered" (Isaiah 8:8–9). For we who are from the nations have been conquered and overcome, and we who bend our necks beneath His grace stand forth as a kind of spoils of His victory. Moreover, the place of His birth was predicted by Micah the prophet, who said: "And you, O Bethlehem, land of Judah, are by no means least among the rulers of Judah; for from you shall come a ruler who will govern my people Israel" (Micah 5:2; Matthew 2:6). Also, the weeks of years up to the time of Christ, the leader that Daniel the prophet predicted, were fulfilled (Daniel 9:24). No less, there is also present the one predicted by Job who "would destroy the giant monster" (Job 3:8) and who gave authority to His intimate disciples "to tread upon serpents and scorpions and over all the power of the enemy, with nothing from him to hurt them" (Luke 10:19). Moreover, if anyone considers the journeys of Christ's apostles to different

places in which, sent by Him, they preached the Gospel, he will find that what they dared to undertake shows something beyond the human and that their ability to accomplish what they dared shows it was from God. If we consider how men hearing them introduce a new teaching were able to receive them or, on the other hand, that often those who wanted to bring the disciples destruction were restrained by a certain divine power that was present with them, then we shall find nothing in this that can be explained by human powers, but the whole achieved by divine power and providence, by signs manifest beyond doubt, and by miracles bearing witness to their word and teaching (Hebrews 2:4; Acts 5:12).

6 Now that these points have been briefly demonstrated, I mean the divinity of Jesus Christ and the fulfilment of everything that had been prophesied of Him, I think it has also been proved at the same time that the very Scriptures that prophesied of Him were divinely inspired, the ones concerning either His coming or the authority of His teaching or its reception by all nations. To this must be added that, whether it is the prediction of the prophets or the Law of Moses that is asserted to be divine and divinely inspired, the claim is put in the clearest light and is proved by the fact that Christ came to this world. For before what had been predicted by them was fulfilled, even though the predictions were true and inspired by God, nevertheless they could not be demonstrated to be true to the degree that they were not yet proved fulfilled. But the coming of Christ makes clear that what they had said was true and divinely inspired, since before that it might have been held as uncertain whether the conclusion of what had been predicted would be fulfilled.

Moreover, if someone considers the prophetic writings with all the diligence and reverence they are worth, while he reads and examines with great care, it is certain that in that very act he will be struck in his mind and senses by some more divine breath and will recognise that the books he reads have not been produced in a human way, but are words of God. And in himself he will discern that the books have been written not by human art or mortal eloquence but, if I may say so, by the elevated style of God. And so the splendour of the coming of Christ, by illuminating the Law of Moses with the radiance of truth, removed that veil which had been placed over the letter, and laid open for all who believe in Him the good things that were hidden covered within (II Corinthians 3:15–16).

7 It would, however, be too laborious to list one by one how or when the predictions made by the prophets in time past have been fulfilled, so that we might seem in this way to give complete assurance to those who doubt, especially when it is possible for anyone who wishes to gain a more careful knowledge of them to assemble proofs more fully from the books of the truth themselves. But if those who are less trained in divine teachings should see fit to object that the meaning that transcends the human is not immediately evident on the surface of the letter, there is nothing surprising about that, because divine matters are brought down to men somewhat secretly and are all the more secret in proportion to anyone's disbelief or unworthiness. For although it is certain that everything that exists or happens in this world is ordered by God's providence, nevertheless certain things show quite openly that they are arranged by the governance of providence, while others are unfolded in so obscure and incomprehensible a fashion that the reason of divine providence lies hidden deep within them. As a result there are sometimes people who do not believe that these matters have reference to providence, since that reason is hidden from them through which the works of divine providence are ordered by a certain ineffable art. Nevertheless, that reason is not equally obscure in everything. For even among humans themselves it is contemplated, less by one, more fully by another; while whoever it is that dwells in Heaven knows more than any human being. And the reason of bodies is evident in one way, that of trees in another, that of animals in another, but that of souls is hidden in still another way. And in what way the diverse motions of rational minds are ordered by divine providence lies hidden for the most part to human beings and even, I think, to the angels, though not to such a degree.

But just as divine providence is not refuted, especially for those who are sure of its existence, because its works or operations cannot be comprehended by human capacities, so neither will the divine inspiration that extends through the entire body of sacred Scripture be called into question because the weakness of our understanding is not strong enough to discover in each different verse the obscure and hidden meanings. This is because the treasure of divine wisdom is hidden in the base and rude vessel of words, as the apostle points out when he says: "But we have this treasure in earthen vessels" so that the strength of divine power may shine forth all the more, provided no dross of human eloquence is mixed with the truth of the teachings (II Corinthians 4:7). For if our books had enticed people to believe because they were written with rhetorical art or philosophical skill, doubtless our faith would be supposed to depend on the art of words and on human wisdom rather than on the power of God (I Corinthians 2:4–5). But as it is, everyone knows that the word of this preaching has been received by great multitudes in almost the whole world in such a way that they have understood what they came to believe to depend not on plausible words of wisdom, but on the demonstration of the Spirit and of power I Corinthians 2:4). Since we have been brought by a more than heavenly power to faith and belief that we should worship as ours one God, the creator of all, let us strive ourselves to advance earnestly by leaving the elementary doctrines of Christ, which are the first beginnings of knowledge; and let us go on to perfection so that the wisdom that is delivered to the perfect may also be delivered to us (Hebrews 6:1; I Corinthians 2:6). This is what the one to whom the preaching of this wisdom was entrusted promises when he says: "Yet among the perfect we impart wisdom, although it is not a wisdom of this world nor of the rulers of this world, who are doomed to pass away" (I Corinthians 2:6). By this he makes it clear that this wisdom of ours, so far as beauty of speech goes, has nothing in common with the wisdom of this world. This wisdom, therefore, is written more clearly and perfectly in our hearts, if it has been revealed to us according to the revelation of the mystery, which was kept secret for long ages, but is now disclosed through the prophetic writings and through the appearing of our Lord and Saviour Jesus Christ, to whom be glory for ever more. Amen. (Romans 16:25–27; II Timothy 1:10; I Timothy 6:14).

Saint ATHANASIUS: The Incarnation of the Word

Come now, Macarius, true lover of Christ, let us set forth what relates to the Word's becoming man, and to His divine appearing amongst us, which Jews slander and Greeks laugh to scorn, but we worship; in order that, all the more for the seeming low estate of the Word, your piety toward Him may be increased and multiplied. For the more He is mocked among the unbelieving, the more witness does He give of His own Godhead: in as much as what men deride as unseemly, this by His own goodness He clothes with seemliness; and what men in their conceits laugh at us merely human, He by his own power demonstrates to be divine, subduing the pretensions of idols by His supposed humiliation – by the Cross – invisibly winning over to recognise His divinity and power those who mock and disbelieve.

But to treat this subject it is necessary to recall the creation of the universe, and God its artificer, so that it may be understood that the renewal of creation has been the work of the self-same Word that made it at the beginning. For it is fitting for the Father to have wrought its salvation in Him by whose means He made it.

God made the universe to exist through His Word out of nothing, and without its having any previous existence, as He says firstly through Moses: "In the beginning God created the Heaven and the earth"; to which also Paul refers when he says: "By faith we understand that the worlds have been framed by the Word of God, so that what is seen hath not been made out of things which do appear". For God is good or rather is essentially the source of goodness; nor could one that is good be niggardly. Grudging existence to none, He has made all things out of nothing by His own Word, Jesus Christ our Lord. And among these, having taken especial pity, above all things on earth, upon the race of men, He gave them a further gift, and made them after His own image, giving them a portion even of the power of His own Word; so that having as it were a kind of reflection of the Word, and being made rational, they might be able to abide ever in blessedness, living the true life which belongs to the saints in paradise. But knowing how the will of man could sway to either side, He secured the grace given them by a law and by the spot where He placed them. For He brought them into His own garden, and gave them a law: so that, if they kept the grace and remained good, they might still keep the life in paradise without sorrow or pain or care, besides having the promise of incorruption in Heaven; but that if they transgressed and turned back, and became evil, they might know that they were incurring that corruption in death which was theirs by nature: no longer to live in paradise, but cast out of it from that time forth to die and to abide in death and in corruption. Now this is that of which Holy Writ also gives warning, saying in the Person of God: "Of every tree that is in the garden, eating thou shalt eat: but of the tree of the knowledge of good and evil, ye shall not eat of it, but on the day that ye eat, dying ye shall die." But by "dying ye shall die", what else could be meant than not dying merely, but also abiding ever in the corruption of death?

You are wondering, perhaps, for what possible reason, having proposed to speak of the Incarnation of the Word, we are at present considering the origin of mankind. But this, too, properly belongs to the aim of our treatise.

For in speaking of the appearing of the Saviour among us, we must speak also of the origin of men, that you may know that the reason of His coming down was because of us. Our transgression called forth the loving kindness of the Word, that the Lord should both make haste to help us and appear among men. For of His becoming incarnate we were the object, and for our salvation He dealt so lovingly as to appear and be born even in a human body. Thus, then, God has made man, and willed that he should abide in incorruption; but men, having despised and rejected the contemplation of God, and devised and contrived evil for themselves, received the condemnation of death with which they had been threatened; and from thenceforth no longer remained as they were made, but were corrupted according to their devices; and death had the mastery over them as king. For transgression of the commandment was turning them back to their natural state so that, just as they have had their being out of nothing, so also, as might be expected, they might look for corruption into nothing in the course of time.

For if out of a former normal state of non-existence they were called into being by the presence and loving kindness of the Word, it followed naturally that when men were bereft of the knowledge of God and were turned back to what was not (for what is evil is not, but what is good is), they should, since they derive their being from God who is, be everlastingly bereft even of being; in other words, that they should be disintegrated and abide in death and corruption. For man is by nature mortal in as much as he is made out of what is not; but by reason of his likeness to Him that is, he would stay his natural corruption, and remain incorrupt; as wisdom says: "The taking heed to His laws is the assurance of immortality." If he were incorrupt, he would live henceforth as God, to which I suppose the divine Scripture refers, when it says: "I have said ye are gods, and ye are all sons of the most Highest: but ye die like men, and fall as one of the princes."

For God has not only made us out of nothing; but He gave us freely, by the grace of the Word, a life in communication with God. But men rejected things eternal and, by counsel of the devil, turned to the things of corruption and so became the cause of their own corruption.

But because of the Word dwelling with them, even their natural corruption did not come near them, as wisdom also says: "God made man for incorruption, and as an image of His own eternity; but by envy of the devil death came into the world." But when this came to pass, men began to die, while corruption thenceforward prevailed against them, gaining power over the whole race. For in their misdeeds men had not stopped short at any set limits; but gradually pressing forward, have passed on beyond all measure: exceeding all lawlessness and stopping at no one evil but devising all manner of new evils in succession, they have become insatiable in sinning. For there were adulteries everywhere and thefts, and the whole earth was full of murders and plunderings. And as to corruption and wrong, no heed was paid to law, but all crimes were being practised everywhere, both individually and jointly. Cities were at war with cities, and nations were rising up against nations; and the whole earth was rent with civil commotions and battles, each man vying with his fellows in lawless deeds. Nor were even crimes against nature far from them, but, as the apostle and witness of Christ says: "For their women changed the natural use into that which is against nature; and likewise also the men, leaving the natural use of the women, burned in their lust one toward another, receiving in themselves that recompense of their error which was meet."

The Word saw that no otherwise could the corruption of men be undone save by death as a necessary condition; while it was impossible for the Word to suffer death, being immortal, the Son of the Father, He took to Himself a body capable of death, that it might be worthy to die in the stead of mankind and might, because of the Word which was come to dwell in it, remain incorruptible, and that thenceforth corruption might be stayed from all by the grace of the Resurrection. So by offering unto death the body He Himself had taken, as an offering and sacrifice free from any stain, straightway He put away death from all His men by the offering of an equivalent. Because He was the Word of God, by offering His own temple for the life of all men, He satisfied the debt by His death. And thus He, the incorruptible Son of God, clothed all men with incorruption by the promise of the Resurrection. For corruption in death no longer has any hold on men, by reason of the Word which came to dwell among them. And as when a great king has entered into some large city and taken up his abode in one of the houses there, such city is at all events held worthy of high honour, nor does any enemy or bandit any longer descend upon it and subject it but, on the contrary, it is thought entitled to all care, because of the king's having taken up his residence in a single house there: so, too, has it been with the Monarch of all. For now that He has come to our realm, and taken up His abode in one body among His peers, the whole conspiracy of the enemy against mankind is checked, and the corruption of death which was prevailing against them is done away. For the race of men has gone to ruin, had not the Lord and Saviour of all, the Son of God, come among us to meet the end of death.

Saint BASIL THE GREAT: Prayer must come first

1 Dearly beloved, each word and deed of Our Saviour Jesus Christ is for us a lesson in virtue and piety. For this end also did He assume our nature, so that every man and every woman, contemplating as in a picture the practice of all virtue and piety, might strive with all their hearts to imitate His example. For this He bore our body, so that as far as we could we might repeat within us the manner of His life. And so therefore, when you hear mention of some word or deed of His, take care not to receive it simply as something that incidentally happened, but raise your mind upwards towards the sublimity of what He is teaching, and strive to see what has been mystically handed down to us.

Martha did indeed welcome the Lord; but Mary sat at His feet. In each sister was an earnest good will. Yet note what each does. Martha served Him by preparing what would be needed for the refreshment of His body; Mary, seated at His feet, listened to His words. The one ministered to the visible man; the other bowed down before the invisible. And the Lord who was there as both God and man was pleased with the good dispositions of both women.

But Martha, busy with her task, cried out to the Lord to speak for her to her sister that she should come and help her. "Speak to her therefore," she said, "that she may get up and help me." But the Lord said to her: "Martha, Martha, thou art careful, and art troubled about many things. But one thing is necessary. Mary hath chosen the best part, which shall not be taken away from her" (Luke 10:38–42). We have not come here for this purpose, to sit at ease at the table, to fill our stomachs. We are here to nourish you, with the word of truth, and by the contemplation of heavenly mysteries. Yet though He did not turn the one away from her task He praised the other because of that to which she had devoted herself.

Here we see the two states placed before us by means of the two women; the lower, choosing to serve Him in corporeal ministrations which also is most profitable, and that which, ascending to the contemplation of the sacred mysteries, is the more spiritual. Take these things spiritually, you who listen, and choose that which you wish. And should you choose the way of service, render your service in the name of Christ. For He said: " As long as you did it to one of these my least brethren, you did it unto me" (Matthew 25:40). And so whether you receive the stranger, or feed the poor, or comfort the afflicted, or give help to those who are in need and in pain, or take care of the sick, Christ receives your service as bestowed on Him. But should you choose to imitate Mary who, putting aside the service of bodily need, ascended to the contemplation of the divine glories, seek truly to do this. Leave the body, leave the tilling of the earth, and the preparation of what is eaten with bread. Sit at the feet of the Lord, and give your mind to His words, that you may become a sharer of the mysteries of the divine nature which Christ reveals. For to contemplate that which Christ teaches is a work above the service of corporeal need.

2 You have then, beloved, received both divine teaching and an example of life. Strive for whichever you will, and be either a servant of the needy of this world, or a zealous lover of the words of Christ. And if it be that you strive after both, then from both gather the fruit of salvation. But the spiritual motive is the first, all the rest come second: "For Mary", He says, "has chosen the better part". If then you would enter into the mysteries of Christ, let you sit by His feet, and receive His Gospel, and abandoning your way of life let you live apart from men and free from all concern, let you have no further thought for your body, and then you will be enabled to enter into mystic converse with Him in contemplation of His truth and so imitate Mary and gain the highest glory.

And, when you pray, see that you ask not for what is alien to your life and provoke the Lord. Ask not for money, nor for human glory, nor power, nor for any of the things that pass away. But seek for the Kingdom of God, and all that is needed for your body will be provided; as the Lord Himself has said: "Seek ye the kingdom of God, and His justice, and all these things will be added unto you" (Matthew 6:33).

Twofold, beloved, are the methods of prayer. One is to give praise to God from a humble heart; the other, the lower, is the prayer of petition. Therefore, when you pray, do not immediately begin with petitions; otherwise you may then be accused of praying to God only when in need. So when you come to pray, leave self behind, leave wife and children. Let the earth go, and rise up to Heaven. Leave behind every creature, the visible and the invisible, and begin with the praise and glory of Him who has made all things. And as often as you offer Him praise be not wandering here and there in your mind. And choose not your words from fables, like the Greeks, but from the holy Scriptures, and say: O Lord, patient and forbearing, I praise Thee because Thou hast spared me who offend Thee daily; giving to all a season for repentance; and because of this Thou art silent, and art patient with us, O Lord, that we may offer glory and praise to Thee who hast care for the salvation of all men. Thou dost help us, now by fear, now by counsel, now through the prophets, and last of all through the coming of Thy anointed; "for thou has made us, and not we ourselves" (Psalms 100:3).

3 And when you have praised and glorified God from the Scriptures, with all your heart, then begin with humility to say: Lord, I am not worthy to praise Thee, for I have sinned most grievously. And though you may not be conscious of any fault, yet so must you speak to Him. For, save God alone, there is no one without sin. We commit many sins, and the greater part of them we forget. Because of this the apostle said: "I am not conscious to myself of anything, yet I am not thereby justified" (I Corinthians 4:4); that is, "I have committed many

sins, and taken no notice of them". And because of this the prophet also says: "Who can understand sins?" (Psalms 19:13). So you do not speak falsely when you say you are a sinner. And if you do know that you are one, you also sin when you say: "I am not a sinner". Say rather: "I have sinned more than other sinners, for I have broken the commandment which says: 'When you have done all things commanded of you, say: we are unprofitable servants; we have done that which it was our duty to do'" (Luke 17:10). So must you think to yourself: "I am a profitless servant."

And again: "In humility let each esteem others better than himself" (Philippians 2:3). Pray to the Lord therefore with fear and humility. And when you pray to Him from a humble heart, say, "I give Thee thanks, O Lord, because Thou hast borne with my sins in patience, and hast left me even till now without chastisement. For I have long deserved to suffer many afflictions; and to be banished from Thy sight; but Thy most clement mercy has borne with me in patience. I thank Thee again, although I am unable to render Thee such thanks as are due Thy mercy."

And when you have fulfilled in turn the duty of praise and of humility, then ask for what you ought to ask for; not for riches, as I said, not for the glory of this earth, not for health of body: for He made you and your health is His care, and He knows which state is profitable to each one, to be healthy or to be infirm. But let you seek, as He has told us, for the Kingdom of Heaven. For, as I said before, He will provide for your body's needs. For our King is of infinite dignity, and it is unfitting that anyone should ask of Him what is not becoming. Be mindful therefore when you pray that you do not bring upon yourself the anger of God; but seek from Him the things that are worthy of God our King. And when you pray for the things that are worthy of being asked of God, cease not from praying till you receive them. For the Lord has intimated this to us where He says in the gospel: "Which of you shall have a friend, and shall go to him at midnight, and shall say to him: 'Friend, lend me three loaves, because a friend of mine is come off his journey to me, and I have not what to set before him'. And he from within should answer, and say: 'Trouble me not, the door is now set shut, and my children are with me in bed; I cannot rise and give thee'. Yet if he shall continue knocking, I say to you, although he will not rise and give him, because he is his friend; yet because of his importunity, he will rise, and give him as many as he needeth" (Luke 11:5–8).

4 Our Lord put this example before us to teach us that we should be strong and persistent in faith. He takes the example of one man's prayer to another man, that you may learn never to be discouraged, so that when you pray and do not receive the answer to your prayer, you should not cease from praying till you do receive it; provided that, as I said, you ask for what God wishes you to ask. And do not say: "I am a sinner, and therefore He does not listen to me". That you may not lost heart on this account He says to us: "Although he will not give him, because he is a friend; yet because of his importunity he will give him as many as he needs".

So henceforth, if a month goes by, or a year, or three years, or four, or many years, do not give up praying until you receive what you ask for; but ask on in faith, and be at the same time steadfast in doing good. It will happen often that someone in his youth strives earnestly for chastity. Then pleasure begins to undermine his resolution, desires awaken his nature, he grows weak in prayer, wine overcomes his youth, modesty perishes, and the man becomes another man. So we change because we have not with high courage of soul stood firm against our passions. It behoves us therefore to resist all things, yet we must cry out to God that He may bring us aid.

For if a man through folly gives way to evil desires, and betrays himself to his enemies, God will not aid him, nor hear him, because through sin he has turned away from God. He who hopes to be helped by God should have no part with what is unworthy. But he who does not betray what he owes to God will never be in want of the divine aid. It is just and fitting that in nothing should we be condemned by our own conscience. Only then may we cry out for divine aid and cry earnestly, and not with minds wandering here and there. For one who so prays, not alone shall he continue unheard by God, but he will also provoke the Lord yet more. For if a man stands in the presence of a king, and speaks with him, he will stand there with great trepidation of mind, careful not to let either his eyes or his mind go wandering. With what greater fear and trembling should we stand in the presence of God, having our whole mind intent on Him alone, and on nothing else whatsoever? For He beholds our inward life; not merely the outward one which men see.

Standing then in God's presence, in a manner truly worthy, and laying before Him all the desires of your heart, cease not to pray till you receive what you ask for. But should your conscience tell you that you are praying unworthily, and should you stand in prayer while your mind goes wandering, then venture not to stand thus in the presence of the Lord for fear your prayer becomes an offence. Should it be however that your soul has become weak through sin, and that you are unable to pray without distraction, strive with yourself as best as you can. Strive manfully before the Lord, having your mind steadfast on Him, and calling upon Him, and God will have compassion on you, since it is not because of indifference but through infirmity that you cannot pray as you ought when you kneel before God. Let him who so strives with himself in every good work cease not to pray till he obtains what he asks for; but in making his request let him knock patiently at the door: "For everyone", He says, "that asketh, receiveth; and he that seeketh, findeth; and to him that knocketh, it shall be opened"; for that which you desire to obtain, what is it but salvation in God?

5 Do you desire to know, beloved, how the saints endured in patience, and yielded not to despair? The Lord called Abraham when he was still a young man, and brought him out of the land of the Assyrians into Palestine, and said to him: "I shall give this land to thee, and to thy seed after thee, and as the stars of heaven shall thy seed be, which shall not be numbered" (Genesis 13:15,16). And the number of his many years went on, and his nature died, and death stood by his door, and yet he did not say: "Lord, You promised me many children, and You foretold that I would be the father of many peoples. And the impulses of nature have withered away; and to my wife because of her age nothing remains of the nature of woman. So Your prophecy was false. For what hope have we since we are both old?" But he did not say this, nor did he think it in his heart, but remained unshaken in faith; and while his body grew old his hope grew young. As his body became weaker and gave him grounds for despairing, his faith gave strength to his soul and his body. "It is God," he said, "who has promised, He is the Lord of nature; otherwise it could not come to pass. It is He who makes possible what is impossible; for He has made all things; and all that is He changes as He wills."

Imitate the faith of Abraham. After his nature had withered, and its powers were at an end, then the promise of the Lord took life. Let us consider ourselves for example. We pray earnestly for a year; and then we cease. We fast for two years; and then we cease to fast. Let us not grow faint in the face of the promise of God. For He who promised this man that his seed would be multiplied has promised us that He will give us what we ask for. For He says: "Come to me, all you that labour, and are burdened, and I will refresh you" (Matthew 11:28). For when you were far from Him He pitied you as you toiled under the weary burden of your sins, and called you and relieved you of it, and then gave you rest. And you, have you no faith in Him? Even should we keep silence our conscience would not suffer us. For we do not doubt that He has power to relieve us; but we care not to take upon us His yoke, which is light and sweet; nor enter by the narrow way to the Kingdom of Heaven; but prefer rather to carry the burden of our sins, and to walk by the broad way of the pleasures of the senses, and to enter in at the wide gate that leads to destruction.

But, you will say, how often have I prayed, and have not been answered? Because you have always prayed badly; either without faith, or with a distracted mind, or for the things that were not expedient for you. And if at times you prayed for what was expedient for you, you did not persevere. For it is written: "In patience shall you possess your souls" (Luke 21:19), and again: "He that shall persevere unto the end, he shall be saved" (Matthew 10:22).

6 God sees into the hearts of those who pray. What need then, someone will say,

that we should ask God for what we need? Does He not know already what we need? Why then should we pray? God does indeed know what things we need, and with generosity provides all we need for the refreshment of our bodies, and since He is good, He sends down His rains upon the just and the unjust alike, and causes His sun to shine upon the good and the bad (Matthew 5:45), even before we ask Him. But faith, and the power of virtue, and the Kingdom of Heaven, these you will not receive unless you ask for them in labouring and steadfastness.

We must first long for these things. Then when you desire them, you must strive with all your heart to obtain them, seeking them with a sincere heart, with patience, and with faith, not being condemned by your conscience as praying without attention or without reverence, and so in time, when God wills, you will obtain your request. For He knows better than you when these things are expedient for you. And perhaps He is delaying in giving them to you, designing to keep your attention fixed upon Him; and also that you may know that this is a gift of God, and may safeguard with fear what is given to you. For what we come by with much labour we are zealous to defend; as losing it we lose also our labour; and treating lightly the gift of God we become unworthy of life eternal. For what did it profit Solomon so quickly to receive the gift of wisdom and then lose it?

7 Do not then lose heart if you do not speedily obtain your request. For if it were known to our good Master that were you at once to receive this favour you would not lose it, He would have been prepared to give it to you unasked. But being concerned for you, He does not do this. For if he who received a single talent and hid it safely, was condemned because he did not put it to profit, how much more would he have been condemned had he lost it? Keeping this in mind, let us continue to give thanks to the Lord whether we receive speedily or slowly that which we pray for. For all things whatsoever the Lord may do He orders all to the end of our salvation; only let us not through faintheartedness cease from our prayers. It was because of this the Lord spoke the parable of the widow who persuaded the judge through her steadfastness (Luke 18:2–5): that we also through our steadfastness in prayer may obtain what we ask for.

By this we also show our faith, and our love of God, since though we do not quickly receive what we ask for, yet we remain steadfast in praising Him and giving thanks. Then let us give Him thanks at all times, so that we may be found worthy of receiving His everlasting gifts; since to Him all praise and glory is due for ever and ever. Amen.

Saint BASIL THE GREAT: The Spirit

Let us now investigate what are our common ideas about the Spirit, as well as those which have been gathered by us from holy Scripture and those which we have received from the unwritten tradition of the fathers. First of all we ask, who on hearing the titles of the Spirit is not lifted up in soul, who does not raise his mind to the supreme One? Sometimes called "Spirit of God", "Spirit of truth which proceedeth from the Father", "right Spirit", "a leading Spirit", its proper title is "Holy Spirit" which is a name specially appropriate to everything that is incorporeal, purely immaterial, and indivisible. So our Lord, when teaching the woman who thought God to be an object of local worship, said "God is a spirit". When we try to form an idea of it we are compelled to advance in our conceptions to the highest, and to think of an intelligent essence, in power infinite, in magnitude unlimited, unmeasured by times or ages, generous with its good gifts, to whom turn all things needing sanctification, after whom reach all things that live in virtue, as being watered by its inspiration and helped on toward their natural and proper end; perfecting all other things but itself in nothing lacking; living not as needing restoration but as suplier of life; not growing by additions but straightway full, self-established, omnipresent origin of sanctification, light perceptible to the mind, supplying illumination to every faculty in the search for truth; by nature unapproachable, apprehended by reason of goodness, filling all things with its power, but communicated only to the worthy: not shared in one measure, but distributing its energy according to "the proportion of faith"; in essence simple, in powers various, wholly present in each and being wholly everywhere; impassively divided, shared without ceasing to be entire, after the likeness of the sunbeam, whose kindly light falls on him who enjoys it as though it shone for him alone, yet illumines land and sea and mingles with the air. So too is the Spirit to everyone who receives, as though given to him alone, and yet it sends forth grace sufficient and full for all mankind, and is enjoyed by all who share it, according to the capacity, not of its power, but of their nature.

Now the Spirit is not brought into intimate association with the soul by physical nearness. How indeed could there be a corporeal approach to the incorporeal? This association results from the withdrawal of the passions which have alienated the soul from its close relationship with God. Only then, after a man is purified from the shame whose stain he took through his wickedness, and has come back again to his natural beauty, and as it were cleaning the royal image and restoring its ancient form, only thus is it possible for him to draw near to the Holy Spirit. And He, like the sun, will by the aid of thy purified eye show thee in Himself the image of the invisible, and in the blessed spectacle of the image thou shalt behold the unspeakable beauty of the Archetype. Through His aid hearts are lifted up, the weak are held by the hand and they who are advancing are brought to perfection. Shining upon those that are cleansed from every spot, He makes them spiritual by fellowship with Himself. Just as when a sunbeam falls on bright and transparent bodies, they themselves become brilliant too, and shed forth a fresh brightness from themselves, so souls wherein the Spirit dwells, illuminated by the Spirit, themselves become spiritual, and send forth their grace to others. Hence comes foreknowledge of the future, understanding of mysteries, apprehension of what is hidden, distribution of good gifts, the heavenly citizenship, a place in the chorus of angels, joy without end, abiding in God, the being made like to God, and, highest of all, the being made God.

But we must proceed to attack our opponents, in the endeavour to confute those "oppositions" advanced against us which are derived from "knowledge" falsely so-called.

It is not permissible, they assert, for the Holy Spirit to be ranked with the Father and Son, on account of the difference of His nature and the inferiority of His dignity. Against them it is right to reply in the words of the apostles, "We ought to obey God rather than men".

For if our Lord, when enjoining the baptism of salvation, charged His disciples to baptise all nations in the name "of the Father and of the Son and of the Holy Ghost", not disdaining fellowship with Him, and these men allege that we must not rank Him with the Father and the Son, is it not clear that they openly oppose the commandment of God?

But all the apparatus of war has been got ready against us; every intellectual missile is aimed at us; and now blasphemers' tongues shoot and hit and hit again, yet harder than Stephen of old was smitten by the killers of the Christ. And do not let them succeed in concealing the fact that, while an attack on us serves as a pretext for the war, the real aim of these proceedings is higher. It is against us, they say, that they are preparing their snares; against us that they are shouting. But the object of attack is faith. The one aim of the whole band of opponents and enemies of sound doctrine is to shake down the foundation of the faith of Christ by levelling apostolic tradition to the ground, and utterly destroying it. So they clamour for written proof, and reject as worthless the unwritten tradition of the Fathers. But we will not slacken in our defence of the truth. We will not abandon the cause. The Lord has delivered to us as a necessary and saving doctrine that the Holy Spirit is to be ranked with the Father.

Our opponents think differently, and see fit to divide and rend asunder, and relegate Him to the nature of a ministering spirit. Is it not then indisputable that they make their own blasphemy more authoritative than the law prescribed by the Lord? Come, then, set aside mere contention. Let us consider the points before us, as follows:

How is it that we are Christians? "Through our faith" is the universal answer. And in what way are we saved? Plainly because we were born again through the grace given in our baptism. How else could we be? And after recognising that this salvation is established through the Father and the Son and the Holy Ghost, shall we fling away "that form of doctrine" which we received? Would it not rather be ground for great groaning if we are found now further off from our salvation "than when we first believed", and deny now what we then received? Whether a man has departed this life without baptism, or has received a baptism lacking in some of the requirements of the tradition, his loss is equal. And whoever does not always and everywhere keep to and hold fast as a sure protection the confession which we recorded at our first admission, when, being delivered "from the idols", we came to the living God", constitutes himself a "stranger" from the "promises" of God, fighting against his own handwriting, which he put on record when he professed the faith. For if to me my baptism was the beginning of life, and that day of rebirth the first of days, it is plain that the utterance uttered in the grace of the moment of adoption was the most honourable of all. Can I then, perverted by these men's seductive words, abandon the tradition which guided me to the light, which bestowed on me the boon of the knowledge of God, whereby I, so long a foe by reason of sin, was made a child of God? But, for myself, I pray that with this confession I may depart hence to the Lord, and them I charge to preserve the faith secure until the day of Christ, and to keep the Spirit undivided from the Father and the Son, preserving the doctrine taught them at their baptism.

Saint GREGORY OF NAZIANZUS: The Necessity of the Trinity

In those who dwell on high I note two states of existence, namely, that of ruling and that of serving. This division is not of the same kind as that which we find among us, which either tyranny has driven between us, or poverty has made, but that which nature makes, if it is right to use this word. For the first of these is also above nature. Of the two this former is creative, ruling, unmoving; the other created, subject to rule and subject to change. Or, to speak more precisely, the one is above time, the other subject to time. The first is called God and subsists in the three greatest; namely, the Cause, the Maker, the Perfector, that is, in the Father, the Son, and the Holy Ghost. But they are not so separate from each other that they are divided in nature; and neither are they so confined in their nature as to be restricted to one person. But it is yet more single than what is completely divided, and yet richer than what is wholly undivided. The other kind is round about us, and is called creature; though among created beings one may be raised above the other, according to the degree of its nearness to God.

And since this is so, "if any man be on the Lord's side, let him join with us" (Exodus 32:26), and let us adore the one Godhead in three persons; not attributing a title of humiliation to the unapproachable glory, but having ever on our lips "the high praise of the one God" in three persons (Psalms 149:6). For since to speak of its greatness, of its nature, infinite and undefined, is beyond us, how can we attribute lowliness to it? But if anyone be a stranger to God, and because of this divide the one and supreme Being into different natures, it is a wonder that such a man is not sundered by the sword, "and his portion appointed with unbelievers" (Luke 12:46), reaping both now and hereafter the evil fruit of his evil mind.

And of the Father, what shall we say, whom all who are ruled by natural reason by common consent forbear to affront, although He has endured the beginnings of an affront through being divided as it were into two, the Good and the Creator by earlier innovators? Of the Son and Holy Ghost you will see how simply and briefly we shall speak. If any one can say of either of these, that He was subject to change, or changeable, or that He was subject to limitation, either of time or place or of power or action, or that He was not good by nature, or not self-moved, or not free, or that He was but a minister of God, or that He sang before Him, or was subject to fear, that he was given freedom, or that he was not to be numbered with the Father, let him prove this and we shall bear with it, and we shall endure it that we are glorified by the dignity of our fellow servants; though we suffer the loss of one who is God.

But if all the Father has belongs also to the Son, save being unbegotten, and all the Son has belongs to the Holy Ghost, save sonship, as well as what is said of Him through being made man, for my salvation, so that taking what was mine He might give me what was His, through this new union, then make an end of your babbling, O ye makers of empty phrases, that at once fall to the ground. "Why will you die, O house of Israel" (Ezekiel 18:31), if I may mourn for you from the Scriptures!

For my part I hold in reverence all the titles of the Word, so many, so great, and so exalted, that even the demons revere them. I reverence the equal majesty of the Holy Ghost, and I am fearful of the punishment threatened those who blaspheme Him (Matthew 12:31). The blasphemy is not in speaking of Him as God, but in the taking away of His divinity. And here we must note that He who is blasphemed is the Lord. He that is to be avenged, the Holy Spirit, is manifestly avenged as Lord. After my illumination, my baptism, I cannot suffer darkness with patience, forging another stamp than that of the three in whom I was baptised; thus to be truly buried in water, not indeed to new life, but unto very death.

O Trinity, I rashly dare to proclaim something, and may I be forgiven for my rashness, for the danger to my soul. I also am an image of God, of the glory that is on high, though I dwell on earth. And I cannot be persuaded that I am redeemed by my equal. If the Holy Ghost is not God, let him first be made God, and let him then make me his equal.

What now is this manipulation of grace, or rather of those who communicate grace, to make as it were a profession of believing God, and come away without God? To profess one thing, to be taught another? What sort of juggling with words is this, asking and receiving the confession of one thing, and teaching something else? Alas for this enlightenment, if after my baptism I have become black again, if I am to see those who are not yet washed whiter than myself, if I am to be endangered by the false belief of my baptiser; if I am to seek a mightier Spirit, and not find him!

Give me a different baptism, and think as you will of this first. Why should you begrudge me a perfect regeneration? Why do you change me, who am a temple of the Holy Spirit, into the dwelling place of something that was created? Why do you partly honour, partly dishonour, what belongs to me, judging falsely of the divinity, that you may cut off the divine gift, or rather, cut me off from the divine gift? Either give honour to the whole divinity, O new teacher of divine truth, or deny honour to it, so that if you must be blasphemous, you may also be consistent: you who set forth unequally a nature that is to be held in equal honour in each who shares it.

To sum up my discourse to you: give praise to God with the cherubim, who join the three most holy into one Lordship (Isaiah 6:3), and reveal to us the first being they they open their wings to men of good will. With David be enlightened, who said to the Light: "In Thy light we shall see light" (Psalms 36:9), that is, in the Spirit we shall see the Son, than whom who can be more far-shining? Thunder with John, "the son of thunder" (Mark 3:17), giving forth no sound that is mean or earthly, but only what is of Heaven and exalted regarding the majesty of God, namely, the Word that was in the beginning, and was with God, and was God (John 1:1), knowing God, true God from the true Father; and not a good fellow-servant honoured with the name of Son. And the other comforter, other from the one who spoke: for it was the Word of God who spoke, and when you hear His words: "I and the Father are one" (John 10:30), understand and keep before your mind unity of nature. And when you read: "We will come and make our abode with Him" (John 14:23), think then of the distinction of persons. And when you hear the names of Father, Son, and Holy Ghost, think of three separate persons.

As you read the acts of the apostles let you with Luke be also inspired. Why should you associate yourself with Ananias and Saphira, with this new kind of thief (for stealing what is your own is new indeed), and this by stealing, not money, nor any other thing of small value, as a golden tongue (Joshua 7:21), a soldier's cloak, like a certain greedy soldier, but stealing the divinity itself; and lying, "not to men, but to God", as you have heard (Acts 5:4)? Who does not revere the authority of the Holy Spirit, who breathes upon whom He wills, and when and where He wills (John 3:8)? He came down upon Cornelius before baptism, to others when they were baptised by the Apostles (Acts 10:44; 19:2), that testimony might be given to the divinity of the Spirit, in that He enters as Lord, and not as servant, and in that He is sought for unto perfection.

Speak with Paul of the things of God, with one who was caught up to the third heaven (II Corinthians 12:2), who frequently numbers for us the three persons, and this in various ways, not keeping to the same order, but placing the same person now first then second, and again third. Why? To make plain to us their equality of nature. Sometimes he speaks of three persons, sometimes of two, sometimes of one; as though the others are wholly inseparable.

And sometimes he attributes a work of God to the Spirit of God (I Corinthians 12:11), as though He were in no way different from Him. Sometimes in place of the Spirit he speaks of Christ (Romans 8:9). And when he distinguishes one person from another, he uses such words as these: "One God, from whom are all things, and we unto him; and one Lord Jesus Christ, by whom are all things, and we by him" (I Corinthians 8:6). At another time he unites the divinity in oneness, as when he says: "for of Him, and by Him, and in Him, are all things" (Romans 11:36); that is, through the Holy Ghost, as is proved from many places in Scripture. To Him be glory for ever and ever. Amen.

Saint GREGORY OF NYSSA: Purgatory and the Resurrection

There is such an instinctive and deep-seated abhorrence of death in all! Those who look on a death-bed can hardly bear the sight; and those whom death approaches recoil from it all they can. Why, even the law that controls us puts death highest on the list of crimes, and highest on the list of punishments. By what device, then, can we bring ourselves to redard as nothing a departure from life, even in the case of a stranger, not to mention that of relations, when they cease to live? We see before us the whole course of human life aiming at this one thing, that is, how we may continue in this life; indeed it is for this purpose that houses have been invented by us to live in; in order that our bodies may not be prostrated in their environment by cold or heat. Again, what is agriculture but the providing of our sustenance? In fact all thought about how we are to go on living is occasioned by the fear of dying. Why is medicine so honoured amongst men? Because it is thought to carry on the combat with death to a certain extent by its methods.

Why do we have long shields, and greaves, and helmets, and all the defensive armour, and enclosures of fortifications, and iron-barred gates, except that we fear to die? Death then being naturally so terrible to us, how can it be easy for a survivor to obey the command to remain unmoved over friends departed?

What is the especial pain we feel, in the mere necessity itself of dying?

How can there not be occasion for grieving, when we see one who lately lived and spoke becoming all of a sudden lifeless and motionless, with the sense of every bodily organ extinct, with no sight or hearing in operation, or any other faculty of apprehension that sense possesses; and if you apply fire or steel to him, even if you were to plunge a sword into the body, or cast it to the beasts of prey, or bury it beneath a mound, that dead man is alike unmoved at any treatment? Seeing, then, that this change is observed in all these ways, and that principle of life, whatever it might be, disappears all at once out of sight, as the flame of an extinguished lamp which burnt the moment before neither remains upon the wick nor passes to some other place, but completely disappears, how can such a change be borne without emotion by one who has no clear ground to rest upon? We hear the departure of the spirit, we see the shell that is left; but of the part that has been separated we are ignorant, both as to its nature and as to the place whither it has fled; for neither earth, nor air, nor water, nor any other element can show as residing within itself this force that has left the body, at whose withdrawal a corpse only remains, ready for dissolution.

How are we to get an unmovable belief in the soul's continuance?

Many hints are interspersed in our Lord's narrative about those who are in Hell to excite the skilled enquirer. I mean that He who parts the good from the bad by a great gulf, and makes the man in torment crave for a drop to be conveyed by a finger, and the man who has been ill-treated in this life rest on a patriarch's bosom, and who relates their previous death and consignment to the tomb, takes an intelligent searcher of His meaning far beyond a superficial interpretation. For what sort of eyes has the rich man to lift up in Hell, when he has left his bodily eyes in that tomb?

And how can a disembodied spirit feel any flame? And what sort of tongue can he have to be cooled with the drop of water, when he has lost his tongue of flesh? What is the finger that is to convey to him this drop? What sort of place is the bosom of repose? The bodies of both of them are in the tomb, and their souls are disembodied, and do not consist of parts either; and so it is impossible to make the framework of the narrative correspond with the truth, if we understand it literally; we can do that only by translating each detail into an equivalent in the world of ideas. Thus we must think of the gulf as that which keeps ideas which may not be confounded from running together, not as a chasm of the earth. Such a chasm, however vast, could be crossed with no difficulty by a disembodied intelligence; since intelligence can in no time be wherever it wishes.

What then are the fire and the gulf and the other features in the picture? Are they not that which they are said to be?

I think that the Gospel signifies by means of each of them certain doctrines with regard to the question of the soul. For when the patriarch first says to the rich man, "Thou in thy lifetime receivedst thy good things," and in the same way speaks of the poor man, that he has done his duty in bearing his share of life's evil things, and then, after that, adds with regard to the gulf that it is a barrier between them, he evidently by such expressions intimates a very important truth; and to my thinking it is as follows. Once man's life had but one character; and by that I mean that it was to be found only in the category of the good and had no contact with evil. The first of God's commandments attests the truth of this; that which gave to man unstinted enjoyment of all the blessings of Paradise, forbidding that which was a mixture of good and evil, and making death the penalty for transgressing in that particular. But man, acting freely by a voluntary impulse, deserted the lot that was unmixed with evil, and drew upon himself that which was a mixture. Yet Divine Providence did not leave that recklessness of ours without a corrective. Death indeed, as the fixed penalty for breaking the law, necessarily fell upon its transgressors; but God divided the life of man into two parts, this present life, and that "out of the body" hereafter; and He placed on the first a limit of the briefest possible time, while He prolonged the other into eternity; and in His love for man He gave him his choice, to have the one or the other of those things, good or evil. I mean, in which of the two parts he liked: either in this short and transitory life, or in those endless ages, whose limit is infinity. Now these expressions "good" and "evil" are equivocal. They are used in two senses, one relating to mind and the other to sense; some classify as good whatever is pleasant to feeling: others are confident that only that which is perceptible by intelligence is good and deserves that name. Those, then, whose reasoning powers have never been exercised, and who have never had a glimpse of the better way, soon use up on gluttony in this fleshly life the dividend of good which their constitution can claim, and they reserve none of it for the after life; but those who by a discreet and sober-minded calculation economise the powers of living are afflicted by things painful the sense here, but they reserve their good for the succeeding life, and so their happier lot is lengthened out to last as long as that eternal life. This in my opinion is the "gulf"; which is not made by the parting of the earth, but by those decisions in this life which result in a separation. The man who has once chosen pleasure in this life, and has not cured his inconsiderateness by repentance, places the land of the good beyond his own reach; for he has dug against himself the yawning impassable abyss of necessity that nothing can break through. This is the reason, I think, that the name of Abraham's bosom is given to that good situation of the soul in which Scripture makes the athlete of endurance repose. For it is related of this patriarch first, of all up to that time born, that he exchanged the enjoyment of the present in the hope of the future; he was stripped of all the surroundings in which his life at first was passed, and resided amongst foreigners, and thus purchased by present annoyance future blessedness. As then figuratively we call a particular circuit of the ocean a "bosom" so does Scripture seem to me to express the idea of those measureless blessings above by the word "bosom", meaning a place into which all virtuous voyagers of this life are, when they have put in from hence, brought to anchor in the waveless harbour of that gulf of blessings. Meanwhile the denial of these blessings which they witness becomes in the others a flame which burns the soul and causes the craving for the refreshment of one drop out of that ocean of blessings wherein the saints are affluent, which nevertheless they do not get.

What then is the doctrine here? Lazarus's soul is occupied with his present blessings and turns round to look at nothing that he has left, while the rich man is still attached, with a cement as it were, even after death, to the life of feeling, of which he does not divest himself even when he has ceased to live, still keeping flesh and blood in his thoughts (for in his entreaty that his kindred may be exempted from his sufferings he plainly shows that he is not freed yet from fleshly feeling), in such details of the story, I think our Lord teaches us this; that those still living in the flesh must as much as they can separate and free themselves from its attachments by virtuous conduct, in order that after death they may not need a second death to cleanse them from the remnants that are owing to this cement of the flesh, and, when once the bonds are loosed from around the soul, her soaring up to the Good may be swift and unimpeded, with no anguish of the body to distract her.

For if any one becomes wholly and thoroughly carnal in thought, such a one, with every motion and energy of the soul absorbed in fleshly desires, is not parted from such attachments, even in the disembodied state; just as those who have lingered long in noisome places do not part with the unpleasantness contracted by that lengthened stay, even when they pass into a sweet atmosphere. So it is that, when the change is made into the impalpable unseen, not even then will it be possible for the lovers of the flesh to avoid dragging away with them some fleshly foulness; and thereby their torment will be intensified, their soul having been materialised by such surroundings. I think too that this view of the matter harmonises with the assertion made by some persons that shadowy phantoms of the departed are often seen around their graves. If this is really so, an inordinate attachment of that particular soul to the life in the flesh is proved to have existed, causing it to be unwilling, even when expelled from the flesh, to fly clean away and to admit the complete change of its form into the impalpable; it remains near the body even after the dissolution of the body, and though now outside it, hovers regretfully over the place where its material is, and continues to haunt it.

If, then, whether by forethought here, or by purgation hereafter, our soul becomes free from any emotional connection with the physical creation, there will be nothing to impede its contemplation of the beautiful; for this last is essentially capable of attracting every being that looks towards it. If the soul is purified of every vice, it will most certainly be in the sphere of beauty. The deity is in very substance beautiful; and to the deity the soul will in its state of purity have affinity, and will embrace it as like itself. Moreover, as every being is capable of attracting its like, and humanity is, in a way, like God, as bearing within itself some resemblances to its prototype, the soul is by a strict necessity attracted to the kindred deity. In fact what belongs to God must by all means and at any cost be preserved for Him. If then, on the one hand, the soul is unencumbered with superfluities and no trouble connected with the body presses it down, its advance towards Him who draws it to Himself is sweet and congenial.

But suppose on the other hand that it has been transfixed with the nails of character so as to be held down to a habit connected with material things, a case like that of those in the ruins caused by earthquakes, whose bodies are crushed by the mounds of rubbish; and let us imagine by way of illustration that these are not only pressed down by the weight of the ruins, but have been pierced as well with some spikes and splinters discovered with them in the rubbish. What, then, would naturally be the plight of those bodies, when they were being dragged by relatives from the ruins to receive the holy rites of burial, mangled and torn entirely, disfigured in the most direful manner conceivable, with the nails beneath the heap harrowing them by the very violence necessary to pull them out?

Such I think is the plight of the soul as well, when the divine force, for God's very love of man, drags that which belongs to Him from the ruins of the irrational and material. Not in hatred or revenge for a wicked life, to my thinking, does God bring upon sinners those painful dispensations; He is only claiming and drawing to Himself whatever, to please Him, came into existence. But while for a noble end He is attracting the soul to Himself, the fountain of all blessedness, it is necessarily the occasion to the being so attracted of a state of torture. Just as those who refine gold from the dross which it contains not only get this base alloy to melt in the fire, but are obliged to melt the pure gold along with the alloy, and then while this last is being consumed the gold remains, so, while evil is being consumed in the purgatorial fire, the soul that is welded to this evil must inevitably be in the fire too, until the spurious material alloy is consumed and annihilated by this fire.

If clay is deeply plastered round a rope, and then the end of the rope is put through a narrow hole, and then someone on the further side violently pulls it by that end, the result must be that, while the rope itself obeys the force exerted, the clay that has been plastered upon it is scraped off it with this violent pulling and is left outside the hole and, moreover, is the cause why the rope does not run easily through the passage, but has to undergo a violent tension at the hands of the puller. In such a manner, I think, we may imagine the agonised struggle of that soul which has wrapped itself up in earthy material passions, when God is drawing it, His own one, to Himself, and the foreign matter which has somehow grown into its substance has to be scraped from it by brute force and so occasions it that keen intolerable anguish.

Therefore it seems that it is not punishment chiefly and principally that the deity, as judge, afflicts sinners with, but He operates, only to get the good separated from the evil and to attract it into the communion of blessedness.

That is my meaning; and also that the agony will be measured by the amount of evil there is in each individual. For it would not be reasonable to think that the man who has remained long in evil known to be forbidden, and the man who has fallen only into moderate sins, should be tortured to the same amount in the judgment upon their vicious habit; but according to the quantity of material will be the longer or shorter time that an agonising flame will be burning; that is as long as there is fuel to feed it. In the case of the man who has acquired a heavy weight of material, the consuming fire must necessarily be very searching; but where that which the fire has to feed upon has spread less far, there the penetrating fierceness of the punishment is mitigated so far as the amount of evil in the subject is diminished. In any and every case evil must be removed out of existence, so that, as we said above, the absolutely non-existent should cease to be at all. Since it is not in its nature that evil should exist outside the will, does it not follow that when every will rests in God, evil will be reduced to complete annihilation, owing to no receptacle there being left for it?

But what help can one find in this devout hope, when one considers the greatness of the evil in undergoing torture even for a single year; and if this intolerable anguish be prolonged for the interval of an age, what grain of comfort is left from any subseqent expectation to him whose purgation is thus commensurate with an entire age?

Why, either we must plan to keep the soul absolutely untouched and free from any stain of evil; or, if our passionate nature makes that quite impossible, then we must plan that our failures in excellence consist only in mild and easily-curable derelictions. For the gospel in its teaching distinguishes between a debtor of ten thousand talents and a debtor of five hundred pence, and of fifty pence and of a farthing, which is the "uttermost" of coins; it proclaims that God's just judgment reaches to all, and enhances the payment necessary as the weight of the debt increases, on the other hand does not overlook the very smallest debts. But the gospel tells us that this payment of debts was not effected by the refunding of money, but that the indebted man was delivered to the tormentors until he had paid the whole debt; and that means nothing else than paying in the coin of torment the inevitable recompense; the recompense, I mean, that consists in taking the share of pain incurred during his lifetime, when he inconsiderately chose mere pleasure, undiluted with its opposite; so that having put off from him all that foreign growth which sin is, and discarded the shame of any debts, he might stand in liberty and fearlessness.

Now liberty is the coming up to a state which owns no master and is self-regulating; it is that which we were given by God at the beginning, but which has been obscured by the feeling of shame arising from indebtedness. Liberty too is in all cases essentially the same; it has a natural attraction to itself. It follows, then, that as everything that is free will be united with its like, and as virtue is a thing that has no master, that is it is free, everything that is free will be united with virtue. But, further, the Divine Being is the fountain of all virtue. Therefore, those who have parted with evil will be united with Him; and so, as the apostle says, God will be "all in all". This utterance seems to me plainly to confirm the opinion we have already arrived at, for it means that God will replace all other things, and be in all.

For while our present life is active among a variety of multiform conditions, and the things we have relations with are numerous, for instance, time, air, locality, food and drink, clothing, sunlight, lamplight, and other necessities of life, none of which is God, that blessed state which we hope for is in need of none of these things, but the Divine Being will become all, and instead of all, to us, distributing Himself proportionately to every need of that existence. It is plain, too, from the holy Scripture, that God becomes, to those who deserve it, locality, and home, and clothing, and food, and drink, and light, and riches, and dominion, and everything thinkable and nameable makes our life happy. But He that becomes "all" things will be "in all" things too; and here it appears to me that Scripture teaches the complete annihilation of evil. If, that is, God will be "in all" existing things, evil, plainly, will not then be amongst them; for if anyone was to assume that it did exist then, how could the belief that God will be "in all" be kept intact? The excepting of that one thing, evil, mars the comprehensiveness of the term "all". But He that will be "in all" will never be in that which does not exist.

What then are we to say to those whose hearts fail at these calamities?

We will say to them this: "It is foolish, good people, for you to fret and complain of the chain of this fixed sequence of life's realities; you do not know the goal towards which each single dispensation of the universe is moving. You do not know that all things have to be assimilated to the divine nature in accordance with the artistic plan of their author, in a certain regularity and order. Indeed, it was for this that intelligent beings came into existence; namely, that the riches of the divine blessings should not lie idle. The all-creating wisdom fashioned these souls, these receptacles with free wills, as vessels as it were, for this very purpose, that there should be some capacities able to receive His blessings and become continually larger with the inpouring of the stream. Such are the wonders that the participation in the divine blessings works: it makes Him into whom they come larger and more capacious; from his capacity to receive it gets for the receiver an actual increase in bulk as well, and he never stops enlarging. The fountain of blessings wells up unceasingly, and the partaker's nature, finding nothing superfluous and without a use in that which it receives, makes the whole influx an enlargement of its own proportions, and becomes at once more wishful to imbibe the nobler nourishment and more capable of containing it; each grows along with each, both the capacity which is nursed in such abundance of blessings and so grows greater, and the nurturing supply which comes on in a flood, answering to the growth of those increasing powers. It is likely, therefore, that this bulk will mount to such a magnitude as there is no limit to check, so that we should never grow into it. With such a prospect before us, are you angry that our nature is advancing to its goal along the path appointed for us? Why, our career cannot be run thitherward, except that which weighs us down, I mean this encumbering load of earthiness, be shaken of the soul; nor can we be domiciled in purity with the corresponding part of our nature, unless we have cleansed ourselves by a better training from the habit of affection which we have contracted in life towards this earthiness. But if there be in you any clinging to this body, and the being unlocked from this darling thing give you pain, let not this either make you despair. You will behold this bodily envelopment, which is now dissolved in death, woven again out of the same atoms, not indeed into this organisation with its gross and heavy texture, but with its threads worked up into something more subtle and ethereal, so that you will not only have near you that which you love, but it will be restored to you with a brighter and more entrancing beauty.

We have not yet touched the most vital of all the questions relating to our faith. I mean, that the inspired writings, both in the New and in the Old Testament, declare most emphatically not only that, when our race has completed the ordered chain of its existence as the ages lapse through their complete circle, this current streaming onward as generation succeeds generation will cease altogether, but also that then, when the completed universe no longer admits of further increase, all the souls in their entire number will come back out of their invisible and scattered condition into tangibility and light, the identical atoms (belonging to each soul) reassembling together in the same order as before; and this reconstitution of human life is called, in these writings which contain God's teaching, the Resurrection.

First, I think, we must briefly run over the scattered proclamations of this doctrine in holy Scripture; they shall give the finishing touch to our discourse. Observe, then, that I can hear David, in the midst of his praises in the divine songs, where he has taken for his theme God's administration of the world, saying: "Thou shalt take away their breath, and they shall die, and return to their dust: Thou shalt send forth Thy Spirit, and they shall be created: and Thou shalt renew the face of the earth." (Psalm 104:29–30). He says that a power of the Spirit which works in all vivifies the beings into whom it enters and deprives those whom He abandons of their life. Seeing, then, that the dying is declared to occur at the Spirit's departure, and the renewal of these dead ones at His appearance, and seeing moreover that in the order of the statement the death of those who are to be thus renewed comes first, we hold that in these words that mystery of the Resurrection is proclaimed to the Church, and that David in the spirit of prophecy expressed this very gift.

One might select many other passages of holy Scripture to establish the doctrine of the Resurrection. For instance, Ezekiel leaps in the spirit of prophecy over all the intervening time, with its vast duration; he stands, by his powers of foresight, in the actual moment of the Resurrection and, as if he had really gazed on what is still to come, brings it in his description before our eyes. He saw a mighty plain, unfolded to an endless distance before him, and vast heaps of bones upon it flung at random, some this way, some that; and then under an impulse from God these bones began to move and group themselves with their fellows that they once owned, and adhere to the familiar sockets, and then clothe themselves with muscle, flesh and skin (which was the process called "decorating" in the poetry of the Psalms); a Spirit in fact was giving life and movement to everything that lay there. But as regards our apostle's description of the wonders of the Resurrection, why should one repeat it, seeing that it can easily be found and read? How, for instance, with "a shout" and the "sound of trumpets" (in the language of the Word) all dead and prostrate things shall be "changed in the twinkling of an eye" into immortal beings.

The expressions in the gospels also I will pass over; for their meaning is quite clear to everyone; and our Lord does not declare in word alone that the bodies of the dead shall be raised up again; but He shows in action the Resurrection itself, making a beginning of this work of wonder from things more within our reach and less capable of being doubted. First, that is, He displays His life-giving power in the case of the deadly forms of disease, and chases those maladies by one word of command; then He raises a little girl just dead; then He makes a young man, who is already being carried out, sit up on his bier, and delivers him to his mother; after that He calls forth from his tomb the four-days-dead and already decomposed Lazarus, vivifying the prostrate body with His commanding voice; then after three days He raises from the dead His own human body, pierced though it was with the nails and spear, and brings the print of those nails and the spear-wound to witness to the Resurrection. But I think that a detailed mention of these things is not necessary; for no doubt about them lingers in the minds of those who have accepted the written accounts of them.

But still the question remains: Is the state which we are to expect to be like the present state of the body? Because if so, then men had better avoid hoping for any Resurrection at all. For if our bodies are to be restored to life again in the same sort of condition as they are in when they cease to breathe, then all that man can look forward to in the Resurrection is an unending calamity. For what spectacle is more piteous than when in extreme old age our bodies shrivel up and change into something repulsive and hideous, with the flesh all wasted in the length of years, the skin dried up about the bones till it is all in wrinkles, the muscles in a spasmodic state from being no longer enriched with their natural moisture, and the whole body consequently shrunk, the hands on either side powerless to perform their natural work, shaken with an involuntary trembling? What a sight again are the bodies of persons in a long consumption! They differ from bare bones only in giving the appearance of being covered with a worn-out veil of skin. What a sight too are those of persons swollen with the disease of dropsy! What words could describe the unsightly disfigurement of sufferers from leprosy? Gradually over all their limbs and organs of sensation rottenness spreads and devours them. What words could describe that of persons who have been mutilated in earthquake, battle, or by any other visitation, and live on in such a plight for a long time before their natural deaths? Or of those who from any injury have grown up from infancy with their limbs awry? What can one say of them? What is one to think about the bodies of new-born infants who have been either exposed, or strangled, or died a natural death, if they are to be brought to life again just such as they were? Are they to continue in that infantile state? What condition could be more miserable than that? Or are they to come to the flower of their age? Well, but what sort of milk does Nature have to suckle them again?

It comes then to this: that, if our bodies are to live again in every respect the same as before, this thing that we are expecting is simply a calamity; whereas if they are not the same, the person raised up will be another than he who died. If, for instance, a little boy was buried, but a grown man rises again, or the reverse, how can we say that the dead in his very self is raised up, when he has had someone substituted for him by virtue of this difference in age? Instead of the child, one sees a grown-up man. Instead of the old man, one sees a person in his prime. In fact, instead of the one person another entirely. The cripple is changed into the able-bodied man; the consumptive sufferer into a man whose flesh is firm; and so on of all possible cases. If, then, the body will not come to life again just such in its attributes as it was when it mingled with the earth, that dead body will not rise again; but on the contrary the earth will be formed into another man. How, then, will the Resurrection affect myself, when instead of me someone else will come to life?

But why dwell longer on these the less forcible objections to the Resurrection, and neglect the strongest one of all? For who has not heard that human life is like a stream, moving from birth to death at a certain rate of progress, and then only ceasing from that progressive movement when it ceases also to exist? This movement indeed is not one of spatial change; our bulk never exceeds itself; but it makes this advance by means of internal alteration; and as long as this alteration is that which its name implies, it never remains at the same stage from moment to moment; for how can that which is being altered be kept in any sameness? There is influx and efflux going on in it in an alternating progress until the moment that the body ceases to live; as long as it is living it has no stay; for it is either being replenished, or it is discharging in vapour, or it is being kept in motion by both of these processes combined. If, then, a particular man is not the same even as he was yesterday, but is made different by this transmutation, when the Resurrection shall restore our body to life again, that single man will become a crowd of human beings, so that with his rising again there will be found the babe, the child, the boy, the youth, the man, the father, the old man, and all the intermediate persons that he once was. But further; chastity and profligacy are both carried on in the flesh; those also who endure the most painful tortures for their religion, and those on the other hand who shrink from such, both one class and the other reveal their character in relation to fleshly sensations; how then can justice be done at the judgment? Let me say something else also from amongst the objections made by unbelievers to this doctrine. No part, they urge, of the body is made by nature without a function. Some parts, for instance, are the efficient causes within us of our being alive; without them our life in the flesh could not possibly be carried on; such are the heart, liver, brain, lungs, stomach, and the other vitals; others are assigned to the activities of sensation; others to those of handing and walking; others are adapted for the transmission of a posterity. Now if the life to come is to be in exactly the same circumstances as this, the supposed change in us is reduced to nothing; but if the report is true, as indeed it is, which represents marriage as forming no part of the economy of that after-life, and eating and drinking as not then preserving its continuance, what use will there be for the members of our body, when we are no longer to expect in that existence any of the activities for which our members now exist? If, for the sake of marriage, there are now certain organs adapted for marriage, then, whenever the latter ceases to be, we shall not need those organs; the same may be said of the hands for working with, the feet for running with, the mouth for taking food with, the teeth for grinding it with, the organs of the stomach for digesting, the evacuating ducts for getting rid of that which has become superfluous. When, therefore, all those operations will be no more, how or wherefore will their instruments exist?

The truth does not lie in these arguments, even though we may find it impossible to give a rhetorical answer to them, couched in equally strong language. The true explanation of all these questions is still stored up in the hidden treasure-rooms of wisdom, and will not come to the light until that moment when we shall be taught the mystery of the Resurrection by the reality of it; and then there will be no more need of phrases to explain the things which we now hope for. Just as many questions might be started for debate amongst people sitting up at night as to the kind of thing that sunshine is, and then the simple appearing of it in all its beauty would render any verbal description superfluous, so every calculation that tries to arrive conjecturally at the future state will be reduced to nothingness by the object of our hopes, when it comes upon us. But since it is our duty not to leave the arguments brought against us in any way unexamined, we will expound the truth as to these points as follows. First let us get a clear notion as to the scope of this doctrine; in other words, what is the end that holy Scripture has in view in promulgating it and creating the belief in it. Well, to sketch the outline of so vast a truth and to embrace it in a definition, we will say that the Resurrection is "the reconstitution of our nature in its original form." But in that form of life, of which God Himself was the Creator, it is reasonable to believe that there was neither age nor infancy nor any of the sufferings arising from our present various infirmities, nor any kind of bodily affliction whatever.

It is reasonable, I say, to believe that God was the Creator of none of these things, but that man was a thing divine before his humanity got within reach of the assault of evil; that then, however, with the inroad of evil, all these afflictions also broke in upon him. Accordingly, a life that is free from evil is under no necessity whatever of being passed amid the things that result from evil. It follows that when a man travels through ice he must get his body chilled; or when he walks in a very hot sun that he must get his skin darkened; but if he has kept clear of the one or the other he escapes these results entirely, both the darkening and the chilling; no one, in fact, when a particular cause was removed, would be justified in looking for the effect of that particular cause. Just so our nature, becoming passionate, had to encounter all the necessary results of a life of passion: but when it shall have started back to the state of passionless blessedness, it will no longer encounter the inevitable results of evil tendencies. Seeing, then, that all the infusions of the life of the brute into our nature were not in us before our humanity descended through the touch of evil into passions, most certainly, when we abandon those passions, we shall abandon all their visible results. No one, therefore, will be justified in seeking in that other life for the consequences in us of any passion. Just as if a man, who, clad in a ragged tunic, has divested himself of the garb, feels no more its disgrace upon him, so we too, when we have cast off that dead unsightly tunic made from the skins of brutes and put upon us (for I take the "coats of skins" to mean that conformation belonging to a brute nature with which we were clothed when we became familiar with passionate indulgence), shall, along with the casting off of that tunic, fling from us all the belongings that were round us of that skin of a brute; and such accretions are sexual intercourse, conception, parturition, impurities, suckling, feeding, evacuation, gradual growth to full size, prime of life, old age, disease and death. If that skin is no longer round us, how can its resulting consequences be left behind within us? It is folly, then, when we are to expect a different state of things in the life to come, to object to the doctrine of the Resurrection on the ground of something that has nothing to do with it. I mean, what has thinness or corpulence, a state of consumption or of plethora, or any other condition supervening in a nature that is ever in a flux, to do with the other life, stranger as it is to any fleeting and transitory passing such as that?

One thing, and one thing only, is required for the operation of the Resurrection; namely that a man should have lived, by being born; or, to use the gospel words, that "a man should be born into the world"; the length or briefness of the life, the manner of the death, is an irrelevant subject of enquiry in connection with that operation. Whatever instance we take, howsoever we suppose this to have been, it is all the same; from these differences in life there arises no difficulty, any more than any facility, with regard to the Resurrection. He who has once begun to live must necessarily go on having once lived, after his intervening dissolution in death has been repaired in the Resurrection. As to the how and the when of his dissolution, what do they matter to the Resurrection? Consideration of such points belongs to another line of enquiry altogether. For instance, a man may have lived in bodily comfort, or in affliction, virtuously or viciously, renowned or disgraced; he may have passed his days miserably, or happily. These and such like results must be obtained from the length of his life and the manner of his living; and to be able to pass a judgment on the things done in his life, it will be necessary for the judge to scrutinise his indulgences, as the case may be, or his losses, or his disease, or his old age, or his prime, or his youth, or his wealth, or his poverty: how well or ill a man, placed in either of these, concluded his destined career; whether he was the recipient of many blessings, or of many ills in a length of life; or tasted neither of them at all, but ceased to live before his mental powers were formed. But whenever the time comes that God shall have brought our nature back to the primal state of man, it will be useless to talk of such things, and to based upon such things can prove God's power to be impeded in arriving at His end. His end is one, and one only; it is this: when the complete whole of our race shall have been perfected from the first man to the last, some having at once in this life been cleansed from evil, others having afterwards in the necessary periods been healed by the fire, others having in their life here been unconscious equally of good and of evil, to offer to every one of us participation in the blessings which are in Him, which, the Scripture tells us, "eye hath not seen, nor ear heard," nor thought ever reached. But this is nothing else, as I at least understand it, but to be in God Himself; for the Good which is above hearing and eye and heart must be that Good which transcends the universe.

But the difference between the virtuous and the vicious life led at the present time will be illustrated in this way: in the quicker or more tardy participation of each in that promised blessedness. According to the amount of the ingrained wickedness of each will be computed the duration of his cure. This cure consists in the cleansing of his soul, and that cannot be achieved without an excruciating condition, as has been expounded in our previous discussion. But anyone would more fully comprehend the futility and irrelevance of all these objections by trying to fathom the depths of our apostle's wisdom. When explaining this mystery to the Corinthians, who, perhaps, were themselves bringing forward the same objections to it as its impugners today bring forward to overthrow our faith, he proceeds on his own authority to chide the audacity of their ignorance, and speaks thus: "Thou wilt say, then, to me, how are the dead raised up, and with what body do they come? Thou fool, that which thou sowest does not live without first dying. And that which thou sowest, thou sowest not that body that shall be, but bare grain, it may chance of wheat or of some other grain. But God giveth it a body as it hath pleased Him." In that passage, it seems to me, he gags the mouths of men who display their ignorance of the fitting proportions in nature, and who measure the divine power by their own strength, and think that only so much is possible to God as the human understanding can take in, and that what is beyond it surpasses also the divine ability. For the man who had asked the apostle, "how are the dead raised up?" evidently implies that it is impossible when once the body's atoms have been scattered that they should again come in concourse together; and this being impossible, and no other possible form of body, besides that arising from such a concourse, being left, he, after the fashion of clever controversialists, concludes the truth of what he wants to prove, by a species of syllogism, thus: If a body is a concourse of atoms, and a second assemblage of these is impossible, what sort of body will those have who rise again? This conclusion, seemingly involved by this artful contrivance of premises, the apostle calls "folly," as coming from men who failed to perceive in other parts of the creation the masterliness of the divine power. For, omitting the sublime miracles of God's hand, by which it would have been easy to place his hearer in a dilemma (for instance he might have asked "how or whence comes a heavenly body, that of the sun for example, or that of the moon, or that which is seen in the constellations; whence the firmament, the air, water, the earth?"), he, on the contrary, convicts the objectors of lack of reason by means of objects which grow alongside us and are very familiar to all. "Does not even husbandry teach thee," he asks, "that the man who in calculating the transcendent powers of the Deity limits them by his own is a fool?" Whence do seeds get the bodies that spring up from them? What precedes this springing up? Is it not a death that precedes? (At least, if the dissolution of a compacted whole is a death.) For indeed it cannot be supposed that the seed would spring up into a shoot unless it had been dissolved in the soil, and so become spongy and porous to such an extent as to mingle its own qualities with the adjacent moisture of the soil, and thus become transformed into a root and shoot; not stopping even there, but changing again into the stalk with its intervening knee-joints that gird it up like so many clasps, to enable it to carry with erect figure the ear with its load of corn. Where, then, were all these things belonging to the grain before its dissolution in the soil? And yet this result sprang from that grain; if that grain had not existed first, the ear would not have arisen. Just, then, as the "body" of the ear comes to light out of the seed, God's artistic touch of power producing it all out of that single thing, and just as it is neither entirely the same thing as that seed, nor something altogether different, so by these miracles performed on seeds you may now interpret the mystery of the Resurrection.

The divine power, in the superabundance of omnipotence, does not only restore you that body once dissolved, but makes great and splendid additions to it, whereby the human being is furnished in a manner still more magnificent. "It is sown," he says, "in corruption; it is raised in incorruption: it is sown in weakness; it is raised in power: it is sown in dishonour; it is raised in glory: it is sown a natural body; it is raised a spiritual body." The grain of wheat, after its dissolution in the soil, leaves behind the slightness of its bulk and the peculiar quality of its shape, and yet it has not left and lost itself, but, still self-centred, grows into the ear, though in many points it has made an advance upon itself, in size, in splendour, in complexity, in form. In the same fashion the human being deposits in death all those peculiar surroundings which it has acquired from passionate propensities; dishonour, I mean, and corruption and weakness and characteristics of age; and yet the human being does not lose itself. It changes as it were into an ear of corn; into incorruption, that is, and glory and honour and power and absolute perfection; into a condition in which its life is no longer carried on in the ways peculiar to mere nature, but has passed into a spiritual and passionless existence. For it is the peculiarity of the natural body to be always moving in a stream, to be always altering from its state for the moment and changing into something else; but none of these processes, which we observe not only in man but also in plants and brutes, will be found remaining in the life that shall be then. Further, it seems to me that the words of the apostle in every respect harmonise with our own conception of what the Resurrection is. They indicate the very same thing that we have embodied in our own definition of it, in which we said that the Resurrection is no other thing than "the reconstitution of our nature in its original form." For, whereas we learn from Scripture in the account of the first creation, that first the earth brought forth "the green herb" (as the narrative says), and that then from this plant seed was yielded, from which, when it was shed on the ground, the same form of the original plant again sprang up, the apostle, it is to be observed, declares that this very same thing happens in the Resurrection also; and so we learn from him the fact, not only that our humanity will be then changed into something nobler, but also that what we have then to expect is nothing else than that which was at the beginning. In the beginning, we see, it was not an ear rising from a grain, but a grain coming from an ear, and, after that, the ear grows round the grain: and so the order indicated in this similitude clearly shows that all that blessed state which arises for us by means of the Resurrection is only a return to our pristine state of grace. We too, in fact, were once in a fashion in a full ear; but the burning heat of sin withered us up, and then on our dissolution by death the earth received us: but in the spring of the Resurrection she will reproduce this naked grain of our body in the form of an ear, tall, well-proportioned and erect, reaching to the heights of Heaven, and, for blade and beard, resplendent in incorruption, and with all the other godlike marks.

For "this corruptible must put on incorruption"; and this incorruption and glory and honour and power are those distinct and acknowledged marks of deity which once belonged to him who was created in God's image, and which we hope for hereafter. The first man, Adam, was the first ear; but with the arrival of evil human nature was diminished into a mere multitude; and, as happens to the grain on the ear, each individual man was denuded of the beauty of that primal ear, and mouldered in the soil: but in the Resurrection we are born again in our original splendour; only instead of that single primitive ear we become the countless myriads of ears in the cornfields. Then every one of the things which make up our conception of the good will come to take their place; incorruption, and life, and honour, and grace, and glory, and everything else that we conjecture is to be seen in God, and in His Image, man, as he was made.

The Sayings of Saint ANTHONY THE GREAT

1 When the holy Abba Anthony lived in the desert he was beset by despair, and attacked by many sinful thoughts. He said to God, "Lord, I want to be saved but these thoughts do not leave me alone; what shall I do in my affliction? How can I be saved?" A short while afterwards, when he got up to go out, Anthony saw a man like himself sitting at his work, getting up from his work to pray, then sitting down and plaiting a rope, then getting up again to pray. It was an angel of the Lord sent to correct and reassure him. He heard the angel saying to him, "Do this and you will be saved."

At these words, Anthony was filled with joy and courage. He did this, and he was saved.

2 When the same Abba Anthony thought about the depth of the judgments of God, he asked, "Lord, how is it that some die when they are young, while others drag on to extreme old age? Why are there those who are poor and those who are rich? Why do wicked men prosper and why are the just in need?" He heard a voice answering him, "Anthony, keep your attention on yourself; these things are according to the judgment of God, and it is not to your advantage to know anything about them."

3 Someone asked Abba Anthony, "What must one do in order to please God?" The old man replied, "Pay attention to what I tell you: whoever you may be, always have God before your eyes; whatever you do, do it according to the testimony of the holy Scriptures; in whatever place you live, do not easily leave it. Keep these three precepts and you will be saved."

4 Abba Anthony said to Abba Poemen, "This is the great work of a man: always to take the blame for his own sins before God and to expect temptation to his last breath."

5 He also said, "Whoever has not experienced temptation cannot enter into the Kingdom of Heaven." He even added, "Without temptations no one can be saved."

6 Abba Pambo asked Abba Anthony, "What ought I to do?" and the old man said to him, "Do not trust in your own righteousness, do not worry about the past, but control your tongue and your stomach."

7 Abba Anthony said, "I saw all the snares that the enemy spreads out over the world and I said groaning, What can get through from such snares?" Then I heard a voice saying to me, "Humility".

8 He also said, "Some have afflicted their bodies by asceticism, but they lack discernment, and so they are far from God."

9 He also said, "Our life and our death is with our neighbour. If we gain our brother, we have gained God, but if we scandalise our brother, we have sinned against Christ."

10 He said also, "Just as fish die if they stay too long out of water, so the monks who loiter outside their cells or pass their time with men of the world lose the intensity of inner peace. So like a fish going towards the sea, we must hurry to reach our cell, for fear that if we delay outside we will lose our inner watchfulness."

11 He said also, "He who wishes to live in solitude in the desert is delivered from three conflicts: hearing, speech, and sight; there is only one conflict for him and that is with fornication."

12 Some brothers came to find Abba Anthony to tell him about the visions they were having, and to find out from him if they were true or if they came from the demons. They had a donkey which died on the way. When they reached the place where the old man was, he said to them before they could ask him anything, "How was it that the little donkey died on the way here?" They said, "How do you know about that, Father?" And he told them, "The demons showed me what happened." So they said, "That was what we came to question you about, for fear we were being deceived, for we have visions which often turn out to be true." Thus the old man convinced them, by the example of the donkey, that their visions came from the demons.

13 A hunter in the desert saw Abba Anthony enjoying himself with the brethren and he was shocked. Wanting to show him that it was necessary sometimes to meet the needs of the brethren, the old man said to him, "Put an arrow in your bow and shoot it." So he did. The old man then said, "Shoot another", and he did so. Then the old man said, "Shoot yet again", and the hunter replied, "If I bend my bow so much I will break it." Then the old man said to him, "It is the same with the work of God. If we stretch the brethren beyond measure they will soon break. Sometimes it is necessary to come down to meet their needs." When he heard these words the hunter was pierced by compunction and greatly edified by the old man he went away. As for the brethren, they went home strengthened.

14 Abba Anthony heard of a very young monk who had performed a miracle on the road. Seeing the old men walking with difficulty along the road, he ordered the wild asses to come and carry them until they reached Abba Anthony. Those who

had been carried told Abba Anthony about it. He said to them, "This monk seems to me to be a ship loaded with goods but I do not know if he will reach harbour." After a while, Anthony suddenly began to weep, to tear his hair and lament. His disciples said to him, "Why are you weeping, Father?" and the old man replied, "A great pillar of the Church has just fallen (he meant the young monk) but go to him and see what has happened." So the disciples went and found the monk sitting on a mat and weeping for the sin he had committed. Seeing the disciples of the old man he said, "Tell the old man to pray that God will give me just ten days and I hope I will have made satisfaction." But in the space of five days he died.

15 The brothers praised a monk before Abba Anthony. When the monk came to see him, Anthony wanted to know how he would bear insults; and seeing that he could not bear them at all, he said to him, "You are like a village magnificently decorated on the outside, but destroyed from within by robbers."

16 A brother said to Abba Anthony, "Pray for me". The old man said to him, "I will have no mercy upon you, nor will God have any, if you yourself do not make an effort and if you do not pray to God."

17 One day some old men came to see Abba Anthony. In the midst of them was Abba Joseph. Wanting to test them, the old man suggested a text from the Scriptures, and, beginning with the youngest, he asked them what it meant. Each gave his opinion as he was able. But to each one the old man said, "You have not understood it." Last of all he said to Abba Joseph, "How would you explain this saying?" and he replied, "I do not know." Then Abba Anthony said, "Indeed, Abba Joseph has found the way, for he has said: "'I do not know.'"

18 Some brothers were coming from Scetis to see Abba Anthony. When they were getting into a boat to go there, they found an old man who also wanted to go there. The brothers did not know him. They sat in the boat, occupied by turns with the words of the fathers, scripture and their manual work. As for the old man, he remained silent. When they arrived on shore they found that the old man was also going to the cell of Abba Anthony. When they reached the place, Anthony said to them, "You found this old man a good companion for the journey?" Then he said to the old man, "You have brought many good brethren with you, father." The old man said, "No doubt they are good, but they do not have a door to their house and anyone who wishes can enter the stable and loose the ass." He meant that the brethren said whatever came into their mouths.

19 The brethren came to the Abba Anthony and said to him, "Speak a word; how are we to be saved?" The old man said to them, "You have heard the Scriptures. That should teach you how." But they said, "We want to hear from you too, Father." Then the old man said to them, "The gospel says, 'If anyone strikes you on one cheek, turn to him the other also.'" (Matthew 5:39) They said, "We cannot do that." The old man said, "If you cannot offer the other cheek, at least allow one cheek to be struck." "We cannot do that either," they said. So he said, "If you are not able to do that, do not return evil for evil," and they said, "We cannot do that either." Then the old man said to his disciple, "Prepare a little brew of corn for these invalids. If you cannot do this, or that, what can I do for you? What you need is prayers."

20 A brother renounced the world and gave his goods to the poor, but he kept back a little for his personal expenses. He went to see Abba Anthony. When he told him this the old man said to him, "If you want to be a monk, go into the village, buy some meat, cover your naked body with it and come here like that." The brother did so, and the dogs and birds tore at his flesh. When he came back the old man asked him whether he had followed his advice. He showed him his wounded body, and Saint Anthony said, "Those who renounce the world but want to keep something for themselves are torn in this way by the demons who make war on them."

21 It happened one day that one of the brethren in the monastery of Abba Elias was tempted. Cast out of the monastery, he went over the mountain to Abba Anthony. The brother lived near him for a while and then Anthony sent him back to the monastery from which he had been expelled. When the brothers saw him they cast him out yet again, and he went back to Abba Anthony saying, "My Father, they will not receive me." Then the old man sent them a

message saying, "A boat was shipwrecked at sea and lost its cargo; with great difficulty it reached the shore; but you want to throw into the sea that which has found a safe harbour on the shore." When the brothers understood that it was Abba Anthony who had sent them this monk, they received him at once.

22 Abba Anthony said, "I believe that the body possesses a natural movement, to which it is adapted, but which it cannot follow without the consent of the soul; it only signifies in the body a movement without passion. There is another movement, which comes from the nourishment and warming of the body by eating and drinking, and this causes the heat of the blood to stir up the body to work. That is why the apostle said, 'Do not get drunk with wine for that is debauchery' (Ephesians 5:18). And in the Gospel the Lord also recommends this to his disciples: 'Take heed to yourselves lest your hearts be weighed down with dissipation and drunkenness' (Luke 21:34). But there is yet another movement which afflicts those who fight, and that comes from the wiles and jealousy of the demons. You must understand what these three bodily movements are: one is natural, one comes from too much to eat, the third is caused by the demons."

23 He also said, "God does not allow the same warfare and temptations to this generation as he did formerly, for men are weaker now and cannot bear so much."

24 It was revealed to Abba Anthony in his desert that there was one who was his equal in the city. He was a doctor by profession and whatever he had beyond his needs he gave to the poor, and every day he sang the Sanctus with the angels.

25 Abba Anthony said, "A time is coming when men will go mad, and when they see someone who is not mad, they will attack him saying, 'You are mad, you are not like us.'"

26 The brethren came to Abba Anthony and laid before him a passage from Leviticus. The old man went out into the desert, secretly followed by Abba Ammonias, who knew that this was his custom. Abba Anthony went a long way off and stood there praying, crying in a loud voice, "God, send Moses, to make me understand this saying." Then there came a voice speaking with him. Abba Ammonias said that although he heard the voice speaking with him, he could not understand what it said.

27 Three fathers used to go and visit blessed Anthony every year and two of them used to discuss their thoughts and the salvation of their souls with him, but the third always remained silent and did not ask him anything. After a long time, Abba Anthony said to him, "You often come here to see me, but you never ask me anything," and the other replied, "It is enough for me to see you, father."

28 They said that a certain old man asked God to let him see the fathers and he saw them all except Abba Anthony. So he asked his guide, "Where is Abba Anthony?" He told him in reply that in the place where God is, there Anthony would be.

29 A brother in a monastery was falsely accused of fornication and he arose and went to Abba Anthony. The brethren also came from the monastery to correct him and bring him back. They set about proving that he had done this thing, but he defended himself and denied that he had done anything of the kind. Now Abba Paphnutius, who is called Cephalos, happened to be there, and he told them this parable: "I have seen a man on the bank of the river buried up to his knees in mud and some men came to give him a hand to help him out, but they pushed him further in up to his neck." Then Abba Anthony said this about Abba Paphnutius: "Here is a real man, who can care for souls and save them." All those present were pierced to the heart by the words of the old man and they asked forgiveness of the brother. So, admonished by the fathers, they took the brother back to the monastery.

30 Some say of Saint Anthony that he was "spirit-borne", that is, carried along by the Holy Spirit, but he would never speak of this to men. Such men see what is happening in the world, as well as knowing what is going to happen.

31 One day Abba Anthony received a letter from the Emperor Constantius, asking him to come to Constantinople and he wondered whether he ought to go. So he said to Abba Paul, his disciple, "Ought I to go?" He replied, "If you go, you will be called Anthony; but if you stay here, you will be called Abba Anthony."

32 Abba Anthony said, "I no longer fear God, but I love Him. For 'love casts out fear'." (I John 4: 18).

33 He also said, "Always have the fear of God before your eyes. Remember Him who gives death and life. Hate the world and all that is in it. Hate all peace that comes from the flesh. Renounce this life, so that you may be alive to God. Remember what you have promised God, for it will be required of you on the day of judgment. Suffer hunger, thirst, nakedness, be watchful and sorrowful; weep and groan in your heart; test yourself, to see if you are worthy of God; despise the flesh, so that you may preserve your souls."

34 Abba Anthony once went to visit Abba Amoun in Mount Nitria and when they met, Abba Amoun said, "By your prayers the number of the brethren increases, and some of them want to build more cells where they may live in peace. How far away from here do you think we should build the cells?" Abba Anthony said, "Let us eat at the ninth hour and then let us go out for a walk in the desert and explore the country." So they went out into the desert and they walked until sunset and then Abba Anthony said, "Let us pray and plant the cross here, so that those who wish to do so may build here. Then when those who remain there want to visit those who have come here, they can take a little food at the ninth hour and then come. If they do this, they will be able to keep in touch with each other without distraction of mind." The distance is twelve miles.

35 Abba Anthony said, "Whoever hammers a lump of iron first decides what he is going to make of it, a scythe, a sword, or an axe. Even so we ought to make up our minds what kind of virtue we want to forge or we labour in vain."

36 He also said, "Obedience with abstinence gives men power over wild beasts."

37 He also said, "Nine monks fell away after many labours and were obsessed with spiritual pride, for they put their trust in their own works and being deceived they did not give due heed to the commandment that says, 'Ask your Father and He will tell you.'" (Deuteronomy 32:7).

38 And he said this, "If he is able, a monk ought to tell his elders confidently how many steps he takes and how many drops of water he drinks in his cell, in case he is in error about it."

The Epistle of Saint JEROME to Heliodorus

With what great eagerness and love I urged that we should remain together in the desert, your heart, conscious of our affection for each other, fully realises. With what lamentations, with what grief, with what groaning I pursued your departure, even this letter to you is a witness; you see it is blotted with tears. But you, like a spoiled child, softened with flattering words your contemptuous refusal of my request. And I in my abstraction did not know at the time what to do.

Should I have kept still? But because of my burning eagerness I could not hide my feelings and control myself. Should I have besought you more earnestly? But you were unwilling to listen, because you did not love me as I loved you. My spurned affection has done the one thing it could. Unable to keep you when you were present, it seeks you when absent. So, since you yourself when on the point of departure asked me to send you a letter of invitation after I had moved to the desert, I promised that I would do so. I am inviting you. Now make haste.

I do not want you to remember old privations: the desert loves the naked. I do not want the difficulty of our pilgrimage of other days to dismay you. Since you believe in Christ, believe also in His words: "Seek first the Kingdom of God, and all these things shall be added unto you." You need not take wallet or staff. He is rich enough who is poor with Christ.

But what am I about? Am I again rashly entreating you? Away with prayers. An end to persuasion. Slighted love should become angry. You, who ignored me when I importuned, will perhaps give ear to my reproof. What are you doing in your ancestral home, luxury-loving soldier? Where is the wall, the ditch, the winter spent under tents of skins? Lo, the trumpet sounds from Heaven. Lo, our commander, fully armed, comes forth surrounded by clouds, to conquer the world. Lo, a sharp two-edged sword goes forth from the king's mouth and cuts down all that stands in its way. And do you come forth, pray, from bedchamber to battle, from the shade to the sunlight?

A body accustomed to a tunic cannot bear the weight of a coat of mail. A head covered with a linen cap refuses a helmet. A hard sword hilt chafes a hand soft from idleness. Hear the pronouncement of your king: "He that is not with me is against me; and he that does not come with me scatters." Remember the day of your enlistment when, buried with Christ in baptism, you took the oath of allegiance: that for His name's sake you would spare neither mother nor father.

Lo, the adversary within your very breast is attempting to kill Christ. Lo, the camp of the enemy pants for the donation which you received when about to set forth on military service. Even if your little nephew is clinging to your neck, although your mother with dishevelled hair and torn garments is displaying the breasts with which she nurtured you, although your father lies on the threshold, trample your father underfoot and set forth. Fly with dry eyes to the standard of the cross. Cruelty is a kind of dutiful conduct in these circumstances.

Later the day will come when you will return to your own country, when you will walk about the heavenly Jerusalem, crowned as a brave man. Then you will take up your citizenship with Paul; then you will seek rights in that same city for your parents; then you will make intercession on my behalf, since I incited you to conquer. Nor, indeed, am I ignorant of the fetters by which you are now impeded.

I have no breast of iron, no heart of stone, I was not born of flint, nor did Hyrcanian tigers suckle me. I, too, have passed through all this. Now your widowed sister clings to you with caressing arms. Now those house slaves with whom you grew up say: "To whom will you leave us as servants?" Now, too, your one time nurse, already old, and her spouse, second only to your own father in claims on your affection, exclaim: "Wait a little for us to die, and then bury us."

Perhaps your foster mother, with pendulous breasts, her brow furrowed with wrinkles, recalling an old lullaby, may repeat it for you. Your teachers of grammar, if they wish, may say: "On you the whole house turns and leans." The love of Christ and the fear of Hell can easily burst these bonds.

But (you say) the Scriptures teach that we must obey our parents. But whoever loves parents more than Christ loses his own soul. The enemy grasps his sword to slay me: and shall I think of my mother's tears? Shall I desert the ranks for the sake of my father, to whom for Christ's sake I do not owe burial, although for His sake I owe it to all men? Peter, by his cowardly advice, was a scandal to the Lord before His passion.

When his brethren sought to prevent Paul from going to Jerusalem, he replied, "What do you mean weeping and afflicting my heart? For I am ready not only to be bound but to die also in Jerusalem for the name of our Lord Jesus Christ."

That battering-ram of affection, by which faith is shaken, must be beaten back by the wall of the gospel. "My mother and my brethren are those who do the will of my Father who is in heaven." If they believe in Christ, they should support me when I am about to fight for His name; if they do not believe, "let the dead bury their dead."

"But this", you say, "holds true only of martyrdom." You are greatly mistaken, brother, if you think a Christian is ever free from persecution. Even now you are being fiercely attacked even if you are not aware of being attacked. Our adversary, as a roaring lion, goes about seeking someone to devour, and do you think this is peace? "He lies in ambush with the rich in private places, that he may kill the innocent; his eyes are upon the poor man; he lies in wait as a lion in his den. He lies in ambush that he may catch the poor man." And do you, destined to be his prey, enjoy soft slumbers, protected by the shade of a leafy tree?

On this side luxury assails me, on that avarice seeks to burst in, on another my belly desires to be my god instead of Christ. Lust constrains me to drive away the Holy Spirit that dwells within me, to violate His temple. An enemy "who has a thousand names, a thousand deadly arts", pursues me, I say. And shall I, poor wretch, deem myself the victor even while I am being taken captive?

I would not, my dearest brother, have you weigh transgressions against each other and judge these which I have mentioned to be less than the sin of idolatry. Nay, give heed to the opinion of the apostle, who says: "For know you this and understand, that no fornicator, or unclean, or covetous person (who serves idols), has inheritance in the Kingdom of God and of Christ." And although in general whatever is of the devil savours of hostility to God, and what is of the devil is idolatry, for all idols are subject to him, yet in another passage he makes a definite statement, saying specifically: "Mortify your members upon the earth: fornication, uncleanness, evil concupiscence and covetousness which are in the service of idols, for which things the wrath of God comes."

The service of an idol consists not merely in this, that one takes a pinch of incense between two fingers and casts this upon an altar fire, or pours a libation of wine from a saucer. Let him deny that avarice is idolatry who can describe as justice the selling of the Lord for thirty pieces of silver. Let him deny that there is sacrilege in lust who has polluted the members of Christ and the living sacrifice pleasing to God by shameful intercourse with the victims of public vice. Let him not admit that they who in the acts of the apostles kept back part of their inheritance, perishing by an immediate punishment, are idolators; but only in case he is like them.

Observe, brother, it is not permitted you to keep any of your possessions. "Everyone who does renounce all that he possesses," says the Lord, "cannot be my disciples."

Why are you, a Christian, so lacking in spirit? Remember him who left his father as well as his nets; remember the publican who arose from the custom house, becoming an apostle at once. "The Son of Man has nowhere to lay his head," and do you measure out wide porticoes and buildings of great extent? Do you, "a joint heir with Christ," expect an inheritance in this world? Translate the word "monk": that is your proper title. What are you, a "solitary", doing in a crowd?

I am no experienced sailor, with ship and cargo intact, addressing warnings suited to those unacquainted with the waves. But as one lately cast ashore after shipwreck, I give advice, with timid voice, to those about to set sail. In that boiling flood the Charybdis of luxury swallows up our salvation. There lust, with a smile like that of Scylla on her girlish lips, by flattery seeks to lure us to make shipwreck of our chastity. Here is a savage shore, here the pirate devil with his comrades carries fetters for his captives-to-be.

Do not be credulous. Do not be unconcerned. Although the smooth surface of the sea, spread out like a pond, smiles at you, this great plain contains mountains within it. Danger is concealed within it. The enemy is within. Let out the sheets, raise the sails. Let the cross fashioned by the yard-arm be set up in front. This stillness portends a storm.

But you say: "What do you mean? Are not all in the city Christians?" Your case is not the same as that of the rest. Give ear to the Lord when He says: "if you will be perfect, go, sell what you have, and give to the poor . . . and come follow me." Now you have promised to be perfect. For when you forsook military service and made yourself a eunuch for the Kingdom of Heaven's sake, what else did you seek to achieve than the perfect life? But the perfect servant of Christ has nothing but Christ; for, if he has anything but Christ, he is not perfect. And if he is not perfect, he lied in the first place when he promised God that he would be perfect. "And the mouth that lies, kills the soul."

Therefore, to conclude, if you are perfect, why do you long for your hereditary goods? If you are not perfect, you have deceived the Lord. The gospel thunders in divine accents: "You cannot serve two masters"; and does anyone dare make Christ a liar by serving Mammon and the Lord? He often cries: "If any man will come after me, let him deny himself, and take up his cross, and follow me." "Do I, when laden with gold, think I am following Christ?" He that says he lives in Christ ought himself also to walk even as He walked.

But if you have nothing (as I know you will say in reply), as you are so well prepared for war why do you not start your campaign? Unless perhaps you think you can do so in your own country, although the Lord made no signs in His. And why was this? Take this explanation on His own authority: "No prophet has honour in his own country." "I do not seek honour," you will say, "my conscience is enough for me." Neither did the Lord seek it; for He fled lest He be made a king by the crowds.

But where there is no honour, there is contempt; where there is contempt, violence is frequent; and where there is violence, there also is indignation, there is no rest; where there is no rest, there the mind is often diverted from its purpose. Moreover, where something is taken away from enthusiasm by restlessness, enthusiasm is made less by as much as is taken away, and when anything is made less, it cannot be called perfect. From this course of reasoning the conclusion is that a monk cannot be perfect in his own country. And not to wish to be perfect is a sin.

But when driven from this position you will appeal to the clergy. How can I presume to say anything of these who surely remain in their cities? Far be it from me to say anything unfavourable of these who, succeeding to the status of the apostles, partake of Christ's body with holy lips, through whom we too are Christians, who hold the keys of the Kingdom of Heaven. They judge us, in a certain measure, before the day of judgment, who in sober chastity guard the Lord's bride. But as I have previously set forth, the status of a monk is one thing, that of the clergy another.

The clergy feed the sheep; I am fed. They get their living from the altar; if I bring no gift to the altar, the axe is laid to my roots as a barren tree. I cannot make poverty my excuse, since in the gospel I see the old woman giving the two copper coins which were all she had left. For me to sit in the presence of a priest is not permitted. He, if I have sinned, is permitted to deliver me to Satan for the destruction of the flesh, that my soul be saved.

And, indeed, under the old law, whoever was disobedient to the priests was either thrust outside the camp and stoned by the people, or else a sword was put to his throat and he expiated his contempt with his blood. But now the disobedient is either cut off by the sword of the Spirit or he is cast out of the Church and torn asunder by the jaws of infuriated demons.

But if the pious flatteries of the brethren invite you to take holy orders, I shall rejoice at your elevation, and shall fear a fall. "If a man desires the office of a bishop, he desires a good work." We know that; but add to the statement the words that follow: "It behoves, therefore, a man of this station to be blameless, the husband of one wife, sober, chaste, prudent, of good behaviour, given to hospitality, teachable, not given to wine, no striker, but modest."

And after setting forth other points that follow from this, he used no less care in speaking of clergy of the third degree, saying: "Deacons in like manner chaste, not double-tongued, not given to much wine, not greedy of filthy lucre, holding the mystery of faith in a pure conscience. And let these also first be proved; and so let them minister, having no crime."

Woe to that man who enters the feast not having a wedding garment! Nothing remains for him but that he hear straightway: "Friend, how did you come here?" And when he is speechless, the servants will be told: "Lift him by his hands and feet, and cast him into the exterior darkness; there shall be weeping and gnashing of teeth."

Woe to him who having received a talent ties it in a napkin, merely keeping what he had received, while others make a profit! Straightway he shall be assailed by the cry of his angry lord: "You wicked servant, why did you not give my money into the bank, that at my coming I might have exacted it with usury?" That is, "You might have laid down at the altar what you could not use. For while you, a poor businessman, held on to the money, you took the place of another man who might have doubled his principal." Therefore, just as he that ministers well purchases to himself a good degree, so he who approaches the chalice of the Lord unworthily shall be guilty of the body and of the blood of the Lord.

Not all bishops are bishops. You observe Peter, but consider Judas also. You regard Stephen, but note Nicholas also, whom the Lord in His apocalypse hates. He devised such base and impious things that from this root grew the heresy of the Ophites. Let every man prove himself and so draw near. Ecclesiastical rank does not make a Christian. Cornelius the centurion, while still a pagan, is filled with the gift of the Holy Spirit. Daniel, a young boy, judges the elders. Amos, while plucking blackberries, is suddenly a prophet. David, a shepherd, is chosen king. Jesus loves most the least of His disciples.

Sit down in a lower place, brother, that when a lesser person comes you may be bidden to go up higher. Upon whom does our Lord lean save on the lowly and the quiet and on him who trembles at His words? To whom more is entrusted, from him more is demanded. "The mighty shall be mightily tormented." Nor let anyone applaud himself for the chastity of a body only that is pure, since every idle word that men shall speak, they shall render an account for in the day of judgment, because even a reproach against a brother is an offence of murder.

It is not easy to stand in Paul's place, to hold the rank of those already reigning with Christ, lest perchance an angel come to rend the veil of your temple, who shall move your candlestick out of its place. If you have a mind to build a tower, reckon the charges of the future work. Salt that has lost its savour is good for nothing but to be cast out and to be trodden on by swine. If a monk has fallen, a priest will pray for him; but who will pray over the fall of a priest?

But as my speech has sailed out from the rocky places, and my frail boat has proceeded into the deep from among rocks hollowed out by the foaming breakers, my sails must be spread to the winds. Having passed beyond the reefs of controversy, I must now, like rejoicing sailors, sing out a glad word of command as epilogue.

O desert of Christ, burgeoning with flowers! O solitude, in which those stones are produced of which in the apocalypse the city of the great king is constructed! O wilderness that rejoices in intimacy with God! What are you doing in the world, brother, you who are greater than the world? How long will the shadows of houses oppress you? How long will the smoky prison of these cities close you in? Believe me, I behold a little more light. It is a delight to cast aside the burden of the flesh and to fly to the sheer glory of the ether.

Do you fear poverty? But Christ calls the poor blessed. Are you afraid to work? But no athlete is crowned without exertion. Are you thinking of food? But faith perceives nor famine. Do you dread bruising on the ground your limbs made lean by fasting? But the Lord lies at your side. Does the unkempt hair of a neglected head cause you to shudder? But Christ is your head. Does the boundless expanse of the wasteland terrify you? Then you walk in Paradise in your imagination. As often as you ascend there in thought, so often shall you not be in the desert. Is your skin made scabrous without baths? But he who is once washed in Christ need not wash again.

And, that you may hear the apostle replying concisely to all these things: "The sufferings of this time are not worthy to be compared with the glory to come, that shall be revealed in us." You are a voluptuary, my dearest, if you wish both to rejoice with the world and afterwards to reign with Christ.

It will come, that day will come, on which this corruptible mortal will put on incorruption and immortality. Blessed is the servant whom his Lord shall find watching. Then at the sound of the trumpet the earth with its peoples shall quake with fear; you shall rejoice. The universe will groan mournfully when the Lord is about to judge; tribe by tribe, men will beat their breasts. Kings once most mighty will tremble with naked flanks. Then Jupiter with his offspring will be displayed truly on fire. Foolish Plato will be brought forward also with his disciples. The reasoning of Aristotle will not avail.

Then you, the illiterate and the poor, shall exult. You shall laugh and say: "Behold my God, who was crucified, behold the Judge. This is He who whimpered as a babe wrapped in swaddling clothes, in a manger. This is that son of a labouring man and a working woman. It was He who, carried in His mother's bosom, fled into Egypt, a God from a man. This is He that was clothed in scarlet, He it is that was crowned with thorns. This is the magician, the man possessed of a devil, the Samaritan. Behold, O Jew, the hands which you nailed. Behold, O Roman, the side that you pierced. Look at this body, whether it is the same as that you said the disciples carried off secretly by night."

O my brother, what labour now can be too hard, that it may fall to your lot to say these words and to be present on that occasion?

Saint John CHRYSOSTOM: The Joys of Christmas

I behold a new and wondrous mystery. My ears resound to the shepherd's song, piping no soft melody, but chanting full forth a heavenly hymn. The angels sing. The archangels blend their voice in harmony. The cherubim hymn their joyful praise. The seraphim exalt His glory. All join to praise this holy feast, beholding the Godhead here on earth, and man in Heaven. He who is above, now for our redemption dwells here below; and he that was lowly is by divine mercy raised.

Bethlehem this day resembles Heaven; hearing from the stars the singing of angelic voices; and in place of the sun, enfolding within itself on every side, the Sun of Justice. And ask not how: for where God wills, the order of nature yields. For He willed, He had the power, He descended, He redeemed; all things move in obedience to God. This day He who is, is born; and He who is, becomes what He was not. For when He was God, He became man; yet not departing from the Godhead that is His. Nor yet by any loss of divinity became He man, nor through increase became He God from man; but being the Word He became flesh, His nature, because of impassibility, remaining unchanged.

When He was born the Jews denied His extraordinary birth; the Pharisees began to interpret falsely the sacred writings; the scribes spoke in contradiction of that which they read. Herod sought Him out who was born, not that he might adore, but to put Him to death. Today all things proclaim the opposite. "For they have not been", that I may speak with the psalmist, "hidden from their children, in another generation" (Psalms 78:4). And so the kings have come, and they have seen the heavenly King that has come upon the earth, not bringing with Him angels, nor archangels, nor thrones, nor dominations, nor powers, nor principalities, but, treading a new and solitary path, He has come forth from a spotless womb.

Yet He has not forsaken His angels, nor left them deprived of His care, nor because of His incarnation has he departed from the Godhead. And behold kings have come, that they might adore the heavenly King of glory; soldiers, that they might serve the Leader of the hosts of Heaven; women, that they might adore Him who was born of a woman so that He might change the pains of childbirth into joy; virgins, to the Son of the Virgin, beholding with joy, that He who is the giver of milk, who has decreed that the fountains of the breast pour forth in ready streams, receives from a Virgin Mother the food of infancy; infants, that they may adore Him who became a little child, so that "out of the mouth of infants and of sucklings", He might perfect praise; children, to the Child who raised up martyrs through the rage of Herod; men, to Him who became man, that He might heal the miseries of His servants; shepherds, to the Good Shepherd who has laid down His life for His sheep; priests, to Him who has become a high priest according to the order of Melchizedek; servants, to Him who took upon Himself the form of a servant that He might bless our servitude with the reward of freedom (Philippians 2:7); fishermen, to Him who from amongst fishermen chose catchers of men; publicans, to Him who from amongst them named a chosen evangelist; sinful women, to Him who exposed His feet to the tears of the repentant; and that I may embrace them all together, all sinners have come, that they may look upon the Lamb of God who takes away the sins of the world.

Since therefore all rejoice, I too desire to rejoice. I too wish to share the choral dance, to celebrate the festival. But I take my part, not plucking the harp, not with the music of the pipes, nor holding a torch, but holding in my arms the cradle of Christ. For this is all my hope, this my life, this my salvation, this my pipe, my harp. And bearing it I come, and having from its power received the gift of speech, I too, with the angels, sing: "Glory to God in the highest"; and with the shepherds, "and on earth peace to men of good will".

This day He who was ineffably begotten of the Father, was for me born of the Virgin, in a way no tongue can tell. Begotten according to His nature before all ages from the Father: in what manner He knows who has begotten Him; born again this day from the Virgin, above the order of nature, in what manner the power of the Holy Spirit knows. And His heavenly generation is true, and His generation here on earth is true. As God He is truly begotten of God; so also as man is He truly born from the Virgin. In Heaven He alone is the only begotten of the one God; on earth He alone is the only begotten of the unique Virgin.

And as in the heavenly generation, to imply a mother is heretical, so in this earthly generation, to speak of a father is blasphemy. The Father begot in the Spirit, and the Virgin brought forth without defilement. The Father begot without the limitations of flesh, since He begot as became the Godhead; so neither did the Virgin endure corruption in her childbearing, since she brought forth miraculously. Hence, since this heavenly birth cannot be described, neither does His coming amongst us in these days permit of too curious scrutiny. Though I know that a virgin this day gave birth, and I believe that God was begotten before all time, yet the manner of this generation I have learned to venerate in silence, and I accept that this is not to be probed too curiously with wordy speech. For with God we look not for the order of nature, but rest our faith in the power of His works.

It is indeed the way of nature that a woman in wedlock brings forth; when an unwed virgin, after she has born a child, is still a virgin, then nature is here surpassed. Of that which happens in accord with nature we may enquire; what passes above it we honour in silence; not as something to be avoided, passed over, but as that which we venerate in silence, as something sublime, beyond all telling.

What shall I say to you; what shall I tell you? I behold a mother who has brought forth; I see a child come to this light by birth. The manner of His conception I cannot comprehend. Nature here is overcome, the boundaries of the established order set aside, where God so wills. For not according to nature has this thing come to pass. Nature here rested, while the will of God laboured. O ineffable grace! The only begotten, who is before all ages, Who cannot be touched or be perceived, who is simple, without body, has now put on my body, which is visible and liable to corruption. For what reason? That coming amongst us he may teach us, and teaching, lead us by the hand to the things that men cannot see. For since men believe that the eyes are more trustworthy than the ears, they doubt of that which they do not see, and so He has deigned to show Himself in bodily presence, that He may remove all doubt.

And He was born from a virgin, who knew not His purpose; neither had she laboured with Him to bring it to pass, nor contributed to that which He had done, but was the simple instrument of His hidden power. That alone she knew which she had learned by her question to Gabriel: "How shall this be done, because I know not a man?": Then said he: "The Holy Spirit shall come upon thee, and the power of the Most High shall overshadow thee."

And in what manner was the Almighty with her, who in a little while came forth from her? He was as the craftsman, who coming on some suitable material, fashions to himself a beautiful vessel; so Christ, finding the holy body and soul of the Virgin, builds for Himself a living temple, and as He had willed, formed there a man from the Virgin; and, putting Him on, this day came forth; unashamed of the lowliness of our nature. For it was to Him no lowering to put on what He Himself had made. Let that handiwork be forever glorified, which became the cloak of its own creator. For as in the first creation of flesh, man could not be made before the clay had come into His hand, so neither could this corruptible body be glorified, until it had first become the garment of its maker.

What shall I say! And how shall I describe this birth to you? For this wonder fills me with astonishment. The Ancient of Days has become an infant. He who sits upon the sublime and heavenly throne, now lies in a manger. And He who cannot be touched, who is simple, without complexity, and incorporeal, now lies subject to the hands of men. He who has broken the bonds of sinners, is now bound by an infant's bands. But He has decreed that ignominy shall become honour, infamy be clothed with glory, and total humiliation the measure of His goodness. For this He assumed my body, that I may become capable of His word; taking my flesh, He gives me His spirit; and so He bestowing and I receiving, He prepares for me the treasure of life. He takes my flesh, to sanctify me;

He gives me His spirit, that He may save me.

But what can I say? And of what shall my feeble tongue speak? "Behold, a virgin shall conceive" (Isaiah 7:14). This is no longer said of something that is to be, but received as something fulfilled. And it was fulfilled among the Jews, to whom it was foretold; it is believed by us, to whom it was not at any time announced. "Behold a virgin shall conceive." The deed was given to the synagogue, but to the Church was given possession. The one found a document, the other a pearl of great price. The one was clothed in wool, the other in a royal robe. Judah brings Him forth, the whole world acclaims Him. The synagogue nourished and instructed Him, the Church seized Him and holds Him fast. The synagogue has the vine branch, I have the fruit of truth. Israel garnered the grapes, the Gentiles drink the mystical wine. The one sowed the seed wheat in Judea, and the Gentiles have reaped the harvest with the sickle of faith. The Gentiles have reverently plucked the rose, and to the Jews remain the thorn of hard-heartedness. The nestling has taken wing, but the foolish still wait by the empty nest. Israel still ponders the leaves of the Book, while the Gentiles enjoy the fruit of the Spirit.

"Behold, a virgin shall conceive." Tell, O Judah, whom he has brought forth? Confide it to me as you did to Herod. But you confide not in men. I know the reason. Because of treachery. You spoke to Herod, but that Herod might destroy Him. To me you are silent, lest I adore Him.

Whom has she brought forth? Whom? The Lord of nature. For though thou art silent, nature cries out. For she has brought forth as He who was born decreed to be born. Not as nature decreed, but He as nature's lord has made for Himself a new and unheard of birth, that He may show Himself as man; but not brought forth as men are born, but born as God. For from a virgin He came forth this day, He who hath set nature aside, and risen above the ways of nuptials.

It was fitting that the giver of all holiness should enter this world by a pure and holy birth. For He it is that of old formed Adam from the virgin earth, and from Adam without help of woman formed woman. For us without woman Adam produced woman, so did the Virgin without man this day bring forth a man. "For it is a man", says the Lord, "and who shall know him" (Jeremiah 17:9). For since the race of women owed to me a debt, as from Adam without woman woman came, therefore without man the Virgin this day brought forth, and on behalf of Eve repaid the debt to man.

That Adam might not take pride, that he without woman had engendered woman, a woman without man has begotten man; so that by the similarity of the mystery is proved the similarity in nature. For as before the Almighty took a rib from Adam, and by that Adam was not made less; so in the Virgin He formed a living temple, and the holy virginity remained unchanged. Sound and unharmed Adam remained even after the deprivation of a rib; unstained the Virgin though a child was born of her.

Not elsewhere did He form for Himself a living temple; nor other body did He take than this, so that men should not remain branded with dishonour. For man being deceived became the devil's slave. So him that was thus supplanted, He took as His own living temple, that being joined to his maker, man might then be wrested from this bond, and from subjection to the devil.

Yet in becoming man He was born, not as man is born, but as God. If He had been born from an ordinary union, as I was, He would have been reckoned a fraud. And for this cause He is now born of a virgin, but in being born He preserves undefiled this womb, and protects that spotless virginity; so that this unheard of manner of bringing forth is for me a pledge of its sublime truthfulness.

So should Gentile or Jew ask me, whether Christ who is God by nature, became man in a manner above nature, I answer, "that is so", and call as witness the unstained seal of virginity. It is God alone who can so rise above nature; for He is the maker of the womb, the author of virginity, who has thus without stain preserved the manner of His own birth, and in a mysterious way has formed there, according to His will, a temple unto Himself.

Tell me, O Judah, has a virgin brought forth, or has she not? If she has, then acknowledge this wondrous birth. If she has not, why did you lead Herod astray?

Why did you, to his urgent inquiry as to where the Christ is to be born, answer: "In Bethlehem of Judah." Did I know the village, or the place? How have I learned of the dignity of His lineage? Was it not Isaiah who spoke of it, as being of God Himself? "Behold, a Virgin shall conceive, and bear a son, and His name shall be called Emmanuel" (Isaiah 7:14).

Is it not you, O wicked enemies, that have brought forth the truth? Have you not, scribes and pharisees, diligent custodians of the law, taught us these things? Did we know the Hebrew tongue?

Was it not you who interpreted the Scriptures? After the Virgin brought forth, and before she brought forth, lest these words be interpreted in praise of God, did you not, when questioned by Herod, bring forward the witness of the prophet Micah, that he might confirm your words?" "And thou Bethlehem of the land of Judah, are not the least among the princes of Judah: for out of thee shall come forth the captain that shall rule my people Israel" (Matthew 2:6; Micah 5:2).

Rightly did the prophet say, "out of thee". He has gone out from thee, and gone into the whole world. He who is, has gone forth. He who is not, is created, or becomes. And of Himself He was, and before was, and always was: but always as God, governing the world. This day He comes forth; as man He rules the people, as God He saves all men.

O kindly enemies! O modest and gentle accusers! Who, without knowing it, proclaimed that God was born in Bethlehem; who made known that He was laid in a manger; who unwittingly pointed out the cave where He lay hidden, and, against their own will, laid on us a debt of gratitude. For they made known that which they strove to keep hidden. Behold them! The foolish teachers! That which they teach, they themselves know not; consumed with hunger, they feed others; thirsting, they give to drink; needy, they yet enrich.

Come, then, let us observe the feast. Come, and we shall commemorate the solemn festival. It is a strange manner of celebrating a festival; but truly wondrous is the whole chronicle of the nativity. For this day the ancient slavery is ended, the devil confounded, the demons take to flight, the power of death is broken, paradise is unlocked, the curse is taken away, sin is removed from us, error driven out, truth has been brought back, the speech of kindliness diffused, and spreads on every side, a heavenly way of life has been implanted on the earth, angels communicate with men without fear, and men now hold speech with angels.

Why is this? Because God is now on earth, and man in Heaven; on every side all things commingle. He has come on earth, while being whole in Heaven; and while complete in Heaven, He is without diminution on earth. Though He was God, He became man; not denying Himself to be God. Though being the impassable Word, He became flesh; that He might dwell amongst us, He became flesh. He did not become God. He was God. Wherefore He became flesh, so that He whom Heaven did not contain, a manger would this day receive. He was placed in a manger, so that He, by whom all things are nourished, might receive an infant's food from His Virgin mother. So, the Father of all ages, as an infant at the breast, nestles in the virginal arms, that the Magi might more easily see Him. Since this day the Magi too have come, and made a beginning of withstanding tyranny; and the heavens give glory, as the Lord is revealed by a star.

"And sitting upon the swift cloud" of His body the Lord flies into Egypt; to escape the treachery of Herod without doubt, but also that the words of Isaiah may be fulfilled (Isaiah 19:24–25): "In that day shall Israel be third to the Egyptian and the Assyrian, and blessed be my people of Egypt, and the work of my hands to the Assyrian". What dost thou say, O Judah, who was first and has become third? The Egyptians and Assyrians are placed before thee, and Israel, the firstborn, is last?

Rightly shall the Assyrians be first, since they through the Magi first adored Him. The Egyptians after the Assyrians, since it was they who received Him flying from the treachery of Herod. Israel is numbered in the third place, as only after His ascent from the Jordan was He acknowledged by His apostles. He entered Egypt, deliberately causing the idols of Egypt to tremble, and after He had closed the porches of Egypt by the destruction of her firstborn.

And so as firstborn He enters Egypt this

day, that He may end the mourning over her ancient grief. Luke has testified that Christ shall be called a firstborn: "And she brought forth her firstborn son." He enters therefore that He may dissolve the ancient sorrow, and instead of plagues bring joy. In place of night and darkness, He brings the light of salvation. The stream of young life was stained by the slaughter of the innocents. He has therefore entered the land of Egypt, who of old made her rivers red. Now He grants the flowing river the power to give salvation; and cleanses their stains and afflictions with the power of His Holy Spirit. The Egyptians had been punished, and turning with fury they had denied God. He went therefore into Egypt, and filled religious souls with the knowledge of God, and disposed that the river should nourish martyrs more numerous than its reeds.

But what shall I say? What shall I utter? "Behold an infant wrapped in swaddling clothes and lying in a manger." Mary is present, who is both virgin and mother. Joseph is present, who is called father. He is called husband, she is called wife. The names indeed are lawful, but there is no other bond. We speak here of words, not of things. He was espoused to her, but the Most High overshadowed her. Hence, Joseph, doubting, knew not what to call the infant. He would not dare to say that it was conceived in adultery; he could not speak harshly against the Virgin; he shrank from calling the child his own. He knew well that here was something unknown to him; how or whence was this child born? And being anxious because of this, there came to him a message, by the voice of an angel, which said: "Fear not to take unto thee Mary thy wife, for that which is conceived in her, is of the Holy Ghost."

The Holy Ghost overshadowed the Virgin. Wherefore was He born of a virgin, and wherefore was her virginity preserved? Because the devil had deceived the virgin Eve; accordingly, to Mary, who was a virgin, Gabriel bore a message of joy. As Eve, being deceived, uttered a word that was the cause of death, so Mary, receiving good tidings, brought forth in the flesh a Word that gave us eternal life. The word of Eve led to the tree, because of which Adam was driven from Paradise; the Word which the Virgin brought forth led to the cross, because of which the thief, standing in the place of Adam, was led into Paradise.

As neither the Gentiles, nor the Jews, nor heretics, believed that God begot as man, accordingly, coming forth this day from a passible body, the impassible preserved inviolate the passible body, that He might show, that just as He was born of a virgin, while she remained a virgin, so likewise God, His sacred substance remaining unchanged, as God, and as befitted God, begot God.

Seeing that men, abandoning Him, fashioned for themselves statues, to which, offending God, they gave adoration, for which cause, on this day, the Word of God, being truly God, appeared in the form of man, that He might set aright this falsehood; and in a veiled manner, has turned all adoration unto Himself. To Him, then, who out of confusion has wrought a clear path, to Christ, to the Father, and to the Holy Ghost, we offer all praise, now and for ever. Amen.

Saint JOHN CHRYSOSTOM: The Happiness of Acting out our Love

Consider how great a blessing it is to exercise love. What cheerfulness it produces! With what great grace it fills the soul! For the other parts of virtue have each their troubled guilt yoked to them. As he that gives up his possessions is often puffed up on this account; the eloquent is affected with a wild passion for glory: the humble-minded, on this very ground, not seldom thinks highly of himself. But love alone with its benefits has great pleasure too and no trouble: and like an industrious bee, gathering the sweets from every flower, it deposits delight in the soul of him who loves it.

Though anyone be a slave, it renders slavery sweeter than liberty. For he who loves rejoices not so much in commanding as in being commanded; although to command is sweet, love changes the nature of things, and presents herself with all blessings in her hands, gentler than any mother, wealthier than any queen, and makes difficulties light and easy, showing virtue to be easy, but vice to be bitter.

See now: to give seems grievous, yet love makes it pleasant; to receive other men's goods seems pleasant; and to love it does not appear pleasant, but frames our minds to avoid it as evil. Again, to speak evil seems pleasant to all, but love, while she makes this out to be bitter, causes speaking well to be pleasant: for nothing is so sweet to us as to be praising one whom we love. Again, anger has a kind of pleasure, but in love it no longer seems so. Though he that is beloved should grieve him who loves him, anger nowhere shows itself, but in tears, and expostulations, and entreaties; and should love behold one in error, she mourns and is in pain: yet even this pain itself brings pleasure, for the very tears and the grief of love are sweeter than any mirth and joy. For instance, they that laugh are not so refreshed as they that weep for friends. And if you doubt it, stop their tears, and see how they become angry like persons intolerably ill-used. "But there is" says one, "a profane pleasure in love." Begone and hold your peace, whoever you are! For nothing is so pure from such pleasure as genuine love. Imagine one single person loved and loving genuinely, as he ought to love. Why, he will so live on earth as if it were Heaven, everywhere enjoying calm and weaving for himself innumerable crowns. For both from envy, and wrath, and jealousy, and pride, and vainglory, and lust and every profane love, such a man will keep his soul pure. Yea, even as no one would do himself an injury, so neither would this man his neighbours. And being such, he will stand with Gabriel himself even while he walks on earth.

Yea, and if this were duly observed by all, there would be neither slave nor free, neither ruler nor ruled, neither rich nor poor, neither small nor great; nor would any devil ever have been known: I say not Satan only, but whatever such spirit there may be, nay, rather were there a hundred or ten thousand such, they would have no power while love existed. For sooner would grass endure the application of fire than the devil the flame of love. She is stronger than any wall, she is firmer than any adamant; or if you can name any material stronger than this, the firmness of love transcends them all. Her, neither wealth nor poverty overcome: nay, rather there would be no poverty, no unbounded wealth, if there were such love, but the good parts only from each situation. For from the one we should reap its abundance, and from the other its freedom from care: and we should neither have to undergo the anxieties of riches, nor the dread of poverty. For tell me not of this ordinary sort, the vulgar and low-minded and really a sort of disease rather than love, but of that which Paul seeks after, which considers the profit of them that are loved, and you shall see that no fathers are so affectionate as persons of this stamp. And even as they that love money cannot endure to spend it, but would rather live uncomfortably than see their wealth diminishing; so too, he that is kindly affected towards everyone would choose to suffer ten thousand evils than see his beloved one injured. Let us then possess ourselves of the love which is above all gifts, that we may obtain both the present and the future blessings which we may all obtain through the grace and mercy of our Lord Jesus Christ. Amen.

Saint AMBROSE: The Hymns of the Little Hours

PRIME

The star of morn to night succeeds;
We therefore meekly pray,
May God in all our words and deeds,
Keep us from harm this day;
May He in love restrain us still
From tones of strife and words of ill,
And wrap around and close our eyes
To earth's absorbing vanities.

May wrath and thoughts that gender
shame
Ne'er in our breasts abide;
And cheerful abstinences tame
Of wanton flesh the pride:
So, when the weary day is o'er,
And night and stillness come once more,
Strong in self-conquering purity,
We may proclaim, with choirs on high:

TERCE

Come, Holy Ghost, who, ever one,
Reignest with Father and with Son,
It is the hour, our souls possess
With Thy full flood of holiness
Let flesh and heart, and lips and mind,
Sound forth our witness to mankind;
And love light up our mortal frame
Till others catch the living flame.
Now to the Father, to the Son,
And to the Spirit, three in one,
Be praise and thanks and glory given,
By men on earth, by saints in Heaven.

SEXT

O God, who cannot change nor fail,
Guiding the hours as they roll by;
Brightening with beams the morning pale,
And burning in the midday sky.
Quench Thou the fires of hate and strife,
The wasting fever of the heart
From perils guard our feeble life,
And to our souls Thy peace impart.

NONE

O God unchangeable and true,
Of all the light and power,
Dispensing light in silence through
Every successive hour;
Lord, brighten our declining day,
That it may never wane,
Till death, when all things round decay,
Brings back the morn again.

COMPLINE

Now that the daylight dies away,
By all Thy grace and love,
Thee, Maker of the world, we pray
To watch our bed above.
Let dreams depart and phantoms fly,
The offspring of the night,
Keep us, like shrines, beneath Thine eyes,
Pure in our foe's despite.
This grace on Thy redeemed confer,
Father, coequal Son,
And Holy Ghost, the Comforter,
Eternal, Three in One.

Te Deum and Gloria in Excelsis

We praise thee, O God: we acknowledge thee to be the Lord.
All the earth doth worship thee, the Father everlasting.
To thee all angels cry aloud: the Heavens, and all the powers therein.
To thee cherubim and seraphim continually do cry,
Holy, holy, holy: Lord God of Sabaoth;
Heaven and earth are full of the Majesty of thy glory.
The glorious company of the apostles praise thee.
The goodly fellowship of the prophets praise thee.
The holy Church throughout all the world doth acknowledge thee;
The Father of an infinite Majesty;
Thine honourable, true, and only Son;
Also the Holy Ghost, the Comforter.

Thou art the King of glory, O Christ.
Thou art the everlasting Son of the Father.
When thou tookest upon thee to deliver man
Thou didst not abhor the Virgin's womb.
When thou hadst overcome the sharpness of death thou didst open the kingdom of heaven to all believers.
Thou sittest at the right hand of God in the glory of the Father.
We believe that Thou shalt come to be our Judge.
We therefore pray Thee, help Thy servants whom Thou hast redeemed with Thy precious blood.
Make them to be numbered with thy Saints in glory everlasting.

O Lord, save Thy people: and bless Thine heritage.
Govern them, and lift them up for ever.
Day by day we magnify thee;
And we worship Thy name, ever world without end.
Vouchsafe, O Lord, to keep us this day without sin.
O Lord, have mercy upon us, have mercy upon us.
O Lord, let Thy mercy lighten upon us, as our trust is in Thee.
O Lord, in Thee have I trusted, let me never be confounded.

Glory be to God on high, and on earth peace, good will towards men. We praise Thee, we bless Thee, we worship Thee, we glorify Thee, we give thanks to Thee for Thy great glory, O Lord God, heavenly King, God the Father Almighty.

O Lord, the only-begotten Son Jesus Christ; O Lord God, Lamb of God, Son of the Father, that takest away the sins of the world, have mercy upon us. Thou that takest away the sins of the world, have mercy upon us. Thou that takest away the sins of the world, receive our prayer. Thou that sittest at the right hand of God the Father, have mercy upon us.

For Thou only art holy; Thou only art the Lord; Thou only, O Christ, with the Holy Ghost, art most high in the glory of God the Father. Amen.

Hymns from the Liturgy of Saint JAMES

I

Let all mortal flesh keep silence, and with fear and trembling stand;
Ponder nothing earthly-minded, for with blessing in His hand,
Christ our God to earth descendeth, our full homage to demand.
King of kings, yet born of Mary, as of old on earth He stood,
Lord of lords, in human vesture – in the body and the blood –
He will give to all the faithful His own self for heavenly food.
Rank on rank the host of Heaven spreads its vanguard on the way,
As the Light of Light descendeth from the realms of endless day
That the powers of Hell may vanish as the darkness clears away.
At His feet the six-winged seraph; cherubim with sleepless eye,
Veil their faces to the Presence, as with ceaseless voice they cry,
Alleluia, alleluia, alleluia, Lord most high.

II

From glory to glory advancing, we praise Thee, O Lord;
Thy name with the Father and Spirit be ever adored.
From strength unto strength we go forward on Zion's highway,
To appear before God in the city of infinite day.
Thanksgiving, and glory and worship, and blessing and love,
One heart and one song have the saints upon earth and above.
Ever more, O Lord, to Thy servants Thy presence be nigh;
Ever fit us by service on earth for Thy service on high.

The Conversion of Saint AUGUSTINE

O Lord You are great, and greatly to be praised. Great is Your power and Your wisdom is infinite. And man, who is a part of what You have created, wants to praise You; this man, carrying about his own mortality, carrying about him a testimony to his own sin, this part of what You have created, wants to praise You. You stir him so deeply that he can only find delight in praising You. For You have created us for Yourself, and our hearts can find no peace till they rest in You.

Men who look for the Lord should praise Him, for those that seek will find. And finding, they shall praise Him. You will I seek, O Lord, calling on You; and I will call on You believing in You, because Your word has been preached to me. My faith, O Lord, calls on You, the faith You have given me, which you have inspired in me, by the humanity of Your Son, and by the ministry of Your preachers.

Who shall plead for me, that I may find rest in You? Who shall plead with You to enter into my heart and so to fill it that I may forget my own evils, and embrace You, my only good? What are You to me? Give me the grace to speak to You. What am I to You, that You should command me to love You, and be angry with me, yes and threaten me with great mischiefs, unless I love You? Is not loving You misery enough? Woe is me! Be merciful, O Lord my God, and explain why You mean so much to me. Say to my soul, I am your salvation. Speak so that I may hear You. Behold, the ears of my heart are before you, O Lord, open them and say to my soul, "I am your salvation." I will run after that voice, and take hold of You. Do not hide Your face from me, let me die to death so that I may see it.

My soul's house is too small for You to come into. Enlarge it for me. Repair it, for it is in ruins. I confess and know there are many things in me that may offend Your eyes, but who can clean it? Or to whom but You shall I cry "Cleanse me, O Lord, from my secret sins, and from strange sins deliver Your servant." I believe, and this is why I speak in this way. You know O Lord that I have confessed my sins, and You forgave the iniquity of my heart. I will not plead with You, who are truth and I will try not to deceive myself, for fear that my self-delusion will betray me. I will not therefore plead with You, for if You, Lord, will mark down all our sins, O Lord, O Lord, who will be able to bear it?

I must now call to mind my forgotten impurities, and the fleshly corruptions of my soul, not because I love them, but so that I may love You, O my God. For love of Your love I would do it, summoning up my most bitter memories so that You may grow sweet to me. O Lord, You happy and secure sweetness, I must piece together my shattered life, shattered when I squandered away my life on worldly vanities. For in my youth I burned with lust, and desired hellish pleasures. And I dared to grow wild, and to pursue foul loves. My beauty withered away, and I stank in Your eyes.

And what was it that I delighted in, but to love and to be loved? But my love did not keep to the moderation of one mind loving another mind but became clouded by fleshly lusts that overcast my heart, so that I could not discern the beauty of a true affection from the fog of impure desire. My youth was ravished away in a whirlpool of impurities. Meanwhile You grew angry towards me, and I did not see it. I had grown deaf by the continual crashing of the chain of my frailty, and I struggled further from You, and You left me alone, and I was ravaged and torn apart, and I boiled over with lust, and You held Your peace. How slow You were in revealing to me that You are my joy. You continued to hold Your peace, and I wandered further and further from You, into more and more fruitless fatigue, proud in my dejectedness and restless in my weariness.

O for somebody who would then have sweetened my misery, who would have converted my love of beauty to some good use; but instead, wretched that I was, I was too set in my ways, pursuing still the violent course of my own will, having left You utterly. I was carried away by my own desires. I broke all Your laws, but I did not escape Your censure. For what mortal can avoid it? For You were with me at every turn most mildly rigorous, always embittering my unlawful pastimes with discontent, all to draw me on to seek for such pleasures as were without discontent, and that I might light upon none but You, O Lord. You hurt us in order to heal us and kill us so that we do not die away from You. Where was I then, and how far was I banished from the happiness of Your house in my sixteenth year? The madness of my raging lust exercised its supreme dominion in me, draining me of all my energy.

Woe unto that audacious soul of mine, which hoped that, forsaking You, it would find some better thing! Turning this way and that from side to side, backwards and forwards, yet it found all places hard and uncomfortable. Only in You can the soul find rest. And behold, You are near at hand, and from our wretched errors You deliver us, and You settle us in your own way, and You do comfort us, and say to us: "Run on, I will carry you, yes, I will bring you to your journey's end, I will carry you to the very end."

You, Lord, are always the same, and You are not angry with us forever, because You have pity on dust and ashes. And it was pleasing in Your sight to reform my deformities. And by inward goadings You startled me, so that I should be disquieted and I should enjoy no peace until I recognised You. So, by the secret hand of Your healing, my pride began to abate and gradually the eyes of my soul began to clear, and the suffering You gave me brought health.

O eternal truth! And true charity! And dear eternity! You are my God, to You I sigh day and night. When I first saw You, You showed me there was something which I might see, but that I was not yet the man to see it. Your darting beams of light dazzled me, and I trembled with love and horror. And I saw myself to be far off from You in a region utterly foreign to You and I heard Your voice speaking to me from on high, saying, "I am the food of strong men, grow and you shall feed on me. Nor shall you change me, like ordinary food, into your substance, but you will be changed into mine." And so I learned how You correct man with rebukes. You purged my soul. And I said: "Is truth therefore nothing at all, since it is neither limited by infinite space nor by finite?" But You cried to me from far off saying "Yes, truly I am that I am." I heard this voice, as things are heard in the heart, and I had no doubts at all about hearing it. I should sooner doubt that I lived than that God is truth and that His creation tells us so.

Then I set myself to seek a way of gaining sufficient strength to enjoy You, but I could not find it, until I embraced that mediator between God and man, the man Jesus Christ, who is over all, blessed by God for ever more, who was calling to me, and saying: "I am the way, the truth, and the life", who mingled that food which I was unable to take, His own flesh, with our own flesh. For the Word was made flesh, so that by Your wisdom, by which You created all things, He might suckle our infancy, for I, not yet humble enough, did not apprehend my Lord Jesus Christ who had made Himself humble; nor did I yet know, what lesson His Humility should teach us. For the Word, the eternal truth, is so highly exalted above the highest of Your creatures, that it raises up those who have been cast down unto itself. Having here below built for itself a lowly cottage of our clay, He caused those who had abandoned Him to be reunited with Him, healing them of their pride and replacing it with love, so that they might become aware of their own weakness and trust no longer in their own strength, and seeing the divinity itself enfeebled by taking our coats of skin upon Him, they might realise their own humanity, and then discard it within Him.

Still the devil was the master of my will. He made a chain out of it, and bound me with it. Lust grew out of this perverted will, and lust repeatedly obeyed became an unbreakable habit. As for that new will which I now began to have towards the free worshipping and enjoying of You, O God, the only assured sweetness, it was not able as yet to overcome my former wilfulness, now hardened in me by so long an indulgence. So my two wills, one new and the other old, the carnal and the spiritual, tried to win mastery over me, and their warfare laid waste my soul. Now, O my Lord, my helper and my redeemer, I will declare and confess to Your name the manner in which You delivered me from the bonds of desire and from the drudgery of worldly business. My disquiet grew more and more, and I daily sighed for You. I began to go to church whenever I was able.

I lashed my soul with accusations, trying to make it follow You. And it drew back, it refused, but gave no reason to excuse its refusal. The rebelliousness of my soul was exhausted, and there remained a silent trembling. It feared the ending of the old habits that were killing it as much as death itself.

Then, in the middle of this storm in my inner being, troubled both in mind and in countenance, I turned to my old friend Alypius, crying out: "What is the matter with us? What is the meaning of this?" Some such words as these I uttered, and then I turned away, while he looked at me in silence and in astonishment. For I was speaking in a way he had never heard before. My forehead, my cheeks, my eyes, my colour, and the tone of my voice, expressed my confusion more strongly than my words. There was a garden at the back of the house where we lodged. The storm within my breast now hurried me there, where no man might interrupt me until I had come to terms with myself. How I was going to do that, God only knew.

I was most insanely mad, and dying to death that I might live, sensible enough to know how utterly miserable I was for the present, but utterly ignorant of how good I shortly was to grow. Into that garden I went, and Alypius followed me step by step. He could not have forsaken me in such a state. I was angry with myself, furious that I did not do Your will and accept Your covenant, my God, which all my bones cried out for me to do, praising You to the very skies. The journey I wanted to take was not one that could be achieved by means of ships or chariots or even by my own legs. It required no more than an act of will, but a thorough and resolute act of will, not a hesitant one, a broken-winged wish fluttering hither and thither, rising with one pinion, struggling and falling with the other. In the midst of my indecisiveness, I was doing many things which men sometimes want to do but cannot because they have lost a limb or because their limbs are bound with fetters, or enfeebled by disease, or incapacitated in some other way. So I did many things in which will to do and power to do were not the same, yet did not that one thing which seemed infinitely more desirable, which, before long, I would have power to will, because before long, I should certainly will to will it. For in this the power of willing is the power of doing, and yet I could not do it. And so my body lent a ready obedience to the slightest desire of the soul, moving its limbs in instant compliance, while my soul could not aid itself in carrying out its great resolve, which needed but resolve to accomplish it.

Sick and tormented, I reproached myself more bitterly than ever, rolling and writhing in my chain so that it almost snapped, but still held me fast. And You, O Lord, were urgent in my inmost heart, applying with austere mercy the scourges of fear and shame, to prevent me failing once more, and the remnant of my worn and slender fetter, instead of breaking, growing strong again, and binding me harder than ever. For I kept saying to myself, "O let it be now, let it be now", and as I spoke I was on the verge of resolution. I was on the point of action, but did not act; but I did not slip back into my former indifference. I tried again, and came a little nearer and still nearer, I could all but touch and reach the goal, yet I did not quite reach or touch it, because I still shrank from dying to death and coming alive to life, and the worse, which was engrained, was stronger in me than the better, which was untrained. And the moment which was to make me different frightened me more the nearer it drew, but it no longer repelled or daunted, it only chilled me.

Trifles of trifles and vanities of vanities, my old mistresses held me back; they caught hold of me and whispered in my ear, "Can you let us go? From that instant we shall see you no more for ever; and from that instant this and that will be forbidden you for ever." What did they mean, O my God, what did they mean by "this and that"? O let Your mercy guard the soul of Your servant from the vileness, the shame that they meant! As I heard them, they seemed to have shrunk to half their former size. No longer did they meet me face to face with open contradiction, but muttered behind my back, and when I moved away plucked at my coat to make me look back. Yet such was my indecision that they prevented me from breaking loose, and shaking myself free, and running after the voice that called me away; for strong habit supported them, asking me, "Do you think you can live without them?"

But the voice of habit had lost its persuasiveness. For there dawned in me the chaste dignity of continence, calm and cheerful but not wanton, modestly alluring me to come and doubt not, offering to welcome and embrace me. And she smiled upon me with a challenging smile, as if she would say, "Cast on Him; fear not; He will not fail, and you will not fall. Cast yourself boldly upon Him; He will sustain you, and heal you." And I blushed, for still I heard the whispers of the daughters of vanity, and still I hung in the wind. And again she seemed to say, "Stop your ears against the whisperings of desire. They tell you of delights, but not according to the law of the Lord your God." Such was the debate that raged in my heart, myself battling against myself. Alypius kept close to my side and waited in silence to see the outcome of my strange agitation.

Now the whole cloud of my misery piled up in my heart, and there rose within me a whirlwind, carrying with it a violent burst of tears. And I rose and left Alypius, for solitude seemed fitter for tears. So I went farther off, till I could feel that his presence was no restraint, and he guessed my feelings. I suppose I had said something before I started up; and he noticed that my voice was fraught with tears, so he remained upon the bench. I flung myself down under a fig tree, and gave my tears free course, and the floods of my eyes broke forth, an acceptable sacrifice in Your sight. And I cried out to You incessantly, not in these words, but with this meaning, "And You, O Lord, how long? How long, O Lord; will You be angry for ever? O remember not our iniquities of old times." For I felt that I was held fast by them, and I went on wailing, "How long, how long? To-morrow and to-morrow? Why not now? Why not this hour make an end of my vileness?"

I spoke, weeping in bitter contrition of heart when, suddenly, I heard a voice from the neighbouring house. It seemed as if some boy or girl, I knew not which, was repeating in a kind of chant the words, "Take and read, take and read." Immediately, I tried to remember intently whether there was any kind of game in which children sang those words; but I could not recollect that I had ever heard them. I stemmed the rush of tears, and rose to my feet; for I could only think it was a divine command to open the Bible, and read the first passage I lighted upon. For I had heard that Antony had happened to enter a church at the moment when this verse of the gospel was being read, "Go, sell all that you have and give to the poor, and you shall have treasure in Heaven; and come and follow me," and by this oracle he had been converted to You on the spot.

I ran back then to the place where Alypius was sitting; for, when I left him, I had left the book of the apostle lying there. I took it up, opened it, and read in silence the passage on which my eyes first fell, "Not in rioting and drunkenness, not in fornication and wantonness, not in strife and envying; but put on the Lord Jesus Christ, and do not waste yourself in nature's desires." No further would I read, nor was it necessary. As I reached the end of the sentence, the light of peace seemed fall upon my heart, and every shadow of doubt melted away. I put my finger, or some other mark, between the leaves, closed the volume, and with calm countenance told Alypius. And then he revealed to me his own feelings which were unknown to me. He asked to see what I had read. I showed him the text, and he read a little further than I had done, for I did not know what followed. What followed was this: "Him that is weak in the faith receive." This he explained to me as applying to himself. These words of warning gave him strength, and with good purpose and resolve, following the inclination of his moral character, which had always been much better than mine, without any painful hesitation, he cast in his lot with me. Immediately we went in to my mother, and to her great joy told her what had happened. But, when we explained to her how it had come to pass, she was filled with exultation and triumph, and blessed You, who are able to do above what we ask or think. For she saw that You had granted her far more than she had ever asked for me in all her tearful lamentations. For so completely did You convert me to Yourself that I desired neither wife nor any hope of this world, but set my feet on the rule of faith, as she had seen me in a vision of many years ago. So You turned her mourning into joy, joy fuller by far than she had ventured to pray for, dearer and purer by far than that which she had hoped to find in the children of my flesh.

O Lord, I am Your servant; I am Your servant and the son of Your handmaid. You burst my bonds asunder; to You will I offer the sacrifice of praise. Let my heart and my tongue praise You, and let all my bones say, "O Lord, who is like You?" Let them speak, and You say unto my soul, "I am your salvation." Who am I, and what am I? What evil is there not in me and my deeds? Or if not in my deeds, in my words? Or if not in my words, in my will? But You, O Lord, are good and merciful. Your right hand drained dry the sea of corruption in my heart. How sweet did it seem to me to taste no more the sweetness of folly; it was joy to cast away what I had feared to lose. For You cast it out, You true and sovereign sweetness. You cast it out and filled its place, You who are sweeter than any pleasure, brighter than any light, though hidden behind the inmost veil; exalted above all honour, though not to them that are exalted in their own eyes. Henceforth my soul was delivered from the gnawing anxieties of ambition and gain, from wallowing in the mud and scratching the swinish itch of lust; and I prattled like a child to You, O Lord my God, my light, my wealth, my salvation. You had pierced the heart with the arrows of Your love, and Your words stuck fast in our flesh, and the examples of Your servants, whom You had changed from black to shining white and from death to life, heaped themselves up in the bosom of our reflection, and burned up all our sluggish irresolution, so that we could not fall into the pit again; yes, they kindled in us so strong a flame that every breath of contradiction from the deceitful tongue served only to fan the fire.

Too late came I to love You, beauty both so ancient and so fresh, yes too late came I to love You. And behold, You were within me, and I was out of myself, where I looked for You: ugly, I rushed headlong upon those beautiful things You have made. You indeed were with me; but I was not with You: these beauties kept me far enough from You: even those, which unless they were in You, should not be at all. You called and cried to me, You even broke open my deafness: Your beams shone on me, and You chased away my blindness: You blew on me most fragrantly and I drew in my breath and now I pant after You; I tasted You, and now hunger and thirst after You; You touched me, and I burn again to enjoy Your peace.

O Love ever burning, and never quenched! O Charity, my God! Kindle me, I beseech You. You command me to be continent: tell me what You command, and command what You will.

Saint AUGUSTINE: On Anger

1 **Voyaging in this world.** I shall with God's help speak to you upon the portion of the gospel that has just been read and in its light I exhort you that you sleep not in your hearts amid the storms and distresses of this world. Perhaps the Lord had not power over death, nor had He sleep within His power? And it may be that sleep overpowered the omnipotent, as He sailed upon the water? If you have so believed, then He sleeps in you: if Christ keeps watch in you, your faith keeps watch.

The apostle says: "That Christ may dwell by faith in your hearts" (Ephesians 3:17). Therefore the sleep of Christ is also a sign of mysery. Those in the boat are those crossing the world upon the wood. Even this ship prefigures the Church. And each soul is itself a world of God, and each one voyages within his own heart; nor is he shipwrecked, if he dwells on the things that are worthy.

2 **Christ must be awakened in the storms of anger.** Have you received an insult? It is the wind. Are you provoked to anger? It is the buffeting of the waves. As the wind rises, and the waves mount up, your ship is in peril; your heart is buffeted by waves, your soul is endangered. Swift on the insult you are eager for revenge: and lo! you are revenged, and yielding to a new disaster, you are shipwrecked. And why? Because in you Christ sleeps. What does this mean: in you Christ sleeps? It means you have forgotten Christ. Then awaken Christ, bring Him to mind; let Christ keep watch in you: look upon Him.

What was it you desired? To be revenged. Has it gone from your memory what He said while they crucified Him: "Father, forgive them, for they know not what they do" (Luke 23:34)? He who was sleeping in your heart sought not to be revenged. Awaken Him, remember Him. Remembrance of Him is remembrance of His word: and to remember Him is to obey Him. And should Christ awaken in you, you will say to yourself: "What kind of man am I that I should seek to be revenged? Who am I that I should utter threats against another?"

It may be that I shall die before I can be revenged. And when breathing my last, on fire with anger, thirsting for revenge, I go forth from this body, He shall not receive me who desired no revenge. He shall not receive me who said: "Forgive, and you shall be forgiven. Give, and it shall be given unto you" (Luke 6:37–38). Therefore shall I bridle my anger, and return to the peace of my heart. Christ commanded the sea, and there came a great calm.

3 **At the command of Christ there is calm.** What I have said to you regarding anger, observe in every temptation. A temptation arises, it is the wind; you are troubled, it is the waves. Awaken Christ, let Him speak with you. Who is this, for "the winds and the sea obey Him?" Who is this whom the sea obeys?" "The sea is His, and He made it" (Psalms 95:5). "All things were made by Him" (John 1:3). Be then as the winds and the sea: obey your Creator. When Christ spoke, the sea gave ear: and will you be deaf? The sea listens to His voice, and the winds cease: and will you keep blowing? What mean you? I keep on talking, I keep on doing, I keep on contriv-

ing: what is this but to keep on blowing, and refusing to be still at the command of Christ?

Let not the sea master you in this tempest of the heart. Yet, since we are men, should the wind beat hard against you, and should it awaken passion in the soul, let us not lose hope. Let us awaken Christ that we may sail on in peace, and come safely home. Turning then to the Lord Our God, the Father Almighty, in pureness of heart, let us at best we can give thanks with all our hearts; beseeching Him that in His goodness he will graciously hear our prayers, and by His power drive evil from our thoughts and actions, increase our faith, guide our minds, grant to us His holy inspirations, and bring us to unending joy through His Son, Our Lord and Saviour Jesus Christ. Amen.

Saint AUGUSTINE: The Love of God

Love God. You will not find anything more worthy of love. You love silver, because it is more precious than iron or bronze. You love gold still more, because it is more precious than silver. Still more, precious stones, for they are prized above gold. Last, you love this light; which all who dread death fear to leave. You love light, I say, as he loved it, with deep longing, who cried to Jesus: "Son of David, have mercy on me".

The blind man cried out, as Jesus was passing by. He heard He might pass by, and not heal him. And how earnestly he cried. Though the crowd rebuked him, he would not be silent. He overcame his rebukers, and held our saviour. While the crowd clamoured against him, and forbade him cry out, Jesus stood, and called him, and said: "What wilt thou that I do to thee?" "Lord", replied the blind man, "that I may see". "Receive thy sight: thy faith hath made thee whole."

Love Christ: Seek the light that is Christ. If he longed for the light of the body, how much more ought you to long for the light of the soul? Let us cry out to Him, not with words, but with virtuous living. Let us live in virtue, and esteem not the world: all that is transitory to us is nothing. They will rebuke us should we live as "worthy" men and lovers of ourselves, and lovers of the earth, delighting in the games, drawing nothing from Heaven, unbridled in heart, and testing all delights: they will, and without any doubt, rebuke us; and should they see us despise what is human, what is earthly, they will say: "Why do you wish to suffer? Why are you foolish?"

The crowd clamours, that the blind man shall not cry out. There are not a few Christians who seek to hinder us from living as Christians: like the crowd that walked with Christ, and hindered the man crying out to Christ, and hungering for light from the kindness of Christ. There are such Christians: but let us overcome them, and live in virtue: and our life shall be the voice of our cry to Christ.

For here is a great mystery. He was passing by when this man began to cry out: when He healed him He stood still. Let Christ's passing by make us prepared to cry out. What is Christ's passing by? Whatsoever He has endured for us here is His passing by. He was born, He passed by: for is he yet being born? He grew up, He passed by; is He yet growing up? He was suckled: is He yet suckled? When weary He slept: does He yet sleep? He ate and He drank: does He yet do this? At the last He was seized, He was bound with ropes, He was beaten, He was crowned with thorns, He was struck by blows, He was defiled with spittle, He was hung on a cross, He was put to death, He was pierced by a lance, He was buried, He rose again. Till then He passes by.

He ascended into Heaven, He sits at the right hand of the Father: He stands still. Cry out all you can: now He will give you light because in Him the "Word was with God". He has of a surety stood still; since He was not changed. " And the Word was God: and the Word was made flesh." The flesh has wrought many things through passing by, and suffered many. The Word has stood still. By this word the soul is enlightened; as by this word the flesh which He took on is adorned. Take away the Word, what then of the flesh? It is as yours. That the flesh of Christ be honoured, the "Word was made flesh, and dwelt among us". Let us live virtuously, and so cry out to Him.

Saint LEO THE GREAT: The Mystery of the Nativity

I

Our Saviour, dearly beloved, was born today: let us be glad. For there is no proper place for sadness, when we keep the birthday of the life which destroys the fear of mortality and brings to us the joy of promised eternity. No one is kept from sharing in this happiness. There is for all one common measure of joy, because as our Lord the destroyer of sin and death finds none free from charge, so is He come to free us all. Let the saint exult in that he draws near to victory. Let the sinner be glad in that he is invited to pardon. Let the Gentile take courage in that he is called to life. For the Son of God, in the fullness of time which the inscrutable depth of the divine counsel has determined, has taken on him the nature of man, thereby to reconcile it to its author: in order that the inventor of death, the devil, might be conquered through that which he has conquered.

And in this conflict undertaken for us, the fight was fought on great and wondrous principles of fairness; for the Almighty Lord enters the lists with His savage foe, not in His own majesty, but in our humility, opposing him with the same form and the same nature, which shares indeed our mortality though it is free from all sin. Truly foreign to this nativity is that which we read of all others, "No one is clean from stain, not even the infant who has lived but one day upon earth." Nothing therefore of the lust of the flesh has passed into that peerless nativity, nothing of the law of sin has entered. A royal virgin of the stem of David is chosen, to be impregnated with the sacred seed and to conceive the divinely-human offspring in mind first and then in body. And lest in ignorance of the heavenly counsel she should tremble at so strange a prediction, she learns from conversation with the angel that what is to be wrought in her is of the Holy Ghost. Nor does she believe it loss of honour that she is soon to be the mother of God. For why should she be in despair over the novelty of such conception, when the power of the Most High has promised to effect it? Her implicit faith is confirmed also by her witness of a miracle, Elizabeth receives unexpected fertility, that there might be no doubt that He who had given conception to the barren, would give it even to a virgin.

II

Therefore the Word of God, Himself God, the Son of God who "in the beginning was with God", through whom "all things were made" and "without" whom "was nothing made", with the purpose of delivering man from eternal death became man: so bending Himself to take on Him our humility without decrease in His own majesty, remaining what He was and assuming what He was not, He united the true form of a slave to that form in which He is equal to God the Father, and joined both natures together by such a compact that the lower should not be swallowed up in its exaltation nor the higher impaired by its new associate. Without detriment therefore to the properties of either substance, which then came together in one person, majesty took on humility, strength weakness, eternity mortality: and for the paying off of the debt belonging to our condition, inviolable nature was united with perishable nature, and true God and true man were combined to form one Lord, so that, as suited the needs of our case, one and the same mediator between God and men, the man Christ Jesus, could both die with the one and rise again with the other.

Rightly therefore did the birth of our salvation impart no corruption to the Virgin's purity, because the bearing of the truth was the keeping of honour. Such then, beloved, was the nativity which became the power of God and the wisdom of God, in Christ, whereby He might be one with us in manhood and surpass us in Godhead. For unless He were true God. He would not bring us a remedy; unless He were true man, He would not give us an example. Therefore the exulting angels' song when the Lord was born was this, "Glory to God in the highest", and their message, "peace on earth to men of good will". For they see that the heavenly Jerusalem is being built up out of all the nations of the world: and over that indescribable work of the divine love how ought the humbleness of men to rejoice, when the joy of the lofty angels is so great?

III

Let us then, dearly beloved, give thanks to God the father, through His Son, in the Holy Spirit, who "for His great mercy, wherewith He has loved us," has had pity on us: and "when we were dead in sins, has quickened us together in Christ," that we might be in Him a new creation and a new production. Let us put off then the old man with his deeds: and having obtained a share in the birth of Christ let us renounce the works of the flesh. Christian, acknowledge your divinity, and becoming a partner in the divine nature, refuse to return to the old baseness by degerate conduct. Remember the head and the body of which you are a member. Recollect that you were rescued from the power of darkness and brought out of God's light and kingdom. By the mystery of baptism you were made the temple of the Holy Ghost: do not put such a being to flight from you by base acts, and subject yourself once more to the devil's thraldom: because your purchase money is the blood of Christ, because He shall judge you in truth who ransomed you in mercy, who with the Father and the Holy Spirit reigns for ever and ever. Amen.

Saint LEO THE GREAT: The Passion

I

The Feast of the Lord's Passion that we have longed for and that the whole world desires, has come, and requires us not to keep silence in our joys: because though it is difficult to speak about this thing worthily and appropriately, yet the priest is not free to withhold from the people's ears instruction on this great mystery of God's mercy, inasmuch as the subject itself, being unspeakable, gives him ease of utterance, and what is said cannot altogether fail where what is said can never be enough. Let human frailty, then, succumb to God's glory, and ever acknowledge itself unequal to the unfolding of His works of mercy. Let us struggle in our thoughts, fail in insight, falter in utterance: it is fitting that even our most perceptive thoughts about the Lord's Majesty should be insufficient. For, remembering what the prophet says, "Seek ye the Lord and be strengthened: seek His face always," no one must assume that he has found all he seeks, or he will fail to come anywhere near success in his endeavours. And amid all the works of God which weary out man's wondering contemplatioı , what so delights and so baffles our mind's gaze as the Saviour's passion? Ponder as we may upon His omnipotence, which is of one and equal substance with the Father, the humility in God is more stupendous than the power, and it is harder to grasp the complete emptying of the divine majesty than the infinite uplifting of the "slave's form" in Him. But we are much aided in our understanding of it by the remembrance that though the Creator and the creature, the inviolable God and the perishable flesh, are absolutely different, yet the properties of both substances meet together in Christ's one person in such a way that alike in His acts of weakness and of power the degradation belongs to the same person as the glory.

II

In that rule of faith, dearly beloved, which we have received in the very beginning of the Creed, on the authority of apostolic teaching, we acknowledge our Lord Jesus Christ, whom we call the only Son of God the Father Almighty, to be also born of the Virgin Mary by the Holy Ghost. Nor do we reject His majesty when we express our belief in His crucifixion, death, and resurrection on the third day. For all that is God's and all that is man's are simultaneously fulfilled by His manhood and His Godhead, so that in virtue of the union of the perishable with the eternal, His power cannot be affected by His weakness, nor His weakness overcome by His power. And rightly was the blessed apostle Peter praised for confessing this union, who when the Lord was enquiring what the disciples knew of Him, quickly anticipated the rest and said, "Thou art the Christ, the Son of the living God." And this assuredly he saw, not by the revelation of flesh or blood, which might have hindered his inner sight, but by the very spirit of the Father working in his believing heart, that in preparation for ruling the whole Church he might first learn what he would have to teach, and for the solidification of the faith, which he was destined to preach, might receive the assurance, "Thou art Peter, and upon this rock I will build my Church, and the gates of Hell shall not prevail against it." The strength, therefore, of the Christian faith, which, built upon an impregnable rock, fears not the gates of death, acknowledges the one Lord Jesus Christ to be both true God and true man, believing Him likewise to be the Virgin's Son, who is His mother's creator: born also at the end of the ages, though He is the creator of time: Lord of all power, and yet one of mortal stock: ignorant of sin, and yet sacrificed for sinners after the likeness of sinful flesh.

III

And in order that He might set the human race free from the bonds of deadly transgression, He hid the power of His majesty from the raging devil, and opposed him with our frail and humble nature. For if the cruel and proud foe could have known the counsel of God's mercy, he would have aimed at soothing the Jews' minds into gentleness, rather than at firing them with unrighteous hatred, lest he should lose the thraldom of all his captives in assailing the liberty of one who owed him nothing. Thus he was foiled by his malice: he inflicted a punishment on the Son of God, which was turned to the healing of all the sons of men. He shed righteous blood, which became the ransom and the drink for the world's atonement.

The Lord undertook that which He chose according to the purpose of His own will. He permitted madmen to lay their wicked hands upon Him: hands which, in ministering to their own doom, were of service to the Redeemer's work. And yet so great was His loving compassion for even His murderers, that He prayed to the Father on the cross, and begged not for His own vengeance but for their forgiveness, saying: "Father, forgive them, for they know not what they do." And such was the power of that prayer that the hearts of many of those who had said, "His blood be on us and on our sons", were turned to penitence by the apostle Peter's preaching, and on one day there were baptised about three thousand Jews and they all were "of one heart and of one soul", being ready now to die for Him whose crucifixion they had demanded.

IV

To this forgiveness the traitor Judas could not attain: for he, the son of perdition, at whose right hand the devil stood, gave himself up to despair before Christ accomplished the mystery of universal redemption. For in that the Lord died for sinners, perhaps even he might have found salvation if he had not hastened to hang himself. But that evil heart, which was now given up to thievish frauds, and now busied with treacherous designs, had never accepted anything of the proofs of the Saviour's mercy. Those wicked ears had heard the Lord's words, when He said, "I came not to call the righteous but sinners", and "the Son of Man came to seek and to save that which was lost". But they conveyed not to his understanding the clemency of Christ, which not only healed bodily infirmities, but also cured the wounds of sick souls, saying to the paralytic man, "Son, be of good cheer, thy sins are forgiven thee"; saying also to the adulteress that was brought to Him, "neither will I condemn thee; go and sin no more", to show in all His works that He had come as the saviour, not the judge of the world.

But the wicked traitor refused to understand this, and took measures against himself, not in the self-condemnation of repentance, but in the madness of perdition, and thus he who had sold the author of life to His murderers, even in dying increased the amount of sin which condemned him.

V

Accordingly that which false witnesses, cruel leaders of the people, wicked priests did against the Lord Jesus Christ, through the agency of a cowardly governor and an ignorant band of soldiers, has been at once the abhorrence and the rejoicing of all ages.

For though the Lord's cross was part of the cruel purpose of the Jews, yet it is of wondrous power through Him they crucified. The people's fury was directed against one, and the mercy of Christ is for all mankind. That which their cruelty inflicts He voluntarily undergoes, so that the work of His eternal will may be carried out through their unhindered crime.

And hence the whole order of events which is most fully narrated in the gospels must be received by the faithful in such a way that by implicit belief in the events of the Lord's passion, we should understand that not only was the remission of sins accomplished by Christ, but also the standard of justice satisfied. God's grace, we hope, will be vouchsafed at your entreaties to help us to fulfil our promise: through Jesus Christ our Lord. Amen.

The Definition of CHALCEDON

1 The holy, great, and ecumenical synod, by the grace of God and the command of our most orthodox and Christ-loving emperors, Marcian and Valentinian Augusti, assembled in the metropolis of Chalcedon, in the Bithynian province, in the martyry of the holy triumphant martyr Euphemia, has decreed as follows:

2 Our Lord and Saviour Jesus Christ, confirming the knowledge of the faith to His disciples, said: "My peace I leave with you, my peace I give to you", to the end that no one should differ from his neghbour in the doctrines of religion, but that the preaching of the truth should be shown forth equally by all.

But since the evil one does not cease, by means of his own seeds, to supplant the seeds of orthodoxy, and ever invents something new against the truth, therefore the Lord, in His care for the human race, excited to zeal this orthodox and most faithful emperor, and called together to himself the chiefs of the priesthood from all parts, in order that, by the action of the grace of Christ the Lord of us all, we might remove every noxious element from the sheep of Christ, and enrich them with the food of truth.

And this, in fact, we have accomplished, having by a unanimous vote driven away the dogmas of error, and having renewed the undeviating creed of the fathers, proclaim the Nicene Creed:

"We believe in one God, the Father Almighty, maker of heaven and earth, and of all things visible and invisible.

"And in one Lord Jesus Christ, the only-begotten Son of God, begotten of the Father before all worlds; light of light, very God of very God; begotten, not made; co-essential with the Father; by whom all things were made; who for us men and for our salvation came down from the heavens, and was incarnated of the Holy Spirit and the Virgin Mary, and was made man; was crucified also for us under Pontius Pilate, and suffered, and was buried, and rose the third day according to the Scriptures; and ascended into the heavens, and sitteth on the right hand of the Father; and shall come again with glory to judge both the quick and the dead, of whose kingdom there shall be no end:

"And in the Holy Spirit, the Lord and life-giver, who proceedeth from the Father; who with the Father and the Son is together worshipped and glorified; who spoke by the prophets. And in one Holy Catholic and Apostolic Church.

"We acknowledge one baptism for the remission of sins. We look for a resurrection of the dead, and life of the world to come. Amen."

3 Although this wise and saving symbol of the divine grace would have been sufficient for complete knowledge and confirmation of orthodoxy, for it both teaches the perfect doctrine concerning the Father and the Son and the Holy Spirit, and sets forth the incarnation of the Lord to those who receive it faithfully; yet, for as much as those who attempt to set aside the preaching of the truth have produced foolish utterances through their own heresies, some daring to corrupt the mystery of the Lord's incarnation and denying the title Mother of God to the Virgin; others introducing confusion by shamelessly imagining the nature of the flesh and of the Godhead to be one, and absurdly maintaining that the divine nature of the only-begotten is by this confusion perishable; therefore the present holy, great, and ecumenical synod, being determined to exclude all their machinations against the truth, affirming the doctrine as unchangeable from the first, has decreed first of all that the Nicene Creed of the holy fathers should remain inviolate; and, because of those who strug-

gle against the Holy Spirit, it ratifies the teaching subsequently set forth by the Council of Constantinople concerning the essence of the Spirit, but making distinct by scriptural testimonies their conception of the Holy Spirit in order to discredit those who were trying to set aside His Sovereignty.

4 It opposes those who presume to degrade the mystery of the incarnation to a mere duality of sons; and it expels from the company of the priests those who dare to say that the Godhead of the only-begotten is perishable, and it denounces those who imagine a mixture or confusion of the two natures of Christ, and it drives away those who fancy that the form of a servant, taken by Him of us, is of a heavenly or any other essence; and it anathematises those who imagine two natures of the Lord before the union, but imagine one after the union. Following, then, the holy fathers, we all unanimously teach that our Lord Jesus Christ is to us one and the same Son, the self-same perfect in Godhead, the self-same perfect in manhood; truly God and truly man; the self-same of a reasonable soul and body; co-essential with the Father according to the Godhead, the self-same co-essential with us according to the manhood; like us in all things, sin apart; before the ages begotten of the Father as to the Godhead, but in the last days, the self-same, for us and for our salvation born of Mary the Virgin, Mother of God, as to the manhood; one and the same Christ, Son, Lord, only-begotten; acknowledged in two natures unconfusedly, unchangeable, indivisible, inseparable; the difference of the natures being in no way removed because of the union, but rather the properties of each nature being preserved, and both concurring into one person and one substance; not as though He were parted or divided into two persons, but one and the self-same Son and only-begotten, God, Word, Lord, Jesus Christ; even as from the beginning the prophets have taught concerning Him, and as the Lord Jesus Christ Himself has taught us, and as the symbol of the fathers has handed down to us.

5 These things having been defined by us with all possible accuracy and care, the holy and ecumenical synod hath decreed that it is unlawful for any one to present, write, compose, devise, or teach to others any other creed; but that those who dare to compose another creed, shall be anathematised.

The Breastplate of Saint PATRICK

I awake today to strong virtue,
I call upon the power of the Trinity,
I believe in its threeness,
I believe in its oneness,
I believe it is the creator of the universe.
I awake today to the power of Christ's
birth and baptism,
To the power of His crucifixion
And his burial,
To the power of His resurrection
And his Ascension,
To the power of his second coming
And the judgment of Doom.
I awake today to the strengths of the rank
of the cherubim,
To the obedience of angels,
To the service of archangels,
To the hope of my reward at resurrection,
To the prayers of patriarchs,
To the predictions of prophets,
To the preachings of apostles,
To the faiths of confessors,
To the innocence of holy virgins,
To the deeds of righteous men.
I awake today to the glory of Heaven,
To the light of the sun,
To the brightness of snow,
To the splendour of fire,
To the speed of lightning,
To the swiftness of wind,
To the depth of sea,
To the stability of earth,
To the compactness of rock.
I awake today to God's power to guide me,
God's might to uphold me,
God's wisdom to teach me,
God's eye to look out for me,
God's ear to hear me,
God's word to speak for me,
God's hand to guard me,
God's way to lie before me,
God's shield to protect me,
God's host to secure me,
Against snares of demons,

Against seduction of vices,
Against lusts of nature,
Against everyone who wishes ill to me,
Far and near
Alone and in a crowd.
So I call upon all these virtues to protect me
Against every cruel, merciless power
Which may come against my body and my soul,
Against incantations of false prophets,
Against blast laws of heathenry,
Against false laws of heretics,
Against craft of idolatry,
Against spells of women and smiths and druids,
Against every knowledge that defiles men's souls.
I call upon Christ to protect me today,
Against poison, against burning, against drowning, against death-wound,
Until a multitude of rewards come to me!
Christ with me, Christ before me, Christ behind me, Christ in me!
Christ below me, Christ above me,
Christ at my right, Christ at my left!
Christ in breadth, Christ in length, Christ in height!
Christ in the heart of everyone who thinks of me,
Christ in the mouth of everyone who speaks to me,
Christ in every eye that sees me,
Christ in every ear that hears me!
I awake today to a strong virtue, an invocation of the Trinity.
I believe in a threeness with confession of a oneness, in the Creator of the universe.
Salvation is the Lord's, salvation is the Lord's, salvation is Christ's.
May Thy salvation, O Lord, be always with us.

Collects from the Sacramentary of GELASIUS

I

O God, who is the author of peace and lover of concord, in knowledge of whom stands our eternal life, whose service is perfect freedom; defend us Your humble servants in all assaults of our enemies; that we, surely trusting in Your defence, may not fear the power of any adversaries; through the might of Jesus Christ our Lord. Amen.

II

O Lord, our heavenly Father, almighty and everlasting God, who has safely brought us to the beginning of this day; defend us in the same with Your mighty power; and grant that this day we fall into no sin, neither run into any kind of danger; but that our doings may be ordered by Your governance, to do always that which is righteous in Your sight; through Jesus Christ our Lord. Amen.

III

O God, from whom all holy desires, all good counsels, and all just works do proceed; give to Your servants that peace which the world cannot give; that both our hearts may be set to obey Your commandments, and also that by You we being defended from the fear of our enemies may pass our time in rest and quietness; through the merits of Jesus Christ our Saviour. Amen.

IV

Lighten our darkness, we beseech You, O Lord; and by Your great mercy defend us from all perils and dangers of this night; for the love of Your only Son, our Saviour, Jesus Christ. Amen.

V

Almighty and everlasting God, who hates nothing that You have made, and does forgive the sins of all them that are penitent; create and make in us new and contrite hearts, that we, worthily lamenting our sins, and acknowledging our wretchedness, may obtain of You, the God of all mercy, perfect remission and forgiveness; through Jesus Christ our Lord. Amen.

VI

O Lord, from whom all good things do come; grant to us Your humble servants, that by Your holy inspiration we may think those things that be good, and by Your merciful guiding may perform the same; through our Lord Jesus Christ. Amen.

VII

O God, who has prepared for them that love You such good things as pass man's understanding; pour into our hearts such love toward You, that we, loving You above all things, may obtain Your promises, which exceed all that we can desire; through Jesus Christ our Lord. Amen.

VIII

Almighty and everlasting God, who is always more ready to hear than we to pray, and is wont to give more than either we desire or deserve; pour down upon us the abundance of Your mercy; forgiving us those things of which our conscience is afraid, and giving us those good things which we are not worthy to ask, but through the merits and mediation of Jesus Christ, Your Son, our Lord. Amen.

IX

Lord, we beseech You, grant Your people grace to withstand the temptations of the world, the flesh, and the devil, and with pure hearts and minds to follow You the only God; through Jesus Christ our Lord. Amen.

X

O God, for as much as without You we are not able to please You; mercifully grant, that Your Holy Spirit may in all things direct and rule our hearts; through Jesus Christ our Lord. Amen.

XI

Grant, we beseech You, merciful Lord, to Your faithful people pardon and peace, that they may be cleansed from all their sins, and serve You with a quiet mind; through Jesus Christ our Lord. Amen.

DIONYSIUS the Areopagite: The Mystical Theology

I

Most exalted Trinity, divinity above all knowledge, whose goodness passes understanding, who guides Christians to divine wisdom; direct our way to the summit of Your mystical oracles, most incomprehensible, most lucid and most exalted, where the simple and pure and unchangeable mysteries of theology are revealed in the darkness, clearer than light; a darkness that shines brighter than light, that invisibly and intangibly illuminates with splendours of inconceivable beauty the soul that sees not. Let this be my prayer.

But give yourself diligently to mystical contemplation, leave the senses, and the operations of the intellect, and all things sensible and intelligible, and things verifiable, that you may rise by ways above knowledge to union with Him who is above all knowledge and all being; that in freedom and abandonment of all you may be carried through pure, entire and absolute abstraction of yourself from all things, into the supernatural radiance of the divine darkness.

But see that none of the uninitiated hear these things. I mean those who trust to created things, and suppose not that anything exists in a supernatural manner, above nature; but imagine that by their own natural understanding they know Him who has made darkness His secret place. But if the principles of the divine mysteries are above the understanding of these, what is to be said of those yet more untaught, who rank the absolute first cause of all after the lowest things in nature, and say that He is in no way above the images which they fashion. Instead they should declare and affirm that in Him as the cause of all, is all that may be predicated positively of created things; while yet they might with more propriety deny these assertions about Him, as being far above all; holding that in this case denial is not contrary to affirmation, since He is infinitely above all notion of definition, and above all affirmation and negation.

Thus the divine Bartholomew says that theology is both much and very little, and that the gospel is great and ample, and yet short. His sublime meaning is, I think, that the beneficent cause of all things says much and says little, and is altogether silent, as having neither human speech nor human understanding, since He is essentially above all created things, and manifests Himself unveiled and as He truly is only to those who pass beyond all that is either pure or impure, who rise above the highest height of holy things, who abandon all divine light and sound and heavenly speech, and are absorbed into the darkness where, as the Scripture says, He truly is, who is beyond all things.

It was not without a deeper meaning that the divine Moses was commanded first to be himself purified, and then to separate himself from the impure; and after all this purification he heard many voices of trumpets, and saw many lights shedding manifold pure beams: and he was thereafter separated from the multitude, and together with the elect priests came to the height of the holy mountains. Yet hereby he did not attain to the presence of God Himself; he saw not Him (for He cannot be looked upon), but the place where He was. This, I think, signifies that the most divine and most exalted of visible and intelligible things are, as it were, manifestations of those that are immediately beneath Him who is above all, whereby is indicated the presence of Him who passes all understanding, and stands, as it were, in that spot which is conceived by the intellect as the highest of His holy places; then they who are free and untrammelled by all that is seen, and all that sees, enter into the true mystical darkness of ignorance, whence all perception of understanding is excluded, and abide in that which is intangible and invisible, being wholly absorbed in Him who is beyond all things, and belong no more to any, neither to themselves nor to another, but are united in their higher part to Him who is wholly unintelligible, and whom, by not understanding at all, they understand in a manner above all intelligence.

II

We desire to abide in this most luminous darkness, and without sight or knowledge, to see that which is above sight or knowledge, by means of that very fact that we see not and know not. For this is truly to see and know, to praise Him who is above nature by the abstraction of all that is natural; as those who would make a statue out of the natural stone remove all the surrounding material which hinders the sight of the shape lying concealed within, and by that abstraction reveal its hidden beauty. It is needful, I think, to make this abstraction in a manner precisely opposite to that in which we deal with the divine attributes; for we add them together, beginning with the primary ones, and passing from them to the secondary, and so to the last; but here we ascend from the last to the first, removing all, so as to unveil and know that which is beyond knowledge, and which in all things is hidden from our sight by that which can be known, and so to behold that supernatural darkness which is hidden by all such light as is in created things.

III

Those matters which are properly the subject of positive theology are these; in what sense the holy divine nature is one, and in what sense three; what it is that is there called paternity, and what filiation; and what the doctrine of the Holy Ghost signifies; how from the uncreated and undivided good those blessed and perfect lights have come forth, yet remained one with the divine nature, with each other, and in themselves, undivided by co-eternal abiding in propagation; how Jesus though immaterial became material in the truth of human nature; and other things taken from Scripture we have expounded positively.

Again God is called good, being, life and wisdom and virtue, with other names spiritually applied to Him. Names are transferred to Him from sensible things. This is what is meant by the divine forms and figures, limbs, instruments, localities, adornments, fury, anger and grief; oaths and curses, sleep and waking, with other modes of sacred and symbolic nomenclature. Because in proportion as we ascend higher our speech is contracted to the limits of our view of the purely intelligible, and so now, when we enter that darkness which is above understanding, we pass not merely into brevity of speech, but even into absolute silence, and the negation of thought. Now we rise from beneath to that which is the highest, and accordingly our speech is restrained in proportion to the height of our ascent; but when our ascent is accomplished, speech will cease altogether, and be absorbed into the ineffable.

IV

We say that the cause of all things, who is Himself above all things, is neither without being nor without life, nor without reason nor without intelligence; nor is He a body; nor has He form or shape, or quality or quantity or mass; He is not localised or visible or tangible; He is neither sensitive nor sensible; He is subject to no disorder or disturbance arising from material passion; He is not subject to failure of power, nor to the accidents of sensible things; He needs no light; He suffers no change or corruption or division, or privation or flux; and He neither has nor is anything else that belongs to the senses.

V

Again, ascending, we say that He is neither soul nor intellect; nor has He imagination, nor opinion or reason; He has neither speech nor understanding, and is neither declared nor understood; He is neither number nor order, nor greatness nor smallness, nor equality nor likeness nor unlikeness; He does not stand or move or rest; He neither has power nor is power; nor is He light, nor does He live, nor is He life; He is neither being nor age nor time; nor is He subject to intellectual contact; He is neither knowledge nor truth, nor royalty nor wisdom; He is neither one nor unity, nor divinity, nor goodness; nor is He spirit, as we understand spirit; He is neither sonship nor fatherhood nor anything else known to us or to any other beings, either of the things that are or the things that are not; nor does anything that is know Him as He is, nor does He know anything that is as it is; He has neither word nor name nor knowledge; He is neither darkness nor light nor truth nor error; He can neither be affirmed nor denied; nay, though we may affirm or deny the things that are beneath Him, we can neither affirm nor deny Him; for the perfect and only cause of all is above all affirmation and all subtraction and beyond all that is.

The Spiritual Practices of Saint BENEDICT

PROLOGUE

Listen, O my son, to the teaching of your master, and open the ear of your heart; willingly receive and faithfully fulfil the admonition of your loving father, so that you may return by the labour of obedience to Him from whom you had departed through the sloth of disobedience. To you, therefore, my words are now addressed, whoever you are that, renouncing your own will, you take up the strong and bright weapons of obedience, in order to fight for the Lord Christ, our true king. In the first place, whatever good work you begin to do, beg of Him with most earnest prayer to perfect; that He who has now vouchsafed to count us in the number of His children may not at any time be grieved by our evil deeds. For we must always so serve Him with the good things He has given us, that not only may He never, as an angry father, disinherit His children, but also may never, as a dreadful Lord incensed by our sins, deliver us to everlasting punishment, as most wicked servants who would not follow Him to glory.

Let us then awake, since the Scripture speaks to us saying: "It is time now for us to rise from sleep". And our eyes being opened to the deifying light, let us hear with wondering ears what the divine voice tells us, daily crying out: "Today if you hear His voice, harden not your hearts." And again: "He who has ears to hear, let him hear what the Spirit says to the churches." And what does he say? "Come, my children, hearken to me, I will teach you the fear of the Lord. Run while you have the light of life, lest the darkness of death seize hold of you."

And the Lord, seeking His own workman in the multitude of the people to whom He spoke, says again: "Who is the man that will have life, and desire to see good days?" And if you, hearing Him answer, "I am he", God will say to you: "If you will have true and everlasting life, keep your tongue from evil and your lips that they speak no guile. Turn from evil, and do good: seek peace and pursue it. And when you have done these things, my eyes will be upon you, and my ears will be open to your prayers; and before you call upon me, I will say to you, behold, I am here". What can be sweeter to us, dearest brethren, than this voice of the Lord inviting us? Behold in His loving kindness the Lord shows us the way of life.

Having girded ourselves with faith and the performance of good works, let us walk in His paths by the guidance of the Gospel, that we may deserve to see Him who has called us to His kingdom. And if we wish to dwell in the tabernacle of His kingdom, we shall by no means reach it unless we do so by our good deeds. The Lord is waiting daily for us to respond by our deeds to His holy admonitions. The days of our life are lengthened for the amendment of our evil ways; as the apostle says, "Know you not that the patience of God is leading you to repentance?" And the merciful Lord says "I do not will the death of a sinner, but that he should be converted and live."

Brothers, we have asked of the Lord who is to inhabit His temple, and we have heard His commands to those who are to dwell there: and if we fulfil those duties, we shall be heirs of the kingdom of Heaven. Therefore our hearts and our bodies must be made ready to fight under the holy obedience of His commands; and let us ask God to supply by the help of His grace what by nature is not possible to us. And if we would arrive at eternal life, escaping the pains of hell, then while there is yet time, while we are still in the flesh, and are able to fulfil all these things by the light which is given us we must hasten to do now what will profit us for all eternity.

We must therefore establish a school of the Lord's service, in the organising of which we hope to order nothing that is harsh. But if anything be somewhat strictly laid down, according to the dictates of sound reason, for the amendment of vices or the preservation of charity, do not therefore fly in dismay from the way of salvation, whose beginning cannot be difficult. But as we go forward in our life and in faith, we shall with hearts enlarged and unspeakable sweetness of love run in the way of God's commandments; so that never departing from His guidance, but persevering in His teaching in the monastery until death, we may by patience share in the sufferings of Christ, that we may deserve to be partakers of His kingdom. Amen.

CALLING THE BRETHREN TO COUNCIL

As often as any important matters have to be transacted in the monastery, let the abbot call together the whole community, and declare what is the question to be settled. And, having heard the counsel of the brethren, let him consider within himself, and then do what he judges most expedient. We have said that all should be called to council, because it is often to the younger that the Lord reveals what is best. But let the brethren give their advice with all humility, and not presume stubbornly to defend their own opinions; but rather let the matter rest with the abbot's discretion, and let all submit to whatever he judges to be best. Yet, even as it becomes disciples to obey their master, so does it become him to order all things prudently and with justice.

Let all, therefore, follow the rule in all things as their guide, and let no man rashly turn aside from it. Let no one in the monastery follow the will of his own heart: nor let any one presume to argue with his abbot. But if he should so presume, let him be subjected to the discipline appointed by the rule. The abbot himself, however, must do everything in the fear of God and in observance of the rule, knowing that he will have without doubt to render to God, the most just judge, an account of all his judgments.

THE INSTRUMENTS OF GOOD WORKS

In the first place, to love the Lord God with all one's heart, all one's soul, and all one's strength.

2 To love one's neighbour as oneself.
3 Not to kill.
4 Not to commit adultery.
5 Not to steal.
6 Not to covet.
7 Not to bear false witness.
8 To honour all men.
9 Not to do to another what one would not have done to oneself.
10 To deny oneself in order to follow Christ.
11 To chastise the body.
12 Not to seek the comfortable life.
13 To love fasting.
14 To relieve the poor.
15 To clothe the naked.
16 To visit the sick.
17 To bury the dead.
18 To help in affliction.
19 To console the sorrowing.
20 To keep aloof from worldly actions.
21 To prefer nothing to the love of Christ.
22 Not to give way to anger.
23 Not to harbour a desire of revenge.
24 Not to foster guile in one's heart.

25 Not to make a feigned peace.
26 Not to forsake charity.
27 Not to swear, for fear of perjury.
28 To utter truth from heart and mouth.
29 Not to render evil for evil.
30 To do no wrong to anyone, and to bear patiently wrong done to oneself.
31 To love one's enemies.
32 Not to render cursing for cursing, but rather blessing.
33 To bear persecution for justice's sake.
34 Not to be proud.
35 Not given to wine.
36 Not a glutton.
37 Not drowsy.
38 Not slothful.
39 Not a grumbler.
40 Not a detractor.
41 To put one's hope in God.
42 To attribute any good that one sees in oneself to God and not to oneself.
43 But to recognise and always impute to oneself the evil that one does.
44 To fear the day of judgment.
45 To dread Hell.
46 To desire everlasting life with all spiritual longing.
47 To keep death daily before one's eyes.
48 To keep guard at all times over the actions of one's life.
49 To know for certain that God sees one everywhere.
50 To dash down on the rock of Christ one's evil thoughts, the instant that they come into the heart:
51 And to lay them open to one's spiritual father.
52 To keep one's mouth from evil and wicked words.
53 Not to love much speaking.
54 Not to speak foolish words or such as move to laughter.
55 Not to love much or excessive laughter.
56 To listen willingly to holy reading.
57 To apply oneself frequently to prayer.
58 Daily to confess one's past sins with tears and sighs to God, and to amend them for the time to come.
59 Not to fulfil the desires of the flesh: to hate one's own will.
60 To obey in all things the commands of the abbot, even though he himself (which God forbid) should act otherwise: being mindful of that precept of the Lord: "Follow what they say, but not what they do."
61 Not to wish to be called holy before one is so: but first to be holy, that one may be truly so called.
62 Daily to fulfil by one's deeds the commandments of God.
63 To love chastity.
64 To hate no man.
65 Not to give way to jealousy and envy.
66 Not to give strife.
67 To fly from vainglory.
68 To revere the seniors.
69 To love the juniors.
70 To pray for one's enemies in the love of Christ.
71 To make peace after a quarrel before the setting of the sun.
72 Never to despair of the mercy of God.

These are the tools of the spiritual craft, which, if they are constantly employed day and night, and duly given back on the day of judgment, will gain for us from the Lord that reward which He Himself hath promised, "which eye has not seen, nor ear heard; nor has it entered into the heart of man to conceive what God has prepared for those that love Him". And the workshop where we are to labour at all these things is the cloister of the monastery, and stability in the community.

OF OBEDIENCE

The first degree of humility is obedience without delay. Those who hold nothing dearer to them than Christ, and who on account of the holy servitude which they have accepted, either for fear of Hell or for the glory of life everlasting, as soon as anything is ordered by the superior, must no more delay in doing it than if it had been commanded by God Himself. It is of these that the Lord says: "At the hearing of the ear he hath obeyed me." And, again, to teachers He says: "He that hears you hears me".

Such brothers, leaving immediately their own occupations and forsaking their own will, and leaving unfinished what they were about, with the speedy step of obedience follow by their deeds the voice of him who commands; and so at the same instant the bidding of the master and the perfect fulfilment of the disciple are joined together in the swiftness of the fear of God, by those who are moved with the desire of attaining eternal life. These brothers choose the narrow way, of which the Lord says: "Narrow is the way which leads to life"; so that living not by their own will, nor obeying their own desires and pleasures, but walking according to the judgment and command of another, and dwelling in community, they desire to have an abbot over them. Such as these without doubt fulfil that saying of the Lord: "I came not to do my own will, but the will of Him who sent me."

But this very obedience will only be acceptable to God and sweet to men if what is commanded be done not fearfully, tardily, nor coldly, nor with grumbling, nor with answering back, showing unwillingness; for the obedience which is given to superiors is given to God, since He Himself has said: "He that hears you, hears Me." And it ought to be offered by disciples with a good will, because, "God loves a cheerful giver". For if the disciple obeys with ill will, and complains not only with his lips but even in his heart, he may fulfil the command, but it will not be accepted by God, who watches the heart of the grumbler. And for such an action he shall gain no reward; nay, rather, he shall incur the punishment due to those who complain unless he amends and makes satisfaction.

THE PRACTICE OF SILENCE

Let us do as the prophet says: "I said I will take heed to my ways. So that I sin not with my tongue, I have placed a watch over my mouth; I became dumb and was silent, and held my peace even from good things." Here the prophet shows that if we ought at times to refrain even from good words for the sake of silence, how much more ought we to abstain from evil words, because of the punishment due to sin. Therefore, let permission to speak be seldom granted even to perfect disciples, although their conversation be good and holy; because it is written: "In much speaking you shall not avoid sin", and elsewhere: "Death and life are in the power of the tongue." For it is fitting for the master to speak and to teach, but the disciple should be silent and listen. Therefore, if anything has to be asked of the superior, let it be done with all humility and reverence. But as for buffoonery or idle words, such as move to laughter, we utterly condemn them in every place.

HUMILITY

The Holy Scripture cries out to us, brethren, saying: "Everyone that exalts himself shall be humbled, and he who humbles himself shall be exalted." In saying this, it teaches us that all exaltation is a kind of pride, against which the prophet shows himself to be on his guard when he says: "Lord, my heart is not exalted nor my eyes lifted up; nor have I walked in great things, nor in wonders above me." And why? "If I did not think humbly, but exalted my soul like a child that is weaned from his mother, so will You repay my soul." So, brethren, if we wish to arrive at the highest point of humility, and speedily to reach that heavenly exaltation to which we can only ascend by the humility of this present life, we must by our ever-ascending actions erect such a ladder as that which Jacob saw in his dream, by which the angels appeared to him descending and ascending. This descent and ascent signifies nothing else than that we descend by self-exaltation and ascend by humility. And the ladder thus erected is our life in the world, which, if the heart be humbled, is lifted up by the Lord to Heaven. The sides of the same ladder we understand to be our body and soul, in which our divine vocation has placed various rungs of humility or discipline, which we must ascend.

The first degree of humility is that a man always keeps the fear of God before his eyes, avoiding all forgetfulness; and that he is ever mindful of all that God has commanded, reminding himself that those who despise God will be consumed in Hell for their sins, and that life everlasting is prepared for those that fear Him. And keeping himself at all times from sin and vice, whether of the thoughts, the tongue, the hands, the feet, or his own will, let him hasten to cut off the desires of the flesh.

Let him consider that he is always watched from Heaven by God, and that his actions are everywhere seen by the eye of the divine majesty, and are every hour reported to Him by His angels. This the prophet tells us, when he shows how God is ever present in our thoughts, saying: "God searches the heart and the veins." And again: "The Lord knows the thoughts of men." And he also says: "You have understood my thoughts afar off", and "The thought of man shall confess to You." In order, therefore, that he may be on his guard against evil thoughts, let the humble brother say always in his heart: "Then shall I be unspotted before Him, if I have kept myself from iniquity."

We are, indeed, forbidden to do our own will by Scripture, which says to us: "Turn away from your own will." And so too we beg of God in prayer that His will may be done in us. Rightly therefore are we taught not to do our own will, if we heed the warning of Scripture: "There are ways which to men seem right, but the ends of which lead to the depths of Hell", or, again, when we tremble at what is said of the careless: "They are corrupt and have become abominable in their pleasures." And in regard to the desires of the flesh, we must believe that God is always present to us, as the prophet says to the Lord: "O Lord, all my desire is before You."

Let us be on our guard then against evil desires, since death has its seat close to the entrance of delight; so the Scripture commands us, saying: "Go not after concupiscence." Since, therefore, the eyes of the Lord note the good and the evil; and the Lord is looking down from Heaven upon the children of men, to see who is seeking God; and since the works of our hands are reported to Him day and night by the angels appointed to watch over us, we must be always on the watch, brethren, lest, as the prophet says in the psalm, God should see us at any time turning to evil and becoming unprofitable; and though He might spare us now, because He is merciful and expects our conversion, He will say to us hereafter: "These things you did and I held my peace."

The second degree of humility is that a man loves not his own will, nor delights in gratifying his own desires, but carries out in his deeds that saying of the Lord: "I came not to do my own will, but the will of Him that sent me." And again Scripture says: "Self-will brings punishment, but necessity wins a crown."

The third degree of humility is that a man for the love of God submits himself to his superior in all obedience; imitating the Lord, of whom the apostle says: "He was made obedient even unto death."

The fourth degree of humility is that if hard and contrary things, even injuries, are done to him, he should embrace them patiently with a quiet conscience, and not grow weary or give in, for as the Scripture says: "He that shall persevere to the end shall be saved." And again: "Let your heart be comforted, and wait for the Lord." And showing how the faithful man ought to bear all things, however contrary, for the Lord's sake it says: "For You we suffer death all the day long; we are esteemed as sheep for the slaughter." And secure in their hope of the divine reward, they go on with joy, saying: "But in all these things we overcome, through Him who has loved us." And in another place Scripture says: "You have proved us, O God; You have tried us as silver is tried by fire; You have led us into the snare, and have laid tribulation on our backs." Moreover, fulfilling the precept of the Lord by patience in adversities and injuries, they who are struck on one cheek offer the other: to him who takes away their coat they leave also their cloak; and being forced to walk one mile, they go two. With Paul the apostle they bear with false brethren, and bless those that curse them.

The fifth degree of humility is not to hide from one's abbot any of the evil thoughts that invade one's heart, or the sins committed in secret, but humbly to confess them. Scripture says: "Make known your way to the Lord, and hope in Him." And again: "Confess to the Lord, for He is good, and His mercy endures for ever." So also the prophet says: "I have made known to you my offence, and my iniquities I have not hidden. I will confess against myself my iniquities to the Lord: and you have forgiven the wickedness of my heart."

The sixth degree of humility is for a monk to be contented with the meanest and worst of everything, and in all that is enjoined him to esteem himself a bad and worthless labourer, saying with the prophet: "I have been brought to nothing, and I knew it not: I have become as a beast before You, yet I am always with You."

The seventh degree of humility is that he should not only call himself with his tongue lower and viler than all, but also believe himself in his inmost heart to be so, humbling himself, and saying with the prophet: "I am a worm and no man, the shame of men and the outcast of the people; I have been exalted, and cast down, and confounded." And again: "It is good for me that You have humbled me, that I may learn Your commandments."

The eighth degree of humility is for a monk to do nothing except what is authorised by the common rule of the monastery, or the example of his seniors.

The ninth degree of humility is that a monk keeps silence until a question is asked him, as the Scripture shows: "In much talking you shall not avoid sin" and, "The talkative man shall not be directed upon the earth."

The tenth degree of humility is that he is not easily moved and prompted to laughter; because it is written: "The fool lifts up his voice in laughter."

The eleventh degree of humility is that when a monk speaks, he does so gently and without laughter, humbly, gravely, with few words, and that he is not noisy, as it is written: "A wise man is known by the fewness of his words."

The twelfth degree of humility is that the monk, not only in his heart but also in his very exterior always shows his humility to all who see him; that is, in the work of God, in the oratory, in the monastery, in the garden, on the road, in the field, or wherever he may be, whether sitting, walking or standing, with head always bent down, and eyes fixed on the earth. He always thinks of the guilt of his sins, and imagines himself already present before the terrible judgment seat of God; he is always saying in his heart what the publican in the gospel said with his eyes fixed on the earth: "Lord, I, a sinner, am not worthy to raise my eyes to Heaven." And again, with the prophet: "I am bowed down and humbled on every side."

Having, therefore, ascended all these degrees of humility, the monk will presently arrive at that love of God which, being perfect, casts out fear: so he shall begin to keep, without labour, and as it were naturally and by custom, all those precepts which he had hitherto observed through fear: no longer through dread of Hell, but for the love of Christ, and from a good habit and a delight in virtue. God will grant these things by the Holy Spirit working in his labourer, now he is cleansed from vice and sin.

OF THE DISCIPLINE OF SAYING THE DIVINE OFFICE

We believe that the divine presence is everywhere, and that the eyes of the Lord behold the good and the evil in every place. Especially should we believe this, without any doubt, when we are doing the work of God. Let us, then, remember what the prophet says: "Serve the Lord in fear", and again, "Sing wisely", and, "In the sight of the angels I will sing praises to You." Therefore let us consider how we ought to behave ourselves in the presence of God and His angels, and so assist at the divine office, that our mind and our voice may accord together.

OF REVERENCE AT PRAYER

If, when we wish to make any request to men in power, we presume not to do so except with humility and reverence, how much more ought we with all lowliness and purity of devotion to offer our prayers to the Lord God of all things? And let us remember that not for our words, but for our purity of heart and tears of repentance shall we be heard. Our prayer, therefore, ought to be short and pure, unless it is prolonged by the inspiration of divine grace. But let communal prayer always be short: and at the signal given by the superior, let all rise together.

WHETHER MONKS OUGHT TO HAVE ANYTHING OF THEIR OWN

The vice of private ownership is above all to be cut off from the monastery at the roots. Let none presume to give or receive anything without the permission of the abbot, nor to keep anything as their own, either book or writing-tablet or pen, or anything whatsoever. But all that is necessary they may hope to receive from the father of the monastery: nor are they allowed to keep anything which the abbot has not given, or at least permitted them to have. Let all things be common to all, as it is written: "Neither did anyone say that anything which he possessed was his own." But if anyone shall be found to indulge in this most baneful vice, and after one or two admonitions does not behave, let him be subjected to correction.

WHETHER ALL OUGHT ALIKE TO RECEIVE WHAT IS NEEDFUL

As it is written: "Distribution was made to every man, according to his need." We do not mean that there should be respecting of persons, God forbid, but consideration for infirmities. Let him, therefore, who has need of less give thanks to God, and not be grieved; and let him who requires more be humbled, and not made proud by the kindness shown to him: and so all the members of the family shall be at peace. Above all, let not the evil of grumbling show itself by the slightest word or sign whatsoever. If anyone is found guilty, let him be subjected to very severe punishment.

THE DAILY MANUAL LABOUR

Idleness is an enemy to the soul; and hence the brethren ought to divide their time between the labour of their hands, and holy reading.

RECEIVING GUESTS

Let all guests that come be received like Christ Himself, who said: "I was a stranger and you took me in." And let fitting honour be shown to all, especially to such as are of the faith, and to strangers. When, therefore, a guest is announced, let him be met by the superior or the brethren, with all due charity. Let them first pray together, and so associate with one another in peace; but the kiss of peace must not be offered until after prayer, to avoid the delusions of the devil. In this salutation let all humility be shown. At the arrival or departure of all guests, let Christ, who indeed is received in their persons, be adored in them, by bowing the head or even prostrating on the ground.

THE GOOD ZEAL WHICH MONKS OUGHT TO HAVE

As there is an evil zeal of bitterness, which separates from God, and leads to Hell, so there is a good zeal, which keeps us from vice, and leads to God and to life everlasting. Let monks, therefore, exert this zeal with most fervent love; that is, "in honour preferring one another." Let them most patiently endure one another's infirmities, whether of body or of mind. Let them vie with one another in obedience. Let no one do what he thinks good for himself, but rather what is good for another. Let them cherish fraternal charity with chaste love, fear God, love their abbot with sincere and humble affection, and prefer nothing whatever to Christ. And may He bring us all alike to life everlasting.

GREGORY THE GREAT to John, Bishop of Constantinople, on Christian leadership

Gregory, to John of Constantinople, Eulogius of Alexandria, Gregory of Antioch, John of Jerusalem, and Anastasias, ex-patriarch of Antioch.

When I consider how, unworthy as I am, and resisting with my whole soul, I have been compelled to bear the burden of pastoral care, a darkness of sorrow comes over me, and my sad heart sees nothing but shadows. For to what end is a bishop chosen by the Lord but to be an intercessor for the offences of the people? With what confidence, then, can I come as an intercessor for the sins of others to Him before whom I am not secure about my own? If anyone should ask me to become his intercessor with a great man who was angry with him, and to myself unknown, I should at once reply, "I cannot go to intercede for you, having no knowledge of that man from familiar acquaintance with him." If then, as man with man, I should properly blush to become an intercessor with one on whom I had no claim, how great is the audacity of my obtaining the place of intercessor for the people with God, whose friendship I am not assured of through the merit of my life! And in this matter I find a still more serious cause of alarm, since we all know well that, when one who is in disfavour is sent to intercede with an angry person, the mind of the latter is provoked to still greater severity. And I am greatly afraid lest the community of believers, whose offences the Lord has so far indulgently borne with, should perish through the addition of my guilt to theirs. But, when in one way or another I suppress this fear, and with mind consoled give myself to the care of my pontifical office. I am deterred by consideration of the immensity of this very task.

For indeed I consider with myself what watchful care is needed that a ruler may be pure in thought, sovereign in action, discreet in keeping silence, profitable in speech, a near neighbour to everyone in sympathy, exalted above all in contemplation, a companion of good livers through humility, and unbending against the vices of evildoers through zeal for righteousness. All of which things, when I try to search them out with subtle investigation, the very wideness of the consideration cramps me in examining the particulars. For, as I have already said, there is need of the greatest care that the ruler should always be pure in thought, because as no impurity ought to pollute the man who has undertaken the office of wiping away the stains of pollution in the hearts of others; for the hand that would cleanse from dirt must be clean, lest, being itself sordid with clinging mire, it soils whatever it touches all the more. For on this account it is said through the prophet: "Be ye clean that be the vessels of the Lord" (Isaiah 52:11). For they bear the vessels of the Lord who undertake, on the surety of their own worth, to conduct the souls of their neighbours to the eternal sanctuary. Let them therefore perceive within themselves how purified they ought to be who carry in the bosom of their own personal responsibility living vessels to the temple of eternity.

Lax cognitions should not possess the priestly heart; nor should he cogitate anything indiscreet or unprofitable, who, constituted as he is for example to others, ought to show in the gravity of his life what store of reason he carries in his breast. And on this breastplate it is further carefully prescribed that the names of the twelve patriarchs should be engraved. For to carry always the fathers registered on the breast is to think without intermission on the lives of the ancients. For the priest walks blamelessly when he pores continually on the examples of the fathers that went before him, when he considers without cease the footsteps of the saints, and keeps down unlawful thoughts, lest he advance beyond the limit of order.

Again, when I betake myself to consider the works required of the pastor, I weigh within myself what intent care is to be taken that he be sovereign in action, that by his living he may point out the way of life to those who are put under him, and that the flock, which follows the voice and manners of the shepherd, may learn how to walk better through example than through words. For he who is required by the necessity of his position to speak the highest things is compelled by the same necessity to exemplify the highest things. For that voice more readily penetrates the hearer's heart which the speaker's life commends, since what he commands by speaking he helps the doing of by showing. Hence it is said through the prophet: "Get thee up into the high mountain, thou that bringest good tidings to Zion" (Isaiah 40:9): which means that he who is engaged in heavenly preaching should already have forsaken the low level of earthly works, and appear as standing on the summit of things, and so the more easily should draw those who are under him to better things as by the merit of his life he cries aloud from heights above. He must let neither prosperity elate nor adversity perturb him; let neither smooth things coax him to the surrender of his will, nor rough things press him down to despair. The divine law also decrees that the priestly vestment is to be made of gold, blue, purple, twice-dyed scarlet, and the fine twined linen (Exodus 28:8), that it may be shown by what great diversity of virtues the priest ought to be distinguished.

Thus in the priest's robe before all things gold glitters, to show that he should shine forth principally in the understanding of wisdom. And with it blue, which is resplendent with aerial colour, is conjoined, to show that through all that he penetrates with his understanding he should rise above earthly favours to the love of celestial things; lest, while caught unawares by his own praises, he is emptied of his very understanding of the truth. With gold and blue, purple also is mingled: which means that the priest's heart, while hoping for the high things which he preaches, should repress in itself even the suggestions of vice, and, as it were, by virtue of a royal power, rebut them, in that he has regard ever to the nobility of inward regeneration, and by his manners guards his right to the robe of the heavenly kingdom. For it is of this nobility of the spirit that it is said through

Peter: "You are a chosen generation, a royal priesthood" (I Peter 2:9). With respect also to this power, whereby we subdue vices, we are fortified by the voice of John, who says: "As many as received Him, to them gave He power to become the sons of God" (John 1:12). This dignity of fortitude the psalmist has in view when he says: "But with me greatly honoured have been Thy friends, O God; greatly strengthened has been the principality".

For truly the mind of saints is exalted to princely eminence while outwardly they are seen to suffer abasement. But with gold, blue and purple, twice-dyed scarlet is conjoined, to show that all excellences of virtue should be adorned with charity in the eyes of the judge within; and that whatever glitters before men may be lighted up in sight of the hidden arbiter with the flame is inward love. And, further, this charity, since it consists in love at once of God and of our neighbour, has, as it were, the lustre of a double dye. He then who so pants after the beauty of his maker as to neglect the care of his neighbours, or so attends to the care of his neighbours as to grow languid in divine love, whichever of these two things it may be that he neglects, knows not what it is to have twice dyed scarlet in the adornment of his body. But, while the mind is intent on the precepts of charity, it undoubtedly remains that the flesh is worn down through abstinence. Hence, with twice-dyed scarlet fine twined linen is conjoined. For fine linen springs from the earth with glittering show, and what is designated by fine linen but bodily chastity shining white in the comeliness of purity? And it is also twisted for being interwoven into the beauty of the vestment, since the habit of chastity then attains to the perfect whiteness of purity when the flesh is worn by abstinence. And, since the merit of affliction of the flesh profits among the other virtues, fine twined linen shows white, as it were, in the diverse beauty of the priestly garment.

Again, when I betake myself to consider the duty of the pastor as to speech and silence, I weigh within myself with trembling care how very necessary it is that he should be discreet in keeping silence and profitable in speech, lest he either utters what ought to be suppressed, or suppresses what he ought to utter. For, as incautious speaking leads into error, so indiscreet silence leaves in error those who might have been instructed. For often improvident rulers, fearing to lose human favour, shrink timidly from speaking freely the things that are right; and, according to the voice of the truth (John 10:12), serve the flock by no means with the zeal of shepherds, but like hirelings, since they fly when the wolf comes if they hide themselves under silence. For the Lord complains, saying: "You have not gone up against the enemy, neither opposed a wall for the house of Israel, to stand in the battle in the day of the Lord" (Ezekiel 13:5). To go up against the enemy is to go with free voice against the powers of this world for defence of the flock; and to stand in the battle in the day of the Lord is to resist bad men when they contend against us out of love of justice.

Again to the sinful people it is said, "Thy prophets have seen false and foolish things for thee: neither did they discover thine iniquity, to provoke thee to repentance" (Lamentations 2:14). For in sacred language teachers are sometimes called prophets, for, by pointing out how fleeting are present things, they make manifest the things that are to come. And such the divine discourse convinces of seeing false things because, while fearing to reprove faults, they flatter evildoers by promising security; neither do they at all cover the iniquity of sinners, since they refrain from chiding. For the language of reproof is the key of discovery, because by chiding it discloses the fault of which even he who has committed it is often himself unaware. Hence Paul says: "That he may be able by sound doctrine even to convince the gainsayers" (Titus 1:9). Hence through Malachi it is said: "The priest's lips keep knowledge, and they shall seek the law at his mouth" (Malachi 2:7). Through Isaiah the Lord admonishes, saying: "Cry aloud, spare not, lift up thy voice like a trumpet" (Isaiah 58:1). For it is true that whosoever enters on the priesthood undertakes the office of a herald, before the coming of the judge who follows terribly. Wherefore, if the priest knows not how to preach, what shall the mute herald utter? This is why the Holy Spirit entered the first pastors in the form of tongues (Acts 2:3); because whomsoever He has filled, He himself at once makes eloquent. But, when the ruler prepares himself for speaking, let him bear in mind with what studious caution he ought to speak, lest, if he be hurried inordinately into speaking, the hearts of hearers be smitten with the wound of error, and, so he, desiring to seem wise, severs the bond of unity. For on this account the Truth says: "Have salt in yourselves, and have peace one with another" (Mark 9:49). Now by salt is denoted the word of wisdom. Let him, therefore, who strives to speak wisely fear greatly, lest by his eloquence the unity of his hearers be disturbed. Paul says: "Not to be more wise than behoveth to be wise, but to be wise unto sobriety" (Romans 12:3).

Again, when I betake myself to consider what manner of man the ruler ought to be in sympathy, and what in contemplation, I weigh within myself that he should be a near neighbour to everyone in sympathy, and exalted above all in contemplation, to the end that through the bowels of loving kindness he may transfer the infirmities of others to himself, and by loftiness of speculation transcend even himself in his aspiration after the invisible; lest either in seeking high things he despise the weak things of his neighbours, or in suiting himself to the weak things of his neighbours he relinquish his aspiration after high things. For so it is that Paul is caught up into paradise (II Corinthians 12:3) and explores the secrets of the third heaven. Yet, though borne aloft in that contemplation of things invisible, recalls the vision of his mind to the bed of the carnal, and directs how they should have intercourse with each other in their hidden privacy, saying: "But on account of fornication let every man have his own wife, and let every woman have her own husband. Let the husband render unto the wife her due, and likewise the wife unto the husband" (I Corinthians 7:2). And after (verse 5): "Defraud ye not one the other, except it be with consent for a time, that ye may give yourselves to prayer, and come together again, that Satan tempt you not." Lo, he is already initiated into heavenly secrets, and yet through condescension he searches the bed of the carnal; and the same eye of the heart which in his elevation he lifts to the invisible, he bends in his compassion upon the secrets of those who are subject to infirmity. In contemplation he transcends Heaven, and yet in his anxious care deserts not the couch of the carnal; because, being joined at once to the highest and to the lowest by the bond of charity, though in himself mightily carried up in the power of the Spirit into the heights above, yet among others, in his loving kindness, he is content to become weak. Hence he says: "Who is weak, and I am not weak? Who is offended, and I burn not?" (II Corinthians 11:29).

Though in contemplation aspiring to the highest things, good rulers should mingle in sympathy with the necessities of the infirm; since charity rises wonderfully to high things when it is compassionately drawn to the low things of neighbours; and the more kindly it descends to the weak things of this world, the more vigorously it returns to the things on high. But those who are over others should show themselves to be such that their subjects may not blush to disclose even their secrets to them; that the little ones, vexed with the waves of temptation, may have recourse to their pastor's heart as to a mother's breast, and wash away their defilement in the tears of his prayer.

Whosoever is striving to enter the gate of eternity may show his temptations to his pastor's heart. And for the most part it comes to pass that, while the ruler's mind becomes aware, through sympathy, of the trials of others, it is itself also attacked by the temptations of which it hears; since the same water in which a multitude of people is cleansed is undoubtedly itself defiled. For, in receiving the pollutions of those who wash, it loses, as it were, the calmness of its own purity. But of this the pastor ought by no means to be afraid, since, under God, who precisely balances all things, he is the more easily rescued from his own temptations as he is more compassionately distressed by those of others.

Again, when I betake myself to consider what manner of man the ruler ought to be in humility, and what in strictness, I weigh within myself how necessary it is that the ruler should be, through humility, a companion of good livers, and, through the zeal of righteousness, rigid against the vices of evildoers; so that in nothing he prefer himself to the good, and yet, when the fault of the bad requires it, he be at once conscious of the power of his priority; to the end that, while among his subordinates who live well he waives his rank and accounts them as his equals, he may not fear to execute the laws of rectitude towards the perverse. For Peter who had received from God the principality of the holy Church, from Cornelius, acting well and prostrating himself humbly before him, refused to accept immoderate veneration, saying: "Stand up; do it not; I myself also am a man" (Acts 10:26). But, when he discovers the guilt of Ananias and Sapphira, he soon shows with how great a power he had been made eminent above all others. For by his word he smote their life, which he detected by the penetration of his spirit; and he recollected himself as chief within the Church against sins, though he did not acknowledge this, when honour was eagerly paid him, before his brethren who acted well. In one case holiness of conduct merited the communion of equality; in the other avenging zeal brought out to view the just claims of authority. Paul, too, knew not himself as preferred above his brethren who acted well, when he said: "Not for that we have dominion over your faith, but are helpers of your joy" (II Corinthians 1:24). And he straightway added: "For by faith ye stand", as if to explain his declaration by saying: "For this cause we have not dominion over your faith, because by faith ye stand; for we are your equals in that wherein we know you to stand." He knew not himself as preferred above his brethren, when he said: "We became babes in the midst of you" (I Thessalonians 2:7); and again: "But ourselves your servants through Christ" (II Corinthians 4:5). But, when he found a fault that required to be corrected, straightway he recollected himself as a master, saying: "What will ye? Shall I come unto you with a rod?" (I Corinthians 4:21).

Supreme rule, then, is ordered well, when he who presides lords it over vices, rather than over his brethren. He orders well the authority he has received who has learnt to maintain it and to keep it in check. He orders it well who knows how through it to tower above sins and with it to set himself on an equality with other men.

Moreover, the virtue of humility ought to be so maintained that the rights of governments relaxed; lest, when any prelate has lowered himself more than is becoming, he is unable to restrain the life of his subordinates under the bond of discipline; and the severity of discipline is to be so maintained that gentleness be not wholly lost through the over-kindling of zeal. For often vices show themselves off as virtues, so that niggardliness would fain appear as frugality, extravagance as liberality, cruelty as righteous zeal, laxity as loving kindness. So both discipline and mercy are far from what they should be, if one is maintained without the other. But there ought to be kept up with great skill both mercy justly considerate, and discipline smiting kindly.

For hence it is that, as the truth teaches (Luke 10:34), the man is brought by the care of the Samaritan half dead into the inn, and both wine and oil are applied to his wounds; the wine to make them smart, the oil to soothe them. For whosoever superintends the healing of wounds must needs administer in wine the smart of pain, and in oil the softness of loving kindness to the end that through wine what is festering may be purged, and through oil what is curable may be soothed. Gentleness, then, is to be mingled with severity; a sort of compound is to be made of both; so that subjects be neither paralysed by too much asperity, nor relaxed by too great kindness. Which thing, according to the words of Paul (Hebrews 9:4), is well signified by that ark of the tabernacle, in which, together with the tables, there is a rod and manna; because, if with knowledge of sacred Scripture in the good ruler's breast there is the rod of constraint, there should be also the manna of sweetness.

Thus, having undertaken the burden of pastoral care, when I consider all these things and many others of like kind, I seem to be what I cannot be, especially as in this place whosoever is called a pastor is onerously occupied by external cares; so that it often becomes uncertain whether he exercises the function of a pastor or of an earthly noble. And indeed whosoever is set over his brethren to rule them cannot be entirely free from external cares; and yet there is need of exceeding care lest he be pressed down by them too much.

Hence it is well said to Ezekiel: "The priests shall not shave their heads, nor allow their locks to grow long, but simply trim their hair" (Ezekiel 44:20). For they are rightly called priests who are set over the faithful for affording them sacred guidance. But the hairs outside the head are thoughts in the mind; which, as they spring up insensibly above the brain, denote the cares of the present life, which, owing to negligent perception, since they sometimes come forth unseasonably, advance, as it were, without our feeling them. Since, then, all who are over others ought indeed to have external anxieties, and yet should not be vehemently bent upon them, the priests are rightly forbidden either to shave their heads or to let their hair grow long; that so they may neither cut off from themselves entirely thoughts of the flesh for the life of those who are under them, nor again allow them to grow too much. The cares of temporal anxiety should both extend themselves as far as need requires, and yet be cut short soon, lest they grow to an immoderate extent. When, therefore, through provident care for bodies applied externally, life is protected and again, through moderate intentness of heart, is not impeded, the hairs on the priest's head are both preserved to cover the skin, and cut short so as not to veil the eyes.

But in this place I see that no such discreet management is possible, since cases of such importance hang over me daily as to overwhelm the mind, while they kill the bodily life. Wherefore, most holy brother, I beseech you by the judge who is to come, by the assembly of many thousand angels, by the Church of the firstborn who are written in Heaven, help me, who am growing weary under this burden of pastoral care, with the intercession of thy prayer, lest its weight oppress me beyond my strength. But, being mindful of what is written: "Pray for one another, that ye may be healed" (James 5:16), I give also what I ask for. But I shall receive what I give. For, while we are joined to you through the aid of prayer, we hold, as it were, each other by the hand while walking through slippery places, and it comes to pass, through a great provision of charity, that the foot of each is the more firmly planted in that one leans upon the other.

Besides, since with the heart man believeth unto righteousness, and with the mouth confession is made unto salvation, I confess that I receive and revere, as the four books of the gospel so also the four councils, to wit: the Nicene, in which the perverse doctrine of Arius is overthrown; the Constantinopolitan also, in which the error of Eunomius and Macedonius is refuted; further, for the first Ephesine, in whch the impiety of Nestorius is condemned; and the Chalcedonian, in which the depravity of Eutyches and Dioscorus is reprobated.

These with full devotion I embrace, and adhere to with most entire approval; since on them, as on a four-square stone, rises the structure of the holy faith; and whosoever, of whatever life and behaviour he may be, holds not fast to their solidity, even though he is seen to be a stone, yet he lies outside the building. The fifth council also I equally venerate, in which the epistle which is called that of Ibas, full of error, is reprobated; Theodorus, who divides the mediator between God and men into two subsistences, is convicted of having fallen into the perfidy of impiety; and the writings of Theodoritus, in which the faith of the blessed Cyril is impugned, are refuted as having been published with madness.

But all persons whom the aforesaid venerable councils repudiate I repudiate; those whom they venerate I embrace; since, they having been constituted by universal consent, he overthrows not them but himself whosoever presumes either to loose those whom they bind, or to bind those whom they loose. Whosoever, therefore, thinks otherwise let him be anathema. But whosoever holds the faith of the aforesaid synods, peace be to him from God the Father, through Jesus Christ His Son, who lives and reigns consubstantially God with Him in the unity of the Holy Spirit for ever and ever. Amen.

Collects from the Sacramentary of Saint GREGORY

I

Almighty God, unto whom all hearts be open, all desires known, and from whom no secrets are hid; cleanse the thoughts of our hearts by the inspiration of Thy Holy Spirit, that we may perfectly love Thee, and worthily magnify Thy holy name; through Christ our Lord. Amen.

II

O God, our refuge and strength, who art the author of all godliness; be ready, we beseech Thee, to hear the devout prayers of Thy Church; and grant that those things which we ask faithfully we may obtain effectually; through Jesus Christ our Lord. Amen.

III

O everlasting God, who hast ordained and constituted the services of angels and men in a wonderful order; Mercifully grant that as Thy holy angels always do Thee service in Heaven, so by Thy appointment they may succour and defend us on earth; through Jesus Christ our Lord. Amen.

IV

O Lord, we beseech Thee mercifully to hear us; and grant that we, to whom Thou hast given a hearty desire to pray, may by Thy mighty aid be defended and comforted in all dangers and adversities; through Jesus Christ our Lord. Amen.

V

O Lord, we beseech Thee mercifully to receive the prayers of Thy people which call upon Thee; and grant that they may both perceive and know what things they ought to do, and also may have grace and power faithfully to fulfil the same; through Jesus Christ our Lord. Amen.

VI

O almighty Lord, and everlasting God, vouchsafe, we beseech Thee, to direct, sanctify, and govern both our hearts and bodies, in the ways of Thy laws, and in the works of Thy commandments; that through Thy most mighty protection, both here and ever, we may be preserved in body and soul; through our Lord and Saviour Jesus Christ. Amen.

AGNUS DEI

O Lord God, Lamb of God, Son of the Father, that takest away the sins of the world, have mercy upon us. Thou that takest away the sins of the world, have mercy upon us. Thou that takest away the sins of the world, receive our prayer. Thou that sittest at the right hand of God the Father, have mercy upon us.

For Thou only art holy; Thou only art the Lord; Thou only, O Christ, with the Holy Ghost, art most high in the glory of God the Father. Amen.

Saint ANSELM: Praise and Thanksgiving to God and a prayer to Christ for his enemies

I give Thee thanks and praise, O my God, my mercy, who hast vouchsafed to lead me unto the conception of Thee, and by the washing of holy baptism to number me among Thy children by adoption. I give Thee thanks and praise, for that Thou hast patience with me in Thine unbounded goodness, waiting for amendment of life in me, who have abounded in sins from my childhood even unto this hour. Thee I praise, Thee I glorify, who by the arm of Thy might hast often delivered me out of many distresses, calamities and miseries, and hitherto hast spared me eternal pains and bodily torments. I praise Thee and glorify Thee, for that Thou hast vouchsafed to grant unto me soundness of body, a quiet life, the love, affection and charity of Thy servants toward me, for all these things are the gifts of Thy goodness. Holy of holies, who makest all things holy, I bless Thee, I glorify Thee, I worship Thee, I give thanks to Thee. Let all Thy creatures bless Thee, let all Thine angels and saints bless Thee. Let me bless Thee in all the actions of my life. Let all my frame, without and within, glorify and bless Thee. My salvation, my light, my glory, let mine eyes see Thee, which Thou hast created and prepared to look upon the beauty of Thine excellency. My music, my delight, let mine ears bless Thee, which Thou hast created and prepared to hear the voice of Thy cheerful salvation. My sweetness, ny refreshment, let my nostrils bless Thee, which Thou has made to live and take pleasure in the sweet odour of Thine ointments. My praise, my new song, my rejoicing, let my tongue bless and magnify Thee, which Thou hast created and prepared to tell forth Thy wonderful works. My wisdom, my meditation, my counsel, let my heart adore and bless Thee for ever, which Thou hast prepared and given unto me to discern Thine unspeakable mercies. My life, my happiness, let my soul, sinful though she be, bless Thee, which Thou hast created and prepared to enjoy Thy goodness.

Father adorable and terrible, worthy of worship and of fear, I bless Thee, whom I have loved, whom I have sought, whom I have ever desired. My God, my lover, I thirst after Thee, I hunger for Thee, I pour out my supplications to Thee, with all the groanings of my heart I crave for Thee. Even as a mother, when her only son is taken from her, sitteth weeping and lamenting continually beside his sepulchre, even so I also, as I can, not as I ought, having in mind Thy passion, Thy buffetings, Thy scourgings, Thy wounds, remembering how Thou wast slain for my sake, how Thou wast embalmed, how and where Thou wast buried, sit with Mary at the sepulchre in my heart, weeping. Where faith hath laid Thee, hope seeketh to find Thee, love to anoint Thee. Most gracious, most excellent, most sweet, who will bring me to find Thee without the sepulchre, to wash Thy wounds with my tears, even the marks of the nails. Ye "daughters of Jerusalem, tell my beloved that I am sick of love". Let Him show Himself to me, let Him make Himself known unto me. Let Him call me by my name; let Him give me rest from my sorrow.

For my sorrow can take no rest while I am an exile from Thy presence, O my God. Come now, O Lord, reveal Thy face to me, show Thy mercy to those that implore it. We know that Thy resurrection is accomplished, manifest to our eyes Thy blessed incorruption. O Thou wonderful one, above all estimation and comparison, I desired Thee, I hoped for Thee, I sought Thee. Lo, Thou Thyself comest, clothed in purple; Thou art "red in Thine apparel". Thou hast "washed Thy garments in wine and Thy clothes in the blood of grapes". "Thou woundedst the head out of the house of the wicked", when "Thou wentest forth for the salvation of Thy people".

Abide with us, abide with us until the morning. Let us enjoy Thy presence; let us be glad and rejoice in Thy resurrection. The darkness thickens, the evening cometh fast. May our sun, the light eternal, Christ our God "shows us the light of His countenance"!

But what is this? Alas, my Lord, alas, my soul! Thou liftest up Thine hands. Lo, Thou goest upon Thy way. The heavens meet Thee, the skies are bowed under Thee, a cloud is prepared to receive Thee in Thine ascension. Now "shall my tears be my meat day and night". I will feed upon my griefs, I will give my soul to drink of my sorrows. "My life shall wax old in heaviness, and my years in mourning." "Whom have I in Heaven but Thee; and there is none upon earth that I desire in comparison of Thee? With my soul will I desire Thee in the night: yea with my spirit within me will I seek Thee early." Yet in the meanwhile wilt Thou come unto us, O Lord, because Thou art gracious, and "will not tarry", because Thou art good. To Thee be glory, world without end. Amen.

PRAYER TO CHRIST FOR MY ENEMIES

Lord Jesus Christ, Lord of all power and goodness, whom I pray to be gracious to my friends, Thou knowest what my heart desireth for mine enemies. For Thou, O "God, who tries the very hearts and reins", Thou knowest the secrets of my heart within me, for it is not hidden from Thee. If Thou hast sown in the soul of Thy servant what he may offer to Thee, and if that enemy and I have sown there likewise what is to be burned with fire, that also is before Thine eyes. Despise not, most gracious God, that which Thou hast sown, but cherish it and give it increase and bring it to perfection and preserve it for ever. For as I could begin no good thing without Thee, so can I neither finish it nor keep it in safety except by Thy help. Judge me not, O merciful God, according to that which displeaseth Thee in me, but take away what Thou hast not planted, and save my soul which Thou hast created. For I cannot amend myself without Thee, because if we be good "it is Thou that dost make us and not we ourselves". Neither can my soul endure Thy judgment, if Thou wilt judge her according to her wickedness. Thou therefore, O Lord, who alone art mighty, whatsoever Thou makest me to desire for mine enemies, be that Thy gift unto them, and Thine answer to my prayer. And if I at any time ask for them anything which transgresseth the rule of love, whether through ignorance or through infirmity or through wickedness, neither do that to them, nor fulfil my petition therein. Thou who art "the true light", enlighten their blindness. Thou who art supreme truth, amend their error. Thou who art the true life, quicken their souls. For Thou hast said by Thy beloved disciple, "He that loveth not his brother, abideth in death". I pray therefore, O Lord, that Thou grant to them so much love of Thee and of their neighbour as Thou commandest us to have, lest they should have sin before Thee concerning their brother.

Forbid it, O good Lord, forbid it that I should be to my brethren an occasion of death, that I should be to them "a stone of stumbling and rock of offence". For it is enough and more than enough that I should be an offence unto myself; mine own sin is sufficient for me. Thy servant entreateth Thee for his fellow servants that they should not on my account offend so great and good a master, but be reconciled to Thee and agree with me according to Thy will for Thy sake. This is the vengeance which my inmost heart desireth to ask of Thee upon my fellow servants, mine enemies and fellow sinners. This is the punishment which my soul asketh upon my fellow servants and enemies, that they should love Thee and one another, according to Thy will and as is expedient for us, so that we may satisfy our common master both as concerning ourselves and as concerning one another, and serve our common Lord in unity by the teaching of charity to the common good. This vengeance I, Thy sinful servant, pray may be prepared against all those that wish me evil and do me evil. Do Thou prepare this also, most merciful Lord, against Thy sinful servant likewise.

Come then, O my good creator and merciful Judge, and by Thy mercy which passeth all reckoning, forgive me all my debts as I in Thy presence forgive all my debtors. And if not yet, because hitherto my spirit doth not so forgive perfectly according to Thy measure but willeth so to do and accomplisheth by Thy help what it can, doing violence to itself, this imperfect forgiveness I offer to Thee as it is, that Thou mayest be pleased perfectly to forgive me my sins and according to Thy power be gracious unto my soul.

Hearken unto me, hearken unto me, O great and good Lord, with desire for the love of whom my soul is fain to feed herself, but cannot satisfy her hunger for Thee, to call upon whom my mouth findeth no name that sufficeth my heart. For there is no word that expresseth unto me that which by Thy grace my heart conceiveth concerning Thee. I have prayed, O Lord, as I could, but my will was greater than my power. Hearken unto me, hearken unto me, according to Thy power, who canst do whatsoever Thou dost will. I have prayed as one weak and sinful, hear me, O hear me, as one mighty and merciful; and grant unto my friends and unto mine enemies not only what I have prayed, but what Thou knowest to be expedient for each one, and agreeable to Thy will. Grant to all, both living and dead, the help of Thy mercy; and ever hear me not according to the desires of my heart or the requests of my lips, but as Thou knowest and willest that I ought to will and to ask, O saviour of the world, who with the Father and the Holy Ghost livest and reignest, God, world without end. Amen.

Saint BERNARD OF CLAIRVAUX: The Benefits of Loving God

Let us consider what profit we shall gain from loving God. Even though our knowledge of this is limited, still it is better to enquire than to ignore it altogether. For although God should not be loved for the sake of reward, He will not leave love unrewarded. True charity is never left destitute, even though she is unselfish and does not seek her own. Love is a state of the soul, not a contract: it cannot result from a mere agreement, nor is it so to be acquired. It is spontaneous in its origin and impulse; and true love is its own satisfaction. It has its reward, but that reward is the beloved object. For whatever you seem to love, if it is because of something else, what you really love is that something else, not the apparent object of desire. St Paul did not preach the gospel in order to earn his bread; he ate that he might be strengthened for his ministry. What he loved was, not bread, but the gospel. True love does not demand a reward, but it deserves one. Surely, no one offers to pay for love; yet some recompense is due to one who loves, and if his love endures, he will doubtless receive it.

On a lower plane of action, it is the reluctant, not the eager, who we urge by promises of reward. Who would think of paying a man to do what he was yearning to do already? For instance, no one would hire a hungry man to eat, or a thirsty man to drink, or a mother to nurse her own child? Who would think of bribing a farmer to tend his own vineyards, or to dig his orchard, or to rebuild his house? So, all the more, one who loves God truly asks no other compensation than God Himself; for if he should demand something else, it would be the prize that he loved, and not God.

It is natural for a man to desire what in his judgment is better than that which he has already, and to be satisfied with nothing which lacks that special quality he misses. So, if it is for her beauty that he loves his wife, he will look longingly at a fairer woman. If he is clad in a rich garment, he will covet a costlier one and, no matter how rich he may be, he will envy a man richer than himself. Do we not see people every day, endowed with vast estates, who keep on joining field to field, dreaming of wider boundaries for their lands? Those who dwell in palaces are always adding house to house, continually building up and tearing down, remodelling and changing. Men in high places are driven by insatiable ambition to get their hands on still greater prizes. And nowhere is there any final satisfaction, because nothing can be defined as absolutely the best or highest. Nothing will content a man except the very best, as he reckons it. Is it not, then, mad folly always to be craving for things which can never lessen our longings, much less satisfy them? No matter how many such things a man has, he is always lusting after what he has not; never at peace, he sighs for new possessions. Discontented, he spends himself in fruitless toil, and finds only weariness in the evanescent and unreal pleasures of the world. In his greediness, he counts all that he has clutched as nothing in comparison with what is beyond his grasp, and loses all pleasure in his actual possessions by longing after what he does not have, yet wants. No man can ever hope to own everything. The little one does possess is gained only with toil, and is held in fear; since each is certain to lose what he has when God's day, appointed though unrevealed, comes. But the perverted will struggles towards the ultimate good by devious ways, yearning after satisfaction, yet being led astray by vanity and being deceived by wickedness. Ah, if you wish to attain to the consummation of all desire, so that nothing unfulfilled will be left, why weary yourself with fruitless efforts, running hither and thither, only to die long before the goal is reached?

In this way the ungodly wander in a circle, longing after something to gratify their yearnings, yet madly rejecting that which alone can bring them to their desired end, not by exhaustion but by attainment. They wear themselves out in useless effort, without reaching their blessed reward, because they delight in creatures, not in the creator. They want to explore creation, trying all things one by one, rather than think of coming to Him who is Lord of all. And if their utmost longing were realised, so that they had all the world for their own, yet did not possess Him who is the author of all being, then the same law of their desire would make them despise what they had, and restlessly seek Him whom they still lacked, that is, God Himself. Rest is in Him alone. Man knows no peace in the world, but nothing disturbs him when he is with God. And so the soul says with confidence: "Whom have I in heaven but Thee; and there is none upon earth that I desire in comparison to Thee. God is the strength of my heart, and my portion for ever. It is good for me to hold me fast by God, to put my trust in the Lord God." By this method anyone would eventually come to God, if only he might have time to test all lesser goods in turn.

But life is too short, strength too feeble, and competitors too many for that course to be practicable. No one could ever reach the end, though he were to weary himself with the long effort and fruitless toil of testing everything that might seem desirable. It would be far easier and far better to make the attempt in imagination rather than in experiment. For the mind is swifter in operation and keener in discrimination than the bodily senses, for this very purpose, that it may go before the senses so that they may be attracted by nothing which the mind has found worthless. And so it is written: "Prove all things: hold fast to that which is good." Which is to say that right judgment should prepare the way for the heart. Otherwise, we may not ascend the hill of the Lord, nor go up to His holy place. We should not profit from possessing a rational mind if we were to follow the impulses of the senses, like beasts, with no regard at all to reason. Those whom reason does not guide may indeed run, but not in the appointed race-track, neglecting the apostolic counsel: "So run that ye may obtain." For how could they obtain the prize, who give it last priority, and run around after everything else first?

But as for the righteous man, he remembers the condemnation pronounced on the multitude who wander after vanity, who travel the broad way that leads to death; and he chooses the King's highway, turning aside neither to the right hand nor to the left, just as the prophet says: "The way of the just is uprightness." Warned, he shuns the perilous road, and takes the direction which shortens the search, which forbids covetousness and commands that he sell all that he has and gives to the poor. Blessed, truly, are the poor, for theirs is the kingdom of Heaven. All who run in a race count as racers, but distinction is made among them. "The Lord knows the way of the righteous: and the way of the ungodly shall perish." "A small thing that the righteous have is better than great riches of the ungodly." As the preacher says, and the fool discovers: "He who loves silver shall not be satisfied with silver." But Christ says, "Blessed are they who hunger and thirst after righteousness for they shall be filled." Righteousness is the natural and essential food of the soul, which can no more be satisfied by earthly treasures than the hunger of the body can be satisfied by air. If you should see a starving man standing with mouth open to the wind, inhaling draughts of air as if in hope of gratifying his hunger, you would think him a lunatic. But it is no less foolish to imagine that the soul can be satisfied with worldly things. What have spiritual gifts to do with carnal appetites, or carnal with spiritual? Praise the Lord, O my soul: Who fills your mouth with good things and bestows bounty immeasurable; He inspires you to good, He preserves you in goodness; He prevents, He sustains, He fills you. He moves you to longing, and it is He for whom you long. Let frequent troubles drive us to frequent prayers; for in this way, we must experience how gracious the Lord is. His goodness once realised draws us to love Him unselfishly, even more than our own needs impel us to love Him selfishly: in the same way that the Samaritans told the woman who had announced that it was Christ who was at the well: "Now we believe, not because of your saying: for we have heard Him ourselves and know that this is indeed the Christ, the saviour of the world." We likewise bear the same witness to our own fleshly nature, saying: "No longer do we love God because of our necessity, but because we have tasted and seen 'how gracious the Lord is'." Our temporal wants have a speech of their own, proclaiming the benefits they have received from God's favour. Once this is recognised, it will not be hard to fulfil the commandment concerning love to our neighbours; for whoever loves God aright loves all God's creatures. Such love is pure, and finds no discomfort in the precept bidding us to purify our souls. Loving as he ought, he counts that command only just. Such love is thankworthy, since it is spontaneous; pure, since it is shown not in word nor tongue, but in deed and truth; just, since it repays what it has received. Whoever loves in this way loves even as he is loved, and seeks no more his own but the things which are Christ's, as Jesus sought not His own welfare, but ours, or rather ourselves. Such was the psalmist's love, when he sang: "O give thanks unto the Lord, for He is gracious." Whoever praises God for His essential goodness, and not merely because of the benefits He has bestowed, does really love God for God's sake, and not selfishly.

I have said already that the motive for loving God is God Himself. And I spoke truly, for He is the efficient cause as well as the final object of our love. He creates the occasion for love, He creates the affection, He brings the desire to good effect. He is such that love to Him is a natural due; and so hope in Him is natural, since our present love would be vain if we did not hope to love Him perfectly some day. Our love is prepared and rewarded by His. He loves us first, out of His great tenderness; then we are bound to repay Him with love; and we are permitted to cherish exultant hopes in Him. He is generous to all that call upon Him, yet He has no gift for them better than Himself. He gives Himself as prize and reward; He is the refreshment of holy souls, the ransom of those in captivity. "The Lord is good to them that wait for Him." What will He be, then, to those who gain His presence? But here is a paradox, that no one can seek the Lord who has not already found Him. It is Your will, O God, to be found, so that people may seek You, to be sought so that You may the more truly be found. But though You can be sought and found, You cannot be preempted. For if we say, "Early shall my prayer come before You", all prayer would be lukewarm unless it was animated by Your inspiration.

The Scripture says God has made all for His own glory, so surely His creatures ought to conform, as much as they can, to His will! In Him should all our affections centre, so that in all things we should seek only to do His will, not to please ourselves. And real happiness will come, not in gratifying our desires, or in gaining transient pleasures, but in accomplishing God's will for us; even as we pray every day: "Your will be done on earth, as it is in Heaven." O chaste and holy love! O sweet and gracious affection! O pure and cleansed purpose, thoroughly washed and purged from any content of selfishness, and sweetened by contact with the divine will! To reach this state is to become godlike. As a drop of water, poured into wine, loses itself, and takes the colour and savour of wine; or as a bar of iron, heated red-hot, becomes like fire itself, forgetting its own nature; or as the air, radiant with sunbeams, seems not so much to be illuminated as to be light itself; so, in the saints, all human affections melt away, by some unspeakable transmutation, into the will of God. For how could God be all in all, if anything merely human remained in man? The substance will endure, but in another beauty, a higher power, a greater glory. When will that be? Who will see, who shall possess it? "When shall I come to appear before the presence of God?" "My heart has talked of You, seek You my face: Your face, Lord, will I seek."

Saint BERNARD OF CLAIRVAUX: Annunciation Dialogue

The evangelist says: "The angel came in unto her", that is to Mary, and he said: "Hail, thou that art full of grace: the Lord is with thee." How did he get in? I imagine that it was into the retirement of the modest chamber, where she with the door fast closed was praying perhaps in secret to her Father. Angels are wont to stand by those who pray, and to take delight in those whom they see lifting up holy hands in their worship: it rejoices them to present unto God the offering of a secret savour, the pure burnt offering of a saintly devotion. The angel indicates how acceptable the prayers of Mary were in the sight of the most high, by saluting her so reverently on his entrance. And it was not difficult for him to enter into the retirement of the virgin though the door were shut; since the nature and fineness of his material substance is such, that iron bars cannot hinder it, wherever it wills to go. Thus walls are no obstacle to angelic spirits, but all things visible give them way, and all bodies, however thick or solid, are penetrable and passable to them. It is not to be supposed, therefore, that the angel entered at some little door which the virgin had left open; since undoubtedly it was her purpose to escape from the society, and to avoid the converse, of men, so that the silence of her devotion might not be troubled, nor her purity offended.

In that hour then, the virgin, most prudently, had closed her small dwelling around her against men; but not against angels. For although an angel was able to enter, to no man would an entrance have been easy.

"Hail", he says, "O full of grace; the Lord is with thee." He did not say, the Lord is "in" thee; but the Lord is with thee. For God, who is wholly in every place equally in His uncompounded nature, yet is in rational creatures after one manner, and in others after another manner; and of the former He dwells effectively in the good, otherwise than in the evil. With the good alone it is the case, that He is with them because of the agreement of their will with His. For when they thus subject their wills to righteousness, that what God thinks fit to will, that is what they also will; in as much as they disagree in no respect from the will of God, they join themselves specially to Him. This is the case with all saints, but in an especial degree with Mary; since so complete was her devotion, that she associated with the divine purpose not only her will but also her body; and of her virgin substance was formed, or rather came into being, the one Christ, who although He was not wholly from God, nor wholly from the virgin; yet was wholly of God, and wholly of the virgin, nor were there two sons, but one son of both the one and the other.

He said therefore: "Hail, O full of grace, the Lord is with thee." Not only the Son, whom you clothe with your human body, but also the Holy Ghost, by whom you conceive: and the Father, by whom He was begotten whom you conceived. The Father, I say, is with you, who makes His Son to be also yours. The Son is with you, who in order to bring about in you a wonderful mystery, miraculously opens for Himself the womb, and yet preserves in you the sign of virginity. The Holy Spirit is with you, who with the Father and the Son sanctifies your womb. Truly the Lord is with you.

"Blessed", I say, "art thou among women" who has escaped that universal curse, by which it was said, "In sorrow thou shalt bring forth children" (Genesis 3:16); and nevertheless are free of that other: "Cursed is the barren in Israel" (Exodus 23:26 and Deuteronomy 7:14): who has obtained that unique blessing, of not remaining barren, and of at the same time, bringing forth without sorrow. Hard the necessity, and heavy the yoke, that lies upon all the daughters of Eve! If they bring forth, they endure anguish, and if they do not, they incur malediction. The pang renders painful their bearing, and the curse forbids them to be barren. Hearing this and reading this, O prudent Virgin, which of the two will you choose? Difficulties, she said, surround me: but it is better for me to remain chaste, though under the curse of barrenness, than first to conceive by lust, what afterwards I shall deservedly bring forth in sorrow. In the one I see malediction, but no sin; in the other both sin and suffering.

For is this malediction anything other than the contempt of men? Is the barren woman in fact called cursed for anything but this, that she is exposed to contempt, as unfruitful and useless? But with me it is a very small thing that I should displease men, while I am able to present myself as a chaste virgin to Christ. O Virgin prudent and devoted, who has taught you that virginity is pleasing to God? What law, what righteousness, what page of the Old Testament has taught or exhorted, or counselled you to live in the flesh not according to the flesh, but to lead upon the earth an angelic life? Where did you read, O blessed Virgin: "The wisdom of the flesh is death" (Romans 8:6), and "Make not provision for the flesh, to fulfil its desire" (Romans 13:14)?

Where did you read of virgins that "they sing a new song, which none can sing, but they who follow the Lamb wherever He goes" (Revelation 14:4)? Where did you read that they are praised, "who have made themselves eunuchs for the Kingdom of Heaven's sake" (Matthew 19:12)? Where did you read: "Though we walk in the flesh we do not war after the flesh" (II Corinthians 10:3), and: "He who gives his virgin to marriage, does well; but he who does not, does better" (I Corinthians 7:38)? Or, "I would that all men were even as I myself" and "It is good for a man to remain thus, according to my counsel"? Of virgins, he says: "I have no precept, but I give a counsel" (I Corinthians 7:25). In fact you had no precept, nor counsel, nor even an example: only a revelation taught you about all things, and the Word of God, quick and powerful, was a teacher to you before your Son, and informed your mind, before He clad Himself with your flesh. You chose to be despised in Israel; so that you might please Him to whom you had committed yourself, to incur the curse of unfruitfulness: but behold the curse is changed into blessing, the sterility into fruitfulness.

Open, O Virgin, your bosom, prepare your womb: for He who is mighty shall do for you great things, so that instead of being a curse in Israel, all generations shall call you blessed. Do not, O prudent Virgin, distrust your fruitfulness, since it shall not take away chastity. You shall conceive, but without sin: shall be with child, but without the burden and fatigues of that state: shall give birth, but not with sorrow: you shall not know a man, yet shall bear a son! And what a son! You shall be the mother of Him whose Father is God. The Son of the brightness of the Father shall be in the crown of chastity. The Wisdom of the heart of the divine Father shall be the fruit of a virgin womb. You shall conceive of God, and shall bring forth Him who is God. Be of good comfort then, O fruitful Virgin, chaste giver-of-birth, spotless mother: for you shall no longer be held a disgrace in Israel, nor numbered among the barren. And if you are still spoken ill of by Israel according to the flesh, not because they see you barren, but because they envy your fruitfulness: remember that Christ also endured the curse of the cross, who blessed thee His mother, in Heaven; but even on earth you are blessed by the angel, and by all generations of the earth you shall deservedly be called blessed. Blessed then are you among women, and blessed is the fruit of your womb.

"When she had heard this, she was troubled at his saying, and cast in her mind what manner of salutation this might be." Virgins who are really virginal are always apprehensive, never secure: they shrink from what is harmless, and are fearful of what is safe, knowing that they have a precious treasure in earthen vessels, that it is difficult to live the angelic life among men, to dwell on earth in a heavenly manner, and while in the flesh to live unwedded. And consequently in whatever is new or sudden they suspect a snare, and think that the whole is directed against them. Therefore Mary also was troubled at the saying of the angel. Troubled, but not overwhelmed. "I am so troubled", says one, "that I cannot speak: I have considered the days of old, and borne in mind the eternal years" (Psalms 77:4–5). In this way Mary too was troubled and did not speak, but considered what manner of salutation this might be. That she was troubled was a mark of virginal modesty: that she was not overwhelmed, of fortitude; that she held her peace and pondered, of prudence. She knew, as a prudent virgin, that often a messenger of Satan transforms himself into an angel of light: and in as much as she was humble and full of simplicity, she hoped nothing at all of such a kind from the holy angel, and therefore pondered what manner of salutation this might be.

Then the angel, very easily comprehending the doubtful looks of the virgin, understanding that she was revolving various thoughts in her mind, calms her fear, removes her doubts, and calling her familiarly by her name, persuades her not to be afraid. "Fear not, Mary", he said "for thou hast found favour with God." Here is no snare, no deception. Suspect not here any fraud or artifice. I am not a man, but a spirit: an angel of God, not of Satan. "Thou hast found favour with God." If you knew how pleasing is your humility to the Most High, how high it raises you before Him, you would consider yourself unworthy neither of angelic address nor respect. For why should you consider that the favour of angels is not due to you, who has found favour with God? You have found that which you sought, that which none before you was able to find, you have found favour with God. What favour? Peace between God and men, the destruction of death, the renewal of life. This then is the favour which you have found with God. And this is the sign of it to you: "Behold thou shalt conceive and bear a son, and thou shalt call His name Jesus." Learn then, prudent virgin, from the name of your promised son, how great and special is the favour which you have obtained before God. "Thou shalt call His name Jesus." Another evangelist states the reason for this name, an angel thus explaining it: "For He shall save His people from their sins" (Matthew 1:21).

I read that two saviours preceded Him of whom we are now speaking, of whom they were types, and that both were of great service to their nation. One one of these led forth his people from Babylon (Haggai 1; Ezra 5:1–5), the other introduced his people into the land of promise (Joshua 1). They indeed defended from their enemies those over whom they ruled; but it could not be said that they saved them from their sins. But He, our Jesus, both saved His people from their sins, and has brought them into the land of the living. Who is this, who even forgives sins? Would that the Lord Jesus would deign to number me, a sinner, among His people, that He may save me from my sins!

For truly blessed are my people whose Lord God is Jesus, because He shall save them from their sins. But I fear that many call themselves His people, whom He will not own: I fear that there are many more, who seem to be even among the more devout of his people, to whom He will one day say: "This people honoureth me with their lips, but their heart is far from me" (Matthew 15:8). For the Lord Jesus knows those who are His: He knows who He has chosen from the beginning. "Why call ye me Lord, Lord," He says, and "do not the things which I say?" (Luke 6:46). Do you then wish to know whether you belong to His people, or rather do you desire to belong to them? Do what Jesus commands; and He will count you among His. Do what He bids in the gospel, in the law and the prophets, and by the mouth of His ministers who are in the Church: submit yourself to His vicars who are set over you, not only the good and gentle, but also the wayward. Learn from Jesus Himself, for He is meek and lowly of heart; and you shall belong to the happy and honourable company of His people, whom He has chosen to be His inheritance; whom the Lord of Hosts has blessed, saying: "Thou art the work of my hands, Israel mine inheritance" (Isaiah 19:25) to whom, lest you should envy Israel according to the flesh, He bears witness, saying: "A people whom I have not known, have served me; as soon as they heard me, they obeyed me" (Psalms 18:43–44).

But let us hear what the same angel thinks respecting Him upon whom, while not yet conceived, He bestows such a name. For he says: "He shall be great, and shall be called the Son of the Highest." He may well say that one shall be great who shall merit to be called the Son of the Highest; "and of whose greatness there is no end" (Psalms 145:3). And "who is great", he says, "as is our God?" (Psalms 77:13). He is evidently great, whose greatness is as the highest, because He is the highest. The son of the highest will judge it no robbery to be of equal nature with the highest (Philippians 2:6).

For God the Father, who is the highest, although He is omnipotent, is not able either to make a creature equal to Himself or to beget a Son unequal. He has indeed made the angel great, but not as great as Himself: and therefore not the highest. But the son alone He has not made, but begotten, the omnipotent by the omnipotent, the highest by the highest, the coeternal by the eternal; and He is able without usurpation or injury to compare Himself in all things with God. It is rightly said therefore that He shall be great, who shall be called the Son of the Highest.

But, why is it said He "shall be" and not rather He "is" great; since He is always great equally, so that He can increase in nothing, nor can be greater after His conception than He is, or has been, before it? Perhaps the angel said He shall be, in order to indicate that He who was great as God shall be great as man? Yes, He shall be truly great; great as man, as teacher, as prophet. For thus it is spoken of Him in the gospel: "That a great prophet has risen up among us" (Luke 7:16). And in fact, that a great prophet should come was promised by a prophet of lesser rank: "Behold, a great prophet shall come, and He shall renew Jerusalem." And you indeed, O Virgin, shall bear, and nourish, and bring up a little child: but seeing Him little, reflect that He is great. For He shall be great, because God shall so magnify Him that all kings and peoples shall worship and do Him service. Let your soul too magnify the Lord, because "He shall be great and shall be called the Son of the Highest". He shall be great, and He who is mighty shall do for thee great things, and holy is His name. For what name can He be called by more holy than the Son of the Highest? And we also who are humble shall glorify the Lord who is great; who, that He might make us great, Himself became a child. "Unto us", says the prophet, a child is born: unto us a son is given" (Isaiah 9:6). Yes, He is born for us, not for Himself; and having received before time a birth much more noble from His Father, He needed not be born in time of a mother. Nor did the angels, who beheld Him in His greatness, need that He should become a little child. For us then He was born, to us He was given, since to us He was necessary.

It only remains that we should do for Him who was born for us and given to us, that for which end He was born and given. Let us avail ourselves of our saviour to our own good; let us work out, by the saviour, our salvation. Behold. He is brought into our midst as a little child. O Child, the desire of all children! Truly childlike, but in wisdom, not in malice! Let us study to become such as He is: let us learn of Him, for He is meek and lowly in heart: so that He who is the great God may not have become a humble man, have been crucified, and died, all to no purpose. Let us learn His humility, let us imitate His gentleness, let us embrace His love, let us partake His passion and be cleansed by His blood. Let us present Him as the propitiation for our sins; since for this it is that He is born for us and given to us, let us present Him before the eyes of His Father and before His own. For the Father "spared not His own son, but delivered Him up for us all" (Romans 8:32) and the Son emptied Himself of His glory and "took upon Him the form of a servant" (Philippians 2:7). He gave us His soul to death, He was counted with the transgressors. He bore the sins of many, and made intercession for the transgressors (Isaiah 53:12). Those cannot perish for whom the Son intercedes, and that they might live, the Father delivered up His Son unto death. Pardon may then be hoped for equally from the one and from the other, since the mercy of each is equal in goodness, the power equal in will, and one the divine nature in which, in the unity of the Holy Spirit, God liveth and reigneth for ever and ever. Amen.

There is no doubt that whatever we say to the praise of the mother, we say also to that of the son: and again, when we honour the Son, we do not detract from the glory of the mother. For if, according to Solomon: "A wise son is the glory of his father" (Proverbs 10:1), how much more glorious is rendered the mother of Him who is wisdom itself! But why do I venture upon the praises of one whom the prophets extol as praiseworthy, whom an angel distinguishes, and with whom the evangelist fills his page? I do not then praise, because I do not dare to do so: I am content to repeat with reverence what the Holy Spirit has explained by the mouth of the evangelist. He goes on to say: "And the Lord God shall give to Him the throne of His father David." These are the words of the angel to the Virgin concerning the Son promised to her: and who, he assures her, shall possess the kingdom of David. That the Lord Jesus came of the house of David His ancestor, no one doubts. But how, I ask, did God give to Him the throne of David His ancestor, seeing that He did not reign in Jerusalem, that when the crowd desired to make Him king, He did not yield to their wishes (John 6:15), and that before Pilate He protested: "My kingdom is not of this world" (John 18:36)? And after all, what great matter was it to promise to Him who sits throned upon the cherubim (Psalms 80:1), whom the prophet saw seated upon a throne high and lifted up (Isaiah 6:1), that He should sit upon the throne of David His father? But we know that here another Jerusalem is signified, much more noble and more rich than that city which is now, and in which David once reigned. That therefore I suppose to be meant here, according to the habitual usage of the sacred writers, who constantly put the sign for the thing signified. Then God truly gave to Him the throne of His father David, when "He set His king upon His holy hill of Zion" (Psalms 2:6).

Here the prophet seems to have indicated more distinctly of what kingdom he had spoken, in saying not "in" Zion, but "upon" Zion. Therefore perhaps the word "upon" was used, because David indeed reigned "in" Zion: but His realm is "over" Zion, of whom it was said to David: "Of the fruit of thy body will I set upon thy seat" (Psalms 132:11); and of whom it was said by another prophet: "Upon the throne of David and upon his kingdom he shall sit" (Isaiah 9:7). Now do you see why you find this word "upon" everywhere? "Upon Zion, upon the throne, upon the seat, upon the kingdom." The Lord God will then give to Him the throne of David his father, not a symbolic, but a real one; but eternal and heavenly, not temporal and earthly. And that is called, as it is here, the throne of David, because that upon which David sat in this world was a symbol of that eternal and heavenly one.

"And He shall reign over the house of Jacob for ever; and His kingdom shall have no end." Here also, if we take the words of the temporal house of Jacob, how can He reign for ever in it, since it does not endure for ever? We must then look for another house of Jacob, which shall endure for ever, in which he shall reign with a never-ending dominion. And did not that (former) house of Jacob in its fury deny Him, and in its foolishness repudite Him before Pilate, when that governor said to them: "Shall I crucify your King?" (John 19:15). And did they not reply with one voice: "We have no king but Caesar"? Inquire then of the apostle, and he will enable you to distinguish between him who is a Jew and from him who is one openly: the circumcision in the spirit from that which is only in the flesh; those who are sons of the faith of Abraham from those who are his sons only according to the flesh. "For they are not all Israel, who are of Israel: neither, because they are the seed of Abraham, are they all children." (Romans 9:6–7). Apply the same principle then and say: not all who are of the blood of Jacob are to be reckoned as of the house of Jacob. Jacob himself is he who was called Israel. Only those, then, who shall be found perfect in the faith of Jacob shall be counted as of his house; or rather it is only those who are truly of the spiritual and everlasting house of Jacob over whom the Lord Jesus shall reign eternally. Who is there of us who, according to this meaning of the word Jacob, will cast out of his heart the devil, will struggle with his vices and concupiscences, so that sin may not reign in his mortal body but that, on the contrary, Jesus shall reign in him now through grace, and through eternity in glory? Happy are those in whom Jesus shall for ever reign, for they shall reign at the same time with Him; and His kingdom shall have no end. O how glorious is that kingdom in which kings are gathered to praise and glorify Him who above all others is King of kings and Lord of lords; in the glorious beholding of whom the righteous "shall shine forth in the kingdom of their Father" (Matthew 13:43). O! if the blessed Jesus would deign to remember me, a sinner, when He shall come into His Kingdom! O if He, on that day when He shall deliver up the kingdom to God His Father, if He would visit me with His salvation, that I may see the felicity of His chosen ones and rejoice in the joy of His people, that I too may praise Him with His inheritance! (Psalms 106: 4–5). But come, Lord Jesus, even now, take away the offences of Your kingdom, that is, my soul; so that You mayest reign in it, as it is Your right to do. For avarice has come and claimed a throne in me: boastfulness seeks to rule over me: pride desires to be my lord: luxury says, I will reign: ambition, detraction, envy and anger strive within me, whose shall I be? As for me, I resist them as far as I am able, and struggle against them to the best of my power. I call upon Jesus my Lord; I defend myself for Him, because I feel that His is the right over me. I hold to Him as my Lord and my God, and I say: "I have no king but Jesus. Come then, O Lord, scatter them in Your strength, and rule over me, for You are my Lord and my God, who is the salvation of Jacob."

Then said Mary to the angel, "How shall this be, seeing I know not a man?" First she prudently held her peace, while she pondered in doubt of what nature that salutation was; preferring humbly not to reply than to speak rashly of what she knew not. But having well reflected and being reassured (for while the angel addressed her outwardly, God influenced her inwardly) and thus strengthened, faith having put fear to flight, and joy diffidence, she asked of the angel: "How shall this be?" She did not doubt the fact; but she enquired respecting the manner and the order in which it would take place: not whether it should do so, but in what way. It is as if she had said: As my Lord, who is the witness of my conscience, is aware of the vow of His servant not to know a man, by what means, and in what order, will it please Him that this shall take place? If it shall be needful that I should break my vow, in order to become the mother of such a son, though I rejoice for the son, yet I grieve for the means proposed: yet His will be done. But if as a virgin I may conceive and bring forth a son, which will not be impossible for Him, if He shall so please: then I know in truth, that He has had respect for the lowliness of His servant. And the angel answered her: "The Holy Ghost shall come upon you, and the power of the Highest shall overshadow you." She was just now said to be "full of grace": and now in what way it is said "the Holy Ghost shall come upon you"? How could she be filled with grace, and yet not have the Holy Spirit, who is the bestower of graces? If on the contrary, she already had the Holy Spirit, how could the angel promise that the Holy Spirit should come upon her, as it were, anew? Perhaps it was on this account that it was not said simply, "He shall come", but, "He shall come upon", because He was indeed already in her through much grace, but is now announced to superabound because of the fullness of more abundant grace, which He was about to pour upon her? But how could she receive more grace, being already filled? If on the contrary, she was able to receive more, how can she be understood to have been previously filled? Could it be that formerly grace filled her mind, but is now to sanctify her womb for its appointed function: in as much as the fullness of the divinity which was in her previously, as in many of the saints, dwelt in her spiritually; but was now about to dwell in her corporeally, as it had done in none of the saints?

He continues then: "And the power of the highest shall overshadow you." He who is able to comprehend the meaning of this, let him do so. For who (she alone being excepted who had the immense happiness of knowing by her own experience what is signified) is capable of understanding or even of forming an idea of how that brightness inaccessible was poured into the chaste womb of the virgin; and how the latter was able to endure the approach of the inaccessible, when the Spirit vivified instantaneously a minute portion of the same body, of which He overshadowed the whole? And perhaps because of this chiefly it was said, "shall overshadow thee", because the matter was altogether a mystery, which the Holy Trinity willed to bring about alone and with Mary alone; and which was given to her alone to know, to whom alone it was given to be experienced. Let then the words, "the Holy Ghost shall come upon you", be thus explained: "shall render you fruitful by His power"; and "the power of the Highest shall overshadow you" as thus: "the manner in which you shall conceive of the Holy Ghost, Christ, the power of God and the wisdom of God, shall be so closely veiled and so deeply hidden in the impenetrable shadow of His secret counsels, that the mystery shall be known only to Himself and you. It is as if the angel had replied to the virgin: "Why do you question me upon a matter which you shall soon have experience of? You shall indeed know it, and that happily; but He who brings about the mystery shall be the teacher to bring it to your knowledge. I have been sent only to announce to you your virginal conception, not to bring it about. It can be taught only by Him who effects it; none but she in whom it shall be brought about can comprehend it." "Therefore also that holy thing which shall be born of you shall be called the Son of God." That is to say: "Since you shall conceive, not of man, but of the Holy Spirit, you shall conceive the very power of the Highest, that is, the Son of God; 'therefore, that Holy Thing which shall be born of you, shall be called the Son of God'. That is to say, not only He who is in the bosom of the Father, coming into your womb, shall overshadow you, but He shall also, taking of your substance, unite it with Himself; and from this He shall then be called Son of God. Even as it is He who was begotten by the Father before all worlds, and therefore called Son of God; so He shall hereafter be called your son. For thus He who was born of the Father is your son, and His Son shall be born of you; yet not that there are two sons, but one Son. And although one be of you, another of Him, yet shall there not be to each His own, but one son, both of the one and of the other."

Notice, I pray you, how reverently the angel spoke it: "that holy thing which shall be born of you". Why does he say simply that holy thing, without adding more? I believe because there was no name by which he could properly and worthily designate that noble, exalted and revered being to be formed by the uniting of the soul and the body drawn from the most pure flesh of the Virgin, with the only begotten son of the Father. If he had said "the holy body", "the holy man" or "the holy child" or any expression of that kind, he would seem to have spoken inadequately. Therefore no doubt he used the indefinite expression, "that holy thing", because whatever the fruit born of the Virgin, it was without doubt holy and even uniquely so, both through the sanctification by the Spirit, and through its assumption by the Word.

Then the angel added: "Behold, thy cousin Elizabeth has also conceived a son in her old age." Why was it necessary to announce to the virgin that this barren woman had also conceived a son? Was it perhaps in order to convince, by the news of a miracle so recent, the virgin, whom he saw to be still doubtful and incredulous? By no means. For we read that Zechariah was punished for such incredulity by this very angel: but we do not read that Mary was in any respect blamed. On the contrary, we know that her faith was praised by Elizabeth speaking prophetically. "Blessed is she that believed: for there shall be a performance of those things which were told her from the Lord." But the reason that the angel made known to Mary the conception of her cousin, hitherto barren, was to complete her joy by adding miracle to miracle. Moreover, it was needful that she who was soon to conceive the son of the Father's affection, with the joy of the Holy Spirit, should in the first place be animated by no slight degree of love and joy: since it was only a heart as full of gladness as of perfect devotedness that was capable of receiving the fullness of happiness and joy. Or it may be that the conception of Elizabeth was announced to Mary, because it was fitting that a fact which was soon to be known to all should be declared beforehand to the Virgin by an angel, rather than made known to her by the mouths of men, and the mother of God appear to be a stranger to the counsels of her son, if she had remained in ignorance of the events which were taking place so near her upon earth. Or, more probably, the conception of Elizabeth was announced to Mary in order that, being made aware already of the coming of the Saviour, and now of that of His forerunner, and knowing the order and the time of each, she would better be able at a later period to declare the truth to the sacred writers and the preachers of the Gospel, as having been fully instructed from on high in all these mysteries from the very beginning. Finally, it is possible that it was made known so that Mary, on learning that a relative already advanced in age was pregnant, she who was still young should hasten as a matter of dutiful attention to visit her; and thus occasion be given to that infant prophet, to pay to his Lord, still younger than he, the first fruits of his duty; and that while the two mothers met, the consciousness felt by the children of each other's presence should add to one miracle another still more marvellous.

But take care not to suppose that all these events so wonderful, which you hear foretold by the angel, are to be brought to pass by him. If you enquire by whom, listen to the angel himself. "For with God", he says,"nothing is impossible". As if he had said: "All these things that I promise you so faithfully rest not upon my power, but upon His by whom I have been sent. And with Him nothing is impossible: for what can be impossible to Him who has done all things by His Word? And I am struck by this in the angel's speech; that he markedly says not "no action", but "no word" is impossible with God.

Does he employ this phrase in order to enable us to understand that while men are easily able to say all that they please, but by no means able to do what they please, God is able as easily and with incomparably greater ease to carry out in action whatever they are able to express in words? I will explain myself. If it were as easy for men to do what they wished as to say it, then to them also no word would be impossible. But now, according to a saying as ancient as well known, "there is a great difference between saying and doing"; and that is so with men, but not with God; for with God alone it is the same thing to do what He says, and to express what He wills; most truly then "no word" shall be impossible with God. For example, the prophets were able to foresee and foretell that a sterile virgin should conceive and bring forth; but were they able to cause her to do so? But God, who gave them the power to foresee, as easily as He was able to predict what He pleased through them, just so easily was able now when it pleased Him to fulfil what He had caused to be predicted. And in fact with God, the word does not differ from the intention, because he is Truth; nor the act from the word, because He is Power; nor is the manner unsuitable to the act, because He is Wisdom. Thus it is that with God no word is impossible.

You have heard, O Virgin, the announcement of that which is about to take place; and the manner in which it will take place; in each there is matter for wonder and rejoicing. Rejoice then, daughter of Zion, daughter of Jerusalem. And since you have heard news of gladness and joy, let us too hear from you the glad response for which we wait, so that the bones which have been humbled by sorrow may leap for joy. You have heard, I say, the fact and have believed, believe also in the manner in which it shall be accomplished. By the operation of the Holy Spirit, not of a man, you shall conceive and bear a son; and the angel waits only for the reply, to return to God who sent him. We too, O Lady, we who are weighed down by the sentence of condemnation, wait for the word of pity. The price of our salvation is offered to you: soon shall we be freed, if you consent to give yourself to the divine plan. Alas! we, who all are the creatures of the eternal word of God, are perishing; we are to be restored by your brief response, and recalled to life. Unhappy Adam with his miserable progeny exiled from paradise, Abraham also and David, entreat this, O pious Virgin, of you. Others join in the entreaty, holy fathers and ancestors of your own, who also dwell in the valley of the shadow of death. The whole world, prostrate at your knees waits for your consent; and not without reason; since upon your lips hangs the consolation of the unhappy, the redemption of the captives, the freedom of the condemned; in short, the safety of the children of Adam, of the whole human race. Reply quickly, O Virgin: give the word which the earth, hell and the heavens themselves wait for. He, the King and Lord of all things, waits for the word of your consent, by means of which He has proposed to save the world, in as much as He has approved of your graces. He whom in silence you have pleased, you will please still more by speech, since He cries to you from Heaven: "O fairest among women, let me hear thy voice" (Canticles 2:14).

If then you do this, He will cause you to see our salvation. Is not this what you desire, what you long for, what you sigh for in daily and nightly prayers? What then! Are you she to whom this was promised, or do we look for another? On the contrary, it is you yourself and not another. You, I say, are that promised, expected and desired one, from whom your holy ancestor Jacob, already drawing near to death, hoped for everlasting life, saying: "I wait for Your salvation, O Lord" (Genesis 49:18). In whom, in short, and by means of whom, our God and King Himself intended before time began to bring about a salvation on earth. Why do you hope for that from another woman, which is offered to you? Why do you expect that to be done by means of another woman, which will be speedily made manifest by means of you, provided you reply and yield your assent? Reply then quickly to the angel, or rather by the angel to the Lord. Speak a word, and receive the Word, utter your transitory word, and conceive the Word divine and eternal. Why do you fear and delay? Believe, consent and conceive. Let humility become bold, let your timidity have confidence. In no way is it needful even now, that virginal simplicity should forget prudence. In this matter alone, O prudent Virgin, you need not fear presumption; for although reserve is prized by its silence, yet now charity should speak. Open, blessed Virgin, your heart to confidence, your lips to consent, your bosom to its Creator. Behold, the desire of all nations knocks at its door. If He should pass away while you are delaying, and you should begin again with grief to seek Him whom your soul loves! Arise then, hasten and open to Him. Rise by faith, hasten by devotion, open by giving consent.

"Behold", she said, "the handmaid of the Lord. Be it unto me according to Your word." The virtue of humility is always found closely associated with divine grace: for God resists the proud, but gives grace to the humble (James 4:6). She replies then with humility, that the dwelling of grace may be prepared. "Behold", she says, "the handmaid of the Lord." How sublime is this humility, which is incapable of yielding to the weight of honours, or of being rendered proud by them! The mother of God is chosen, and she declares herself His handmaid. It is in truth a mark of no ordinary humility that even when so great an honour is done to her, she does not forget to be humble. It is no great thing to be humble when in a low condition; but humility in one that is honoured is a great and rare virtue. If, for my sins or for those of others, God should permit that the Church, deceived by my pretensions, should elevate such a miserable and humble man as I to any even the most ordinary honour, should not I immediately, forgetful of what I am, begin to think myself such a one as men (who do not see the heart) imagine me to be? I should believe in the public opinion, not regarding the testimony of my conscience, not estimating honour by virtues, but virtue by honours; I should believe myself to be the more holy, the higher was the position I occupied. You may frequently see in the Church men sprung from the lower ranks who have attained to the higher, and from being poor have become rich, beginning to swell with pride, forgetting their low extraction, being ashamed of their family and disdaining their parents because they are in a humble condition. You may see also wealthy men attaining rapidly to ecclesiastical honours, and then at once regarding themselves as men of great holiness, though they have changed their clothes only and not their minds; and persuading themselves that they are worthy of a dignity to which they have attained by solicitation: and that which they owe (if I dare to say so) to their wealth, they ascribe to their merits. I do not speak of those whom ambition blinds, and for whom even honour is a matter for pride.

But I see (much to my regret) some who, after having despised and renounced the pomp of this world in the school of humility, habituating themselves still more to pride, and under the wings of a master who is meek and humble in heart, become more and more insolent and impatient in the cloister than they had been in the world. And, which is a thing still more perverse, there are very many who, while in their own homes would have had to bear contempt, cannot endure to do so in the house of God. They would not have been able to obtain honours in the world, where all desire to possess them, and yet they expect to be loaded with honours, where all have made profession to despise them. I see others (and it is a thing not to be seen without grief) after having enrolled themselves in the army of Christ, entangling themselves anew in the affairs of the world, and plunging again into wordly objects: with earnest zeal they build up walls, but neglect to build up their own characters; under pretext of the general good, they sell their words to the rich and their salutations to matrons; but in spite of the formal order of their sovereign, they cast covetous eyes on the goods of others, and do not shrink from lawsuits to maintain their own rights; not listening to the proclamation made by the apostle, as a herald bidden by the King: "This is the very fault among you, that you go to law one with another. Why do you not rather endure wrong?" (I Corinthians 6:7). Is it so that they have crucified themselves to the world, and that the world is crucified to them, that those who before had scarcely been known in their town or village are now seen traversing provinces, frequenting courts, cultivating a knowledge of kings and the friendship of the great? What shall I say of their religious habit itself? In it they require not so much warmth as colour: and they have more care of the cleanness of their vestment than the culture of their virtues. I am ashamed to say it, but women are surpassed in their study of dress by monks, when costliness in clothing is studied more than utility. At length every appearance of the religious state is laid aside, and the soldiers of Christ strive to be adorned, not to be armed. Even when they are preparing for the struggle, and ought to oppose to the powers of the air the ensign of poverty (which those adversaries greatly fear), they rather prefer to present themselves in carefully studied dress, the sign of peace, and thus, willing to give themselves unarmed and without the striking of a blow to their enemies. All these evils only come when, renouncing those sentiments of humility which have caused us to quit the world, and finding ourselves thus drawn back to the unprofitable tastes and desires for worldly things, we become like dogs returning to their vomit.

Whoever we are who find such inclinations in ourselves, let us mark well what was the reply of her who was chosen to be the mother of God, but who did not forget humility. "Behold", she said, "the handmaid of the Lord; let it be to me according to your word." "Let it be to me" is the expression of a desire, not the indication of a doubt. Even those words "according to your word" are to be understood more as the feeling of one wishing for and desiring, than as the expression of the doubt of one uncertain. We may understand "let it be to me" as words of prayer.

And certainly no one prays for anything unless he believes that it exists, and hopes to obtain it. But God wills that what He has promised should be asked of Him in prayer. And perhaps therefore He in the first place promises many things which He has resolved to give us, that our devotion may be excited by the promise: and that thus our earnest prayer may merit what He had been disposed to bestow upon us freely. This is was that the prudent Virgin understood, when she joined the merit of her prayer with the previous gift of the promise freely bestowed upon her, saying: "let it be to me according to your word." Let it be to me according to Your word concerning the Word. Let the Word which was in the beginning with God become flesh from my flesh.

Let the Word, I pray, be to me, not as a word spoken only to pass away but conceived and clothed in flesh, not in air, that He may remain with us. Let Him be, not only to be heard with the ears, but to be seen with the eyes, touched with the hands and borne on the shoulders. Let the Word be to me, not as a word written and silent, but incarnate and living: that is, not traced with dead signs upon dead parchments; but livingly impressed in human form upon my chaste womb: nor by the tracing of a pen of lifeless reed, but by the operation of the Holy Spirit. Finally, let it thus be to me, as was never done to anyone before me, nor after me shall be done. God has indeed formerly spoken in various manners to the fathers by the prophets: and the word of God is recorded to have been produced in the ear of some, in the mouth of others and in others, again, by the hand: but I pray that the Word of God may be formed in my womb according to Your word.

I desire that He may be formed, not as the word in preaching, not as a sign in figures, or as a vision in dreams: but silently inspired, personally incarnated, found in the body, in my body. Let the Word therefore deign to do in me and for me what He needed not to do, and could not do, for Himself; according to Your word. Let it be done indeed generally for the sake of the whole world, but specially let it be done unto me, according to Your word.

AELRED, Abbot of RIEVAULX: The Pastoral Prayer

1 O Good Shepherd Jesus, good, gentle, tender Shepherd, behold a shepherd, poor and pitiful. A shepherd of Your sheep indeed, but weak and clumsy and of little use, cries out to You. To You, I say, Good Shepherd, this shepherd, who is not good, makes his prayer. He cries to You, troubled upon his own account, and troubled for Your sheep.

ACT OF CONTRITION

2 For when in bitterness of soul I view my former life, it scares and frightens me that I should be called shepherd, for I am surely mad if I do not know myself unworthy of the name. Your holy mercy is upon me, to snatch my wretched soul out of the nether hell. You show mercy as You will, Your pity succours him whom You are pleased to pity; and such is Your forgiveness of my sin, that You do not avenge Yourself by damning me, nor do You even overwhelm me with reproaches; and, even when You do accuse, You love me no less. Nevertheless, I am disturbed and troubled, for I am mindful of Your goodness, yes – but I am not unmindful of my own ingratitude. See, then, before You is my heart's confession of the countless sins from which Your mercy has been pleased to free my hapless soul. My whole heart renders thanks and praise to You with all its might for all these benefits. But I am no less in Your debt for all the evil things I have not done. For, most assuredly, whatever evil thing I have not done, it was Your guiding hand that made me abstain from doing it; since either You did take away the means thereto, or else You did correct my inclination, or gave me the power to resist. But what am I to do, O Lord my God, about the ills whereby, in Your just judgment, You suffer Your servant, the son of Your handmaiden, still to be wearied and

be overcome? The things concerning which my sinful soul is troubled in Your sight, O Lord, cannot be counted; yet, for all that, neither my sorrow for them nor my care to shun their repetition is as great as they demand, and as my will desires.

FACING HIS OFFICE

3 To You, my Jesus, I confess, therefore; to You, my Saviour and my hope, to You, my comfort and my God, I humbly own that I am not as contrite and as fearful as I ought to be for my past sins; nor do I feel enough concern about my present ones. And You, sweet Lord, have set a man like this over Your family, over the sheep of Your pasture. Me, who takes all too little trouble with myself, You bid to be concerned on their behalf; and me, who never prays enough about my own sins, You would have pray for them. I, who have taught myself so little too, have also to teach them. Wretch that I am, what have I done? What have I undertaken? What was I thinking of? Or rather, sweetest Lord, what were You thinking of regarding this poor wretch?

Sweet Lord, I pray You, is not this Your family, Your own people, which you have led out of the second Egypt, and which have been created and redeemed by You? And lastly, You have gathered them together out of all parts, and made them live together in a house where all men follow a common way of life. Why then, O fount of mercy, have You willed to put such people, souls so dear to You, into the charge of such an outcast from Your face?

Was it to satisfy my appetites, to give free rein to my desires, in order that You might have the more against me, and sentence me with more severity, and punish me for others' sins, as well as for my own? O God most holy, if this were the case, was it then fair to let so many souls, souls of such quality, suffer such risk, solely that there might be more obvious reason for one man's severer punishment? For to what greater peril can subjects be exposed, than to a stupid and sinful superior?

Or, and this it is more seemly to expect, more pleasant to experience from kindness such as Yours, did You set such a person over Your household, Lord, in order that, if it should please Your goodness to rule it well through him, Your mercy might be shown, Your wisdom known, the excellence of Your power declared thereby as Yours alone, not man's; and so the wise, the righteous, and the strong should never glory in their wisdom, righteousness and strength as though they were their own; for, when such persons rule Your people well, it is not they, but You, that rule them. Give not the glory to us, O Lord, if this is so, but to Your own name.

INTRODUCTION TO THE PRAYERS THAT FOLLOW

4 Yet, Lord, whatever the reason why You have put my unworthy, sinful self into this office, or have allowed others to appoint me to it, the fact remains that You command me, so long as You allow me to hold the same office, to be concerned for those set under me, and to pray for them most particularly. Wherefore, O Lord, I lay my prayers before You, trusting not in my own righteousness, but in Your great mercy, and where no merit of my own can lift its voice, duty is eloquent. Let Your eyes, therefore, be upon me, Lord, and let Your ears be open to my prayers. But since, according to the divine law, a priest is bound to offer sacrifice first for himself, then for his people, I make an oblation to Your majesty first of the sacrifice of prayer for my own sins.

PRAYER FOR HIS OWN NEEDS

5 Lord, look at my soul's wounds. Your living and effective eye sees everything. It pierces like a sword, even to part soul and spirit. Assuredly, my Lord, You see in my soul the traces of my former sins, my present perils, and also motives and occasions for others yet to be. You see these things, Lord, and I would have You see them. You know well, O searcher of my heart, that there is nothing in my soul that I would hide from You, even had I the power to escape Your eyes. Woe to the souls that want to hide themselves from You. They cannot make themselves not to be seen by You, but only miss Your healing and incur Your punishment. So see me, sweet Lord, see me.

My hope, most merciful, is in Your loving kindness; for You will see me, either as a good physician sees, intent upon my healing, or else as a kind master, anxious to correct, or a forbearing father, longing to forgive. This, then, is what I ask, O fount of pity, trusting in Your mighty mercy and merciful might: I ask You, by the power of Your most sweet name, and by Your holy manhood's mystery, to put away my sins and heal the languors of my soul, mindful only of Your goodness, not of my ingratitude.

Further, against the vices and the evil passions which still assault my soul, (whether they come from past bad habit, or from my immeasurable daily negligence, whether their source is in the weakness of my corrupt and vitiated nature, or in the secret tempting of malignant spirits) against these vices, Lord, may Your sweet grace afford me strength and courage; that I may not consent to them, nor let them reign in my mortal body, nor yield my members to be instruments of wickedness. And as I thus resist, heal all my weakness perfectly, cure all my wounds, and put back into shape all my deformities. Lord, may Your good, sweet Spirit descend into my heart, and make there a dwelling for Himself, cleansing it from all defilement both of flesh and spirit, pouring into it the increment of faith, and hope, and love, disposing it to penitence and love and gentleness. May He quench with the dew of his blessing the heat of my desires, and with this power put to death my carnal impulses and fleshly lusts. In labours, and in watchings, and in fastings, may He give me fervour and discretion, to love and praise You, to pray and think of You; and may he give me power and devotion to order every act and thought according to Your will, and also perseverance in these virtues to my life's end.

SPECIAL PRAYER FOR WISDOM

6 These things, my hope, I need for my own sake. But there are others that I need not only for myself, but for the sake of those to whom You bid me be a power for good, rather than merely a superior. There was a wise king once, who asked that wisdom might be given him to rule Your people. His prayer found favour in Your eyes, You did hear him; and at that time You had not met the cross, nor shown Your people that amazing love. But now, sweet Lord, behold before Your face Your own people, whose eyes are ever on Your cross, and who themselves are signed with it. You have entrusted to Your sinful servant the task of ruling them. My God, You know what a fool I am, my weakness is not hidden from Your sight. Therefore, sweet Lord, I ask You not for gold, I ask You not for silver, nor for jewels, but only that You would give me wisdom, that I may know how to rule Your people well. O fount of wisdom, send her from Your throne of might, to be with me, to work with me, to act in me, to speak in me, to order all my thoughts and words and deeds and plans according to Your will, and to the glory of Your name, to further their advance and my salvation.

PRAYER FOR THE GOOD OF ALL

7 You know my heart, Lord; You know that my will is that whatever You have given Your servant should be devoted wholly to their service, and spent for them in its entirety; and I myself would be freely spent for them. So may it be, O Lord, so may it be. My powers of perception and of speech, my work time and my leisure, my doing and my thinking, the times when things go well with me, the times when they go ill, my life, my death, my good health and my weakness, each single thing that makes me what I am, the fact that I exist and think and judge, let all be used, let all be spent for those for whom You deigned to be spent Yourself.

Teach me Your servant, therefore, Lord, teach me, I pray You, by Your Holy Spirit, how to devote myself to them and how to spend myself on their behalf. Give me, by Your unutterable grace, the power to bear their shortcomings with patience, to share their griefs in loving sympathy, and to help them according to their needs. Taught by Your Spirit, may I learn to comfort the sorrowful, confirm the weak and raise the fallen; to be myself one with them in their weakness, one with them when they burn at causes of offence, one in all things with them, all things to all of them, that I may gain them all.

Give me the power to speak the truth straightforwardly, and yet acceptably; so that they all may be built up in faith and hope and love, in chastity and lowliness, in patience and obedience, in spiritual fervour and submissiveness of mind. And, since You have appointed this blind guide to lead them, this untaught man to teach, this ignorant one to rule them, for their sakes, Lord, if not for mine, teach him whom You have made to be their teacher, lead him who You have bidden to lead them, rule him who is their ruler. Teach me, therefore, sweet Lord, how to restrain the restless, comfort the discouraged, and support the weak. Teach me to suit myself to everyone according to his nature, character and disposition, according to his power of understanding or his lack of it, as time and place require, in each case, as You would have me do. And since the weakness of my flesh, or it may be my lack of courage and my heart's corruption, prevent my edifying them by labours of watching and fasting, I beg Your bounteous mercy that they may be edified by my humility and charity, my patience and my pity. May my words and teaching build them up, and may they always be assisted by my prayers.

PRAYER FOR SUBORDINATES

8 Hear me yet further, God most merciful, for those for whom I am compelled and drawn to pray to You, both by my duty and by my heart's love. Remembering Your kindness, I am bold. For You, sweet Lord, know how much I love them, how I yearn over them, and how my heart goes out to them. You know, Lord, I do not want to rule them harshly or self-assertively, but to help them in charity, rather than command, and to be subject to them in humility, while being always one of them in sympathy.

Hear me, therefore, hear me, O Lord my God, and let Your eyes be open on them day and night. Spread Your wings, most loving Lord, and shield them. Stretch forth Your holy right hand, Lord, and bless them; and pour into their hearts Your Holy Spirit, that He may keep them in unity of spirit and the bond of peace, chaste in their bodies and lowly in their minds. May He be there to help them when they pray, and fill them with the unction and the riches of Your love.

May He renew their minds with sweet compunction, enlighten their hearts with the light of Your grace, cheer them with hope, humble them with fear and kindle them with love. May it be he who prompts them to such prayers as You will gladly hear. May He, Your same sweet Spirit, be in them, when they make meditation; so that enlightened, by Him they may know You, and ever cherish in their hearts the thought of Him; so that in trouble they will call on Him, and turn to Him in all perplexity. May the same loving Comforter, when they are being tempted, come swiftly to their aid; and may He help their weakness in all the straits and troubles of this life. By the same Spirit make them, Lord, to be, within themselves, with one another and towards myself, peaceable and equable and kind, obedient, serviceable, helpful to each other. May they be fervent in spirit, rejoicing in hope, enduring steadfastly through poverty and fasting, toils and vigils, silence and repose. Drive far from them, O Lord, the spirit of pride and of vainglory, of envy and of gloom, of weariness and slander, of distrust and despair, of fornication and uncleanness, of discord and presumption. Be in their midst, according to Your faithful promise.

And, since You know what each of them needs, I pray You, strengthen what is weak in them. Spurn not their fraility, heal that which is diseased, give joy for sorrow, kindle what is lukewarm, establish what is insecure in them, that each of them may know he does not lack Your grace in any of his trials and temptations.

PRAYER FOR TEMPORAL NEEDS

9 Lord, as You shall see fit, provide Your servants also with those temporal goods with which the weakness of this wretched body is in this life sustained. This one thing only do I crave, my Lord, from Your sweet pity: namely, that whether it be much or little that You give You would make me, Your servant, a good and faithful steward in respect to all, a wise and fair distributor, a sensible provider. Inspire them too, my God, to bear it patiently when You withhold things; and, when You do bestow, to use Your gifts with temperance and restraint. Inspire them, O Lord, also to have of me, who am Your servant, and their servant for Your sake, such an opinion as may profit them, such love and fear of me, as You, Lord, see to be good for them.

CONCLUSION

10 I, for my part, commit them into

Your holy hands and loving providence. May no one snatch them from Your hand, nor from Your servant's, unto whom You have committed them. May they persevere with gladness in their holy purpose, unto the attainment of everlasting life with You, our most sweet Lord, their helper always, who lives and reigns to ages of ages. Amen.

Saint FRANCIS OF ASSISI: The Canticle of the Sun

1 Most high, most great and good Lord, to You belong praises, glory and every blessing; to You alone do they belong, most high, and no one is worthy to name You.

2 Bless You, my Lord, for the gift of all Your creatures and especially for our brother sun, by whom the day is enlightened. He is radiant and bright, of great splendour, bearing witness to You, O my God.

3 Bless You, my Lord, for our sister the moon and the stars; You have formed them in the heavens, fair and clear.

4 Bless You, my Lord, for my brother the wind, for the air, for cloud and calm, for every kind of weather, for by them You sustain all creatures.

5 Blessed be my Lord for our sister water, which is very useful, humble, chaste and precious.

6 Bless You, my Lord, for brother fire, gay, noble and beautiful, untamable and strong, by whom You illumine the night.

7 Bless You, my Lord, for our mother the earth, who sustains and nourishes us, who brings forth all kinds of fruit, herbs and bright-hued flowers.

8 Bless You, my Lord, for those who pardon for love of You, and who patiently bear infirmity and tribulation. Happy are those who abide in peace, for by You, Most High, they will be crowned.

9 Bless You, my Lord, for our sister, death of body, from whom no living man can escape. Woe to him who dies in a state of mortal sin. Happy are they who at the hour of death are found in obedience to Your holy will, for the second death cannot hurt them.

10 Praise you and bless you my Lord; give Him thanks and serve Him with great humility.

Saint BONAVENTURE: The Goodness and Greatness of Saint Francis

HIS KINDLY PIETY

1 True godliness had so filled the heart of Francis and entered his inmost parts, that it seemed to have established its sway over the man of God. It was this piety that, through devotion, uplifted him towards God; through compassion, transformed him into the likeness of Christ; through humility, inclined him towards his neighbour, and, through his all-embracing love for every creature, set forth a new picture of man's condition before the fall. And as by this piety he was touched with kindly feeling for all things, so above all, when he saw souls redeemed by the precious blood of Christ Jesus being defiled by any stain of sin, he would weep over them with such tenderness of compassion that he seemed, like a mother in Christ, to suffer for them daily. And this was the chief cause of his veneration for the ministers of the word of God: because with devout care they raise up seed to the brother who is dead, that is, to Christ crucified for sinners, by converting them, and cherishing the same seed with careful devotion. This ministry of compassion, he maintained, was more acceptable to the father of mercies than all sacrifice, especially if it were performed with the zeal of perfect charity, so that this end might be striven after by example rather than by command, by tearful prayer rather than by eloquent speech.

2 Accordingly, he would say that that preacher should be deplored as one without true piety, who in his preaching did not seek the salvation of souls, but his own glory, or who by the sins of this life pulled down that which he built up by the truth of his teaching. He would say that the brother who is simple and unready of speech, who by his good example incites others to good,

should be preferred to such a one. That saying: "The barren has borne many", he would expound; "The barren", he said "is the little poor brother, who has not the function of begetting sons in the Church. He in the judgment shall bear many, for those whom he now converts to Christ by his secret prayers shall be then added to his glory by the judge. And 'she that has many children has become feeble', for the empty preacher of many words who now boasts of many begotten, as it were, by his power, shall then see that there is nothing of his own in them."

3 Since he looked with heartfelt piety and glowing zeal for the salvation of souls, he would say that he was filled with the sweetest fragrance, and anointed as if with precious ointment whenever he heard of many being led into the way of truth by the sweet savour of the reputation of the holy brothers scattered throughout the world. Hearing such reports, he would rejoice in spirit, heaping with blessings those brothers who, by word or deed, were bringing sinners to the love of Christ. Likewise, those who were transgressing against holy religion by their evil works fell under the heaviest sentence of his curse. "By You," said he, "O Lord most holy, by the entire company of Heaven, and by me, Your little one, curse them who by their evil example bring to nothing and destroy that which through the holy brothers of this order You have built up, and continue to build." Often he was affected by such sadness because of this stumbling-block of the weak brethren that he thought his strength would fail him, were he not sustained by the comfort of the divine mercy.

But when once he was disturbed by evidence of evil, and with troubled spirit was praying, praying to the merciful Father for his sons, he obtained this answer from the Lord: "Why do you fret, poor little mortal? Have I set you as a shepherd over my religion that you should forget I am its chief protector? I have appointed you, simple as you are, for this very end, that the things that I shall perform through you may be ascribed, not to man's working, but to grace from above. I have created this religion, I will keep it and feed it, and, when some fall away, I will raise up others in their place, so that, if none were born, I would cause them to be born. And by whatever shocks this little poor religion may be shaken, it shall always remain unscathed under my guard."

4 The vice of slander, hateful to the fount of goodness and grace, Francis shrank from as from a serpent's tooth, declaring it to be a most hateful plague, and an abomination to the most holy God, for the slanderer feeds on the blood of those souls that he has slain by the sword of his tongue. On one occasion hearing a certain brother blacken the reputation of another, he turned to his vicar, and said: "Rise, rise, make careful enquiry, and, if you find the accused brother to be guiltless, with stern discipline make the accuser known to all." At times, indeed, he would sentence someone who had deprived his brother of his good reputation to be himself deprived of his habit, and deemed that he ought not to be able to lift up his eyes unto God unless first he had exerted himself to restore, as best he might, that which he had taken away. "The sin of slanderers," he would say, "is more heinous than that of robbers, in as much as the law of Christ, which is fulfilled in the observance of godliness, binds us to desire more the salvation of the soul than of the body."

5 To those afflicted with bodily suffering of any sort, he would minister with a marvellous tenderness of sympathy; if he perceived any destitution or lack, he would in the gentleness of his devout heart carry it to Christ. Mercy, truly, was inborn in him, and redoubled by the shedding upon it of the piety of Christ. So his soul was melted over the poor and the weak, and, when he could not open his hand to any, he opened his heart. It happened that one of the brothers had made a somewhat harsh reply to a poor man that persistently asked for alms. When the devout lover of the poor heard it, he told that brother to throw himself, naked, at the poor man's feet, declare himself at fault, and beg the favour of his prayer and his forgiveness. When he had humbly done this, the father gently added: "When you see a poor man, O brother, a mirror is set before you of the Lord, and of His mother in her poverty. In the infirm, you can see the infirmities that He took upon Himself." In all the poor, he, himself the most Christlike of all poor men, beheld the image of Christ, and so he judged that all things that were provided

for himself, were they even the necessities of life, should be given up to any poor folk whom he met, and not only as largesse, but as if they were their own property.

It happened that a certain beggar met him, as he was returning from Siena, when because of sickness he was wrapped in a cloak over his habit. Noticing with pitiful eye the poor man's misery, "It is our duty", said he to his companion, "to restore the cloak to this poor man, for his own it is. For we received it only as a loan, until we should happen to find another poorer than ourselves." But his companion, thinking of the need of the kindly father, urgently tried to prevent him from providing for another, leaving himself uncared for.

'I think", said he, "the great Almsgiver would account it a theft in me if I did not give what I wear to one needing it more." Accordingly he used to ask from those that had given him necessities for the succour of his body permission to give them away if he should meet a needier person, so that he might do so with their sanction. He withheld nothing, neither cloak, nor habit, nor books, nor the very ornaments of the altar, but all these he would, while he could, give to the needy, so that he might fulfil the ministry of charity. Often when he met on the road poor folk carrying burdens, he would lay their burdens upon his own weak shoulders.

6 When he thought of the first beginning of all things, he was filled with a yet more overflowing charity, and would call the dumb animals, however small, by the names of brother and sister, because he recognised in them the same origin as in himself. Yet he loved with a special warmth and tenderness those creatures that imitate by the similarity of their nature the holy gentleness of Christ, and in the interpretation of Scripture are symbols of Him. Often he would buy back lambs that were being taken to be killed, in remembrance of that most gentle lamb who allowed himself to be brought to the slaughter for the redemption of sinners.

One night, when the servant of God was lodging at the Monastery of San Verecondo in the diocese of Gubbio, a ewe gave birth to a lamb. Near by there was a very fierce sow, and she, not sparing the innocent life, murdered him with her greedy jaws. When the gentle father heard of this he was moved with wonderful pity, and, remembering that lamb without blemish, mourned over the dead lamb in the presence of all, saying: "Woe is me, brother little lamb, innocent creature, symbolising Christ to men! Curse that evil beast that has devoured you, and let neither man nor beast eat her flesh immediately." Marvellous to relate, the cruel sow began to languish, and in three days paid the penalty in her own body, and suffered death as her retribution. Her carcass was thrown into a ditch near the monastery, and lay there for a long time, dried up like a board, and food for no famished beast. Let human evil-doing, then, take note, by what a punishment it shall be overtaken at the last, if the savageness of a brute beast was smitten by a death so awful; let faithful devotion also consider how in the servant of God was shown a piety of such marvellous power and abundant sweetness, that even the nature of beasts in their own way, acclaimed it.

7 While he was travelling near the city of Siena, he came upon a great flock of sheep in the pastures. And when he had greeted them graciously, as was his habit, they left their feeding and all ran towards him, raising their heads, and gazing fixedly at him with their eyes. So eagerly did they acclaim him that both the shepherds and the brothers marvelled, seeing around him the lambs, and the rams too, so wonderfully filled with delight.

At another time, at St Mary of the Little Portion, a lamb was brought to the man of God, which he thankfully received, because of the love of guilelessness and simplicity that the lamb's nature exhibits. The holy man exhorted the lamb that it should praise God instantly, and avoid offending the brothers; the lamb, on its part, as though it had observed the piety of the man of God, diligently obeyed his instructions. For when I heard the brothers chanting in the choir, it too would enter the church, and, unbidden by anyone, would bend the knee, bleating before the altar of the Virgin Mother of the Lamb, as though it wanted to greet her. Furthermore, at the elevation of the most holy body of Christ in the solemn mass, it would bend its knee and bow, as though the sheep, in its reverence, would reprove the irreverence of the undevout, and would incite Christ's devout people to revere the sacrament.

At one time he had with him in Rome a lamb, because of his reverence for that most gentle Lamb, and he entrusted it to a noble matron, the lady Jacoba di Settesoli, to be cared for in her bower. This lamb, like one instructed in spiritual things by the saint, when the lady went into church kept closely by her side in going and in returning. If in the early morning the lady delayed her rising, the lamb would rise and would butt her with its little horns, and rouse her by its bleatings, admonishing her with gestures and nods to hurry to church. Because of this, the lamb that had been a pupil of Francis and had now become a teacher of devotion, was cherished by the lady as a marvellous and loveworthy creature.

8 At another time, at Greccio, a live leveret was brought to the man of God, which, when set down free on the ground so that it might escape wherever it wanted, at the call of the kindly father leapt with flying feet into his bosom. He, fondling it in the instinctive tenderness of his heart, seemed to feel for it as a mother, and, bidding it in gentle tones beware of being recaptured, let it go free. But although it was set on the ground many times to escape it always returned to the father's bosom, as though by some hidden sense it perceived the tenderness of his heart; and so at length, by his command, the brothers carried it away to a safer and more remote spot.

Similarly, on an island on the lake of Perugia, a rabbit was caught and brought to the man of God, and, although it fled from others, it entrusted itself to his hands and bosom with the confidence of a tame creature.

As he was hurrying by the lake of Rieti to the hermitage of Greccio, a fisherman out of devotion brought him a water-fowl, which he gladly received and then, opening his hands, told it to go; however, it would not leave him. Then he, lifting his eyes to Heaven, remained for a long time in prayer and, after a long hour returning to himself as though from afar, gently told the little bird to go and praise the Lord. Then, having thus received his blessing and leave, it flew away, showing joy by the movement of its body.

Similarly, from the same lake there was brought to him a fine, live fish, which he called, as was his way, by the name of brother, and put back into the water near the boat. Then the fish played in the water near the man of God, and, as though drawn by love of him, would not leave the boatside until it had received his blessing and leave.

9 Another time, when he was walking with a certain brother through the Venetian marshes, he chanced upon a great host of birds that were sitting and singing among the bushes. Seeing them, he said to his companion: "Our sisters the birds are praising their creator, let us too go among them and sing to the Lord praises and the canonical hours." When they went among them, the birds did not stir from the spot, and when, because of their twittering, they could not hear each other in reciting the hours, the holy man turned to the birds, saying: "My sisters the birds, cease from singing while we give our due praises to the Lord." Then the birds held their peace, and remained silent until, having said his hours at leisure and rendered his praises, the holy man of God again gave them leave to sing. And, when he had done so they at once took up their song again after their usual fashion.

At St Mary of the Little Portion, near the cell of the man of God, a cicada sat on a fig-tree and chirped; and often by her song she stirred up the servant of the Lord to divine praises, who had learnt to marvel at the glorious handiwork of the creator even as seen in little things. One day he called her, and she, as though divinely taught, alighted upon his hand. When he said to her, "Sing, my sister cicada, and praise the Lord your creator with your glad song," she obeyed at once, and began to chirp, nor did she cease until, at the father's bidding, she flew back to her own place. There she stayed for eight days she stayed, on any day coming at his call, singing, and flying back, as he bade her. At length the man of God said to his companions: "Let us now give our sister cicada leave to go, for she has gladdened us enough with her song, stirring us up these eight days past to the praises of God." And at once, his leave given, she flew away, and was never seen there again, as though she dared not in any way transgress his command.

10 Once while he was lying ill at Siena a fresh-caught pheasant was sent to him, alive, by a certain nobleman. The bird, as soon as it saw and heard the holy man, pressed near him with such friendliness that it would in no way allow itself to be parted from him. For, although it was set down several times in a vineyard outside the home of the brothers, so that it might escape if it would, it still ran back in haste to the father as though it had always been brought up by his hand. Then, when it was given to a certain man who used out of devotion to visit the servant of God, it seemed as though it grieved to be out of the sight of the gentle father, and refused all food. At last, it was brought back to the servant of God, and, as soon as it saw him, testified to its delight by its gestures, and ate eagerly.

When he had come to the solitudes of Alverna, to keep a lent in honour of the Archangel Michael, birds of many kinds fluttered about his cell, and seemed by their tuneful chorus and joyful movements to rejoice at his coming, and to invite and entice the holy father to linger there. Seeing this, he said to his companion: "I perceive, brother, that it is in accordance with the divine will that we should stay here for a while, so greatly do our sisters the little birds seem to take comfort in our presence." While, accordingly, he was staying in that place, a falcon that had its nest there bound itself to him by close ties of friendship. For always at that hour of night when the holy man used to rise for the divine office, the falcon was first with its song and cries. And this was most acceptable to the servant of God, the more because the great concern which the bird showed for him shook from him all drowsiness of sloth. But when the servant of Christ was unusually weighed down by infirmity, the falcon would spare him, and would not mark for him so early an awakening. At such times, as though taught by God, he would strike the bell of his voice about dawn with a light touch. Truly, there would seem to have been a divine omen, alike in the gladness of the birds of myriad species and in the cries of the falcon, as that praiser and worshipper of God, borne up on the wings of contemplation, was at that very place and time to be exalted by the vision of the seraph.

11 At one time, while he was staying in the hermitage of Greccio, the natives of that place were plagued by many evils. For a herd of ravening wolves was devouring not only beasts but also men, and every year a hailstorm laid waste their corn and vineyards. And so, when the herald of the holy gospel was preaching to them under these afflictions, he said: "I promise you, pledging the honour and glory of almighty God, that all this plague shall go from you, and that the Lord will look upon you, and multiply your property if only, believing me, you will take pity on yourselves, and will first make true confession, then bring forth fruits worthy of repentance. But again, I declare to you that if, unthankful for His benefits, you turn again to your vomit, the plague will be renewed, the punishment will be redoubled, and greater wrath will be showered upon you." Then from that very hour, they turned at his admonition to repentance, and the disasters ceased, the perils passed, and nothing of havoc was wrought by wolves or hailstorms. But what is yet more marvellous, if a hailstorm ever fell on their neighbours' lands, as it neared their borders it stopped, or changed its course to some another region. Both hail and wolves observed the pact made with the servant of God; nor did they attempt any more to break the law of natural piety by raging against men that had turned to piety, as long as men in their turn did not act wickedly against the most holy laws of God.

With holy affection, then, must we think on the holiness of this blessed man, that was of such wonderful sweetness and might that he conquered wild beasts, tamed woodland creatures, and taught tame ones, and inclined the nature of the brutes that had revolted from fallen man, to obey him. For certainly it is this piety which is profitable to all things, having promise of the life that now is, and of that which is to come.

THE SACRED STIGMATA

1 It was the custom of that angelic man, Francis, never to be slothful in doing good, but rather, like the heavenly spirits on Jacob's ladder, to be always ascending towards God or stooping towards his neighbour. For he had learnt so wisely to apportion the time granted to him for merit that one part of it he would spend in

labouring for the benefit of his neighbours, the other he would devote to the peaceful ecstasies of contemplation. And so, when according to the demands of time and place he had managed to secure the salvation of others, he would leave behind the disturbances of crowds, and seek a hidden solitude and a place for silence, in which, giving himself up more freely to the Lord, he might brush off any dust that was clinging to him from his conversation with men.

Accordingly, two years before he gave up his spirit to Heaven, led by the divine counsel he was brought after many and varied toils to a high mountain, called Mount Alverna. When, as was his habit, he began to keep a lent there, fasting in honour of St Michael Archangel, he was filled to overflowing, as never before, with the sweetness of heavenly contemplation, and was kindled with a yet more burning flame of heavenly longings, and began to feel the gifts of the divine bestowal heaped upon him. He was carried into the heights, not like a curious examiner of the divine majesty who is weighed down by the glory of it, but as a faithful and wise servant, searching out the will of God, to whom it was always his fervent and greatest desire to conform himself in every way.

2 So by the divine oracle it was instilled into his mind that by opening the book of the gospels it should be revealed to him by Christ what would be most pleasing to God in him and from him. And so, having first prayed very devoutly, he took the holy book of the gospels from the altar, and had it opened, in the name of the Holy Trinity, by his companion, a man devoted to God, and holy. As in three openings of the book the Lord's passion was discovered each time, Francis, full of the Spirit of God, truly understood that, as he had imitated Christ in the deeds of his life, so it was necessary to be made like Him in the trials and sufferings of His passion before he should depart from this world. And, although by reason of the great austerity of his past life and continual sustaining of the Lord's cross, he was now frail in body, he was not at all afraid, but was even more valiantly inspired to endure a martyrdom. For in him the all-powerful kindling of the love of the good Jesus had increased into coals of fire, which had a most vehement flame, so that many waters could not quench his love, so strong was it.

3 When, therefore, by a seraphic glow of longing he had been uplifted towards God, and by his sweet compassion had been transformed into the image of He Who by His exceeding love endured to be crucified, on a certain morning about the feast of the Exaltation of Holy Cross, while he was praying on the side of the mountain, he saw a seraph with six wings, flaming and resplendent, coming down from the heights of Heaven. When in his flight most swift he had reached the space of air near the man of God, there appeared between the wings the figure of a man crucified, with his hands and feet stretched forth in the shape of a cross, and fastened to a cross. Two wings were raised above His head, two were spread forth to fly, while two hid His whole body. Beholding this, Francis was mightily astonished, and joy, mingled with sorrow, filled his heart. He rejoiced at the gracious expression with which he saw Christ, under the guise of the seraph, regard him, but His crucifixion pierced his soul with a sword of pitying grief. He marvelled exceedingly at the appearance of a vision so unfathomable, knowing that the infirmity of the passion does in no way accord with the immortality of a seraphic spirit.

At last he understood, the Lord revealing it to him, that this vision had been presented to his gaze by the divine providence, that the friend of Christ might have foreknowledge that he was to be totally transformed in the image of Christ crucified, not by martyrdom of body, but by kindling of heart. Accordingly, as the vision disappeared, it left in his heart a wonderful glow, but on his flesh also it imprinted a no less wonderful image of its tokens. For immediately there began to appear on his hands and feet the marks of the nails, as he had just seen them in that figure of the crucified. For his hands and feet seemed to be pierced through the middle with nails, the heads of the nails showing in the palms of the hands and upper side of the feet, and their points showing on the other side; the heads of the nails were round and black in the hands and feet, while the points were long, bent, and turned back, being formed of the flesh itself, and protruding from it. The right side was, as if it had been pierced by a lance, seamed with a red scar, from which the sacred blood welled often, staining his habit and breeches.

4 Now the servant of Christ realised that the stigmata so manifestly imprinted on his flesh could not be hidden from his intimate friends; nevertheless, fearing to make public the holy secret of the Lord, he was set in a great strife of questioning, as to whether he should tell what he had seen, or should keep it silent. And so he called some of the brothers, and, speaking to them in general terms, set before them his doubt, and asked their advice. Then one of the brothers, Illuminato by name, and illuminated by grace, realising that he had seen some marvellous things, in that he seemed almost stricken dumb with amazement, said to the holy man: "Brother, you know that at times the divine secrets are shown to you, not only for your own sake, but for the sake of others also. Therefore, I think you would have reason to fear that you will be judged guilty of hiding your talent, if you keep hidden that which you have received and which would be profitable to many." At this speech, the holy man was moved so that, although at other times he used to say, "My secret to me", he did then, with much fear relate the vision, adding that He who had appeared to him had said some words which, so long as he lived, he would never reveal to any man. Truly we must believe that those utterances of that holy seraph marvellously appearing on the cross were so secret that perhaps it was not lawful for a man to utter them.

5 Now after the true love of Christ had transformed His lover into the same image, and after he had spent forty days in solitude, as he had determined, when the feast of St Michael Archangel came, this angelic man, Francis, descended from the mountain, bearing with him the image of the crucified engraved, not on tablets of stone or wood by the craftsman's hand, but written on his flesh by the finger of the living God. And for as much as it is good to keep close the secret of a king, the man who shared this royal secret always hid those sacred signs as best he could. However, since it pertains to God to reveal the great things that He does for His glory, the Lord Himself, who had imprinted those seals upon him in secret, wrought various miracles openly by them so that the hidden and wonderful power of those stigmata might be demonstrated by the well known fame of the signs that followed.

6 So, in the province of Rieti, there had prevailed a very terrible plague, which devoured all oxen and sheep so cruelly that no help had been of any avail. But a certain man that feared God was warned at night by a vision to go in haste to a hermitage of the brothers, and obtain some water that had washed the hands and feet of the servant of God, Francis, who at that time was staying there, and to sprinkle it over all the animals. Accordingly, he rose at dawn, and came to the place, and, having secretly obtained this water from the companions of the holy man, he sprinkled the sheep and oxen that were diseased with it. Wonderful to relate, as soon as the sprinkling, were it but a drop, fell upon the sick animals as they lay on the ground, they recovered their former strength, and got up immediately, and, as though they had felt no sickness, hurried to the pastures! So it happened through the marvellous virtue of that water that had touched the sacred wounds that the whole plague was at once stopped, and the contagious sickness banished from the flocks and herds.

7 In the neighbourhood of the aforesaid Mount Alverna, before the holy man had stayed there, a cloud used to arise from the mountain and a fierce hailstorm to lay waste the fruits of the earth. But after that blessed vision, to the amazement of the inhabitants, the hail ceased, so that the excellence of that heavenly apparition and the virtue of the stigmata that were imprinted by it there might be attested by the very face of the heavens, made calm beyond its habit.

It happened one winter season that, because of his bodily infirmity and the roughness of the roads, he was riding on a poor man's ass, and was obliged to pass the night under the edge of an overhanging rock, so that he might by any means escape the inconveniences of the snow and night that had overtaken them, and which hindered him so that he was not able to reach the place in which he was to lodge. And when Francis realised that this man was muttering, sighing, and complaining, and was tossing himself to and fro, like one thinly clad, and unable to sleep by reason of the bitter cold, he, kindled with the glow of the love divine, touched him with his outstretched hand. Marvellous to relate, as soon as that holy hand that bore the burning of the live coal of the seraph touched the man, his sense of cold was utterly banished, and as great a warmth came upon him within and without as if the flaming breath from the mouth of a furnace had blown upon him. Strengthened by it in mind and body, he slept more sweetly until the morning among the rocks and snow than he had ever done resting in his own bed, as he himself declared afterwards.

And so it is proved by sure tokens that those sacred seals were imprinted by the might of He who by the ministry of seraphs purifies, enlightens, and kindles, so that they brought health out of pestilence by driving it forth, and with wonderful efficacy bestowed ease and warmth upon men's bodies. After his death this was shown by clearer portents which shall be told later in their proper place.

8 Francis himself, although he strove with great diligence to hide the treasure found in the field, could nevertheless not conceal it so that some people should not behold the stigmata in his hand and feet, although he almost always kept his hands covered, and from that time forth wore sandals on his feet. For, while he lived, many brothers saw them, who, although they were men worthy of all trust because of their special holiness, did still for the removal of all doubt swear a solemn oath, laying their hands on thrice-holy things, that it was so and that they had seen it. Also, some cardinals, during the intimate communication that they held with the holy man, saw them, and these composed truthful praises of the sacred stigmata, in prose and verse and anthems, which they published in his honour, giving their witness both in word and in writing to the truth. The supreme pontiff, moreover, the lord Alexander, when he was preaching in the presence of many brothers, myself among them, declared that he, during the lifetime of the saint, had seen with his own eyes those sacred stigmata. At the time of death, more than fifty brothers saw them, as did Clare, that virgin most devoted to God, with the rest of her sisters, and countless seculars, many of whom both kissed them with devout emotion and touched them with their hands, to confirm their witness.

However, the wound in his side he carefully concealed so that during his lifetime no one might see it, except by stealth. So one of the brothers who used solicitously to tend him, having prevailed on him with holy caution to take off his habit so that it might be shaken out, by looking closely saw the wound, and moreover, by laying three fingers upon it with a quick touch, learnt the extent of it both by sight and by touch.

With a similar precaution the brother that was then his vicar saw it. And a brother of wonderful simplicity, who was his companion, while he was rubbing the shoulder-blades of the holy man because of a pain and weakness that he suffered there, put his hand inside his hood, and by an accident let it fall on the sacred wound, inflicting great pain on him. From then on Francis wore his under-garments made so that they reached right up to his armpits, to cover the wound in the side. And so the brothers who washed these, or shook out his habit as occasion demanded, finding them stained with blood, by this clear sign arrived at a certain knowledge of the sacred wound, whose appearance, revealed afterwards at his death, they too, in company with very many others, gazed upon and venerated.

9 Up then, most valiant knight of Christ! Bear the armour of that most invincible Captain, equipped and adorned with which you shall overcome all enemies. Bear the standard of the King most high, to look upon which inspires all the warriors of the host of God. Bear no less the seal of the chief priest, Christ, by which your words and deeds shall be deservedly received as blameless and authoritative by all men. For from now on, because of the marks of the Lord Jesus which you bear in your body, let no man trouble you, but rather, let whoever is the servant of Christ be constrained to deepest devotion and love for you. For these most clear tokens, proven, not by the two or three witnesses that are enough to establish a matter, but by a multitude, over and above what was necessary, the witness of God in you, and the things done through you are worthy of all belief. They take from the infidels every pretext or excuse, while they strengthen believers in

faith, uplift them by confidence of hope, and kindle them with the fire of charity.

10 Now, truly, is that first vision fulfilled which you saw, that you should become a captain in the warfare of Christ, and should be clothed with heavenly armour, marked with the sign of the cross. Now that vision of the crucified, which at the outset of your conversion pierced your soul with a sword of pitying sorrow, and the sound of the voice from the cross, proceeding as though from the exalted throne of Christ and His hidden place of atonement, as you declared in your holy converse, are shown to have been true beyond a doubt. Now, too, the cross that, as you made progress in your conversion, was seen by brother Silvester marvellously coming forth from your mouth, the swords, too, that the holy Pacifico saw laid crosswise upon you, piercing your heart, and your appearance uplifted in the air with arms outstretched in the manner of a cross, while the holy Anthony was preaching on the title of the Cross, as that angelic man, Monaldo, saw; these are all truly shown and proved to have been seen, not in imaginations of the brain, but by revelation from Heaven. Now, finally, that vision that was promised you towards the end of your life, that is, the exalted image of the seraph, and the lowly image of Christ shown together kindling you inwardly and marking you outwardly like another angel ascending from the sunrise, with the seal of the living God in you, gives a confirmation of faith to those visions, and likewise receives from them a witness to its own truth. By these seven appearances of the cross of Christ in you and about you, marvellously set forth and shown in order of time, you have attained, as though by six steps, to the seventh, where you make an end, and rest. For the cross of Christ was at the outset of your conversion both set before you, and taken up by you, and then as you made progress in your conversion, it was unceasingly sustained by you throughout your most holy life, and was shown as an example to others with such clearness and certainty that it demonstrates that at the end you arrived at the summit of gospel perfection; thus no one who is truly devout will reject this showing forth of Christ-like wisdom written in your mortal dust, no one who is a true believer will impeach it, no one who is truly humble will lightly esteem it, seeing that it is truly the work of God.

Eucharistic Hymns of THOMAS AQUINAS

HYMN FOR THE BLESSED SACRAMENT

The Word at God's right hand came
 forth,
And shining still as God on high,
Descended to the gloom of earth,
For man's redemption doomed to die.

Betrayed by one He loved, and led
To cruel death at treason's hand,
Upon the latest eve, He fed
With His own flesh the chosen band.

He giveth in its twofold kind
The saving flesh, the cleansing blood,
That every man His love may find,
And fill his soul with heavenly food.

Born man, He makes Himself our kin,
He gives His body at the board,
He dies and is the price of sin,
He reigns, and is our sweet reward.

O fount of life! O saving host,
That Heaven's high door has open laid,
War presses hard, our hope is lost
Without Thy strength and powerful aid.

Omnipotent Trinity,
To Thee be endless glory given;
Grant us eternal life with Thee
In our sweet fatherland of Heaven.

THE NEW PASCH

Sing, my tongue, the saving story,
Earth's redeeming mystery sing;
Sing the blood, that fount of glory,
Shed by man's all gracious king,
Blessed be the womb that bore Thee,
Thou that camest, our hope to bring

Given while yet the young creation
Sang with all the stars of morn,
Jesus came for our salvation,

From a stainless virgin born;
And His closing ordination
Doth the world with love adorn.

At the paschal table leaning
He, beside His chosen band,
Words of wonder intervening,
While He closed the law's command
Kept the pasch with newer meaning,
Gave Himself with His own hand,

By His word the bread He breaketh
To His very flesh he turns;
In the chalice which he taketh,
Man the cleansing blood discerns,
Faith to loving bosoms maketh
Clear the mystic truth she learns.

Let us then this rite of wonder
With our prostrate souls adore;
Let each ancient law surrender
To the Christ for ever more,
To the saviour sweet and tender,
Fount of grace, of love the store.

To the Father's glory leading,
Sound the holy jubilee;
To the Son, our sorrows heeding,
Sing the love that made us free,
To the Lord from both proceeding
Let the self-same praises be.

MORNING HYMN FOR CORPUS CHRISTI

Let joy abound with us on every side,
The sacred feast proclaiming far
and wide;
Come, let our souls, renewed in love,
arise,
In thought, word, action, purged and
purified.

We celebrate the supper of that night,
When Christ Himself, the Lord of love
and light,
Lamb and unleavened bread, gave to
the twelve
His body, and fulfilled the ancient rite.

Our souls in joy receive His solemn
word,
The lamb of God, the bread of life,
the Lord,
His body broke and gave to each
and all,
God's flesh by God's hand given at the
board.

Thus breaking to the sorrowing ones
the bread,
He took and blessed the chalice, and
He said:
"Take ye the cup and drink; this is
my blood,
That unto man's redemption shall be
shed."

So did the Christ the sacrifice ordain,
And gave His priests the duty to
maintain.
The rite; 'tis theirs alone to take and give
That love that ever shall with man remain.

The bread of angels is to man restored;
All figures end in Heaven's sublime
reward;
O wondrous thought! the poor, the weak,
the low
Feast on the body of the living Lord.

Thou triune deity, to Thee we pray,
Honoured upon the altar day by day,
Visit our souls, and by Thy holy light
Lead us to Heaven, and be Thy paths our
way.

HYMN FOR PRIVATE MEDITATION

Devoutly I adore Thee, O my Lord,
Who art concealed in figures at the board;
To Thee my heart bows down in voiceless
faith;
I see Thee not, but I believe Thy word.

Sight, touch and taste are easily deceived;
Thy word alone can safely be believed;
I grant, O Son of God, whate'er to me
Thou sayest; in Thee have I all faith
achieved.

Upon the cross was Thy divinity
Concealed, nor here Thy human form
we see,
Yet I, in faith confessing, seek Thee, Lord,
Like the repentant thief upon the tree.

I do not ask, as Thomas did, dear Lord,
To see Thy wounds; sufficient is Thy word;
O, fill my soul with firmer faith, that still
In hope and love with Thee it may accord.

O sweet memorial of the saviour's death,
True bread that brings to man the living breath,
Grant that my soul Thy holy law may know,
And live with Thee in everlasting faith.

A pitying pelican, dear Jesus, be;
Save by the blood Thou sheddest on the tree,
My starving soul, Thy precious blood, whereof
One drop from every crime the world can free.

Jesus, whom here in figures I behold,
I hunger for the time to see unrolled
The veil from Thy sweet features; let me be
Blest with the vision in Thy halls of gold.

HYMN FOR HOLY COMMUNION

O food of life eternal!
O bread of choirs supernal!
O manna from on high!
Fill all that hunger for Thee;
To seekers, who adore Thee,
Thy sweetness ne'er deny.

We seek Thy holy dwelling,
O fount of love, outwelling
From Jesus' tender heart;
Lord, bring Thy cup of healing
To all before Thee kneeling;
Our hope, our life Thou art.

O Jesus, saviour tender,
To Thee, the bread, we render
All reverence and all love;
Lord, lead our lives before Thee,
To see Thee and adore Thee
In vision clear above.

SEQUENCE FOR CORPUS CHRISTI

Sing aloud, O Zion, praising
Christ, thy royal shepherd, raising
Hymns of love and songs of joy;
Let the music sound forever,
Never ceasing, tiring never,
All thy powers of praise employ.

Lo, the theme of all thanksgiving,
Vivifying bread and living,
On the holy altar shown!
Yea, the selfsame bread of Heaven,
At the sacred supper given
To the twelve by Christ the Son.

Sing aloud in song sonorous,
Sing His praise in swelling chorus,
Sing in love and sweet accord;
Men of every race and nation
Hold the feast of Christ's creation,
Founded by His holy word.

Lo, the king upon his table
Lays a pasch more new and stable,
Ending every ancient rite;
Older laws give place to newer,
Shadows fly, and worship truer
Cometh with the wondrous light.

And today, as Christ ordaineth,
To his memory still remaineth
Joy, descending from above,
Still remain for our salvation
Bread and wine in consecration,
Making earth a home of love.

To the faithful Jesus giveth,
In His love, this truth that liveth,
To His blood is changed the wine;
Bread unto His body turneth;
Man by living faith discerneth
All the mystery divine.

Here, two different species under,
Hides in signs awaking wonder,
Christ's best gift, most excellent,
From His flesh and blood He giveth
Food and drink; in each He liveth
Whole within the sacrament.

Never by partaking groweth
Less the gift which He bestoweth,
Comes to all the sweet reward;
Whether single or in union,
Few or thousands at communion,
Every soul receives the Lord,

And the good and bad receive Him,
They who doubt and who believe Him;
But with what a different end!
To the worthy soul, salvation;
To the impenitent, damnation, –
Death to foe and life to friend.

Though the sacrament ye sever
Into fragments, fear ye never,
In each part remaineth ever
What the whole contained before;
In the sign alone obtaineth
Change; but as the Lord ordaineth,
He, the signified, remaineth
Whole and perfect evermore.

Lo, the bread of angels, bearing
Strength to souls in sorrow wearing,
With the sons of mercy sharing,
Not the unregenerate;
Food prefigured and foretold in
Sacred signs and symbols olden,
Bringing unto man the golden
Hour of glory consecrate.

Gentle Jesus, shepherd tender,
Bread of life, in mercy render
Peace, and blessed hope engender;
Saviour, be our sure defender,
Make us worthy of Thy love;
Thou all-knowing and all-heeding
Save Thy flock with care and feeding;
Let us follow in Thy earnest pleading,
Hear us in our earnest pleading,
Give us to the fold above.

The Golden Legends of JACOBUS DE VORAIGNE

OF SAINT SEBASTIAN

St Sebastian was a man of great faith, a good Christian, and was born in Narbonne, and was later taught and learned doctrine in the city of Milan. He was so well loved by Diocletian and Maximian, emperors of Rome, that they made him a duke, and wanted him with them always. He wore the habit of a knight, and was girded with a girdle of gold. All this Sebastian did not do for jollity nor because he dreaded death, nor because he wished to die for the love of Jesus Christ. He did it in order to strengthen the Christians in their belief when they were threatened with physical torment and tempted to deny the faith.

It happened that two German brothers, Marcus and Marcellianus, very Christian men and noble of lineage, were taken and compelled by the emperor to worship and sacrifice to idols. They were given thirty days in prison before the sentence of death for their Christian faith would be carried out, during which time they should counsel and advise themselves whether they would sacrifice to the idols or die, and their friends might come to them in prison to entreat and turn them from their faith. Their parents and friends came to them, and said: "Why this hardness of heart? Do you despise the old age of your father and mother? You bring them new sorrows; the great pain that they had at your birth was not as great as the sorrow that they have now, and the sorrow that your mother suffers is beyond words. Therefore, dear friends, we beg you to remedy these sorrows, and to leave the error of the Christians." After these words their mother came to them, crying and tearing her hair and showing her breasts, and said, weeping: "Alas! I am despairing and unhappy that I may lose my two sons whom I have suckled and nourished so sweetly. You, fair son", she said to one of them, "were sweet and charming to me." And to the other, she said: "You were like your father. Alas! to what mischief and sorrow am I delivered by you, my fair sons; I lose my sons who by their own will choose to die. My most dear children, have mercy on your sorrowful mother. I am in such great distress and such great misery for you; O poor wretch that I am, what shall I do if I lose my two sons? I see them go to death by their own free will. Alas! to desire death is a new thing." Then their father was brought between two servants, who showed his grey hair to his sons, and cried: "Alas! I, sorrowful wretch, come to the death of my two sons, who will die by their own agreement. O my dearest sons who were the sustenance and staff of my old age, sweetly nourished and taught and learned in science, what is this open foolishness and passion that comes on you and causes you to love and desire death? There was never such folly nor passion seen in the world. O, my friends, come forth and help me to weep for my children, you who have hearts of pity. Weep, old and young, and I will weep so much that I will not see the death of my sons."

While the father was weeping and saying these things, the wives of the two sons came, carrying their children. Weeping and crying, they said: "See, our dear husbands, in what state you leave us and your children! Alas, what will become of us, our children, and our goods, that shall be lost for your sake? Have you hearts of iron? How can you be so hard, so unnatural and so cruel as to despise your father and mother, refuse all your friends, chase away your wives, deny and forsake your children, and voluntarily deliver yourselves to die so shamefully?" Then Marcus and Marcellianus were so ashamed and moved that they were almost turned from the Christian faith, and would for the sake of their parents and friends have sacrificed to the idols.

However, at these words, St Sebastian seeing them in such distress, and their determination so softened, came to them and said: "O noble knights of Jesus Christ, wise and hardy, who have come to the victory and now go back; for a few beseeching words, you will lose the enduring victory. Do not lose everlasting life for the entreating words of women; be an example to other Christians and be strong in the faith, address your hearts to the world above, and do not lose your crown for the weeping of your wives and children. They that weep now would be glad and joyous if they knew what you know. They believe that there is no other life but this which they see before their eyes, which after this life shall come to nothing: if they knew what is that other life without death and without heaviness, in which is joy everlasting, without doubt they would hurry to go with you and would reject this life as nothing.

"For it is full of misery and is also false, and from the beginning has deceived all who trust in the world. Daily more harm is done in this life, for it makes gluttons and lechers; it makes thieves kill, and the angry cruel, and the liars false and deceivable; it puts discord between married people, and debate among the peaceable; through the world comes all malice and felony. This evil is done in this life by those who expect to live long, and when they have spent their life doing evil, then she gives to them her daughter, death perpetual. That is the reward that the life of this world gives to her servants, who depart from it dispossessed, and take nothing with them but their sins."

After this St Sebastian turned to the parents and friends of Marcus and Marcellianus and said to them: "O friends, that is the life of this world which deceives you in such ways that you turn your friends from the everlasting life; you trouble your children by your foolish words and your false weepings so that they should not come to the company of Heaven, to permanent honour and the fellowship of the celestial emperor. If they should assent to your appeal, they would be with you only a little while, and then would depart from your company and you would see them in torments that would never end. There cruel flame devours the souls of disbelievers and worshippers of idols, dragons eat the lips of the cursed, and the serpents destroy the evil. There nothing is heard but wailings, weepings, and horrible cries of souls which burn continually in the fire of Hell, and shall burn forever without dying. Allow your sons to escape their torments, and think how you may let them suffer death for the love of Jesus Christ. Remember that they, when they have departed from you, will make ready your place and your mansion in Heaven, where you and your children may be in perpetual joy."

When St Sebastian, who was in the habit of a knight clad with a mantle and girt with a girdle of gold, had said these words there came a great light, in which appeared a youngling clad with a white mantle among seven angels. He gave to St Sebastian peace saying: "You shall always be with me." The wife of Nicostratus, named Zoe, in whose house Marcus and Marcellianus were in prison, saw this. She had been mute and dumb for six years but she understood what St Sebastian had said, and she had seen the light about him, and she fell down at his feet and by signs of her hands made prayers to him. After St Sebastian knew that she had lost her speech, he said to her: "If I am the servant of Jesus Christ and if all that I have said is true, then I pray that He will render to you your speech again who opened the mouth of Zechariah the prophet." And this woman cried out, saying: "The word that you have said is very true. Blessed be you and the word of your mouth, and blessed be all they that through you believe in Jesus Christ, the Son of God, for I have certainly seen seven angels before you holding a book in which was written all that you have said. Cursed be they that do not believe you." And Nicostratus, and the father and mother, and all the friends of Marcellianus and Marcus, received the Christian faith. Seventy-eight persons, men, women and children were baptised in all by Polycarp the priest. For ten days they abode together in prisons and prayers, and thanked God for His benefits.

Among them was Tranquillinus, father of the holy martyrs, who had had gout in his feet and hands for eleven years. As soon as Polycarp had baptised him he became as whole and sound in his feet and hands as a child. After the ten days, Agrestin and Chromatius, provosts of Rome, had Tranquillinus brought before them, and demanded how his sons were advised and counselled. He answered: "You did much good when you gave them respite, for in the meantime they that should have died have found life and joy." The provost supposed that his sons had been turned, and said: "Tomorrow I shall see how your sons will make sacrifice to the idols, by whom you and they may dwell in peace." Tranquillinus said: "Gentle man, if you will justly adore and work about me and my sons you will find that the name of Christian men is of great virtue." And the provost said: "Tranquillinus, are you insane?" He answered: "I have been out of my senses, but as soon as I believed in Jesus Christ I received health of body and soul." The provost said: "I see well that the respite of your sons has brought you into error." Tranquillinus said: "Do you know from what works come error?"

The provost bade him say, and he said: "The first error is to leave the way of life and go by the way of death to dispute that men who are dead are gods and to adore their images made of wood and stone." The provost said: "Then there are no gods that we adore?" Tranquillinus said: "It is read in our books what kind of men they were that you adore for gods, how evilly they lived, and how wickedly they died. Saturnus, whom you worship for a god, was lord of Crete and ate the flesh of his children. is he not one of your gods? And Jupiter, his son, whom you adore, slew his father, and took his sister for his wife. What evil was this? It is you who are in great error, adoring this cursed man and saying to the image of stone: 'Thou art my god', and to the piece of wood: 'Help me'."

The provost said: "If there is only one, invisible, God that you adore, why then do you adore Jesus Christ whom the Jews crucified?" Tranquillinus answered: "If you knew of a ring of gold in which was a precious stone lying in the mire of a valley, you would send your servants to find it. And if they could not lift it you would take off your clothes of silk, put on a coarse coat and help to unearth the ring, and make a great feast." The provost said: "Why have you put forward this proposition now?" Tranquillinus answered: "To show you that we adore only one God." The provost said: "What do you understand by this ring?" Tranquillinus said: "The gold of the ring is the human body, and the precious stone signifies the soul enclosed in the body. The body and the soul make a man like the gold and precious stone make a ring, and much more precious is the man to Jesus Christ than the ring is to you. You send your servants to take up this ring out of the dirt or mire, and they cannot.

"So did God send the prophets into this world to draw the human lineage out of the ordure of sin, and they were unable to do it. As you should leave your rich clothes and clothe yourself with a coarse coat, and would descend into the privy, and put your hands into foul ordure to take up the ring, so the majesty of God hid the light of the divinity by a carnal vestment. He took our human nature and clad Himself with it and descended from Heaven. He came here into the privy of this world, and put His hand into the ordure of our miseries by suffering hunger and thirst, and took us up out of the filth and washed us from our sins by the water of baptism. Thus he who despises you because you descend in a foul habit to take up the ring might well be put to death by you; and all that deny or despise Jesus Christ because He humbled Himself to save man may not escape the death of Hell."

The provost said: "I can see that these are just fables; you have taken respite for your sons, do you not know well that the emperor our lord is cruel towards Christian men?" Tranquillinus said: "It is folly to doubt human power more than divine power. They that are cruel to us may well torment our bodies but they cannot take Jesus Christ from our hearts." Then the provost put Tranquillinus in the hands of the sergeant, saying: "Show me the medicine by which you are healed of your gout, and I shall give you gold without number." Tranquillinus said: "You know that much evil will come to them that sell and buy the grace of God, but if you want to be cured of gout, believe in Jesus Christ and you shall be as whole as I am." The provost said: "Bring him to me who has healed you." Tranquillinus went to Polycarp and told him all this, and brought him with St Sebastian to the provost.

Polycarp instructed the provost in the faith and prayed that he might have his health, and St Sebastian said that he must first deny his idols and give him licence to destroy them. Chromatius said that his servants should break up the idols but St Sebastian said: "They are afraid and dare not, and if the fiends hurt any of them on any occasion the misbelievers would say it was because of what they had done." So Polycarp and St Sebastian destroyed more than two hundred idols and then they said to the provost: "Why have you not received health now that we have broken the idols? Either you still have your misbelief or you still have some idols." And Chromatius showed them a chamber which was as light as though it were lit by stars, on which his father had spent two hundred pois of gold, and St Sebastian said: "As long as you keep this whole you will never have health."

Chromatius then agreed that the chamber should be destroyed, but Tiburtius, his son, a noble young man, said plainly that so great a work should be preserved. "However, I will not be against my father's health," he said, "so I will ordain that there are two furnaces of fire burning, and then I wish you to destroy this work. If my father has his health, I shall be content. If he does not, I shall order you to be burnt in the furnaces." St Sebastian said: "Be it as you have said." Forthwith they went and destroyed the chamber, and in the meanwhile the angel of our Lord appeared to the provost and said his health was given to him. He was whole, and ran after the angel to kiss his feet, but he denied him for he had not received baptism. And then he and Tiburtius and one thousand four hundred of their family were baptised.

Then Zoe was taken by the misbelievers and tormented for so long that she gave up the ghost. When Tranquillinus heard this he came forth and said: "Alas! Why do we live so long? Women go before us to the crown of martyrdom." Within a few days he was stoned to death. And Tiburtius was commanded to go barefoot upon burning coals or else make sacrifice to the idols, and he made the sign of the cross upon the coals and walked on them, saying: "Methinks I tread upon rose flowers in the name of our Lord Jesus Christ." To which Fabian the provost said: "It is not unknown to us that your Jesus Christ is a teacher of sorcery." Tiburtius replied: "Hold your peace, you cursed wretch, for you are not worthy to a name so worthy, so holy and so sweet a name." The provost was very angry and commanded that Tiburtius's head be smitten off, and so he was martyred.

Then Marcus and Marcellianus were sorely tormented and bound to a pillar, and as they were so bound they said: "Lo! How good and joyful it is, brethren, to dwell together." The provost said: "You wretches, do away with your madness and deliver yourselves." They said: "We were never so well fed, we would that you would let us stand here until the spirits depart from our bodies." And then the provost commanded that they should be pierced through the body with spears, and so Marcus and Marcellianus fulfilled their martyrdom.

After this St Sebastian was reported to the emperor of Rome as a Christian, wherefore Diocletain made him come before him, and said: "I have always loved you well and have made you master of my palace; how then have you been Christian secretly against my health, and in spite of our gods?" St Sebastian replied: "Always have I worshipped Jesus Christ for your health and for the sake of Rome and I think to pray and demand help of idols of stone is a great folly." With these words Diocletain was enraged, and commanded St Sebastian to be led to the field and there to be bound to a stake and shot. The archers shot at him until he was as full of arrows as an urchin is full of pricks, and left him there for dead.

The night after a Christian woman came to take St Sebastian's body and to bury it, but she found him alive and brought him to her house and took charge of him until he was better. Many Christian men came to him and counselled him to leave the place, but St Sebastian was strengthened and stood upon a step which the emperor would pass by, and said to him: "The bishops of the idols deceive evilly you who accuse the Christian men of being contrary to the common profit of the city, who pray for your estate and for the health of Rome." Diocletian said: "Are you not Sebastian, whom we commanded to be shot to death?" And St Sebastian said: "Our Lord has rendered to me life to the end so that I might tell you that you persecute Christian men wickedly and cruelly." Then Diocletian had him brought into prison in his palace and beaten sorely with stones until he died. The tyrants threw his body into a great privy, so that the Christian men might make no feast of burying his body, or of his martyrdom. But St Sebastian appeared afterwards to St Lucy, a glorious widow, and said to her: "In such a privy will you find my body hanging on a hook, which is not defouled with any ordure. When you have washed it, you will bury it at the catacombs by the apostles." And the same night she and her friends accomplished all that Sebastian had commanded her. He was martyred in the year of our Lord two hundred and eighty-seven.

St Gregory tells in the first book of his Dialogues that a woman of Tuscany who was newly wedded was prayed for to go with other women to the dedication of the church of St Sebastian. The night before, she was so moved in her flesh that she could not abstain from her husband, and in the morning, having greater shame of men than of God, she went there. As she entered the oratory where the relics of St Sebastian were, the fiend took her and tormented her, before all the people. The priest took the coverture off the altar and covered her, and the devil then assailed the priest. The woman's friends took her to the enchanters so that the fiend might be exorcised, but as soon as they began the enchantment a legion of devils entered into her, that is six thousand six hundred and sixty-six, and vexed her more sharply than before. A holy man named Fortunatus healed her by his prayers.

The stories of the Lombards say that in the time of King Gumbet all Italy was smitten with a great pestilence and this pestilence was mostly at Rome and Pavia. Then the good angel was seen visibly by many, and an evil angel following, bearing a staff which he used to smite and slay, and as many strokes as he smote a house so were that number of dead borne out of it. At last it was shown to one of the angels by God's grace that the plague would not end until they made an altar to St Sebastian at Pavia. This they did in the church of St Peter and then the plague ceased. From Rome relics of St Sebastian were brought, and St Ambrose in his preface said this: "O Lord, the blood of Thy blessed martyr St Sebastian was shed for the confession of Thy name. He has shown that in infirmity Thy marvels profit virtue, they give benefit to our studies, and to them not steadfast to Thee they give aid and help. Let us pray to this holy martyr St Sebastian that he may pray to our Lord for our delivery from all pestilence and from sudden death that we may come to everlasting joy and glory in Heaven."

Of SAINT GEORGE, MARTYR

St George was a knight and born in Cappadocia. One day he came to the province of Libya, a city called Silene. By this city was a pond like a sea, in which was a dragon which envenomed the whole country. Once people were assembled to slay him but when they saw him they fled. And when the dragon came near the city he venomed the people with his breath, so they gave him every day two sheep to eat in order that he would not harm the people. When the sheep failed, a man and a sheep were given daily. Then was an ordinance made in the town that there should be taken a draw of the children and young people in the town, and each one, were he gentle or poor, should be delivered when the lot fell on him or her. So it was that many of those in the town were delivered to the dragon. Then the lot fell upon the king's daughter, about which he was exceedingly unhappy and he said to the people: "For the love of the gods take gold and silver and all that I have, and let me have my daughter." They said: "How sir! You have made and ordained the law, and our children are now dead. Your daughter shall be given, or else we shall burn you and your houses."

When the king saw that he might do no more, he began to weep, and said to his daughter: "Now I shall never see your wedding." He returned to the people and demanded eight days' respite, which they granted to him. When the eight days had passed, they came to him and said: "You see that the city perishes." Then the king arrayed his daughter as though she were to be wedded, embraced her and kissed her and gave her his benediction, and led her to the place where the dragon was.

While she was there St George passed by, and when he saw the lady he demanded of her what she was doing there. She said: "Go your way, fair young man, so that you do not perish also." He asked further, "Why do you weep?" When she saw that he was determined to know, the king's daughter told him that she was to be delivered to the dragon. Then St George said: "Fair daughter, doubt you nothing, for I shall help you in the name of Jesus Christ." She said: "For God's sake, go, knight, go your way, and abide not with me, for you cannot deliver me." As they spoke together the dragon appeared and came quickly towards them. St George was on his horse, and he drew out his sword and garnished the dragon with the sign of the cross and rode hardily against him. He smote him with his spear and hurt him badly and threw him to the ground. And afterwards St George said to the maid: "Deliver to me your girdle and bind it around the neck of the dragon and be not afraid." When she had done this the dragon followed her as if he were a meek and gentle beast. Then she led him into the city, and the people fled to the mountains and valleys, and said: "Alas, alas! We shall all be dead." But St George said to them: "Doubt you nothing. Believe in God and Jesus Christ and be baptised and I shall slay the dragon." Then the king was baptised, and all his people, and St George slew the dragon and smote off his head, and commanded that he should be thrown into the fields, and four carts with oxen drew him out of the city.

Then were fifteen thousand men baptised, without women and children, and the king made a church there of our Lady and of St George, in which still springs up a healing fountain of living water. After this the king offered St George as much money as might be numbered but he refused all and commanded that it should be given to poor people for God's sake. He proposed to the king four things, that he should have charge of the churches, that he should honour the priests and hear their services diligently, and that he should have pity on the poor people, and afterwards he kissed the king and departed.

Now it happened that in the time of the emperors Diocletian and Maximian there was so great a persecution of Christian men that within a month at least twenty-two thousand were martyred. Some became so frightened that they denied and forsook God and made sacrifice to the idols. When St George saw this, he left the habit of a knight and sold all that he had and gave it to the poor, and took the habit of a Christian man and went into the middle of the heathens and began to cry: "All the gods of the heathens and gentiles are devils, my God made the heavens and is very God." Then the provost said to him: "Why is it that you say our gods are devils? And say to us who you are and what your name is." He answered and said: "I am named George, I am a gentleman, a knight of Cappadocia, and have left all to serve the God of Heaven."

The provost tried to draw him into his faith with fair words, and when he could not succeed he raised him onto gallows; and beat him so much with great staves and rods of iron that his body was badly hurt. Afterwards he took brands of iron and joined them to his sides, and his bowels which then appeared he rubbed with salt, and then he sent him to prison. But our Lord appeared to him the same night with great light and comforted him sweetly and from this great consolation St George took such encouragement that he feared no torment they might make him suffer. When Dacian, the provost, saw that he might not overcome him, he called his enchanter and said to him: "I see that these Christian people doubt our torments." The enchanter took strong venom and mixed it with wine, and invoked the names of his false gods, and gave it to St George to drink. St George took it and made the sign of the cross on it, and drank it without harming himself. Then the enchanter made it stronger than it had been with venom, and gave it to him to drink, and it still did not harm him. When the enchanter saw that, he knelt at the feet of St George and prayed to him that he would make him Christian.

When Dacian knew that he was becoming Christian he went to smite off his head. And afterwards in the morning he had St George set between two wheels which were full of swords, sharp and cutting on both sides. After a while the wheels broke and St George escaped without hurt. Then Dacian commanded that he be put in a cauldron full of molten lead, but when St George entered into it by virtue of our Lord it seemed that he was in a bath well at ease. Dacian, seeing this, began to assuage his wrath, and to flatter St George with fair words, saying to him: "George, the patience of our gods is great to you who have blasphemed them, and shown to them great contempt. Then fair and right sweet son, I pray you that you return to our law and make sacrifice to the idols, and leave your folly, and I shall raise you to great honour and worship." St George began to smile, and said to him: "Why did you not say so at the beginning? I am ready to do as you say." Then was Dacian glad and had it cried all over the town that the people should assemble to see George make sacrifice which so much had striven against. The city was arrayed and feast kept throughout the town, and all came to the temple to see him.

When St George was on his knees, and they supposed that he was worshipping the idols, he prayed to our Lord God of Heaven that He would destroy the temple and the idol in honour of His name, to make the people converted. And fire descended from Heaven and burnt the temple and the idols, and their priests, and then the earth opened and swallowed all the cinders and ashes that were left. Then Dacian had St George brought before him, and said to him: "What are the evil deeds that you have done, and the great untruths you have told?" Then said St George to him: "Ah, sir, believe it not, but come with me and see how I shall sacrifice." Dacian said to him: "I see well your fraud, you will make the earth swallow me as you have the temple and my gods." St George replied: "O villain, tell me how your gods can help you when they cannot help themselves!"

Dacian was so angry that he said to his wife: "I shall die of anger if I cannot surmount and overcome this man." She said in reply: "Evil and cruel tyrant! Do you not see the great virtue of the Christian people? I said to you that you should do no harm to them for their God fights for them, and you know well that I will become Christian." Then was Dacian much abashed and said to her: "Will you be Christian?" He took her by the hair, and beat her cruelly. Then she demanded of St George: "What may I become because I am not christened?" The blessed George answered: "Doubt you nothing, fair daughter, for you shall be baptised in your blood." She began to worship our Lord Jesus Christ, and so she died and went to Heaven. On the morrow, Dacian gave his sentence that St George should be drawn through all the city, and after his head should be smitten off. St George prayed to our Lord that all they that desired any favour might get it in the name of our Lord God, and a voice came from Heaven which said that what St George desired was granted. And after he had made his orison his head was smitten off, about the year of our Lord two hundred and eighty-seven. When Dacian went home from the place where St George was beheaded, fire fell down from Heaven upon him and burnt him and all his servants.

Gregory of Tours tells that there were some who bore relics of St George who came to a certain oratory in a hospital, and on the morning when they went to depart they could not move the door until they had left there part of their relics. It is also found in the history of Antioch that when the Christian men went overseas to conquer Jerusalem, one, a right fair young man, appeared to a priest of the host and counselled him that he should carry with him a little of the relics of St George, for he was conductor of the battle. He was so insistent that the priest took some. And when they had besieged Jerusalem and dare not mount or go up on the walls, because of the defence of the Saracens, they saw what appeared to be St George with white arms and a red cross. He led them on to the walls and so was Jerusalem taken with his help.

And between Jerusalem and Port Jaffa, by a town called Ramys, is a chapel of St George which is now desolate and uncovered, and therein dwell Christian Greeks. In the said chapel lies the body of St George, but not the head. And there lie his father and mother and uncle, not in the chapel but under the wall of the chapel; and the keepers will not allow pilgrims to enter the chapel unless they pay two ducats, so few come in but offer outside instead at an altar. And there are seven years and seven lents of pardon; and the body of St George lies in the middle of the choir of the said chapel, and in his tomb is a hole into which a man put his hand. And when a Saracen who is mad is brought there, he may put his head in the hole and be made pefectly whole, and have his wit again.

The blessed and holy martyr St George is patron of the realm of England and the cry of men of war. In the worship of him is founded the noble order of the garter. Also a noble college in the castle of Windsor in which the heart of St George which Sigismund, the emperor of Almayne, brought and gave for a great and precious relic of King Harry V. The college is nobly endowed to the honour and worship of Almighty God and his blessed martyr St George. Let us pray to him that he be special protector and defender of the English realm.

Prayer of Saint RICHARD OF CHICHESTER

DAY BY DAY

Thanks be to Thee, Lord Jesus Christ,
for all the benefits which Thou hast won
for us, for all the pains and insults
which Thou has borne for us. O most
merciful redeemer, friend and
brother, may we know Thee more
clearly, love Thee more dearly,
and follow Thee more nearly, day by day.

JOHN TAULER: Mary Magdalene

"Martha, Martha, thou art careful and art troubled about many things. But one thing is necessary; Mary hath chosen the best part, which shall not be taken away from her."

In our dear Lord Jesus Christ, and in His holy and fruitful coming, I greet you, faithful children of God, who are assembled here to learn of the divine word, and of the best way to eternal salvation. Amen.

Dearly beloved and elect, listen to the voice of God in your hearts, earnestly and diligently, so that you may not be led astray and blinded by transitory things and your own natural tendencies. If you heartily desire to become the dearest friends and disciples of our beloved Lord Jesus Christ, you must rid yourselves of all that pertains to the creature, and especially free yourselves, as much as possible, of all that can be rightly and honestly called necessary. You must look to Him alone as the source of all things, for He needs the help of none. You must keep yourselves cut off and freed from all superfluous and unnecessary conversation and outward delight in human beings, and from all images, both external and internal, that are pleasing in any way to the natural man, or of which you are conscious. You must do this, like the beloved Mary Magdalene; so that God may work His wonderful works in you, according to His dear will, and may pour out upon you His fervent, ardent love and divine grace, that you may acknowledge, as you fall at His sacred feet, that all that may befall you is needful and His divine decree.

Now mark, if we were inwardly conscious of it, we should well understand how very often we may be blinded, to our own disadvantage, by unnecessary and external works of love, which prevent our perceiving the divine inspiration and our own infirmities. Although such works may have been done in love, both great and godlike, and may not be really evil in themselves, still they are not that which is best and most perfect. Our Lord Jesus Christ praised Mary Magdalene for her absolute separation from all such things, when He said: "She has chosen the best part" and He rebuked Martha, because she was too careful in her anxiety and great and loving service, for she loved Him and His chosen disciples with ardent, fervent love; and that in itself was right and proper. Therefore, if we especially desire to receive from God consolation and teaching that will be useful to us and bear fruit in us, and a true and perfect separation from all needful things, both bodily and spiritual, it is very necessary that we should decide at once to cut ourselves off from all unnecessary works and habits, in our words, works and all things that are more than absolutely necessary, either in bodily or spiritual matters, so following the teachings of God and of our own consciences. It is especially necessary that we should shun and flee from all those persons who desire to lead us astray, and suggest thoughts to us of outward things, however holy those persons may be, or may seem to be; for they are not our true friends in sincerity and truth, whether they be father confessors or whoever they may be, either spiritual or worldly-minded people. We shall never find God anywhere so perfectly, so fruitfully and so truly as in retirement and in the wilderness; like the Blessed Mother of God, St John the Baptist, and Mary Magdalene, and other saints and patriarchs. They all fled from the world, from society, and all the cares and anxieties of the creature, and went into the forests and into the desert, or wherever they could find the greatest solitude.

O! much intercourse and society, and much outward conversation and necessary business, lead up to an evil old age, and drive out God, however good our intentions may have been. For, when we fill our hearts with the creature, and with strange useless images, God must of necessity remain outside, neither does He desire to enter there. A barrel that has been filled with refuse or with decaying matter cannot afterwards be used for good, generous wine or any other pure drink. O! truly, we may turn where and to whoever we will in this life, and, in all outward things, we shall find nothing but falsity, unfaithfulness and dissension. Where we imagine we shall be able to seek and to find great consolation and delight, we lose entirely all inward consolation, and are robbed entirely of that peace of mind which it had taken us a long time to attain in solitude. We cannot regain it, and we become greatly discontented, offending by unnecessary, superfluous and untrue words; we waste our time, and do many other things which cause our hearts to grow cold and extinguish our love. Conscience pricks us, and we are easily stirred up and urged on to impatience and anger. Woe be to us! If we could only realise this, we should find that in God only can we have peace and consolation, or truly perfect joy and delight.

Let us turn to God with all our hearts, and wait for Him in meekness and patience, as did the holy prophets and patriarchs, in the Old Testament; for they indeed waited patiently for His coming in Hades, for many thousands of years before they were redeemed. O! surely, we ought to be more ready to wait for Him, when, for a time, He withdraws His consolation and sweetness, of which we are quite unworthy, and hides Himself from us. He thinks only of what is best and most useful for us, so that He may kindle and stir up our love and our longing for Him, ever more and more. For in His love and great mercy He neither wills nor desires to refuse or to take from us anything that is useful and necessary either in body or spirit; He knows surely what is best for us.

O God, how greatly we need Your mercy! for we are so foolish and senseless that we often allow little things to keep us back, imagining that we are pleasing God, when we sing His praise with many high-sounding words; though the words used by the Saviour and His dear disciples were short and simple. Or again, we think we are pleasing God and helping our neighbour by an unjustifiable waste of time and much outward sorrow. Or again, we think it is good and useful for us to carry on much unnecessary business and to delight in our fellow-creatures (however holy they may be or appear to be). Thus even the blessed form of our dear Lord Jesus Christ, and His faithful, fatherly and fruit-bringing presence, became harmful to His dear disciples and hindered them and led them astray, as He Himself said: "It is expedient for you that I go away: for if I do not go away, the Comforter will not come to you." Or again, we think we may have and hold many things with delight, and as our own, without spiritual harm; either temporal goods, company, familiar intercourse with relations or spiritual friends, while at the same time we are pleasing our dear Lord and continuing in His love; though He was despised, He was sorrowful and poor, and said Himself: "There is no man that hath left house, or brethren, or sisters, or father, or mother, or wife, or children, or land for my sake, but he shall receive a hundredfold now in this time, and in the world to come eternal life."

He says also in another place: "He who hateth not his father and mother and wife and children, and brethren and sisters, yea, and his own life also, he cannot be my disciple."

O God! Could we but see into the depths of the loving teaching of our dear Lord, we should surely acknowledge at once that all our life is unholy, and that it is not at all that which we imagine it to be.

If we ever are to attain to true divine peace, and be completely united with God, all that is not absolutely necessary, either bodily or spiritually, must be cast off; everything that could interpose to an unlawful extent between us and Him, and lead us astray; for He alone will be Lord in our hearts, and none other; for divine love can admit of no rival.

O! let us praise the death of our dear Lord Jesus Christ and his inestimable merit, and ponder on the short transitory nature of this miserable life, and the delusions of this faithless, treacherous and deceitful world. Remember how dangerous it is to hold intercourse with any, whether clergy or laity, and how short our time is here, and that we must be preparing for the day of our death which is ever drawing nearer. If you keep watch over your hearts, and listen for the voice of God and learn of Him, in one short hour you can learn more from Him than you could learn from man in a thousand years. Dear children, use this short but most precious time wisely and profitably; and let none cause you to err, not to deceive you, so that you may not, to your own disadvantage, neglect your own salvation. We may lose much of our worldly goods, but we may also recover them again, though they will be of no further use to us when this short fleeting life is over. But if we lose but one little hour of this precious time, or vainly waste it, we can never recover it again; and we shall be in need of it throughout eternity, and be deprived of the exceedingly great and eternal joy and reward, which we might otherwise have earned.

I fear, indeed, that there is great cause for anxiety, both on my account and on that of all those who cling too much to their fellow creatures, and who are led astray and needlessly troubled by asking, hearing and talking too much about strange and useless tales. It comes to pass, too, that when through His great and endless mercy God preserves us from great and coarse sins, He nevertheless allows us to persist in fruitless outward imaginings, in a cold, thoughtless, foolish state of blindness, so that we neither can make, nor desire to make, any progress towards a state of perfection, and shall have in consequence to endure the fires of purgatory. We are like foolish asses, which never learn any form of speech but their own braying, or seek any other comfort or sweetness but rough, tasteless thistles, while they have to endure scorn and many a hard and cruel blow, which they really do not deserve. Surely this is so, if we are not willing to give up outward attachments and distractions, simply for the sake of God and our own eternal salvation, yet we ought to be able to do so readily for the sake of that great peace of heart, which, even in this world, would be ours; and because we should be freed from much painful and unmerited oppression and perplexity. Truly, the man who wishes to prove himself always in the right, in everything that he does, sees, hears and discusses, and who will not give way and be silenced, will never be at peace with himself, and will have a barren, sullen and wandering mind; he will prey upon himself, even if he is left in peace by all, and is tried by no outward pressure. We must commend all that we possess both in body and spirit in full confidence to God, and allow Him to work in us according to His will; and then we shall attain perfect peace. He can guide and prepare us far better in all things, both bodily and spiritual, and for our own good both in body and spirit, if He finds that we have desired and sought honestly His praise and glory alone in all things. This indeed should suffice us; we need no longer be careworn or troubled about anything, either without or within, but must seek only to give ourselves into His keeping entirely, in all humility. If it seems good to Him, He can show us in many ways what we ought to do and what we ought to leave undone; for He only knows what is really needful for us, and He only desires that which is best for us, if we would only trust ourselves entirely to Him.

But we want to order our own ways, and to do that which we think best, just as we fancy and it pleases us, perhaps solely in the light of nature. We want to be wiser than God, who is the source of all wisdom, and we imagine that, could we but rid ourselves of this sorrow or of that person, or could we be at such and such a court or society, it would be to our profit and advantage. Truly, if we could but see it, we should find that the evil spirit willingly deceives us and leads our hearts astray, making us restless and discontented. Steadfastness is not only one of the sources of virtue, but also shares in all other virtues; therefore the evil one always endeavours, whenever he gets a chance, to prevent men from holding fast to this virtue. But if we strove more diligently to find him out, we should realise that we are seeking secretly and ignorantly by the light of nature. We imagine things, and lie to ourselves, and are ready to flee from the cross, and to cast it away, before God sees fit to remove it. Truly, this should not and ought not to be so; for our dear Lord, in His great love and mercy towards His chosen ones, afflicts and crucifies them unceasingly in this world, in many secret, strange ways, often unknown to them. He would not have them love anything too well in this life, so that evil spirits may never gain any power over them. Our dear Lord afflicts and crucifies one man in one way, and another man in another way; one more, another less, according to the needs of each, and according to the power of each to receive the grace of God, and to draw nearer to His own will in all things. Therefore we must be ready to suffer and submit, as much in one kind of suffering and need as in another, just as God sees fit to afflict us. We must not think at once that if we could have some really divine witness or testimony from God, or from His friends, that we then should be more at peace; for often, when we strive to avoid some slight suffering or discipline, we only fall into it all the more deeply.

Woe to us! Were we only not so foolish, but recognised instead how very much the smallest suffering or affliction purifies us and unites us to God, and brings us to God; how great our eternal reward will be, and how quickly it drives and chases away the evil spirit from us, so that he can have no power over us. Surely we should be ready to run miles to the cross, and should earnestly thank all those who in any way afflicted or tried us. We should turn towards the road that they take from real joy and thankfulness, and we should be glad, beyond all measure, that we had been able to find and to carry so heavy a cross. So did the holy apostle, St Andrew; he rejoiced exceedingly in the cross, and longed for it with fervent love and desire; because he craved in some measure to be like his God and Lord who was crucified for our sakes. Oh! even in this life how great and enduring is the reward that we might gain, if we only yielded ourselves wholly and joyfully to the will of God. Suffering and all kinds of affliction are indeed most precious and fruitful and make men so like Him, that our Lord will not leave any of His friends without suffering. For, rather than that His chosen ones should be undisciplined and unprepared, He is ready to create suffering out of nothing, and allows them to be tried by all sorts of irrational and dishonest things, that by means of them they may be prepared.

But, alas! in these times, we are altogether unworthy of these fruitful gifts of God; we are careless and unreceptive. We protect ourselves from them, and struggle against them as much as lies in our power; for we will not suffer anyone to try us or to afflict us either by word or deed. When anyone attacks us, we fly at him at once, like angry dogs; we assert ourselves, and excuse ourselves in words, or in our own minds, by thinking that we were right or wrong, and that we ought not to allow ourselves to be oppressed in any way. Alas! why is our nature so untamed, so wild and unmortified; and why are we so foolish? We ought to think of suffering and affliction as necessary for us, though we are unworthy of them, and we should at all times thankfully and humbly receive the good gifts of God in silence, humility, meekness and patience, like the upright and steadfast Job. We should always feel that we are guilty and suffer justly, however unjustly we may have been treated according to our own view; neither ought we to justify ourselves. Thus we may attain to true divine peace and stir up our fellow-men to all virtues. This would be more praiseworthy and well-pleasing to God, than any outward discipline that we could devise or carry out for ourselves.

Know this, my dear children, that if all our teachers were buried, and all our books were burned, we should still find enough teaching and contrast to ourselves in the life and example of our Lord Jesus Christ, wherever we might need it, if we would only diligently and earnestly learn how He went before, in silent patience, in gentleness, in adversity, in temptations of the evil one, in resignation, in scorn, in poverty, and in all manner of bitter suffering and pain. Surely, if we examined ourselves more often in this most useful and salutary mirror, we should more readily and joyfully suffer affliction and adversity, and be better able to overcome and resist temptations and evil suggestions, in whatever form they attacked us or encountered us. All suffering and all work would be much lighter and easier to suffer and to bear, and then all the things that we see and hear would tend only to our good.

For, if we wish to attain to great and fruitful peace in God, in nature, but not in this world, we must first diligently and earnestly learn to make the best of all things, and to endure, kindly and meekly, the behaviour of all kinds of men, their ways and customs; for they will often try and afflict us. The behaviour of other men and their ways will often vex and displease us; it will seem to us as though one person talked too much, another too little; one was too indolent, another too energetic; one erring in one way, another in another. Customs and fashions are so many and so various, that they assail us in many secret and unsuspected ways. We must learn to withstand them all vigorously, that they may take no root in us. By reason of weakness we cannot always keep our hearts free; yet we can at least vigorously check any outbreak in words, so that we shall neither condemn nor judge others, nor talk much of the lives and doings of others, either openly or in secret, however much we may be tempted. By acting thus we shall be great gainers; we shall be much less likely to break out in anger; for we shall be more inclined to peace and kindliness, and be better able to endure. Our dear Lord Jesus Christ set us an example by so gently and meekly allowing the traitor Judas, and all those who hated Him, to remain near Him, although He knew all the hatred and unfaithfulness that they bore towards Him, and for which He, who was Himself without guilt and sin, might justly have punished them. No one is so perfect that if he were to examine his own heart he would not find some sin of which he should rid himself, so that he might not justly reprove others.

Therefore, dear children, learn from my weaknesses to know your own, and rid yourselves of them. Take all my words, not my works, as from God; for I have studied them all in the book of my transgressions; take them earnestly to heart as a gentle warning and exhortation, not as an instruction; for I know that I need really to be taught by you and all men. He who does not occupy himself at home with a collected mind and pure heart in true humility cannot withstand temptation vigorously, nor acknowledge truth in all sincerity. Voluntary poverty is better than all the goods of this world, and union with God than Heaven and earth full of blessings given by the command of God. May the everlasting peace of God be with you throughout all time and eternity. Amen.

THOMAS À KEMPIS: How to Imitate Christ

BOOK I

"He that followeth Me, walketh not in darkness," saith the Lord. These are the words of Christ, by which we are admonished how we ought to imitate His life and manners, if we will be truly enlightened, and be delivered from all blindness of heart. Let therefore our chief endeavour be to meditate upon the life of Jesus Christ.

The doctrine of Christ exceedeth all the doctrines of holy men; and he that hath the

Spirit will find in it hidden manna. But it happens that many who often hear the gospel of Christ are yet but little affected, because they are void of the spirit of Christ. But whoever would fully and feelingly understand the words of Christ, must endeavour to conform his life wholly to the life of Christ.

What will it avail thee to dispute profoundly the Trinity, if thou be void of humility, and art thereby displeasing to the Trinity? Surely high words do not make a man holy and just; but a virtuous life maketh him dear to God. I would rather feel forgiveness, than understand its definition. If thou didst know the whole Bible by heart, and the sayings of all the philosophers, what would all that profit thee without the love of God and without grace? Vanity of vanities, and all is vanity, except to love God, and to serve Him only. This is the highest wisdom, by contempt of the world to tend towards the Kingdom of Heaven.

It is vanity therefore to seek after perishing riches, and to trust in them. It is also vanity to hunt after honours, and to climb to high degree. It is vanity to follow the desires of the flesh, and to labour for that for which thou must afterwards suffer more grievous punishment. Vanity it is, to wish to live long, and to be careless to live well. It is vanity to care only for this present life, and not to foresee those things which are to come. It is vanity to set thy love on that which speedily passeth away, and not to hasten to where everlasting joy abideth.

Call often to mind that proverb, "That the eye is not satisfied with seeing, nor the ear filled with hearing." Endeavour therefore to withdraw thy heart from the love of visible things, and to turn thyself to the invisible. For they that follow their sensuality, stain their own consciences, and lose the favour of God.

All men naturally desire to know; but of what use availeth knowledge without the fear of God? Surely, a humble husbandman who serveth God is better than a proud philosopher who, neglecting himself, laboureth to understand the course of the heavens. Whoever knoweth himself well, groweth more mean in his own conceit, and delighteth not in the praises of men. If I understood all things in the world, and had not charity, how would that help me in the sight of God, who will judge me according to my deeds?

Cease from an inordinate desire of knowing, for therein is much distraction and deceit. The learned are well-pleased to seem so to others, and to be accounted wise. There are many things, which to know profits the soul little or nothing: and he is very unwise, who is intent upon other things than those that may avail him for his salvation. Many words do not satisfy the soul; but a good life comforteth the mind and a pure conscience giveth great assurance in the sight of God.

How much the more thou knowest and how much the better thou understandest, so much the more grievously shalt thou therefore be judged, unless thy life be also more holy. Be not therefore extolled in thine own mind for any art or science which thou knowest, but rather let the knowledge given thee make thee more humble and cautious. If thou thinkest that thou understandest and knowest much; know also that there are many things more which thou knowest not. Affect not to be over-wise, but rather acknowledge thine own ignorance. Why wilt thou prefer thyself before others, since there be many more learned, and more skilful in the Scripture than thou art? If thou wish to know or learn anthing profitable, desire to be unknown, and to be little esteemed by man.

The highest and most profitable reading is the true knowledge and consideration of ourselves. It is great wisdom and perfection to esteem nothing of ourselves, and to think always well and highly of others. If thou shouldest see another sin openly, or commit some heinous offence, yet oughtest thou not to esteem the better of thyself; for thou knowest not how long thou shalt be able to remain in good estate. We are all frail, but thou oughtest to esteem none more frail than thyself.

Happy is he who is taught truth by itself, not by figures and words that pass away; but as it is in itself. Our own opinion and our own sense often deceives us, and they discern but little. What does it avail to cavil and dispute much about dark and hidden things; when for being ignorant of them we shall not be so much as reproved at the day of judgment? It is a great folly to neglect the things that are profitable and necessary, and give our minds to that which is curious and hurtful: we have eyes and see not.

And what have we to do with the dry notions of logicians? He to whom the eternal Word speaketh, is delivered from a world of unnecessary conceptions. From that one Word come all things, and all speak that one; and this is the beginning, which also speaketh unto us. No man without that Word understandeth or judgeth rightly. He to whom all things are one, he who reduceth all things to one, and seeth all things in one, may enjoy a quiet mind, and remain peaceable in God. O God, who art the truth, make me one with Thee in everlasting charity. It is tedious to me often to read and hear many thngs: In Thee is all that I would have and can desire. Let all doctors hold their peace; let all creatures be silent in Thy sight; speak Thou alone unto me.

The more the man is united within himself, and becometh inwardly simple and pure, so much the more and higher things doth he understand without labour; for he receiveth intellectual light from above. A pure, sincere, and stable spirit is not distracted, though it be employed in many works; for it works all to the honour of God, and inwardly being still and quiet, seeks not itself in any thing it doth. Who hinders and troubles thee more than the unmortified affections of thine own heart? A good and godly man disposeth within himself beforehand those things which he is outwardly to do: neither do they draw him according to the desires of an inordinate inclination, but he ordereth them according to the prescript of right reason. Who hath a greater combat than he that laboureth to overcome himself? This ought to be our endeavour, to conquer ourselves, and daily to wax stronger, and to make a further growth in holiness.

All perfection in this life hath some imperfection mixed with it; and no knowledge of ours is without some darkness. A humble knowledge of thyself is a surer way to God than a deep search after learning. Yet learning is not to be blamed, nor the mere knowledge of any thing whatsoever to be disliked, it being good in itself, and ordained by God; but a good conscience and a virtuous life is always to be preferred before it. But because many endeavour rather to get knowledge than to live well, therefore they are often deceived, and reap either nothing, or a very slender profit from their labours.

O, if men bestowed as much labour in the rooting out of vices, and planting of virtues, as they do in moving of questions, neither would there so much hurt be done, nor so great scandal be given in the world, nor so much looseness be practised in religious houses. Truly, at the day of judgment we shall not be examined on what we have read, but what we have done; not how well we have spoken, but how religiously we have lived. Tell me now, where are all those doctors and masters, with whom thou wast well acquainted, whilst they lived and flourished in learning? Now others possess their livings and perhaps scarcely ever think of them. In their lifetime they seemed something, but now they are not spoken of.

O, how quickly doth the glory of the world pass away! O that their life had been answerable to their learning! Then had their study and reading been to good purpose. How many perish by reason of vain learning in this world, who take little care of the serving of God: and because they choose rather to be great than humble, therefore they become vain in their imaginations. He is truly great, that is great in charity. He is truly great, that is little in himself, and that maketh no account of any height of honour. He is truly wise, that accounteth all earthly things as dung, that he may gain Christ. And he is truly learned, that doeth the will of God, and forsaketh his own will.

We must not give ear to every saying or suggestion, but ought warily and leisurely to ponder things according to the will of God. But alas; such is our weakness, that we often rather believe and speak evil of others than God. Those that are perfect men do not easily give credit to everything one tells them; for they know that human frailty is prone to evil, and subject to fail in words.

It is great wisdom not to be rash in thy proceedings, nor to stand stiffly in thine own conceits; and also not to believe everything which thou hearest nor presently to relate again to others what thou hast heard or dost believe. Consult with him that is wise and conscientious, and seek to be instructed by a better than thyself, rather than to follow thine own inventions. A good life maketh a man wise according to God, and giveth him experience in many things. The more humble a man is in himself, and the more subject and resigned unto God; so much the more prudent shall he be in all his affairs, and enjoy greater peace and quiet of heart.

Truth, not eloquence, is to be sought for in Holy Scripture. Each part of the Scripture is to be read with the same spirit in which it was written. We should rather search after our spiritual profit in the Scriptures, than subtlety of speech. We ought to read plain and devout books as willingly as high and profound. Let not the authority of the writer offend thee, whether he be of great or small learning; but let the love of pure truth draw thee to read. Search not who spoke this or that, but mark what is spoken.

Men pass away, but the truth of the Lord remaineth for ever. God speaks unto us in sundry ways without respect of persons. Our own curiosity often hindereth us in reading of the Scriptures, when we examine and discuss that which we should rather pass over without more ado. If thou desire to reap profit, read with humility, simplicity, and faithfulness; and never desire the estimation of learning. Enquire willingly, and hear with silence the words of holy men; dislike not the parables of the elders, for they are not recounted without cause.

Whensoever a man desireth any thing inordinately, he is presently disquieted in himself. The proud and covetous can never rest. The poor and humble in spirit live together in all peace. The man that is not yet perfectly dead to himself, is quickly tempted and overcome in small and trifling things. The weak in spirit, and he that is yet in a carnal state and prone to the senses, can hardly withdraw himself altogether from earthly desires: and therefore he is often afflicted when he goeth about to withdraw himself from them; and easily falleth into indignation when any opposition is made against him.

And if he hath followed therein his appetite, he is presently disquieted with remorse of conscience; because he yielded to his passion, which profiteth him nothing in the obtaining of the peace he sought. True quietness of heart therefore is achieved by resisting our passions, not by obeying them. There is then no peace in the heart of a carnal man, nor in him that is addicted to outward things, but in the spiritual and fervent man.

He is vain that putteth his trust in man, or creatures. Be not ashamed to serve others for the love of Jesus Christ; nor to be esteemed poor in this world. Presume not upon thyself, but place thy hope in God. Do what lieth in thy power and God will assist thy good will. Trust not in thine own knowledge, nor in the subtlety of any living creature; but rather in the grace of God, who helpeth the humble and humbleth those that are self-presuming.

Glory not in wealth if thou have it, nor in friends who are powerful; but in God who giveth all things, and above all desireth to give thee Himself. Extol not thyself for the height of thy stature or beauty of thy person, which may be disfigured and destroyed with a little sickness. Take not pleasure in thy natural gifts, or wit, lest thereby thou displease God, to whom appertaineth all the good whatsoever thou hast by nature.

Esteem not thyself better than others, lest perhaps in the sight of God, who knoweth what is in man, thou be accounted worse than they. Be not proud of well-doing; for the judgment of God is far different from the judgment of men, and that often offendeth Him which pleaseth them. If there be any good in thee, believe that there is much more in others, that so thou mayest conserve humility within thee. It is no prejudice unto thee to debase thyself under all men; but it is very prejudicial to thee to prefer thyself before any one man. The humble enjoy continual peace, but in the heart of the proud is envy and frequent indignation.

Lay not thy heart open to everyone; but talk of thy affairs with the wise, and such as fear God. Converse not much with young people and strangers. Flatter not the rich: neither must thou appear willingly before great personages. Keep company with the humble and plain ones, with the devout and virtuous; and confer with them of those things that may edify. Be not familiar with any woman; but in general commend all good women to God. Desire to be familiar with God alone and His angels, and avoid the acquaintance of men.

We must have charity towards all, but familiarity with all is not expedient. Sometimes it falleth out, that a person unknown to us is much esteemed of, from the good report given him by others; whose presence notwithstanding is not grateful to the eyes of the beholders. We think sometimes to please others by our company, and we rather displease them with those bad qualities which they discover in us.

It is a great matter to live in obedience, to be under a superior, and not to be at our own disposing. It is much safer to obey, than to govern. Many live under obedience, rather for necessity than for charity; such are discontented, and do easily pine and murmur. Neither can they attain to freedom of mind, unless they willingly and heartily put themselves under obedience for the love of God. Go whither thou wilt, thou shalt find no rest but in humble subjection under the government of a superior. The imagination and change of places have deceived many.

True it is, that every one willingly doth that which agreeth with his own sense and liking; and is apt to affect those most that are of his own mind; but if God be amongst us, we must sometimes cease to adhere to our own opinion for the sake of peace. Who is so wise that he can fully know all things? Be not therefore too confident in thine own opinion, but be willing to hear the judgment of others. If that which thou thinkest be not amiss, and yet thou partest with it for God, and followest the opinion of another, it shall be better for thee.

I have often heard that it is safer to hear and take counsel, than to give it. It may also happen that each one's opinion may be good; but to refuse to yield to others when reason or a special cause requireth it, is a sign of pride and stiffness.

Fly the tumultuousness of the world as much as thou canst; for the talk of worldly affairs is a great hindrance, although they be discoursed of with sincere intention. For we are quickly defiled, and enthralled with vanity. Often I might wish that I had held my peace when I have spoken; and that I had not been in company. Why do we so willingly speak and talk one with another, when notwithstanding we seldom return to silence without hurt of conscience? The reason why we so willingly talk is because in discoursing one with another, we seek to receive comfort one of another, and desire to ease our mind over-wearied with sundry thoughts: and we very willingly talk and think of those things which we most love or desire; or of those which we feel most contrary and troublesome unto us.

But alas, this is often in vain, and to no end; for this outward comfort is the cause of no small loss of inward and divine consolation. Therefore we must watch and pray, lest our time pass away idly. If it be lawful and expedient for thee to speak, speak those things that may edify. An evil custom and neglect of our own good doth give too much liberty to inconsiderate speech. Yet religious discourses of spiritual things do greatly further our spiritual growth, especially when persons of one mind and spirit are gathered together in God.

We might enjoy much peace, if we would not busy ourselves with the words and deeds of other men, with things which are nothing to do with us. How can he abide long in peace, who thrusts himself into the cares of others, who seeks occasions abroad, who little or seldom recollects himself within his own breast? Blessed are the single-hearted; for they shall enjoy much peace.

What is the reason that some of the saints were so perfect and contemplative? Because they laboured to mortify themselves wholly to all earthly desires; and therefore they could with their whole heart fix themselves upon God, and be free for holy retirement. We are too much led by our passions, and too solicitous for transitory things. We also seldom overcome any one vice perfectly, and are not inflamed with a fervent desire to grow better every day; and therefore we remain cold and lukewarm in religion.

If we were perfectly dead unto ourselves, and not entangled within our own breasts; then should we be able to taste divine things, and to have some experience of heavenly contemplation. The greatest and indeed the whole impediment is that we are not disentangled from our passions and lusts, neither do we endeavour to enter into that path of perfection which the saints have walked before us; and when any small adversity befalleth us, we are too quickly dejected, and turn ourselves to human comforts.

If we would endeavour like men of courage to stand in the battle, surely we should feel the favourable assistance of God from Heaven. For He who giveth us occasion to fight, to the end that we may get the victory, is ready to succour those that fight manfully, and trust in His grace. If we esteem our progress in religious life to consist only in some exterior observances, our devotion will quickly be at an end. But let us lay the axe to the root, that being freed from passions, we may find rest to our souls.

If every year we would root out one vice, we should sooner become perfect men. But how often we perceive it goes contrary, and that we were better and purer at the beginning of our conversion than after many years of our profession. Our fervour and profiting should increase daily: but now it is accounted a great matter, if a man can retain but some part of his first zeal. If we would but a little force ourselves at the beginning, then should we be able to perform all things afterwards with ease and delight.

It is a hard matter to leave off that to which we are accustomed, but it is harder to go against our own wills. But if thou dost not overcome little and easy things, how wilt thou overcome harder things? Resist thy inclination in the very beginning, and unlearn evil customs, lest perhaps little by little they draw thee to greater difficulty. O if thou didst but consider how much inward peace unto thyself, and joy unto others, thou shouldst procure by demeaning thyself well, I suppose thou wouldest be more careful of thy spiritual progress.

It is good that we have sometimes some troubles and crosses; for they often make a man enter into himself, and consider that he is here in banishment, and ought not to place his trust in any wordly thing. It is good that we are sometimes contradicted, and that there be an evil or a lessening conceit of us although we do and intend well. These things often help to the attaining of humility, and defend us from vainglory: for then we chiefly seek God for our inward witness, when outwardly we be condemned by men, and when there is no credit given unto us.

And therefore a man should settle himself so fully in God, that he need not seek many comforts of men. When a good man is afflicted, tempted, or troubled with evil thoughts, then he understandeth better the great need he hath of God, without whom he perceiveth he can do nothing that is good. Then also he sorroweth, lamenteth, and prayeth, by reason of the miseries he suffereth. Then he is weary of living longer and wisheth that death would come, that he might be dissolved and be with Christ. Then also he well perceiveth that perfect security and full peace cannot be had in this world.

So long as we live in this world we cannot be without tribulation and temptation. According as it is written in Job, "The life of man upon earth is a life of temptation." Every one therefore ought to be careful about his temptations, and to watch in prayer, lest the devil find an advantage to deceive him; who never sleepeth, but goeth about seeking whom he may devour. No man is so perfect and holy, but he hath sometimes temptations; we cannot be and altogether without.

Nevertheless temptations are often very profitable to us, though they be troublesome and grievous; for in them a man is humbled, purified, and instructed. All the saints passed through many tribulations and temptations, and profited thereby. And they that could not bear temptations, became reprobate, and fell away. There is no order so holy nor a place so secret where there are no temptations, or adversities.

There is no man that is altogether free from temptations whilst he liveth, being born with an inclination to evil. When one temptation or tribulation goeth away, another cometh; and we shall always have something to suffer, because we are fallen from the state of our felicity. Many seek to fly temptations, and do fall more grievously into them. By flight alone we cannot overcome, but by patience and true humility we become stronger than all our enemies.

He that only avoideth them outwardly, and doth not pluck them up by the roots, shall profit little; temptations will the sooner return unto him, and he shall feel himself in a worse case than before. By little and little, and by patience with long-suffering, through God's help, thou shalt more easily overcome, than with violence and thine own importunity. Often take counsel in temptations, and deal not roughly with him that is tempted; but give him comfort, as thou wouldest wish to be done to thyself.

The beginning of all evil temptations is inconstancy of mind, and small confidence in God. For as a ship without a helm is tossed to and fro with the waves; so the man who is remiss, and apt to leave his purpose, is many ways tempted. Fire tests iron, and temptation the just man. We know not often what we are able to do, but temptations show us what we are. Yet we must be watchful, especially in the beginning of the temptation; for the enemy is then more easily overcome, if he is not allowed to enter the door of our hearts, but is resisted outside the gate at this first knock. Wherefore one said, "Withstand the beginnings, for afterwards remedy comes often too late." For first there cometh to the mind a bare thought of evil, then a strong imagination of it, afterwards delight, and evil motion, and then our wicked enemy getteth complete entrance, whilst he is not resisted in the beginning. And the longer a man is negligent in resisting, so much the weaker does he become daily in himself, and the enemy stronger against him.

Some suffer great temptations in the beginning of their conversion; others in the latter end. Others again are much troubled almost through the whole time of their life. Some are but easily tempted, according to the wisdom and equity of the divine appointment, which weigheth the states and deserts of men, and ordaineth all things for the welfare of His own chosen ones.

We ought not therefore to despair when we are tempted, but so much the more fervently to pray unto God, that He will vouchsafe to help us in all tribulations; who surely, according to the words of St Paul, will give with the temptation such issue that we may be able to bear it. Let us therefore humble our souls under the hand of God in all temptations and tribulations, for He will save and exalt the humble spirit.

In temptations and afflictions, a man is tested in how much he hath profited; and his reward is thereby the greater, and his grace more eminently shines forth. Neither is it any such great thing if a man is devout and fervent, when he feeleth no affliction; but if in time of adversity he bear himself patiently, there is hope then of great proficiency in grace. Some are kept from great temptations, and in small ones which do daily occur are often overcome; to the end that, being humbled, they may never presume on themselves in great matters, who are baffled in small things.

Turn thine eyes unto thyself, and beware thou judge not the deeds of other men. In judging of others a man laboureth in vain, often erreth, and easily sinneth; but in judging and discussing of himself, he always laboureth fruitfully. We often judge things according to how we fancy them; for private affection berefts us easily of true judgment. If God were always the pure intention of our desire, we should not be so easily troubled, through the repugnance of our carnal mind.

But often something lurketh within, or else occurreth from without, which draweth us after it. Many secretly seek themselves in what they do, and know it not. They seem also to live in peace of mind, when things are done according to their will and opinion; but if things happen otherwise than they desire, they are straightway moved and much vexed. The diversities of judgments and opinions often cause times dissensions between friends and countrymen, between religous and devout persons.

An old custom is broken with difficulty and no man is willing to be led farther than he can see. If thou dost rely more upon thine own reason or industry than upon that power which brings thee under the obedience of Jesus Christ, it will be long before thou become illuminated; for God will have us perfectly subject unto Him, that, being inflamed with His love, we may transcend the narrow limits of human reason.

For no wordly thing, nor for the love of any man, is any evil to be done; but yet, for the profit of one that standeth in need, a good work is sometimes to be intermitted without any scruple, or changed also for a better. For by doing this, a good work is not lost, but changed into a better. Without charity the exterior work profiteth nothing; but whatsoever is done in charity, be it never so little and contemptible in the sight of the world, it becomes wholly fruitful. For God weigheth more with how much love a man worketh, than how much he doeth.

He doeth much, that doeth a thing well. He doeth well that rather serveth the community, than his own will. Often it seemeth to be charity, and it is rather carnality; because natural inclination, self-will, hope of reward, and desire of our own interests, will seldom be far away.

He that hath true and perfect charity, seeketh himself in nothing, but only desireth in all things that the glory of God should be exalted. He also envieth none; because he affecteth no private good; neither will he rejoice in himself; but wisheth above all things to be made happy in the enjoyment of God. He attributeth nothing that is good to any man, but wholly referreth it unto God from whom as from a fountain all things proceed; in whom finally all the saints rest as in their highest fruition. O he that hath but one spark of true charity would certainly discern that all earthly things are full of vanity.

Those things that a man cannot amend in himself or in others, he ought to suffer patiently, until God orders things otherwise. Think that perhaps it is better so for thy trial and patience, without which all our good deeds are not much to be esteemed. Thou oughtest to pray even when thou hast such impediments, that God would vouchsafe to help thee, and that thou mayest bear them kindly.

If one that is once or twice warned will not give over, contend not with him: but commit all to God, that His will may be fulfilled, and His name honoured in all His servants, who well knoweth how to turn evil into good. Endeavour to be patient in bearing with the defects and infirmities of others, of whatever sort they be; because thyself also hast many failings which must be borne with by others. If thou canst not make thyself such a one as thou wouldest, how canst thou expect to have another in all things to thy liking? We would willingly have others perfect, and yet we amend not our own faults.

We will have others severely corrected, and will not be corrected outselves. The large liberty of others displeaseth us; and yet we will not have our own desires denied us. We will have others kept under by strict laws; but in no way will ourselves be restrained. And thus it appeareth, how seldom we weigh our neighbour in the same balance with ourselves. If all men were perfect, what should we have to suffer on behalf of our neighbour for God?

But now God hath thus ordered it, that we may learn to bear one another's burdens; for no man is without fault; no man but hath his burden; no man sufficient of himself; no man wise enough of himself; but we ought to bear with one another, comfort one another, help, instruct, and admonish one another. Occasions of adversity best reveal how great virtue or strength each one hath. For occasions do not make a man frail, but they show what he is.

Thou must learn to break thy own will in many things if thou wilt have peace and concord with others. It is no small matter to dwell in a religious community, or congregation, to converse therein faithfully unto death. Blessed is he that hath there lived well, and ended happily. If thou will persevere in grace as thou oughtest, and grow therein, esteem thyself as a banished man, and a pilgrim upon earth. Thou must be contented for Christ's sake to be esteemed as a fool in this world, if thou desire to lead a religious life.

The wearing of a religious habit, and shaving of the crown, do little profit; but change of manners, and perfect mortification of passions, make a true religious man. He that seeketh anything else but merely God, and the salvation of his soul, shall find nothing but tribulation and sorrow, Neither can he remain long in peace, that laboureth not to be the least, and subject unto all.

Thou camest to serve, not to rule. Know that thou wast called to suffer and to labour, not to be idle or to spend thy time in talk. Here therefore men are proved as gold in the furnace. Here no man can stand, unless he humble himself with his whole heart for the love of God.

Consider the lively examples of the holy fathers, in whom true perfection and religion shined; and thou shalt see how little it is, and almost nothing, which we do now in these days. Alas! what is our life, if it be compared to them! The saints and friends of Christ served the Lord in hunger and thirst, in cold and nakedness, in labour and weariness, in watchings and fastings, in prayer and holy meditations, in many persecutions and reproaches.

O how many and grievous tribulations suffered the apostles, martyrs, confessors, virgins, and all the rest that endeavoured to follow the steps of Christ! For they hated their lives in this world that they might keep themselves until life eternal. O how strict and self-renouncing a life, led those holy fathers in the wilderness! What long and grievous temptations they suffered! How often were they assaulted by the enemy! What frequent and fervent prayers offered they to God! What rigorous abstinences did they use! What great zeal and care had they in their spiritual proficiency! How strong a combat they fought for the overcoming of their lusts! What pure and upright intentions kept they towards God! In the day they laboured, and in the night they attended to continual prayer: although when they laboured even, they ceased not from mental prayer.

They spent all their time with profit; every hour seemed short for the service of God. And by reason of the great sweetness they felt in contemplation, they forgot the necessity of corporal refreshments. They renounced all riches, dignities, honours friends, and kinsfolk; they desired to have nothing which appertained to the world; they scarcely even took things necessary for the sustenance of life; they grieved to serve their bodies even in necessity. Therefore they were poor in earthly things, but very rich in grace and virtues. Outwardly they were destitute, but inwardly they were refreshed with grace and divine consolation.

They were strangers to the world, but near and familiar friends to God. They seemed to themselves as nothing, and to this present world despicable; but they were precious and beloved in the eyes of God. They were grounded in true humility, lived in simple obedience, walked in love and patience: and therefore they profited daily in the spirit, and obtained great grace in God's sight. They were given as an example to all religious men; and they should more provoke us to endeavour after spiritual proficiences, than the number of the lukewarm should prevail to make us remiss.

O how great was the fervour of all religious persons in the beginning of their holy institution! How great was their devotion to prayer! What ambition to excel others in virtue! What exact discipline then flourished! What great reverence and obedience, under the rule of their superiors, observed they in all things! Their footsteps yet remaining testify that they were indeed holy and perfect men; who, fighting so valiantly, trod the world under their feet. Now, he is greatly accounted of who is not a transgressor, and who can with patience endure that which he hath undertaken.

O the lukewarmness and negligence of our times, that we so quickly decline from the ancient fervour, and are come to that state that our sloth and lukewarmness of spirit maketh our own life tedious unto us. Would to God the desire to grow in virtues did not wholly sleep in thee, who hast often seen the many examples of devout and religious persons!

The life of a good religious person ought to be adorned with all virtues; that he may inwardly be such as outwardly he seemeth to men. And with reason there ought to be much more within than is perceived without. For God beholdeth us; whom we are bound most highly to reverence wheresoever we are, and to walk in purity like angels in His sight. Daily ought we to renew our purposes, and to stir ourselves to greater fervour, as though this were the first day of our conversion; and to say, "Help me, my God, in this my good purpose, and in Thy holy service; and grant that I may now this day begin perfectly; for that which I have done hitherto is as nothing."

According to our purpose shall be the success of our spiritual profiting; and much diligence is necessary to him that will profit much. And if he that firmly proposeth often faileth, what shall he do that seldom proposeth any thing, or with little resolve; it may happen in sundry ways that we leave off our purpose; yet the light omission of spiritual exercises seldom passes without some loss to our souls. The purpose of just men depends not upon their own wisdom, but upon God's grace; on whom they always rely for whatsoever they take in hand. For man proposes, but God disposes; neither is the way of man in himself.

If an accustomed exercise be sometimes omitted either for some act of piety, or profit to my brother, it may easily afterwards be recovered again. But if out of a slothful mind, or out of carelessness, we lightly forsake the same, it is a great offence against God, and will be found to be prejudicial to ourselves. Let us do the best we can, we shall still too easily fail in many things. Yet must we always purpose some certain course, and especially against those failings which do most of all molest us. We must diligently search into, and set in order both the outward and the inward man, because both of them are of importance to our progress in godliness.

If thou canst not continually recollect thyself, yet do it sometimes, at the least once a day, namely, in the morning or at night. In the morning fix thy good purpose; and at night examine thyself what thou hast done, how thou hast behaved thyself in word, deed, and thought; for in these perhaps thou hast often offended both God and thy neighbour. Gird up thy loins like a man against the vile assaults of the devil; bridle thy riotous appetite, and thou shalt be the better able to keep under all the unruly motions of the flesh. Never be entirely idle; but either be reading, or writing, or praying, or meditating, or endeavouring something for the public good. As for bodily exercises, they must be used with discretion, neither are they to be practised by all men alike.

Those exercises which are not common are not to be exposed to public view; for things private are practised more safely at home. Nevertheless, thou must beware thou neglect not those which are common, being more ready for what is private. But having fully and faithfully accomplished all which thou art bound and enjoined to do, if thou hast any spare time, betake thee to thyself, as thy devotion shall desire. All cannot use one kind of spiritual exercise, but one is more useful for this person, another for that. According to the season of times also, different exercises are fitting; some suit us better on working days, others on holy days. In the time of temptation, we have need of some, and of others in time of peace and quietness. Some we need when we are pensive, and some when we rejoice in the Lord.

About the time of the chief festivals, good exercises are to be renewed, and the prayers of holy men more fervently to be implored. From festival to festival we should make some good purpose, as though we were then to depart out of this world, and to come to the everlasting feast in Heaven. Therefore ought we carefully to prepare ourselves at holy times, and to live more devoutly, and to keep more exactly all things that we are to observe, as though we were shortly at God's hands to receive the reward to our labours.

But if it be deferred, let us think within ourselves that we are not sufficiently prepared, and unworthy yet of such great glory, which shall be revealed in us in due time; and let us endeavour to prepare ourselves better for our departure. "Blessed is that servant," said the evangelist St Luke, "whom his Lord when He cometh shall find watching: Verily, I say unto you, He shall make him ruler over all His goods".

Seek a convenient time to retire into thyself, and meditate often upon God's loving-kindness. Meddle not with curiosities; but read such things as may rather yield compunction to thy heart, than occupation to thy head. If thou wilt withdraw thyself from speaking vainly, and from gadding idly, as also from hearkening after novelties and rumours, thou shalt find leisure enough and suitable for meditation on good things. The greatest saints avoided the society of men, when they could conveniently do so, and did rather choose to live to God, in secret.

One said, "As often as I have been among men, I returned home less a man than I was before." And this we find true, when we talk long together. It is easier for a man to keep well at home, than to keep himself well when abroad. He therefore that intends to attain to the more inward and spiritual things of religion must with Jesus depart from the multitude and press of people. No man doth safely appear abroad but he who gladly can abide at home, out of sight. No man speaks securely but he that holds his peace willingly. No man securely commands but he that hath learned readily to obey.

No man rejoiceth securely, unless he hath within him the testimony of a good conscience. And yet always the security of the saints was full of the fear of God. Neither were they the less anxious and humble in themselves, because they shone outwardly with grace and great virtues. But the security of bad men ariseth from pride and presumption, and in the end it deceiveth them. Although thou seem to be a good religious man, or a devout solitary, never promise thyself security in this life.

Often those who have been in the greatest esteem and account amongst men have fallen into the greatest danger, by over-much self-confidence. To many it is more profitable not to be altogether free from temptations, but to be often assaulted, lest they should be too secure, and so perhaps be puffed up with pride; or else too freely give themselves to worldly comforts. O how good a conscience should he keep that would never seek after transitory joy, nor ever entangle himself with the things of this world! O what great peace and quietness should he possess who would cut off all vain anxiety, and think only upon divine things, and such as are profitable for his soul, and who would place all his confidence in God.

No man is worthy of heavenly comfort, unless he has diligently exercised himself in holy compunction. If thou desirest true contrition of heart, enter into thy secret chamber and shut out the tumults of the world, as it is written, "In your chamber be ye grieved." In thy chamber thou shalt find what abroad thou shalt too often lose. The more thou visitest thy chamber, the more thou wilt like it; the less thou comest there, the more thou wilt loathe it. If in the beginning of thy conversion thou art content to remain in it, and keep to it well, it will afterwards be to thee a dear friend, and a most pleasant comfort.

In silence and in stillness a religious soul advantageth herself, and learneth the mysteries of Holy Scripture. There she findeth rivers of tears, wherein she may every night wash and cleanse herself; that she may be so much the more familiar with her Creator, by how much the farther off she liveth from all worldly disquiet. Whoever therefore withdraweth himself from his acquaintance and friends, God will draw near unto him with His holy angels. It is better for a man to live privately, and to take care of himself, than to neglect his soul, even if he could work wonders in the world. It is commendable in a religious person seldom to go abroad and to be unwilling to see or to be seen.

Why art thou desirous to see that which it is unlawful for thee to have? The world passeth away and the lust thereof. Our sensual desires draw us to roam abroad; but when the time is past, what carriest thou home with thee but a burdened conscience and distracted heart? A merry going out bringeth often a mournful return home; and a joyful evening often makes a sad morning. So all carnal joy enters gently, but in the end it bites and stings to death. What canst thou see elsewhere, which thou canst not see here? Behold the heaven and the earth and all the elements; for of these are all things created.

What canst thou see anywhere that can long continue under the sun? Thou thinkest perchance to satisfy thyself, but thou canst never attain satisfaction. Shouldst thou see all things present before thine eyes, what were it but a vain and unprofitable sight? Lift up thine eyes to God in the highest, and pray Him to pardon thy sins and negligences. Leave vain things to the vain; but be thou intent upon those things which God hath commanded thee. Shut thy door upon thee, and call unto thee Jesus, thy beloved. Stay with Him in thy closet; for thou shalt not find so great peace anywhere else. If thou hadst not gone abroad and listened to idle rumours, thou wouldest the better have preserved a happy peace of mind. But since thou delightest sometimes to hear novelties, it is but fit thou suffer for it some disquietude of heart.

If thou wilt make any progress in godliness, keep thyself in the fear of God, and affect not too much liberty. Restrain all thy senses under the severity of discipline, and give not thyself over to foolish mirth. Give thyself to compunction of heart, and thou shalt gain much devotion by it. Compunction layeth open much good, which dissoluteness is wont quickly to destroy. It is a wonder that any man can ever perfectly rejoice in this life if he duly consider and thoroughly weigh his state of banishment, and the many perils with which his soul is surrounded.

Through levity of heart, and small care for our failings, we become insensible of the real sorrows of our souls; and so we often vainly laugh, when we have just cause to weep. There is no true liberty nor right joy but in the fear of God accompanied with a good conscience. Happy is he, who can cast off all distracting impediments, and bring himself to the one single purpose of holy compunction. Happy is he, who can abandon all that may defile his conscience or burden it. Let others alone in their matters, they likewise shall not hinder thee in thine.

Do not busy thyself in matters which appertain to others; neither entangle thyself with the affairs of thy betters. Still have an eye to thyself first, and be sure most especially to admonish thyself before all thy beloved friends. If thou hast not the favour of men, be not grieved at it; but take this to heart, that thou behave thyself so warily and circumspectly as it becometh the servant of God, and a devout religious man. It is often better and safer that a man should not have many consolations in this life, especially such as are according to the flesh. But if we have not divine consolations at all, or do very seldom taste them, the fault is ours, because we seek not after compunction of heart, nor do altogether forsake the vain and outward comforts of this world.

Know that thou art unworthy of divine consolation, and that thou hast rather deserved much tribulation. When a man hath perfect contrition, then is the whole world grievous and bitter unto him. A good man findeth always sufficient cause for mourning and weeping. For whether he consider his own or his neighbour's estate, he knoweth that none liveth here without tribulation. And the more narrowly a man looks into himself, so much the more he sorroweth. Our sins and wickedness, wherein we lie so enwrapt that we can seldom apply ourselves to heavenly contemplations, minister unto us matters of just sorrow and inward compunction.

If thou think more often of thy death than of thy living long, there is no question but thou wouldst be more zealous to amend. If also thou didst but consider within thyself the infernal pains in the other world, I believe thou wouldst willingly undergo any labour or sorrow in this world, I believe thou wouldst willingly undergo any labour or sorrow in this world, and not be afraid of the greatest austerity. But because these things enter not to the heart, and we still love those things only that delight us, therefore it is we remain cold and very dull in religion.

It is often our want of spirit which maketh our miserable body so easily complain. Pray therefore unto the Lord with all humility, that He will vouchsafe to give thee the spirit of compunction. And say with the prophet, "Feed me, O Lord, with the bread of tears, and give me plenteousness of tears to drink."

Miserable thou art, wherever thou be, or whither thou turnest, unless thou turn thyself unto God. Why art thou troubled when things succeed not as thou wouldest or desirest? For who is he that hath all things according to his mind? Neither I nor thou, nor any man upon earth. There is none in this world, even though he is king or bishop, without some tribulation or perplexity. Who is then in the best case or condition? Even he who is able to suffer something for God.

Many weak and infirm persons say Behold! What a happy life such a one leads; how wealthy, how great he is, in what power and dignity! But lift up thine eyes to the riches of Heaven, and thou shalt see that all the goods of this life are to be accounted nothing. They are very uncertain, and rather burdensome than otherwise, because they are never possessed without anxiety and fear. Man's happiness consisteth not in having abundance of temporal goods; moderate portion is sufficient for him. Truly it is misery enough even to live upon the earth. The more spiritual a man desires to be, the more bitter does this present life become to him; because he sees more clearly and perceives more sensibly the defects of human corruption. For to eat and to drink, to sleep and to watch, to labour and to rest, and to be subject to other necessities of nature, is doubtless a great misery and affliction to a religious man, who would gladly be set loose, and free from all sin.

For the inward man is much weighed down with these outward and corporal necessities whilst we live in this world. Therefore the prophet prayeth with great devotion to be enabled to be free from them, saing, "Bring me, O Lord, out of my necessities." But woe be to them that know not their own misery; and a greater woe to them that love this miserable and corruptible life! For there are some who dote so much upon it, that although by labour or by begging they can scarce get mere necessaries, yet if they might be able to live here always, they would care nothing at all for the Kingdom of God.

O how senseless are those men, and unbelieving in heart, who lie so deeply sunk in the earth that they can relish nothing but carnal things! But miserable as they are, they shall in the end feel to their cost how vile and empty was that which they loved. Whereas the saints of God and all the devout friends of Christ regarded not those things which pleased the flesh nor those which flourished in this life, but longed after the everlasting riches with their whole hope and earnest intention. Their whole desire was carried upward to things durable and invisible, that the desire of things visible might not draw them to things below.

O my brother, lose not the confidence of making progress in godliness; there is yet time, the hour is not yet past. Why wilt thou defer thy good purpose from day to day? Arise and begin and say, now is the time to be doing, to be striving, now is the fit time to amend thyself. When thou art ill at ease and much troubled, then is the time of deserving best. Thou must pass through fire and water before thou come to the place of refreshment. Unless thou dost earnestly force thyself, thou shalt never get the victory over sin. So long as we carry about this frail body of ours, we can never be without sin, or live without weariness and pain. We would gladly be quiet and freed from all misery, but seeing that by sin we have lost our innocence, we have together with that lost also the true felicity. Therefore it becomes us to have patience, and to wait for the mercy of God, till this iniquity pass away, and mortality be swallowed up in life.

O how great is human frailty, which is always prone to evil! Today thou confessest thy sins, and tomorrow thou committest the very same thou hast confessed. Now, thou are purposed to look well unto thy ways, and within a while thou so behavest thyself, as though thou hadst never any such purpose at all. Good cause have we therefore to humble ourselves, and never to have any great conceit of ourselves: since we are so frail and so inconstant. Besides, by our own negligence, we may quickly lose that which, by the grace of God, with much labour we have scarce at length obtained.

What will become of us in the end, who begin so early to wax lukewarm! Woe be unto us, if we will so soon give ourselves unto ease, as if all were in peace and safety, when as yet there appeareth no sign of true holiness in our conversation! We have much need like young beginners to be newly instructed again to good life, if perhaps there is some hope of future amendment, and greater proficiency in things spiritual.

Very quickly there will be an end of thee here; look what will become of thee in another world. Today the man is here; tomorrow he hath disappeared. And when he is out of sight, quickly also is he out of mind. O the stupidity and darkness of man's heart, which thinketh only upon the present, and doth not rather care for what is to come! Thou oughtest so to order thyself in all thy thoughts and actions, as if today thou were about to die. If thou hadst a good conscience, thou wouldst not greatly fear death. It is better to avoid sins than to fly death. If today thou art not prepared, how wilt thou be so tomorrow? Tomorrow is uncertain, and how knowest thou that thou shalt live till tomorrow!

What availeth it to live long, when there is so small amendment in our practice! Alas! length of days doth more often make our sins the greater, than our lives the better! O that we had spent but one day in this world thoroughly well! Many there are who count how long it is since their conversion; and yet often slender is the fruit of amendment of life. If to die is accounted dreadful, to live long may perhaps prove more dangerous. Happy is he that always hath the hour of his death before his eyes, and daily prepareth himself to die. If at any time thou hast seen another man die, make account thou must also pass the same way.

When it is morning, think thou mayest die before night; and when evening comes, dare not to promise thyself the next morning. Be thou therefore always in readiness, and so lead thy life that death may never take thee unprepared. Many die suddenly and when they look not for it; for the Son of Man will come at an hour when we think not. When that last hour shall come, thou wilt begin to have a greatly different opinion of thy whole life that is past, and be exceedingly sorry thou has been so careless and remiss.

O how wise and happy is he that now laboureth to be such a one in his life as he wisheth to be found at the hour of death! A perfect contempt of the world, a fervent desire to go forward in all virtue, the love of discipline, the painfulness of repentance, the readiness of obedience, the denying of ourselves, and bearing any affliction whatever for the love of Christ, will give us great confidence that we shall die happily. Whilst thou art in health thou mayest do much good; but when thou art sick, I see not what thou wilt be able to do. Few by sickness grow better and more reformed; as also they who wander much abroad seldom thereby become holy.

Trust not to friends and kindred, neither put off the care of thy soul's welfare till hereafter; for men will forget thee sooner than thou art aware of. It is better to look to it now, and do some good beforehand, than to trust to other men's help. If thou art not careful for thee now, who will be careful for thee hereafter? The time that is now present is very precious: now are the days of salvation; now is the acceptable time. But alas! that thou shouldest spend thy time so idly here, when thou mightest purchase to live eternally hereafter. The time will come when thou shalt desire one day or hour in which to amend, and I cannot say that it will be granted thee.

O beloved, from what great danger mightest thou deliver thyself, from what great fear free thyself, if thou wouldst ever be fearful and mindful of death! Labour now so to live that at the hour of death thou mayest rather rejoice than fear. Learn now to die to the world that thou mayest then being to live with Christ. Learn now to disdain all things that thou mayest then freely go to Christ. Chastise thy body now by repentance that thou mayest then have assured confidence.

Ah! fool, why dost thou think to live long when thou canst not promise to thyself one day. How many have been deceived and suddenly snatched away! How often dost thou hear the reports that such a man is slain, another man is drowned, a third breaks his neck with a fall from some high place, this man died eating, and that man playing! One perished by fire, another by the sword, another of the plague, another was slain by thieves. Thus death is the end of all, and man's life suddenly passeth away like a shadow.

Who shall remember thee when thou art dead? Do, do now, my beloved, whatever thou art able to do; for thou knowest not when thou shalt die, nor yet what shall befall thee after thy death. Now, whilst thou hast time, heap unto thyself everlasting riches. Think on nothing but the salvation of thy soul, care for nothing but the things of God. Make now friends to thyself by honouring the saints of God, and imitating their actions, that when thou failest in this life they may receive thee into everlasting habitations.

Keep thyself as a stranger and pilgrim upon the earth, and as one to whom the affairs of this world do not affect. Keep thy heart free, and lifted up to God, because thou hast here no abiding city. Send thither thy daily prayers and sighs together with thy tears, that after death thy spirit may be found worthy with much happiness to pass to the Lord.

In all things have a special aim to thy end, and how thou wilt be able to stand before that severe judge from whom nothing is hidden, who is not pacified with gifts, nor admitteth any excuses, but will judge according to right and equity. O wretched and foolish sinner, who sometimes fearest the countenance of an angry man, what answer wilt thou make to God who knoweth all thy wickedness! Why dost thou not provide for thyself against that great Day of Judgment, when no man can excuse or answer for another, but every one shall have enough to answer for himself? Now are thy pains profitable, thy tears acceptable, thy groans audible, thy grief pacifieth God, and purgeth thy soul.

The patient man hath a great and wholesome purgatory, who though he received injuries, yet grieveth more for the malice of another than for his own wrong; who prayeth willingly for his adversaries, and from his heart forgiveth their offences; he delayeth not to ask forgiveness of whomsoever he hath offended; he is sooner moved to compassion than to anger; he often offereth a holy violence to himself, and laboureth to bring the body wholly into subjection to the spirit. It is better to purge our sins, and cut off our vices here, than to keep them to be punished hereafter. We do but deceive ourselves through an inordinate love of the flesh.

What is there that the infernal fire shall feed upon, but thy sins? The more thou sparest thyself now and followest the flesh, the more severe hereafter shall be thy punishment, and thou storest up greater fuel for that flame. In what things a man hath sinned, in the same things shall he be grievously punished. There shall the slothful be pricked forward with burning goads, and the glutton be tormented with extreme hunger and thirst. There shall the luxurious and lovers of pleasure be bathed in burning pitch and stinking brimstone, and the envious, like mad dogs, shall howl for very grief.

There is no sin but shall have its own proper torment. There the proud shall be filled with all confusion; the covetous shall be pinched with miserable penury. One hour of pain there shall be more bitter than a thousand years of the sharpest penance here! There is no quiet, no comfort for the damned there; yet here we have some intermission of our labours, and enjoy the comfort of our friends. Be now solicitous and sorrowful because of thy sins, that at the Day of Judgment thou mayest be secure with the company of blessed souls. For then shall the righteous with great boldness stand against such as have vexed and oppressed them. Then shall he stand to judge them, who doth now humbly submit himself to the censures of men. Then shall the poor and humble have great confidence, but the proud man shall be compassed with fear on every side.

Then will it appear that he was wise in this world who had learned to be a fool and to be despised for Christ's sake. Then shall every affliction patiently undergone delight us, when the mouth of all iniquity shall be stopped. Then shall all the devout rejoice and all the profane mourn. Then shall he more rejoice that hath beaten down his own flesh than he that hath abounded in all pleasure and delight. Then shall the poor attire shine gloriously and the precious robes seem vile and contemptible. Then the poor cottage shall be more commended than the gilded palace. Then will constant patience more avail us than all earthly power. Then simple obedience shall be exalted above all worldly wisdom.

Then shall a good and clear conscience more rejoice a man than all the learning of philosophy. Then shall the contempt of riches weigh more than all the worldling's treasure. Then wilt thou be more comforted that thou hast prayed devoutly than that thou hast fared daintily. Then wilt thou be more glad thou hast kept silence, than that thou hast talked much. Then will good works avail more than many goodly words. Then a strict life and severe repentance will be more pleasing than all earthly delights. Accustom thyself now to suffer a little, that thou mayest then be delivered from more grievous pains. Test first here what thou canst endure hereafter. If now thou canst endure so little, how wilt thou then be able to support eternal torments? If now a little suffering make thee so impatient, what will hell fire do hereafter. Assure thyself thou canst not have two paradises; it is impossible to enjoy delights in this world, after that to reign with Christ.

Suppose thou hast hitherto lived always in honours and delights, what would all this avail thee if thou wert to die at this instant? All therefore is vanity, except to love God and serve Him only. For he that loveth God with all his heart is neither afraid of death, nor of punishment, nor of judgment, nor of Hell; for perfect love gives secure access to God. But he that takes delight in sin, what marvel is it if he be afraid, both of death and judgment? Yet it is good, although love be not yet strong enough to withhold thee from sin, at least the fear of Hell should restrain thee. But he that layeth aside the fear of God can never continue long in good estate, but falleth quickly into the snares of the devil.

Be watchful and diligent in the service of God; and often think to thyself why thou camest here, and why thou hast left the world. Was it not that thou mightest live for God, and become a spiritual man? Be fervent then in going forward, for shortly thou shalt receive the reward of thy labours; there shall not be then any more fear or sorrow in thy coasts. Labour but now a little, and thou shalt find great rest, yea, perpetual joy to thy soul. If thou continuest faithful and fervent in doing good, there is no doubt that God will be faithful and liberal in rewarding thee. Thou oughtest to have a good hope of getting the victory; but thou must not be secure, lest thou wax either negligent or proud.

When one that was in anxiety of mind, often wavering between fear and hope, did once, being oppressed with grief, humbly prostrate himself in a church before the altar in prayer, and said within himself, O if I knew that I should yet persevere!, he presently heard within him an answer from God, which said, What if thou didst know it, what wouldest thou do? Do now what thou wouldest do then, and thou shalt be secure. And being herewith comforted and strengthened, he committed himself wholly to the will of God, and that worrying anxiety ceased: neither had he the mind to search curiously any farther, to know what should befall him; but rather laboured to understand what was the perfect and acceptable will of God for the beginning and accomplishing of every good work.

"Hope in the Lord, and do good," saith the prophet, "and inhabit the land, and thou shalt be fed in the riches thereof." One thing there is, that draweth many back from spiritual progress, and the diligent amendment of their lives; namely, extreme fear of the difficulty or the labour of the combat. However, they above others improve most in all virtue who endeavour most to overcome those things which are most grievous and contrary unto them. For there a man improveth most and obtaineth greater grace, where he most overcometh himself and mortifieth himself in spirit.

But all men have not equally much to overcome and mortify. Yet he that is zealous and diligent, though he have more passions, shall profit more than another that is of a more temperate disposition, if he is less fervent in the pursuit of all virtue. Two things especially further our amendment, to wit, to withdraw ourselves violently from that to which nature is viciously inclined, and to labour earnestly for that good which we most want. Be careful also to avoid with great diligence those things in thyself which do commonly displease thee in others.

Gather some profit to thy soul wheresoever thou art; so if thou seest or hearest of any good examples, stir up thyself to the imitation thereof. But if thou observe anything worthy of reproof, beware thou do not the same. And if at any time thou has done it, labour quickly to amend thyself. As thine eye observeth others, so art thou also noted again by others. O how sweet and pleasant a thing it is to see Christian brethren fervent and devout, well-mannered and well-disciplined! And on the contrary, how sad and grievous a thing it is to see them live in a dissolute and disordered way, not applying themselves to that for which they are called! How hurtful a thing is it when they neglect the good purposes of their vocation, and busy themselves in that which is not committed to their care!

Be mindful of the profession thou hast made and have always before the eyes of thy soul the remembrance of thy Saviour crucified. Thou hast good cause to be ashamed in looking upon the life of Jesus Christ, seeing that thou hast not as yet endeavoured to conform thyself more unto Him, even though thou hast been a long time in the way of God. A religious person that exerciseth himself seriously and devoutly in the most holy life and passion of our Lord shall there abundantly find whatever is necessary and profitable for him; neither shall he need to seek any better thing, away from Jesus. O if Jesus crucified would come into our hearts, how quickly and fully should we be instructed in all truth!

A fervent religious person taketh and beareth all that is commanded him. But he that is negligent and lukewarm hath tribulation upon tribulation and on all sides is afflicted: for he is void of inward consolation, and is forbidden to seek external comforts. A religious person that liveth not according to discipline lies open to great mischief to the ruin of his soul. He that seeketh liberty and ease shall ever live in disquiet; for one thing or another will displease him.

O that we had nothing else to do, but always with our mouth and whole heart to praise our Lord God! O that thou mightest never have need to eat, or drink, or sleep; but mightest always praise God, and only employ thyself in spiritual exercises; thou shouldest then be much more happy than now thou art, when for so many necessities thou art constrained to serve thy body! Would God there were not these necessities, but only the spiritual refreshments of the soul, which, alas, we taste of too seldom!

When a man cometh to that estate that he seeketh not his comfort from any creature, then doth he begin perfectly to relish God. Then shall he be contented with whatsoever doth befall him in this world. Then shall he neither rejoice in great matters nor be sorrowful for small; but entirely and confidently commit himself to God, who shall be unto him all in all; to whom nothing doth perish nor die, but all things do live unto Him, and serve Him without delay.

Remember always thy end, and how lost time never returns. Without care and diligence thou shalt never achieve virtue. If thou begin to wax lukewarm, it will begin to be evil with thee. But if thou give thyself to fervour of spirit, thou shalt find much peace, and feel less labour, through the assistance of God's grace and the love of virtue. The fervent and diligent man is prepared for all things. It is harder work to resist vices and passions than to toil in bodily labours. He that avoideth not small faults, by little and little falleth into greater. Thou wilt always rejoice in the evening if thou spend the day profitably. Be watchful over thyself, stir up thyself, admonish thyself and whatever becomes of others neglect not thyself. The more holy violence thou usest against thyself, the greater shall be thy spiritual profit.

BOOK II

"The Kingdom of God is within you," saith the Lord. Turn with thy whole heart unto the Lord, and forsake this wretched world, and thy soul shall find rest. Learn to despise outward things, and to give thyself to things inward, and thou shalt perceive the Kingdom of God to come in thee. "For the Kingdom of God is peace and joy in the Holy Ghost," which is not given to the unholy. Christ will come unto thee, and show thee His own consolation, if thou prepare for Him a worthy mansion within thee. All his glory and beauty is from within, and there He delighteth Himself. The inward man He often visiteth; and hath with him sweet discourses, pleasant solace, much peace, familiarity exceedingly wonderful.

O faithful soul, make ready thy heart for this bridegroom, that he may vouchsafe to come unto thee, and to dwell within thee. For thus saith He, "If any love Me, he will keep My words, and We will come unto him and will make our abode with him." Give therefore admittance unto Christ, and deny entrance to all others. When thou hast Christ, thou art rich, and hast enough. He will be thy faithful and provident helper in all things, so that thou shalt not need to trust in men. For men soon change, and quickly fail; but Christ remaineth for ever, and standeth by us firmly unto the end.

There is no great trust to be put in a frail and mortal man, even though he is profitable and dear unto us: neither ought we to be much grieved if sometimes he crosses and contradicts us. They that today take thy part, tomorrow may be against thee; and often do they turn right round like the wind. Put all thy trust in God, let Him be thy fear and thy love: He shall answer for thee, and will do in all things what is best for thee. Thou has not here an abiding city; and wherever thou mayest be, thou art a stranger and pilgrim: neither shalt thou ever have rest, unless thou be inwardly united unto Christ.

Why dost thou here gaze about, since this is not the place of thy rest? In Heaven ought to be thy home, and all earthly things are to be looked upon as unimportant. All things pass away, and thou together with them. Beware thou cleave not unto them, lest thou be caught, and so perish. Let thy thought be on the Highest, and thy prayer for mercy directed unto Christ without ceasing. If thou canst not contemplate high and heavenly things, rest thyself in the passion of Christ, and dwell willingly in His sacred wounds. For if thou fly devoutly unto the wounds and precious marks of the Lord Jesus, thou shalt feel great comfort in tribulation: neither wilt thou much care for the slights of men, and wilt easily bear words of detraction.

Christ was also in the world, despised of men, and in great need, forsaken by His acquaintances and friends, in the midst of slanders. Christ was willing to suffer and be despised; and darest thou complain of any man? Christ had adversaries and backbiters; and dost thou wish to have all men thy friends and benefactors? Whence shall thy patience attain her crown if no adversity befall thee? If thou art willing to suffer no opposition, how wilt thou be the friend of Christ? Suffer with Christ, and for Christ, if thou desire to reign with Christ.

If thou hadst but once perfectly entered into the secrets of the Lord Jesus, and tasted a little of His ardent love, then wouldest thou not have regard for thine own convenience or inconvenience, but rather wouldest rejoice at slanders, if they should be cast upon thee; for the love of Jesus maketh a man despise himself. A lover of Jesus and of the truth, and a true inward Christian, and one free from inordinate affections, can freely turn himself unto God, and lift himself above himself in spirit, and with joy remain at rest.

He that judgeth of all things as they are, and not as they are said or esteemed to be, is truly wise, and taught rather of God than men. He that can live inwardly, and make small reckoning of external things, neither requireth places, nor expecteth times, for performing religious exercises. A spiritual man quickly recollecteth himself, because he never poureth out himself wholly to outward things. He is not hindered by outward labour, or business, which may be necessary for the time; but as things fall out, so he accommodates himself to them. He that is well ordered and disposed within himself, cares not for the strange and perverse behaviour of men. A man is hindered and distracted in proportion as he draweth external matters towards himself.

If it were well with thee, and thou wert well purified from sin, all things would fall out to thee for good, and to thy advancement in holiness. But many things displease and often trouble thee, because thou art not yet perfectly dead unto thyself, nor separated from all earthly things. Nothing so defileth and entangleth the heart of man, as the impure love of others. If thou refuse outward comfort, thou wilt be able to contemplate the things of Heaven and often to receive internal joy.

Pay no attention who is for thee, or against thee; but mind what thou art about, and take care that God may be with thee in everything thou doest. Have a good conscience, and God will defend thee. For whom God will help, no man's perverseness shall be able to hurt. If thou canst be silent and suffer without doubt thou shalt see that the Lord will help thee. He knoweth the time and manner in which to deliver thee, and therefore thou oughtest to resign thyself unto Him. It belongs to God to help, and to deliver from all confusion. It is often very profitable to keep us humble, so that others know and rebuke our faults.

When a man humbleth himself for his failings, then he easily pacifieth others, and quickly satisfieth those that are angry with him. God protecteth the humble and delivereth him; the humble He loveth and comforteth; unto the humble man He inclineth Himself; unto the humble He giveth great grace; and after his humiliation He raiseth him to glory. Unto the humble He revealeth His secrets, and sweetly draweth and inviteth him unto Himself. The humble person, though he suffer confusion, is yet tolerably well in peace; for he rests on God and not on the world. Do not think that thou hast made any progress, unless thou esteem thyself inferior to all.

First keep thyself in peace, and then thou shalt be able to pacify others. A peaceable man doth more good than he that is well learned. A passionate man draweth even good into evil, and easily believeth the worst. A good peaceable man turneth all things to good. He that is content in peace is not suspicious of any. But he that is discontented and troubled is tossed with many suspicions: he is neither quiet himself, nor suffereth others to be quiet. He often speaketh that which he ought not to speak, and omitteth that which it would be more expedient for him to do. He considereth what others are bound to do, and neglecteth that which he is bound to do himself. First, therefore, have a careful zeal over thyself, and then thou mayest justly show thyself zealous also of thy neighbour's good.

Thou knowest well how to excuse and colour thine own deeds, but thou art not willing to receive the excuses of others. It were more just that thou shouldest accuse thyself, and excuse thy brother. If thou wilt be borne withal, bear also with another. Behold how far off thou art yet from true charity and humility, which knoweth not how to be angry with any, nor to be moved with indignation, except against its own self. It is no great matter to associate with the good and gentle; for this is naturally pleasing to all, and every one willingly enjoyeth peace, and loveth those best that agree with him. But to be able to live peaceably with hard and perverse persons, or with the disorderly, or with such as go contrary to us, is a great grace, and a most commendable and manly thing.

Some there are that keep themselves in peace, and are in peace also with others. And there are some that neither are in peace themselves, nor suffer others to be in peace: they are troublesome to others, but always more troublesome to themselves. And others there are that keep themselves in peace, and study to bring others unto peace. Nevertheless, our whole peace in this miserable life consisteth rather in humble sufferance than in not feeling adversities. He that can best tell how to suffer will best keep himself in peace. That man is conqueror of himself, and lord of the world, the friend of Christ, and heir of Heaven.

By two wings, a man is lifted up from things earthly, namely, by simplicity and purity. Simplicity ought to be in our intention; purity in our affections. Simplicity doth tend towards God; purity doth apprehend and, as it were, taste Him. No good action will hinder thee, if thou art inwardly free from inordinate affection. If thou intend and seek nothing else but the will of God and the good of thy neighbour, thou shalt thoroughly enjoy internal liberty. If thy heart were sincere and upright, then every creature would be unto thee a looking-glass of life and a book of holy doctrine. There is no creature so small and abject that it representeth not the goodness of God.

If thou wert inwardly good and pure, then wouldest thou be able to see and understand all things well without impediment. A pure heart penetrateth Heaven and Hell. Such as every one is inwardly, so he judgeth outwardly. If there be joy in the world, surely a man of pure heart possesseth it. And if there by anywhere tribulation and affliction, an evil conscience best knows it. As iron put into the fire loseth its rust, and becometh clearly red hot, so he that wholly turneth himself unto God puts off all slothfulness, and is transformed into a new man.

When a man beginneth to grow lukewarm, then he is afraid of a little labour, and willingly receiveth external comforts. But when he once beginneth to overcome himself perfectly, and to walk manfully in the way of God, then he esteemeth those things to be light which before seemed grievous unto him.

We cannot trust much to ourselves, because grace is often wanting in us, and understanding also. There is but little light in us, and that which we have we quickly lose by our negligence. Often, too, we do not perceive our own inward blindness nor see how great it is. We often do evil, and, worse, excuse it. We are sometimes moved with passion and we think it to be zeal. We reprehend small things in others and pass over greater matters in ourselves. We quickly enough feel and weigh what we suffer at the hands of others; but we mind not what others suffer from us. He that well and rightly considereth his own works, will find little cause to judge harshly of another.

The inward Christian preferreth the care of himself before all other cares. And he that diligently attendeth unto himself, can easily keep silence concerning others. Thou wilt never be thus inwardly religious unless thou pass over other men's matters with silence, and look especially to thyself. If thou attend wholly unto God and thyself, thou wilt be but little moved with whatsoever thou seest abroard. Where art thou when thou art not with thyself? And when thou hast run over all, what hast thou then profited, if thou hast neglected thyself? If thou desirest peace of mind and true unity of purpose, thou must still put all things behind thee, and look only upon thyself.

Thou shalt then make great progress, if thou keepest thyself free from all temporal care. Thou shalt greatly fall back, if thou esteem anything temporal as of value. Let nothing be great unto thee, nothing high, nothing pleasing, nothing acceptable, but only God himself, or that which comes from God. Esteem as vain all comfort which thou receivest from any creature. A soul that loveth God despiseth all things that are inferior to God. God alone is everlasting, and of infinite greatness, filling all creatures; the soul's solace, and the true joy of the heart.

The glory of a good man is the testimony of a good conscience. Have a good conscience, and thou shalt ever have joy. A good conscience is able to bear very much, and is very cheerful in adversities. An evil conscience is always fearful and unquiet. Thou shalt rest sweetly, if thy heart does not reprehend thee. Never rejoice, but when thou hast done well. Sinners never have true joy, nor feel inward peace; because "there is no peace to the wicked," saith the Lord. And if they should say, "We are in peace, no evil shall fall upon us, and who shall dare to hurt us?" believe them not; for upon a sudden will arise the wrath of God, and their deeds shall be brought to nothing and their thoughts shall perish.

To glory in tribulation is no hard thing for him that loveth; for so to glory, is to glory in the cross of the Lord. That glory is short, which is given and received from men. Sorrow always accompanieth the world's glory. The glory of the good is in their consciences, and not in the tongues of men. The gladness of the just is of God, and in God; and their joy is of the truth. He that desireth true and everlasting glory careth not for that which is temporal. And he that seeketh temporal glory, or despiseth it not from his soul, showeth himself to have but little esteem of the glory of Heaven. He enjoyeth great tranquillity of heart that careth neither for the praise nor blame men.

He will easily be content and at peace, whose conscience is pure. Thou art not the more holy, though thou be commended; nor the more worthless, though thou be found fault with. What thou art, that thou art; not by words canst thou not be made greater than what thou art in the sight of God. If thou consider what thou art within thee, thou wilt not care what men say of thee. Man looketh on the countenance, but God on the heart. Man considereth the deeds, but God weigheth the intentions. To be always doing well, and to esteem little of oneself, is the sign of a humble soul. To refuse to be comforted by any creature is a sign of great purity and inward confidence.

He that seeketh no witness for himself from without, doth show that he hath wholly committed himself unto God. "For not he that commendeth himself, the same is approved," saith blessed Paul, "but whom God commendeth." To walk inwardly with God, and not to be kept abroad by any outward affection, is the state of a spiritual man.

Blessed is he that understandeth what it is to love Jesus, and who despiseth himself for Jesus's sake. Thou oughtest to leave thy beloved for thy Beloved; so that Jesus will be loved alone above all things. The love of things created is deceitful and inconstant; the love of Jesus is faithful and persevering. He that cleaveth unto creatures shall fall with that which is subject to fall; he that embraceth Jesus shall stand firmly for ever. Love Him, and keep Him for thy friend, who, when all others go away, will not forsake thee, nor suffer thee to perish in the end. Some time or other thou must be separated from all, whether thou wilt or not.

Keep close to Jesus both in life and in death, and commit thyself unto his trust, who, when all fail, can alone help thee. Thy Beloved is of that nature that he will admit of no rival; but will have thy heart alone, and sit on His own throne as King. If thou couldst empty thyself perfectly from all creatures, Jesus would willingly dwell with thee. Whatever thou reposest in men, not in Jesus, is all little better than lost. Trust not nor lean upon a reed shaken by the wind; for all flesh is grass, and all the glory thereof shall wither away as the flower of the field.

Thou shalt quickly be deceived, if thou only look to the outward appearance of men. For if in others thou seekest thy comfort and profit, thou shalt too often feel loss. If thou seekest Jesus in all things, thou shalt surely find Jesus. But if thou seekest thyself, thou shalt also find thyself, but to thine own destruction. For man doth more hurt himself if he seek not Jesus, than the whole world and all his adversaries could injure him.

When Jesus is present, all is well, and nothing seems difficult; but when Jesus is absent, everything is hard. When Jesus speaks not inwardly to us, all other comfort is nothing worth; but if Jesus speaks but one word, we feel great consolation. Did not Mary Magdelene rise immediately from the place where she wept, when Martha said to her, "The Master is come, and calleth for thee?" Happy hour! when Jesus calleth from tears to spiritual joy. How dry and hard art thou without Jesus! How foolish and vain if thou desire anything out of Jesus! Is not this a greater loss, than if thou shouldest lose the whole world?

What can the world profit thee without Jesus? To be without Jesus is a grievous hell; and to be with Jesus a sweet paradise. If Jesus be with thee, no enemy shall be able to hurt thee. He that findeth Jesus findeth a good treasure, a good above all good. And he that loseth Jesus loseth much indeed, more than the whole world! Most poor is he who liveth without Jesus; and he most rich who is well with Jesus.

It is a matter of great skill to know how to converse with Jesus; and to know how to keep Jesus, a point of great wisdom. Be thou humble and peaceable, and Jesus will be with thee. Be devout and quiet, and Jesus will stay with thee. Thou mayest soon drive away Jesus, and lose His favour, if thou wilt turn aside to outward things. And if thou shouldest drive Him from thee, and lose Him, unto whom wilt thou flee and who wilt thou then seek for thy friend? Without a friend thou canst not well live; and if Jesus be not above all a friend to thee, thou shalt be indeed sad and desolate. Thou actest therefore like an idiot if thou trust or rejoice in any other. It is preferable to have all the world against us, rather than to have Jesus offended with us. Amongst all therefore that be dear unto us, let Jesus alone be specially loved.

Love all for Jesus, but Jesus for Himself. Jesus Christ alone is singularly to be loved; who alone is found good and faithful above all friends. For Him, and in Him, let friends as well as foes be dear unto thee; and all these are to be prayed for, that He would make them all know and love Him. Never desire to be singularly commended or beloved, for that appertaineth only unto God, who hath none like unto Himself. Neither do thou desire that the heart of any should be set on thee, nor do thou set thy heart on the love of any; but let Jesus be in thee, and in every good man.

Be pure and free within, and entangle not thy heart with any creature. Thou oughtest to be naked and open before God, ever carrying thy heart pure towards Him, if thou wouldest be free to consider and see how sweet the Lord is. And truly, unless thou be prevented and drawn by His grace, thou shalt never attain to that happiness to forsake and take leave of all, that thou alone mayest be united to Him alone. For when the grace of God cometh unto a man, then he is made able to do all things. And when it goeth away, then is he poor and weak, and as it were left only for the lash and the scourge. In this case thou oughtest not to be dejected, nor to despair; but at God's will to stand steadily, and, whatever comes upon thee, to endure it for the glory of Jesus Christ; for after winter followeth summer, after night the day returneth, and after a tempest comes a great calm.

It is no hard matter to despise human comfort when we have divine comfort. It is much, very much, to be able to want both human and divine comfort; and, for God's honour, to be willing cheerfully to endure banishment of heart; and to seek oneself in nothing, nor to regard one's own merit. What great matter is it, if at the coming of grace thou be cheerful and devout? This hour is wished for by all men. He rideth easily enough whom the grace of God carrieth. And what marvel if he feel not his burden, he who is borne up by the Almighty, and led by the sovereign guide?

We are always willing to have something for our comfort; and a man doth not without difficulty strip himself of self. The holy martyr Laurence, with his priest, overcame the world, because whatsoever seemed delightsome in the world, he despised; and for the love of Christ he patiently suffered God's chief priest Sixtus, whom he most dearly loved, to be taken away from him for ever. He therefore overcame the love of man by the love of the Creator; and he rather chose what pleased God than human comfort. So also must thou learn to part even with a near and dear friend, for the love of God. Nor must thou take it hard when thou art deserted by a friend, as knowing that we all at last must be separated one from another.

A man must strive long and mightily within himself, before he can learn fully to master himself, and to draw his whole heart unto God. When a man trusteth in himself, he easily slideth unto human comforts. But a true lover of Christ, and a diligent follower of all virtue, does not fall back on comforts, nor seek such sensible sweetnesses; but rather prefers hard exercises and to sustain severe labours for Christ.

When therefore spiritual comfort is given thee from God, receive it with thankfulness; but understand that it is the gift of God, not any deserving of thine. Be not puffed up, be not too joyful nor vainly presumptuous; but rather be all the more humble for that gift, more wary too and fearful in all thine actions; for that hour will pass away, and temptation will follow. When consolation is taken from thee, do not immediately despair; but with humility and patience wait for the heavenly visitation; for God is able to give thee back again even more ample consolation. This is nothing new nor strange unto them that have experience in the way of God; for the great saints and ancient prophets had often experienced such kind of vicissitudes.

For which cause, one under the enjoyment of divine grace said, "I said in my prosperity, I shall never be moved." But in the want of this grace, what he found in himself he goes on thus to speak of, "Thou didst turn Thy face from me, and I was troubled." Yet in the midst of all this he doth not by any means despair, but more earnestly beseecheth the Lord, and saith, "Unto Thee, O Lord, will I cry, and I will pray unto my God." At length he receives the fruit of his prayer and testifies that he was heard, saying, "The Lord hath heard me, and taken pity on me; the Lord hath become my helper." But in what way? "Thou hast turned," saith he, "my sorrow into joy and thou hast compassed me about with gladness." If great saints were so dealt with, we that are weak and poor ought not to despair if we are sometimes fervent and sometimes cold; for the Spirit cometh and goeth, according to the good pleasure of His own will. For which cause blessed Job saith, "Thou visiteth early in the morning, and suddenly thou provest him."

Upon what then can I hope, or wherein ought I to trust, save in the great mercy of God alone, and in the only hope of heavenly grace? For whether I have with me good men, either religious brethren or faithful friends; whether holy books or beautiful treatises, or sweet chanting and hymns; all these help but little, and have but little savour, when grace forsaketh me and I am left in mine own poverty. At such time there is no better remedy than patience, and the denying of myself according to the will of God.

I never found anyone so religious and devout, that he had not sometimes a withdrawing of grace, or felt not some decrease of zeal. There was never a saint so highly wrapped in God and so illuminated, who first or last was not tempted. For he is not worthy of the high contemplation of God, who hath not been exercised with some tribulation for God's sake. For temptation going before is often a sign of ensuing comfort. For unto those that are proved by temptations, heavenly comfort is promised. "He that shall overcome," saith He, "I will give him to eat of the Tree of Life."

But divine consolation is given, that a man may be bolder to bear adversities. There followeth also temptation, lest he should wax proud of any good. The devil sleepeth not, neither is the flesh as yet dead; therefore cease not to prepare thyself for the battle; for on thy right hand and on thy left are enemies who never rest.

Why seekest thou rest, since thou art born to labour? Dispose thyself to patience rather than to comfort, and to the bearing of the cross rather than to gladness. What secular person is there that would not willingly receive spiritual joy and comfort, if he could always have it? For spiritual comforts exceed all the delights of the world and pleasures of the flesh. For all worldly delights are either vain or unclean; but spiritual delights are only pleasant and honest, sprung from virtue, and infused by God into pure minds. But no man can always enjoy these divine comforts according to his desire; for the time of temptation is not long away.

But false freedom of mind and great confidence of ourselves is very contrary to heavenly visitations. God doeth well for us in giving the grace of comfort but man doeth evil in not returning again unto God with thanksgiving. And therefore the gift of grace cannot flow in us, because we are unthankful to the giver, and return them not wholly to the head fountain. For grace ever attendeth him that is duly thankful; and from the proud shall be taken that which is usually given to the humble.

I desire not that consolation that taketh compunction from me; nor do I affect that contemplation which leadeth to haughtiness of mind. For all that is high, is not holy; nor all that is sweet, good; nor every desire, pure; nor is everything that is dear unto us pleasing to God. Willingly do I accept that grace, whereby I may ever be found more humble, and more affected with holy fear, and may become more ready to renounce myself. He that is taught by the gift of grace, and schooled by the scourge of the withdrawing of it, will not dare to attribute any good to himself, but will rather acknowledge himself poor and naked. Give unto God that which is God's, and ascribe unto thyself that which is thine own; that is, give thanks to God for His grace; and acknowledge to thyself alone what is attributed to sin and the punishment due to sin.

Set thyself always in the lowest place and the highest shall be given thee; for the highest cannot stand without the lowest. The greatest saints before God are the least in their own judgments; and the more glorious they are, so much the humbler they are within themselves. Those that are full of truth and heavenly glory are not desirous of vain glory. Those that are firmly settled and grounded in God, can in no way be proud. And they that ascribe unto God, whatever good they have received, seek not glory one of another, but wish for that glory which is from God alone; and desire above all things that God may be praised in Himself, and in all His saints; and are always tending to this very thing.

Be therefore thankful for the least gift, so that thou shalt be meet to receive greater. Let the least be unto thee even as the greatest, the most contemptible gift as of especial value. If thou consider the worth of the giver, no gift will seem little, or of too small esteem. For that cannot be little which is given by the most high God. If He should give punishment and stripes, it ought to be a matter of thankfulness; because He doth it always for our welfare, whatever He permitteth to happen unto us. He that desireth to keep the grace of God, let him be thankful for grace given, and patient for the taking away of it: let him pray that it may return: let him be cautious and humble, lest he lose it.

Jesus hath now many lovers of His heavenly kingdom, but few bearers of His cross. He hath many who are desirous of consolation, but few of tribulation. He findeth many companions of His table, but few of His abstinence. All desire to rejoice with Him, few are willing to endure anything for Him, or with Him. Many follow Jesus to the breaking of bread; but few to the drinking of the cup of His Passion. Many revere His miracles, few follow the ignominy of His cross. Many love Jesus so long as no adversities befall them. Many praise and bless Him so long as they receive any consolations from Him. But if Jesus hides Himself and leaves them but a little while, they fall either into complaining or into too much dejection of mind.

But they who love Jesus for the sake of Jesus and not for some special comfort of their own, bless Him in all tribulation and anguish of heart, as well as in the state of highest comfort. Yea, although He should never be willing to give them comfort, they nevertheless would ever praise Him and wish to be always giving thanks.

O how powerful is the pure love of Jesus, which is mixed with no self-interest or self-love! Are not all those to be called mercenary, who are ever seeking consolations? Do they not show themselves to be rather lovers of themselves than of Christ, who are always thinking of their own profit and advantage? Where shall one be found who is willing to serve God for nothing?

Rarely is any one found so spiritual as to be strippped of the love of all earthly things. For where is any man to be found who is indeed poor in spirit, and thoroughly empty of all affection for creatures? "From afar, yea, from the ends of the earth, is his value." If a man should give all his substance, yet is it nothing. And if he should practise great repentance, still it is little. And if he should attain to all knowledge, he is still far off. And if he should be of great virtue and of very fervent devotion, yet there is much wanting: especially one thing which is most necessary for him. What is that? That leaving all, he forsake himself, and go wholly from himself, and retain nothing out of self-love. And when he hath done all that is to be done so far as he knoweth, let him think that he hath done nothing.

Let him not weigh that much which might be much esteemed; but let him pronounce himself to be in truth an unprofitable servant, as the truth Himself saith, "When you shall have done all things that are commanded you, say 'We are unprofitable servants.'" Then may he be truly poor and naked in spirit, and say with the prophet, "I am alone and poor." Yet no man is richer than he, no man more powerful, no man more free; for he is able to leave himself in the lowest place.

Unto many this seemeth a hard saying, "Deny thyself, take up thy cross, and follow Jesus." But much harder will it be to hear that last word, "Depart from Me, ye cursed, into everlasting fire." For they who now willingly hear and follow the word of the cross, shall not then fear to hear the sentence of everlasting damnation. This sign of the cross shall be in Heaven, when the Lord shall come to judgment. Then all the servants of the cross, who in their lifetime conformed themselves to Christ crucified, shall draw near to Christ the judge with great confidence.

Why therefore fearest thou to take up the cross which leadeth thee to a kingdom? In the cross is salvation, in the cross is life, in the cross is protection against our enemies, in the cross is infusion of heavenly sweetness, in the cross is strength of mind, in the cross joy of spirit, in the cross the height of virtue, in the cross the perfection of sanctity. There is no everlasting life but in the cross. Therefore take up thy cross and follow Jesus, and thou shalt go into life everlasting. He went before, bearing His cross, and died for thee on the cross; that thou mayest also bear thy cross and desire to die on the cross with Him. For if thou be dead with Him, thou shalt also live with Him. And if thou be His companion in punishment, thou shalt be partaker with Him also in glory.

Behold! in the cross all doth consist, and all lieth in our dying thereon; for there is no other way unto life and unto true inward peace, but the way of the holy cross, and of daily mortification. Go where thou wilt, seek whatsoever thou wilt, thou shalt not find a higher way above nor a safer way below, than the way of the holy cross. Dispose and order all things according to thy will and judgment; yet thou shalt ever find that of necessity thou must suffer somewhat, either willingly or against thy will, and so thou shalt ever find the cross. For either thou shalt suffer pain in thy body or in thy soul tribulation of spirit.

Sometimes thou shalt be forsaken of God, sometimes thou shalt be troubled by thy neighbours; and, more often, thou shalt be wearisome to thyself. Neither canst thou be delivered or eased by any remedy or comfort; but as long as it pleaseth God, thou oughtest to bear it. For God will have thee learn to suffer tribulation without comfort; and that thou subject thyself wholly to Him, and by tribulation become more humble. No man hath so sympathetic feeling of the passion of Christ, as he who hath suffered the like himself. The cross, therefore, is always ready, and everywhere waits for thee. Thou canst not escape it wherever thou goest, thou carriest thyself with thee, and shalt ever find thyself. Both above and below, without and within, whichever thou dost turn, everywhere thou shalt find the Cross; and everywhere of necessity thou must hold fast patience, if thou wilt have inward peace, and enjoy an everlasting crown.

If thou bear the cross cheerfully, it will bear thee, and lead thee to the desired end, namely, where there shall be an end of suffering, though here that shall not be. If thou bear it unwillingly, thou makest for thyself a new burden, and increasest thy load, and yet notwithstanding thou must bear it. If thou cast away one cross, without doubt thou shalt find another, and that perhaps a heavier one.

Thinkest thou to escape that which no mortal man could ever avoid? Which of the saints in the world was without crosses and tribulation? For not even our Lord Jesus Christ was ever one hour without the anguish of His passion, so long as He lived. "Christ," saith He, "must needs suffer, and rise again from the dead, and so enter into His glory." And how dost thou seek any other way than this royal way, which is the way of the holy cross?

Christ's whole life was a cross and martyrdom: and dost thou seek rest and joy for thyself? Thou art deceived, thou art deceived if thou seek any other thing than to suffer tribulations; for this whole mortal life is full of miseries, and lined on every side with crosses. And the higher a person advances in spirit, so much the heavier crosses he often findeth; because the grief of his banishment increases with his love of God.

Nevertheless this man, though so many ways afflicted, is not without refreshing comfort, for he perceiveth very much benefit to accrue unto him by the enduring of his own cross. For whilst he willingly putteth himself under it, all the burden of tribulation is turned into the confidence of divine comfort. And the more the flesh is wasted by affliction, so much the more is the spirit strengthened by inward grace. And sometimes he is so comforted with the desire of tribulation and adversity, for the love of conformity to the cross of Christ, that he would not wish to be without grief and tribulation; because he believes that he shall be unto God so much the more acceptable, the more grievous things he can suffer for Him. This is not the power of man, but it is the grace of Christ, which can and doth so much in frail flesh; so that what it naturally abhors and flees from, that by fervour of spirit it encounters and loves.

It is not according to man's inclination to bear the cross, to love the cross, to chastise the body, and bring it into subjection, to flee honours, willingly to suffer, scorn to despise himself and to wish to be despised, to endure all adversities and damages and to desire no prosperity in this world. If thou look, thou shalt be able to thyself to accomplish nothing of this kind. But if thou trust in the Lord, fortitude shall be given thee from Heaven, and the world and the flesh shall be made subject to thy command. Neither shalt thou fear thy enemy the devil, if thou be armed with faith, and signed with the cross of Christ.

Set thyself, therefore, like a good and faithful servant of Christ, to bear manfully the cross of thy Lord, who out of love was crucified for thee. Prepare thyself to bear many adversities and many kinds of troubles in this miserable life; for so it must be with thee, wherever thou art, and so surely thou shalt find it, wherever thou hide thyself. So it must be; nor is there any remedy or means to escape from tribulation and sorrow, but only to endure thyself. Drink of the Lord's cup with hearty affection, if thou desire to be His friend, and never to part with Him. As for comforts, leave them to God; let Him do therein as shall best please Him. But do not set thyself to suffer tribulations, and account them the greatest comforts; for the sufferings of this present time, although thou alone couldest suffer them all, cannot worthily deserve the glory which is to come.

When thou shalt come to this estate, that tribulation shall seem sweet, and thou shalt relish it for Christ's sake; then think it to be well with thee, for thou hast found a paradise upon earth. As long as it is grievous to thee to suffer, and that thou desirest to flee it, so long shalt thou be ill at ease, and the desire of escaping tribulation will follow thee everywhere.

It thou dost set thyself to that which thou oughest, namely to suffering, and to death, it will quickly be better with thee, and thou shalt find peace. Although thou shouldest have been carried unto the third heaven with Paul, thou art not so secure that thou shalt suffer no adversity. "I will show him," saith Jesus, "what great things he must suffer for My name." It remaineth, therefore, that thou must suffer, if it please thee to love Jesus, and to serve Him perpetually.

O that thou wert worthy to suffer something for the name of Jesus! How great glory would remain unto thyself; what joy would arise to all God's saints; what great edification also to thy neighbour! For all men recommend patience; few, however, are willing to suffer. With great reason oughtest thou cheerfully to suffer some little for Christ's sake; since many suffer more grievous things merely for the world.

Know for certain that thou oughtest to lead a dying life. And the more any man dieth to himself, so much the more doth he begin to live unto God. No man is fit to comprehend heavenly things, unless he submit himself to the bearing of adversities for Christ's sake. Nothing is more acceptable to God, nothing more wholesome to thee in this world, than to suffer cheerfully for Christ. And if thou couldest choose, thou oughtest rather to wish to suffer adversities for Christ, than to be refreshed with many consolations; because thou wouldest thus be more like unto Christ, and more conformable to all the saints. For our worthiness, and the proficiency of our spiritual estate consisteth not in many sweetnesses and comforts; but rather in thoroughly enduring great afflictions and tribulations.

Indeed, if there had been any better thing, and anything more profitable to man's salvation, than suffering, surely Christ would have shown it by word and example. For both the disciples that followed Him, and also all who desire to follow Him, He plainly exhorteth to bear of the cross, and saith, "If any will come after Me, let him deny himself, and take up his cross, and follow Me." So that when we have thoroughly read and searched all, let this be the final conclusion, "That through many tribulations we must enter into the Kingdom of God."

BOOK III

"I will hearken what the Lord God will

speak in me." Blessed is the soul which heareth the Lord speaking within her, and receiveth from His mouth the word of consolation. Blessed are the ears that gladly receive the pulses of the divine whisper, and give no heed to the many whisperings of this world. Blessed indeed are those ears which listen not after the voice which is sounding without, but for the Truth teaching inwardly. Blessed are the eyes which are shut to outward things, but intent on things eternal. Blessed are they that enter far into things internal, and endeavour to prepare themselves more and more, by daily exercises, for the receiving of heavenly secrets. Blessed are they who are glad to have time to spare for God, and who shake off all wordly impediments.

Consider these things, O my soul, and shut up the door of thy sensual desires, that thou mayest hear what the Lord thy God shall speak in thee. Thus saith thy Beloved, I am thy salvation, thy peace, and thy life: keep thyself with Me, and thou shalt find peace. Let go all transitory things, and seek those which are everlasting. What are all temporal things but seducing snares? and what can all creatures avail thee if thou art forsaken by the Creator? Bid farewell, therefore, to all other things, and labour to please thy Creator and to be faithful unto Him, that so thou mayest be able to attain unto true blessedness.

Speak, O Lord, for Thy servant heareth. I am Thy servant, grant me understanding, that I may know Thy testimonies. Incline my heart to the words of Thy mouth: let Thy speech distil as the dew. The children of Israel in times past said unto Moses, "Speak thou unto us, and we will hear: let not the Lord speak unto us, lest we die." Not thus, Lord, not thus, I beseech Thee: but rather, with the prophet Samuel, I humbly and earnestly entreat, "Speak, Lord, for Thy servant heareth." Let not Moses speak unto me, nor any of the prophets, but rather do Thou speak, O Lord God, inspirer and enlightener of all the prophets; for Thou alone without them canst perfectly instruct me, but they without Thee can profit nothing.

They indeed may sound forth words, but they cannot give the Spirit. Most beautifully do they speak, but if Thou art silent, they inflame not the heart. They teach the letter, but Thou openest the sense: they bring forth mysteries, but Thou unlockest the meaning of sealed things. They declare Thy commandments, but Thou helpest us to fulfil them. They point out the way, but Thou givest strength to walk in it. What they can do is only external, but Thou instructest and enlightenest the heart. They water outwardly, but Thou givest fruitfulness. They cry aloud in words, but Thou impartest understanding to the hearing.

Let not Moses therefore speak unto me but Thou, O Lord my God, the everlasting truth; lest I die, and prove unfruitful, if I be only warned outwardly, and not inflamed within. Lest it turn to my condemnation, – the word heard and not fulfilled, known and not loved, believed and not observed. Speak therefore, Lord, for Thy servant heareth: for Thou hast the words of eternal life. Speak Thou unto me, to the comfort, however imperfect, of my soul, and to the amendment of my whole life, and to Thy praise and glory and honour everlasting.

My son, hear My words, words of greatest sweetness, surpassing all the knowledge of the philosophers and wise men of this world. "My words are Spirit and Life," and not to be weighed by the understanding of man. They are not to be drawn forth for vain approbation, but to be heard in silence, and to be received with all humility and great affection. And I said, Blessed is the man whom Thou shalt instruct, O Lord, and shalt teach out of Thy law, that Thou mayest give him rest from the evil days, and that he be not desolate upon earth.

I taught the prophets from the beginning, saith the Lord, and cease not, even to this day, to speak to all; but many are hardened, and deaf to My voice. The majority of people do more willingly listen to the world than to God; they would rather follow the desires of their own flesh than God's good pleasure. The world promiseth things temporal and mean, and is served with great eagerness: I promise things most high and eternal, and yet the hearts of men remain torpid and insensible. Who is there that in all things serveth and obeyeth Me with such great care as the world and its lords are served withal? "Be ashamed, O Sidon, saith the sea." And if thou ask the cause, hear why. For a small fee, a long journey is undertaken; for everlasting life, many will scarce once lift a foot from the ground. The most pitiful reward is sought after; for a single bit of money sometimes there is shameful contention; for a vain matter and slight promise, men fear not to toil day and night.

But, alas! For an unchangeable good, for an inestimable reward, for the highest honour, and glory without end, they grudge even the least fatigue. Be ashamed, therefore, thou slothful and complaining servant, that they are found to be more ready to destruction than thou to life. They rejoice more in vanity than thou dost in the truth. Sometimes, indeed, they are frustrated of their hope; but My promise deceiveth none, nor sendeth anyone away empty who trusteth in Me. What I have promised, I will give; what I have said, I will fulfil; if only any man remains faithful in My love even to the end. I am the rewarder of all good men, and the strong approver of all who are devoted to Me.

Write thou My words in thy heart, and meditate diligently on them; for in time of temptation they will be very needful for thee. What thou understandest not when thou readest, thou shalt know in the day of visitation. In two ways I visit my elect, namely, with temptation and with consolation. And I daily read two lessons to them, one in reproving their vices, another in exhorting them to the increase of all virtues. He that hath My words and despiseth them, hath One that shall judge him in the last day.

A Prayer to implore the grace of Devotion. O Lord my God! Thou art to me whatsoever is good. And who am I, that I should dare speak to Thee? I am Thy poorest, meanest servant, and a most vile worm, much more poor and contemptible than I can or dare express. Yet do Thou remember me, O Lord, because I am nothing, I have nothing, and I can do nothing. Thou alone art good, just, and holy; Thou canst do all things; Thou accomplishest all things, Thou fillest all things, only the sinner Thou leavest empty. Remember Thy mercies, and fill my heart with Thy grace, Thou who wilt not that Thy works should be void and in vain. How can I bear up myself in this miserable life, unless Thou strengthen me with Thy mercy and grace? Turn not Thy face away from me; delay not Thy visitation; withdraw not Thy consolation, lest my soul become as a thirsty land unto Thee. Teach me, O Lord, to do Thy will; teach me to live worthily and humbly in Thy sight; for Thou art my wisdom, Thou dost truly know me, and didst know me before the world was made, and before I was born in the world.

My son, walk thou before Me in truth, and ever seek Me in simplicity of thy heart. He that walketh before Me in truth, shall be defended from evil incursions, and the truth shall set him free from seducers, and from the slanders of unjust men. If the truth has made thee free, thou shalt be free indeed, and shalt not care for the vain words of men. O Lord, it is true. According as Thou sayest, so, I beseech Thee, let it be with me; let Thy truth teach me, guard me, and preserve me safe to the end. Let it set me free from all evil affection and inordinate love; and I shall walk with Thee in great liberty of heart.

I will teach thee, saith the Truth, those things which are right and pleasing in My sight. Reflect on thy sins with great displeasure and grief; and never esteem thyself because of any good works. In truth thou art a sinner; thou art subject to and encumbered with many passions. Of thyself thou always tendest to nothing; speedily art thou cast down, speedily overcome, speedily disordered, speedily dissolved. Thou hast nothing in which thou canst glory, but many things for which thou oughtest to account thyself vile; for thou art much weaker than thou art able to comprehend.

And therefore let nothing seem much unto thee whatever thou doest. Let nothing seem great, nothing precious and wonderful, nothing worthy of estimation, nothing high, nothing truly commendable and to be desired but only that which is eternal. Let the eternal truth be above all things pleasing to thee. Let thy own extreme unworthiness be always displeasing to thee. Fear nothing, blame nothing, flee nothing, so much as thy vices and sins; which ought to be more unpleasing to thee than any losses whatsoever of earthly things. Some walk insincerely in My sight, but led by a certain curiosity and pride wish to know My secrets, and to understand the high things of God, neglecting themselves and their own salvation. These people, when I resist them, for their pride and curiosity, often fall into great temptations and sins.

Fear the judgments of God and dread the wrath of the Almighty. Do not however discuss the works of the Most High, but search diligently thine own iniquities, and see in how many great things thou hast offended, and how many good things thou hast neglected. Some carry their devotion only in books, some in pictures, some in outward signs and figures. Some have Me in their mouths, but little in their hearts. Others there are who, being illuminated in their understandings and purged in their affection, do always breathe after things eternal, are unwilling to hear of the things of this world, and to serve the necessities of nature with grief; and these perceive what the Spirit of Truth speaketh in them. For He teacheth them to despise earthly, and to love heavenly, things, to neglect the world, and to desire Heaven all the day and night.

I bless thee, O Heavenly Father, Father of my Lord Jesus Christ, for Thou hast vouchsafed to remember me, a poor creature. O Father of mercies and God of all comfort, thanks be to Thee, who sometimes with Thy comfort refreshest me, unworthy as I am of all comfort. I will always bless and glorify Thee, with Thy only-begotten Son, and the Holy Ghost, the Comforter, for ever and ever. Ah, Lord God, Thou holy lover of my soul, when Thou comest into my heart, all that is within me shall rejoice. Thou art my glory, and the exultation of my heart: Thou art my hope and refuge in the day of my trouble.

But because I am as yet weak in love, and imperfect in virtue, I need to be strengthened and comforted by Thee; therefore visit me often, and instruct me with all holy discipline. Set me free from evil passions, and heal my heart of all inordinate affections; that being inwardly cured and thoroughly cleansed, I may be made fit to love, courageous to suffer, steady to persevere.

Love is a great thing, a great and thorough good; by itself it makes every thing that is heavy, light; and it bears evenly all that is uneven. For it carries a burden which is no burden, and makes everything that is bitter, sweet and tasteful. The noble love of Jesus impels a man to do great things, and stirs him up to be always longing for what is more perfect. Love desires to be aloft, and will not be kept back by anything low and mean. Love desires to be free, and estranged from all worldly affections, so that its inward sight may not be hindered; that it may not be entangled by any temporal prosperity, or subdued by any adversity. Nothing is sweeter than love, nothing more courageous, nothing higher, nothing wider, nothing more pleasant, nothing fuller nor better in Heaven and earth; because love is born of God, and cannot rest but in God, above all created things.

He that loveth, flieth, runneth, and rejoiceth; he is free, and cannot be held in. He giveth all for all, and hath all in all; because he resteth in One highest above all things, from whom all that is good flows and proceeds. He respecteth not the gifts, but turneth himself above all goods unto the giver. Love knoweth no measure, but is fervent beyond all measure. Love feels no burden, thinks nothing of trouble, attempts what is above its strength, pleads no excuse of impossibility; for it thinks all things lawful for itself and all things possible. It is therefore able to undertake all things, and it completes many things, and warrants them to take effect where he who does not love would faint and lie down.

Love is watchful and, sleeping, slumbereth not. Though weary, it is not tired; though pressed, it is not straightened; though alarmed, it is not confounded: but as a lively flame and burning torch, it forces its way upwards, and securely passes through all. If any man love, he knoweth what is the cry of this voice. For it is a loud cry in the ears of God, the mere ardent affection of the soul, when it saith, "My God, my Love, Thou art all mine, and I am all Thine."

Enlarge Thou me in love that with the inward palate of my heart I may taste, how sweet it is to love, and to be dissolved, and, as it were, to bathe myself in Thy love. Let me be possessed by love, mounting above myself, through excessive fervour and admiration. Let me sing the song of love, let me follow Thee, my Beloved, on high; let my soul spend itself in Thy praise, rejoicing through love. Let me love Thee more than myself, nor love myself but for Thee: and, in Thee, love all that truly love Thee, as the law of Love commandeth, shining out from Thyself.

Love is active, sincere, affectionate, pleasant, and amiable; courageous, patient, faithful, prudent, long-suffering, and never seeking itself. For in whatever instance a person seeketh himself, there he falleth from love. Love is circumspect, humble and upright: not yielding to softness or to levity, nor attending to vain things; it is sober, chaste, steady, quiet, and guarded. Love is subject and obedient to its superiors, to itself mean and despised, to God devout and thankful, trusting and hoping always in Him even when God imparteth no relish of sweetness unto it: for without sorrow none liveth in love.

He that is not prepared to suffer all things, and to stand to the will of his Beloved, is not worthy to be called a lover of God. A lover ought to embrace willingly all that is hard and distasteful for the sake of his Beloved; and not to turn away from Him for any contrary accidents.

My son, thou art not yet a courageous and considerate lover. Wherefore sayest Thou this, O Lord? Because for a slight opposition thou givest over thy undertakings, and too eagerly seekest consolation. A courageous lover standeth firm in temptations, and giveth no credit to the crafty persuasions of the enemy. As I please him in prosperity, so in adversity I am not unpleasant to him.

A considerate lover regardeth not so much the gift of Him who loves him, as the love of the giver. He esteems the good will rather than the value of the gift, and sets all gifts below Him who he loves. A noble-minded lover resteth not in the gift, but in Me above every gift. All therefore is not lost, if sometimes thou hast less feeling for Me or My saints than thou wouldest. That good and sweet affection which thou sometimes feelest, is the effect of grace present, and a sort of foretaste of thy heavenly home: but thou must not lean too much on this for it comes and goes. But to strive against evil thoughts which may occur to thee, and to reject with scorn the suggestions of the devil, is a notable sign of virtue, and shall have great reward.

Let no strange fancies therefore trouble thee, which on any subject whatever may crowd into thy mind. Keep to thy purpose with courage and an upright intention towards God. Neither is it an illusion that sometimes thou art suddenly rapt on high, and presently returnest again unto the accustomed vanities of thy heart. For these thou dost rather unwillingly suffer, than commit: and so long as they displease thee, and thou strivest against them, it is matter of reward, and no loss.

Know that the ancient enemy doth strive by all means to hinder thy desire for good, and to keep thee clear of all religious exercises; particularly from the reverent estimation of God's saints, from the devout commemoration of My passion, from the profitable remembrance of sins, from the guard of thine own heart, and from the firm purpose of advancing in virtue. Many evil thoughts does he suggest to thee, so that he may cause a wearisomeness and horror in thee, to call thee back from prayer and holy reading. Humble confession is displeasing unto him; and if he could, he would cause thee to cease from Holy Communion. Trust him not, nor care for him, although he will often set snares of deceit to entrap thee. Charge him with it, when he suggesteth evil and unclean thoughts unto thee; say unto him, "Away thou unclean spirit! Blush, thou miserable wretch! Most unclean art thou that bringest such things unto mine ears. Begone from me, thou wicked seducer! thou shalt have no part in me: but Jesus shall be with me as a strong warrior, and thou shalt stand confounded. I would rather die, and undergo any torment, than consent unto thee. Hold thy peace, and be silent; I will hear thee no more, though thou shouldest work me many troubles. "The Lord is my light and my salvation, whom then shall I fear?" If whole armies should stand together against me, my heart shall not fear. The Lord is my helper and my redeemer."

Fight like a good soldier: and if thou sometimes fall through frailty, take again greater strength than before, trusting in My more abundant grace: and take great care of pleasing thyself, and of pride. This brings many into error, and makes them sometimes fall into almost incurable blindness. Let the fall of the proud, thus foolishly presuming of themselves, warn thee and keep thee ever humble.

My son, it is more profitable and safer for thee, to conceal the grace of devotion; not to lift thyself on high, nor to speak much of it or to dwell much upon it; but rather to despise thyself, and to fear it, as given to one unworthy of it. This affection must not be too earnestly cleaved unto, for it may be quickly changed to the contrary. Think when thou art in grace, how miserable and needy thou art without grace. Nor is it in this only that thy progress in spiritual life consists, when thou hast the grace of comfort; but rather when with humility, self-denial, and patience, thou endurest the withdrawing of it; provided thou do not then become listless in the exercise of prayer, nor suffer the rest of thy accustomed duties to be at all neglected. Rather do thou cheerfully perform what lieth in thee, according to the best of thy power and understanding; and do not wholly neglect thyself because of the dryness or anxiety of mind which thou feelest.

For there are many who, when things do not succeed well with them, presently become impatient or slothful. For the way of man is not always in his power, but it belongeth to God to give, and to comfort, when He will, and how much He will, and whom He will; as it shall please Him, and no more. Some unadvised persons, in their over earnest desire of the grace of a devoted life, have destroyed themselves; because they attempted more than they were able to perform, not weighing the measure of their own weakness, but following the desire of their heart rather than the judgment of their reason. And because they presumed on greater matters than was pleasing to God, they therefore quickly lost His grace. They who had built themselves nests in Heaven were made helpless and vile outcasts; to the end that being humbled and impoverished, they might learn not to fly with their own wings, but to trust under My feathers. They that are yet but novices and inexperienced in the way of the Lord, unless they govern themselves by the counsel of discreet persons, may easily be deceived and broken to pieces.

And if they will rather follow their own notions than trust to others who are more experienced, their end will be dangerous, at least if they are unwilling to be drawn away from their own foolish conceit. It is seldom the case that they who are self-wise endure humbly to be governed by others. Better it is to have a small portion of good sense with humility, and a slender understanding, than great treasures of many sciences with vain self-complacency. Better it is for thee to have little of that which may make thee proud. He acts not very discreetly, who wholly gives himself over to spiritual joy, forgetting his former helplessness, and that chastened fear of the Lord which is afraid of losing the grace which hath been offered. Nor again is he very valiantly wise who, in time of adversity or any heaviness, at once yields too much to despairing thoughts, and reflects and thinks of Me less confidingly than he ought.

He who in time of peace is willing to be over-secure often shall be found in time of war too much dejected and full of fears. If thou hadst the wit always to continue humble and moderate within thyself, and also thoroughly to moderate and govern thy spirit, thou wouldest not so quickly fall into danger and offence. It is good counsel, that when fervour of spirit is kindled within thee, thou shouldest consider how it will be when that light shall leave thee. And when this does happen, then remember that the light may return again, which as a warning to thyself and for Mine own glory, I have withdrawn for a time.

Such trials are often more profitable than if thou shouldest always have things prosper according to thy will. For a man's worthiness is not to be estimated by the number of visions and comforts which he may have, or by his skill in the scriptures, or by his being placed in a higher station than others. But the proof is if he be grounded in true humility, and full of divine charity; if he be always purely and sincerely seeking God's honour; if he think nothing of, and unfeignedly despise, himself, and even rejoice more to be despised and put low by others, than to be honoured by them.

Shall I speak unto my Lord since I am but dust and ashes? If I esteem myself to be anything more, behold, Thou standest against me, and my iniquities bear true witness, and I cannot contradict it. But if I abase myself, and reduce myself to nothing, and shrink from all self-esteem, and grind myself to what I am, dust, Thy grace will be favourable to me, and Thy light near unto my heart; and all self-esteem, however little, shall be swallowed up in the valley of my nothingness, and perish for ever. There Thou showest Thyself unto me, what I am, what I have been, and from where I come; for I am nothing, and I knew it not. If I am left to myself, behold! I become nothing but mere weakness; but if Thou for an instant look upon me, I am forthwith made strong, and am filled with new joy. And a great marvel it is, that I am so suddenly lifted up, and so graciously embraced by Thee, who of mine own weight am always sinking downward.

Thy love is the cause of this, freely preventing me, and relieving me from so many necessities, guarding me from pressing dangers, and snatching me, as I may truly say, from inumerable. For indeed by loving myself amiss, I lost myself; and by seeking Thee alone, and purely loving Thee, I have found both myself and Thee, and by that love have more deeply reduced myself to nothing. Because Thou, O sweetest Lord, dealest with me above all desert, and above all that I dare hope for or ask.

Blessed be Thou, my God: for although I am unworthy of any benefits, yet Thy noble bounty and infinite goodness never ceaseth to do good even to the ungrateful, and to those who are turned away far from Thee. Turn Thou us unto Thee, that we may be thankful, humble, and devout; for Thou art our salvation, our courage, and our strength.

My son, I ought to be thy supreme and ultimate end, if thou desire to be truly blessed. With this intention thy affections will be purified, which are too often inordinately inclined to selfishness and unto creatures. For if in anything thou seekest thyself, immediately thou faintest and driest up. I would therefore thou shouldest refer all things unto Me in the first place, for I am He who have given all. Consider everything as flowing from the Highest Good; and therefore all must be reduced unto Me as their original.

From Me, as from a living fountain, the small and the great, the poor and the rich, draw the water of life; and they that willingly and freely serve Me, shall receive grace for grace. But he who desires to glory in things out of Me, or to take pleasure in some private good, shall not be grounded in true joy, nor be enlarged in his heart, but shall in many ways be encumbered and straitened. Thou oughtest therefore to ascribe nothing of good to thyself, nor do thou attribute goodness unto any man; but give all unto God, without whom man hath nothing. I have bestowed all, and My will is to have thee all again; and with great strictness do I require a return of thanks.

This is the truth whereby vainglory is put to flight. And if heavenly grace enter in and true charity, there will be no envy nor narrowness of heart, neither will self-love busy itself. For divine charity overcometh all things, and enlargeth all the powers of the soul. If thou rightly judge, thou wilt rejoice in Me alone, in Me alone thou wilt hope; for none is good save God alone, who is to be praised above all things, and in all to be blessed.

Now I will speak again, O Lord, and will not be silent; I will say in the ears of my God, my Lord and my King, who is on high: "O how great is the abundance of Thy goodness, O Lord, which Thou hast laid up for them that fear Thee." But what art Thou to those who love Thee? What to those who serve Thee with their whole heart? Truly unspeakable is the sweetness of contemplating Thee, which Thou bestowest on them that love Thee. In this especially Thou hast showed me the sweetness of Thy charity; that when I was not, Thou madest me, when I went far astray from Thee, Thou broughtest me back again that I might serve Thee, and hast commanded me to love Thee.

O Fountain of love unceasing, what shall I say concerning Thee? How can I forget Thee, who hast vouchsafed to remember me, even after I have wasted away and perished? Thou hast shown mercy to Thy servant beyond all expectation; and hast exhibited favour and loving kindness beyond all desert. What return shall I make to Thee for this grace? For it is not granted to all to forsake all, to renounce the world, and to undertake a life of religious seclusion. Is it any great thing that I should serve Thee, whom the whole creation is bound to serve? It ought not to seem much to me, to serve Thee; but rather this doth appear much to me and wonderful, that Thou vouchsafest to receive into Thy service one so poor and unworthy, and to make him one with Thy beloved servants.

Behold! all things are Thine which I have, and whereby I serve Thee. And yet on the other hand, Thou rather servest me than I Thee. Behold! Heaven and earth, which Thou hast created for the service of man, are ready at hand, and do daily perform whatever Thou hast commanded. And this is little; Thou has moreover also appointed angels to minister to man. But that which excelleth all this is that Thou Thyself hast vouchsafed to serve man, and hast promised that Thou wouldest give Thyself unto him.

What shall I give Thee for all these thousands of benefits? I would I could serve Thee all the days of my life. I would I were able, at least for one day, to do Thee some worthy service. Truly Thou art worthy of all service, of all honour and everlasting praise. Truly Thou art my Lord, and I Thy poor servant, who am bound to serve Thee with all my might, neither ought I ever to be weary of praising Thee. And this I wish to do, this I desire; and whatsoever is lacking to me, do Thou, I beseech Thee, vouchsafe to supply.

It is a great honour and a great glory to serve Thee, and despise all things for Thee. For great grace shall be given to those who have willingly subjected themselves to Thy most holy service. Those who for Thy love have renounced all carnal delights shall find the sweetest consolations of the Holy Ghost. They shall attain great freedom of mind, who for Thy name's sake enter into the narrow way, and have left off all worldly care.

O sweet and delightful service of God, by which a man is made truly free and holy! O sacred state of religious servitude, which makes a man equal to the angels, pleasing to God, terrible to devils, and worthy to be commended of all the faithful! O welcome service, ever to be desired, in which we are rewarded with the greatest good and attain to joy which shall endlessly remain with us!

My son, it is needful for thee still to learn many things more, which thou hast not even yet well learned. What are these, O Lord? That thou frame thy desires wholly according to My good pleasure; and that thou be not a lover of thyself, but an earnest follower of My will. Various longings and desires often inflame thee and drive thee forwards with vehemence; but do thou consider whether thou be not thus moved rather for thine own advantage, than for My honour. If I Myself be the cause, thou wilt be well content with whatever I shall ordain; but if there lurk in thee any self-seeking, behold, this it is that hindereth thee and weigheth thee down.

Beware therefore thou lean not too much upon any preconceived desire, without asking My counsel, lest perhaps afterwards it repent thee, or thou be displeased with that which at first pleased thee, and which thou wast earnestly zealous for, as being the best. For not every affection which seems good is immediately to be followed; nor again is every contrary affection at the first to be avoided. It is sometimes expedient to use restraint even in good desires and endeavours, lest through importunity thou incur distraction of mind; lest by thy want of self discipline thou beget a scandal unto others: or again being by others thwarted and resisted, thou become suddenly confounded, and so fall.

Sometimes, however, thou must use violence, and resist manfully thy sensual appetite, not regarding what the flesh would, or would not; but rather taking pains that it may be made subject to the Spirit; and it ought to be chastised and to be forced to remain under servitude, until it be prepared for everything, and learn to be content with a little, and to be pleased with plain and simple things, nor to murmur against any inconvenience.

O Lord my God, patience is very necessary for me, as I plainly see, for many things in this life happen contrary to us. For whatever plans I devise for my own peace, my life cannot be without war and affliction. It is so, My son. But My will is, that thou seek not that peace which is void of temptations, or which feeleth nothing contrary; but rather think that thou hast then found peace, when thou art exercised with sundry tribulations, and tried in many adversities.

If thou say that thou art not able to suffer much, how then wilt thou endure the fire hereafter? Of two evils the lesser is always to be chosen. That thou mayest therefore avoid future everlasting punishment, endeavour to endure present evils patiently for God's sake. Dost thou think that the men of this world suffer nothing, or but a little? Ask even of those who enjoy the greatest delights, and thou shalt find it otherwise. But, thou wilt say, they have many delights, and follow their own wills, and therefore they do not much weigh their own afflictions. It is so, that they have whatever they want; but how long dost thou think it will last?

Behold, the wealthy of this world shall fade away like smoke, and there shall be no memory of their past joys! Yea, even while they are alive, they do not have peace in themselves without bitterness, weariness, and fear. For from the self-same thing in which they imagine their delight to be, often they receive the penalty of sorrow. Nor is it anything but just, that having inordinately sought and followed after pleasures, they should not enjoy them without shame and bitterness.

O how brief, how false, how extreme and filthy are all those pleasures. Yet so drunken and blind are men that they do not understand; but like dumb beasts, for the poor enjoyment of this corruptible life, they incur the death of the soul. Thou therefore, My son, "go not after thy lusts, but refrain thyself from thine appetites." "Delight thyself in the Lord, and He shall give thee the desires of thine heart."

For if thou desire true delight, and to be more fully comforted by Me; behold, in the contempt of all worldly things, and in the cutting off all base delights, shall be thy blessing, and abundant consolation shall be given thee. And the more thou withdrawest thyself from all solace of creatures, how much sweeter and more powerful consolations shalt thou find in Me. But at the first, thou shalt not without some sadness, nor without a laborious conflict, attain unto these consolations. Old inbred habits will make resistance, but they shall be entirely overcome by better habits. The flesh will murmur against thee; but with fervency of spirit thou shalt restrain it. The old serpent will incite and trouble thee, but by prayer he shall be put to flight; moreover, by any useful employment thou shalt greatly stop the way against him.

My son, he that endeavoureth to withdraw himself from obedience, withdraweth himself from grace: and he who seeketh for himself private benefits, loseth those which are common. He that doth not cheerfully and freely submit himself to his superior, it is a sign that his flesh is not as yet perfectly obedient unto him, but often kicketh and murmureth against him. Learn thou therefore quickly to submit thyself to thy superior, if thou desire to keep thine own flesh under the yoke. For the outward enemy is more speedily overcome, if the inward man is not laid waste. There is no worse enemy, nor one more troublesome to the soul, than thou art unto thyself, if thou art not in harmony with the Spirit. It is altogether necessary that thou take up a true contempt for thyself, if thou desire to prevail against flesh and blood.

Because as yet thou lovest thyself too much, therefore thou art afraid to resign thyself wholly to the will of others. And yet, what greater matter is it, if thou, who art but dust and nothing, subject thyself to a man for God's sake, when I, the Almighty and the Most Highest, who created all things of nothing, humbly subjected Myself to man for thy sake? I became of all men the most humble and the most abject, that thou mightest overcome thy pride with My humility. O dust, learn to be obedient. Learn to humble thyself, thou earth and clay, and to bow thyself down under the feet of all men. Learn to break thine own wishes, and to yield thyself to all subjection.

Be fiercely hot against thyself, and suffer no pride to dwell in thee: but show thyself so humble and so very small, that all may be able to walk over thee, and to tread thee down as the dust of the streets. Vain man, what hast thou to complain of? What canst thou answer, foul sinner, to them that upbraid thee, thou who hast so often offended God, and so many times deserved hell? But Mine eye spared thee, because thy soul was precious in My sight; that thou mightest know My love, and ever be thankful for My benefits; that thou mightest continually give thyself to true subjection and humility, and endure patiently the contempt which belongs to thee.

Thou, O Lord, thunderest forth Thy judgments over me, Thou shakest all my bones with fear and trembling, and my soul is sorely afraid. I stand astonished; and I consider "that the Heavens are not pure in Thy sight." If in angels Thou didst find wickedness, and didst not spare even them, what shall become of me? Even stars fell from Heaven, what then can I presume who am but dust? They whose works seemed commendable have fallen into the lowest misery; and those who did eat the bread of angels, I have seen delighting themselves with the husks of swine.

There is therefore no sanctity, if Thou, O Lord, withdraw Thine hand. No wisdom availeth, if Thou cease to guide. No courage helpeth, if Thou cease to defend. No chastity is secure, if Thou do not protect it. No custody of our own availeth, if Thy sacred watchfulness is not present with us. For, if we are left to ourselves, we sink and perish; but being visited by Thee, we are raised up and live. Truly we are unstable, but through Thee we are strengthened: we wax lukewarm, but by Thee we are inflamed.

O how humbly and meanly ought I to think of myself! How ought I to esteem it as nothing, if I should seem to have any good quality! With what profound humility ought I to submit myself to Thy unfathomable judgments, O Lord, where I find myself to be nothing else than nothing, and still nothing! O unmeasurable weight! O sea that can never be passed over, where I can discover nothing of myself but only and wholly nothing! Where then is the hiding-place of glory? Where is the confidence conceived of virtue? All vain glorying is swallowed up in the depth of Thy judgments over me.

What is all flesh in Thy sight? Shall the clay glory against Him that formeth it? How can he be lifted up with vain words whose heart is truly subject to God? Not all the world can lift up him whom the truth hath subjected unto itself: neither shall he who hath firmly settled his whole hope in God be moved with tongues of any who praise him. For even they themselves who speak, are nothing, for they will pass away with the sound of their own words; but the truth of the Lord remaineth for ever.

My son, say thou thus in everything: "Lord, if this be pleasing unto Thee, so let it be. Lord, if it be to Thy honour, in Thy name let this be done. Lord, if Thou seest it expedient, and allowest it to be profitable for me, then grant unto me that I may use this to Thine honour. But if Thou knowest it will be hurtful unto me, and profit nothing to the health of my soul, take away any such desire from me." For every desire proceedeth not from the Holy Spirit, even though it seem unto a man right and good. It is difficult to judge truly whether a good spirit or the contrary drive thee to desire this or that; or whether by thine own spirit thou be moved to it. Many have been deceived in the end, who at the first seemed to be led on by a good spirit.

Therefore whatever occurs to the mind as desirable, must always be desired and prayed for in the fear of God and with the humility of heart; and chiefly thou must commit the whole matter to Me with special resignation of thyself, and thou must say, "O Lord, Thou knowest what is best for us, let this or that be done, as Thou shalt please. Give what Thou wilt, and how much Thou wilt, and when Thou wilt. Deal with me as Thou thinkest good, and as best pleases Thee, and is most for Thy honour. Set me where Thou wilt, and deal with me in all things just as Thou wilt. I am in Thy hand: turn me round, and turn me back again, whichever way Thou please. Behold, I am Thy servant, prepared for all things; for I desire not to live unto myself, but unto Thee; and O that I could do it worthily and perfectly!"

A prayer that the will of God may be fulfilled. O most merciful Jesus, grant to me Thy grace, that it may be with me, and labour with me, and persevere with me even to the end. Grant that I may always desire and will that which is to Thee most acceptable and most dear. Let Thy will be mine and let my will ever follow Thine, and agree perfectly with it. Let my will be all one with Thine, and let me not be able to will or not to will any thing else but what Thou willest or dost not will.

Grant that I may die to all things that are in the world, and for Thy sake love to be condemned, and not known in this generation. Grant to me above all things that can be desired to rest in Thee, and in Thee to have my heart at peace. Thou art the true peace of the heart, Thou its only rest; out of Thee all things are hard and restless. In this very peace, that is, in Thee, the one chief eternal Good, I will sleep and rest.

Whatever I can desire or imagine for my comfort, I look for it not here but hereafter. For if I might alone have all the comforts of the world, and were able to enjoy all the delights thereof, it is certain that they could not long endure. Wherefore, O my soul, thou canst not be fully comforted, nor have perfect refreshment, except in God, the comforter of the poor, and patron of the humble. Wait a little while, O my soul, wait for the divine promise, and thou shalt have abundance of all good things in Heaven. If thou desire inordinately the things that are present, thou shalt lose those which are heavenly and eternal. Use temporal things, and desire eternal. Thou canst not be satisfied with any temporal good, because thou art not created to enjoy them.

Although thou shouldest possess all created good, yet couldest thou not be happy thereby nor blessed; but in God, who created all things, consisteth thy whole blessedness and felicity; not such as is seen and commended by the foolish lovers of the world, but such as the good and faithful servants of Christ wait for, and of which the spiritual and pure in heart, whose conversation is in Heaven, sometimes have a foretaste. Vain and brief is all human consolation. Blessed and true is the consolation which is received inwardly from the truth. A devout man beareth everywhere about with him his own comforter Jesus, and saith unto Him, "Be Thou present with me, O Lord Jesus, in every time and place. Let this be my consolation, to be cheerfully willing to do without all human comfort. And if Thy consolation be wanting, let Thy will and just trial of me be unto me as the greatest comfort; for Thou wilt not always be angry, neither wilt Thou threaten for ever."

My son, suffer Me to do with thee what I please; I know what is expedient for thee. Thou thinkest as a man; thou judgest in many things as human feelings persuade thee. O Lord, what Thou sayest is true. Thy anxiety for me is greater than all the care that I can take for myself. For he standeth but very totteringly, who casteth not all his anxiety upon Thee. O Lord, if only my will may remain right and firm towards Thee, do with me whatsoever it shall please Thee. For it cannot be any thing but good, whatsoever Thou shalt do with me. If it be Thy will I should be in darkness, be Thou blessed; and if it be Thy will I should be in light, be Thou again blessed. If Thou vouchsafe to comfort me, be Thou blessed; and if Thou wilt have me afflicted, be Thou ever equally blessed.

My son, such as this ought to be thy state, if thou desire to walk with Me. Thou oughtest to be as ready to suffer as to rejoice. Thou oughtest as cheerfully to be destitute and poor, as full and rich.

O Lord, for Thy sake, I will cheerfully suffer whatever shall come on me with Thy permission. From Thy hand I am willing to receive equally good and evil, sweet and bitter, joy and sorrow, and for all that befalleth me I will be thankful. Keep me safe from all sin, and I shall fear neither death nor Hell. So as Thou dost not cast me from Thee for ever, nor blot me out of the book of life, whatever tribulation may befall me shall not hurt me.

My son, I descended from Heaven for thy salvation; I took upon Me thy miseries, not necessity but charity drawing Me to them; that thou thyself mightest learn patience, and bear temporal miseries without grudging. For from the hour of My birth, even until My death on the cross, I was not without suffering or grief. I suffered great want of things temporal; I often heard many complaints against Me; I endured with benignity disgraces and revilings; in return for benefits I received ingratitude; for miracles, blasphemies; for heavenly doctrine, reproofs.

O Lord, because Thou wert patient in Thy lifetime, herein especially fulfilling the commandment of Thy Father, it is reason that I, a most miserable sinner, should bear myself patiently according to Thy will, and for my soul's welfare endure the burden of this corruptible life as long as Thou Thyself shall choose for me. For although this present life be burdensome to our feelings, yet notwithstanding it is now by Thy grace made very gainful; and by Thy example and the footsteps of Thy saints, more bright and endurable to the weak. It is, too, much more full of consolation than it was formerly in the old law, when the gate of Heaven remained shut: and the way also to Heaven seemed more obscure, when so few took care to seek after the Kingdom of Heaven. Moreover also they who then were just, and such as should be saved, could not enter into the heavenly kingdom, before Thy passion, and the due satisfaction of Thy holy death.

O what great thanks am I bound to render unto Thee, that Thou hast vouchsafed to show unto me and to all faithful people the good and the right way to Thine eternal kingdom. For Thy life is our way, and by holy patience we walk toward Thee, who art our crown. If Thou hadst not gone before us and taught us, who would have cared to follow? Alas, how many would remain behind and far off, if they considered not Thy most noble example!

Behold, we are even yet lukewarm, though we have heard of so many of Thy miracles and doctrines; what would become of us, if we had not such great light by which to follow Thee!

What is that thou sayest, My son? Cease to complain when thou considerest My passion, and the sufferings of other holy persons. Thou hast not yet made resistance unto blood. It is but little which thou sufferest, compared with those who suffered so much, who were so strongly tempted, so grievously afflicted, so many ways tried and exercised. Thou oughtest therefore to call to mind the heavier sufferings of others so that thou mayest the easier bear thy own very small troubles. And if they seem unto thee not very small, then beware lest thy impatience be the cause thereof. However, whether they are small, or whether they are great, endeavour patiently to undergo them all.

The better thou disposest thyself to suffering, so much the more wisely thou doest, and so much the greater reward shalt thou receive; thou shalt also more easily endure it, if both in mind and by habit thou art diligently prepared for it. Do not say, "I cannot endure to suffer these things at the hands of such a one, nor ought I to endure things of this sort; for he hath done me great wrong, and reproacheth me with things which I never thought of; but of another I will willingly suffer, that is, if they are also things which I shall see I ought to suffer." Such a thought is foolish; it considereth not the virtue of patience, nor by whom it will be crowned; but rather weigheth too exactly the persons and the injuries offered to itself.

He is not truly patient, who is willing to suffer only so much as he thinks good, and from whom he pleases. But the truly patient man minds not by whom he is exercised, whether by his superiors, by one of his equals or by an inferior; whether by a good and holy man, or by one that is perverse and unworthy. But indifferently from every creature, however much or how ever often anything adverse befalls him, he takes it all thankfully as from the hands of God, and esteems it a great gain: for with God it is impossible that any thing, however small, if only it suffered for God's sake, should pass without its reward.

Be thou therefore always prepared for the fight, if thou wilt have the victory. Without a combat thou canst not attain to the crown of patience. If thou art unwilling to suffer, thou refusest to be crowned. But if you desire to be crowned, fight manfully, endure patiently. Without labour there is no arriving at rest, nor without fighting can the victory be reached. O Lord, let that become possible to me by Thy grace, which by nature seems impossible to me. Thou knowest that I am able to suffer but little, and that I am quickly cast down, when a slight adversity ariseth. For Thy name's sake, let every exercise of tribulation be made amiable and desirable to me; for to suffer and to be disquieted for Thy sake is very wholesome for my soul.

I will confess against my mine own unrighteousness; I will confess my weakness unto Thee, O Lord. It is often a small matter that makes me sad and dejected. I resolve that I will act with courage, but when even a small temptation comes, I am at once in a great strait. It is sometimes a very trifle from which a great temptation arises. And whilst I am thinking myself tolerably safe, and when I least expect it, I sometimes find myself almost entirely overcome by a slight breath.

Behold therefore, O Lord, my low state, and my frailty which is in every way known to Thee. Have mercy on me, and deliver me from the mire, that I may not stick fast in it, may not remain utterly cast down for ever. This is that which often strikes me backwards, and confounds me in Thy sight, that I am so subject to fall and so weak in resisting my passions. And although I do not altogether consent, yet their continued assaults are troublesome and grievous to me; and it is exceedingly irksome to live thus daily in conflict. From hence my weakness becomes known unto me, in that hateful fancies do always much more easily rush into my mind than depart from it.

Most mighty God of Israel, Thou zealous lover of faithful souls! O that Thou wouldst consider the labour and sorrow of Thy servant, and assist him in all things whatsoever he undertaketh. Strengthen me with heavenly courage, lest the old man, the miserable flesh, not as yet fully subject to the Spirit, prevail and get the upper hand; against which it will be needful for me to fight as long as I breathe in this miserable life. Alas, what a kind of life is this, where tribulation and miseries are never wanting; where all is full of snares and enemies! For when one tribulation or temptation retreateth, another cometh on; and while the first conflict is yet lasting, many others come unexpectedly one after another.

And how can a life be loved that hath so many embitterments, and is subject to so many calamities and miseries? How, too, can it be called a life, that begetteth so many deaths and plagues? And yet it is the object of men's love, and many seek to delight themselves therein. The world is often blamed for being deceitful and vain, and yet men do not easily part with it, because the desires of the flesh bear so great a sway. But some things draw us to love the world; others to condemn it. The lust of the flesh, the lust of the eyes, and the pride of life, draw us to the love of the world; but the pains and miseries that justly follow them cause a hatred and loathing of the world.

But alas, the fondness for vicious pleasures overcometh the mind of him who is addicted to the world; and he esteemeth it a delight to be under thorns, because he hath neither seen nor tasted the sweetness of God and the inward pleasantness of virtue. But they who completely condemn the world, and study to live to God under holy discipline, are not ignorant of the divine sweetness promised to those who truly forsake the world; they also very clearly see how grievously the world erreth, and how it is in many ways deceived.

Above all things, and in all things, O my soul, thou shalt rest in the Lord always, for He Himself is the everlasting rest of the saints. Grant me, O most sweet and loving Jesus, to rest in Thee above all creatures, above all health and beauty, above all glory and honour, above all power and dignity, above all knowledge and subtelty, above all riches and arts, above all joy and gladness, above all fame and praise, above all sweetness and comfort, above all hope and promise, above all desert and desire: above all gifts and favours that Thou canst give us, above all mirth and exultation that the mind of man can receive and feel: finally, above angels and archangels, and above all the heavenly host, above all things visible and invisible, and above all that Thou art not, O my God.

Because Thou, O Lord my God, art supremely good above all; Thou alone art most high, Thou alone most powerful, Thou alone most full and sufficient, Thou alone most sweet and most full of consolation: Thou alone art most lovely and loving, Thou alone most noble and glorious above all things, in whom all good things together both perfectly are, and have been, and shall be. And therefore it is too small and unsatisfying, whatsoever Thou bestowest on me besides Thyself, or revealest unto me of Thyself, or promisest, whilst Thou art not seen, and not fully obtained. For surely my heart cannot truly rest, nor be entirely contented, unless it rest in Thee, and surmount all gifts and all creatures whatsoever.

O Thou most beloved spouse of my soul, Jesus Christ, Thou most pure lover, Thou Lord of all creation: O that I had the wings of true liberty that I might flee away and rest in Thee! O when shall it be fully granted me to consider in quietness of mind and see how sweet Thou art, my Lord God? When shall I fully gather up myself into Thee, that by reason of my love for Thee I may not feel myself, but Thee alone, above all sense and measure, in a manner not known unto every one! But now I often groan and bear my infelicity with grief. Because many evils occur in this vale of miseries, which do often trouble, grieve, and overcloud me; often hinder and distract me, allure and entangle me, so that I can have no free access unto Thee, nor enjoy the sweet welcomings which are ever ready with the blessed spirits. O let my sighs move Thee, and my manifold desolation here on earth move Thee.

O Jesus, Thou brightness of eternal glory, Thou comfort of the pilgrim soul, with Thee is my tongue without voice, and my very silence speaketh unto Thee. How long doth my Lord delay to come? Let Him come unto me, His, poor despised servant, and let Him make me glad. Let Him put forth His hand, and deliver a poor wretch from all anguish. Come, O come; for without Thee I shall have no joyful day nor hour; for Thou art my joy, and without Thee my table is empty. A wretched creature am I, and imprisoned and loaded with fetters, until Thou refresh me with the light of Thy presence, and grant me liberty, and show a friendly countenance toward me.

Let others seek what they please instead of Thee; but for me, nothing else doth nor shall delight me, but Thou only, my God, my hope, my everlasting salvation. I will not hold my peace, nor cease to pray, until Thy grace return again, and Thou speak inwardly unto me, Behold, here I am. Behold, I come unto thee, because thou hast called upon Me. Thy tears and the desire of thy soul, thy humiliation and thy contrition of heart, have inclined and brought Me unto thee. And I said, "Lord I have called upon Thee, and have desired to enjoy Thee, being ready to refuse all things for Thy sake. For Thou first hast stirred me up that I might seek Thee. Blessed be Thou therefore, O Lord, that hast showed this goodness to Thy servant, according to the multitude of Thy mercies." What hath Thy servant more to say before Thee? He can only greatly humble himself in Thy sight, ever mindful of his own iniquity and vileness. For there is none like Thee in all the wonderful things of Heaven and earth. Thy works are very good, Thy judgments true, and by Thy providence the universe is governed. Therefore praise and glory be unto Thee, O wisdom of the Father: let my mouth, my soul, and all creatures together, praise and bless Thee.

Open, O Lord, my heart in Thy law, and teach me to walk in Thy commandments. Grant me to understand Thy will, and with great reverence and diligent consideration to remember Thy benefits, as well in general as in particular, that hencefoth I may be able worthily to give Thee thanks. But I know, and confess, that I am not able, even in the least point, to give Thee due thanks for the favours which Thou bestowest upon me. I am less than the least of all Thy benefits: and when I consider Thine excellence, the greatness of it maketh my spirit faint.

All that we have in soul and in body, and whatever we posses outwardly or inwardly, naturally or supernaturally, are Thy benefits, and proclaim Thee bountiful, merciful, and good, from whom we have received all good things. Although one has received more, another less, all notwithstanding are Thine, and without Thee not even the least blessing can be had. He that hath received the greatest cannot glory in his own desert, nor extol himself above others, nor insult the lesser; for he is the greatest and the best, who ascribeth least unto himself, and who in rendering thanks is the most humble and the most devout. And he that esteemeth himself viler than all men, and judgeth himself most unworthy, is fittest to receive the greater blessings.

But he that hath received fewer ought not to be out of heart, nor to take it grievously, nor envy them that are enriched with greater store; but rather he should turn his mind to Thee, and exceedingly praise Thy goodness, because Thou bestowest Thy gifts so bountifully, so freely, and so willingly, without respect of persons. All things proceed from Thee, and therefore in all Thou art to be praised. Thou knowest what is fit to be given to everyone; and why this man should have less and that more, it is not for us to judge, but for Thee who dost exactly mark everyone's deserts.

Wherefore, O Lord God, I even esteem it a great mercy not to have much of that which outwardly and in the opinion of men seems worthy of glory and applause. For so it is, that he who considers the poverty and unworthiness of his own person, should be so far from conceiving grief or sadness, or from being cast down at it that he should rather take great comfort, and be glad; because Thou, O God, hast chosen the poor and humble and the despised of this world for Thyself, for Thy familiar and domestic attendants. Examples are Thy apostles themselves, whom Thou hast made princes over all the earth. And yet they lived in the world without complaint, so humble and simple, without all malice and deceit, that they even rejoiced to suffer approach for Thy name; and what the world abhorreth, they embraced with great affection.

When, therefore, a man loveth Thee and acknowledgeth Thy benefits, nothing ought to please him much as Thy will toward him, and the good pleasure of Thine eternal appointment. And herewith he ought to be so contented and comforted, that he would as willingly be the least, as another would wish to be the greatest. He would, too, be as peaceable and contented in the last place as in the first; as willing to be a despised castaway, of no name or character, as to be preferred in honour before others, and to be greater in the world than they. For Thy will and the love of Thy glory ought to be preferred before all things, and to comfort him more, and please him better, than all the benefits which he either hath received, or may receive.

My son, now will I teach thee the way of peace and true liberty. O Lord, I beseech Thee, do as Thou sayest, for this is delightful to me to hear. Be desirous, My son, to do the will of another rather than thine own. Choose always to have less rather than more. Seek always the lowest place, and to be inferior to everyone. Wish always, and pray, that the will of God may be wholly fulfilled in thee. Behold, such a man entereth within the borders of peace and rest.

O Lord, this short discourse of Thine containeth within itself much perfection. Although it is short, it is yet full of meaning, and abundant in fruit. For if it could faithfully be kept by me, I ought not to be so easily disturbed. For as often as I feel myself unquiet and weighed down, I find that I have gone back from this doctrine. But Thou who canst do all things, and ever lovest the profiting of my soul, increase in me Thy grace, that I may be able to fulfil Thy words, and to work out mine own salvation.

A Prayer against evil thoughts. O Lord my God, be not Thou far from me; my God, have regard to help me: for there have risen up against me sundry thoughts and great fears, afflicting my soul. How shall I pass through unhurt? How shall I break them to pieces? "I will go before thee," saith He, "and will humble the great ones of the earth; I will open the doors of the prison, and reveal unto thee hidden secrets." Do, O Lord, as Thou sayest, and let all my evil thoughts fly from before Thy face. This is my hope, my only consolation, to flee unto Thee in every tribulation, to trust in Thee, to call upon Thee from my inmost heart, and to wait patiently for Thy consolation.

A Prayer for mental illumination. O merciful Jesus, enlighten Thou me with a clear shining inward light, and remove all darkness from the habitation of my heart. Repress Thou my wandering thoughts, and break in pieces those temptations which violently assault me. Fight Thou strongly for me, and vanquish the evil beasts, I mean the alluring desires of the flesh; that peace may be obtained by Thy power, and that Thine abundant praise may resound in Thy holy court, that is, in a pure conscience. Command the winds and tempests; say unto the sea: Be still. Say to the north wind: Blow not; and there shall be a great calm.

Send out Thy light and Thy truth, that they may shine upon the earth; for until Thou enlighten me, I am but as earth without form and void. Pour forth Thy grace from above, imbue my heart with heavenly dew, supply fresh streams of devotion to water the face of the earth, that it may bring forth good and excellent fruit. Lift Thou up my mind which is pressed down by a load of sins, and draw up my whole desire to things heavenly; that, having tasted the sweetness of supernal happiness, it may be irksome to me even to think about earthly things.

Pluck me away, and deliver me from all transitory consolation of creatures; for no created thing can give full comfort and rest to my desires. Join me to Thyself with an inseparable bond of love; for Thou alone dost satisfy him that loveth Thee, and without Thee all things are vain and frivolous.

My son, be not curious, nor trouble thyself with idle anxieties. What is this or that to thee? Follow thou Me, for what is it to thee whether that man be such or such, or whether this man do or speak this or that? Thou shalt not need to answer for others, but shalt give account for thyself; why therefore dost thou entangle thyself? Behold, I know everyone, and see all things that are done under the sun; also I understand how it is with everyone, what he thinks, what he wishes, and at what his intentions aim. Unto Me therefore all things are to be committed; but keep thyself gently at peace, and allow the unquiet, to be as unquiet as they will. Whatever they have done or said, shall come upon themselves, for Me they cannot deceive.

Be not careful for the shadow of a great name, or for the familiar friendship of many, or for the private affection of men, for these things both distract the heart and greatly darken it. Willingly would I speak

My word, and reveal My secrets unto thee, if thou wouldest diligently observe My coming, and open unto Me the door of thine heart. Be thou circumspect, and watchful in prayer, and in all things humble thyself.

My son, I have spoken; "Peace I leave with you, My peace I give unto you: not as the world giveth, give I unto you." Peace is what all desire, but all do not care for the things that appertain to true peace. My peace is with the humble and gentle of heart; in much patience shall thy peace be. If thou wilt hear Me and follow My voice, thou shalt be able to enjoy much peace. What then shall I do, Lord? In every matter look to thyself, what thou doest and what thou sayest; and direct thy whole attention unto this, that thou mayest please Me alone, and neither desire or seek any thing besides Me. But of the words or deeds of others judge nothing rashly; neither entangle thyself with things not committed unto thee; and doing thus thou mayest be little or seldom disturbed.

But never to feel any disturbance at all, nor have any trouble of mind or body, belongs not to this life, but the state of eternal rest. Think not therefore that thou hast found true peace, if thou feel no heaviness; nor that all is well, if thou art vexed with no adversary; nor that "to be perfect" is to have all things done according to thy desire. Neither esteem thyself at all highly, or account thyself to be specially beloved, if thou art in a state of great devotion and sweetness; for it is not by these things that a true lover of virtue is known, nor doth the spiritual progress and perfection of a man consist in these things.

"Wherein then, O Lord, doth it consist?" In giving thyself over with all thy heart to the divine will, not seeking thine own interest, either in great matters or in small, either in time or in eternity. So shalt thou keep one and the same countenance, always with thanksgiving, both in prosperity and adversity, weighing all things with an equal balance. Be thou of such courage, and so patient in hope, that when inward comfort is withdrawn, thou mayest prepare thy heart to suffer even greater things; and do not justify thyself, as though thou oughtest not to suffer these afflictions or any so great, but justify Me in whatsoever I appoint, and still praise My holy name. Then shalt thou walk in the true and right way of peace, and thou shalt have undoubted hope to see My face again with great delight. For if thou attain to the full contempt of thyself, know that thou shalt then enjoy abundance of peace, as great as this thy state of sojourning is capable of.

O Lord, it is the business of a perfect man never to relax his mind from attentive thought of heavenly things, and thus to pass amidst many cares, as it were, without care; not as one destitute of all feeling, but by the privilege of a free mind, cleaving to no creature with inordinate affecion.

I beseech Thee, my most gracious God, preserve me from the cares of this life, lest I should be too much entangled therein; also from the many necessities of the body, lest I should be ensnared by pleasure; and from whatever is an obstacle to the soul, lest being broken with troubles I should be overthrown. I speak not of those things which worldly vanity so earnestly desireth, but of those miseries, which as punishments and as the common curse of mortality, weigh down and hinder the soul of Thy servant, that it cannot enter into the freedom of the Spirit so often as it would.

O my God, Thou sweetness ineffable, make bitter for me all carnal comfort, which draws me away from the love of things eternal, and in an evil manner allures me to itself by the view of some present delightful good. Let me not be overcome, O Lord, let me not be overcome by flesh and blood; let not the world and the brief glory of it deceive me; let not the devil and his subtle fraud supplant me. Give me strength to resist, patience to endure, and constancy to persevere. Give me, instead of all the comforts of the world, the most sweet unction of Thy Spirit, and in place of carnal love pour in the love of Thy name.

Behold! Meat, drink, clothes, and other necessaries for the maintenance of the body, are burdensome to a fervent spirit. Grant me to use such refreshments moderately, and not to be entangled with an overgreat desire of them. It is not lawful to cast away all things, because nature is to be sustained; but to require superfluïties, and those things that are merely pleasurable, the holy law forbiddeth us; for then the flesh would rebel against the Spirit. Herein, I beseech Thee, let Thy hand govern me and teach me, that I may not exceed the due bounds.

My son, thou oughtest to give all for all, and to be nothing of thyself. Know thou that the love of thyself doth thee more hurt than anything in the world. According to the love and affection which thou bearest towards anything, so doth it more or less cleave to thee. If thy love be pure, simple, and well-ordered, thou shalt be free from the bondage of things. Do not covet that which it is not lawful for thee to have. Do not have that which may entangle thee, and deprive thee of inward liberty. Strange it is that thou committest not thyself wholly unto Me, from the bottom of thy heart, with all things thou canst have or desire.

Why dost thou consume thyself with vain grief? Why weary thyself with superfluous cares? Stand to My good will, and thou shalt suffer no detriment at all. If thou seek this or that, and wouldest be in such or such a place, the better to enjoy thy own profit and pleasure, thou shalt never be at quiet, nor free from trouble of mind; for in every instance something will be lacking, and in every place there will be some one to cross thee.

Man's welfare, then, lies not in obtaining and multiplying any external things, but rather in despising them, and utterly rooting them out from the heart. And this thou must understand refers not only to income and wealth, but also to seeking after honour also, and the desire of vain praise, all of which must pass away with this world. The place availeth little if the spirit of fervour is wanting, neither shall that peace long continue, which is sought from without; if the state of thy heart be destitute of a true foundation (that is, unless thou stand steadfast in Me), thou mayest change but not better thyself. For when occasion arises, and is laid hold of, thou shalt find what thou didst flee from, and more too.

A Prayer for a clean heart, and Heavenly Wisdom. Strengthen me, O God, by the grace of Thy Holy Spirit. Grant me to be strengthened with might in the inner man, and to empty my heart of all useless care and anguish; not to be drawn away with sundry desires of any thing whatever, whether mean or precious, but to look on all things as passing away, and on myself also as no less about to pass away with them. For nothing is permanent under the sun, where all things are vanity and vexation of spirit. O how wise is he that so considereth them!

O Lord, grant me heavenly wisdom, that I may learn above all things to seek and to find Thee, above all things to relish and to love Thee, and to think of all other things as being, as indeed they are, at the disposal of Thy wisdom. Grant me prudently to avoid him that flatters me, and to endure patiently him that contradicts me. Because it is a great part of wisdom not to be moved with every wind of words, nor to give ear to an ill-flattering siren; for thus we shall go on securely in the way in which we have begun.

My son, take it not grievously if some think ill of thee, and speak that which thou wouldest not willingly hear. Thou oughtest to judge the worst of thyself, and to think no man weaker than thyself. If thou dost walk inwardly, thou wilt not much weigh fleeting words outwardly. It is no small prudence to keep silence in an evil time, and inwardly to turn thyself to Me, and not to be troubled by the judgment of men.

Let not thy peace be in the tongues of men; for whether they interpret well or ill of thee thou art still man. Where are true peace and true glory? Are they not in Me? And he that neither coveteth to please men, nor feareth to displease them, shall enjoy much peace. From inordinate love and vain fear ariseth all disquiet of heart and distraction of the mind.

Blessed be Thy Name, O Lord, for ever; for it is Thy will that this temptation and tribulation should come upon me. I cannot escape it, but must flee to Thee, that Thou mayest help me, and turn it to my good. Lord, I am now in affliction, and my heart is ill at ease, for I am much troubled with the present suffering. And now, O beloved Father, what shall I say? I am caught amidst straits; save Thou me from this hour. Yet therefore came I unto this hour, that Thou mayest be glorified when I shall have been greatly humbled, and by Thee delivered. Let it please Thee, Lord, to deliver me; for, poor wretch that I am, what can I do, and whither shall I go without Thee? Grant me patience, O Lord, even now in this emergency. Help me, my God, and then I will not fear, however grievously I am be afflicted.

And now amidst these my troubles what shall I say? Lord, Thy will be done; I have well deserved to be afflicted and weighed down. Therefore I ought to bear it; and O that I may bear it with patience, until the tempest pass over, and all be well again, or even better! Thy omnipotent hand is able to take even this temptation from me, and to assuage the violence of it thereof, that I may not utterly sink under it; as often before Thou hast dealt with me, O my God, my mercy! And the more difficult it is to me, so much the more easy to Thee is this change of the right hand of the Most High.

My son, I am the Lord, who giveth strength in the day of tribulation. Come to Me, when it is not well with thee. This is that which most of all hindereth heavenly consolation, that thou art too slow in turning thyself unto prayer. For before thou dost earnestly supplicate Me, thou seekest in the meanwhile many comforts, and refreshest thyself in outward things. And hence it comes to pass that all doth little profit thee, until thou well consider that I am He who rescue them that trust in Me; and that apart from Me there is neither powerful help, nor profitable counsel, nor lasting remedy. But having now recovered breath after the tempest, gather strength again in the light of My mercies; for I am at hand, saith the Lord, to repair all, not only entirely, but also abundantly and in most plentiful measure.

Is there anything hard to Me? Or shall I be like one that saith and doeth not? Where is thy faith? Stand firmly and with perseverance; take courage and be patient; comfort will come to thee in due time. Wait, wait, I say, for Me: I will come and take care of thee. It is a temptation that vexeth thee, and a vain fear that frightens thee. What else doth anxiety about the future bring thee, but sorrow upon sorrow? "Sufficient for the day is the evil thereof." It is a vain thing and unprofitable, to be either disturbed or pleased about future things, which perhaps will never come to pass.

But it is in the nature of man, to be deluded with such imaginations; and a sign of a mind as yet weak, to be so easily drawn away by the suggestions of the enemy. For so that he may delude and deceive thee, he careth not whether it be by true or by false propositions; nor whether he overthrow thee with the love of the present, or the fear of future things. Let not therefore thy heart be troubled, neither let it fear. Trust in Me, and put thy confidence in My mercy. When thou thinkest thyself farthest off from Me, often I am nearest to thee. When thou countest almost all to be lost, then often the greatest gain of reward is close at hand. All is not lost, when any thing falleth out contrary. Thou oughtest not to judge according to present feeling; nor so to take any grief, or give thyself over to it, from wherever it cometh, as though all hopes of escape were quite taken away.

Think not thyself wholly left, although for a time I have sent thee some tribulation, or have even withdrawn thy desired comfort; for this is the way to the Kingdom of Heaven. And without doubt it is more expedient for thee and the rest of My servants, that ye be exercised with adversities, than that ye should have all things according to your desires. I know the secret thoughts of thy heart, and that it is expedient for thy welfare that thou art left sometimes without taste of spiritual sweetness, lest perhaps thou shouldest be puffed up with thy prosperous estate, and shouldest be willing to please thyself in that which thou should not. That which I have given, I can take away; and I can restore it again when I please.

When I give it, it is Mine; when I withdraw it, I take not anything that is thine; for Mine is every good gift and every perfect gift. If I send upon thee affliction, or any cross whatever, repine not, nor let thy heart fail thee; I can quickly succour thee, and turn all thy heaviness into joy. I am righteous, and greatly to be praised when I deal thus with thee.

If thou art wise, and considerest what the truth is, thou oughtest never to mourn dejectedly for any adversity that befalleth thee, but rather to rejoice and give thanks. Yea, thou wilt account this thine especial joy, that I afflict thee with sorrows, and do not spare thee. "As the Father hath loved Me, I also love you," said I unto My beloved disciples; whom certainly I sent out not to temporal joys, but to great conflicts; not to honours, but to contempts; not to idleness, but to labours; not to rest, but to bring forth much fruit with patience. Remember thou these words, O my son!

O Lord, I stand much in need of yet greater grace, if I ought to reach that state, where neither man nor any creature shall be a hindrance unto me. For as long as anything holds me back, I cannot freely take my flight to Thee. He was longing to fly freely who said, "O that I had wings like a dove, and I will flee away and be at rest!" What is more at rest than the single eye? and what is more free than he that desireth nothing upon earth? A man ought therefore to rise over all creatures, and perfectly to go out of himself and stand in a sort of ecstasy of mind, and so see that Thou, the creator of all things, hast nothing amongst creatures like Thyself. Unless, too, a man be disengaged from the affection of all creatures, he cannot with freedom of mind attend to divine things. For that is the reason why there are few contemplative men to be found, because few have the knowledge to withdraw themselves fully from perishing creatures.

To obtain this there is need of much grace, which may elevate the soul, and carry it away above itself. And unless a man be elevated in spirit, and freed from all creatures, and wholly united with God, whatever he knoweth and whatever he hath, is of no great weight. For a long while shall he be small, and lie grovelling below, whoever he art that esteemeth anything great but the one only infinite eternal Good. And whatever is not God, is nothing, and ought to be accounted as nothing. There is a great difference between the wisdom of an illuminated and devout man, and the knowledge of a learned and studious clerk. Far more noble is that learning which floweth from above, from the divine influence, than that which is painfully acquired by the wit of man.

There are many who desire contemplation but have no mind to practise the things that are required for it. It is also a great hindrance that men rest in signs and sensible things, and take little care about the perfect mortification of themselves. I know not what it is, or by what spirit we are led, or what we pretend, we that seem to be called spiritual, that we take so many pains, and are so full of anxiety about transitory and mean things, while we scarcely at all, or but seldom, think of our own inward concern with full recollection of mind.

Alas, presently, after a slight recollection, we break out again, and weigh not our works with diligent and strict examination. We came not where our affections lie, nor bewail the impurity that is in all our actions. For "all flesh had corrupted his way," and therefore did the great deluge ensue. Since then our inward affection is much corrupted, our actions proceeding from there must be corrupted also, giving proof of the want of internal vigour. From a pure heart proceedeth the fruit of a good life.

We ask how much a man has done, but from what degree of virtuous principle he acts is not so carefully weighed. We inquire whether he has been courageous, rich, handsome, skilful, a good writer, a good singer, or a good labourer; but how poor he is in spirit, how patient and meek, how devout and spiritual, is seldom spoken of. Nature respecteth the outward things of a man. Grace turneth itself to the inward. The one is often disappointed; the other hath her trust in God, and so is not deceived.

My son, thou canst not possess perfect liberty unless thou wholly renounce thyself. They are but in fetters, all who merely seek their own interest, and are lovers of themselves; they are covetous, inquisitive, gossiping, always seeking what is soft and delicate, not the things of Jesus Christ, but devising and framing that which will not continue. For all that is not of God shall perish. Keep this short and complete saying: "Forsake all and thou shalt find all." Leave desire and thou shalt find rest. Weigh this thoroughly in thy mind, and when thou hast fulfilled it, thou shalt understand all things.

O Lord, this is not the work of one day nor is it children's sport; rather in this short word is included all the perfection of religious persons.

My son, thou oughtest not to turn away, nor to be cast down, when thou hearest of the way of the perfect; but shouldest rather be stirred up to higher things, at least in desire to sigh after them. I would it were so with thee, and thou had arrived at this, to be no longer a lover of thyself, but didst stand merely at My beck, and at his whom I have appointed a father over thee; then shouldest thou exceedingly please Me, and all thy life would pass away in joy and peace. Thou hast yet many things to part with which unless thou wholly resign up unto Me, thou shalt not attain to that which thou desirest. "I counsel thee to buy of Me gold tried in the fire that thou mayest become rich"; that is, heavenly wisdom, which treadeth under foot all that is mean and low. Set little by earthly wisdom, and care not foolishly to please others or thyself.

I said that mean things must be bought with things which, among men, are precious and of great esteem. For true heavenly wisdom doth seem very mean, of small account, and almost forgotten among men, as having no high thoughts of itself, nor seeking to be magnified upon earth. Many indeed praise it with their mouth, but in their life they are far from it; yet is it the precious pearl, which is hidden from many.

My son, trust not to thy feeling, for whatever it is now, it will quickly be changed into another thing. As long as thou livest, thou art subject to mutability, even against thy will; so as thou seem one person while merry, another while sad; one while quiet, another while troubled; now devout, then indevout; now diligent, then listless; now grave, and then light. But he that is wise and well instructed in the Spirit standeth fast upon these mutable things; not heeding what he feeleth in himself, nor which way the wind of instability bloweth; but so that the whole intention of his mind tendeth to the right and best end. For thus he will be able to continue throughout one and the same, and unshaken; in the midst of so many various events the single eye of his intention being directed unceasingly towards Me.

And the purer the eye of the intention is, with so much the more constancy doth a man pass through the several kinds of storms which assail him. But in many the eye of a pure intention waxes dim, for their regard is quickly drawn aside to some pleasurable object which meets them. For it is rare to find one who is wholly free from all blemish of self-seeking. So of old the Jews came to Bethany to Martha and Mary, not for Jesus's sake only, but also that they might see Lazarus. The eye of our intention therefore is to be purified, that it may be single and right, and directed towards Me, beyond all the various objects which may come between.

"Behold! My God, and all things to me." What more can I wish, and what happier thing can I long for? O sweet and savoury Word! (to him, that is, who loveth the Word not the world nor the things that are in the world). "My God, and all things". To him that understandeth, enough is said; and to repeat it often, is delightful to him that loveth. When Thou art present, all things are delightful, but when Thou art absent, everything becomes irksome. Thou givest quietness of heart, and great peace, and festive joy. Thou makest us to think well of all circumstances, and in all to praise Thee; neither can any thing please long without Thee; but if it must needs be pleasant and tasteful, Thy grace must be present, and it must be seasoned with the seasoning of Thy wisdom.

What will not be tasteful unto him that hath a true relish for Thee? And him that hath no relish for Thee, what shall have power to please? But the wise men of the world, and they also who relish the things of the flesh, are destitute of Thy wisdom; for in the former is found the utmost vanity, and in the latter death. But they that follow Thee by the contempt of worldly things, and mortification of the flesh, are known to be truly wise; for they are brought over from vanity to truth, from the flesh to the spirit. These relish God; and whatsoever good is found in creatures, they wholly refer to the praise of their maker. Great, however, yea, very great, is the difference between the sweetness of the Creator and of the creature, of Eternity and of time, of Light uncreated and of light enlightened.

O Everlasting Light, surpassing all created luminaries, dart Thou the beams of Thy brightness from above, which may penetrate all the most inward parts of my heart. Purify, rejoice, enlighten and enliven my spirit, with all the powers thereof, that I may cleave unto Thee with most exceeding joy and triumph. O when will that blessed and desired hour come, that Thou mayest satisfy me with Thy presence, and be unto me all in all. So long as this is not granted me, I shall not have full joy. Still, alas, the old man doth live in me, he is not wholly crucified, is not perfectly dead. Still lusteth he mightily against the Spirit, and stirreth up inward wars, nor suffereth the kingdom of the soul to be in peace.

But Thou that rulest the power of the sea, and stillest the violent motion of its waves, arise and help me! Scatter the nations that desire war; crush Thou them in Thy might. Display Thy wonderful works, I beseech Thee, and let Thy right hand be glorified; for there is no other hope or refuge for me, save in Thee, O Lord my God.

My son, thou art never secure in this life, but, as long as thou livest, thou shalt always need spiritual armour. Thou dwellest among enemies, and art assaulted on the right hand and on the left. If therefore thou defend not thyself on every side with the shield of patience, thou wilt not be long without a wound. Moreover, if thou set not thy heart fixedly on Me, with a sincere wish to suffer all things for Me, thou wilt not be able to bear the heat of this combat, nor to attain to the palm of the blessed. Thou oughtest therefore manfully to go through all, and to use a strong hand against whatsoever withstandeth thee. For to him that overcometh is manna given, and for the indolent there remaineth much misery.

If thou seek rest in this life, how wilt thou then attain to the everlasting rest? Dispose not thyself for much rest, but for great patience. Seek true peace, not in earth, but in heaven; not in men, nor in any other creature, but in God alone. For the love of God thou oughtest cheerfully to undergo all things, that is to say, all labour and pain, temptation, vexation, anxiety, necessity, infirmity, injury, abuse, reproof, humiliation, confusion, correction, and scorn of every kind and degree. These help to virtue; these are the trial of a novice in Christ; these frame the heavenly crown. I will give an everlasting reward for a short labour, and infinite glory for transitory confusion.

Thinkest thou that thou shalt always have spiritual consolations at thine own will? My saints had not such always, but they had many afflictions, and sundry temptations, and feelings of great desolateness. Nevertheless in all these they bore themselves patiently, and trusted in God rather than in themselves; knowing that the sufferings of this time are not worthy to be compared with the future glory. Wilt thou have that at once, which many after many tears and great labours have hardly obtained? Wait for the Lord, behave thyself manfully, and be of good courage; do not distrust Him, do not leave thy place, but steadily expose body and soul for the glory of God. I will reward thee plentifully and will be with thee in every tribulation.

My son, cast thy heart firmly on the Lord, and fear not the judgment of men, when conscience testifieth of thy dutifulness and innocence. It is a good and happy thing to suffer in such a way; nor will this be grievous to a heart which is humble, and which trusteth in God rather than in itself. Most men are given to talk much, and therefore little confidence is to be placed in what they say. Moreover, also, to satisfy all is not possible. Although Paul endeavoured to please all in the Lord, and was made all things to all men, yet with him it was a very small thing that he should be judged by man's judgment.

He did abundantly for the edification and salvation of others as much as it lay in his power to do; yet could he not hinder but that he was by others sometimes judged, sometimes despised. Therefore he committed all to God, who knew all; and when men spoke unjust things, or thought vanities and lies, and boasted of themselves as they wished, he defended himself, even to their face, with humility and patience. Sometimes, however, he made answer, lest the weak should be offended by his silence.

Who art thou that thou shouldest fear a mortal man? Today he is, and tomorrow he is not seen. Fear God, and thou shalt not shrink from the terrors of men. What harm can the words or injuries of any man do thee? He hurteth himself rather than thee, nor shall he be able to avoid the judgment of God, whoever he is. Do thou have God before thine eyes, and contend not with peevish words. And though for the present thou seem to be worsted, and to suffer shame undeservedly, do not therefore repine, neither lessen thy crown by impatience. But rather lift up thine eyes unto Me in Heaven, who am able to deliver thee fom all shame and wrong, and to render to every man according to his works.

My son, forsake thyself, and thou shalt find Me. Stay where thou art, making no choice, nor appropriating any thing whatever to thyself; and thou shalt always be a gainer. For even greater grace shall be added to thee, the moment thou dost resign thyself, provided thou dost not turn back to take thyself again. Lord, how often shall I resign myself? And wherein shall I forsake myself? Always; every hour; as well in small things as well as in great. I expect nothing, but desire that thou be found naked and void of all things. Otherwise, how canst thou be Mine, and I thine, unless thou be stripped of all self-will, both within and without? The sooner thou doest this, the better it will be with thee; and the more fully and sincerely thou doest it, so much the more shalt thou please Me, and so much the greater shall be thy gain.

There are some who resign themselves, but with certain exceptions: for they put not their full trust in God, and therefore they study how to provide for themselves. Some also at first do offer all, but afterwards being assailed with temptation, they return again to their own ways, and therefore make no progress in the path of virtue. These shall not attain to the true liberty of a pure heart, nor to the favour of My sweetest familiarity, unless they first make an entire resignation and a daily oblation of themselves unto Me. Without this, there neither is nor can be any lasting fruitful union with Me.

I have often said unto thee and now again I say, forsake thyself, resign thyself, and thou shalt enjoy much inward peace. Give all for all; ask for nothing, require back nothing; abide purely and unhesitatingly in Me, and thou shalt possess me; thou shalt be free in heart, and darkness shall not tread thee down. Let this be thy whole endeavour, this thy prayer, this thy desire; that thou mayest be stripped of all selfishness, and with entire simplicity follow Jesus only; mayest die to thyself, and live eternally to Me. Then shalt thou be rid of all vain fancies, causeless perturbations, and superfluous cares. Then also immoderate fear shall leave thee, and inordinate love shall die.

My son, thou oughtest with all diligence to endeavour that, in every place, and in every external action or occupation, thou mayest be inwardly free, and thoroughly master of thyself; and that all things be under thee, and not thou under them. Thou must be lord and master of thine own actions, and not a slave or hireling. Rather thou shouldest be as a freed man and a true Hebrew, passing over into the lot and freedom of the sons of God. For they, standing upon things present, contemplate things eternal. With the left eye they look on transitory things, and with the right on the things of Heaven. They are not drawn by temporal things to cleave unto them; rather they draw temporal things to serve them well, in such ways as they are ordained by God and appointed by the great work-master, who hath left nothing in His creation without due order.

If too, in all circumstances thou stand steadfast, and do not estimate the things which thou seest and hearest by the outward appearance, nor with a carnal eye; but presently in every affair dost enter with Moses into the tabernacle to ask counsel of the Lord; thou shalt sometimes hear the divine oracle, and shalt return instructed concerning many things, both present and to come. For Moses always had recourse to the tabernacle for the deciding of doubts and questions, and fled to the help of prayer, for support under dangers and the iniquity of men. So oughtest thou in like manner to take refuge within the closet of thine heart, earnestly craving the divine favour. For we read, that Joshua and the children of Israel were deceived by the Gibeonites because they asked not counsel beforehand at the mouth of the Lord, but trusting too easily to fair words, were deluded by counterfeit pity.

My son, always commit thy cause to Me, I will dispose well of it in due time. Wait for My ordering of it, and thou shalt find it will be for thy good. O Lord, I do most cheerfully commit all unto Thee, for my care can little avail. Would that I did not so much dwell on future events, but gave myself up without reluctance to Thy good pleasure.

My son, often a man vehemently struggleth for something he desireth, but when he hath arrived at it, he beginneth to be in another mind; for the affections do not long remain on one object, but rather urge us from one thing to another. It is therefore no small benefit for a man to forsake himself even in the smallest things.

The true profiting of a man consisteth in the denying of himself; and he that is thus self-denied, liveth in great freedom and security. But the old enemy, who always sets himself against all that are good, ceaseth at no time from tempting, but day and night lieth grievously in wait, to cause the unwary to fall headlong into the snare of deceit. "Watch ye, and pray," saith the Lord, "that ye enter not into temptation."

"Lord, what is man, that Thou art mindful of him, or the son of man that Thou visitest him?" What hath man deserved that Thou shouldest grant him Thy favour? O Lord, what cause can I have to complain, if Thou forsake me? Or if Thou do not that which I desire, what can I justly say against it? Surely this I may truly think and say; Lord, I am nothing, I can do nothing, I have nothing that is good of myself, but in all thigs I am full of decay. And am ever tending to nothing. And unless Thou help me, and inwardly inform me, become altogether lukewarm and ready to fall to pieces.

But Thou, Lord, art Thyself always the same, and endurest for ever; always good, just, and holy; doing all things well, justly, and holily, and ordering them in wisdom. Whereas I, that am more ready to go backward than forward, do not ever continue in one estate, for "seven times are passed over me." Nevertheless it soon becometh better, when it so pleaseth Thee, and when thou vouchsafest to stretch forth Thy helping hand; for Thou alone canst help me without human aid, and so strengthen me that my countenance shall be no more changed, but my heart shall be turned to Thee alone, and be at rest.

Wherefore, if I could perfectly cast off all human consolation, either for the attainment of devotion, or because of mine own necessities, which enforce me to seek after Thee, for no mortal can comfort me, then might I well hope in Thy grace, and rejoice in the gift of new consolation.

Thanks be unto Thee from whom all proceedeth, whenever it goes well with me. But I am in Thy sight mere vanity and nothing, an inconstant and weak person. Whereof then can I glory; or for what do I desire to be respected? Is it for being nothing? This too is most vain. Mere empty glory is in truth an evil pest, the greatest of vanities; because it draweth a man from true glory, and robbeth him of heavenly grace. For whilst he pleaseth himself, he displeaseth Thee; whilst he gapeth after the praise of men, he is deprived of true virtues.

But the true glory and holy exultation is for a man to glory in Thee, and not in himself; to rejoice in Thy name, not in his own virtue or strength, nor to take delight in any creature except it be for Thy sake. Praised be Thy name, not mine; magnified be Thy work, not mine: let Thy holy name be blessed, but to me let no part of men's praises be given. Thou art my glory, Thou art the joy of my heart. In Thee will I glory and rejoice all day, but as for myself, I will not glory except in my infirmities.

Let the Jews seek honour of one another, I will ask for that which cometh from God alone. Truly all human glory, all temporal honour, all worldly highness, compared to Thy eternal glory, is vanity and folly. O my God, my Truth, and my Mercy, O Blessed Trinity, to Thee alone be praise, honour, power, and glory, for ever and ever.

My son, make it no matter of thine if thou see others honoured and advanced, but thyself condemned and debased. Lift up thy heart unto Heaven to Me, and the contempt of men on earth will not grieve thee. Lord, we are in blindness, and are quickly misled by vanity. If I look rightly into myself, I cannot say that any creature hath ever done me wrong; and therefore I cannot justly complain before Thee.

But because I have often and grievously sinned against Thee, all creatures do justly take arms against me. Unto me, therefore, shame and contempt are justly due, but unto Thee are due praise, honour, and glory. And unless I prepare myself with cheerful willingness to be despised and forsaken of all creatures, and to be esteemed quite entirely nothing, I cannot obtain inward peace and stability, nor be spiritually enlightened, nor be fully united unto Thee.

My son, if thou rest thy peace on any person, because thou hast formed a high opinion of him, and because you are in daily familiar intercourse with each other, thou wilt become entangled and unstable. But if thou have recourse to the ever-living and abiding truth, the desertion or death of a friend will not grieve thee. Thy regard for thy friend ought to be grounded in Me; and for My sake is he to be beloved, whoever he is that thou thinkest well of, and who is dear to thee in this life. Without Me friendship hath no strength, no continuance; neither is that love true and pure, which is not knit by Me. Thou oughtest to be so dead to such affections of beloved friends that, so far as thou art concerned, thou wouldest choose to be without all human sympathy. Man approacheth so much the nearer unto God, the farther he retireth from all earthly comfort. In proportion, too, as he descendeth lower into himself, and is meaner in his own sight, so much the higher he ascendeth to God.

But he that attributeth any good to himself, hindereth God's grace from coming unto him; because the grace of the Holy Spirit seeketh a humble heart. If thou couldest but perfectly annihilate thyself, and empty thyself of all created love, then might I even hold Myself bound to overflow into thee with great grace. When thou lookest to the creatures, the countenance of the Creator is withdrawn from thee. Learn in all things to overcome thyself, for the sake of the Creator; then shalt thou be able to attain unto divine knowledge. How ever mean anything is, if it is inordinately loved and regarded, it keeps back the soul from the chief Good, and corrupts it.

My son, let not the sayings of men move thee, however fair and ingenious they may be. "For the Kingdom of God consisteth not in word, but in power." Give attention to My words, for they inflame the heart, and enlighten the mind; they produce compunction, and they supply abundant variety of consolation. Never read thou the word of God in order to appear more learned or more wise. Be studious for the mortification of thy sins; for this will profit thee more than the knowledge of many difficult questions.

When thou hast read and dost know many things, thou must always return to one beginning and principle. I am He that teacheth man knowledge; and I bestow on little children a clearer understanding than can be taught by man. He to whom I speak shall quickly be wise, and shall profit much in Spirit. Woe be to them that enquire many curious things of men, and take small care about the way of serving Me! The time will come when the Master of masters, Christ the Lord of angels, shall appear to hear the lessons of all, that is, to examine the consciences of everyone. And then will He search Jerusalem with candles, and the hidden things of darkness shall be laid open, and the arguing of men's tongues shall be silent.

I am He who in one instant lifts up the humble mind to comprehend more reasonings of eternal truth, than if he had studied ten years in the schools. I teach without noise of words, without confusion of opinions, without ambition of honour, without the scuffling of arguments. I am He who instructs men to despise earthly things, to loathe things present, to seek things eternal, to relish things eternal; to flee honours, to endure offences, to place all hope in Me, to desire nothing apart from Me, and above all things ardently to love Me.

For a certain person, by loving Me from the bottom of his heart, became instructed in things divine, and was wont to speak admirable truths. He made greater progress by forsaking all things, than by studying subtle niceties. Nevertheless, to some men I speak common things, to others special things; to some I gently show Myself in signs and figures, whilst to some I reveal mysteries in much light. The voice of books is indeed one, but it informs not all alike; for inwardly I am the teacher of the truth, the searcher of the heart, the discerner of the thoughts, the promoter of the actions, distributing to every man as I shall judge fit.

My son, in many things it is thy duty to be ignorant, and to esteem thyself as one dead upon the earth, and one to whom the whole world is crucified. Many things, too, there are which it is thy duty to pass by with a deaf ear, that so thou mayest be more mindful of those which belong to thy peace. It is more profitable to turn away one's eyes from unpleasing subjects, and to leave each person to his own opinion, than to give attendance to contentious discourses. If all stands well between God and thee, and thou hast His judgment in thy mind, thou shalt very easily endure to be as one defeated.

O Lord, to what a pass are we come! Behold, we bewail a temporal loss, for a pitiful gain we toil and run; while the spiritual harm we incur is forgotten, and hardly do we return to a sense of it. That which profit us little or nothing, is minded, and that which is especially necessary, is negligently passed over; because the whole man doth slide off to external things, and unless he speedily recover himself, he settleth down in them, and that willingly.

Grant me help, O Lord, in tribulation, for vain is the help of man! How often have I not met with faithfulness there, where I thought myself sure of it! How often, too, have I found it there, where beforehand I least expected it! It is vain therefore to have hope in men; but the salvation of the righteous is in Thee, O God! Blessed be Thou, O Lord my God, in all things that befall us. We are weak and unstable; we are quickly deceived and quite changed.

Who is he that is able in all things so warily and circumspectly to keep himself, as never to come into any deception or perplexity? But he that trusteth in Thee, O Lord, and seeketh Thee with a single heart, doth not so easily slip. And if he fall into any tribulation, be he never so much entangled, yet shall he quickly either through Thee be delivered, or by Thee be comforted; for Thou wilt not forsake him that hopeth in Thee even to the end. A friend is rarely found that continueth faithful in all his friend's distresses. Thou, O Lord, even Thou alone art most faithful at all times, and there is none other like unto Thee.

O how wise was that holy soul which said, "My mind is firmly settled, and is grounded in Christ." If thus it were with me, the fear of man would not so easily vex me, nor darts of words move me. Who has the power to foresee, who to guard against, all future evils? If even when we do foresee things, they often hurt us, how can unforeseen evils otherwise than grievously wound us? But wretch as I am, why have I not foreseen better for myself? Why, too, have I so easily given credit to others? But we are men, nothing else but frail men, even though by many we were to be reputed and called angels. Whom shall I trust, O Lord? Whom shall I trust but Thee? Thou art the truth, which neither doth deceive, nor can be deceived. And on the other side, "every man is a liar," weak, inconstant, and subject to fall, especially in words; and therefore we must scarcely ever give credit to that which on the face of it seemeth to sound right.

O with what wisdom hast thou warned us to beware of men; and, that a man's foes are they of his own household; and not to give credit if one should say, Lo here, or Lo there. My hurt has been my instructor, and I wish it may make me more cautious, and not more unwise. "Be wary," saith one, "be wary, keep to thyself what I say to thee"; and whilst I hold my peace, and think it is secret, he cannot himself keep that which he desired me to keep, but presently betrays both me and himself, and is gone. From such mischief-making reckless persons protect Thou me, O Lord, that I neither fall into their hands, nor ever commit such things myself. Grant me to observe truth and constancy in my words, and remove far from me a crafty tongue. What I am not willing to suffer I ought by all means beware of doing.

O how good it is, and tending to peace, to be silent about other men, and not to believe indifferently all that is said, nor too easily to hand on reports. Also it is good to lay one's self open to few; and ever to be seeking after Thee as the beholder of the heart: and not to be carried about with every wind of words, but to desire that all things, both within and without, be accomplished according to the pleasure of Thy will. How safe is it, for the keeping of heavenly grace, to avoid appearances, and not to seek those things which seem to cause admiration abroad; but to pursue with all diligence the things which bring amendment of life and godly zeal.

How many have been the worse for having their virtue known and overhastily commended! How truly profitable hath grace been when preserved in silence in this frail life, which we are told is all temptation and warfare!

My son, stand steadily, and put thy trust in Me; for what are words, but words? They fly through the air, but they cannot hurt a stone. If thou art guilty, think that thou wouldest gladly amend thyself; if conscience reproach thee not, consider that thou wouldest gladly suffer this for God's sake. Little enough it is, to suffer sometimes from words, since thou hast not yet the courage to endure hard stripes. And why do such small matters go to thy heart, but because thou art yet carnal, and regardest men more than thou oughtest? For it is because thou art afraid of being despised, that thou art unwilling to be reproved for thy faults, and seekest the shelter of excuses.

But look better into thyself, and thou shalt acknowledge that the world is yet alive in thee, and a vain desire to please men. For when thou shrinkest from being abased and confounded for thy faults, it is evident thou art neither truly humble, nor truly dead to the world, nor the world crucified to thee. But give diligent ear to My word, and thou shalt not care for ten thousand words spoken by men. Behold, if all should be spoken against thee that could be most maliciously invented, what would it hurt thee if thou wouldst suffer it to pass entirely away, and make no more reckoning of it than of a splinter? Could it pluck so much as one hair from thy head?

But he that hath no heart within him, nor hath God before his eyes, is easily moved with a word of dispraise. Whereas he that trusteth in Me, and hath no wish to trust in his own judgment, shall be free from the fear of men. For I am the judge and the discerner of all secrets: I well understand how the matter passed; I know him that offereth the injury, and him that suffereth it. From Me proceedeth that word; by My permission this hath happened; that the thoughts of many hearts may be revealed. I shall judge the guilty and the innocent; but by a secret judgment I have thought fit first to test them both.

The testimony of men often deceiveth: My judgment is true; it shall stand, and shall not be overthrown: it commonly lieth hidden, and is manifest but to a few, and that in special cases: yet it never erreth, nor can err, although to the eyes of the foolish it may seem not right. To Me, therefore, men ought to have recourse in every judgment, and not to rely on their own opinion. For the just man will not be disturbed, whatsoever befalleth him from God. Even if an unjust charge is brought against him, he will not much care. Nor again will he vainly exult, if through others he be justly vindicated. For he considereth that I am He that searchest the heart and being, and judge not according to the outward face and human appearance. For often in My sight is found that which in the judgment of men is thought to be commendable of blame.

O Lord God, the just judge, strong and patient, Thou who knowest the frailty and wickedness of men, be Thou my strength, and all my confidence, for mine own conscience sufficeth me not. Thou knowest what I know not; and therefore under all blame I ought to humble myself, and to bear it meekly. Of Thy mercy then forgive me whenever I have acted otherwise, and when the next trial comes, grant me the grace of more thorough endurance. Because better to me is Thine overflowing pity for the obtaining of pardon, than any fancied righteousness of my own to ward off the latent misgivings of conscience. Although I know nothing by myself, yet I cannot justify myself by this ignorance; for without Thy mercy, in Thy sight shall no man living be justified.

My son, be not wearied out by the labours which thou hast undertaken for My sake, nor let tribulations ever cast thee down; but let My promise strengthen and comfort thee under every circumstance. I am well able to reward thee, above all measure and degree. Thou shalt not long toil here, nor always be oppressed with griefs. Wait a little while, and thou shalt see a speedy end of thine evils. There will come an hour when all labour and trouble shall cease. Poor and brief is all that which passeth away with time.

Do in earnest what thou doest; labour faithfully in My vineyard; I will be thy recompense. Write, read, chant, mourn, keep silence, pray, endure crosses manfully; life everlasting is worth all these conflicts, and greater than these. Peace shall come on a day which is known unto the Lord, and it shall be not day nor night, that is, of this present time, but unceasing light, infinite brightness, steadfast peace, and secure rest. Then thou shalt not say, "Who shall deliver me from the body of this death?" nor cry, "Woe is me, that my sojourning is prolonged!" for death shall be cast down headlong, and there shall be salvation which can never fail, no more anxiety, blessed joy, society sweet and noble.

O if thou hadst seen the everlasting crowns of the saints in Heaven, and with what great glory they now rejoice, who once were esteemed by the world as contemptible, and unworthy of life itself; truly thou wouldest forthwith humble thyself even to the earth, and wouldest rather seek to be under all, than to have command over so much as one person. Neither wouldest thou long for this life's pleasant days, but rather wouldst rejoice to suffer affliction for God, and esteem it thy greatest gain to be reputed as nothing amongst men.

O if thou hadst a relishing of these things, and didst suffer them to sink into the bottom of thy heart, how couldest thou dare to complain so much as once? Are not all painful labours to be endured for the sake of eternal life? It is no small matter to lose or to gain the Kingdom of God. Lift up thy face therefore unto Heaven; behold, I and all My saints with Me, who in this world had great conflicts, do now rejoice, are now comforted, now secure, now at rest, and shall remain with Me everlasting in the kingdom of My Father.

O most blessed mansion of the City which is above! O most clear day of eternity, which night obscureth not, but the highest truth ever englighteneth! O day ever joyful, ever secure, and never changing into a contrary state! O that that day might once appear, and that all these temporal things were at an end! To the saints indeed, it shineth, glowing with uninterrupted brightness, but to those who are pilgrims on the earth it appeareth only far off, and as through a glass.

The citizens of heaven know how joyful that day is, but the banished children of Eve bewail the bitterness and tediousness of this day. The days of this life are few and evil, full of sorrows and hardships. Here a man is defiled with many sins, ensnared with many passions, held fast by many fears, racked with many cares, distracted with many curiosities, entangled with many vanities, compassed about with many errors, worn away with many labours, burdened with temptations, enervated by pleasures, tormented with want.

O when shall these evils be at an end? When shall I be delivered from the miserable bondage of my sins? When shall I be mindful, O Lord, of Thee alone? When shall I fully rejoice in Thee? When shall I enjoy true liberty without any impediment whatsoever, without all trouble of mind and body? When shall I have solid peace, peace secure and undisturbed, peace within and peace without, peace every way assured? O, merciful Jesus, when shall I stand to behold Thee? When shall I contemplate the glory of Thy kingdom? When wilt Thou be unto me all in all? O when shall I be with Thee in Thy kingdom, which Thou hast prepared for Thy beloved ones from all eternity? I am left, a poor and banished man, in the land of my enemies, where daily there are wars and great calamities.

Comfort my banishment, assuage my sorrow; for my whole desire sigheth after Thee. For all is a burden to me, whatsoever this world offereth for consolation. I long to enjoy Thee most inwardly, but I cannot attain it. My desire is that I may be wholly given up to things heavenly, but temporal things and unmortified passions weigh me down. With the mind I wish to be above all things, but with the flesh I am enforced against my will to be beneath them. Thus, unhappy man that I am, I fight against myself, and have become grievous to myself, whilst my spirit seeketh to be above, and my flesh to be below.

O what do I inwardly suffer, whilst in my mind I dwell on things heavenly, and presently whilst I pray, a multitude of carnal temptations and thoughts occur to me! O my God, be not far from me, nor turn away in wrath from Thy servant. Cast forth Thy lightning, and disperse them; shoot out Thine arrows and let all the imaginations of the enemy be confounded. Gather in and call my senses unto Thee; make me forget all worldly things; enable me to cast away speedily, and with scorn, all vicious imaginations. Succour me, O Thou the everlasting truth, that no vanity may move me. Come to me, Thou heavenly sweetness, and let all impurity flee from before Thy face. Pardon me also, and in mercy deal gently with me, whenever as in prayer I think on anything besides Thee. For truly I must confess that I am wont to yield to many distractions. Thus often and often it happens that I am not where I am bodily standing or sitting but rather where my thoughts carry me. Where my thoughts are, there am I; and commonly there are my thoughts, where my affection is. That readily occurs to me, which naturally brings delight, or by custom is pleasing.

And for this cause, Thou that art truth itself hast plainly said, "For where thy treasure is, there thy heart is also." If I love Heaven, I willingly muse on Heavenly things. If I love the world, I rejoice with the felicity of the world, and grieve for the adversity thereof. If I love the flesh, I shall be constantly imagining those things that are pleasing to the flesh. If I love the Spirit, I shall delight to think on things spiritual. For whatever I love, thereof do I willingly speak and hear, and carry home with me the forms, the ideas and representations thereof. But blessed is the man who for Thy sake, O Lord, is willing to part with all creatures, who does violence to his nature, and through fervour of the Spirit crucifieth the lust of the flesh; that so with a serene conscience he may offer pure prayers unto Thee, and all earthly things both outwardly and inwardly being excluded, he may be fit to be admitted into the angelical choirs.

My son, when thou perceivest the desire of eternal bliss to be poured on thee from above, and longest to depart out of the tabernacle of the body, that thou mayest be able to contemplate My brightness without shadow; open thy heart wide, and receive this holy inspiration with thy whole desire. Give greatest thanks to the heavenly goodness, which treateth thee with such condescension, visiting thee mercifully, stirring thee up fervently, sustaining thee powerfully, lest through thine own weight thou sink down to earthly things. For thou dost not obtain this by thy own thought or endeavour, but by the mere condescension of heavenly grace and divine regard; to the end that thou mayest make further progress in all virtue, and in greater humility, and prepare thyself for future conflicts, earnestly striving to cleave unto Me with the whole affection of thy heart, and to serve Me with fervent willingness.

My son, often the fire burneth, but the flame ascendeth not up without smoke. So likewise the desires of some men burn towards heavenly things, and yet they are not free from the temptation of carnal affection. And therefore it is not altogether purely for the honour of God, that they make such earnest requests to Him. Such also often are thy desires, which thou hast pretended to be so serious and earnest. For those desires are not pure and perfect, which are tinctured with the love of thine own special interest and advantage.

Ask not for that which is delightful and profitable to thee, but for that which is acceptable to Me, and tends to My honour; for if thou judgest aright, thou oughtest to prefer and follow My appointment, rather than thine own desire, or anything whatever that is to be desired. I know thy desire, and have often heard thy groanings. Already thou longest to be in the glorious liberty of the sons of God; already dost thou delight in the thought of the everlasting habitation, thy heavenly home full of joy; but that honour is not yet come; still there remaineth another time, a time of war, a time of labour and of trial. Thou desirest to be filled with the chief good, but thou canst not attain it just yet. I am He; wait thou for Me, saith the Lord, until the Kingdom of God shall come.

Thou art still to be tested upon earth, and to be exercised in many things. Comfort shall be sometimes given thee, but it shall not be granted in full. Take courage therefore, and be valiant, as well in doing as in suffering things contrary to nature. It is thy duty to put on the new man, and to be changed into another person. It is thy duty often to do what thou wouldst not; thy duty too to leave undone what thou wouldst do. That which pleaseth others, shall go well forward; that which pleaseth thee, shall not speed. That which others say shall be heard; what thou sayest, shall be accounted nothing: others shall ask and shall receive; thou shalt ask but shalt not obtain.

Others shall be great in the praise of men, but about thee there shall be nothing said. To others this or that shall be committed, but thou shalt be accounted of no use. At this nature will sometimes be troubled, and it is a great thing if thou bear it with silence. In these and many such instances, the faithful servant of the Lord is wont to be tried as to how far he can deny and break himself in all things. There is scarcely any thing which thou hast such need to die to thyself, as in seeing and suffering those things that are adverse to thy will, especially when that is commanded, which seemeth unto thee inconvenient, or useless. And because thou, being under authority, darest not resist the higher power, therefore it seems hard to thee to walk at another's beck, and to give up all thine own opinion.

But consider, My son, the fruit of these labours, the end near at hand, and the reward exceeding great; and thou wilt not grudge to hear them, rather thou wilt have the strongest comfort of thy patience. For instead of that little of thy will which now thou so readily forsakest, thou shalt always have thy will in Heaven. There surely thou shalt find all that thou mayest wish, all that thou shalt be able to desire. There thou shalt have within thy reach all good, without fear of losing it. There shall thy will be ever one with Me; it shall not covet any outward or private thing. There none shall withstand thee, no man shall complain of thee, no man hinder thee, nothing stand in thy way; but all things thou canst desire shall be there together present, and refresh thy whole affection, and fill it up to the brim. There I will give thee glory for the reproach which here you suffer, the garment of praise for heaviness, a kingly throne for ever. There shall the fruit of obedience appear, the labour of repentance shall rejoice, and humble subjection shall be gloriously crowned.

At present, then, bend thyself humbly under all, and care not who said this or commanded it. But take especial care, that whether thy superior, or thy inferior, or thine equal, require anything of thee, or even insinuate their desire, thou take it all in good part, and with a sincere will endeavour to fulfil it. Let one seek this, another that; let this man glory in this, the other in that, and be praised a thousand thousand times; but do thou rejoice neither in this nor in that, but in the contempt of thyself, and in the good pleasure and honour of Me alone. This is what thou art to wish, that whether it be by life or by death God may be always glorified in thee.

O Lord God, Holy Father, be Thou blessed both now and for evermore, because as Thou wilt, so it is done, and what Thou doest is good. Let Thy servant rejoice in Thee, not in himself nor in anything else; for Thou alone art the true gladness, Thou art my hope and my crown, Thou art my joy and my honour, O Lord. What hath Thy servant, but what he hath received from Thee, even without any merit of his? Thine are all things, both what Thou hast given, and what Thou hast made. I am poor, and in troubles, from my youth; and my soul is sorrowful sometimes even unto tears; sometimes also my spirit is of itself disquieted, by reason of impending sufferings.

I long after the joy of peace, I earnestly crave the peace of Thy children, who are fed by Thee in the light of Thy comfort. If Thou give peace, if Thou pour into me holy joy, the soul of Thy servant shall be full of melody, and shall become devout in Thy praise. But if Thou withdraw Thyself, as too many times Thou dost, he will not be able to run the way of Thy commandments; but rather he will bow his knees, and smite his breast, because it is now with him as it was in times past, when Thy candle shone upon his head, and under the shadow of Thy wings he was protected from the temptations which assaulted him.

O righteous Father, and ever to be praised, the hour is come that Thy servant is to be tested. O beloved Father, meet and right it is that in this hour Thy servant should suffer something for Thy sake. O Father, evermore to be honoured, the hour is come, which from all eternity Thou didst foreknow should come; that for a short time Thy servant should outwardly be oppressed, but inwardly should ever live with Thee. The hour is come that he should be for a little while held cheap, and humble, and in the sight of men should fail, and be wasted with sufferings and languors; that he may rise again with Thee in the morning dawn of the new light, and be glorified in Heaven. Holy Father, Thou hast so appointed it, and so wilt have it; and that is fulfilled which Thou thyself hast commanded.

For this is a favour of Thy friend, for Thy love to suffer and be afflicted in the world; however often, and by whomsoever, and in whatever way Thou permittest it to befall him. Without Thy counsel and providence, and without cause, nothing cometh to pass in the earth. It is good for me, Lord, that Thou hast humbled me, that I may learn Thy righteous judgments, and may cast away all haughtiness of heart, and all presumptuousness. It is profitable for me that shame hath covered my face, that I may seek to Thee for consolation rather than to men. I have learned also by this to dread Thy unsearchable judgments, who afflictest the just with the wicked, though not without equity and justice.

I give Thee thanks, because Thou hast not spared my sins, but hast worn me down with bitter stripes, inflicting sorrows and sending anxieties upon me within and without. There is no one else under Heaven who can comfort me, but only Thou, O Lord my God, and heavenly physician of souls, who strikest and healest, who bringest down to hell and bringest back again. Thy discipline is over me, and Thy very rod itself shall instruct me.

Behold, O beloved Father, I am in Thy hands, I bow myself under the rod of Thy correction. Smite my back and my neck, so that I may bend my crookedness to Thy will. Make me a dutiful and humble disciple, as Thou art wont to be kind, that I may be ever ready to go, if Thou does but beckon to me. Unto Thee I commend myself and all that is mine, to be corrected: it is better to be punished here than hereafter. Thou knowest all things generally, and also each separately, and there is nothing in man's conscience which can be hidden from Thee. Before things are done, Thou knowest that they will come to pass; and Thou hast no need that any should teach or admonish Thee of what is going on here on the earth. Thou knowest what is expedient for my spiritual progress, and how greatly tribulation serves to scour off the rust of sins. Do with me according to Thy desired good pleasure, and disdain me not for my sinful life, known to none so thoroughly and clearly as to Thee alone.

Grant me, O Lord, to know that which is worth knowing, to love that which is worth loving, to praise that which pleaseth Thee most, to esteem that highly which to Thee is precious, to abhor that which in Thy sight is filthy and unclean. Suffer me not to judge according to the sight of the outward eyes, nor to give sentence according to the hearing of the ears of ignorant men; but with a true judgment to discern between things visible and spiritual, and above all to be ever searching after the good pleasure of Thy will.

The minds of men are often deceived in their judgments; the lovers of the world too are deceived in loving only things visible. Is a man ever better for being by man esteemed great? The deceitful in flattering the deceitful, the vain man in extolling the vain, the blind in commending the blind, the weak in magnifying the weak, deceiveth him; and in truth doth rather put him to shame, while he so vainly praiseth him. "For what every one is in Thy sight, that is he, and no more," saith humble St Francis.

My son, thou art not able always to continue in the fervent desire of all that is virtuous, nor to persist in the higher pitch of contemplation; but thou must needs sometimes by reason or original corruption descend to inferior things, and bear the burden of this corruptible life, though against thy will, and with weariness. As long as thou carriest a mortal body, thou shalt feel weariness and heaviness of heart. Thou oughtest therefore in the flesh often to bewail the burden of the flesh; for thou canst not employ thyself unceasingly in spiritual studies and divine contemplation.

Then it is expedient for thee to flee to humble and exterior works, and to refresh thyself with good actions; to expect with a firm confidence My coming and heavenly visitation; to bear patiently thy banishment and the dryness of thy mind, till I shall again visit thee, and set thee free from all anxieties. For I will cause thee to forget thy painful toils, and to enjoy thorough inward quietness. I will spread open before thee the pleasant fields of scriptures, that with an enlarged heart thou mayest begin to run the way of My commandments. And thou shalt say, "The sufferings of this present time are not worthy to be compared with the future glory that shall be revealed to us."

O Lord, I am not worthy of Thy consolation, nor of any spiritual visitations; and therefore Thou dealest justly with me when Thou leavest me poor and desolate. For though I could shed a sea of tears, still I should not be worthy of Thy consolation. I am not then worthy of anything but to be scourged and punished; because grievously and often I have offended Thee, and in many things have greatly sinned. Wherefore, in the judgment of truth and reason, I am not worthy even of the least comfort. But thou, O gracious and merciful God, who willest not that Thy works should perish, show the riches of Thy goodness upon the vessels of mercy, vouchsafest even beyond all his desert to comfort Thy servant above the manner of men. For Thy consolations are not like the discourses of men.

What have I done, O Lord, that Thou shouldest bestow any heavenly comfort upon me? I remember not that I have done any good, but that I have been always prone to sin, and slow to amend. This is true, and I cannot deny it. If I should say otherwise, Thou wouldest stand against me, and there would be none to defend me. What have I deserved for my sins, but hell and everlasting fire? I confess in truth that I am worthy of all scorn and contempt nor is it fit that I should be remembered amongst Thy devout servants. And although I be unwilling to hear this, yet I will for the truth's sake lay open my sins, even against myself, that so the more readily I may be accounted worthy to obtain Thy mercy.

What shall I say, in that I am guilty, and full of confusion? My mouth can utter nothing but these words, "I have sinned, O Lord! I have sinned; have mercy on me, pardon me!" Allow me a little time, that I may bewail my griefs, before I go into the land of darkness, a land covered with the shadow of death. What dost Thou require of a guilty and miserable sinner, as that he be contrite, and that he humble himself for his offences? Of true contrition and humbling of the heart ariseth hope of forgiveness; the troubled conscience is reconciled to God; the grace which was lost is recovered; man is preserved from the wrath to come; and God and the penitent soul meet together with a holy kiss.

Humble contrition for sins is an acceptable sacrifice unto Thee, O Lord, giving forth a savour far sweeter in Thy sight than the perfume of frankincense. This is also the pleasant ointment, which Thou wouldest should be poured upon Thy sacred feet; for a contrite and humble heart Thou hast never despised. Here is the place of refuge from the angry face of the enemy; here is amended and washed away whatever defilement and pollution hath been anywhere else contracted.

My son, My grace is precious, it suffereth not itself to be mingled with external things, nor with earthly consolations. Thou oughtest therefore to cast away the hindrance of grace, if thou desire to receive infusion. Look out for a secret place for thyself, love to dwell alone with thyself, desire the conversation of none; but rather pour out devout prayer unto God, that thou mayest keep thy mind in compunction, and thy conscience pure. Esteem thou the whole world as nothing; prefer attendance upon God before all outward things. For thou wilt not be able to attend upon Me, and at the same time to take delight in things transitory. It is meet that thou remove thyself far away from acquaintance and dear friends, and keep thy mind void of all temporal comfort. So the blessed apostle Peter beseecheth that the faithful of Christ would keep themselves in this world as strangers and pilgrims.

O how great a confidence shall we have at the hour of death, whom no affection to anything detaineth in the world. But what it is to have a heart so alienated from all things, the sickly mind doth not as yet comprehend; nor doth the carnal man know the liberty of the spiritual man. Notwithstanding, if he would be truly spiritual, he ought to renounce those who are far off, as well as those who are near unto him, and to beware of no man more than of himself. If thou perfectly overcome thyself, thou shalt very easily bring all else under the yoke. The perfect victory is to triumph over ourselves. For he that keepeth himself subject, in such a way that his sensual affections be obedient to reason, and his reason in all things obedient to Me; that person is truly conqueror of himself, and lord of the world.

If thou desire to mount unto this height, thou must set out courageously, and lay the axe to the root, that thou mayest pluck up and destroy the hidden inordinate inclination to self, and all love of private and earthly good. By this vicious propensity, namely, man's inordinate love of self, almost everything is upheld, which ought thoroughly to be overcome. If this evil be vanquished and subdued, there will presently ensue great peace and tranquillity. But because few labour to be perfectly dead to themselves, or fully go forth from themselves, therefore in themselves they remain entangled, nor can they be lifted up in spirit above themselves. But for he that desireth to walk freely with Me, it is necessary that he mortify all his corrupt and inordinate affections, and that he should not earnestly cleave to any creature with particular love.

My son, mark diligently the motions of nature and of grace; for in a very contrary and subtle manner do they move, and can hardly be distinguished but by him that is spiritually and inwardly enlightened. All men indeed desire that which is good, and pretend somewhat good in their words and deeds; and therefore under the show of good, many are deceived, nature is crafty, and seduceth many, ensnareth and deceiveth them, and hath always self for her end and object: but grace walketh in simplicity, abstaineth from all show of evil, sheltereth not herself under deceits, doeth all things purely for God's sake, in whom also she finally resteth.

Nature is reluctant and loth to die, or to be kept down, or to be overcome, or to be in subjection, or readily to be subdued; but grace studieth self-mortification, resisteth sensuality, seeketh to be in subjection, longeth to be defeated, hath no wish to use her own liberty; she loves to be kept under discipline, and desires not to rule over any, but always to live, remain, and be under God, and for God's sake is ready humbly to bow down to every ordinance of man. Nature striveth for her own advantage, and considereth what profit she may reap by another: grace considereth not what is profitable and commodious to herself, but rather what may be for the good of many. Nature willingly receiveth honour and reverence: but grace faithfully attributeth all honour and glory unto God.

Nature feareth shame and contempt: but grace rejoiceth to suffer reproach for the name of Jesus. Nature loveth leisure and bodily rest: grace cannot be unemployed, but cheerfully embraceth labour. Nature seeketh to have things that are curious and beautiful, and abhorreth those which are cheap and coarse: but grace delighteth in what is plain and humble, despiseth not rough things, nor refuseth to wear that which is old and patched. Nature respecteth temporal things, rejoiceth at earthly gains, sorroweth for loss, is irritated by every little injurious word: but grace looks to things eternal, cleaves not to things temporal, is not disturbed at losses, nor soured with hard words; because she hath placed her treasure and joy in Heaven, where nothing perisheth.

Nature is covetous, doth more willingly receive than give, and loveth to have things private and what she can call her own: but grace is kind-hearted and communicative, shunneth private interest, is content with a little, judgeth that it is more blessed to give than to receive. Nature inclines a man to the creatures, to his own flesh, to vanities, and to vagaries hither and thither: but grace draweth unto God and to every virtue, renounceth creatures, avoideth the world, hateth the desires of the flesh, restraineth wanderings abroad, blusheth to be seen in public. Nature is willing to have some outward solace, wherein she may be sensibly delighted: but grace seeketh consolation in God alone, and to have delight in the highest good above all visible things.

Nature manages everything for her own gain and profit, she cannot bear to do anything gratis, but for every kindness she hopes to obtain either what is equal, or what is better, or at least praise or favour; and is very earnest to have her works and gifts and words much valued: but grace seeketh no temporal thing, nor desireth any other reward than God alone, nor asketh more of temporal necessaries than what may serve her for the obtaining of thing eternal.

Nature rejoiceth to have many friends and family, she glorieth in noble place and noble birth, she relies on the powerful, fawns upon the rich, applauds those who are like herself: but grace loves even her enemies, and is not puffed up with multitudes of friends; nor thinks anything of high birth unless it is joined with more exalted virtue: she favoureth the poor rather than the rich, sympathises more with the innocent than with the powerful, rejoiceth with the true man, not with the deceitful: she is ever exhorting good men to strive for the best gifts, and by all virtue to become like to the Son of God. Nature quickly complaineth of want and of trouble: grace endureth need wth firmness and constancy.

Nature referreth all things to herself, striveth and argueth for herself: but grace bringeth back all to God, from whence originally they proceed; she ascribeth no good to herself, nor doth she arrogantly presume; she contendeth not, nor preferreth her own opinion before others; but in every matter of sense and understanding submitteth herself unto the eternal wisdom and the divine judgment. Nature is eager to know secrets and to hear news; she likes to appear abroad, and to make proof of many things by her own senses; she desires to be acknowledged, and do things for which she may be praised and admired: but grace cares not to hear news, nor to understand curious matters, because all this takes its rise from the old corruption of man; seeing that upon earth there is nothing new, nothing durable. Grace teacheth therefore to restrain the senses, to shun vain complacency and ostentation, humbly to hide those things that are worthy of admiration and praise, and from every matter and in every knowledge to seek profitable fruit, and the praise and honour of God. She will not have herself nor hers publicly praised, but desireth that God should be blessed in His gifts, who of mere love bestoweth all things.

This grace is a supernatural light, and a certain special gift of God, and the proper mark of the elect and pledge of everlasting salvation; it raiseth up a man from earthly things to love the things of Heaven, and from being carnal maketh him a spiritual man. The more therefore nature is depressed and subdued, so much the greater grace is infused, and every day by new visitations the inward man becomes reformed according to the image of God.

O Lord my God, who hast created me after Thine own image and likeness, grant me this grace, which Thou hast shown to be so great and so necessary to salvation; that I may overcome my most evil nature, which draweth me to sin and to perdition. For I feel in my flesh the law of sin contradicting the law of my mind, and leading me captive to the obeying of sensuality in many things; neither can I resist the passions thereof, unless Thy most holy grace fervently infused into my heart, assists me.

There is need of Thy grace, O Lord, and of great degrees thereof, that nature may be overcome, which is ever prone to evil from her youth. For through Adam the first man, nature being fallen and corrupted by sin, the penalty of this stain hath descended upon all mankind, in such a way, that "nature" itself, which by Thee was created good and upright, is now taken for the sin and infirmity of corrupted nature; because its inclination left unto itself draweth to evil and to inferior things. For the small power which remaineth is as it were a spark lying hidden in the ashes. This is natural reason itself, encompassed about with great darkness, yet still retaining power to discern the difference between good and evil, true and false, although it is unable to fulfil all that it approveth, and enjoyeth no longer the full light of the truth, nor soundness of its own affections.

Hence it is, O my God, that I delight in Thy law after the inward man, knowing Thy commandment to be good, just and holy, reproving also all evil and sin, teaching that it is to be avoided. But with the flesh I serve the law of sin, whilst I obey sensuality rather than reason. Hence it is, that the will to do what is good is present with me, but how to perform it I find not. Hence it is that I often purpose many good things, but because grace is lacking to help my infirmity, upon a light resistance I start back and faint. Hence it comes to pass that I know the way of perfection, and see clearly enough how I ought to act; but being pressed down with the weight of my own corruption, I rise not to what is more perfect.

O Lord, how entirely necessary is Thy grace for me, to begin anything good, to proceed with it, and to accomplish it. For without it I can do nothing, but in Thee I can do all things, when Thy grace doth strengthen me. O grace truly celestial! without which our most worthy actions are nothing, nor are any gifts of nature to be esteemed. Neither arts nor riches, beauty nor strength, wit nor eloquence, are of any value before Thee, without Thy grace, O Lord. For gifts of nature are common to good and bad, but the peculiar gift of the elect is grace and love; and they that bear this honourable mark, are accounted worthy of everlasting life. So eminent is this grace, that neither the gift of prophecy, nor the working of miracles, nor any speculation, however high, is of any esteem without it. No, not even faith or hope, or any other virtues, are unto Thee acceptable without charity and grace.

O most blessed grace, that makest the poor in spirit rich in virtues, and renderest him who is rich in many goods humble in heart! Come thou down unto me, come and replenish me early with thy comfort, lest my soul faint with weariness and dryness of mind. I beseech Thee, O Lord, that I may find grace in Thy sight; for Thy grace is sufficient for me, though other things that nature longeth for be not obtained. Although I am be tempted and vexed with many tribulations, yet I will fear no evils, so long as Thy grace is with me. This alone and by itself is my strength; this alone giveth advice and help. This is stronger than all enemies, and wiser than all the wise.

Thy grace is the mistress of truth, the teacher of discipline, the light of the heart, the solace in affliction, the driver away of sorrow, the expeller of fear, the nurse of devotion, the source and fountain of tears. Without this, what am I but a withered piece of wood, and an unprofitable branch only meet to be cast away? Let Thy grace therefore, O Lord, always prevent and follow me, and make me continually given to good works, through Thy Son Jesus Christ. Amen.

My son, the more thou canst go out of thyself, so much the more wilt thou be able to enter into Me. As to be void of all desire of external things produceth inward peace, so the forsaking of thyself inwardly, joineth thee unto God. I wish thee to learn perfect resignation of thyself to My will, without contradiction or complaint. Follow thou Me: "I am the Way, the Truth, and the Life." Without the way there is no going; without the truth, there is no knowing; without the life, there is no living. I am the way, which thou oughtest to follow; the truth, which thou oughtest to trust; the life, which thou oughtest to hope for. I am the inviolable way, the infallible truth, the endless life. I am the straightest way, the supreme truth, the truth, the blessed, the uncreated life. If thou remain in My way, thou shalt know the truth and the truth shall make three free, and thou shalt lay hold on eternal life.

If thou wilt enter into life, keep the commandments. If thou wilt know the truth, believe Me. If thou wilt be My disciple, deny thyself utterly. If thou wilt possess a blessed life, despise this life present. If thou wilt be exalted in heaven, humble thyself in this world. If thou wilt reign with Me, bear the cross with Me. For only the servants of the cross find the way of blessedness and of true light.

O Lord Jesus, since as Thy life was strict, and despised by the world, grant me grace to imitate Thee, though with the world's contempt. For the servant is not greater than his Lord, nor the disciple above his Master. Let thy servant be exercised in the knowledge and practice of Thy life, for therein my salvation and true holiness doth consist. Whatsoever I read or hear apart from it, doth not give me full refreshment or delight.

My son, inasmuch as thou knowest and hast read all these things, happy shalt thou be, if thou do them. "He that hath my commandments and keepeth them, loveth Me; and I will love him, and will manifest Myself unto him," and will make him sit together with Me in My Father's kingdom. O Lord Jesus, as Thou hast said and promised, so truly let it come to pass, and grant that I may not be wholly undeserving of this favour. I have received the cross, I have received it from Thy hand; I will bear it, and bear it even unto death, as Thou hast commanded me. Truly the life of a good religious person is a cross, yet is is also a guide to paradise. We have now begun, it is not lawful to go back, neither is it fit to leave that which we have undertaken.

Let us then take courage, brethren, let us go forward together, Jesus will be with us. For the sake of Jesus we have undertaken this cross; for the sake of Jesus let us persevere in the cross. He will be our helper, who is also our guide and forerunner. Behold, our king entereth in before us, and He will fight for us. Let us follow manfully, let no man fear any terrors; let us be prepared to die valiantly in battle, nor bring such a disgrace on our glory as to flee from the cross.

My son, patience and humility in adversities are more pleasing to Me than much comfort and devotion when things go well. Why art thou so grieved for every little matter spoken against thee? Although it were much more, thou oughtest not to have been moved. But now let it pass; it is not the first that hath happened, nor is it anything new; neither shall it be the last, if thou live long. Thou art courageous enough, so long as nothing adverse befalleth thee. Thou canst give good counsel also, and canst strengthen others with thy words; but when any tribulation suddenly comes to thy door, thou failest in counsel and in strength. Observe then thy great frailty, which thou too often hast experienced in small occurrences. It is notwithstanding intended for thy good, when these are such like trials happen to thee.

Put it out of thy heart as best thou canst, and if tribulation has touched thee, yet let it not cast thee down nor long perplex thee. Bear it at least patiently, if thou canst not joyfully. Although thou be unwilling to bear it, and conceivest indignation at it, yet restrain thyself, and suffer no inordinate word to pass out of thy mouth, whereby Christ's little ones may be offended. The storm which is now raised shall quickly be appeased, and inward grief shall be sweetened by the return of grace. "I yet live", saith the Lord, "and am ready to help thee, and to give thee more than ordinary consolation, if thou put thy trust in Me, and call devoutly upon Me."

Be more patient of soul, and gird thyself to greater endurance. All is not lost, although thou do feel thyself very often afflicted or grievously tempted. Thou art a man, and not God; thou art flesh, not an angel. How canst thou look to continue always in the same state of virtue, when an angel in Heaven hath fallen, as also the first man in Paradise? I am He who lifts up the mourners to safety and soundness, and those that know their own weakness I advance to My own divine nature.

O Lord, blessed be Thy word, more sweet unto my mouth than honey and the honeycomb. What should I do in these so great tribulations and straits, unless Thou didst comfort me with Thy holy discourses? What matter is it, how much or what I suffer, so as I may at length attain to the port of salvation? Grant me a good end, grant me a happy passage out of this world. Be mindful of me, O my God, and direct me in the right way to Thy kingdom. Amen.

My son, beware thou dispute not of high matters, nor of the secret judgments of God, asking why this man is so left, and that man taken into such great favour; why also one is so grievously afflicted, and another so eminently exalted. These things are beyond all reach of man's faculties, neither is it in the power of any reason or diputation to search out the judgments of God. When therefore the enemy suggesteth these things unto thee, or some curious people raise the question, let thy answer be that of the prophet, "Thou art just, O Lord, and Thy judgment is right." And again, "The judgments of the Lord are true and righteous altogether." My judgments are to be feared, not to be discussed; for they are such as cannot be comprehended by the understanding of man.

In like manner I advise thee not to enquire nor dispute of the merits of holy men, as to which of them is holier than the other, or which shall be the greater in the Kingdom of Heaven. Such matters often breed unprofitable strifes and contentions, they also nourish pride and vainglory; from which arise envies and dissensions, whilst one proudly endeavours to put forward one saint, and the other another. To wish to know and search out such things answers no good purpose, rather is displeasing to the righteous souls; for I am not the God of dissension, but of peace; which peace consisteth rather in true humility than in self-exaltation.

Some are carried with zeal of affection towards these saints or those; nevertheless this is rather human love than divine. I am He who made all the saints; I gave them grace; I obtain for them glory. I know what every one hath deserved; I have prevented them with the blessings of My goodness. I foreknew My beloved ones before the beginning of the world. I chose them out of the world, they chose not Me first. I called them by grace, I drew them by mercy, I led them safe through sundry temptations. I poured into them glorious consolations, I gave them perseverance, I crowned their patience.

I acknowledge both the first and the last; I embrace all with love inestimable. I am to be praised in all My saints; I am to be blessed above all things, and to be honoured in every one, whom I have thus gloriously exalted and predestined, without any precedent merits of their own. He therefore that condemneth one of the least of Mine, honoureth not the greatest; for I made both the small and the great. And he that disparageth any of the saints, disparageth Me also, and all others in the Kingdom of Heaven.

These all are one through the bond of charity; their thought is the same, their will is the same, and in love they are all united one to another.

But still, which is a far higher consideration, they love Me more than they do themselves or any merits of their own. For, being raised above self and self-love, they are wholly carried out to love Me, in whom also they rest with entire fruition. Nothing can turn them back, nothing can press them down; for being full of the eternal truth, they burn with the fire of unquenchable charity. Let therefore carnal and natural men who can love nothing but their own selfish joys, forbear to dispute of the state of God's saints. Such men add and take away according to their own fancies, not as it pleaseth the eternal truth.

Many are ignorant, especially those who, being but slenderly enlightened, can seldom love any with a perfect spiritual love. They are as yet much drawn by natural affection and human friendship to this man or to that; and according to the experience they have of themselves in their earthly affections, so do they frame their imaginations of heavenly things. But there is an incomparable distance between the things which the imperfect imagine in their conceits, and those which the illuminated are enabled to behold, through revelation from above.

Beware, therefore, My son, that thou handle not with vain curiosity things which exceed thy knowledge; but rather let this be thy great business and endeavour, to attain, if it be the meanest place, in the Kingdom of God. Even if any man should know who exceeds another in sanctity, or who is accounted the greatest in the Kingdom of Heaven; what would his wisdom profit him, unless he should humble himself the more in My sight, and then should rise up to give the greater praise to My name, in proportion to this his knowledge? Far more acceptable to God is he that thinketh of the greatness of his own sins, and the smallness of his virtues, and how far he is from the perfection of saints, than he who disputeth of their greatness or littleness.

They are well, if men would but content themselves, and refrain from their vain discourses. They glory not of their own merits, inasmuch as they ascribe no goodness to themselves, but attribute all to Me, who of My infinite love have given them all things. They are filled with so great love of the divinity, and with such an overflowing joy, that there is no glory nor happiness that is or can be wanting unto them. All the saints, the higher they are in glory, so much the more humble are they in themselves, and the nearer and dearer unto Me. And therefore thou hast written, "That they did cast their crowns before God, and fell down on their faces before the Lamb, and adored him that liveth for ever and ever".

Many enquire who is the greatest in the Kingdom of God, who know not whether they shall ever be numbered among the least in heaven, where all are great; for they all shall be called, and shall be, the sons of God. "The least shall become a thousand," and "the sinner of a hundred years shall die." For when the disciples asked who should be greatest in the Kingdom of Heaven, they received such an answer as this: "Except ye be converted, and become as little children, ye shall not enter into the Kingdom of Heaven; whosoever therefore shall humble himself as this little child, the same is greatest in the Kingdom of Heaven."

Woe be unto them who disdain to humble themselves willingly with little children; because the low gate of the Kingdom of Heaven will not give them entrance. Woe also to the rich, who have here their consolation; for whilst the poor enter into the Kingdom of God, they shall stand lamenting without. Rejoice ye that art humble, and, ye poor, be filled with joy, for yours is the Kingdom of God if at least ye walk according to the truth.

Lord, what is the confidence I have in this life? Or what is the greatest comfort I can derive from anything under heaven? Is it not Thou, O Lord my God, whose mercies are without number? Where hath it ever been well with me without Thee? Or when could it be ill with me, when Thou wert present? I would rather be poor for Thee, than rich without Thee. I choose rather to be a pilgrim on earth with Thee, than without Thee to possess Heaven. Where Thou art, there is Heaven: and where Thou art not, there is death and hell. Thou art all my desire, and therefore I must sigh and call and earnestly pray unto Thee. In short, there is none whom I can fully trust, none that can seasonably help me in my necessities, but only Thou, my God. Thou art my hope, Thou my confidence; Thou art my comforter, and in all things most faithful unto me.

All men seek their own gain; Thou settest forward my salvation and my profit only, and turnest all things to my good. Although Thou exposest me to many temptations and adversities, yet Thou orderest all this to my advantage, who art wont to try Thy beloved ones a thousand ways. In which trial of me Thou oughtest no less to be loved and praised, than if Thou didst fill me full of heavenly consolations.

In Thee therefore, O Lord God, I place my whole hope and refuge; on Thee I rest all my tribulation and anguish; for I find all to be weak and inconstant, whatever I behold apart from Thee. For many friends cannot profit, nor strong helpers assist, nor prudent counsellors give a profitable answer, nor the books of the learned afford comfort, nor any precious substance deliver, nor any place, however retired and lonely, give shelter, unless Thou Thyself dost assist, help, strengthen, console, instruct, and guard us.

For all things that seem to belong to the attainment of peace and felicity, without Thee, are nothing, and do bring in truth no felicity at all. Thou therefore art the fountain of all that is good, the height of life, the depth of all that can be spoken; and to hope in Thee above all things is the strongest comfort of Thy servants. To Thee therefore do I lift up my eyes; in Thee my God, the Father of mercies, do I put my trust. Bless and sanctify my soul with Thy heavenly blessings, that it may become Thy holy habitation, and the seat of Thine eternal glory; and let nothing be found in this temple of Thy divinity which shall offend the eyes of Thy majesty. According to the greatness of Thy goodness and multitude of Thy mercies, look upon me, and hear the prayer of Thy poor servant, who is far exiled from Thee in the land of the shadow of death. Protect and keep the soul of me, the meanest of Thy servants, and by Thy grace accompanying me direct it along the way of peace to its home of everlasting brightness. Amen.

MARTIN LUTHER: Man is Free

Christian faith has seemed to many an easy thing; not a few even reckon it among the social virtues, as it were; and this they do because they have not examined it experimentally, and have never tasted it. For it is not possible for any man to write well about it, or to understand well what is rightly written, who has not at some time tasted its spirit, under the pressure of tribulation; while he who has tasted of it, even to a very small extent, can never write, speak, think, or hear about it sufficiently. For it is a living fountain, springing up unto eternal life, as Christ calls it (John 4:14).

Now, though I cannot boast of my abundance, and though I know how poorly I am qualified, yet I hope that, after having been vexed by various temptations, I have attained some little drop of faith, and that I can speak of this matter, if not with more elegance, certainly with more solidity, than those literal and over-subtle disputants who have hitherto discoursed upon it without understanding their own words. So I may open an easier way for laymen for these alone I am trying to serve I first lay down these two propositions, concerning spiritual liberty and servitude:

A Christian man is the most free lord of all, and subject to none; a Christian man is the most dutiful servant of all, and subject to everyone.

Although these statements appear contradictory, yet, when they are found to agree together they will serve my purpose excellently. They are both the statements of Paul himself, who says: "Though I be free from all men, yet have I made myself servant unto all" (I Corinthians 9:19), and "Owe no man anything, but to love one another" (Romans 13:8). Now love is by its own nature dutiful and obedient to the beloved object. Thus even Christ, though Lord of all things, was yet made of a woman; made under the law; at once free and a servant; at once in the form of God and in the form of a servant.

Let us examine the subject on a deeper level. Man is composed of a twofold nature, a spiritual and a bodily. The spiritual nature is called the soul, the spiritual, inward new man; the bodily nature is called the flesh, outward, old man. The apostle speaks of this: "Though our outward man perish, yet the inward man is renewed day by day" (II Corinthians 4:16). The result of this diversity is that in the Scriptures opposing statements are made concerning the same man, the fact being that in the same man these two men are opposed to one another; the flesh fighting against the spirit, and the spirit against the flesh (Galatians 5:17).

We first approach the subject of the inward man, so that we may see by what means a man becomes justified, free, and a true Christian; that is, a spiritual, new, and inward man. It is certain that absolutely none among outward things, under whatever name they may be reckoned, has any influence in producing Christian righteousness or liberty, nor, on the other hand, unrighteousness or slavery. This can be shown by an easy argument.

What can it profit the soul that the body should be in good condition, free, and full of life; that it should eat, drink, and act according to its pleasure; when even the most impious slaves of every kind of vice are prosperous in these matters? Again, what harm can ill-health, bondage, hunger, thirst, or any other outward evil, do the soul, when even the most pious of men, and the freest in the purity of their conscience, are harassed by these things? Neither of these states of things has to do with the liberty or the slavery of the soul.

And so it will profit nothing that the body should be adorned with sacred vestments, or dwell in holy places, or be occupied in sacred offices, or pray, fast, and abstain from certain meats, or do whatever works can be done through the body and in the body. Something widely different will be necessary for the justification and liberty of the soul, since the things I have spoken of can be done by an impious person, and only hypocrites are produced by devotion to these things. On the other hand, it will not at all injure the soul that the body should be clothed in profane raiment, should dwell in profane places, should eat and drink in the ordinary fashion, should not pray aloud, and should leave undone all the things above mentioned, which may be done by hypocrites.

And, to cast everything aside, even speculations, meditations, and whatever things can be performed by the exertions of the soul itself, is of no profit. One thing, and one alone, is necessary for life, justification, and Christian liberty; and that is the most holy word of God, the gospel of Christ, as He says, "I am the resurrection and the life; he that believeth in me shall not die eternally" (John 11:25), and also, "If the Son shall make you free, ye shall be free indeed" (John 8:36), and, "Man shall not live by bread alone, but by every word that proceedeth out of the mouth of God" (Matthew 4:4).

Let us therefore hold it as certain and firmly established that the soul can do without everything except the word of God, without which none at all of its wants are provided for. But, having the word, it is rich and wants for nothing, since that is the word of life, of truth, of light, of peace, of justification, of salvation, of joy, of liberty, of wisdom, of virtue, of grace, of glory, and of every good thing. It is on this account that the prophet in a whole Psalm (Psalms 119), and in many other places, sighs for and calls upon the word of God with so many groanings and words.

Again, there is no more cruel stroke of the wrath of God than when He sends a famine of hearing His words (Amos 8:11), just as there is no greater favour from Him than the sending forth of His word, as it is said: "He sent His word and healed them, and delivered them from their destructions" (Psalms 107:20). Christ was sent for no other office than that of the word; and the order of apostles, that of bishops, and that of the whole body of the clergy, have been called and instituted for no object but the ministry of the word.

But you will ask, What is this word, and by what means is it to be used, since there are so many words of God? I answer, the apostle Paul (Romans 1) explains what it is, namely the gospel of God, concerning His Son, incarnate, suffering, risen, and glorified through the Spirit, the sanctifier. To preach Christ is to feed the soul, to justify it, to set it free, and to save it, if it believes the preaching. For faith alone, and the efficacious use of the word of God, brings salvation. "If thou shalt confess with thy mouth the Lord Jesus, and shalt believe in thine heart that God hath raised Him from the dead, thou shalt be saved" (Romans 10:9); and again, "Christ is the end of the law for righteousness to every one that believeth" (Romans 10:4), and "The just shall live by faith" (Romans 1:17). For the word of God cannot be received and honoured by any works, but by faith alone. Hence it is clear that as the soul needs the word alone for life and justification, so it is justified by faith alone, and not by any works. For if it could be justified by any other means, it would have no need of the word, nor consequently of faith.

Since then this faith can reign only in the inward man, as it is said, "With the heart man believeth unto righteousness" (Romans 10:10); and since it alone justifies, it is evident that by no outward work or labour can the inward man be at all justified, made free, and saved. And so, on the other hand, it is solely by impiety and incredulity of heart that he becomes guilty and a slave of sin, deserving condemnation, not by any outward sin or work. Therefore the first care of every Christian ought to be to lay aside all reliance on works, and strengthen his faith alone more and more, and by it grow in the knowledge, not of works, but of Christ Jesus, who has suffered and risen again for him, as Peter teaches (I Peter 5) when he makes no other work to be a Christian one. Thus Christ, when the Jews asked Him what they should do so that they might work the works of God, rejected the multitude of works, with which He saw that they were puffed up, and commanded them one thing only, saying: "This is the work of God: that ye believe on Him whom He hath sent, for Him hath God the Father sealed" (John 6:27–29).

Hence a right faith in Christ is an incomparable treasure, carrying with it universal salvation and preserving from all evil, as it is said, "He that believeth and is baptised shall be saved; but he that believeth not shall be damned" (Mark 16:16). Thus, too, Paul says: "For with the heart man believeth unto righteousness" (Romans 10:10).

It is to be noted that the whole Scripture of God is divided into two parts: precepts and promises. The precepts certainly teach us what is good, but what they teach is not immediately done. For they show us what we ought to do, but do not give us the power to do it. They were ordained, however, for the purpose of showing man to himself, that through them he may learn his own impotence for good and may despair of his own strength. For this reason they are called the Old Testament, and are so.

For example, "Thou shalt not covet", is a precept by which we are all convicted of sin, since no man can help coveting, whatever efforts to the contrary he may make. In order therefore that he may fulfil the precept, and not covet, he is constrained to despair of himself and to seek elsewhere and through another the help which he cannot find in himself; as it is said, "O Israel, thou hast destroyed thyself; but in me is thine help" (Hosea 13:9). Now what is done by this one precept is done by all; for all are equally impossible of fulfilment by us.

Now when a man has through the precepts been taught his own impotence, and become anxious by what means he may satisfy the law, for the law must be satisfied, so that no jot or tittle of it may pass away, otherwise he must be hopelessly condemned then, being truly humbled and brought to nothing in his own eyes, he finds in himself no resource for justification and salvation.

Then comes in that other part of Scripture the promises of God, which declare the glory of God, and say, "If you wish to fulfil the law, and, as the law requires, not to covet, lo! believe in Christ, in whom are promised to you grace, justification, peace, and liberty." All these things you shall have, if you believe, and shall be without them if you do not believe. For what is impossible for you by all the works of the law, which are many and yet useless, you shall fulfil in an easy and summary way through faith, because God the Father has made everything to depend on faith so that whoever has it has all things, and he who has it not has nothing. "For God hath concluded them all in unbelief, that He might have mercy upon all" (Romans 11:32). Thus the promises of God give that which the precepts exact, and fulfil what the law commands; so that all is of God alone, both the precepts and their fulfilment. He alone commands; He alone also fulfils. Hence the promises of God belong to the New Testament; indeed, are the New Testament.

Now, since these promises of God are words of holiness, truth, righteousness, liberty, and peace, and are full of universal goodness, the soul, which holds to them with a firm faith, is so united to them, thoroughly absorbed by them, that it not only partakes in, but is penetrated and saturated by, all their virtues. For if the touch of Christ was healing, how much more does that most tender spiritual touch, that is, absorption of the word, communicate to the soul all that belongs to the word! In this way therefore the soul, through faith alone, without works, is by the word of God justified, sanctified, endowed with truth, peace, and liberty, and filled full with every good thing, and is truly made the child of God, as it is said, "To them gave He power to become the sons of God, even to them that believe on His name" (John 1:12).

From all this it is easy to understand why faith has such great power, and why no good works, nor even all good works put together, can compare with it, since no work can compel the word of God or be in the soul. Faith alone reigns in it; and the soul is made by the word, just as iron exposed to fire glows like fire, on account of its union with the fire. It is clear then that to a Christian man his faith suffices for everything, and that he has no need of works for justification. But if he has no need of works, neither has he need of the law; and if he has no need of the law, he is certainly free from the law, and the saying is true, "The law is not made for righteous man" (I Timothy 1:9). This is Christian liberty, our faith, the effect of which is, not that we should be careless or lead a bad life, but that no one should need the law or works for justification and salvation.

To make what we have said more easily understood, let us explain it in terms of this image. The works of a Christian man, who is justified and saved by his faith out of the pure and unbought mercy of God, ought to be regarded in the same light as would have been those of Adam and Eve in paradise and of all their posterity if they had not sinned. Of them it is said, "The Lord God took the man and put him into the garden of Eden to dress it and to keep it" (Genesis 2:15). Now Adam had been created by God just and righteous, so that he could not have needed to be justified and made righteous by keeping the garden and working in it; but, that he might not be unemployed, God gave him the business of keeping and cultivating paradise. These would indeed have been works of perfect freedom, being done for no object but that of pleasing God, and not in order to obtain justification, which he already had to the full, and which would have been innate in us all.

So it is with the works of a believer. Being by his faith replaced afresh in paradise and created anew, he does not need works for his justification, but that he may not be idle, and so may exercise his own body and preserve it. His works are to be done freely, with the sole object of pleasing God. Only we are not yet fully created anew in perfect faith and love; these require to be increased, not, however, through works, but through themselves.

A bishop, when he consecrates a church, confirms children, or performs any other duty of his office, is not consecrated as bishop by these works; indeed, unless he had been previously consecrated as bishop, not one of those works would have any validity; they would be foolish, childish, and ridiculous. Thus a Christian, being consecrated by his faith, does good works; but he is not by these works made a more sacred person, or more a Christian. That is the effect of faith alone; indeed, unless he were previously a believer and a Christian, none of his works would have any value at all; they would really be impious and damnable sins.

True, then, are these two sayings: "Good works do not make a good man, but a good man does good works"; "Bad works do not make a bad man, but a bad man does bad works." It is always necessary that the substance or person should be good before any good works can be done, and that good works should follow and proceed from a good person. As Christ says, "A good tree cannot bring forth evil fruit, neither can a corrupt tree bring forth good fruit" (Matthew 7:18). Now it is clear that the fruit does not bear the tree, nor does the tree grow on the fruit; but, on the contrary, the trees bear the fruit, and the fruit grows on the trees.

As, then, trees must exist before their fruit, and as the fruit does not make the tree either good or bad, but, on the contrary, a tree of either kind produces fruit of the same kind, so must first the person of the man be good or bad before he can do either a good or a bad work; and his works do not make him bad or good, but he himself makes his works either bad or good.

Since, then, works justify no man, but a man must be justified before he can do any good work, it is most evident that it is faith alone which, by the mere mercy of God through Christ, and by means of His word, can worthily and sufficiently justify and save the person; and that a Christian man needs no work, no law, for his salvation; for by faith he is free from all law, and in perfect freedom does gratuitously all that he does, seeking nothing either of profit or of salvation, since by the grace of God he is already saved and rich in all things through his faith, but solely that which is well-pleasing to God.

This is the truly Christian life, here is faith really working by love when a man applies himself with joy and love to the works of that freest servitude in which he serves others voluntarily and for nothing, satisfied in the fullness and riches of his own faith.

So, when Paul had taught the Philippians how they had been made rich by that faith in Christ in which they had obtained all things, he teaches them further in these words: "If there be therefore any consolation in Christ, if any comfort of love, if any fellowship of the spirit, if any bowels and mercies, fulfil ye my joy, that ye be like-minded, having the same love, being of one accord, of one mind. Let nothing be done through strife or vainglory; but in lowliness of mind let each esteem other better than themselves. Look not every man on his own things, but every man also on the things of others" (Phillippians 2:1–4).

In this we see clearly that the apostle lays down this rule for a Christian life: that all our works should be directed to the advantage of others, since every Christian has such abundance through his faith that all his other works and his whole life remain over and above that, with which to serve and benefit his neighbour from spontaneous goodwill.

Lo! my God, without merit on my part, of His pure and free mercy has given to me, an unworthy, condemned, and contemptible creature, all the riches of justification and salvation in Christ. For such a Father, who has overwhelmed me with these inestimable riches of His, why should I not freely, cheerfully, and with my whole heart, and from voluntary zeal, do all that I know will be pleasing to Him and acceptable in His sight? I will therefore give myself, as a sort of Christ, to my neighbour, as Christ has given Himself to me; and will do nothing in this life except what I see will be needful, advantageous, and wholesome for my neighbour, since by faith I abound in all good things in Christ.

Thus from faith flow forth love and joy in the Lord, and from love a cheerful, willing, free spirit, disposed to serve our neighbour voluntarily, without taking any account of gratitude or ingratitude, praise or blame, gain or loss. Its object is not to lay men under obligations, nor does it distinguish between friends and enemies, or look to gratitude or ingratitude, but most freely and willingly spends itself and its goods, whether it loses them through ingratitude, or gains goodwill. For thus did its Father, distributing all things to all men abundantly and freely, making His sun to rise upon the just and the unjust. Thus, too, the child does and endures nothing except the free joy with which it delights through Christ in God, the giver of such great gifts.

You see, then, that if we recognise those great and precious gifts, as Peter says, which have been given to us, love is quickly diffused in our hearts through the Spirit, and by love we are made free, joyful, all-powerful, active workers, victors over all our tribulations, servants to our neighbour, and nevertheless lords of all things. But, for those who do not recognise the good things given to them through Christ, Christ has been born in vain; such persons walk by works, and will never attain the taste and feeling of these great things. Therefore just as our neighbour is in want, and has need of our abundance, so we too in the sight of God were in want, and had need of His mercy. And as our heavenly Father has freely helped us in Christ, so ought we freely to help our neighbour by our body and works, and all should become to each other a sort of Christ, so that we may be mutually Christ, and that the same Christ may be in all of us; that is, that we may be truly Christians.

Who, then, can comprehend the riches and glory of the Christian life? It can do all things, has all things, and is in want of nothing; is lord over sin, death, and hell, and at the same time is the obedient and useful servant of all. But alas! it is at this day unknown throughout the world; it is neither preached nor sought after, so that we are quite ignorant about our own name, why we are and are called Christians. We are certainly called so from Christ, who is not absent, but dwells among us, provided, that is, that we believe in Him and are reciprocally and mutually one the Christ of the other, doing to our neighbour as Christ does to us. But now, in the doctrine of men, we are taught only to seek merits, rewards, and things which are already ours, and we have made Christ a taskmaster far more severe than Moses.

The blessed Virgin, beyond all others, affords us an example of the same faith, in that she was purified according to the law of Moses, and like all other women, though she was bound by no such law and had no need of purification. Still she submitted to the law voluntarily and of free love, making herself like the rest of women, that she might not offend or throw contempt on them. She was not justified by doing this; but, being already justified, she did it freely and gratuitously. Thus ought our works too to be done, and not in order to be justified by them; for, being first justified by faith, we ought to do all our works freely and cheerfully for the sake of others.

Any man believing these things may easily keep clear of danger among those innumerable commands and precepts of the Pope, of bishops, of monasteries, of churches, of princes, and of magistrates, which some foolish pastors urge on us as being necessary for justification and salvation, calling them precepts of the Church, when they are not so at all. For the Christian freeman will speak thus: "I will fast, I will pray, I will do this or that which is commanded me by men, not as having any need of these things for justification or salvation, but that I may thus comply with the will of the Pope, of the bishop, of such a community or such a magistrate, or of my neighbour as an example to him; for this cause I will do and suffer all things, just as Christ did and suffered much more for me, though He needed not at all to do so on His own account, and made Himself for my sake under the law, when He was not under the law. And although tyrants may do me violence or wrong in requiring obedience to these things, yet it will not hurt me to do them, so long as they are not done against God."

From all this every man will be able to attain a sure judgment and faithful discrimination between all works and laws, and to know who are blind and foolish pastors, and who are true and good ones. For whatever work is not directed to the sole end either of keeping under the body, or of doing service to our neighbour provided he requires nothing contrary to the will of God, is no good or Christian work. Hence I greatly fear that at this day few or no colleges, monasteries, altars, or ecclesiastical functions are Christian ones. I fear that in all these nothing is being sought but what is already ours; while we fancy that by these things our sins are purged away and salvation is attained, and thus utterly do away with Christian liberty. This comes from ignorance of Christian faith and liberty.

This ignorance and this crushing of liberty are diligently promoted by the teaching of very many blind pastors, who stir up and urge the people to a zeal for these things, praising them and puffing them up with their indulgences, but never teaching faith. Now I would advise you, if you have any wish to pray, to fast, or to make foundations in churches, as they call it, to take care not to do so with the object of gaining any advantage, either temporal or eternal. You will thus wrong your faith, which alone bestows all things on you, and the increase of which, either by working or by suffering, is alone to be cared for. What you give, give freely and without price, that others may prosper and have increase from you and from your goodness. Thus will you be truly good and a Christian.

We give this rule: the good things which we have from God ought to flow from one to another, and become common to all, so that every one of us may, as it were, put on his neighbour, and so behave towards him as if he were himself in his place. They flowed and continue to flow from Christ to us; He put us on, and acted for us as if He Himself were what we are. From us they flow to those who have need of them; so that my faith and righteousness ought to be laid down before God as a covering and intercession of the sins of my neighbour, which I am to take on myself, and so labour and endure servitude in them, as if they were my own; for this has Christ done for us. This is true love and the genuine truth of Christian life. But it is true and genuine only where there is true and genuine faith. Hence the apostle attributes to charity this quality: that she seeks not her own.

We conclude therefore that a Christian man does not live in himself, but in Christ and in his neighbour, or else is no Christian: in Christ by faith; in his neighbour by love. By faith he is carried upwards above himself to God, and by love he sinks back below himself to his neighbour, still always abiding in God and His love, as Christ says, "Verily I say unto you, hereafter ye shall see Heaven open, and the angels of God ascending and descending upon the Son of Man" (John 1:51).

Thus much concerning liberty, which, as you see, is a true and spiritual liberty, making our hearts free from all sins, laws, and commandments, as Paul says, "The law is not made for a righteous man" (I Timothy 1:9), and one which surpasses all other external liberties, as far as Heaven is above earth. May Christ make us to understand and preserve this liberty. Amen.

JOHN CALVIN: How to Endure Persecution

"Let us go forth out of the tents after Christ, bearing his reproach" (Hebrews 13:13).

All the exhortations which can be given us to suffer patiently for the name of Jesus Christ, and in defence of the gospel, will have no effect if we do not feel assured of the cause for which we fight. For when we are called to part with life, it is absolutely necessary to know on what grounds. We cannot possess the necessary firmness, unless it be founded on certainty of faith.

It is true that persons may be found who will foolishly expose themselves to death in maintaining some absurd opinions and reveries conceived by their own brain, but such impetuosity is more to be regarded as frenzy than as Christian zeal; and, in fact, there is neither firmness nor sound sense in those who thus cast themselves away. It is only in a good cause that God can acknowledge us as his martyrs. Death is common to all, and the children of God are condemned to ignominy and tortures just as criminals are; but God makes the distinction between them, becauses he cannot deny His truth. On our part, then, it is requisite that we have sure and infallible evidence of the doctrine which we maintain; and hence, as I have said, we cannot be rationally impressed by any exhortations which we receive to suffer persecution for the gospel, if no true certainty of faith has been imprinted in our hearts. For to hazard our life is not natural, and though we were to do it, it would only be rashness, not Christian courage. In a word, nothing that we do will be approved by God if we are not thoroughly persuaded that it is for Him and His cause that we suffer persecution, and the world is our enemy.

What then should be done in order to inspire our breasts with true courage? We have, in the first place, to consider how precious the confession of our faith is in the sight of God. We little know how much God prizes it.

A heathen could say, "What a miserable thing to save life by giving up the only things which make life desirable!" And yet he and others like him never knew for what end men are placed in the world, and why they live in it. It is true they knew enough to say that men ought to conduct themselves honestly and without reproach; but all their virtues were mere paint and smoke. We know far better what the chief aim of life should be, namely, to glorify God, in order that He may be our glory. When this is not done, woe to us! And we cannot continue to live for a single moment upon the earth without heaping additional curses on our heads. Still we are not ashamed to purchase a few days of pleasure here below, renouncing the eternal kingdom by separating ourselves from Him.

Were we to ask the most ignorant, not to say the most brutish, persons in the world why they live, they would not venture to answer simply that it is to eat, and drink, and sleep; for all know that they have been created for a higher and holier end. And what end can we find if it be not to honour God, and allow ourselves to be governed by Him, like children by a good parent; so that after we have finished the journey of this corruptible life, we may be received into His eternal inheritance? Such is the principal, indeed the sole, end. When we do not take it into account, and are intent on a brutish life, which is worse than a thousand deaths, what can we find for our excuse? To live and not know why is unnatural. To reject the causes for which we live, under the influence of a foolish longing for a respite of some few days, during which we are to live in the world, while separated from God, such infatuation and madness defy description!

But as persecution is always harsh and bitter, let us consider how and by what means Christians may be able to fortify themselves with patience, so as unflinchingly to expose their life for the truth of God. The apostle says, "Let us go forth from the city after the Lord Jesus, bearing his reproach." In the first place, he reminds us that although the swords are not to be drawn over us nor the fires kindled to burn us, we cannot be truly united to the Son of God while we are rooted in this world. So, a Christian, even in repose, must always have one foot lifted to march to battle, and not only so, but he must have his affections withdrawn from the world, although his body is dwelling in it. At first sight this seems hard, still we must be satisfied with the words of St Paul, (I Thessalonians 3:3,) "We are called and appointed to suffer." As if he had said, such is our condition as Christians; this is the road by which we must go, if we would follow Christ.

Meanwhile, to solace our infirmity and mitigate the vexation and sorrow which persecution might cause us, a good reward is offered. In suffering for the cause of God, we are walking step by step after the Son of God, and have Him for our guide. When we are commanded to follow the Lord Jesus, His guidance is too good and honourable to be refused. Now in order that we may be more deeply moved, not only is it said that Jesus Christ walks before us as our captain, but that we are made in his image; as St Paul speaks (Romans 8:29,) "God hath ordained all those whom he hath adopted for His children, to be made conformable to Him who is the pattern and head of all."

Are we so delicate as to be unwilling to endure anything? Then we must renounce the grace of God by which He has called us to the hope of salvation. For there are two things which cannot be separated: to be members of Christ, and to be tried by many afflictions. We certainly ought to prize such a conformity to the Son of God much more than we do. It is true that in the world's judgment there is disgrace in suffering for the gospel. But since we know that unbelievers are blind, ought we not to have better eyes than they? It is ignominy to suffer at the hands of the worldly authorities, but St Paul shows us by his example that we have to glory in scourgings for Jesus Christ, as marks by which God recognises us and avows us for his own. And we know what St Luke narrates of Peter and John (Acts 5:41,) namely that they rejoiced to have been "counted worthy to suffer infamy and reproach for the name of the Lord Jesus."

Ignominy and dignity are two opposites: so says the world which, being infatuated, judges against all reason and in this way converts the glory of God into dishonour. But, for our part, let us not refuse to be vilified in the world's eyes, in order to be honoured before God and His angels. We see what pains the ambitious take to receive the commands of a king, and what a boast they make of it. The Son of God presents His commands to us, and everyone stands back! Tell me, pray, whether in so doing we are worthy of having anything in common with Him? There is nothing here to attract our sensual nature, but such notwithstanding are the true marks of nobility in the heavens. Imprisonment, exile, evil report, imply in men's imagination whatever is to be vituperated; but what hinders us from viewing things as God judges and declares them, save our unbelief? Wherefore, let the name of the Son of God have all the weight with us which it deserves, that we may learn to count it honour when He stamps His mark upon us: if we act otherwise our ingratitude is insupportable!

Were God to deal with us according to our deserts, would He not have just cause to chastise us daily in a thousand ways? Even more, a hundred thousand deaths would not suffice for a small portion of our misdeeds! Now, if in His infinite goodness He puts all our faults under His foot and abolishes them, and instead of punishing us according to our demerit, devises an admirable means to convert our afflictions into honour and a special privilege, so that through them we are taken into partnership with His Son, must it not be said, when we disdain such a happy state, that we have indeed made little progress in Christian doctrine?

Accordingly St Peter, after exhorting us (I Peter 4:15) to walk so purely in the fear of God, as "not to suffer as thieves, adulterers, and murderers", immediately adds, "if we must suffer as Christians, let us glorify God for the blessing which he thus bestows upon us." It is not without cause he speaks thus. For who are we, I pray, to be witnesses of the truth of God, and advocates to maintain His cause? Here we are poor worms of the earth, creatures full of vanity, full of lies, and yet God employs us to defend His truth, an honour which pertains not even to the angels of Heaven! May not this consideration alone greatly inspire us to offer ourselves to God to be employed in any way in such honourable service?

When the prophets and apostles went to death, it was not without feeling within some inclination to recoil. "They will lead thee whither thou wouldst not", said our Lord Jesus Christ to Peter. (John 21:18). When such fears of death arise within us, let us gain mastery over them, or rather let God gain it; and meanwhile, let us feel assured that we offer Him a pleasing sacrifice when we resist and do violence to our inclinations for the purpose of placing ourselves entirely under His command: this is the principal war in which God would have His people to be engaged. He would have them strive to suppress every rebellious thought and feeling which would turn them aside from the path to which He points. And the consolations are so ample, that it may well be said, we are more than cowards if we give way!

In ancient times vast numbers of people, to obtain a simple crown of leaves, refused no toil, no pain, no trouble; nay, it even cost them nothing to die, and yet every one of them fought for adventure, not knowing whether he was to gain or lose the prize. God holds forth to us the immortal crown by which we may become partakers of His glory: He does not mean us to fight haphazardly, but all of us have a promise of the prize for which we strive. Have we any cause then to decline the struggle? Do we think it has been said in vain, "If we die with Jesus Christ we shall also live with Him"? (II Timothy 2:11). Our triumph is prepared, and yet we do all we can to shun the combat.

It is a monstrous thing that persons who make a boast of having heard a little of the gospel can venture to open their lips to give utterance to quibbling. Some will say, what do we gain by confessing our faith to obstinate people who have deliberately resolved to fight against God? Is not this to cast pearls before swine? As if Jesus Christ had not distinctly declared (Matthew 10:16,) that He wishes to be confessed among the perverse and malignant. If they are not instructed by this, they will at all events remain confounded; and hence confession is of a sweet smell before God, even though it is deadly to the reprobate. There are some who say, what will our death profit? Will it not rather prove an offence? As if God had left them the choice of dying when they should see it good and find the occasion opportune. On the contrary, we approve our obedience by leaving in His hand the profit which is to accrue from our death.

In the first place, then, the Christian man, wherever he may be, must resolve, notwithstanding dangers or threatenings, to walk in simplicity as God has commanded. Let him guard as much as he can against the ravening of the wolves. Above all, let him place his life in the hands of God. Has he done so? Then if he happens to fall into the hands of the enemy, let him think that God, having so arranged, is pleased to have him for one of the witnesses of His Son; and therefore that he has no means of drawing back without breaking faith with Him to whom we have promised all duty in life and in death, Him whose possessions we are and to whom we belong, even though we should have made no promise.

I explained above how little prepared we shall be to suffer martyrdom, if we are not armed with the divine promises. It now remains to show somewhat more fully what the meaning and aim of these promises are. Now there are three promises. The first is, that in as much as our life and death are in His hand, He will so preserve us by His might that not a hair will be plucked out of our heads without His leave. Believers, therefore, ought to feel assured that into whatever hands they may fall, God is not divested of the guardianship which He exercises over them. Were such a persuasion well imprinted on our hearts, we should be delivered from the greater part of the doubts and perplexities which torment us and obstruct us in our duty.

We see tyrants let loose: therefore it seems to us that God no longer possesses any means of saving us, and we are tempted to provide for our own affairs as if nothing more were to be expected from Him. On the contrary, His providence, as He unfolds it, ought to be regarded by us as an impregnable fortress. Let us labour, then, to learn the full meaning of the expression, that our bodies are in the hands of Him who created them. For this reason He has sometimes delivered His people in a miraculous manner, and beyond all human expectation, as Shedrach, Meshach, and Abednego, from the fiery furnace, Daniel from the den of lions, Peter from Herod's prison, where he was locked in, chained, and guarded so closely. By these examples He meant to testify that He holds our enemies in check, although it may not seem so to us, and has power to withdraw us from the midst of death when He pleases: not that He always does it; but in reserving authority to Himself to dispose of us for life and for death, He would have us to feel fully assured that He has us under His charge; so that whatever tyrants attempt, and with whatever fury they may rush against us, it belongs to Him alone to order our life.

If He permits tyrants to slay us, it is not because our life is not dear to Him, and held in greater honour a hundred times more than it deserves. Such being the case, having declared by the mouth of David (Psalms 116:15,) that the death of the saints is precious in His sight, He says also by the mouth of Isaiah (26:21), that the earth will discover the blood which seems to be concealed. Let the enemies of the gospel, then, be as prodigal as they will of the blood of martyrs, they shall have to render a fearful account of it even to its last drop! In the present day, they indulge in proud derision while consigning believers to the flames; and after having bathed in their blood, they are intoxicated by it to such a degree as to count all the murders which they commit mere festive sport. But if we have patience to wait, God will show in the end that it is not in vain He has taxed our life at so high a value. Meanwhile, let it not offend us that it seems to confirm the gospel which in worth surpasses Heaven and earth!

To be better assured that God does not leave us as it were forsaken in the hands of tyrants, let us remember the declaration of Jesus Christ, when He says (Acts 9:4) that He Himself is persecuted in His members. God had indeed said before, by Zechariah, (2:8): "He who touches you touches the apple of mine eye." But here it is said much more expressly, that if we suffer for the gospel, it is as much as if the Son of God were suffering in person. Let us know, therefore, that Jesus Christ must forget Himself before He can cease to think of us when we are in prison, or in danger of death for His cause; and let us know that God will take to heart all the outrages which tyrants commit upon us, just as if they were committed on His own Son.

Let us now come to the second point which God declares to us in His promise for our consolation. It is that He will so sustain us by the energy of His Spirit that our enemies, do what they may, even with Satan at their head, will gain no advantage over us. And we see how He displays His gifts in such an emergency; for the invincible constancy which appears in the martyrs, abundantly and beautifully demonstrates that God works in them mightily. In persecution there are two things grievous to the flesh, the vituperation and insult of men, and the tortures which the body suffers. Now God promises to hold out His hand to us so effectually that we shall overcome both by patience. What He thus tells us He confirms by fact. Let us take this shield, then, to ward off all fears by which we are assailed, and let us not confine the working of the Holy Spirit within such narrow limits as to suppose that He will not easily surmount all the cruelties of men.

Of this we have had, among other examples, one which is particularly memorable. A young man who once lived with us here, having been apprehended in the town of Tournay, was condemned to have his head cut off if he recanted, and to be burned alive if he continued steadfast to his purpose! When he was asked what he meant to do, he replied simply, "He who will give me grace to die patiently for His name, will surely give me grace to bear the fire!" We ought to take this expression not as that of a mortal man, but as that of the Holy Spirit, to assure us that God is not less powerful to strengthen us, and render us victorious over tortures, than to make us submit willingly to a milder death. Moreover, we often see what firmness He gives to unhappy malefactors who suffer for their crimes. I speak not of the hardened, but of those who derive consolation from the grace of Jesus Christ, and by this means with a peaceful heart undergo the most grievous punishment which can be inflicted. One beautiful instance is seen in the thief who was converted at the death of our Lord. Will God, who thus powerfully assists poor criminals when enduring the punishment for their misdeeds, be so wanting to His own people, while fighting for His cause, as not to give them invincible courage.

The third point for consideration in the promises which God gives his martyrs is, the fruit which they ought to hope for from their sufferings, and in the end, if need be, from their death. Now this fruit is that after having glorified his name, after having edified the Church by their constancy, they will be gathered together with the Lord Jesus into His immortal glory. Let believers, then, learn to lift up their heads towards the crown of glory and immortality to which God invites them, that they may not feel reluctant to leave the present life for such a recompense; and, to feel well assured of this inestimable blessing, let them have always before their eyes the likeness which they have to our Lord Jesus Christ seeing death in the midst of life, just as He, by the reproach of the cross, attained to the glorious resurrection, wherein consists all our felicity, joy, and triumph!

The Ecstasies of Saint TERESA OF AVILA

One day, when I was at prayer, the Lord was pleased to reveal to me nothing but His hands, the beauty of which was so great as to be indescribable. This made me very fearful, as does every new experience that I have when the Lord is beginning to grant me some supernatural favour. A few days later I also saw the divine face, which seemed to leave me completely absorbed. I could not understand why the Lord revealed Himself gradually like this since He was later to grant me the favour of seeing Him fully, until at length I realised that His Majesty was leading me according to my natural weakness. May He be blessed for ever, for so much glory all at once would have been more than so base and wicked a person could bear: knowing this, the Lord prepared me for it by degrees.

You may suppose that it would have needed no great effort to behold those hands and that beauteous face. But there is such beauty about glorified bodies that the glory which illumines them throws all who look upon such supernatural loveliness into confusion. I was so much afraid, then, that I was plunged into turmoil and confusion, though later I began to feel such certainty and security that my fear was lost.

One year, on St Paul's Day, when I was at Mass, I saw a complete representation of this most sacred humanity, just as in a picture of His resurrected body, in very great beauty and majesty; this I described in detail to you in writing, at your very insistent request. It distressed me terribly to have to do so, for it is impossible to write such a description without a disruption of one's very being, but I did the best I could and so there is no reason for me to repeat the attempt here. I will only say that, if there were nothing else in Heaven to delight the eyes but the extreme beauty of the glorified bodies there, that alone would be the greatest bliss. A special bliss, then, will it be to us when we see the humanity of Jesus Christ; for, if it is like this even on earth, where His Majesty reveals Himself according to what our wretchedness can bear, what will it be like where the fruition of that joy is complete? Although this vision is imaginary, I never saw it, nor any other vision, with the eyes of the body, but only with the eyes of the soul.

Those who know better than I say that this type of vision is much nearer perfection; more so than those which are seen with the eyes of the body. The last-named type, they say, is the lowest and the most open to delusions from the devil. At that time I was not aware of this, and wished that as this favour was being granted me, it could have been of such a kind as was visible to the eyes of the body, and then my confessor would not tell me I was imagining it. And no sooner had the vision faded, the very moment, indeed, after it had gone, than I began to think the same thing myself, that I had imagined it and was worried at having spoken about it to my confessor and wondered if I had been deceiving him. Here was another cause for distress, so I went to him and consulted him about it. He asked me if I had told him what the vision really looked like to me or if I had meant to deceive him. I said I had told him the truth, for I felt sure I had not been lying or had had any such intention; I would not think one thing and say another for the whole world.

This he well knew, and so he managed to calm me. It worried me so much to have to go to him about these things that I cannot imagine how the devil could ever have suggested to me that I must be inventing them and thus be torturing myself. But the Lord made such haste to grant me this favour and to make its reality plain, that my doubt about its being fanciful left me immediately and since then it has become quite clear to me how silly I was. For, if I were to spend years and years imagining how to invent anything so beautiful, I could not do it, and I do not even know how I should try for, even in its whiteness and radiance alone, it exceeds all that we can imagine.

It is not a radiance which dazzles, but a soft whiteness and an infused radiance which, without wearying the eyes, causes them the greatest delight; nor are they wearied by the brightness which they see in seeing this divine beauty. So different from any earthly light is the brightness and light now revealed to the eyes that, by comparison with it, the brightness of our sun seems quite dim and we should never want to open our eyes again for the purpose of seeing it. It is as if we were to look at a very clear stream in a bed of crystal, reflecting the sun's rays, and then to see a very muddy stream, in an earthy bed and overshadowed by clouds. Not that the sun, or any other such light, enters into the vision: on the contrary, it is like a natural light and makes all other kinds of light seem artificial. It is a light which never gives place to night, and, being always light, is disturbed by nothing. It is of such a kind, indeed, that no one, however powerful his intellect, could ever imagine it as it is. And so quickly does God reveal it to us that, even if we needed to open our eyes in order to see it, there would not be time for us to do so. But it is all the same whether they are open or closed: if the Lord is pleased for us to see it, we shall do so even against our will. There is nothing powerful enough to divert our attention from it, and we can neither resist it nor attain to it by any diligence or care of our own. This I have conclusively proved by experience, as I shall relate.

I should like now to say something of the way in which the Lord reveals Himself through these visions. I do not mean that I shall describe how it is that He can introduce this strong light into the inward sense and give the understanding an image so clear that it seems like reality. That is a matter for learned men to explain. The Lord has not been pleased to grant me to understand how it is; and I am so ignorant, and my understanding is so dull that, although many attempts have been made to explain it to me, I have not yet succeeded in understanding how it can happen. There is no doubt about this: I have not a keen understanding; again and again I have proved that my mind has to be spoon-fed, as they say, if it is to retain anything.

Occasionally my confessor used to be astounded at the depths of my ignorance, and it never became clear to me how God did this and how it was possible that He should; nor, in fact, did I want to know, so I never asked anyone about it, though, as I have said, I have for many years been in touch with men of sound learning. What I did ask them was whether certain things were sinful or not: as for the rest, all I needed was to remember that God did everything and then I realised that I had no reason to be afraid and every reason to praise Him. Difficulties like that only arouse devotion in me, and, the greater they are, the greater is the devotion.

I will describe, then, what I have discovered by experience. How the Lord effects it, learned men will explain better than I and will make clear everything obscure of which I do not know the explanation. At certain times it really seemed to me that it was an image I was seeing; but on many other occasions I thought it was no image, but Christ Himself, such was the brightness with which He revealed Himself to me. Sometimes, because of its indistinctness, I would think the vision was an image, though it was like no earthly painting, however perfect, and I have seen a great many good ones. It is ridiculous to think that the one thing is any more like the other than a living person is like his portrait: however well the portrait is done, it can never look completely natural: one sees, in fact, that it is a dead thing. But let us pass over that, apposite and literally true though it is.

I am not saying this as a comparison, for comparisons are never quite satisfactory: it is the actual truth. The difference is similar to that between something living and something painted, neither more so nor less. For if what I see is an image, it is a living image, not a dead man but the living Christ. And He shows me that He is both Man and God, not as He was in the sepulchre, but as He was when He left it after rising from the dead. Sometimes He comes with such majesty that no one can doubt it is the Lord Himself; this is especially so after Communion, for we know that He is there, since the faith tells us so. He reveals Himself so completely as the Lord of that inn, the soul, that it feels as though it were wholly dissolved and consumed in Christ. O my Jesus, if one could but describe the majesty with which You reveal Yourself! How completely are You Lord of the whole world, and of the heavens, and of a thousand other worlds, and of countless worlds and heavens that You have created! And the majesty with which You reveal Yourself shows the soul that to be Lord of this is nothing for You.

Here it becomes evident, my Jesus, how trifling is the power of all the devils in comparison with Yours, and how he who is pleasing to You can trample upon all the hosts of Hell. Here we see with what reason the devils trembled when You descended into Hades: well might they have longed for a thousand deeper hells in order to flee from such great majesty! I see that You are pleased to reveal to the soul the greatness of Your majesty, together with the power of this most sacred humanity in union with the divinity. Here is a clear picture of what the day of judgment will be, when we shall behold the majesty of this king and see the rigour of His judgment upon the wicked. Here we find true humility, giving the soul power to behold its own wretchedness, of which it cannot be ignorant. Here is shame and genuine repentance for sin; for, though it sees God revealing His love to it, the soul can find no place to hide itself and thus is utterly confounded. I mean that, when the Lord is pleased to reveal to the soul so much of His greatness and majesty, the vision has such exceeding great power that I believe it would be impossible to endure, unless the Lord were pleased to help the soul in a most supernatural way by sending it into a rapture or an ecstasy, during the fruition of which the vision of that divine presence is lost. Though it is true that afterwards the vision is forgotten, the majesty and beauty of God are so deeply imprinted upon the soul that it is impossible to forget these, save when the Lord is pleased for the soul to suffer the great loneliness and aridity that I shall describe later; for then it seems even to forget God Himself. The soul is now a new creature: it is continuously absorbed in God; it seems to me that a new and living love of God is beginning to work within it to a very high degree; for, though another type of vision, revealing God without presenting any image of Him, is of a higher kind, yet, if the memory of it is to last, despite our weakness, and if the thoughts are to be well occupied, it is a great thing that so divine a presence should be presented to the imagination and should remain within it. These two kinds of vision almost invariably occur simultaneously, and so the eyes of the soul see the excellence and the beauty and the glory of the most holy humanity. And in the other way it is revealed to us how He is God, and that He is powerful, and can do all things, and commands all things, and rules all things, and fills all things with His love.

The vision is to be very highly esteemed, and, in my view, there is no peril in it, as its effects show that the devil has no power over it. Three or four times, I think, he has attempted to present the Lord Himself to me in this way, by making a false image of Him. He takes the form of flesh, but he cannot counterfeit the glory which the vision has when it comes from God. He makes these attempts in order to destroy the effects of the genuine vision that the soul has experienced; but the soul, of its own accord, resists them: it then becomes troubled, despondent and restless; loses the devotion and joy which it had before; and is unable to pray. At the beginning of my experiences, as I have said, this happened to me three or four times. It is so very different from a true vision that I think, even if a soul has experienced only the prayer of quiet, it will become aware of the difference. The thing is very easy to recognise; and, unless a soul wants to be deceived, I do not think the devil will deceive it if it walks in humility and simplicity. Anyone, of course, who has had a genuine vision from God will recognise the devil's work almost at once; he will begin by giving the soul consolations and favours, but it will thrust them from it. And further, I think, the devil's consolations must be different from those of God: there is no suggestion in them of pure and chaste love and it very soon becomes easy to see from where they come. So, in my view, where a soul has had experience, the devil will be unable to do it any harm.

Of all impossibilities, the most impossible is that these true visions should be the work of the imagination. There is no way in which this could be so: by the mere beauty and whiteness of a single one of the hands which we are shown, the imagination is completely transcended. In any case, there is no other way in which it would be possible for us to see in a moment things of which we have no recollection, which we have never thought of, and which, even in a long period of time, we could not invent with our imagination, because, as I have already said, they far transcend what we can comprehend on earth. Whether we could possibly be in any way responsible for this will be clear from what I shall now say. If, in a vision, the representation proceeded from our own understanding, quite apart from the fact that it would not bring about the striking effects which are produced when a vision is of God, the position would be like that of a man who wants to put himself to sleep but stays awake because sleep has not come to him. He needs it, perhaps his brain is tired, and so is anxious for it; and he settles down to doze, and does all he can to go off to sleep, and sometimes thinks he is succeeding, but if it is not real sleep it will not restore him or refresh his brain, indeed, the brain sometimes grows wearier. Something like that will be the case here: instead of being restored and becoming strong, the soul will grow wearier and become tired and peevish. It is impossible for human tongue to exaggerate the riches which a vision from God brings to the soul: it even bestows health and refreshment on the body.

I used to put forward this argument, together with others, when they told me, as they often did, that I was being deceived by the devil or that it was all the work of my imagination. I also drew such comparisons as I could and as the Lord revealed to my understanding. But it was all to little purpose, because there were some very holy persons in the place, by comparison with whom I was a lost creature; and, as God was not leading these persons by that way, they were afraid and thought that what I saw was the result of my sins. They repeated to one another what I said, so that before long they all got to know about it, though I had spoken of it only to my confessor and to those with whom he had commanded me to discuss it.

I once said to the people who were talking to me in this way that if they were to tell me that a person whom I knew well and had just been speaking to was not herself at all, but that I was imagining her to be so, and that they knew this was the case, I should certainly believe them rather than my own eyes. But, I added, if that person left some jewels with me, which I was actually holding in my hands as pledges of her great love, and if, never having had any before, I were to find myself rich instead of poor, I could not possibly believe that this was delusion, even if I wanted to. And, I said, I could show them these jewels – for all who knew me were well aware how my soul had changed: my confessor himself testified to this, for the difference was very great in every respect, and no fancy, but such as all could clearly see. As I had previously been so wicked, I concluded, I could not believe that, if the devil were doing this to delude me and drag me down to Hell, he would make use of means which so completely defeated their own ends by taking away my vices and making me virtuous and strong; for it was quite clear to me that these experiences had immediately made me a different person.

My confessor, who, as I have said, was a very holy father of the company of Jesus, gave them, so I learned, the same reply. He was very discreet and a man of deep humility, and this deep humility brought great trials upon me; for, being a man of great prayer and learning, he did not trust his own opinion, and the Lord was not leading him by this path. Very great trials befell him on my account. I knew they used to tell him that he must be on his guard against me, lest the devil should deceive him into believing anything I might say to him, and they gave him similar examples of what had happened with other people. All this worried me. I was afraid that there would be no one left to hear my confession, and that everyone would flee from me: I did nothing but weep.

By the providence of God, this father consented to persevere with me and hear me: so great a servant of God was he that for His sake he would have exposed himself to anything. So he told me that I must not offend God or depart from what he said to me, and if I were careful about that I need not be afraid that He would fail me. He always encouraged me and soothed me. And he always told me not to hide anything from him, in which I obeyed him. He would say that, if I did this, the devil, assuming it to be the devil, would not hurt me, and that in fact, out of the harm which he was trying to do my soul, the Lord would bring good. He did his utmost to lead my soul to perfection. As I was so fearful, I obeyed him in every way, though imperfectly. For the three years and more during which he was my confessor, I gave him a great deal of trouble with these trials of mine, for during the grievous persecutions which I suffered, and on the many occasions when the Lord allowed me to be harshly judged, often undeservedly, all kinds of tales about me were brought to him and he would be blamed on my account when he was in no way blameworthy.

Had he not been a man of such sanctity, and had not the Lord given him courage, he could not possibly have endured so much, for he had to deal with people who did not believe him, but thought I was going to destruction. At the same time he had to soothe me and deliver me from the fears which were oppressing me, though these he sometimes only intensified. He had also to reassure me; for, whenever I had a vision involving a new experience, God allowed me to be left in great fear. This all came from my having been, and my still being, such a sinner. He would comfort me most compassionately, and, if he had had more trust in himself, I should have had less to suffer, for God showed him the truth about everything and I believe the sacrament itself gave him light.

Those of God's servants who were not convinced that all was well would often come and talk to me. Some of the things I said to them I expressed carelessly and they took them in the wrong sense.

To one of them I was very much attached: he was a most holy man, my soul was infinitely in his debt and I was infinitely distressed at his misunderstanding me when he was so earnestly desirous that I should advance in holiness and that the Lord should give me light. Well, as I have said, I spoke without thinking what I was saying and my words seemed to these people lacking in humility. When they saw any faults in me, and they must have seen a great many, they condemned me outright. They would ask me certain questions, which I answered plainly, though carelessly; and they then thought I was trying to instruct them and considered myself a person of learning. All this reached the ears of my confessor (for they were certainly anxious to improve me), whereupon he began to find fault with me.

This state of things went on for a long time and I was troubled on many sides; but, thanks to the favours which the Lord granted me, I endured everything. I say this so that it may be realised what a great trial it is to have no one with experience of this spiritual road; if the Lord had not helped me so much, I do not know what would have become of me. I had troubles enough to deprive me of my reason, and I sometimes found myself in such a position that I could do nothing but lift up my eyes to the Lord. For though the opposition of good people to a weak and wicked woman like myself, and a timid one at that, seems nothing when described in this way, it was one of the worst trials that I have ever known in my life, and I have suffered some very severe ones. May the Lord grant me to have done His majesty a little service here; for I am quite sure that those who condemned and accused me were doing Him service and that it was all for my good.

I have strayed far from my intention, for I was trying to give the reasons why this kind of vision cannot be the work of the imagination. How could we picture Christ's humanity merely by studying the subject, or form any impression of His great beauty by means of the imagination? No little time would be necessary if such a reproduction were to be in the least like the original. One can indeed make such a picture with one's imagination, and spend time in regarding it, and considering the form and brilliance of it; little by little one may even learn to perfect such an image and store it up in the memory. Who can prevent this? Such a picture can undoubtedly be fashioned with the understanding. But with regard to the vision which we are discussing, there is no such way of doing this: we have to look at it when the Lord is pleased to reveal it to us, to look as He wills and at whatever He wills. And there is no possibility of our subtracting from it or adding to it, nor any way in which we can obtain it, whatever we may do, nor look at it when we like or refrain from looking at it. If we try to look at any particular part of it, we at once lose Christ.

For two and a half years things went on like this, and it was quite usual for God to grant me this favour. It must now be more than three years since He took it from me as a continually recurring favour by giving me something else of a higher kind, which I shall describe later. Though I saw that He was speaking to me, and though I was looking upon that great beauty of His, and experiencing the sweetness with which He uttered those words – sometimes stern words – with that most lovely and divine mouth, and though, too, I was extremely desirous of observing the colour of His eyes, or His height, so that I should be able to describe it, I have never been sufficiently worthy to see this, nor has it been of any use for me to attempt to do so; if I tried, I lost the vision altogether. Though I sometimes see Him looking at me compassionately, His gaze has such power that my soul cannot endure it and remains in so sublime a rapture that it loses this beauteous vision in order to have the greater fruition of it all. So there is no question here of our wanting or not wanting to see the vision. It is clear that the Lord wants of us only humility and shame, our acceptance of what is given us and our praise of its giver.

This refers to all visions, none excepted. There is nothing that we can do about them; we cannot see more or less of them at will; and we can neither call them up nor banish them by our own efforts. The Lord's will is that we shall see quite clearly that they are produced, not by us but by His majesty. Still less can we be proud of them: on the contrary, they make us humble and fearful, when we find that, just as the Lord takes from us the power of seeing what we desire, so He can also take from us these favours and His grace, with the result that we are completely lost. So while we live in this exile let us always walk with fear.

Almost invariably the Lord showed Himself to me in His resurrection body, and it was thus, too, that I saw Him in the Host. Only occasionally, to strengthen me when I was in tribulation, did He show me His wounds, and then he would appear sometimes as He was on the cross and sometimes as in the garden. On a few occasions I saw Him wearing the crown of thorns and sometimes He would also be carrying the cross, because of my necessities and those of others, but always in His glorified flesh. Many are the affronts and trials that I suffered through telling this and many are the fears and persecutions that it has brought me. So sure were those whom I told of it that I had a devil that some of them wanted to exorcise me. This troubled me very little, but I was sorry when I found that my confessors were afraid to hear my confessions or when I heard that people were saying things to them against me. Nonetheless, I could never regret having seen these heavenly visions and I would not exchange them for all the good things and delights of this world. I always considered them a great favour from the Lord, and I think they were the greatest of treasures; often the Lord Himself would reassure me about them. I found my love for Him growing exceedingly: I used to go to Him and tell Him about all these trials and I always came away from prayer comforted and with new strength. I did not dare to argue with my critics, because I saw that that made things worse, as they thought me lacking in humility. With my confessor, however, I did discuss these matters; and whenever he saw that I was troubled he would comfort me greatly.

As the visions became more numerous, one of those who had previously been in the habit of helping me and who used sometimes to hear my confessions when the minister was unable to do so, began to say that it was clear I was being deceived by the devil. So, as I was quite unable to resist it, they commanded me to make the sign of the cross whenever I had a vision, and to snap my fingers at it so as to convince myself that it came from the devil, whereupon it would come again: I was not to be afraid, they said, and God would protect me and take the vision away. This caused me great distress: as I could not help believing that my visions came from God, it was a terrible thing to have to do; and, as I have said, I could not possibly wish them to be taken from me. However, I did as they commanded me. I besought God often to set me free from deception; indeed, I was continually doing so, and with many tears. I would also invoke St Peter and St Paul, for the Lord had told me (it was on their festival that he had first appeared to me) that they would prevent me from being deluded; and I used often to see them very clearly on my left hand, though not in an imaginary vision. These glorious saints were in a very real sense my lords.

To be obliged to snap my fingers at a vision in which I saw the Lord caused me the sorest distress. For, when I saw Him before me, I could not have believed that the vision had come from the devil even if the alternative were my being cut to pieces. So this was a kind of penance to me, and a heavy one. In order not to have to be so continually crossing myself, I would carry a cross in my hand. This I did almost invariably; but I was not so particular about snapping my fingers at the vision, for it hurt me too much to do that. It reminded me of the way the Jews had insulted Him, and I would beseech Him to forgive me, since I did it out of obedience to him who was in His own place, and not to blame me, since he was one of the ministers whom He had placed in His Church. He told me not to worry about it and said I was quite right to obey, but He would see that my confessor learned the truth. When they made me stop my prayer He seemed to me to have become angry, and He told me to tell them that this was tyranny. He used to show me ways of knowing that the visions were not of the devil.

Once, when I was holding in my hand the cross of a rosary, He put out His own hand and took it from me, and, when He gave it back to me, it had become four large stones, much more precious than diamonds, incomparably more so, for it is impossible, of course, to make comparisons with what is supernatural, and diamonds seem imperfect counterfeits beside the precious stones which I saw in that vision. On the cross, with exquisite workmanship, were portrayed the five wounds. He told me that henceforward it would always look to me like that, and so it did: I could never see the wood of which it was made, but only these stones.

To nobody, however, did it look like this except to myself. As soon as they had begun to order me to test my visions in this way, and to resist them, the favours became more and more numerous. In my efforts to divert my attention from them, I never ceased from prayer; even when asleep I used to seem to be praying, for this made me grow in love. I would address my complaints to the Lord, telling Him I could not bear it. Desire and strive to cease thinking of Him as I would, it was not in my power to do so. In every respect I was as obedient as I could be, but about this I could do little or nothing, and the Lord never gave me leave to disobey. But, though He told me to do as I was bidden, He reassured me in another way, by teaching me what I was to say to my critics; and this He does still. The arguments with which He provided me were so conclusive that they made me feel perfectly secure.

Shortly after this, His majesty began to give me clearer signs of His presence, as He had promised to do. There grew within me so strong a love of God that I did not know who was inspiring me with it, for it was entirely supernatural and I had made no efforts to obtain it. I found myself dying with the desire to see God and I knew no way of seeking that life save through death. This love came to me in vehement impulses, which, though less unbearable, and of less worth, than those of which I have spoken previously, took from me all power of action. For nothing afforded me satisfaction and I was incapable of containing myself: it really seemed as though my soul were being torn from me. O sovereign artifice of the Lord, with what subtle diligence do You work upon Your miserable slave! You hid Yourself from me, and out of Your love oppressed me with a death so delectable that my soul's desire was never to escape from it.

No one who has not experienced these vehement impluses can possibly understand this: it is no question of physical restlessness within the breast, or of uncontrollable devotional feelings which occur frequently and seem to stifle the spirit. That is prayer of a much lower kind, and we should check such quickenings of emotion by endeavouring gently to turn them into inward recollection and to keep the soul hushed and still. Such prayer is like the violent sobbing of children: they seem as if they are going to choke, but if they are given something to drink their excess emotion is checked immediately. So it is here: reason must step in and take the reins, for it may be that this is partly accounted for by temperament. On reflection comes a fear that there is some imperfection, which may be largely due to the senses. So this child must be hushed with a loving caress which will move it to a gentle kind of love; it must not, as they say, be driven at the point of the fist. Its love must find an outlet in interior recollection and not be allowed to boil right over like a pot to which fuel has been applied indiscriminately. The fire must be controlled at its source and an endeavour must be made to quench the flame with gentle tears, not with tears caused by affliction, for these proceed from the emotions already referred to and do a great deal of harm. I used at first to shed tears of this kind, which left my brain so distracted and my spirit so wearied that for a day or more I was not fit to return to prayer. Great discretion, then, is necessary at first so that everything may proceed gently and the operations of the spirit may express themselves internally, great care should be taken to prevent operations of an exterior kind.

These other impulses are very different. It is not we who put on the fuel; it seems rather as if the fire is already kindled and it is we who are suddenly thrown into it to be burned up. The soul does not try to feel the pain of the wound caused by the Lord's absence. Rather an arrow is driven into the very depths of the entrails, and sometimes into the heart, so that the soul does not know either what is the matter with it or what it desires. It knows quite well that it desires God and that the arrow seems to have been dipped in some drug which leads it to hate itself for the love of this Lord so that it would gladly lose its life for Him. No words will suffice to describe the way in which God wounds the soul and the sore distress which He causes it, so that it hardly knows what it is doing. Yet so delectable is this distress that life holds no delight which can give greater satisfaction. As I have said, the soul would gladly be dying of this ill.

This distress and this bliss between them bewildered me so much that I was never able to understand how such a thing could be. Oh, what it is to see a wounded soul – I mean when it understands its condition sufficiently to be able to describe itself as wounded for so excellent a cause! It sees clearly that this love has come to it through no act of its own, but that, from the exceeding great love which the Lord bears it, a spark seems suddenly to have fallen upon it and to have set it wholly on fire. Oh, how often, when in this state, do I remember that verse of David: "As the hart panteth after the fountains of water, so my soul panteth after Thee, O God," which I seem to see fulfilled literally in myself!

When these impulses are not very strong they appear to calm down a little, or, at any rate, the soul seeks some relief from them because it knows not what to do. It performs certain penances, but is quite unable to feel them, while the shedding of its blood causes it no more distress than if its body were dead. It seeks ways and means whereby it may express something of what it feels for the love of God; but its initial pain is so great that I know of no physical torture which can drown it. There is no relief to be found in these medicines: they are quite inadequate for so sublime an ill. A certain alleviation of the pain is possible if the soul begs God to grant it relief from its ill, though it sees none save death, by means of which it believes it can have complete fruition of its good. At other times the impulses are so strong that the soul is unable to do either this or anything else. The entire body contracts and neither arm nor foot can be moved. If the subject is on his feet, he remains as though transported and cannot even breathe: all he does is to moan, not aloud, for that is impossible, but inwardly, out of pain.

It pleased the Lord that I should sometimes see the following vision. I would see beside me, on my left hand, an angel in bodily form, a type of vision which I am not in the habit of seeing, except very rarely. Though I often see representations of angels, my visions of them are of a different type.

I saw this angel in the following way. He was not tall, but short, and very beautiful, his face so aflame that he appeared to be one of the highest types of angel, who seem to be all afire. They must be those who are called cherubim: they do not tell me their names but I am well aware that there is a great difference between certain angels and others, of a kind that I could not possibly explain. In his hands I saw a long golden spear and at the end of the iron tip I seemed to see a point of fire. With this he seemed to pierce my heart several times so that it penetrated to my entrails. When he drew it out, I thought he was drawing Himself out with it; and he left me completely afire with a great love for God. The pain was so sharp that it made me utter several moans; and so excessive was the sweetness caused me by this intense pain that one can never wish to lose it, nor will one's soul be content with anything less than God. It is not bodily pain, but spiritual, though the body has a share in it, indeed, a great share. So sweet are the colloquies of love which pass between the soul and God that if anyone thinks I am lying I beseech God, in His goodness, to give him the same experience.

During the days that this continued, I went about as if in a stupor. I had no wish to see or speak with anyone, but only to hug my pain, which caused me greater bliss than any that can come from the whole of creation. I was like this on several occasions when the Lord was pleased to send me these raptures, and so deep were they that, even when I was with other people, I could not resist them; so, greatly to my distress, they began to be talked about. Since I have had them, I do not feel this pain so much. But when it does begin, the Lord seems to transport the soul and to send it into an ecstasy, so that it cannot possibly suffer or have any pain because it immediately begins to experience fruition. May He be blessed for ever, who bestows so many favours on one who so ill deserves such great benefits.

Saint IGNATIUS LOYOLA: Prayers of Obedience

DEDICATION

Teach us, Lord,
to serve You as You deserve,
to give and not to count the cost,
to fight and not to heed the wounds,
to labour and not to ask for any reward
save that of knowing that we do Your will.

SURRENDER

Take, Lord, all my liberty,
my memory, my understanding,
and my whole will.
You have given me all that I have,
all that I am,
and I surrender all to Your Divine will,
You have given me all that I have,
all that I am,
and I surrender all to Your divine will,
That You dispose of me.
Give me only Your love and Your grace.
With this I am rich enough,
and I have no more to ask.

Saint JOHN OF THE CROSS: Poems of Love

THE DARK NIGHT

1 I departed in the darkness
With the pains of love oppressed,
Happy lot! for none observed me;
All my house was then at rest.

2 By the ladder that is secret,
In the darkness on I pressed,
Through the night, disguised in
safety,
All my house was then at rest.

3 Unobserved and unobserving
In the silent blissful night;
And in my heart the fire burning
Was my only guide and light.

4 To the place where He was waiting,
Safely guided on the way,
On I went; the light was brighter
Than the sunshine of midday.

5 Night that led to my Beloved,
Guide and light upon the way
And made us one; night more lovely
Than the dawn of coming day.

6 On my breast with flowers covered,
Which for Him alone I kept,
I caressed Him; and the cedars
Waving fanned Him while He
slept.

7 When his tresses were disordered
By the motion of the air,
Then I fainted, and He struck me
With His hand so soft and fair.

8 Self-forgetting, there I rested
On my love reclined my head,
All anxieties discarded
'Mid the lilies round me spread.

THE LIVING FLAME OF LOVE

1 O living flame of love,
How painless is the smart,
Thy tender wounds create
Within my very heart;
O end at last the weary strife
And break the web of this my life.

2 O gentle hand and touch,
O wound in sweetness rife,
O burning, a foretaste
Of everlasting life.
The debt is paid that long was due,
And death by death brings life anew.

3 O lamps of fire that burn,
Illumining the night,
Sense in its caverns glows
With unaccustomed light.
They once were dark but now are
bright,
And to my love give warmth and
light.

4 How loving Thou dost lie
Awake within my breast,
And by Thyself alone,
In secret there at rest.
The sweetness of Thy blissful breath
Makes strong my love; and strong
as death.

THE EXILED SOUL

1 My God, my Lord, do Thou remember
That I by faith have gazed upon Thy
face
Lacking which sight no bliss exists for me!

2 For since I saw Thee, live I in such sort
That there is naught can bring
Joy to my soul but for an hour, or moment!

3 God of my life! nothing can make me
glad,
For all my gladness springs from sight
of Thee,
And faileth me because I have Thee not.

4 If 'tis Thy will, my God, I live forlorn
I'll take my longings even for my comfort
While dwelling in this world.

5 With me no happiness in aught shall
bide
Except the hope of seeing Thee, my God,
Where I shall never dread to lose Thee
more.

6 When shall there dawn that most
delicious day.
When, O my Glory, may I joy in Thee,
Delivered from this body's heavy load?

7 There will my bliss be measureless,
entire,
At witnessing how glorious Thou art,
Wherein will lie the rapture of my life.

8 What will it be when I shall dwell with
Thee,
Since suffering doth bring such happiness?
Upraise me, now, O Lord, into Thy
Heaven!

9 Yet if my life can bring increase of
glory
To Thine eternal being,
In truth I do not wish that it should end.

10 The unending moment of the bliss
of heaven
Will end my pain and anguish
So that I shall remember them no more.

11 I went astray because I served Thee
not,
As I have gained by knowing Thee, my
God!
Henceforth I crave to love Thee ever
more!

CRANMER'S "Exhortation" and "Confession"

Dearly beloved brethren, the Scripture moveth us in sundry places to acknowledge and confess our manifold sins and wickedness; and that we should not dissemble nor cloke them before the face of Almighty God our heavenly Father; but confess them with an humble, lowly, penitent, and obedient heart; to the end that we may obtain forgiveness of the same, by his infinite goodness and mercy. And although we ought at all times humbly to acknowledge our sins before God; yet ought we most chiefly so to do, when we assemble and meet together to render thanks for the great benefits that we have received at his hands, to set forth his most worthy praise, to hear his most holy Word, and to ask those things which are requisite and necessary, as well for the body as the soul. Wherefore I pray and beseech you, as many as are here present, to accompany me with a pure heart, and humble voice, unto the throne of the heavenly grace, saying after me;

Almighty and most merciful Father; we have erred, and strayed from thy ways like lost sheep. We have followed too much the devices and desires of our own hearts. We have offended against thy holy laws. We have left undone those things which we ought to have done; and we have done those things which we ought not to have done; and there is no health in us. But thou, O Lord, have mercy upon us, miserable offenders. Spare thou them, O God, which confess their faults. Restore thou them that are penitent; according to thy promises declared unto mankind in Christ Jesu our Lord. And grant, O most merciful Father, for his sake; that we may hereafter live a godly righteous, and sober life, to the glory of thy holy Name. Amen.

REYNOLDS' "General Thanksgiving"

Almighty God, father of all mercies, we thine unworthy servants do give thee most humble and hearty thanks for all thy goodness and loving-kindness to us, and to all men; we bless thee for our creation, preservation, and all the blessings of this life: but above all, for thine inestimable love in the redemption of the world by our Lord Jesus Christ; for the means of grace, and for the hope of glory.

And, we beseech thee, give us that due sense of all thy mercies, that our hearts may be unfeignedly thankful, and that we show forth thy praise, not only with our lips, but in our lives; by giving up ourselves to thy service, and by walking before thee in holiness and righteousness all our days; through Jesus Christ our Lord, to whom with thee and the Holy Ghost be all honour and glory, world without end. Amen.

JOHN DONNE: Jesus Wept

"Jesus wept" (John 11:35)

I am now but upon the compassion of Christ. There is much difference between his compassion and his passion, as much as between the men that are to handle them here. But "The tear of Christ's passion is a vicarious one": a great personage may speak of his passion, of his blood; my vicarage is to speak of his compassion and his tears. Let me chafe the wax, and melt your souls in a bath of his tears now, let him set to the great seal of his effectual passion, in his blood, then. It is a commonplace, I know, to speak of tears: I would you know as well, it were a common practice to shed them. Though it be not so, yet bring St Bernard's patience. Be willing to hear him, that seeks not your acclamation to himself, but your humiliation to his and your God; not to make you praise with them that praise, but to make you weep with them that weep, and Jesus wept.

The Masorites (the Masorites are the critics upon the Hebrew Bible, the Old Testament) cannot tell us, who divided the chapters of the Old Testament into verse; neither can any other tell us, who did it in the New Testament. Whoever did it seems to have stopped in an amazement in this text, and by making an entire verse of these two words, Jesus wept, and no more, to intimate that there needs no more for the exalting of our devotion to a competent height, than to consider how, and where, and when, and why Jesus wept. There is not a shorter verse in the Bible, nor a larger text. There is another as short; Rejoice evermore, and of that holy joy, I may have leave to speak here hereafter, more seasonably, in a more festival time, by my ordinary service. This is the season of general compunction and mortification, and no man privileged, for Jesus wept.

In that letter which Lentulus is said to have written to the senate of Rome, in which he gives some characters of Christ, he says, that Christ was never seen to laugh, but to weep often. Now in what number he limits his often, or upon what testimony he grounds his number, we know not. We take knowledge that He wept thrice. He wept here, when He mourned with them that mourned for Lazarus; He wept again, when He drew near to Jerusalem, and looked upon that city; and He wept a third time, in His passion. There is but one evangelist, but this St John, that tells us of these first tears, the rest say nothing of them; there is but one evangelist, St Luke, that tells us of His second tears, the rest speak not of those; there is no evangelist, but there is an apostle that tells us of his third tears, St Paul says, That in the days of His flesh, He offered up prayers with strong cries, and tears; and those tears, expositors of all sides refer to His passion, though some to His agony in the garden, some to His passion on the cross; and these in my opinion most fitly; because those words of St Paul belong to the declaration of the priesthood, and of the sacrifice of Christ; and for that function of His, the cross was the altar; and therefore to the cross we fix those third tears. The first were humane tears, the second were prophetical, the third were pontifical, appertaining to the sacrifice. The first were shed in a condolency of a human and natural calamity fallen upon one family; Lazarus was dead: the second were shed in contemplation of future calamities upon a nation; Jerusalem was to be destroyed: the third, in contemplation of sin, and the everlasting punishment due to sin, and to such sinners as would make no benefit of that sacrifice, which He offered in offering Himself. His friend was dead, and then Jesus wept; He justified natural affections, and such offices of piety: Jerusalem was to be destroyed, and then Jesus wept; He commiserated public and national calamities, though a private person: His very giving of Himself for sin, was to become to a great many ineffectual; and then Jesus wept; He declared how indelible the natural stain of sin is that not such sweat as His, such tears, such blood as His could absolutely wash it out of man's nature. The tears of the text are as a spring, a well, belonging to one household, the sisters of Lazarus: the tears over Jerusalem are as a river, belonging to a whole country; the tears upon the cross, are as the sea, belonging to all the world; and though literally there fall no more into our text, than the spring, yet because the spring flows into the river, and the river into the sea, and that wheresoever we find that Jesus wept, we find our text, (for our text is but that, Jesus wept) therefore by the leave and light of his blessed Spirit, we shall look upon those lovely, those heavenly eyes, through this glass of his own tears, in all these three lines, as He wept here over Lazarus, as He wept there over Jerusalem, as He wept upon the cross over all of us. For so often Jesus wept.

First then, Jesus wept as other men do, taking a necessary occasion to show that He was true man. He was now in hand with the greatest miracle that ever He did, the raising of Lazarus, so long dead. Could we but do so in our spiritual raising, what a blessed harvest were that. What a comfort to find one man here today, raised from his spiritual death, this day twelvemonth. Christ did it every year, and every year He improved his miracle. In the first year, He raised the governor's daughter; she was newly dead, and as yet in the house. In the beginning of sin, and whilst in the house, in the house of God in the church, in a glad obedience to God's ordinances and institutions there, for the reparation and resuscitation of dead souls, the work is not so hard. In His second year, Christ raised the widow's son; and him be found without, ready to be buried. In a man grown cold and stiff in sin, impenetrable, inflexible by denouncing the judgments of God, almost buried in a stupidity, and insensibleness of his being dead, there is more difficulty. But in His third year, Christ raised this Lazarus; he had been long dead, and buried, and in probability, putrified after four days.

This miracle Christ meant to make a pregnant proof of the resurrection, which was His principal intentions therein. For the greatest arguments against the resurrection being for the most part of this kind, when a fish eats a man, and another man eats that fish, or when one man eats another, how shall both these men rise again? When a body is resolved in the grave to the first principles, or is passed into other substances, the case is somewhat near the same; and therefore Christ would work upon a body near that state, a body putrified. And truly, in our spiritual raising of the dead, to raise a sinner putrified in his own earth, resolved in his own dung, especially that hath passed many transformations, from shape to shape, from sin to sin (he hath been a salamander and lived in the fire, in the fire successively, in the fire of lust in his youth, and in his age in the fire of ambition; and then he hath been a serpent, a fish, and lived in the waters, in the water successively, in the troubled water of sedition in his youth, and in his age in the cold waters of indevotion) how shall we raise this salamander and this serpent, when this serpent and this salamander is all one person, and must have contrary music to charm him, contrary physic to cure him? To raise a man resolved into divers substances, scattered into divers forms of several sins, is the greatest work. And therefore this miracle (which implied that) St Basil calls a pregnant, a double miracle. For here is a dead man alive again; that had been done before; but Basil says, "He that is fettered, and manacled, and tied with many difficulties, he walks."

And therefore as this miracle raised Him most estimation, so (for they ever accompany one another), it raised Him most envy: envy that extended beyond him, to Lazarus himself, who had done nothing; and yet, "The chief priests consulted how they might put Lazarus to death, because by reason of him, many believed in Jesus". A disease, a distemper, a danger which no time shall ever be free from; that wheresoever there is a coldness, a disaffection to God's cause, those who are any way occasionally instruments of God's glory, shall find cold affections. If they killed Lazarus, had not Christ done enough to let them see that He could raise him again? For "It was a blind malice, if they thought, that Christ could raise a man naturally dead, and could not if he were violently killed". This then being His greatest miracle, preparing the hardest article of the Creed, the resurrection of the body, as the miracle itself declared sufficiently His divinity, that nature, so in this declaration that He was God, he would declare that He was man too, and therefore Jesus wept.

He wept as man doth weep, and He wept as a man may weep; for these tears were proof that He was a true man, but no distrustful, no inordinate man. In Job there is a question asked of God, "Hast Thou eyes of flesh, and dost Thou see, as man sees?" Let this question be directed to God manifested in Christ, and Christ will weep out an answer to that question, I have eyes of flesh, and I do weep as man weeps. Not as sinful man, not as a man, that had let fall his bridle, by which he should turn his horse: not as a man that were cast from the rudder, by which he should steer his ship: not as a man that had lost his interest and power in his affections, and passions; Christ wept not so. Christ might go farther that way, than any other man: Christ might relax Himself, and give more scope and liberty to His passions, than any other man: both because He had no original sin within to drive Him, no inordinate love without to draw Him, when his affections were moved; which all other men have.

God says to the Jews, "That they had wept in his ears"; God had heard them weep: but for what, and how? They wept for flesh. There was a tincture, there was a deep dye of murmuring in their tears. Christ goes as far in the passion, in His agony, and He comes to a passionate deprecation, in His harsh spirit and in the "if it were possible", and in the "let the cup pass from me". But as all these passions were sanctified in the root, from which no bitter leaf, no crooked twig could spring, so they were instantly washed with His ceruntamen, a present and a full submitting of all to God's pleasure, "Yet not my will, O Father, but Thine be done". It will not be safe for any man to come so near an excess of passions, as he may find some good men in the Scriptures to have done: that because he hears Moses say to God, "Blot my name out of the book of life", therefore he may say, "God damn me," or "I renounce God." It is not safe for a man to expose himself to a temptation, because he hath seen another pass through it. Every man may know his own bias, and to what sin that diverts him: the beauty of the person, the opportunity of the place, the importunity of the party, being his mistress, could not shake Joseph's constancy. There is one such example, of one that resisted a strong temptation: but then there are in one place, two men together, that sinned upon their own bodies, Ner and Onan, then when no temptation was offered, nay when a remedy against temptation was ministered to them.

Some man may be chaster in the stews, than another in the church; and some man will sin more in his dreams, than another in his discourse. Every man must know how much water his own vessel draws, and not to think to sail over, wheresoever he hath seen another (he knows not with how much labour) shove over: nor to adventure so far, as he may have reason to be confident in his own strength: for though he may be safe in himself, yet he may sin in another, if by his indiscreet, and improvident example, another be scandalized. Christ was always safe; He was led of the Spirit: of what spirit? His own spirit: Led willingly into the wilderness, to be tempted of the devil. No other man might do that; but He who was able to say to the sun, stand still, sun, was able to say to Satan, Get ye hence, Satan. Christ in another place gave such scope to His affections, and to others' interpretations of His actions, that His friends and kinsfolk thought Him mad, beside Himself: but all this while, Christ had His own actions, and passions, and their interpretations in His own power: He could do what He would. Here in our text, Jesus was troubled, and He groaned; and vehemently, and often, His affections were stirred: but as in a clean glass, if water be stirred and troubled, though it may conceive a little light froth, yet it contracts no foulness in that clean glass, the affections of Christ were moved, but so: in that holy vessel they would contract no foulness, no declination towards inordinateness. But then every Christian is not a Christ; and therefore as he that would fast forty days, as Christ did, might starve; and he that would whip merchants out of the temple, as Christ did, might be knockt down in the temple; so he knowing his own inclinations, or but the general ill inclination of all mankind, as he is infected with original sin, that should converse so much with publicans and sinners, might participate of their sins. The rule is, we must avoid inordinateness of affections; but when we come to examples of that rule, ourselves, well understood by ourselves, must be our own examples; for it is not always good to go so far, as some good men have gone before.

Now though Christ were far from both, yet He came nearer to an excess of passion, than to an indolency, to a senselessness, to a privation of natural affections. Inordinateness of affections may sometimes make some men like some beasts; but indolency, absence, emptiness, privation of affections, makes any man at all times, like stones, like dirt. In the last, saith St Peter, that is, in the worst days, in the dregs, and lees, and tartar of sin, then shall come men, lovers of themselves; and that is ill enough in man; for that is an affection peculiar to God, to love himself. Self-love cannot be called a distinct sin, but the root of all sins, says the school in the mouth of Aquinas. It is true that Justin Martyr says "The end of Christian philosophy is to be wise like God;" but not in this, to love ourselves; for the greatest sin that ever was, and that upon which even the blood of Christ Jesus hath not wrought, the sin of angels, was that, to be like God. To love ourselves, to be satisfied in ourselves, to find an omni-sufficiency in ourselves, is an intrusion, an usurpation upon God: and even God Himself, who had that omni-sufficiency in Himself, conceived a conveniency for His glory, to draw a circumference about that centre, creatures about Himself, and to shed forth lines of love upon all them, and not to love Himself alone. Self-love in man sinks deep: but yet you see, the apostle in his order, casts the other sin lower, that is, into a worse place to be without natural affections.

St Augustine extends these natural affections, to religious affections, because they are natural to a supernatural man, to a regenerate man, who naturally loves those that are of the household of the faithful, that profess the same truth of religion: and not to be affected with their distresses, when religion itself is distressed in them, is impiety. He extends these affections to moral affections; the love of eminent and heroic virtues in any man: we ought to be affected by the fall of such men. And he extends them to civil affections, the love of friends; not to be moved on their behalf, is argument enough that we do not much love them.

For our case in the text, these men whom Jesus found weeping, and wept with them, were not of His family: they were neighbours, and Christ had had a conversation, and contracted a friendship in that family: "He loved Martha, and her sister, and Lazarus", says the story: and He would let the world see that He loved them: for so the Jews argued that saw Him weep, "Behold how He loved them"; without outward declarations, who can conclude an inward love? To assure that, Jesus wept.

To an inordinateness of affections it never came; to a natural tenderness it did; and so far as to tears; and then who needs be ashamed of weeping? "Look away far from me, for I will weep bitterly", says Jerusalem in Isaiah. But "look upon me", says Christ in the Lamentations, "Behold and see if ever there were any sorrow, any tears like mine": not like His in value, but in the root as they proceeded from natural affection, they were tears of imitation, and we may, we must, weep tears like His tears. They scourged Him, they crowned Him, they nailed Him, they pierced Him, and then blood came; but He shed tears voluntarily, and without violence: the blood came from their ill, but the tears from His own good nature: the blood was drawn, the tears were given. We call it a childish thing to weep, and a womanish; and perchance we mean worse in that than in the childish; for therein we may mean falsehood to be mingled with weakness. Christ made it an argument of His being man, to weep, for though the lineaments of man's body, eyes and ears, hands and feet, be ascribed to God in the Scriptures, though the affections of man's mind be ascribed to Him, (even sorrow, nay repentance itself, is attributed to God) I do not remember that ever God is said to have wept: it is for man. And when God shall come to that last act in the glorifying of man, when He promises, to wipe all tears from His eyes, what shall God have to do with that eye that never wept?

He wept out of a natural tenderness in general; and he wept now because of a particular occasion. What was that? That Lazarus was dead. We stride over many steps at once; waive many such considerable circumstaces as these; Lazarus his friend was dead, therefore He wept, Lazarus, the staff and sustentation of that family was dead, he upon whom his sisters relied was dead, therefore He wept. But I stop only upon this one step; that he was dead. Now a good man is not the worse for dying, that is true and capable of a good sense, because he is established in a better world: but yet when he is gone out of this world he is none of us, he is no longer a man. The stronger opinion in the school is that Christ Himself, when he lay dead in the grave, was no man. Though the Godhead never departed from the body, (there was no divorce of that hypostatical union) yet because the human soul had departed from it, He was no man. Hugo de St Victor, who thinks otherwise, that Christ was a man then, thinks so upon a weak ground: he thinks that because the soul is the form of man, the soul is man; and that therefore, the soul remaining, the man remains. But it is not the soul, but the union of the soul, that makes the man. The master of the sentences, Peter Lombard, who thinks so too, that Christ was then a man, thinks so upon as weak a ground: he thinks that it is enough to constitute a man, that there be a soul and body, though that soul and body be not united; but still it is the union that makes the man: and therefore when he is disunited, dead, he is none of us, he is no man; and therefore we weep, however well he be. Abraham was loath to let go his wife, though the king had her: a man has a natural loathness to let go his friend, though God take him to Him.

St Augustine says that he knew well enough that his mother was in Heaven; and St Ambrose, that he knew well enough that his master Theodosius the emperor was in Heaven, but because they saw not in what state they were, they thought that something might be asked at God's hands in their behalf; and so out of a humane and pious officiousness, in a devotion perchance undigested, conconcocted, and retaining yet some crudities, some irresolutions, they strayed into prayers for them after they were dead. Lazarus's sisters had no doubt of their brother's salvation; they believed his soul to be in a good estate: and for his body, they told Christ, as "Lord we know that he shall rise at the last day"; and yet they wept.

Here in this world, we who stay lack those who have gone out of it: we know they shall never come to us; and when we shall go to them, we dispute whether we shall know them or not. They who think that it conduces to the perfection of happiness in Heaven, that we should know one another, think piously if they think we shall. For as for the maintenance of public peace, states and churches may think diversely in points of religion that are not fundamental, and yet both be true and orthodox churches; so for the exaltation of private devotion in points that are not fundamental, various men may think diversely, and both be equally good Christians. Whether we shall know them there, or not, is problematical and equal; that we shall not till then, is dogmatic and certain: therefore we weep. I know there are philosophers that will not let us weep, nor lament the death of any: and I know that in the Scriptures there are rules, and that there are instructions conveyed in that example, that David left mourning as soon as the child was dead; and I know that there are authors of a middle nature, above the philosophers, and below the Scriptures, in the Apocryphal books, and I know it is said there, "Comfort thyself, for thou shalt do him no good that is dead. Thou shalt make thyself worse and worse, in the worst degree." But yet all this is but of inordinate lamentation; for in the same place, the same wise man says, "My son, let thy tears fall down over the dead; weep bitterly and make great moan, as he is worthy." When our Saviour Christ had uttered his "it is finished", all was finished, and their rage could do Him no more harm, when He had uttered His "Into your hands", He had delivered and God had received His soul yet how did the whole frame of nature mourn in eclipses, and tremble in earthquakes, and dissolve and shed in pieces in the opening of the temple, because He was dead.

Truly, to see the hand of a great and mighty monarch, that hand that has governed the civil sword, the sword of justice at home, and drawn and sheathed the foreign sword, the sword of war abroad, to see that hand lie dead, and not be able to nip or fillip away one of his own worms, (and then, what man, though he be one of those men, of whom God has said, "Ye are gods", yet "What man is there that lives, and shall not see death?") to see the brain of a great and religious counsellor (and God bless all from making, all from calling anything great that is not religious) to see that brain that produced means to becalm guests at council tables, storms in parliaments, tempests in popular commotions, to see that brain produce nothing but swarms of worms, and no proclamation to disperse them; to see a reverend prelate that has resisted heretics and schismatics all his life, fall like one of them by death, and perchance be called one of them when he is dead; to recollect all, to see great men made no men, to be sure that they shall never come to us, not to be sure that we shall know them when we come to them; to see the lieutenants and images of God, kings; the sinews of the state, religious counsellors; the spirit of the church, zealous prelates; and then to see vulgar, ignorant, wicked, and wicked men thrown all by one hand of death, into one cart, into one common tide-boat, one hospital, one almshouse, one prison, the grave, in whose dust no man can say, this is the king, this is the slave, this is the bishop, this is the heretic, this is the counsellor, this is the fool; even this miserable equality of such unequal persons, by so foul a hand, is the subject of this lamentation; even, because Lazarus was dead, Jesus wept.

He wept even in that respect, because he was dead, and He wept in this respect too, because those means which in appearance might have saved his life, by His default were not used, for when He came to the house, one sister, Martha, said to Him "Lord if thou hadst been here, my brother had not died"; and then the other sister, Mary, said so too: "Lord if Thou hadst been here, my brother had not died": they all cry out, that He who only, only by coming, might have saved his life, would not come. Our Saviour knew in Himself that He abstained to better purpose, and to the greater glory of God: for when He heard of his death, He said to His disciples, "I am glad for your sakes that I was not there". Christ had certain reserved purposes which conduced to a better establishing of their faith, and to a better advancing of God's kingdom, the working of that miracle. But yet because others were able to say to Him, it was in you to have saved him, and He did not that, affected him; and Jesus wept.

He wept, though they said to Him, "He hath been four days dead, and stinks". Christ does not say, "there is no such matter, he does not stink"; but "though he does, my friend shall not lack my help". Good friends, useful friends, though they may commit some errors, and though for some misbehaviours they may stink in our nostrils, must not be derelicted, abandoned to themselves. Many a son, many a good heir, finds an ill air from his father; his father's life stinks in the nostrils of all the world, and he hears everywhere exclamations upon his father's usury, and extortion, and oppression: yet it becomes him by a better life, and by all other means to rectify and redeem his father's fame. "He is four days dead" is no plea for my negligence in my family; to say, my son, or my servant has proceeded so far in ill courses, that now it is to no purpose to go about to reform him, because "he is four days dead". "Four days dead" is no plea in my pastoral charge, to say that seducers, and practicers, and persuaders, and solicitors for superstition, enter so boldly into every family, that now it is to no purpose to preach religious wariness, religious discretion, religious constancy. "Four days dead" is no plea for my usury, for my simony; to say, I do but as all the world does, and has used to do so a long time. To preach there where reprehension of growing sin is acceptable, is to preach in season; where it is not acceptable, it is out of season; but yet we must preach in season, and out of season too. And when men are so refractory, that they forbear to hear, or hear and resist our preaching, we must pray; and where they despise or forbid our praying, we must lament them, we must weep: he was four days dead, Lazarus was far spent, yet Jesus wept.

He wept, He was moved; though He knew that Lazarus was to be restored, and raised to life again: for as He meant to declare a great good will to him at last, so He would utter some by the way; He would do a great miracle for him, as He was a mighty God; but He would weep for him too, as He was a good-natured man. Truly it is no very charitable disposition, if I give all at my death to others, if I keep all my life to myself. For how many families have we seen shaken, ruined by this distemper, that though the father means to keep nothing of the inheritance from the son at his death, yet because he affords him not a competent maintenance in his life, he submits his son to an encumbering of his fame with ignominious shiftings, and an encumbering of the estate with irrecoverable debts. I may mean to feast a man plentifully at Christmas, and that man may starve before in Lent: great persons may think it in their power to give life to persons and actions by their benefits, when they will, and before that will is up and ready, both may become incapable of their benefits. Jesus would not give this family, whom He pretended to love, occasion of jealousy, of suspicion that He neglected them; and therefore though He came not presently to that great work, which He intended at last, yet He left them not comfortless by the way, Jesus wept.

And so (that we may reserve some minutes for the rest) we end this part, applying to every man that blessed exclamation of St Ambrose, "Lord Jesus be pleased to come to this grave, to weep over this dead Lazarus, this soul in this body": and though I come not to a present rising, a present deliverance from the power of all sin, yet if I can feel the dew of Your tears upon me, if I can discern the eye of Your compassion bent towards me, I have comfort all the way, and that comfort will flow into an infallibility in the end.

And this be the end of this part, to which we are come by these steps. Jesus wept, so that as He showed himself to be God, He might appear to be man too: He wept not inordinately; but He came nearer excess than indolency: He wept because he was dead; and because all means for life had not been used; He wept, though he were far spent; and He wept, though He meant to raise him again.

We pass now from His humane to His prophetical tears, from Jesus weeping in contemplation of a natural calamity fallen upon one family, Lazarus was dead, to His weeping in contemplation of a national calamity foreseen upon a whole people; Jerusalem was to be destroyed. His former tears had some of the spirit of prophecy in them; for therefore says Epiphanius, Christ wept there, because He foresaw how little use the Jews would make of that miracle; His humane tears were prophetical, and His prophetical tears are humane too, they rise from good affections to that people. And therefore the same author says that because they thought it an uncomely thing for Christ to weep for any temporal thing, some men have expunged and removed that verse out of St Luke's gospel, that Jesus when He saw that city, wept: but He is willing to be proposed, and to stand for ever as an example of weeping in contemplation of public calamities; therefore Jesus wept.

He wept first in the midst of the congratulations and acclamations of the people, then when the whole multitude of his disciples cried out, "Blessed be the King, that comes in the name of the Lord", Jesus wept. When Herod took to himself the name of the Lord, when he admitted that gross flattery, "It is a God and not a man that speaks," it was no wonder that present occasion of lamentation fell upon Him. But in the best times, and under the best princes, (first, such is the natural mutability of all worldly things; and then, and that especially, such is the infiniteness, and enormousness of our rebellious sin) there is ever just occasion of fear of worse, and so of tears. Every man is but a sponge, and but a sponge filled with tears: and whether you lay your right hand or your left upon a full sponge, it will weep. Whether God lay his left hand, temporal calamities, or his right hand, temporal prosperity; even that temporal prosperity comes always accompanied with so much anxiety in ourselves, so much uncertainty in itself, and so much envy in others, as that that man who abounds most, that sponge shall weep.

Jesus wept, amid the acclamations, when all went well enough with Him, to show the slipperiness of worldly happiness; and then He wept when He was in the act of denouncing judgments upon them, Jesus wept, to show with how ill a will He inflicted those judgments, and that themselves, and not He, had drawn those judgments upon them. How often do the prophets repeat that phrase, "O the burden of the judgments that I have seen upon this, and this people!" It was a burden that pressed tears from the prophet Isaiah, "I will water thee with my tears, O Heshbon": when he must pronounce judgments upon her, he could not but weep over her. No prophet is so tender as Christ, nor so compassionate; and therefore He never takes rod into His hand, but with tears in His eyes. Alas, did God lack a footstool, that He should make man only to tread and trample upon? Did God lack glory, and could have it no other way, but by creating man therefore, to afflict Him temporally here, and eternally hereafter? Whatsoever Christ weeps for in the way of His mercy, it is likely He was displeased with it in the way of His justice: if He wept for it, He would rather it were not so. If then those judgments upon Jerusalem were only from His own primary, and positive, and absolute decree, without any respect to their sins, could He be displeased with his own act, or weep and lament for that which only Himself had done? Would God ask that question of Israel, "Why will you die, O house of Israel?" if God lay open to that answer, "We die because you have killed us"; Jerusalem would not judge herself, therefore Christ judged her; Jerusalem would not weep for herself, and therefore Jesus wept; but in those tears of His, He showed, that He would rather her own tears had been averted, and washed away those judgments.

He wept, "when Jesus came near the city and saw it, then He wept", according to the text He wept there, and not till then. If we will not come near the miseries of our brethren, if we will not see them, we will never weep over them, never be affected towards them. It was "when He", not "when they", when Christ Himself, not when His disciples, His followers, who could do Jerusalem no good, took knowledge of it. It was not when those people, nor was it not when those things, nor when those judgments drew near; it is not said so; neither is there any time limited in the text, when those judgments were to fall upon Jerusalem; it is only said generally, indefinitely, that these days shall come upon her. And yet Christ did not ease Himself upon that, those calamities were remote and far off, but though they were so, and not to fall till after His death, yet He lamented future calamities then; then Jesus wept. Many such little brooks as these fall into this river, the consideration of Christ's prophetical tears; but let it be enough to have sprinkled these drops out of the river; that Jesus, though a private person, wept in contemplation of public calamities; that He wept in the best times, foreseeing worse; that He wept in their miseries, because He was no author of them: that He wept not till He took their miseries into His consideration; and He did weep a good time before those miseries fell upon them. There remain yet His third tears, His pontifical tears, which accompany His sacrifice; those tears we call the sea, but a sea which must now be bounded with a very little sand.

To sail apace through this sea; these tears, the tears of His cross, were caused by that inestimable weight, the sins of all the world. If all the body were eye, argues the apostle in another place; why, here all the body was eye, every pore of His body made an eye by tears of blood, and every inch of His body made an eye by their bloody scourges. And if Christ's looking upon Peter, made Peter weep, shall not His looking upon us here, with tears in His eyes, such tears in such eyes, springs of tears, rivers of tears, seas of tears, make us weep too? Peter, who wept under the weight of his particular sin, wept bitterly; how bitterly wept Christ under the weight of all the sins of all the world? In the first tears, Christ's humane tears (those we called a spring) we fetched water at one house, we condoled a private calamity in another; Lazarus was dead. In His second tears, His prophetical tears, He wept on the condoling of a whole nation; and those we called a river. In these third tears, His pontifical tears, tears for sin, for all sins (those we call a sea) here is a sea free and open to all; every man may sail home, home to himself, and lament his own sins there.

I am far from concluding all to be impenitent, that do not actually weep and shed tears; I know there are constitutions, complexions, that do not afford them. And yet the worst epithet which the best poet could fix upon Pluto himself, was to call him "a person that could not weep". But to weep for other things, and not to weep for sin, or if not to tears, yet not to come to that tenderness, to that melting, to that thawing, that resolving of the bowels which good souls feel; this is a sponge (I said before, every man is a sponge) this is a sponge dried up into a pumice stone; the lightness, the hollowness of a sponge is there still, but (as the pumice is) dried in the Etnas of lust, of ambition, of other flames in this world.

I have but three words to say of these tears of this weeping. What it is, what it is for, what it does; the nature, the use, the benefit of these tears, is all. And in the first, I forbear to insist upon St Basil's metaphor, sin is my sickness, the blood of Christ Jesus is my cure, tears is the sweat that that produces. I forbear Gregory Nyssa's metaphor too, tears are our best blood, so agitated, so ventilated, so purified, so rarified into spirits, as that thereby I become as one spirit with my God. That is large enough, and embraces all, which St Gregory says, that man weeps truly, that the soul sheds true tears, who considers seriously, first, the blessed state which man was in, in his integrity at first, where he was; and then considers the weak estate that man is in now, in the midst of temptations, where if he had no more, himself would be temptation too much, where he is; and yet considers farther, the insupportable, and for all that, the inevitable, the irreparable, and for all that, undeterminable torments of Hell, where he will be; and lastly, the inexpressible joy and glory which he loses in Heaven where he shall never be. These four to consider seriously, where man was, where he is, where he shall be, where he shall never be, are four such rivers, as constitute a paradise. And as a ground may be a weeping ground, though it have no running river, no constant spring, no gathering of waters in it; so a soul that can pour out itself into these religious considerations, may be a weeping soul, though it have a dry eye: this weeping then is but a true sorrow, (that was our first) and then, what this true sorrow is given us for is our next consideration.

As water is in nature a thing indifferent, it may give life, (so the first living things that were, were in the water) and it may destroy life, (so all things living upon the earth, were destroyed in the water) but yet though water may, though it have done good and bad, yet water does now one good office, which no ill quality that is in it can equal, it washes our souls in baptism; so though there be good tears and bad tears, tears that wash away sin, and tears that are sin, yet all tears have this degree of good in them, that they are all some kind of argument of good nature, of a tender heart; and the Holy Ghost loves to work in wax, and not in marble. I hope that is but merely poetical which the poet says; that some study to weep with a good grace; they make use and advantage of their tears, and weep when they will. But of these who weep not when they would, but when they would not, do half employ their tears upon that for which God has given them that sacrifice, upon sin. God made the firmament, which he called Heaven, after it had divided the waters: after we have distinguished our tears, natural from spiritual, worldly from heavenly, then there is a firmament established in us, then there is a heaven opened to us: and truly, to cast pearls before swine will scarce be better resembled, than to shed tears (which resemble pearls) for worldly losses.

Are there examples of men passionately enamoured upon age? Or if upon age, upon deformity? If there be examples of that, are they not examples of scorn too? Do not all others laugh at their tears? And yet such is our passionate doting upon this world. According to St Augustine, (and even St Augustine himself has scarce said anything more pathetically), the face of the whole world is so defaced, so wrinkled, so ruined, so deformed, as that man might be trusted with this world, and there is no jealousy, no suspicion that this world should be able to minister any occasion of temptation to man. And yet, St Gregory says, as wittily as St Augustine, (as it is easy to be witty, easy to extend an epigram to a satire, and a satire to an invective, in declaiming against this world), that world which finds itself truly in an autumn, in itself, finds itself in a spring, in our imaginations. He farther says: the world passes away, and yet we cleave to it; and when we cannot stay it from passing away, we pass away with it.

To mourn passionately for the love of this world, which is decrepit, and upon the deathbed, or immoderately for the death of any that is passed out of this world, is not the right use of tears. That has good use which Chrysologus notes, that when Christ was told of Lazarus' death, He said He was glad; when He came to raise him to life, then He wept: for though his disciples gained by it, (they were confirmed by a miracle) though the family gained by it, (they had their Lazarus again) yet Lazarus himself lost by it, by being reimprisoned, recommitted, re-submitted to the manifold incommodities of this world. When our Saviour Christ forbade the women to weep for him, it was because there was nothing in Him for tears to work upon; no sin: Christ, says St Bernard, did not absolutely forbid tears, but regulated and ordered their tears, that they might weep in the right place; first for sin. David wept for Absalom; he might imagine that he had died in sin, he wept not for the child by Bathsheba, he could not suspect so much danger in that. "Rivers of waters ran down from mine eyes", says David. Why? "Because they", who are they? not other men, as it is ordinarily taken; but "Because mine own eyes" (so Hilary, and Ambrose, and Augustine take it) "have not kept Thy laws". As the calamities of others, so the sins of others may, but our own sins must be, the object of our sorrow, "Thou shalt offer to me", says God, "the first of thy ripe fruits, and of thy liquors". And of thy tears: thy first tears must be to God for sin: the second and third may be to nature and civility, and such secular offices. But "Will anyone wash his feet in water for sore eyes?", is St Chrysostom's exclamation. Will any man embalm the carcass of the world, which he treads underfoot, with those tears which should embalm his soul? Did Joseph of Arimathaea bestow any of his perfumes (though he brought a superfluous quantity, a hundred pound weight for one body), did he bestow any upon the body of either of the thieves? Tears are true sorrow, that you heard before; true sorrow is for sin, that you have heard now; all that remains is how this sorrow works, what it does.

The fathers have infinitely delighted themselves in this descant, the blessed effect of holy tears. He among them that reminds us that in the old law all sacrifices were washed, he means, that our best sacrifice, even prayer itself, receives an improvement, a dignity, by being washed in tears. He that reminds us, that if any room of our house be on fire, we run for water, means that in all temptations, we should have recourse to tears. He that tells us, that money being put into a basin is seen at a farther distance, if there be water in the basin than if it be empty, means also, that our most precious devotions receive an addition, a multiplication, by holy tears. St Bernard says all that this means is, "A hard heart is a foul heart". Would you shut up the devil in his own channel, his channel of brimstone, and make that worse? St Jerome tells the way, "Thy tears torment him more than the fires of hell"; will you needs have holy water? Truly, true tears are the holiest water. And as for purgatory, it is liberally confessed by a Jesuit, "One tear will do you as much good as all the flames of purgatory". We have said more than once that man is a sponge; and "all our sins are written in God's book", says St Chrysostom: if there I can fill my sponge with tears, and so wipe out all my sins out of that book, it is a blessed use of the sponge.

I might speak upon this, the manifold benefits of godly tears, long; so long, as till you wept, and wept for sin; and that might be very long. I contract all to this one, which is all: to how many blessednesses must these tears, this godly sorrow reach by the way, when as it reaches to the very extreme, to that which is opposed to it, to joy? For godly sorrow is joy. The words in Job are in the Vulgate, "Lord spare me awhile that I may lament my lamentable estate": and so ordinarily the expositors that follow that translation, make their use of them. But yet it is in the original, "Lord spare me awhile, that I may take comfort": that which one calls lamenting, the other calls rejoicing: to conceive true sorrow and true joy, are things not only contiguous, but continual; they do not only touch and follow one another in a certain succession, joy assuredly after sorrow, but they consist together, they are all one, joy and sorrow. "My tears have been my meat day and night," says David: not that he had no other meat, but that none relished so well. It is a grammatical note of a Jesuit, (I do not tell you it is true; I have almost told you that it is not true, by telling you whose it is, but that is but a grammatical note) that when it is said, "The time of singing is come", it might as well be rendered out of the Hebrew, "The time of weeping is come"; and when it is said, "Lord I will sing unto Thy name," it might as well be rendered out of the Hebrew, "I will weep, I will sacrifice my tears unto Thy name". So equal, so indifferent a thing is it, when we come to godly sorrow, whether we call it sorrow or joy, weeping or singing.

To end all, to weep for sin is not a damp of melancholy, to sigh for sin is not a vapour of the spleen, but as Monica's confessor said to her, on behalf of her son St Augustine, "The son of these tears cannot perish"; so wash yourself in these three exemplar baths of Christ's tears, in His humane tears, and be tenderly affected with humane accidents, in His prophetical tears, and avert as much as lies in you, the calamities imminent upon others, but especially in His pontifical tears, tears for sin, and I am your confessor; not I, but the Spirit of God himself is your confessor, and He absolves you, the soul bathed in these tears cannot perish: for this is the threefold dipping which was used in the primitive church in baptism. And in this baptism, you take a new Christian name, you who were but a Christian, are now a regenerate Christian; and as Naaman the leper came cleaner out of the Jordan, than he was before his leprosy (for his flesh became as the flesh of a child), so there shall be better evidence in this baptism of your repentance, than in your first baptism; better in yourself, for then you had no sense of your own estate, in this you have: and you shall have better evidence from others too; for however some others will dispute, whether all children which die after baptism, be certainly saved or not, it never fell into doubt or disputation, whether all that die truly repentant, be saved or not. Weep these tears truly, and God shall perform to you, first that promise which He makes in Isaiah "The Lord shall wipe all tears from your face", all that are fallen by any occasion of calamity here, in the militant church; and he shall perform that promise which he makes in Revelation, "The Lord shall wipe all tears from thine eyes", that is, dry up the fountain of tears; remove all occasion of tears hereafter, in the triumphant Church.

The Sacred Maxims of BLAISE PASCAL

Faith is different from proof. One is human, and the other is a gift from God.

Men despise religion. They hate it and are afraid it may be true.

Man's condition is one of inconstancy, boredom and anxiety.

What astonishes me most is to see that everyone is not astonished at his own weakness.

He who does not see the vanity of the world is pretty vain himself. But who does not see it, apart from the young whose lives are all noise, diversions, and thoughts of the future? But take away their diversion, and you will see them shrivel up with boredom. Then they feel their nothingness without recognising it. But nothing can be more miserable than to be intolerable and depressed as soon as one is reduced to introspection with no sort of diversion.

When I consider the short stretch of my life absorbed into the eternity which comes before and after, "as the remembrance of a guest that tarries but a day", the small space that I occupy and which I see swallowed up in the infinite immensity of spaces of which I know nothing and which know nothing of me, I become rather frightened and become surprised to see myself here rather than there: there is no reason for me to be here rather than there, nor why it should be now rather than then. How did I get here? By whose command was I allotted this time and place?

Ecclesiastes shows that man without God is totally ignorant and in unavoidable misery, for anyone is unhappy who wants to do something but cannot do it. Now he wants to be happy and assured of some truth. Yet he is unable either to know or want to know. He cannot even doubt.

Then what sort of freak is man! How novel, how monstrous, how chaotic, how paradoxical, how prodigious! Judge of all things, foolish earthworm, repository of truth, sewer of doubt and error, glory and refuse of the universe!

You must know, arrogant man, how much of a paradox you are to yourself. Be humble, feeble reason! Be silent, idiot nature; realise that man infinitely transcends man, hear from your master your real condition of which you know nothing. Listen to God.

And so life passes in this way. We seek rest by struggling against certain obstacles, and once we have overcome them, our rest becomes intolerable because of the boredom it produces. We must get away from it and look for excitement. We think either of our present miseries, or those which might come about. And even if we felt quite safe on every side, boredom on its own account would not fail to seep out from the bottom of our hearts, where its natural roots lie, and to poison our entire spirit.

How hollow and foul is the heart of man!

All this craving and this helplessness, what else do they mean but that there was once in man a true happiness, of which all that now remains is an empty shell? In vain, he tries to fill this with everything around him, seeking in things that are not there the help he cannot find in those that are; but they will not be able to help, since this infinite abyss can be filled only with an infinite and immutable object; in other words, by God Himself. Only God is man's true good, and since man abandoned Him, it is a strange thing that nothing in nature has been found to take His place: stars, sky, earth, elements, plants, cabbages, leeks, animals, insects, calves, serpents, fever, plague, war, famine, vice, adultery and incest. Since losing his true good, man has become capable of seeing it in anything, even in his own destruction, even though it is so contrary to God, to reason and to nature.

That is the state men are in today. They retain some slight instinct from the happiness of their first nature, and are plunged into the wretchedness of their blindness and their concupiscence, which has become their second nature.

There is enough light for those who desire only to see, and enough darkness for those of a contrary disposition.

There is enough light to enlighten the elect and enough darkness to humiliate them. There is enough darkness to blind the reprobate, and enough light to condemn them and deprive them of excuse.

Pity the atheists who seek, for are they not unhappy enough? Inveigh against those who boast about it.

Atheism indicates strength of mind, but only up to a certain point.

The last act is bloody, however good the rest of the play. They throw earth over your head and that is it for ever.

There is nothing which conforms so well with reason as the denial of reason.

The last step of reason is to recognise that there is an infinite number of things which are beyond reason. It is merely feeble if it does not go as far as to realise that.

But at the same time we know our own misery, because this God is nothing less than our redeemer from misery. Thus we can know God properly only by knowing our own iniquities.

Anyone who considers himself in the following way will be terrified at the thought that he is upheld in the material being given him by nature, supported between the two abysses of the infinite and nothingness, and he will tremble at the sight of these marvels.

We sail on a vast expanse, ever uncertain, ever drifting, hurried from one to the other goal. If we think to attach ourselves firmly to any point, it totters and fails us; if we follow, it eludes our grasp, and flies from us, vanishing for ever. Nothing stays for us. This is our natural condition, yet always the most contrary to our inclination; we burn with desire to find a steadfast place and an ultimate fixed basis whereon we may build a tower to reach the infinite. But our whole foundation breaks up, and earth opens up to the abysses.

Man is but a reed, the weakest in nature, but a reed which thinks. There is no need for the whole universe to arm itself to crush him; a vapour, a drop of water is enough to kill him. But were the universe to crush him, man would still be more noble than that which has slain him, because he knows that he dies, and that the universe has the better of him. The universe knows nothing of this.

The eternal silence of these infinite spaces fills me with dread.

There are some who see clearly that Man's only enemy is the concupiscence which turns him away from God, and not from his enemies, never the good but God.

Let those who believe that man's good lies in the flesh and that his evil lies in whatever turns him away from sensual pleasures satiate themselves and die of it. But those who seek God with all their hearts, whose only discomfort is to be deprived of the sight of God, whose only desire is to possess Him, whose only enemies are those who turn away from Him, and who grieve at finding themselves surrounded and dominated by such enemies, let them take heart, for I bring them good news. There is one who will set them free, I will show Him to them, I will show them that there is a God for them, and I will not show Him to others.

The incarnation shows the extent of man's wretchedness by the greatness of the remedy required.

No doctrine is better suited to man than that which teaches him his dual capacity for receiving and losing grace, on account of the dual danger of despair or pride to which he is always exposed.

There is no one as happy as a true Christian, nor anyone so reasonable, virtuous and lovable.

To render passion harmless let us behave as though we only had a week to live.

It is wrong that anyone should become attached to me even though they do so gladly and willingly. I would be misleading those in whom I aroused such a desire, for I am no-one's goal nor do I have the means of satisfying anyone. If man was not made for God, why is he only happy in God? If man was made for God, why is he so opposed to God?

Love's effects are terrifying. This indefinable something, so miniscule that we cannot recognise it, upsets the whole earth, princes, armies, the entire world. Cleopatra's nose: if it had been shorter the whole face of the world would have been different.

The only thing that consoles us for our miseries is diversion. Yet it is the greatest of our miseries. For it is that above all which prevents us from thinking about ourselves and leads us imperceptibly to distraction. But for that we should be bored, and boredom drives us to seek a more solid means of escape, but diversion keeps us amused and brings us imperceptibly on to our death.

Apart from Christ there is only vice, wretchedness, error, darkness, death and despair.

Not only do we know God through Jesus Christ, but we only know ourselves through Jesus Christ; we only know life and death through Jesus Christ. Without Him, we cannot know the meaning of our life or our death, of God or of ourselves.

The heart has its reasons of which reason knows nothing: we know this in a thousand ways. I say that it is natural for the heart to love the universal being or itself, according to its allegiance, and it hardens itself against one or the other as it chooses, rejecting one and keeping the other. Is it reason that makes you love yourself?

It is the heart which sees God and not reason. That is what faith is: God seen by the heart, not by reason.

It takes no great elevation of the soul to realise that in this life there is no true and solid satisfaction, that all our pleasures are mere vanity, that our afflictions are infinite, and finally death which threatens us at every moment must in a few years inevitably face us with the inescapable and appalling alternative of being annihilated or miserable throughout eternity. There is nothing more real or more terrible than that. We can be as brave as we like about it: that is the end awaiting even the world's best. Let us consider these things, and let us say whether it is not beyond doubt that the only good thing in this life is the hope of another life, that we are only happy as we come nearer to the other life, and that, just as no more happiness awaits those who have been quite certain of eternity, so there is no happiness for those who have no awareness of it.

There is no surer sign of a feeble heart than failure to desire that the eternal promises be true.

Imagine a number of men in chains, all under sentence of death, some of whose throats are cut each day in the sight of the others; those remaining see their own condition in the condition of their fellows, and looking at each other with grief and despair they await their turn. This is the image of the human condition.

Witty sayings, unkind judgements. He who makes many witticisms has a bad disposition.

Curiosity is mere vanity. Most people only want to know in order to talk, like the doctor who goes on talking for a quarter of an hour when he has already everything, because he is so eager to have his say.

If you want people to think well of you, do not speak well of yourself.

We do not get bored with eating and sleeping every day, since we soon feel hungry or sleepy again; otherwise we would get bored with it. Similarily, if we do not hunger for spiritual things, we find them boring: "Hunger after righteousness" is the eighth beatitude.

The nature of self-love and of this human self is to love only self and consider only self. But what is it for? It cannot help knowing that the object of its love is full of faults and wretchedness: it wants to be great and sees that it is small; it wants to be happy and sees that it is wretched; it wants to be perfect and sees that it is full of imperfections; it wants to be the object of men's love and esteem and sees that its faults deserve only their condemnation.

JOHN BUNYAN: The Pilgrim's Progress

IN THE SIMILITUDE OF A DREAM

As I walked through the wilderness of this world, I lighted on a certain place, where was a den; and I laid me down in that place to sleep: and as I slept I dreamed a dream. I dreamed, and behold I saw a man clothed with rags, standing in a certain place, with his face away from his house, a book in his hand, and a great burden upon his back. I looked, and saw him open the book, and read therein; and as he read, he wept and trembled: and not being able longer to contain himself, he broke out with a lamentable cry, saying, "What shall I do?"

In this plight therefore he went home, and restrained himself as long as he could so that his wife and children should not perceive his distress; but he could not be silent long, because his trouble increased: so at length he spoke his mind to his wife and children; and thus he began to talk to them: "O my dear wife," said he, "and you the children of my bowels, I your dear friend am in myself undone, by reason of a burden that lies hard upon me: moreover, I am for certain informed that this our city will be burned with fire from Heaven, in which fearful overthrow, both myself, with you, my wife, and you, my sweet babes, shall miserably come to ruin; except (the which yet I see not) some way of escape can be found, whereby we may be delivered." At this his relations were sore amazed; not because they believed that what he said to them was true, but because they thought that some frenzy or distemper had got into his head. Therefore, it drawing towards night, and they hoping that sleep might settle his brains, with all haste they got him to bed; but the night was as troublesome to him as the day, wherefore instead of sleeping, he spent it in sighs and tears. So when the morning was come, they would know how he did and he told them worse and worse. He also set to talking to them again, but they began to be hardened; they also thought to drive away his distemper by harsh and surly carriages to him: sometimes they would deride, sometimes they would chide, and sometimes they would quite neglect him, wherefore he began to retire himself to his chamber to pray for, and pity them; and also to condole his own misery. He would also walk alone in the fields, sometimes reading, and sometimes praying, and thus for some days he spent his time.

Now, I saw upon a time, when he was walking in the fields, that he was (as he was wont) reading in his book, and greatly distressed in his mind; and as he read, he burst out, as he had done before, crying, "What shall I do to be saved?"

I saw also that he looked this way, and that way, as if he would run; yet he stood still, because, as I perceived, he could not tell which way to go. I looked then, and saw a man named Evangelist coming to him, and asked, "Wherefore dost thou cry?" He answered, "Sir, I perceive, by the book in my hand, that I am condemned to die, and after that to come to judgment; and I find that I am not willing to do the first, nor able to do the second."

Then said Evangelist, "Why not willing to die, since this life is attended with so many evils?" The man answered, "Because I fear that this burden that is upon my back will sink me lower than the grave; and I shall fall into Hell. And, Sir, if I be not fit to go to prison, I am not fit (I am sure) to go to judgment, and from thence to execution; and the thoughts of these things make me cry."

Then said Evangelist, "If this be your condition, why do you stand still?" He answered, "Because I know not whither to go." Then he gave him a parchment roll, and there was written within, "Fly from the wrath to come."

The man therefore read it, and looking upon Evangelist very carefully, said, "Whither must I fly?" Then said Evangelist pointing with his finger over a very wide field, "Do you see yonder Wicket Gate?" The man said, "No". Then said the other, "Do you see yonder shining light?" He said, "I think I do." Then said Evangelist, "Keep that light in your eye, and go up directly thereto, so shall you see the gate at which, when you knock, it shall be told to you what you should do."

So I saw in my dream that the man began to run. Now he had not run far from his own door, but his wife and children perceiving it began to cry after him to return. But the man put his fingers to his ears, and ran on crying, "Life, life, eternal life". So he looked not behind him, but fled towards the middle of the plain.

The neighbours also came out to see him, and as he ran some mocked, others threatened; and some cried after him to return. Now among those that did so, there were two that were resolved to fetch him back by force. The name of the one was Obstinate, and the name of the other Pliable. Now by this time the man was a good distance from them, but they were resolved to pursue him however, which they did and in little time they overtook him. Then said the man, "Neighbours, wherefore are you come?" They said, "To persuade you to go back with us." But he said, "That can by no means be. You dwell," said he, "in the City of Destruction (the place also where I was born), I see it to be so; and dying there, sooner or later, you will sink lower than the grave, into a place that burns with fire and brimstone; be content, good neighbour, and go along with me."

"What!" said Obstinate, "and leave our friends and our comforts behind us!"

"Yes," said Christian (for that was his name), "because, all that which you shall forsake is not worthy to be compared with a little of that that I am seeking to enjoy, and if you will go along with me, and hold it, you shall fare as I myself; for there where I go is enough and to spare; come away, and prove my words."

Obstinate. What are the things you seek, since you leave all the world to find them?

Christian. I seek an inheritance, incorruptible, undefiled, and that does not fade away; and it is laid up in Heaven, and fast there, to be bestowed at the time appointed on them that diligently seek it. Read it so, if you will, in my book.

Obstinate. Tush, away with your book; will you go back with us, or no?

Christian. No, not I, because I have laid my hand to the plough.

Obstinate. Come then, neighbour Pliable, let us turn again, and go home without him; there is a company of these crazed-headed coxcombs that, when they take a fancy, by the end are wiser in their own eyes than seven men that can render a reason.

Pliable. Don't revile; if what the good Christian says is true, the things he looks after are better than ours; my heart inclines to go with my neighbour.

Obstinate. What! More fools still? Be ruled by me and go back. Who knows whither such a brain-sick fellow will lead you? Go back, go back, and be wise.

Christian. Come with me neighbour Pliable, there are such things to be had which I spoke of, and many more glories besides. if you believe not me, read here in this book; and for the truth of what is expressed therein, behold, all is confirmed by the blood of Him that made it.

Pliable. Well neighbour Obstinate I begin to come to a point; I intend to go along with this good man, and to cast in my lot with him. But my good companion, do you know the way to this desired place?

Christian. I am directed by a man whose name is Evangelist, to speed me to a little gate that is before us, where we shall receive instruction about the way.

Pliable. Come then, good neighbour, let us be going.

Then they went both together.

Obstinate. And I will go back to my place, I will be no companion of such misled fantastical fellows.

Now I saw in my dream, that when Obstinate was gone back, Christian and Pliable went talking over the plain; and thus they began their discourse:

Christian. Come neighbour Pliable, how do you do? I am glad you are persuaded to go along with me, and had even Obstinate himself but felt what I have felt of the powers and terrors of what is yet unseen, he would not thus lightly have given us the back.

Pliable. Come neighbour Christian, since there is none but us two here, tell me now further, what the things are, and how to be enjoyed, whither we are going.

Christian. I can better conceive of them with my mind, than speak of them with my tongue; but yet since you are desirous to know, I will read of them in my book.

Pliable. And do you think that the words of your book are certainly true?

Christian. Yes verily, for it was made by Him that cannot lie.

Pliable. Well said; what things are they?

Christian. There is an endless kingdom to be inhabited, and everlasting life to be given us; that we may inhabit that kingdom for ever.

Pliable. Well said, and what else?

Christian. There are crowns of glory to be given us; and garments that will make us shine like the sun in the firmament of Heaven.

Pliable. This is excellent; and what else?

Christian. There shall be no more crying, nor sorrow; for He that is owner of the place will wipe all tears from our eyes.

Pliable. And what company shall we have there?

Christian. There we shall be with seraphim, and cherubim, creatures that will dazzle your eyes to look on them. There also you shall meet with thousands and ten thousands that have gone before us to that place; none of them are hurtful, but loving, and holy, every one walking in the sight of God and standing in His presence with acceptance for ever. In a word, there we shall see the elders with their golden crowns; there we shall see the holy virgins with their golden harps. There we shall see men that by the world were cut in pieces, burnt in flames, eaten of beasts, drowned in the seas, for the love that they bore to the Lord of the place, all well, and clothed with immortality, as with a garment.

Pliable. The hearing of this is enough to ravish one's heart; but are these things to be enjoyed? How shall we get to be sharers thereof?

Christian. The Lord, the governor of that country, has recorded that in this book, the substance of which is, if we be truly willing to have it, He will bestow it upon us freely.

Pliable. Well, my good companion, glad am I to hear of these things: come on, let us mend our pace.

Christian. I cannot go so fast as I would, by reason of this burden that is upon my back.

Now I saw in my dream, that just as they had ended this talk, they drew near a very miry Slough that was in the midst of the plain, and they, being heedless, did both fall suddenly into the bog. The name of the Slough was Despond. Here therefore they wallowed for a time, being grievously bedaubed with the dirt, and Christian, because of the burden that was on his back, began to sink in the mire.

Then said Pliable, "Ah, neighbour Christian, where are you now?"

"Truly", said Christian, "I do not know."

At that Pliable began to be offended, and angily said to his fellow, "Is this the happiness you have told me all this while of? If we have such ill speed at our first setting out, what may we expect, 'twixt this and our journey's end? If I get out again with my life you shall possess the brave country alone for me." And with that he gave a desperate struggle or two, and got out of the mire on that side of the Slough which was next to his own house. So away he went, and Christian saw him no more.

Wherefore Christian was left to tumble in the Slough of Despond alone; but still he endeavoured to struggle to that side of the Slough that was still further from his own house, and next to the Wicket Gate; the which he did, but could not get out, because of the burden that was upon his back; but I beheld in my dream, that a man came to him, whose name was Help, and asked him what he did there.

Christian. Sir, I was bid go this way by a man called Evangelist, who directed me also to yonder Gate, that I might escape the wrath to come; and as I was going thither, I fell in here.

Help. But why did you not look for the steps?

Christian. Fear followed me so hard, that I fled the next way, and fell in.

Help. Then give me thy hand. So he gave him his hand, and he drew him out, and set him upon sound ground, and bade him go on his way.

Then I stepped to him that plucked him out, and said, "Sir, wherefore, since over this place is the way from the City of Destruction, to yonder Gate, is it, that this ground is not mended, that poor travellers might go thither with more security?" And he said unto me, "This miry Slough is such a place as cannot be mended; it is the descent whither the scum and filth that attends conviction for sin continually runs, and therefore is it called the Slough of Despond: for still as the sinner is awakened about his lost condition, there arises in his soul many fears, and doubts, and discouraging apprehensions, which all of them get together, and settle in this place; and this is the reason for the badness of this ground.

"It is not the pleasure of the king that this place should remain so bad; his labourers also, have, by the direction of his majesty's surveyors, been for above this sixteen hundred years employed about this patch of ground, if perhaps it might have been mended; yea, and to my knowledge," said he, "here have been swallowed up at least twenty thousand cart loads; yea, millions of wholesome instructions, that have at all seasons been brought from all places of the king's dominions (and they that can tell, say they are the best materials to make good ground of the place); if so be it might have beeen mended, but it is the Slough of Despond still, and so will be when they have done what they can.

"True, there are by the direction of the law-giver, certain good and substantial steps, placed even through the very midst of this Slough; but at such time as this place does much spew out its filth, as it does against change of weather, these steps are hardly seen; or if they be, men through the dizziness of their heads step besides; and they they are bemired to purpose, notwithstanding the steps be there; but the ground is good when they are once got in at the Gate."

Now I saw in my dream, that by this time Pliable had got home to his house again. So his neighbours came to visit him; and some of them called him wise man for coming back; and some called him fool for hazarding himself with Christian; others again mocked at his cowardliness, saying, "Surely since you began to venture, I would not have been so base to have given out for a few difficulties." So Pliable sat sneaking among them. But at last he got more confidence, and then they all turned their tales, and began to deride poor Christian behind his back. And thus much concerning Pliable.

Now as Christian was walking alone by himself, he espied one afar off come crossing over the field to meet him; and their chance was to meet just as they were crossing the way of each other. The gentleman's name was Mr Worldly Wiseman, he dwelt in the town of Carnal Policy, a very great town, and also hard by from whence Christian came. This man then meeting with Christian, and having some inkling of him, for Christian's setting forth from the City of Destruction was much noised abroad, not only in the town where he dwelt, but also it began to be the town-talk in some other places, Master Worldly Wiseman therefore, having some guess of him, by beholding his laborious going, by observing his sighs and groans and the like, began thus to enter into some talk with Christian.

Wordly Wiseman. How now, good fellow, whither away after this burdened manner?

Christian. A burdened manner indeed, as ever I think poor creature had. And whereas you ask me, "Whither away?" I tell you, sir, I am going to yonder Wicket Gate before me; for there, as I am informed, I shall be put into a way to be rid of my heavy burden.

Wordly Wiseman. Have you a wife and children?

Christian. Yes, but I am so laden with this burden that I cannot take that pleasure in them as formerly. Methinks I am as if I had none.

Wordly Wiseman. Will you listen to me, if I give you counsel?

Christian. If it be good, I will, for I stand in need of good counsel.

Wordly Wiseman. I would advise you then that you with all speed get yourself rid of your burden; for you will never be settled in your mind till then: nor can you enjoy the benefits of the blessing which God has bestowed upon you till then.

Christian. That is that which I seek, even to be rid of this heavy burden; but get it off myself I cannot. Nor is there a man in our country that can take if off my shoulders; therefore am I going this way, as I told you, that I may be rid of my burden.

Worldly Wiseman. Who bid you go this way to be rid of your burden?

Christian. A man that appeared to me to be a very great and honourable person; his name, as I remember, is Evangelist.

Worldly Wiseman. I invoke evil upon him for his counsel; there is not a more dangerous and troublesome way in the world than that unto which he has directed you, and that you shall find if you will be ruled by his counsel. You have met with something (as I perceive) already; for I see the dirt of the Slough of Despond is upon you; but that Slough is the beginning of the sorrows that do attend those that go on in that way; hear me, I am older than you! You are likely to meet with in the way which you go: wearisomeness, painfulness, hunger, perils, nakedness, sword, lions, dragons, darkness, and in a word, death, and what not? These things are certainly true, having been confirmed by many testimonies. And why should a man so carelessly cast away himself by giving heed to a stranger?

Christian. Why, sir, this burden upon my back is more terrible to me than are all these things which you have mentioned. Nay, methinks I care not what I meet with in the way, so be I can also meet with deliverance from my burden.

Worldly Wiseman. How came you by your burden at first?

Christian. By reading this book in my hand.

Worldly Wiseman. I thought so, and it has happened unto you as to other weak men, who meddling with things too high for them, do suddenly fall into your distractions; which distractions do not only unman men (as yours I perceive has done you), but they run them upon desperate ventures, to obtain they know not what.

Christian. I know what I would obtain, it is ease for my heavy burden.

Wordly Wiseman. But why wilt thou seek for ease this way, seeing so many dangers attend it, especially, since (had you but patience to hear me) I could direct you to the obtaining of what you desire, without the dangers that you in this way will run yourself into. Yea, and the remedy is at hand. Besides, I will add, that instead of those dangers, you shall meet with much safety, friendship, and content.

Christian. Pray, sir, open this secret to me.

Worldly Wiseman. Why, in yonder village (the village is named Morality) there dwells a gentleman, whose name is Legality, a very judicious man (and a man of a very good name) that has skill to help men off with such burdens as yours are, from their shoulders. Yea, to my knowledge he has done a great deal of good this way. Ay, and besides, he has skill to cure those that are somewhat crazed in their wits with their burdens. To him, as I said, you may go, and be helped presently. His house is not quite a mile from this place; and if he should not be at home himself, he has a pretty young man to his son, whose name is Civility, that can do it (to speak on) as well as the old gentleman himself. There, I say, you may be eased of your burden, and if you are not minded to go back to your former habitation, as indeed I would not wish you to do, you may send for your wife and children to this village, where there are houses now standing empty, one of which you may have at reasonable rates; provision there is also cheap and good, and that which will make your life the more happy is, to be sure, there you shall live by honest neighbours, in credit and good fashion.

Now Christian was somewhat at a loss, but presently he concluded: if this be true which this gentleman has said, my wisest course is to take his advice, and with that he thus further spoke.

Christian. Sir, which is my way to this honest man's house?

Worldly Wiseman. Do you see yonder high hill?

Christian. Yes, very well.

Worldly Wiseman. By that hill you must go, and the first house you come at is his.

So Christian turned out of his way to go to Mr Legality's house for help, but behold, when he was got now hard by the hill, it seemed so high, and also that side of it that was next to the wayside did hang so much over, that Christian was afraid to venture further, lest the hill should fall on his head. Wherefore there he stood still, and knew not what to do. Also his burden, now, seemed heavier to him than while he was in his way. There came also flashes of fire out of the hill, that made Christian afraid that he should be burned. Here therefore he sweated, and did quake for fear. And now he began to be sorry that he had taken Mr Worldly Wiseman's counsel; and with that he saw Evangelist coming to meet him; at the sight also of whom he began to blush for shame. So Evangelist drew nearer, and nearer, and coming up to him, he looked upon him with a severe and dreadful countenance, and thus began to reason with Christian.

Evangelist. What do you here?

At which word Christian knew not what to answer. Wherefore, at present, he stood speechless before him. Then said Evangelist further, "Are not you the man that I found crying, without the walls of the City of Destruction?"

Christian. Yes, dear sir, I am the man.

Evangelist. Did not I direct you the way to the little Wicket Gate?

Christian. Yes, dear sir.

Evangelist. How is it then that you are so quickly turned aside, for you are now out of the way?

Christian. I met with a gentleman, as soon as I had got over the Slough of Despond, who persuaded me that I might in the village before me find a man that could take off my burden.

Evangelist. What was he?

Christian He looked like a gentleman, and talked much to me, and got me at last to yield; so I came hither. But when I beheld this hill, and how it hangs over the way, I suddenly made a stand, lest it should fall on my head.

Evangelist. What said that gentleman to you?

Christian. Why, he asked me whither I was going, and I told him.

Evangelist. And what said he then?

Christian. He asked me if I had a family, and I told him. But, said I, I am so laden with the burden that is on my back that I cannot take pleasure in them as formerly.

Evangelist. And what said he then?

Christian. He bid me with speed get rid of my burden and I told him 'twas ease that I sought; and, said I, I am therefore going to yonder gate to receive further direction how I may get to the place of deliverance. So he said that he would show me a better way, and short, not so attended with difficulties as the way, sir, that you set me. "Which way", said he, "will direct you to a gentleman's house that has skill to take off these burdens." So I believed him, and turned out of that way into this, so that I might be soon eased of my burden; but when I came to this place, and beheld things as they are, I stopped for fear (as I said) of danger: but I now know not what to do.

"Then" said Evangelist "stand still a little, that I may show you the words of God". So he stood trembling. Then said Evangelist, "See that you refuse not him that speaks; for if they escaped not who refused him that spoke on earth, much more shall not we escape, if we turn away from Him that speaks from Heaven. He said moreover, 'Now the just shall live by faith; but if any man draw back, my soul shall have no pleasure in him.' He also did thus apply them. You are the man that is running into this misery, you have begun to reject the counsel of the most high, and to draw back your foot from the way of peace, even almost to the hazarding of your perdition."

Then Christian fell down at his foot as if dead, crying, "Woe is me, for I am undone", at the sight of which Evangelist caught him by the right hand, saying, "All manner of sin and blasphemies shall be forgiven unto men; be not faithless, but believing." Then did Christian again a little revive, and stood up trembling, as at first, before Evangelist.

Then Evangelist proceeded, saying, "Give more earnest heed to things that I shall tell you of. I will now show you who it was that deluded you, and who 'twas also to whom he sent you. The man that met you is one Worldly Wiseman, and rightly is he so called; partly, because he favours only the doctrine of this world (therefore he always goes to the town of Morality to church) and partly because he loves that doctrine best, for it saves him from the cross; and because he is of this carnal temper, therefore he seeks to prevent my ways, though right. Now there are three things in this man's counsel that you must utterly abhor.

1 His turning you out of the way.

2 His labouring to render the cross odious to you.

3 And his setting your feet in that way that leads unto the ministration of death.

"First, you must abhor his turning you out of the way; yea, and your own consenting thereto, because this is to reject the counsel of God, for the sake of the counsel of a Wordly Wiseman. The Lord says, 'Strive to enter in at the strait gate', the gate which I sent you, 'for strait is the gate that leads unto life, and few there be that find it.' From this little Wicket Gate, and from the way thereto has this wicked man turned you, to the bringing of you almost to destruction. Hate therefore his turning you out of the way, and abhor yourself for hearkening to him.

"Secondly, you must abhor his labouring to render the cross odious unto you; for you are to prefer it before the treasures in Egypt: besides, the King of Glory has told you, that he that will save his life shall lose it: and he that comes after him, 'and hates not his father and mother, and wife, and children, and brethren, and sisters; yea, and his own life also, he cannot be my disciple.' I say therefore, for a man to labour to persuade you, that that shall be your death, without which the truth hath said, you cannot have eternal life, this doctrine you must abhor.

"Thirdly, you must hate his setting of your feet in the way that leads to the ministration of death. And for this you must consider to whom he sent you, and also how unable that person was to deliver you from your burden.

"He to whom you were sent for ease, being by name Legality, is the son of the bond-woman which now is, and is in bondage with her children, and is in a mystery this Mount Sinai, which you have feared will fall on your head. Now if she with her children are in bondage, how can you expect by them to be made free? This Legality therefore is not able to set you free from your burden. No man was as yet ever rid of his burden by him, no, nor ever is like to be. You cannot be justified by the works of the law; for by the deeds of the law no man living can be rid of his burden, therefore Mr Worldly Wiseman is an alien, and Mr Legality a cheat, and for his son Civility, notwithstanding his simpering looks, he is but an hypocrite, and cannot help you. Believe me, there is nothing in all this noise that you have heard of this sottish man, but a design to beguile you of your salvation, by turning you from the way in which I had set you." After this Evangelist called aloud to the heavens for confirmation of what he had said; and with that there came words and fire out of the mountain under which poor Christian stood, that made the hair of his flesh stand. The words were thus pronounced, "As many as are of the works of the law, are under the curse; for it is written, 'Cursed is every one that continueth not in all things which are written in the book of the law to do them.' "

Now Christian looked for nothing but death, and began to cry out lamentably, even cursing the time in which he met with Mr Worldly Wiseman, still calling himself a thousand fools for hearkening to his counsel: he also was greatly ashamed to think that this gentleman's arguments, flowing only from the flesh, should have that prevalency with him as to cause him to forsake the right way. This done, he applied himself again to Evangelist in words and sense as follows.

Christian. Sir, what think you? Is there hope? May I now go back and go up to the Wicket Gate, shall I not be abandoned for this, and sent back from thence ashamed? I am sorry I have hearkened to this man's counsel, but may my sin be forgiven.

Evangelist. Your sin is very great, for by it you have committed two evils; you have forsaken the way that is good, to tread in forbidden paths: yet the man at the gate will receive you, for he has good will for men. Only take heed that you do not turn aside again, lest you perish from the way when his wrath is kindled but a little.

Then did Christian address himself to go back, and Evangelist, after he had kissed him, gave him one smile, and bid him Godspeed. So he went on with haste, neither did he speak he to any man by the way; nor if any man asked him, would he vouchsafe them an answer. He went like one that was all the while treading on forbidden ground, and could by no means think himself safe, till again he was got into the way which he left to follow Mr Worldly Wiseman's counsel. So in process of time Christian got up to the Gate.

Now over the Gate there was written, "Knock and it shall be opened unto you." He knocked therefore, more than once or twice, saying, "May I now enter here? Will he within open to sorry me, though I have been an undeserving rebel? Then shall I not fail to sing his lasting praise on high."

At last there came a grave person to the gate named Good Will, who asked who was there, and whence he came, and what he would have.

Christian. Here is a poor burdened sinner, I come from the City of Destruction, but am going to Mount Zion, that I may be delivered from the wrath to come. I would therefore, sir, since I am informed that by this gate is the way thither, know if you are willing to let me in.

Good Will. I am willing with all my heart. And with that he opened the Gate.

So when Christian was stepping in, the other gave him a pull. Then said Christian, "What means that?" The other told him, "A little distance from this gate, there is erected a strong castle, of which Beelzebub is the captain. From thence both he, and them that are with him, shoot arrows at those that come up to this gate, if perhaps they may die before they can enter in." Then said Christian, "I rejoice and tremble." So when he was got in, the man of the gate asked him who directed him thither.

Christian. Evangelist bade me come hither and knock (as I did). And he said that you, sir, would tell me what I must do.

Good Will. An open door is set before you, and no man can shut it.

Christian. Now I begin to reap the benefits of my hazards.

Good Will. But how is it that you came alone?

Christian. Because none of my neighbours saw their dangers as I saw mine.

Good Will. Did any of them know of your coming?

Christian. Yes, my wife and children saw me at the first, and called after me to turn again. Also some of my neighbours stood crying, and calling after me to return; but I put my fingers in my ears, and so came on my way.

Good Will. But did none of them follow you to persuade you to go back?

Chirstian. Yes, both Obstinate and Pliable; but when they saw that they could not prevail, Obstinate went railing back, but Pliable came with me a little way.

Good Will. But why did he not come through?

Christian. We indeed came both together, until we came to the Slough of Despond, into the which we also suddenly fell. And then was my neighbour Pliable discouraged, and would not adventure further. Wherefore getting out again, on that side next to his own house, he told me I should possess the brave country alone for him; so he went his way, and I came mine. He after Obstinate, and I to this gate.

Good Will. Alas, poor man, is the celestial glory of so small esteem with him that he counts it not worth running the hazards of a few difficulties to obtain it?

Christian. Truly, I have said the truth of Pliable, and if I should also say all the truth of myself, it will appear there is no betterment 'twixt him and myself. 'Tis true, he went back to his own house, but I also turned aside, to go in the way of death, being persuaded thereto by the carnal arguments of one Mr Worldly Wiseman.

Good Will. Oh, did he light upon you! What, he would have had you seek for ease at the hands of Mr Legality; they are both of them a very cheat: but did you take his counsel?

Christian. Yes, as far as I dared, I went to find out Mr Legality, until I thought that the mountain that stands by his house would have fallen upon my head: wherefore there I was forced to stop.

Good Will. That mountain has been the death of many, and will be the death of many more: 'tis well you escaped being by it dashed in pieces.

Christian. Why, truly I do not know what had become of me there, had not Evangelist happily met me again as I was musing in the midst of my dumps: but 'twas God's mercy that he came to me again, or else I had never come hither. But now I am come, such as one as I am, more fit indeed for death by that mountain, than thus to stand talking with my Lord. But oh, what a favour is this to me, that yet I am admitted entrance here.

Good Will. We make no objections against any, notwithstanding all that they have done before they come hither, they in no wise are cast out; and therefore, good Christian, come a little way with me, and I will teach you about the way you must go. Look before you; do you see this narrow way? That is the way you must go. It was cast up by the patriarchs, prophets, Christ, and His apostles, and it is as straight as a rule can make it. This is the way you must go.

Christian. But are there no turnings nor windings, by which a stranger may lose the way?

Good Will. Yes, there are many ways that lead into this; and they are crooked, and wide; but thus thou may'st distinguish the right from the wrong, only in being straight and narrow.

Then I saw in my dream that Christian asked him further if he could not help him off with his burden that was upon his back; for as yet he had not got rid thereof, nor could he by any means get it off without help.

He told him, "As to the burden, be content to bear it, until you come to the place of deliverance; for there it will fall from your back itself."

Then Christian began to gird up his loins, and to address himself to his journey. So the other told him that by that he was gone some distance from the gate he would come to the House of the Interpreter, at whose door he should knock; and he would show him excellent things. Then Christian took his leave of his friend, and he again bade him Godspeed.

Then he went on, till he came to the House of the Interpreter, where he knocked, over and over. At last one came to the door, and asked who was there.

Christian. Sir, here is a traveller, who was bidden by an acquaintance of the good man of this house, to call here for my profit. I would therefore speak with the master of the house.

So he called for the master of the House, who after a little time came to Christian and asked him what he would have.

Christian. Sir, I am a man that am come from the City of Destruction, and am going to the Mount Zion, and I was told by the man that stands at the gate, at the head of this way that if I called here, you would show me excellent things, such as would be an help to me in my journey.

*Interpreter.*Come in, I will show you that which will be profitable to you.

So he commanded his man to light the candle, and bid Christian follow him; so he had him into a private room, and bade his man open a door, which when he had done, Christian saw a picture of a very grave person hung up against the wall, and this was the fashion of it: it had eyes lifted up to Heaven, the best of books in its hand, the law of truth was written upon its lips, the world was behind its back; it stood as if it pleaded with men, and a crown of gold did hang over its head.

Christian. What means this?

Interpreter. The man whose picture this is is one of a thousand; he can beget children, travail in birth with children, and nurse them himself when they are born. And whereas you see him with his eyes lifted up to Heaven, the best of books in his hand, and the law of truth writ on his lips, it is to show you that his work is to know, and unfold dark things to sinners even as also you see him stand as if he pleaded with men. And whereas you see the world as cast behind him, and that a crown hangs over his head, that is to show you that slighting and despising the things that are present, for the love that he hath to his master's service, he is sure in the world that comes next to have glory for his reward. Now, I have showed you this picture first, because the man whose picture this is, is the only man whom the lord of the place whither you are going has authorised to be your guide in all difficult places you may meet with in the way. Wherefore take good heed to what I have showed you, and bear well in your mind what you have seen, lest in your journey you meet with some that pretend to lead you right, but their way goes down to death.

Then he took him by the hand, and led him into a very large parlour that was full of dust, because never swept which, after he had reviewed a little while, the Interpreter called for a man to sweep. Now when he began to sweep, the dust began so abundantly to fly about that Christian had almost therewith been choked. Then said the Interpreter to a damsel that stood by, "Bring hither water, and sprinkle the room", which when she had done was swept and cleansed with pleasure.

Christian. What means this?

Interpreter. This parlour is the heart of a man that was never sanctified by the sweet grace of the gospel; that dust is his original sin, and inward corruptions that have defiled the whole man. He that began to sweep at first is the law, but she that brought water, and did sprinkle it, is the gospel. Now, whereas you saw that so soon as the first began to sweep, the dust did so fly about that the room by him could not be cleansed, but that you were almost choked therewith, this is to show you that the law, instead of cleansing the heart (by its working) from sin, does revive, put strength into, and increase it in the soul, even as it does discover and forbid it, for it does not give power to subdue.

Again, as you saw the damsel sprinkle the room with water, upon which it was cleansed with pleasure: this is to show you that when the gospel comes in the sweet and precious influences thereof to the heart, then I say, even as you saw the damsel lay the dust by sprinkling the floor with water, so is sin vanquished and subdued, and the soul made clean, through the faith of it; and consequently fit for the King of Glory to inhabit.

I saw moreover in my dream, that the Interpreter took him by the hand, and led him into a little room, where sat two little children, each one in his chair. The name of the eldest was Passion, and of the other, Patience. Passion seemed to be much discontent, but Patience was very quiet. Then Christian asked, "What is the reason of the discontent of Passion?" The Interpreter answered, "The governor of them would have him wait for his best things till the beginning of the next year, but he will have all now. But Patience is willing to wait."

Then I saw that one came to Passion, and brought him a bag of treasure, and poured it down at his feet; the which he took up, and rejoiced therein and withal laughed Patience to scorn. But I beheld but a while, and he had lavished all away, and had nothing left him but rags.

Christian. Expound this matter more fully to me.

Interpreter. These two lads are figures: Passion, of the men of this world, and Patience, of the men of that which is to come. For as here you see, Passion will have all now, this year; that is to say, in this world. So are the men of this world, they must have all their good things now, they cannot stay till next year; that is, until the next world, for their portion of good. That proverb, "A bird in the hand is worth two in the bush," is of more authority with them than are all the divine testimonies of the good of the world to come. But as you saw, that he had quickly lavished all away, and had presently left him nothing but rags; so will it be with all such men at the end of this world.

Christian. Now I see that Patience has the best wisdom, and that upon many accounts.

1 Because he waits for the best things.

2 And also because he will have the glory of his, when the other has nothing but rags.

Interpreter. Nay, you may add another, to wit, the glory of the next world will never wear out, but these are suddenly gone. Therefore Passion had not so much reason to laugh at Patience because he had his good things first, as Patience will have to laugh at Passion because he had his best things last; for first must give place to last, because last must have his time to come, but last gives place to nothing, for there is not another to succeed. He therefore that hath his portion first, must needs have a time to spend it, but he that has his portion last must have it lastingly. Therefore it is said of Dives, "In your life you received your good things, and likewise Lazarus evil things; but now he is comforted, and you are tormented."

Christian. Then I perceive, 'tis not best to covet things that are now, but to wait for things to come.

Interpreter. You say the truth. For the things that are seen are temporal; but the things that are not seen are eternal. But though this be so, yet since things present and our fleshly appetite are such near neighbours one to another, and again, because things to come, and carnal sense, are such stragers one to another, therefore it is that the first of these so suddenly fall into amity, and that distance is so continued between the second.

Then I saw in my dream that the Interpreter took Christian by the hand, and led him into a place where a fire was burning against a wall, and one standing by it always, casting much water upon it to quench it: yet did the fire burn higher and hotter.

Then said Christian, "What means this?"

The Interpreter answered, "This fire is the work of grace that is wrought in the heart. He that casts water upon it, to extinguish and put it out, is the Devil: but in that you see the fire, notwithstanding, burn higher and hotter, you shall also see the reason of that." So he had him about to the other side of the wall, where he saw a man with a vessel of oil in his hand of the which he did also continually cast, but secretly, into the fire. Then said Christian, "What means this?" The Interpreter answered, "This is Christ, who continually with the oil of his grace maintains the work already begun in the heart, by the means of which, notwithstanding what the Devil can do, the souls of his people prove gracious still. And in that you saw that the man stood behind the wall to maintain the fire, this is to teach you that it is hard for the tempted to see how this work of grace is maintained in the soul."

I saw also that the Interpreter took him again by the hand, and led him into a pleasant place where was built a stately palace, beautiful to behold; at the sight of which Christian was greatly delighted. He saw also upon the top thereof certain persons walked who were clothed all in gold. Then said Christian, "May we go in thither?" Then the Interpreter took him, and led him up toward the door of the palace; and behold, at the door stood a great company of men as desirous to go in, but dared not. There also sat a man, at a little distance from the door, beside a table, with a book, and his inkhorn before him, to take the name of him that should enter therein. He saw also that in the doorway stood many men in armour to keep it, being resolved to do to the man that would enter what hurt and mischief they could. Now was Christian somewhat in a muse. At last, when every man started back for fear of the armed men, Christian saw a man of a very stout countenance come up to the man that sat there to write, saying, "Set down my name, sir." Which when he had done, he saw the man draw his sword, and put a helmet upon his head, and rush toward the door upon the armed men, who laid upon him with deadly force; but the man, not at all discouraged, fell to cutting and hacking most fiercely; so after he had received and given many wounds to those that attempted to keep him out, he cut his way through them all, and pressed forward into the palace. At which there was a pleasant voice heard from those that were within, even of the three that walked upon the top of the palace, saying,

Come in, come in;
Eternal Glory thou shalt win.

So he went in, and was clothed with such garments as they. Then Christian smiled, and said, "I think verily I know the meaning of this."

"Now," said Christian, "let me go hence." "Nay, stay", said the Interpreter, "till I have shown you a little more, and after that, you shall go on your way." So he took him by the hand again, and led him into a very dark room, where there sat a man in an iron cage.

Now the man, to look on, seemed very sad. He sat with his eyes looking down to the ground, his hands folded together, and he sighed as if he would break his heart. Then said Christian, "What means this?" At which the Interpreter bid him talk with the man.

Then said Christian to the man, "What are you?"

The man answered, "I am what I was not once."

Christian. What were you once?

Man. I was once a fair and flourishing holy man, both in my own eyes, and also in the eyes of others. I once was, as I thought, likely to reach the Celestial City, and had even then joy at the thoughts that I should get thither.

Christian. Well, but what are you now?

Man. I am now a man of despair, and am shut up in it, as in this iron cage. I cannot get out. O now I cannot.

Christian. But how came you in this condition?

Man. I left off to watch, and be sober; I laid the reins upon the neck of my lusts; I sinned against the light of the world, and the goodness of God. I have grieved the Spirit, and He is gone. I tempted the Devil, and he is come to me. I have provoked God to anger, and He has left me. I have so hardened my heart, that I cannot repent.

Then said Christian to the Interpreter, "But is there no hope for such a man as this?"

"Ask him," said the Interpreter.

Christian. Is there no hope but you must be kept in this iron cage of despair?

Man. No, none at all.

Christian. Why? The Son of the Blessed is very pitiful.

Man. I have crucified Him to myself afresh, I have despised His person, I have despised His righteousness, I have counted His blood an unholy thing, I have done despite to the spirit of grace: therefore I have shut myself out of all the promises and there now remains to me nothing but threatenings, dreadful threatenings, fearful threatenings of certain judgment and fiery indignation, which shall devour me as an adversary.

Christian. For what did you bring yourself into this condition?

Man. For the lusts, pleasures, and profits of this world; in the enjoyment of which I did then promise myself much delight: but now every one of those things also bite me and gnaw me like a burning worm.

Christian. But can you not now repent and turn?

Man. God has denied me repentance; His word gives me no encouragement to believe; yea, Himself has shut me up in this iron cage: nor can all the men in the world let me out. O eternity! eternity! How shall I grapple with the misery that I must meet with in eternity?

Interpreter. Let this man's misery be remembered by you, and be an everlasting caution to you.

Christian. Well, this is fearful; God help me to watch and be sober; and to pray, that I may shun the cause of this man's misery. Sir, is it not time for me to go on my way now?

Interpreter. Tarry till I shall show you one thing more, and then you shalt go on your way.

So he took Christian by the hand again, and led him into a chamber, where there was one arising out of bed; and as he put on his raiment he shook and trembled. Then said Christian, "Why does this man thus tremble?" The Interpreter then bid him tell to Christian the reason of his so doing. So he began, and said, "This night as I was in my sleep, I dreamed, and behold the heavens grew exceeding black; also it thundered and lightened in most fearful wise, that it put me into an agony. So I looked up in my dream and saw the clouds rack at an unusual rate, upon which I heard a great sound of a trumpet, and saw also a man sit upon a cloud, attended with the thousands of Heaven; they were all in flaming fire, also the heavens were on a burning flame. I heard then a voice saying, "Arise you dead, and come to judgment," And with that the rocks rent, the graves opened, and the dead that were therein came forth; some of them were exceeding glad, and looked upward, and some sought to hide themselves under the mountains. Then I saw the man that sat upon the cloud open the book and bid the world draw near. Yet there was, by reason of a fiery flame that issued out and came from before him, a convenient distance betwixt him and them, as betwixt the judge and the prisoners at the bar. I heard it also proclaimed to them that attended on the man that sat on the cloud, "Gather together the tares, the chaff, and stubble, and cast them into the burning lake," and with that the bottomless pit opened, just where I stood; out of the mouth of which there came in an abundant manner smoke, and coals of fire, with hideous noises. It was also said to the same persons, "Gather my wheat into my garner." And with that I saw many catched up and carried away into the clouds, but I was left behind. I also sought to hide myself, but I could not; for the man that sat upon the cloud still kept his eye upon me: my sins also came into mind, and my conscience did accuse me on every side. Upon this I awaked from my sleep.

Christian. But what was it that made you so afraid of this sight?

Man. Why, I thought that the Day of Judgment was come, and that I was not ready for it: but this frightened me most, that the angels gathered up several, and left me behind; also the pit of Hell opened her mouth just where I stood; my conscience too within afflicted me; and as I thought, the Judge had always his eye upon me, showing indignation in his countenance.

Then said the Interpreter to Christian, "Have thou considered all these things?"

Christian. Yes, and they put me in hope and fear.

Interpreter. Well, keep all things so in your mind, that they may be as a goad in your sides, to prick you forward in the way you must go.

Then Christian began to gird up his loins, and to address himself to his journey.

Then said the Interpreter, "The Comforter be always with you, good Christian, to guide you in the way that leads to the City."

So Christian went on his way, saying,

Here I have seen things rare, and profitable;
Things pleasant, dreadful, things to make me stable
In what I have begun to take in hand.
Then let me think on them, and understand
Wherefore they showed me was, and let me be
Thankful, O good Interpreter, to thee.

Now I saw in my dream that the highway up which Christian was to go was fenced on either side with a wall, and that wall is called Salvation. Up this way therefore did burdened Christian run, but not without great difficulty, because of the load on his back.

He ran thus till he came at a place somewhat ascending; and upon that place stood a cross, and a little below in the bottom, a sepulchre. So I saw in my dream, that just as Christian came up with the cross, his burden loosed from off his shoulders, and fell from off his back; and began to tumble, and so continued to do till it came to the mouth of the sepulchre, where it fell in, and I saw it no more.

Then was Christian glad and lightsome, and said with a merry heart, "He has given me rest, by His sorrow, and life, by His death." Then he stood still a while, to look and wonder; for it was very surprising to him that the sight of the cross should thus ease him of his burden. He looked therefore, and looked again, even till the springs that were in his head sent the water down his cheeks. Now as he stood looking and weeping, behold three shining ones came to him, and saluted him, with "Peace be to you." So the first said to him, "Your sins be forgiven." The second stripped him of his rags, and clothed him with change of raiment. The third also set a mark on his forehead, and gave him a roll with a seal upon it, which he bade him look on as he ran, and that he should give it in at the Celestial Gate: so they went their way. Then Christian gave three leaps for joy, and went on singing,

Thus far did I come laden with my sin,
Nor could aught ease the grief that I was in,
Till I came hither. What a place is this!
Must here be the beginning of my bliss?
Must here the burden fall from off my back?
Must here the strings that bound it to me, crack?

Blessed Cross! Blessed Sepulchre! Blessed rather be
The man that there was put to shame for me.

I saw then in my dream that he went on thus, even until he came to a valley, where he saw, a little out of the way, three men fast asleep, with fetters upon their heels. The name of the one was Simple, another Sloth, and the third Presumption.

Christian then seeing them lie in this way went to them, if perhaps he might awake them. And cried, "You are like them that sleep on the top of a mast, for the Dead Sea is under you, a gulf that has no bottom; awake therefore, and come away; be willing also, and I will help you off with your irons." He also told them, "If he that goes about like a roaring lion comes by, you will certainly become prey to his teeth." With that they looked upon him, and began to reply in this sort. Simple said, "I see no danger". Sloth said, "Yet a little more sleep", and Presumption said, "Every tub must stand upon its own bottom, what is the answer else that I should give you?" And so they lay down to sleep again, and Christian went on his way.

Yet was he troubled to think that men in that danger should so little esteem the kindness of him that so freely offered to help them, both by awakening them, counselling them, and proffering to help them off with their irons. And as he was troubled thereabout, he espied two men come tumbling over the wall on the left hand of the narrow way; and they made up a pace to him. The name of the one was Formalist, and the name of the other Hypocrisy. So, as I said, they drew up unto him, who thus entered with them into discourse.

Christian. Gentlemen, whence came you, and whither do you go?

Formalist and Hypocrisy. We were born in the land of Vainglory, and are going for praise to Mount Zion.

Christian. Why came you not in at the gate which stand at the beginning of the way? Know you not that it is written that, "He that comes not in by the door, but climbs up some other way, the same is a thief and a robber."

Formalist and Hypocrisy. To go to the gate for entrance, is by all our countrymen counted too far about; and that therefore our usual way is to make a short cut of it, and to climb over the wall as we have done.

Christian. But will it not be counted a trespass against the lord of the city whither we are bound, thus to violate his revealed will?

Formalist and Hypocrisy. As for that, you need not to trouble your head thereabout, for what we did we had custom for; and could produce, if need were, testimony that would witness it for more than a thousand years.

Christian. But will your practice stand a trial at law?

Formalist and Hypocrisy. Custom, it being of so long a standing as above a thousand years, would doubtless now be admitted as a thing legal, by any impartial judge. And besides, as long as we get into the way, what's matter which way we get in; if we are in, we are in: you are but in the way, who, as we perceive, came in at the gate; and we are also in the way that came tumbling over the wall: wherein now is your condition better than ours?

Christian. I walk by the rule of my master, you walk by the rude working of your fancies. You are counted thieves already by the lord of the way, therefore I doubt you will not be found true men at the end of the way. You come in by yourselves without his direction, and shall go out by yourselves without his mercy.

To this they made him but little answer; only they bade him look to himself. Then I saw that they went on every man in his way, without much conference one with another; save that these two men told Christian, that, as to laws and ordinances, they doubted not, but they should as conscientiously do them as he. "Therefore", said they, "we see not wherein you differ from us, but by the coat that is on your back, which was, as we believe, given to you by some of your neighbours to hide the shame of your nakedness."

Christian. By laws and ordinances you will not be saved, since you came not in by the door. And as for this coat that is on my back, it was given me by the lord of the place whither I go; and that, as you say, to cover my nakedness with. And I take it as a token of his kindness to me, for I had nothing but rags before; and besides, thus I comfort myself as I go, surely, think I, when I come to the gate of the city, the lord thereof will know me for good, since I have his coat on my back; a coat that he gave me freely in the day that he stripped me of my rags. I have moreover a mark in my forehead, of which perhaps you have taken no notice, which one of my lord's most intimate associates fixed there in the day that my burden fell off my shoulders. I will tell you moreover, that I had then given me a sealed roll to comfort me by reading, as I go in the way. I was also bid to give it in at the Celestial Gate in token of my certain going in after it; all which things I doubt you want, and want them because you came not in at the gate.

To these things they gave him no answer, only they looked upon each other, and laughed. Then I saw that they went on all, save that Christian kept before, and had no more talk but with himself, and that sometimes sighingly, and sometimes comfortably: also he would be often reading in the roll that one of the shining ones gave him, by which he was refreshed.

I believe then, that they all went on till they came to the foot of a hill, at the bottom of which was a spring. There was also in the same place two other ways besides that which came straight from the gate; one turned to the left hand, and the other to the right, at the bottom of the hill; but the narrow way lay right up the hill (and the name of the going up the side of the hill is called Difficulty). Christian now went to the spring and drank thereof to refresh himself, and then began to go up the hill, saying,

This hill, though high, I covet to ascend
The difficulty will not me offend,
For I perceive they way to life lies here;
Come, pluck up, heart; let's neither faint
nor fear:
Better, though difficult, the right way to
go,
Than wrong, though easy, where the
end is woe.

The other two also came to the foot of the hill. But when they saw that the hill was steep and high, and that there were two other ways to go; and supposing also that these two ways might meet again with that up which Christian went, on the other side of the hill; therefore they were resolved to go in those ways. Now the name of one of those ways was Danger, and the name of the other Destruction.

So the one took the way which is called Danger, which led him into a great wood, and the other took directly up the way to Destruction, which led him into a wide field full of dark mountains, where he stumbled and fell, and rose no more.

I looked then after Christian, to see him go up the hill, where I perceived he fell from running to walking, and from walking to clambering upon his hands and his knees, because of the steepness of the place. Now about the midway to the top of the hill was a pleasant arbour, made by the lord of the hill, for the refreshing of weary travellers. Thither therefore Christian got, where also he sat down to rest him. Then he pulled his roll out of his bosom, and read therein to his comfort; he also now began afresh to take a review of the coat or garment that was given him as he stood by the cross. Thus pleasing himself a while, he at last fell into a slumber, and thence into a fast sleep, which detained him in that place until it was almost night, and in his sleep his roll fell out of his hand. Now as he was sleeping, there came one to him and awaked him, saying, "Go to the ant, you sluggard, consider her ways, and be wise," and with that Christian suddenly started up, and sped him on his way, and went apace till he came to the top of the hill.

Now when he was got up to the top of the hill, there came two men running fast against him; the name of the one was Timorous, and the name of the other Mistrust. To whom Christian said, "Sirs, what's the matter you run the wrong way?" Timorous answered that they were going to the City of Zion, and had got up that difficult place. "But", said he, "the further we go, the more danger we meet with, wherefore we turned, and are going back again."

"Yes", said Mistrust, "for just before us lie a couple of lions in the way, whether sleeping or waking we know not and we could not think, if we came within reach, but they would presently pull us in pieces."

Christian. You make me afraid, but whither shall I fly to be safe? If I go back to my own country, that is prepared for fire and brimstone, and I shall certainly perish there. If I can get to the Celestial City, I am sure to be in safety there. I must venture, to go back is nothing but death, to go forward is fear of death, and life everlasting beyond it. I will yet go forward. So Mistrust and Timorous ran down the hill, and Christian went on his way. But thinking again of what he heard from the men, he felt in his bosom for his roll that he might read therein and be comforted; but he felt, and found it not. Then was Christian in great distress, and knew not what to do, for he wanted that which used to relieve him, and that which should have been his pass into the Celestial City. Here therefore he began to be much perplexed, and knew not what to do; at last he bethought himself that he had slept in the arbour that is on the side of the hill: and falling down upon his knees, he asked God forgiveness for that his foolish action, and then went back to look for his roll. But all the way he went back, who can sufficiently set forth the sorrow of Christian's heart? Sometimes he sighed, sometimes he wept, and oftentimes he chided himself, for being so foolish as fall asleep in that place which was erected only for a little refreshment from his weariness. Thus therefore he went back, carefully looking on this side and on that, all the way as he went, if happily he might find his roll, that had been his comfort so many times in his journey. He went thus till he came again within sight of the arbour, where he had sat and slept; but that sight renewed his sorrow the more, by bringing again, even afresh, his evil of sleeping unto his mind. Thus therefore he now went on, bewailing his sinful sleep, saying, "O wretched man that I am, that I should sleep in the day-time! That I should sleep in the midst of difficulty! That I should so indulge the flesh as to use that rest for ease to my flesh which the lord of the hill hath erected only for the relief of the spirits of pilgrims! How many steps have I taken in vain! (Thus it happened to Israel for their sin, they were sent back again by the way of the Red Sea.) And I am made to tread those steps with sorrow which I might have trod with delight, had it not been for this sinful sleep. How far might I have been on my way by this time! I am made to tread those steps thrice over which I needed not to have trod but once: Yea, now also I am like to be benighted, for the day is almost spent. O that I had not slept!" Now by this time he was come to the arbour again, where for a while he sat down and wept, but at last (as Christian would have it) looking sorrowfully down under the settle, there he espied his roll, the which he with trembling and haste caught up, and put it into his bosom; but who can tell how joyful this man was, when he had got his roll again! For this roll was the assurance of his life, and acceptance at the desired haven. Therefore he laid it up in his bosom, gave thanks to God for directing his eye to the place where it lay, and with joy and tears betook himself again to his journey. But oh how nimbly now did he go up the rest of the hill! Yet before he got up, the sun went down upon Christian; and this made him again recall the vanity of his sleeping to his remembrance, and thus he again began to condole with himself: "Ah sinful sleep! How for your sake am I like to be benighted in my journey! I must walk without the sun, darkness must cover the path of my feet, and I must hear the noise of doleful creatures, because of my sinful sleep!" Now also he remembered the story that Mistrust and Timorous told him of, how they were frighted with the sight of the lions. Then said Christian to himself again, "These beasts range in the night for their prey, and if they should meet with me in the dark, how should I shift them? How should I escape being by them torn in pieces? Thus he went on his way, but while he was thus bewailing his unhappy miscarriage, he lifted up his eyes, and behold there was a very stately palace before him, the name of which was Beautiful and it stood just by the highway side.

So I saw in my dream that he made haste and went forward, that if possible he might get lodging there. Now before he had gone far, he entered into a very narrow passage, which was about a furlong from the porter's lodge, and looking very narrowly before him as he went, he espied two lions in the way. Now, thought he, I see the dangers that Mistrust and Timorous were driven back by (the lions were chained, but he saw not the chains). Then he was afraid, and thought also himself to go back after them, for he thought nothing but death was before him. But the porter at the lodge, whose name is Watchful, perceiving that Christian made a halt, as if he would go back, cried unto him saying, "Is your strength so small? Fear not the lions, for they are chained, and are placed there for trial of faith where it is; and for discovery of those that have none: keep in the midst of the path, and no hurt shall come unto you."

Then I saw that he went on, trembling for fear of the lions, but taking good heed to the directions of the porter; he heard them roar, but they did him no harm. Then he clapped his hands, and went on till he came and stood before the gate where the porter was. Then said Christian to the porter, "Sir, what house is this? And may I lodge here tonight?" The porter answered, "This house was built by the lord of the hill, and he built it for the relief and security of pilgrims." The porter also asked whence he was, and whither he was going.

Christian. I am come from the City of Destruction, and am going to Mount Zion; but because the sun is now set, I desire, if I may, to lodge here tonight.

Porter. What is your name?

Christian. My name is now Christian; but my name at the first was Graceless; I came of the race of Japhet, whom God will persuade to dwell in the tents of Shem.

Porter. But how does it happen that you come so late? The sun is set.

Christian. I had been here sooner, but that, wretched man that I am! I slept in the arbour that stands on the hillside; nay, I had notwithstanding that, been here much sooner, but that in my sleep I lost my evidence, and came without it to the brow of the hill; and then feeling for it, and finding it not, I was forced with sorrow of heart, to go back to the place where I slept my sleep, where I found it, and now I am come.

Porter. Well, I will call out one of the virgins of this place, who will, if she likes your talk, bring you in to the rest of the family, according to the rules of the house. So Watchful the porter rang a bell, at the sound of which came out at the door of the house, a grave and beautiful damsel named Discretion, and asked why she was called.

The porter answered, "This man is in a journey from the City of Destruction to Mount Zion, but being weary and benighted, he asked me if he might lodge here tonight; so I told him I would call for you, who after discourse had with him, may do as seems good to you, even according to the law of the house."

Then she asked him whence he was, and whither he was going, and he told her. She asked him also, how he got into the way and he told her. Then she asked him what he had seen, and met with in the way, and he told her; and last, she asked his name, so he said, "It is Christian; and I have so much the more a desire to lodge here tonight, because, by what I perceive, this place was built by the lord of the hill for the relief and security of pilgrims." So she smiled, but the water stood in her eyes. And after a little pause she said, "I will call forth two or three more of the family." So she ran to the door, and called out Prudence, Piety and Charity, who after a little more discourse with him, had him in to the family; and many of them meeting him at the threshold of the house said, "Come in, blessed of the lord; this house was built by the lord of the hill on purpose to entertain such pilgrims in." Then he bowed his head, and followed them into the house. So when he was come in, and set down, they gave him something to drink; and consented together that until supper was ready, some one or two of them should have some particular discourse with Christian, for the best improvement of time. And they appointed Piety and Prudence and Charity to discourse with him; and thus they began.

Piety. Come, good Christian, since we have been so loving to you, to receive you in to our house this night, let us, if perhaps we may better ourselves thereby, talk with you of all the things that have happened to you in your pilgrimage.

Christian. With a very good will, and I am glad that you are so well disposed.

Piety. What moved you at first to betake yourself to a pilgrim's life?

Christian. I was driven out of my native country by a dreadful sound that was in my ears, to wit, that unavoidable destruction did attend me, if I stayed in that place where I was.

Piety. But how did it happen that you came out of your country this way?

Christian. It was as God would have it; for when I was under the fears of destruction I did not know whither to go; but by chance there came a man, even to me (as I was trembling and weeping), whose name is Evangelist, and he directed me to the Wicket Gate, which else I should never have found; and so set me into the way that hath led me directly to this house.

Piety. But did you not come by the House of the Interpreter?

Christian. Yes, and did see such things there, the remembrance of which will stick by me as long as I live; specially three things. To wit, how Christ, in despite of Satan, maintains His work of grace in the heart; how the man had sinned himself quite out of hopes of God's mercy; and also the dream of him that thought in his sleep the Day of Judgment was come.

Piety. Why? Did you hear him tell his dream?

Christian. Yes, and a dreadful one it was, I thought. It made my heart ache as he was telling of it, but yet I am glad I heard it.

Piety. Was that all that you saw at the House of the Interpreter?

Christian. No, he took me and he showed me a stately place, and how the people were clad in gold that were in it; and how there came a venturous man, and cut his way through the armed men that stood in the door to keep him out; and how he was bidden to come in, and win eternal glory. Methought those things did ravish my heart. I could have stayed at that good man's house a twelve-month but that I knew I had further to go.

Piety. And what saw you else in the way?

Christian. Saw! Why, I went but a little further, and I saw one, as I thought in my mind, hang bleeding upon the tree; and the very sight of him made my burden fall off my back (for I groaned under a weary burden), but then it fell down from me. 'Twas a strange thing to me, for I never saw such a thing before. Yea, and while I stood looking up (for then I could not forbear looking), three shining ones came to me: one of them testified that my sins were forgiven me; another stripped me of my rags and gave me this broidered coat which you see; and the third set the mark which you see on my forehead, and gave me this sealed roll (and with that he plucked it out of his bosom).

Piety. But you saw more than this, did you not?

Christian. The things that I have told you were the best: yet some other matters I saw as namely I saw three men, Simple, Sloth, and Presumption, lie asleep a little out of the way as I came, with irons upon their heels; but do you think I could awake them! I also saw Formalist and Hypocrisy come tumbling over the wall, to go, as they pretended, to Zion, but they were quickly lost; even as I myself did tell them, but they would not believe. But, above all, I found it hard work to get up this hill, and as hard to come by the lions' mouths, and truly if it had not been for the good man, the porter that stands at the gate, I do not know but that after all, I might have gone back again: but now I thank God I am here, and I thank you for receiving me.

Then Prudence thought good to ask him a few questions, and desired his answer to them.

Prudence. Do you not think sometimes of the country from whence you came?

Christian. Yes, but with much shame and detestation. Truly, if I had been mindful of that country from whence I came out, I might have had opportunity to have returned; but now I desire a better country; that is, a heavenly one.

Prudence. Do you not yet bear away with you some of the things that then you were conversant withal?

Christian. Yes, but greatly against my will; especially my inward and carnal cogitations with which all my countrymen, as well as myself, were delighted. But now all those things are my grief, and might I but choose my own things I would choose never to think of those things more. But when I would be doing of that which is best, that which is worst is with me.

Prudence. Do you not find sometimes, as if those things were vanquished, which at other times are your perplexity?

Christian. Yes, but that is but seldom; but they are to me golden hours, in which such things happen to me.

Prudence. Can you remember by what means you find your annoyances at times as if they were vanquished?

Christian. Yes, when I think what I saw at the cross, that will do it; and when I look upon my broidered coat, that will do it; also when I look into the roll that I carry in my bosom, that will do it; and when my thoughts wax warm about whither I am going, that will do it.

Prudence. And what is it that makes you so desirous to go to Mount Zion?

Christian. Why, there I hope to see Him alive, that did hang dead on the cross; and there I hope to be rid of all those things that to this day are in me an annoyance to me. There they say there is no death, and there I shall dwell with such company as I like best. For to tell you truth, I love Him, because I was by Him eased of my burden, and I am weary of my inward sickness. I would fain be where I shall die no more, and with the company that shall continually cry, holy, holy, holy.

Then said Charity to Christian, "Have you a family? Are you a married man?"

Christian. I have a wife and four small children.

Charity. And why did you not bring them along with you?

Then Christian wept, and said, "Oh how willingly would I have done it, but they were all of them utterly averse to my going on pilgrimage."

Charity. But you should have talked to them, and have endeavoured to have shown them the danger of being left behind.

Christian. So I did, and told them also what God had showed to me of the destruction of our city; but I seemed to them as one that mocked, and they believed me not.

Charity. And did you pray to God that He would bless your counsel to them?

Christian. Yes, and that with much affection; for you must think that my wife and poor children were very dear unto me.

Charity. But did you tell them of your own sorrow and fear of destruction? For I suppose that destruction was visible enough to you?

Christian. Yes, over and over and over. They might also see my fears in my countenance, in my tears, and also in my trembling under the apprehension of the judgment that did hang over our heads; but all was not sufficient to prevail with them to come with me.

Charity. But what could they say for themselves why they came not?

Christian. Why, my wife was afraid of losing this world, and my children were given to the foolish delights of youth; so what by one thing, and what by another, they left me to wander in this manner alone.

Charity. But did you not with your vain life, damp all that you by words used by way of persuasion to bring them away with you?

Christian. Indeed I cannot commend my life; for I am conscious to myself of many failings. Therein, I know also that a man by his conversion, may soon overthrow what by argument or persuasion he does labour to fasten upon others for their good. Yet, this I can say, I was very wary of giving them occasion, by any unseemly action, to make them averse to going on pilgrimage. Yea, for this very thing, they would tell me I was too precise, and that I denied myself things (for their sake) in which they saw no evil. Nay, I think I may say, that, if what they saw in me did hinder them, it was my great tenderness in sinning against God, or of doing any wrong to my neighbour.

Charity. Indeed Cain hated his brother, because his own works were evil, and his brother's righteous; and if thy wife and children have been offended with thee for this they thereby show themselves to be implacable to good; and you have delivered your soul from their blood.

Now I saw in my dream that thus they sat talking together until supper was ready. So when they had made ready they sat down to meat. Now the table was furnished with fat things and with wine that was well refined, and all their talk at the table was about the lord of the hill; as namely about what he had done, and wherefore he did what he did, and why he had built that house; and by what they said I perceived that he had been a great warrior, and had fought with and slain him that had the power of death, but not without great danger to himself, which made me love him the more.

For, as they said, and as I believe (said Christian), he did it with the loss of much blood; but that which put glory of grace into all he did was that he did it of pure love for his country. And besides, there were some of them of the household that said they had seen, and spoke with Him since He did die on the cross; and they have attested that they had it from His own lips, that he is such a lover of poor pilgrims that the like is not to be found from the east to the west.

They moreover gave an instance of what they affirmed, and that was: he had stripped himself of his glory that he might do this for the poor; and that they heard him say and affirm that he would not dwell in the Mountain of Zion alone. They said moreover that he had made many pilgrims princes though by nature they were beggars born, and their origin had been the dunghill.

Thus they discoursed together till late at night; and after they had committed themselves to their Lord for protection, they betook themselves to rest. The pilgrim they laid in a large upper chamber, whose window opened towards the sun rising; the name of the chamber was Peace, where he slept till break of day; and then he woke and sang,

Where am I now? Is this the love
and care
Of Jesus, for the men that pilgrims are
Thus to provide! That I should be
forgiven!
And dwell already the next door to
Heaven.

So in the morning they all got up, and after some more discourse they told him that he should not depart till they had showed him the rarities of that place. And first they had him into the study where they showed him records of the greatest antiquity; in which, as I remember my dream, they showed him first the pedigree of the lord of the hill, that he was the son of the Ancient of Days, and came by an eternal generation. Here also was more fully recorded the acts that he had done, and the names of many hundreds that he had taken into his service; and how he had placed them in such habitations that could neither by length of days, nor decays of nature, be dissolved.

Then they read to him some of the worthy acts that some of his servants had done, how they had subdued kingdoms, wrought righteousness, obtained promises, stopped the mouths of lions, quenched the violence of fire, escaped the edge of the sword, out of weakness were made strong, waxed valiant in fight and turned to fight the armies of the aliens.

Then they read again in another part of the records of the house where it was showed how willing their lord was to receive into his favour any, even any, though they in time past had offered great affronts to his person and proceedings. Here also were several other histories of many other famous things; of all which Christian had a view, as of things both ancient and modern, together with prophecies and predictions of things that have their certain accomplishment, both to the dread and amazement of enemies, and the comfort and solace of pilgrims.

The next day they took him, and had him into the armoury, where they showed him all manner of furniture, which their lord had provided for pilgrims, as sword, shield, helmet, breastplate, All-prayer and shoes that would not wear out. And there was here enough of this to harness out as many men for the service of their Lord as there be stars in the Heaven for multitude.

They also showed him some of the engines with which some of his servants had done wonderful things. They showed his Moses' rod, the hammer and nail with which Jael slew Sisera, the pitchers, trumpets, and lamps too, with which Gideon put to flight the armies of Midian. Then they showed him the ox's goad wherewith Shamgar slew six hundred men. They showed him also the jaw-bone with which Samson did such mighty feats; they showed him moreover the sling and stone with which David slew Goliath of Gath and the sword also with which their lord will kill the man of sin, in the day that he shall rise up to the prey. They showed him besides many excellent things, with which Christian was much delighted. This done, they went to their rest again.

Then I saw in my dream, that on the morrow he got up to go forward, but they desired him to stay till the next day also. "And then", said they, "we will (if the day be clear) show you the Delectable Mountains", which they said would yet further add to his comfort, because they were nearer the desired Heaven than the place where at present he was. So he consented and stayed. When the morning was up they had him to the top of the house, and bade him look south; so he did, and behold, at a great distance he saw a most pleasant mountainous country, beautified with woods, vineyards, fruits of all sorts; flowers also, with springs and fountains, very delectable to behold. Then he asked the name of the country; they said it was Immanuel's Land: "And it is as common", said they, "as this hill is to and for all the pilgrims. And when you come there from thence, you may see to the gate of the Celestial City, as the shepherds that live there will make appear."

Now he bethought himself of setting forward, and they were willing he should: "But first", said they, "let us go again into the armoury", so they did; and when he came there, they harnessed him from head to foot with what was of proof, lest perhaps he should meet with assaults in the way. He being therefore thus dressed walked out with his friends to the gate, and there he asked the porter if he saw any pilgrims pass by, then the porter answered, "Yes".

Charity. Pray, did you know him?

Porter. I asked his name, and he told me it was Faithful.

Christian. O, I know him, he is my townsman, my near neighbour, he comes from the place where I was born: how far do you think he may be before?

Porter. He is got by this time below the hill.

Christian. Well, good porter, the Lord be with you, and add to all your blessings much increase, for the kindness you have showed to me.

Then he began to go forward, but Discretion, Piety, Charity and Prudence would accompany him down to the foot of the hill. So they went on together, reiterating their former discourses till they came to go down the hill. Then said Christian, "As it was difficult coming up, so (so far as I can see) it is dangerous going down." "Yes", said Prudence, "so it is, for it is a hard matter for a man to go down into the Valley of Humiliation, as you are now, and to catch no slip by the way. Therefore", said they, "are we come out to accompany you down the hill." So he began to go down, but very warily, yet he caught a slip or two.

Then I saw in my dream that these good companions (when Christian was gone down to the bottom of the hill) gave him a loaf of bread, a bottle of wine, and a cluster of raisins; and then he went on his way.

But now in this Valley of Humiliation poor Christian was hard put to it for he had gone but a little way before he espied a foul fiend coming over the field to meet him; his name is Apollyon. Then did Christian begin to be afraid, and to cast in his mind whether to go back, or to stand his ground. But he considered again that he had no armour for his back, and therefore thought that to turn the back to him might give him greater advantage with ease to pierce him with his darts; therefore he resolved to venture, and stand his ground. For, thought he, had I no more in my eye than the saving of my life, 'twould be the best way to stand.

So he went on, and Apollyon met him. Now the monster was hideous to behold, he was clothed with scales like a fish (and they are his pride) he had wings like a dragon, feet like a bear, and out of his belly came fire and smoke, and his mouth was as the mouth of a lion. When he was come up to Christian he beheld him with a disdainful countenance and thus began to question with him.

Apollyon. Whence come you, and whither are you bound?

Christian. I come from the City of Destruction, which is the place of all evil, and am going to the City of Zion.

Apollyon. By this I perceive you are one of my subjects, for all that country is mine; and I am the prince and god of it. How is it then that you have ran away from your king? Were it not that I hope you may do me more service, I would strike you now at one blow to the ground.

Christian. I was born indeed in your dominions, but your service was hard, and your wages such as a man could not live on, for the wages of sin is death; therefore when I was come to years, I did as other considerate persons do, look out if perhaps I might mend myself.

Apollyon. There is no prince that will thus lightly lose his subjects, neither will I as yet lose you. But since you complain of your service and wages, be content to go back; what our country will afford I do here promise to give you.

Christian. But I have let myself to another, even to the king of princes, and how can I with fairness go back with you?

Apollyon. You have done in this, according to the proverb, changed a bad for a worse: but it is ordinary for those that have professed themselves his servants, after a while to give him the slip; and return again to me: do you so too, and all shall be well.

Christian. I have given him my faith, and sworn my allegiance to him; how then can I go back from this, and not be hanged as a traitor?

Apollyon. You did the same to me and yet I am willing to pass by all, if now you will yet turn again, and go back.

Christian. What I promised you was in my ignorance; and besides, I count that the prince under whose banner now I stand is able to absolve me; yea, and to pardon also what I did as to my compliance with you.

And besides (O destroying Apollyon), to speak truth, I like his service, his wages, his servants, his government, his company, and country better than yours: and therefore leave off to persuade me further, I am his servant, and I will follow him.

Apollyon. Consider again when you are in cool blood what you are likely to meet with in the way that you go. You know that for the most part his servants come to an ill end, because they are transgressors against me and my ways. How many of them have been put to shameful deaths! And besides, you count his service better than mine, whereas he never came yet from the place where he is to deliver any that served him out of our hands; but as for me, how many times, as all the world very well knows, have I delivered, either by power or fraud, those that have faithfully served me, from him and his, though taken by them; and so I will deliver you.

Christian. His forbearing at present to deliver them is on purpose to try their love, whether they will cleave to him to the end: and as for the ill end you say they come to, that is most glorious in their account: for, for present deliverence, they do not much expect it; for they stay for their glory, and then they shall have it, when their prince comes in his, and the glory of the angels.

Apollyon. You have already been unfaithful in your service to him, and how do you think to receive wages of him?

Christian. Wherein, O Apollyon, have I been unfaithful to him?

Apollyon. You did faint at first setting out, when you were almost choked in the Gulf of Despond. You did attempt wrong ways to be rid of your burden, whereas you should have stayed till your Prince had taken it off. You did sinfully sleep, and lose your choice things: you were also almost persuaded to go back at the sight of the lions; and when you talk of your journey, and of what you have heard and seen, you are inwardly desirous of vainglory in all that you say or do.

Christian. All this is true, and much more, which you have left out; but the prince whom I serve and honour is merciful and ready to forgive. But besides, these infirmities possessed me in your country, for there I sucked them in, and I have groaned under them, been sorry for them, and have obtained pardon of my prince.

Then Apollyon broke out into a grievous rage, saying, "I am an enemy to this prince: I hate his person, his laws, and people. I am come out on purpose to withstand you.

Christian. Apollyon, beware what you do, for I am in the king's highway, the way of holiness, therefore take heed to yourself.

Then Apollyon straddled quite over the whole breadth of the way, and said, "I am void of fear in this matter, prepare yourself to die, for I swear by my infernal den that you shall go no further, here will I spill your soul: and with that he threw a flaming dart at his breast; but Christian had a shield in his hand, with which he caught it, and so prevented the danger of that. Then did Christian draw, for he saw 'twas time to bestir him; and Apollyon as fast made at him, throwing darts as thick as hail by which, notwithstanding all that Christian could do to avoid it, Apollyon wounded him in his head, his hand and foot; this made Christian give a little back: Apollyon therefore followed his work at full force, and Christian again took courage, and resisted as manfully as he could. This sore combat lasted for above half a day, even till Christian was almost quite spent. For you must know that Christian, by reason of his wounds, must needs grow weaker and weaker.

Then Apollyon, espying his opportunity, began to gather up close to Christian, and wrestling with him, gave him a dreadful fall; and with that Christian's sword flew out of his hand. Then said Apollyon, "I am sure of you now," and with that he had almost pressed him to death, so that Christian began to despair of life. But as God would have it, while Apollyon was fetching of his last blow thereby to make a full end of this good man, Christian nimbly reached out his hand for his sword, and caught it, saying, "Rejoice not against me, O mine enemy! When I fall I shall arise," and with that give him a deadly thrust, which made him give back as one that had received his mortal wound, Christian, perceiving that, made at him again, saying, "Nay, in all these things we are more than conquerors through Him that loved us." And with that Apollyon spread forth his dragon's wings, and sped him away, that Christian saw him no more.

In this combat no man can imagine, unless he had seen and heard as I did, what yelling, and hideous roaring Apollyon made all the time of the fight; he spake like a dragon; and on the other side, what sighs and groans burst from Christian's heart. I never saw him all the while give so much as one pleasant look, till he perceived he had wounded Apollyon with his two-edged sword; then indeed he did smile, and look upward, but 'twas the dreadfullest sight that ever I saw.

So when the battle was over, Christian said, "I will here give thanks to him that has delivered me out of the mouth of the lion, to him that did help me against Apollyon." And so he did, saying,

Great Beelzebub, the captain of this fiend,
Designed my ruin; therefore to this end
He sent him harnessed out, and he with rage
That hellish was did fiercely me engage;
But blessed Michael helped me, and I
By dint of sword did quickly make him fly;
Therefore to him let me give lasting praise,
And thank and bless his holy name always.

Then there came to him a hand with some of the leaves of the tree of life, which Christian took, and applied to the wounds that he had received in the battle, and was healed immediately. He also sat down in that place to eat bread, and to drink of the bottle that was given him a little before; so being refreshed, he addressed himself to his journey, with his sword drawn in his hand. For he said, "I know not but some other enemy may be at hand". But he met with no other affront from Apollyon quite through this valley.

Now at the end of this valley was another, called the Valley of the Shadow of Death, and Christian must needs go through it because the way to the Celestial City lay through the midst of it. Now this valley is a very solitary place. The prophet Jeremiah thus describes it, "A wilderness, a land of deserts, and of pits, a land of drought, and of the shadow of death, a land that no man" (but a Christian) "passeth through, and where no man dwelt."

Now here Christian was worse put to it than in his fight with Apollyon, as by the sequel you shall see.

I saw then in my dream, that when Christian was got to the borders of the Shadow of Death there met him two men, children of them that brought up an evil report of the good land, making haste to go back: to whom Christian spoke as follows.

Christian. Whither are you going?

Men. Back, back; and would have you to do so too, if either life or peace is prized by you.

Christian. Why? What's the matter?

Men. Matter! We were going that way as you are going, and went as far as we dared; and indeed we were almost past coming back, for had we gone a little further, we had not been here to bring the news to you.

Christian. But what have you met with?

Men. Why we were almost in the Valley of the Shadow of Death, but that by good luck we looked before us, and saw the danger before we came to it.

Christian. But what have you seen?

Men. Seen! Why the valley itself, which is as dark as pitch; we also saw there the hobgoblins, satyrs, and dragons of the pit; we heard also in that valley a continual howling and yelling, as of a people under unutterable misery who there sat bound in affliction and irons: and over that valley hangs the discouraging clouds of confusion; death also does always spread his wings over it. In a word, it is every whit dreadful, being utterly without order.

Christian. I perceive not yet, by what you have said, but that this is my way to the desired Heaven.

Men. Be it thy way, we will not choose it for ours.

So they parted, and Christian went on his way, but still with his sword drawn in his hand, for fear lest he should be assaulted.

I saw then in my dream so far as this valley reached, there was on the right hand a very deep ditch; that ditch is it into which the blind have led the blind in all ages, and have both there miserably perished. Again, behold on the left hand there was a very dangerous quagmire, into which, if even a good man falls he can find no bottom for his foot to stand on. Into that quagmire King David once did fall, and had no doubt therein been smothered, had not He that is able plucked him out.

The pathway was here also exceeding narrow, and therefore good Christian was the more put to it; for when he sought in the dark to shun the ditch on the one hand, he was ready to tip over into the mire on the other; also when he sought to escape the mire, without great carefulness he would be ready to fall into the ditch. Thus he went on, and I heard him here sigh bitterly, for, besides the dangers mentioned above, the pathway was here so dark that often when he lifted up his foot to set forward he knew not where, or upon what, he should set it next.

About the midst of this valley, I perceived the mouth of Hell to be, and it stood also hard by the wayside. Now, thought Christian, what shall I do? And ever and anon the flame and smoke would come out in such abundance, with sparks and hideous noises (things that cared not for Christian's sword, as did Apollyon before) that he was forced to put up his sword, and betake himself to another weapon called All-Prayer; so he cried in my hearing, "O Lord I beseech Thee deliver my soul." Thus he went on a great while, yet still the flames would be reaching towards him: also he heard doleful voices, and rushing to and fro, so that sometimes he thought he should be torn in pieces, or trodden down like mire in the streets. This frightful sight was seen, and these dreadful noises were heard by him, for several miles together. And coming to a place where he thought he heard a company of fiends coming forward to meet him, he stopped, and began to muse what he had best to do. Sometimes he had half a thought to go back. Then again he thought he might be halfway through the valley; he remembered also how he had already vanquished many a danger: and that the danger of going back might be much more than to go forward; so he resolved to go on. Yet the fiends seemed to come nearer and nearer, but when they were come even almost at him, he cried out with a most vehement voice, "I will walk in the strength of the Lord God"; so they gave back, and came no further.

One thing I would not let slip; I took notice that now poor Christian was so confounded that he did not know his own voice, and thus I perceived it: just when he was come over against the mouth of the burning pit, one of the wicked ones got behind him, and stepped up softly to him, and whisperingly suggested many grievous blasphemies to him which he verily thought had proceeded from his own mind. This put Christian more to it than anything that he met with before, even to think that he should now blaspheme Him that he loved so much before; yet, could he have helped it, he would not have done it: but he had not the discretion either to stop his ears, or to know from whence those blasphemies came.

When Christian had travelled in this disconsolate condition some considerable time, he thought he heard the voice of a man, as going before him, saying, "Though I walk through the Valley of the Shadow of Death, I will fear no ill, for You are with me."

Then was he glad, and that for these reasons.

First, because he gathered from thence, that some who feared God were in this valley as well as himself.

Second, for that he perceived God was with them, though in that dark and dismal state; and why not, thought he, with me, though by reason of the impediment that attends this place I cannot perceive it.

Third, because he hoped (could he overtake them) to have company by and by. So he went on, and called to him that was before; but he knew not what to answer, because he also thought himself to be alone: and by and by, the day broke; then said Christian, "He hath turned the shadow of death into the morning."

Now morning being come he looked back, not of desire to return, but to see by the light of the day what hazards he had gone through in the dark. So he saw more perfectly the ditch that was on the one hand, and the quagmire that was on the other; also how narrow the way was which lay between them both; also now he saw the hobgoblins, and satyrs, and dragons of the pit, but all afar off; for after break of day they came not nigh; yet they were discovered to him, according to that which is written, "He discovers deep things out of darkness, and brings out to light the shadow of death".

Now was Christian much affected with his deliverance from all the dangers of his solitary way, which dangers, though he feared them more before, yet he saw them more clearly now, because the light of the day made them conspicuous to him; and about this time the sun was rising, and this was another mercy to Christian: for you must note, that though the first part of the Valley of the Shadow of Death was dangerous, yet this second part which he was yet to go, was, if possible, far more dangerous. For from the place where he now stood, even to the end of the valley, the way was all along set so full of snares, traps, gins, and nets here, and so full of pits, pitfalls, deep holes, and shelvings down there, that had it now been dark, as it was when he came the first part of the way, had he had a thousand souls, they had in reason been cast away; but, as I said, just now the sun was rising. Then said he, "His candle shines on my head, and by His light I go through darkness."

In this light therefore he came to the end of the valley. Now I saw in my dream that at the end of this valley lay blood, bones, ashes, and mangled bodies of men, even of pilgrims that had gone this way formerly; and while I was musing what should be the reason, I espied a little before me a cave, where two giants, Pope and Pagan, dwelt in old time, by whose power and tyranny the men whose bones, blood, ashes, etc, lay there, were cruelly put to death. But by this place Christian went without much danger, which I somewhat wondered at; but I have learnt since that Pagan has been dead many a day; and as for the other, though he be yet alive he is by reason of age, and also of the many shrewd brushes that he met with in his younger days, grown so crazy and stiff in his joints that he can now do little more than sit in his cave's mouth, grinning at pilgrims as they go by, and biting his nails, because he cannot come at them.

So I saw that Christian went on his way, yet at the sight of the old man that sat in the mouth of the cave, he could not tell what to think, specially because he spoke to him, though he could not go after him, saying, "You will never mend till more of you be burned": but he held his peace, and set a good face on't, and so went by, and catched no hurt. Then sang Christian,

O world of wonders! (I can say no less)
That I should be preserved in that distress
That I have met with here! O blessed be
That hand that from it hath delivered me!
Dangers in darkness, devils, Hell, and sin,
Did compass me, while I this vale was in;
Yea, snares, and pits, and traps, and nets did lie
My path about, that worthless silly I
Might have been catched, entangled, and cast down:
But since I live let Jesus wear the crown.

Now as Christian went on his way he came to a little ascent, which was cast up on purpose that pilgrims might see before them. Up there therefore Christian went, and looking forward he saw Faithful before him, upon his journey. Then said Christian aloud, "Ho, ho, so-ho, stay, and I will be your companion." At that Faithful looking behind him, to whom Christian cried again, "Stay, stay, till I come up to you"; but Faithful answered, "No, I am upon my life, and the avenger of blood is behind me." At this Christian was somewhat moved, and putting to all his strength, he quickly got up with Faithful, and did also over-run him, so the last was first. Then did Christian vaingloriously smile, because he had gotten the start of his brother, but not taking good heed to his feet, he suddenly stumbled and fell, and could not rise again, until Faithful came up to help him.

Then I saw in my dream they went very lovingly on together, and had sweet discourse of all things that had happened to them in their pilgrimage, and thus Christian began.

Christian. My honoured and well-loved brother Faithful, I am glad that I have overtaken you and that God has so tempered our spirits that we can walk as companions in this so pleasant path.

Faithful. I had thought, dear friend, to have had your company quite from our town, but you did get the start of me; wherefore I was forced to come thus much of the way alone.

Christian. How long did you stay in the City of Destruction, before you set out after me on your pilgrimage?

Faithful. Till I could stay no longer; for there was great talk presently after you had gone out that our city would in a short time with fire from Heaven be burned down to the ground.

Christian. What? Did your neighbours talk so?

Faithful. Yes, 'twas for a while in everybody's mouth.

Christian. What, and did no more of them but you come out to escape the danger?

Faithful. Though there was, as I said, a great talk thereabout, yet I do not think they did firmly believe it. For in the heat of the discourse I heard some of them deridingly speak of you, and of your desperate journey (for so they called this your pilgrimage), but I did believe, and do still, that the end of our city will be with fire and brimstone from above, and therefore I have made my escape.

Christian. Did you hear no talk of neighbour Pliable?

Faithful. Yes, Christian, I heard that he followed you till he came to the Slough of Despond; where, as some said, he fell in, but he would not be known to have so done; but I am sure he was soundly bedabbled with that kind of dirt.

Christian. And what said the neighbours to him?

Faithful. He has since his going back been held greatly in derision and that among all sorts of people. Some do mock and despise him, and scarce will any set him on work. He is now seven times worse than if he had never gone out of the city.

Christian. But why should they be so set against him, since they also despise the way that he forsook?

Faithful. Oh, they say, "Hang him, he is a turncoat, he was not true to his profession." I think God has stirred up even his enemies to hiss at him and make him a proverb, because he has forsaken the way.

Christian. Had you no talk with him before you came out?

Faithful. I met him once in the streets, but he leered away on the other side, as one ashamed of what he had done; so I spoke not to him.

Christian. Well, at my first setting out, I had hopes of that man; but now I fear he will perish in the overthrow of the city, for it is happened to him according to the true proverb, "The dog is turned to his vomit again, and the sow that was washed to her wallowing in the mire."

Faithful. They are my fears of him too: but who can hinder that which will be?

Christian. Well, neighbour Faithful, let us leave him, and talk of things that more immediately concern ourselves. Tell me now, what you have met with in the way as you came. For I know you have met with some things, or else it may be writ for a wonder.

Faithful. I escaped the slough that I perceive you fell into, and got up to the gate without that danger; only I met with one whose name was Wanton, that had like to have done me a mischief.

Christian. 'Twas well you escaped her net; Joseph was hard put to it by her, and he escaped her as you did, but it had like to have cost him his life. But what did she do to you?

Faithful. You cannot think (but that you know something) what a flattering tongue she had; she lay at me hard to turn aside with her, promising me all manner of content.

Christian. Nay, she did not promise you the content of a good conscience.

Faithful. You know what I mean, all carnal and fleshly content.

Christian. Thank God you have escaped her; the abhorred of the Lord shall fall into her ditch.

Faithful. Nay, I know not whether I did wholly escape her, or no.

Christian. Why, I think you did not consent to her desires?

Faithful. No, not to defile myself, for I remembered an old writing that I had seen which said, "Her steps take hold of Hell." So I shut my eyes, because I would not be bewitched with her looks. Then she railed at me, and I went my way.

Christian. Did you meet with no other assault as you came?

Faithful. When I came to the foot of the hill called Difficulty, I met with a very aged man, who asked me what I was, and whither bound. I told him that I was a pilgrim, going to the Celestial City. Then said the old man, "You look like an honest fellow; will you be content to dwell with me, for the wages that I shall give you?" Then I asked him his name, and where he dwelt. He said his name was "Adam the First, and I dwell in the town of deceit." I asked him then, what was his work? And what the wages that he would give? He told me that his work was many delights and his wages that I should be his heir at last. I further asked him what house he kept, and what other servants he had. So he told me that his house was maintained with all the dainties in the world, and that his servants were those of his own begetting. Then I asked how many children he had; he said, that he had but three daughters, The Lust of the Flesh, The Lust of the Eyes, and The Pride of Life, and that I should marry them all if I would. Then I asked how long a time he would have me live with him. And he told me, as long as he lived himself.

Christian. Well, and what conclusion came the old man and you to at last?

Faithful. Why, at first I found myself somewhat inclined to go with the man, for I thought he spoke very fair; but looking in his forehead as I talked with him I saw there written, "Put off the old man with his deeds."

Christian. And how then?

Faithful. Then it came burning hot into my mind, whatever he said and however he flattered, that when he got me home to his house he would sell me for a slave. So I bade him forbear to talk, for I would not come near the door of his house. Then he reviled me, and told me that he would send such a one after me, that should make my way bitter to my soul. So I turned to go away from him, but just as I turned myself to go thence, I felt him take hold of my flesh, and give me such a deadly twitch back that I thought he had pulled part of me after himself. This made me cry, "O wretched man!" So I went on my way up the hill.

Now when I had got about halfway up, I looked behind me, and saw one coming after me, swift as the wind; so he overtook me just about the place where the settle stands.

Christian. Just there, did I sit down to rest me; but being overcome with sleep I there lost this roll out of my bosom.

Faithful. But good brother, hear me out. So soon as the man overtook me, he was but a word and a blow; for down he knocked me and laid me for dead. But when I was a little come to myself again, I asked him wherefore he served me so. He said, because of my secret inclining to Adam the First; and with that he struck me another deadly blow on the breast, and beat me down backward; so I lay at his foot as dead as before. So when I came to myself again, I cried him mercy; but he said, "I know not how to show mercy", and with that knocked me down again. He had doubtless made an end of me, but that one came by and bade him forbear.

Christian. Who was that, that bade him forbear?

Faithful. I did not know Him at first, but as He went by, I perceived the holes in His hands, and His side; then I concluded that He was our Lord. So I went up the hill.

Christian. That man that overtook you was Moses, he spares none, neither knows he how to show mercy to those that transgress his law.

Faithful. I know it very well, it was not the first time that he has met with me. 'Twas he that came to me when I dwelt securely at home, and that told me he would burn my house over my head, if I stayed there.

Christian. But did not you see the house that stood there on the top of that hill on the side of which Moses met you?

Faithful. Yes, and the lions too, before I came at it; but for the lions, I think they were asleep, for it was about noon, and because I had so much of the day before me I passed by the porter, and came down the hill.

Christian. He told me indeed that he saw you go by, but I wish you had called at the house; for they would have showed you so many rarities, that you would scarce have forgot them to the day of your death. But pray tell me, did you meet nobody in the Valley of Humility?

Faithful. Yes, I met with one Discontent, who would willingly have persuaded me to go back again with him: his reason was, that the valley was altogether without honour; he told me moreover that there to go was the way to disobey all my friends, as Pride, Arrogance, Self conceit, Wordly Glory, with others, who he knew, as he said, would be very much offended, if I made such a fool of myself, as to wade through this valley.

Christian. Well, and how did you answer him?

Faithful. I told him that although all these that he named might claim kindred of me, and that rightly (for indeed they were my relations, according to the flesh), yet since I became a pilgrim they have disowned me, as I also have rejected them; and therefore they were to me now no more than if they had never been of my lineage. I told him moreover that as to this valley, he had quite misrepresented the thing: for before honour is humility, and a haughty spirit before a fall. Therefore, said I, I had rather go through this valley to the honour that was so accounted by the wisest, than choose that which he esteemed most worth our affections.

Christian. Met you with nothing else in that valley?

Faithful. Yes, I met with Shame, but of all the men that I met with in my pilgrimage, he, I think, bears the wrong name. The other would be said, nay after a little argumentation (and somewhat else) but this bold-faced Shame would never have done.

Christian. Why, what did he say to you?

Faithful. What! Why he objected against religion itself; he said it was a pitiful, low, sneaking business for a man to mind religion; he said that a tender conscience was an unmanly thing, and that for man to watch over his words and ways, so as to tie up himself from that hectoring liberty that the brave spirits of the times accustom themselves unto would make him the ridicule of the times. He objected also that but a few of the mighty, rich, or wise, were ever of my opinion; nor any of them neither, before they were persuaded to be fools, and to be of a voluntary fondness, to venture the loss of all, for nobody else knows what. He moreover objected to the base and low estate and condition of those that were chiefly the pilgrims; also their ignorance of the times in which they lived, and want of understanding in all natural science. Yea, he did hold me to it at that rate also about a great many more things than here I relate; as, that it was a shame to sit whining and mourning under a sermon, and a shame to come sighing and groaning home. That it was a shame to ask my neighbour forgiveness for petty faults, or to make restitution where I had taken from any: he said also that religion made a man grow strange to the great, because of a few vices (which he called by finer names) and made him own and respect the base, because of the same religious fraternity. And is not this, said he, a shame?

Christian. And what did you say to him?

Faithful. Say! I could not tell what to say at the first. Yea, he put me so to it, that my blood came up in my face, even this Shame fetched it up, and had almost beat me quite off. But at last I began to consider, "that which is highly esteemed among men, is had in abomination with God". And I thought again, this Shame tells me what men are, but he tells me nothing of what God or the Word of God is. And I thought moreover that at the day of doom we shall not be doomed to death or life, according to the hectoring spirits of the world, but according to the wisdom and law of the Highest. Therefore, thought I, what God says is best, though all the men in the world are against it. Seeing then that God prefers his religion, seeing God prefers a tender conscience, seeing they that make themselves fools for the Kingdom of Heaven are wisest; and that the poor man that loves Christ is richer than the greatest man in the world that hates him. Shame, depart, you are an enemy to my salvation; shall I entertain you against my sovereign Lord? How then shall I look Him in the face at His coming? Should I now be ashamed of His ways and servants, how can I expect the blessing? But indeed this Shame was a bold villain; I could scarce shake him out of my company; yea, he would be haunting of me, and continually whispering me in the ear, with some one or other of the infirmities that attend religion. But at last I told him, 'twas but in vain to attempt further in this business; for those things that he disdained, in those did I see most glory. And so at last I got past this importunate one.

And when I had shaken him off, then I began to sing:

The trials that those men do meet withal
That are obedient to the heavenly call,
Are manifold and suited to the flesh,
And come, and come, and come again afresh;
That now, or sometime else, we by them may
Be taken, overcome, and cast away.
O let the pilgrims, let the pilgrims then
Be vigilant, and quit themselves like men.

Christian. I am glad, my brother, that you did withstand this villain so bravely; for of all, as you say, I think he has the wrong name; for he is so bold as to follow us in the streets, and to attempt to put us to shame before all men that is, to make us ashamed of that which is good; but if he was not himself audacious, he would never attempt to do as he does. But let us still resist him, for notwithstanding all his bravados, he promotes the fool, and none else. "The wise shall inherit glory", said Solomon, "but shame shall be the promotion of fools".

Faithful. I think we must cry to Him for help against Shame, that would have us be valiant for truth upon the earth.

Christian. You say true. But did you meet nobody else in that valley?

Faithful. No not I, for I had sunshine all the rest of the way, through that, and also through the Valley of the Shadow of Death.

Christian. 'Twas well for you; I am sure it fared far otherwise with me. I had for a long season, as soon almost as I entered into that valley, a dreadful combat with that foul fiend, Apollyon. Yea, I thought verily he would have killed me; especially when he got me down, and crushed me under him as if he would have crushed me to pieces. For as he threw me, my sword flew out of my hand; nay he told me he was sure of me, but I cried to God and He heard me, and delivered me out of all my troubles. Then I entered into the Valley of the Shadow of Death and had no light for almost half the way through it. I thought I should have been killed there, over and over: but at last, day broke, and the sun rose, and I went through that which was behind with far more ease and quiet.

Moreover I saw in my dream that as they went on Faithful, as he chanced to look on one side, saw a man whose name is Talkative, walking at a distance beside them (for in this place there was room enough for them all to walk). He was a tall man, and something more comely at a distance than at hand. To this man, Faithful addressed himself in this manner.

Faithful. Friend, whither away? Are you going to the Heavenly Country?

Talkative. I am going to that same place.

Faithful. That is well. Then I hope we may have your good company.

Talkative. With a very good will will I be your companion.

Faithful. Come on then, and let us go together, and let us spend our time in discoursing of things that are profitable.

Talkative. To talk of things that are good to me is very acceptable, with you or with any other; and I am glad that I have met with those that incline to so good a work. For to speak the truth, there are but few that care thus to spend their time (as they are in their travels) but choose much rather to be speaking of things to no profit, and this has been a trouble to me.

Faithful. That is indeed a thing to be lamented; for what things so worthy of the use of the tongue and mouth of men on earth, as are the things of the God of Heaven.

Talkative. I like you wonderful well, for your saying is full of conviction; and I will add, what thing so pleasant, and what so profitable, as to talk of the things of God?

What things so pleasant, that is, if a man has any delight in things that are wonderful, for instance, if a man does delight to talk of the history or the mystery of things; or if a man does love to talk of miracles, wonders, or signs, where shall he find things recorded so delightful, and so sweetly penned, as in the holy Scripture?

Faithful. That's true: but to be profited by such things in our talk should be that which we design.

Talkative. That is it that I said; for to talk of such things is most profitable, for by so doing, a man may get knowledge of many things; as of the vanity of earthly things, and the benefit of things above: thus in general, but more particularly, by this a man may learn the necessity of the new birth, the insufficiency of our works, the need of Christ's righteousness, etc. Besides, by this a man may learn by talk what it is to repent, to believe, to pray, to suffer, or the like, by this also a man may learn what are the great promises and consolations of the gospel, to his own comfort. Further, by this a man may learn to refute false opinions, to vindicate the truth, and also to instruct the ignorant.

Faithful. All this is true, and glad am I to hear these things from you.

Talkative. Alas! The want of this is the cause that so few understand the need of faith and the necessity of a work of grace in their soul, in order to eternal life, but ignorantly live in the works of the law, by which a man can by no means obtain the Kingdom of Heaven.

Faithful. But by your leave, heavenly knowledge of these is the gift of God; no man attains to them by human industry, or only by the talk of them.

Talkative. All this I know very well. For a man can receive nothing except it be given him from Heaven; all is of grace, not of works. I could give you an hundred scriptures for the confirmation of this.

Faithful. Well then, said Faithful; what is that one thing that we shall at this time found our discourse upon?

Talkative. What you will. I will talk of things heavenly, or things earthly; things moral, or things evangelical; things sacred, or things profane; things past, or things to come; things foreign, or things at home; things more essential, or things circumstantial, provided that all be done to our profit.

Now did Faithful begin to wonder and stepping to Christian (for he walked all this while by himself), he said to him (but softly), "What a brave companion have we got! Surely this man will make a very excellent pilgrim."

At this Christian modestly smiled and said, "This man with whom you are so taken will beguile with this tongue of his twenty of them that know him not."

Faithful. Do you know him then?

Christian. Know him! Yes, better than he knows himself.

Faithful. Pray what is he?

Christian. His name is Talkative, he dwells in our town; I wonder that you should be a stranger to him, only I consider that our town is large.

Faithful. Whose son is he? And whereabout does he dwell?

Christian. He is the son of one Saywell, he dwelt in Prating Row; and he is known of all that are acquainted with him, by the name of Talkative in Prating Row, and notwithstanding his fine tongue, he is but a sorry fellow.

Faithful. Well, he seems to be a very pretty man.

Christian. That is, to them that have not thorough acquaintance with him, for he is best abroad; near home he is ugly enough. Your saying that he is a pretty man, brings to my mind what I have observed in the work of the painter whose pictures shows best at a distance, but very near, more unpleasing.

Faithful. But I am ready to think you do but jest, because you smiled.

Christian. God forbid that I should jest (though I smiled), in this matter, or that I should accuse any falsely; I will give you a further discovery of him: this man is for any company, and for any talk; as he tals now with you, so will he talk when he is on the ale-bench; and the more drink he has in his crown, the more of these things he has in his mouth; religion has no place in his heart, or house, or conversation; all he has lies in his tongue, and his religion is to make a noise therewith.

Faithful. Say you so! Then I am in this man greatly deceived.

Christian. Deceived? You may be sure of it. Remember the proverb, "They say and do not: but the Kingdom of God is not in word, but in powers." He talks of prayer, of repentance, of faith, and of the new birth, but he knows but only to talk of them. I have been in his family, and have observed him both at home and abroad; and I know what I say of him is the truth. His house is as empty of religion, as the white of an egg is of savour. There is there neither prayer nor sign of repentance for sin. Yea, the brute in his kind serves God far better than he. He is the very stain, reproach, and shame of religion to all that know him; it can hardly have a good word in all that end of the town where he dwells, through him. Thus say the common people that know him, "A saint abroad and a devil at home." His poor family finds it so, he is such a churl, such a railer at, and so unreasonable with his servants, that they neither know how to do for or speak to him. Men that have any dealings with him say 'tis better to deal with a Turk than with him, for fairer dealing they shall have at their hands. This Talkative, if it be possible, will go beyond them, defraud, beguile, and overreach them. Besides, he brings up his sons to follow his steps; and if he finds in any of them a foolish timorousness (for so he calls the first appearance of a tender conscience), he calls them fools and blockheads, and by no means will employ them in much, or speak to their commendations before others. For my part I am of opinion that he has, by his wicked life, caused many to stumble and fall; and will be, if God prevent not, the ruin of many more.

Faithful. Well, my brother, I am bound to believe you; not only because you say you know him, but also because like a Christian you make your reports of men. For I cannot think that you speak these things of ill will, but because it is even so as you say.

Christian. Had I known him no more than you, I might perhaps have thought of him as at the first you did. Yea, had he received this report, at their hands only, that are enemies to religion, I should have thought it had been a slander, a lot that often falls from bad men's mouths upon good men's names and professions. But all these things, yea, and a great many more as bad, of my own knowledge I can prove him guilty of. Besides, good men are ashamed of him, they can neither call him brother nor friend: the very naming of him among them makes them blush, if they know him.

Faithful. Well, I see that saying and doing are two things, and hereafter I shall better observe this distinction.

Christian. They are two things indeed, and are as diverse as are the soul and the body. For as the body without the soul is but a dead carcass; so, saying, if it be alone, is but a dead carcass also. The soul of religion is the practical part: "Pure religion and undefiled, before God and the Father, is this, to visit the fatherless and widows in their affliction, and to keep himself unspotted from the world." This Talkative is not aware of; he thinks that hearing and saying will make a good Christian and thus he deceives his own soul. Hearing is but as the sowing of the seed; talking is not sufficient to prove that fruit is indeed in the heart and life; and let us assure ourselves that at the day of doom, men shall be judged according to their fruits. It will not be said then, "Did you believe?" but, "Were you doers, or talkers only?" and accordingly shall they be judged. The end of the world is compared to our harvest, and you know men at harvest regard nothing but fruit. Not that anything can be accepted that is not of faith, but I speak this to show you how insignificant the profession of Talkative will be at that day.

Faithful. This brings to my mind that of Moses, by which he describes the beast that is clean. He is such a one that parts the hoof, and chews the cud only. The hare chews the cud, but yet is unclean, because he parts not the hoof. And this truly resembles Talkative; he chews the cud, he seeks knowledge, he chews upon the Word, but he divides not the hoof, he parts not with the way of sinners; but as the hare he retains the foot of a dog, or bear, and therefore he is unclean.

Christian. You have spoken, for aught I know, the true gospel sense of those texts; and I will add another thing. Paul calls some men, yea, and those great talkers too, "sounding brass, and tinkling cymbals"; that is, as he expounds them in another place, "Things without life, giving sound." Things without life, that is, without the true faith and grace of the gospel; and consequently, things that shall never be placed in the Kingdom of Heaven among those that are the children of life, though their sound by their talk be as if it were the tongue or voice of an angel.

Faithful. Well, I was not so fond of his company at first, but I am sick of it now. What shall we do to be rid of him?

Christian Take my advice, and do as I bid you, and you shall find that he will soon be sick of your company too, except God shall touch his heart and turn it.

Faithful. What would you have me to do?

Christian. Why, go to him, and enter into some serious discourse about the power of religion; and ask him plainly (when he has approved of it, for that he will) whether this thing be set up in his heart, house, or conversation.

Then Faithful stepped forward again and said to Talkative, "Come, what cheer? How is it now?"

Talkative. Thank you, well. I thought we should have had a great deal of talk by this time.

Faithful. Well, if you will, we will fall to it now; and since you left it with me to state the question, let it be this: how does the saving grace of God discover itself, when it is in the heart of man?

Talkative. I perceive then that our talk must be about the power of things; well, 'tis a very good question, and I shall be willing to answer you. And take my answer in brief thus: first, where the grace of God is in the heart, it causes there a great outcry against sin. Secondly . . .

Faithful. Nay, hold, let us consider of one at once. I think you should rather say, it shows itself by inclining the soul to abhor its sin.

Talkative. Why, what difference is there between crying out against and abhorring of sin?

Faithful. Oh! A great deal. A man may cry out against sin, of policy; but he cannot abhor it but by virtue of a godly antipathy against it. I have heard many cry out against sin in the pulpit, who yet can abide it well enough in the heart, and house, and conversation. Joseph's mistress cried out with a loud voice, as if she had been very holy; but she would willingly, notwithstanding that, have committed uncleanness with him. Some cry out against sin even as the mother cries out against her child in her lap, when she calls it slut and naughty girl, and then falls to hugging and kissing it.

Talkative. You try to catch me out, I perceive.

Faithful. No, not I, I am only for setting things right. But what is the second thing whereby you would prove a discovery of a work of grace in the heart?

Talkative. Great knowledge of gospel mysteries.

Faithful. This sign should have been first, but first or last it is also false. Knowledge, great knowledge may be obtained in the mysteries of the gospel, and yet no work or grace in the soul. Yea, if a man have all knowledge, he may yet be nothing, and so consequently be no child of God. When Christ said, "Do you know all these things?" and the disciples had answered, "Yes", He added, "Blessed are you if you do them." He does not lay the blessing in the knowing of them, but in the doing of them. For there is a knowledge that is not attended with doing: he that knows his master's will and does it not. A man may know like an angel and yet be no Christian: therefore your sign is not true. Indeed to know is a thing that pleases talkers and boasters, but to do is that which pleases God. Not that the heart can be good without knowledge; for without that the heart is naught. There is therefore knowledge, and knowledge. Knowledge that rests in the bare speculation of things, and knowledge that is accompanied with the grace of faith and love, which puts a man upon doing even the will of God from the heart. The first of these will serve the talker, but without the other the true Christian is not content. "Give me understanding, and I shall keep thy law, yea, I shall observe it with my whole heart."

Talkative. You try to catch me out again, this is not for edification.

Faithful. Well, if you please, propound another sign how this work of grace discovers itself where it is.

Talkative. Not I, for I see we shall not agree.

Faithful. Well, if you will not, will you give me leave to do it?

Talkative. You may use your liberty.

Faithful. A work of grace in the soul discovers itself, either to him that has it, or to bystanders.

To him that has it, thus. It gives him conviction of sin, especially of the defilement of his nature, and the sin of unbelief (for the sake of which he is sure to be damned, if he finds not mercy at God's hand by faith in Jesus Christ). This sight and sense of things works in him sorrow and shame for sin; he finds moreover revealed in him the saviour of the world, and the absolute necessity of closing with him for life, at the which she finds hungerings and thirstings after Him, to which hungerings and thirstings promise is made. Now according to the strength or weakness of his faith in his saviour, so is his joy and peace, so is his love to holiness, so are his desires to know Him more, and also to serve Him in this world. But though I say it discovers itself thus unto him yet it is but seldom that he is able to conclude that this is a work of grace, because his corruptions now, and his abused reason makes his mind to misjudge in this matter; therefore in him that has this work there is required a very sound judgment before he can with steadiness conclude that this is a work of grace.

To others it is thus discovered:

1 By an experimental confession of his faith in Christ.

2 By a life answerable to that confession, to wit, a life of holiness: heart holiness, family holiness (if he has a family) and by conversation holiness in the world; which in general teaches him inwardly to abhor his sin and himself for that in secret, to suppress it in his family, and to promote holiness in the world; not by talk only, as a hypocrite or talkative person may do, but by a practical subjection in faith and love to the power of the world. And now, sir, as to this brief description of the work of grace, and also the discovery of it, if you have aught to object, object. If not, then give me

leave to propound to you a second question.

Talkative. Nay, my part is not now to object, but to hear; let me therefore have your second question.

Faithful. It is this: do you experience the first part of this description of it? And does your life and conversation testify the same? Or stands your religion in word, or in tongue, and not in deed and truth? Pray, if you incline to answer me in this, say no more than you know that God above will say amen to; and so, nothing but what your conscience can justify you in. "For not he that commends himself is approved, but whom the Lord commends." Besides, to say I am thus and thus when my conversation and all my neighbours tell me I lie, is great wickedness.

Then Talkative at first began to blush, but recovering himself, thus he replied, "You come now to experience, to conscience, and God; and to appeal to him for justification of what is spoken. This kind of discourse I did not expect, nor am I disposed to give an answer to such questions, because I count not myself bound thereto, unless you take it upon you to be a catechiser; and, though you should so do, yet I may refuse to make you my judge; but I pray will you tell me why you ask me such questions?"

Faithful. Because I saw you forward to talk, and because I knew not that you had aught else but notion. Besides, to tell you all the truth, I have heard of you that you are a man whose religion lies in talk, and that your conversation gives this your mouth-profession the lie. They say you are a spot among Christians, and that religion fares the worse for your ungodly conversation, that some already have stumbled at your wicked ways, and that more are in danger of being destroyed thereby; your religion and an ale-house, and covetousness and uncleanness, and swearing and lying and vain company-keeping, etc. will stand together. The proverb is true of you which is said of a whore; to wit, that she is a shame to all women; so you are a shame to all people who profess religion.

Talkative. Since you are ready to take up reports, and to judge so rashly as you do, I cannot but conclude you are some peevish or melancholy man not fit to be discoursed with, and so adieu.

Then came up Christian and said to his brother, "I told you how it would happen, your words and his lusts could not agree; he had rather leave your company than reform his life: but he is gone as I said; let him go; the loss is no man's but his own; he has saved us the trouble of going from him: for he continuing, as I suppose he will do, as he is, he would have been but a blot in our company: besides, the apostle says, 'From such withdraw thyself'."

Faithful. But I am glad we had this little discourse with him, it may happen that he will think of it again; however, I have dealt plainly with him; and so am clear of his blood if he perishes.

Christian. You did well to talk so plainly to him as you did; there is but little of this faithful dealing with men nowadays, and that makes religion so stink in the nostrils of many, as it does. For they are these talkative fools, whose religion is only in word, and are debauched and vain in their conversation, that being so much admitted into the fellowship of the godly do stumble the world, blemish Christianity, and grieve the sincere. I wish that all men would deal with such, as you have done, then should they either be made more comformable to religion, or the company of saints would be too hot for them.

Then did Faithful say,

How Talkative at first lifts up his plumes!
How bravely does he speak! How he presumes
To drive down all before him! But so soon
As Faithful talks of heart-work, like the moon
That's past the full, into the wane he goes;
And so will all, but he that heart-work knows.

Thus they went on talking of what they had seen by the way; and so made the way easy, which would otherwise no doubt have been tedious to them: for now they went through a wilderness.

Now when they were got almost quite out of this wilderness, Faithful chanced to cast his eye back, and espied one coming after them, and he knew him. "Oh!" said Faithful to his brother, "who comes yonder?" Then Christian looked, and said, "It is my good friend Evangelist." "Ay, and my good friend too," said Faithful, "for 'twas he that set me the way to the gate." Now was Evangelist come up unto them, and thus saluted them.

Evangelist. Peace be with you, dearly beloved, and peace be to your helpers.

Christian. Welcome, welcome, my good Evangelist, the sight of your countenance brings to my remembrance your ancient kindness and unwearied labouring for my eternal good.

Faithful. And a thousand times welcome your company, O sweet Evangelist, how desirable is it to us, poor pilgrims!

Evangelist. How has it fared with you, my friends, since the time of our last parting? What have you met with, and how have you behaved yourselves?

Then Christian and Faithful told him of all things that had happened to them in the way; and how, and with what difficulty they had arrived to that place.

Evangelist. Right glad am I, not that you met with trials, but that you have been victors; and for that you have, notwithstanding many weaknesses, continued in the way to this very day.

I say, right glad am I of this thing, and that for my own sake and yours. I have sowed, and you have reaped, and the day is coming when both he that sowed, and they that reaped shall rejoice together; that is, if you hold out. For, in due time you shall reap, if you faint not. The crown is before you, and it is an incorruptible one; so run that you may obtain it. Some there be that set out for this crown, and after they have gone far for it, another comes in and takes it from them. Hold fast therefore as you have, let no man take your crown; you are not yet out of the gun-shot of the Devil: you have not resisted unto blood, striving against sin: let the Kingdom be always before you, and believe steadfastly concerning things that are invisible. Let nothing that is on this side of the other world get within you; and above all, look well to your own hearts, and to the lusts thereof; for they are deceitful above all things, and desperately wicked. Set your faces like a flint, you have all power in heaven and earth on your side.

Then Christian thanked him for his exhortation, but told him withal that they would have him speak further to them for their help in rest of the way; and the rather for that they well knew that he was a prophet, and could tell them of things that might happen unto them; and also how they might resist and overcome them. To which request Faithful also consented. So Evangelist began as follows.

Evangelist. My sons, you have heard in the words of the truth of the gospel, that you must through many tribulations enter into the Kingdom of Heaven. And again, that in every city, bonds and afflictions abide in you; and therefore you cannot expect that you should go long on your pilgrimage without them, in some sort or other. You have found something of the truth of these testimonies upon you already, and more will immediately follow. For now, as you see, you are almost out of this wilderness, and therefore you will soon come into a town that you will by and by see before you, and in that town you will be badly beset with enemies who will strain hard but they will kill you, and be you sure that one or both of you must seal the testimony which you hold, with blood: but be you faithful unto death, and the king will give you a crown of life. He that shall die there, although his death will be unnatural, and his pain perhaps great, he will yet have the better of his fellow; not only because he will be arrived at the Celestial City soonest, but because he will escape many miseries that the other will meet with in the rest of his journey. But when you are come to the town, and shall find fulfilled what I have here related, then remember your friend and acquit yourselves like men; and commit the keeping of your souls to your God, as unto a faithful creator.

Then I saw in my dream that when they were got out of the wilderness they presently saw a town before them, and the name of that town is Vanity; and at the town there is a fair kept called Vanity Fair. It is kept all the year long; it bears the name of Vanity Fair, because the town where 'tis kept is lighter than vanity; and also, because all that is there sold, or that comes thither, is vanity. As is the saying of the wise, "All that comes is vanity."

This fair is no new erected business, but a thing of ancient standing; I will show you the original of it.

Almost five thousand years ago, there were pilgrims walking to the Celestial City, as these two honest persons are; and Beelzebub, Apollyon, and Legion, with their companions, perceiving by the path that the pilgrims made that their way to the city lay through this town of Vanity, they contrived here to set up a fair; a fair wherein should be sold all sorts of vanity, and that it should last all the year long. Therefore at this fair are all such merchandise sold, as houses, lands, trades, places, honours, preferments, titles, countries, kingdoms, lusts, pleasures, and delights of all sorts, as whores, bawds, wives, husbands, children, masters, servants, lives, blood, bodies, souls, silver, gold, pearls, precious stones, and what not.

And moreover, at this fair there is at all times to be seen jugglings, cheats, games, plays, fools, apes, knaves, and rogues, and that of all sorts.

Here are to be seen too, and that for nothing, thefts, murders, adulteries, falsc-swearers, and that of a blood-red colour.

And as in other fairs of less moment there are the several rows and streets under their proper names, where such and such wares are vended: so here likewise, you have the proper places, rows, streets (viz countries and kingdoms), where the wares of this fair are soonest to be found: here is the Britain Row, the French Row, the Italian Row, the Spanish Row, the German Row, where several sorts of vanities are to be sold. But as in other fairs, some one commodity is as the chief of all the fair, so the ware of Rome and her merchandise is greatly promoted in this fair: only our English nation, with some others, have taken a dislike thereat.

Now, as I said, the way to the Celestial City lies just through this town, where this lusty fair is kept; and he that will go to the city, and yet not go through this town, must needs go out of the world. The Prince of Princes himself, when here, went through this town to his own country, and that upon a fair-day too. Yea, and I think it was Beelzebub, the chief lord of this fair, that invited him to buy of his vanities; yea, would have made him lord of the fair, would he but have done him reverence as he went through the town. Yea, because he was such a person of honour, Beelzebub had him from street to street, and showed him all the kingdom of the world in a little time, that he might if possible allure that blessed one, to cheapen and buy some of his vanities. But he had no mind to the merchandise, and therefore left the town without laying out so much as one farthing upon these vanities. This fair therefore is an ancient thing, of long standing, and a very great fair.

Now these pilgrims, as I said, must needs go through this fair: well, so they did; but behold, even as they entered into the fair, all the people in the fair were moved, and the town itself as it were in a hubbub about them; and that for several reasons.

First, the pilgrims were clothed with such kind of raiment as was diverse from the raiment of any that traded at that fair. The people therefore of the fair made a great gazing upon them. Some said they were fools, some they were bedlams, and some "They are outlandish-men."

Second, as they wondered at their apparel so they did likewise at their speech; for few could understand what they said. They naturally spoke the language of Canaan; but they that kept the fair, were the men of this world, so that from one end of the fair to the other, they seemed barbarians each to the other.

Third, but that which did not a little amuse the merchandisers was that these pilgrims set very light by all their wares, they cared not so much as to look upon them; and if they called upon them to buy, they would put their fingers in their ears, and cry, "Turn away my eyes from beholding vanity"; and look upwards, signifying that their trade and traffic was in Heaven.

One chanced mockingly, beholding the carriages of the men, to say to them, "What will you buy?" but they, looking gravely upon him, said, "We buy the truth." At that there was an occasion taken to despise the men the more; some mocking, some taunting, some speaking reproachfully and some calling upon others to smite them. At last things came to a hubbub and great stir in the fair, insomuch that all order was confounded. Now was word presently brought to the great one of the fair, who quickly came down and deputed some of his most trusty friends to take these men into examination about whom the fair was almost overturned. So the men were brought to examination; and they that sat upon them asked them whence they came, whither they went, and what they did there in such an unusual garb? The men told them that they were pilgrims and strangers in the world, and that they were going to their own country, which was the heavenly Jerusalem; and that they had given no occasion to the men of the town nor yet to the merchandisers thus to abuse them, and to stop them in their journey, except it was for that when one asked them what they would buy, they said they would buy the truth. But they that were appointed to examine them did not believe them to be any other than bedlams and mad, or else such as came to put all things into a confusion in the fair. Therefore they took them, and beat them, and besmeared them with dirt, and then put them into the cage, that they might be made a spectacle to all the men of the fair. There therefore they lay for some time, and were made the objects of any man's sport, or malice, or revenge, the great one of the fair laughing still at all that befell them. But the men being patient, and not rendering railing for railing but contrariwise blessing, and giving good words for bad, and kindness for injuries done, some men in the fair that were more observing and less prejudiced than the rest, began to check and blame the baser sort for their continual abuses done by them to the men. They therefore in angry manner let fly at them again, counting them as bad as the men in the cage, and telling them that they seemed confederates, and should be made partakers of their misfortunes. The others replied that for aught they could see, the men were quiet and sober, and intended nobody any harm; and that there were many that traded in their fair that were more worthy to be put into the cage, yea, and pillory too, than were the men that they had abused. Thus after divers words had passed on both sides (the men behaving themselves all the while very wisely and soberly before them), they fell to some blows among themselves and did harm one to another. Then were these two poor men brought before their examiners again, and there charged as being guilty of the late hubbub that had been in the fair. So they beat them pitifully, and hanged irons upon them, and led them in chains up and down the fair, for an example and a terror to others, lest any should further speak on their behalf, or join themselves unto them. But Christian and Faithful behaved themselves yet more wisely, and received the ignominy and shame that was cast upon them with so much meekness and patience, that it won to their side (though but few in comparison of the rest) several of the men in the fair. This put the other party yet into a greater rage, insomuch that they concluded the death of these two men. Wherefore they threatened that neither the cage, nor irons, should serve their turn, but that they should die for the abuse they had done and for deluding the men of the fair.

Then were they remanded to the cage again, until further order should be taken with them. So they put them in, and made their feet fast in the stocks.

Here also they called again to mind what they had heard from their faithful friend Evangelist, and were the more confirmed in their way and sufferings by what he told them would happen to them. They also now comforted each other that whose lot it was to suffer, even he should have the best on't; therefore each man secretly wished that he might have that preferment: but committing themselves to the all-wise disposition of Him that rules all things, with much content they stayed in the condition in which they were, until they should be otherwise disposed of.

Then a convenient time being appointed, they brought them forth to their trial in order to their condemnation. When the time was come, they were brought before their enemies and arraigned; the judge's name was Lord Hategood. Their indictment was one and the same in substance, though somewhat varying in form; the contents whereof was this:

> That they were enemies to, and disturbers of their trade; that they had made commotions and divisions in the town, and had won a party to their own most dangerous opinions, in contempt of the law of their prince.

Then Faithful began to answer that he had only set himself against that which had set itself against Him that is higher than the highest. "And", said he, "as for disturbance, I make none, being myself a man of peace; the party that were won to us were won by beholding our truth and innocence, and they are only turned from the worse to the better. And as to the king you talk of; since he is Beelzebub, the enemy of our Lord, I defy him and all his angels."

Then proclamation was made, that they that had aught to say for their lord the king against the prisoner at the bar should forthwith appear, and give their evidence. So there came in three witnesses, to wit, Envy, Superstition and Pickthank. They were then asked if they knew the prisoner at the bar and what they had to say for their lord the king against him.

Then stood forth Envy and said to this effect: "My lord, I have known this man a long time, and will attest upon my oath before this honourable bench, that he is . . .

Judge. Hold, give him his oath.

So they swore him. Then Envy said, "My lord, this man, notwithstanding his plausible name, is one of the vilest men in our country; he neither regards prince nor people, law nor custom, but does all that he can to possess all men with certain of his disloyal notions, which he in the general calls principles of faith and holiness. And in particular, I heard him once myself affirm that Christianity, and the customs of our town of Vanity were diametrically opposite, and could not be reconciled. By which saying, my lord, he does at once not only condemn all our laudable doings, but us in the doing of them."

Then did the Judge say to him, "Have you any more to say?"

Envy. My lord, I could say much more, only I would not be tedious to the court. Yet if need be, when the other gentlemen have given their evidence, rather than anything shall be wanting that will dispatch him, I will enlarge my testimony against him.

So he was bade stand by. Then they called Superstition, and bade him look upon the prisoner; they also asked what he could say for their lord the king against him. Then they swore him, so he began.

Superstition. My lord, I have no great acquaintance with this man, nor do I desire to have further knowledge of him; however, this I know, that he is a very pestilent fellow, from some discourse that the other day I had with him in this town. For then talking with him, I heard him say that our religion was naught, and such by which a man could by no means please God: which sayings of his, my lord, your lordship very well knows what necessarily thence will follow, to wit, that we still do worship in vain, are yet in our sins, and finally shall be damned; and this is what I have to say.

Then was Pickthank sworn, and bade say what he knew, on behalf of their lord the king against the prisoner at the bar.

Pickthank. My lord, and you gentlemen all, this fellow I have known of for a long time, and have heard him speak things that ought not be spoken. For he has railed on our noble Prince Beelzebub, and has spoken contemptibly of his honourable friends, whose names are the Lord Old Man, the Lord Carnal Delight, the Lord Luxurious, the Lord Desire of Vainglory, my old Lord Lechery, Sir Having Greedy, with all the rest of our nobility; and he has said moreover, that if all men were of his mind, if possible, there is not one of these noblemen should have any longer a being in this town. Besides, he has not been afraid to rail on you, my lord, who are now appointed to be his judge, calling you an ungodly villain, with many other such like vilifying terms, with which he has bespattered most of the gentry of our town.

When this Pickthank had told his tale, the judge directed his speech to the prisoner at the bar, saying, "You renegade, heretic, and traitor, have you heard what these honest gentlemen have witnessed against you?"

Faithful. May I speak a few words in my own defence?

Judge. Sirrah, sirrah, you deserve to live no longer, but to be slain immediately upon the place; yet that all men may see our gentleness towards you, let us hear what you have to say.

Faithful. I say then in answer to what Mr Envy has spoken, I never said aught but this, that what rule, or laws, or custom, or people, were flat against the word of God, are diametrically opposite to Christianity. If I have said amiss in this, convince me of my error, and I am ready here before you to make my recantation.

As to the second, to wit, Mr Superstition, and his charge against me, I said only this, that in the worship of God there is required a divine faith; but there can be no divine faith without a divine revelation of the will of God: therefore whatever is thrust into the worship of God that is not agreeable to divine revelation, cannot be done but by an human faith, which faith will not profit to eternal life.

As to what Mr Pickthank has said, I say (avoiding terms as that I am said to rail, and the like), that the prince of this town, with all the rabble his attendants by this gentleman named, are more fit for a being in Hell than in this town and country; and so the Lord have mercy upon me.

Then the judge called to the jury (who all this while stood by, to hear and observe), "Gentlemen of the jury, you see this man about whom so great an uproar has been made in this town: you have also heard what these worthy gentlemen have witnessed against him; also you have heard his reply and confession: it lies now in your breasts to hang him, or save his life. But yet I think meet to instruct you in our law.

"There was an act made in the days of Pharaoh the Great, servant to our prince, that lest those of a contrary religion should multiply and grow too strong for him, their males should be thrown into the river. There was also an act made in the days of Nebuchadnezzar the Great, another of his servants, that whoever would not fall down and worship his golden image should be thrown into a firey furnace. There was also an act made in the days of Darius, that who so, for some time, called upon any god but his, should be cast into the lions' den. Now the substance of these laws this rebel has broken, not only in thought (which is not to be borne), but also in word and deed, which must therefore needs be intolerable.

"For that of Pharaoh, his law was made upon a supposition, to prevent mischief, no crime being yet apparent; but here is a crime apparent. For the second and third, you see he disputes against our religion; and for the treason he has confessed he deserves to die the death."

Then went the jury out, whose names were Mr Blindman, Mr Nogood, Mr Malice, Mr Lovelust, Mr Liveloose, Mr Heady, Mr Highmind, Mr Enmity, Mr Liar, Mr Cruelty, Mr Hatelight, and Mr Implacable, who every one gave in his private verdict against him among themselves, and afterwards unanimously concluded to bring him in guilty before the judge. And first Mr Blindman, the foreman, said, "I see clearly that this man is a heretic." Then said Mr Nogood, "Away with such a fellow from the earth." "Ay", said Mr Malice, "for I hate the very looks of him." Then said Mr Lovelust, "I could never endure him." "Nor I", said Mr Liveloose, "for he would always be condemning my way." "Hang him, hang him," said Mr Heady. "A sorry scrub", said Mr Highmind. "My heart rises against him," said Mr Enmity. "He is a rogue," said Mr Liar. "Hanging is too good for him," said Mr Cruelty. "Let's dispatch him out of the way," said Mr Hatelight. Then said Mr Implacable, "Might I have all the world given me, I could not be reconciled to him, therefore let us forthwith bring him in guilty of death." And so they did, therefore he was presently condemned to be taken from the place where he was, to the place from whence he came, and there to be put to the most cruel death that could be invented.

They therefore brought him out to do with him according to their law; and first they scourged him, then they buffeted him, they they lanced his flesh with knives; after that they stoned him with stones, then pricked him with their swords, and last of all they burned him to ashes at the stake. Thus came Faithful to his end.

Now, I saw that there stood behind the multitude a chariot and a couple of horses, waiting for Faithful, who (so soon as his adversaries had dispatched him) was taken into it, and straightway was carried up through the clouds, with sound of trumpet, the nearest way to the Celestial Gate. But as for Christian, he had some respite, and was remanded back to prison; so he there remained for a space: but He that overrules all things, having the power of their rage in His own hand, so wrought it about that Christian for that time escaped them, and went his way.

And as he went he sang.

Well Faithful, you have faithfully professed
Unto thy Lord: with Him you shall be blessed;
When faithless ones with all their vain delights
Are crying out under their hellish plights,
Sing, Faithful, sing, and let your name survive,
For though they killed you, you are yet alive.

Now I saw in my dream that Christian went not forth alone, for there was one whose name was Hopeful (being made so by the beholding of Christian and Faithful in their words and behaviour, in their sufferings at the fair) who joined himself unto him, and entering into a brotherly covenant, told him that he would be his companion. Thus one died to make testimony to the truth, and another rises out of his ashes to be a companion with Christian. This Hopeful also told Christian that there were many more of the men in the fair that would take their time and follow after.

So I saw that quickly after they were got out of the fair they overtook one that was going before them, whose name was By Ends; so they said to him, "What countryman, sir, and how far go you this way?" He told them that he came from the town of Fair Speech, and he was going to the Celestial City (but told them not his name).

"From Fair Speech", said Christian, "are there any that be good live there?"

By Ends. Yes, I hope.

Christian. Pray sir, what may I call you?

By Ends. I am a stranger to you, and you to me; if you be going this way, I shall be glad of your company, if not, I must be content.

Christian. This town of Fair Speech, I have heard of it, and, as I remember, they say it's a wealthy place.

By Ends. Yes, I will assure you that it is, and I have very many rich kindred there.

Christian. Pray who are your kindred there, if a man may be so bold?

By Ends. Almost the whole town; and in particular, my Lord Turnabout, my Lord Timeserver, my Lord Fair Speech (from whose ancestors that town first took its name), also Mr Smoothman, Mr Facingbothways, Mr Anything, and the parson of our parish, Mr Twotongues, was my mother's own brother by father's side; and to tell you the truth, I am become a gentleman of good quality; yet my greatgrandfather was but a waterman, looking one way and rowing another; and I got most of my estate by the same occupation.

Christian. Are you a married man?

By Ends. Yes, and my wife is a very virtuous woman, the daughter of a virtuous woman. She was my Lady Faining's daughter, therefore she came of a very honourable family, and is arrived to such a pitch of breeding that she knows how to carry it to all, even to prince and peasant. 'Tis true, we somewhat differ in religion from those of the stricter sort, yet but in two small points: first, we never strive against wind and tide; secondly, we are always most zealous when religion goes in his silver slippers; we love much to walk with him in the street if the sun shines and the people applaud it.

Then Christian stepped a little at one side to his fellow Hopeful, saying, "It runs in my mind that this is one By Ends, of Fair Speech, and if it be he, we have as very a knave in our company as dwells in all these parts." Then said Hopeful, "Ask him: methinks he should not be ashamed of his name." So Christian came up with him again and said, "Sir, you talk as if you knew something more than all the world does, and if I take not my mark amiss, I deem I have half a guess of you: is not your name Mr By Ends of Fair Speech?"

By Ends. That is not my name, but indeed it is a nickname that is given me by some that cannot abide me, and I must be content to bear it as a reproach, as other good men have borne theirs before me.

Christian. But did you never give an occasion to men to call you by this name?

By Ends. Never, never! The worst that ever I did to give them an occasion to give me this name was that I had always the luck to jump in my judgment with the present way of the times, whatever it was, and my chance was to gain thereby; but if things are thus cast upon me, let me count them a blessing, but let not the malicious load me therefore with reproach.

Christian. I thought indeed that you were the man that I had heard of, and to tell you what I think I fear this name belongs to you more properly than you are willing we should think it does.

By Ends. Well, if you will thus imagine, I cannot help it. You shall find me a fair company-keeper, if you will still admit me your associate.

Christian. If you will go with us you must go against wind and tide, the which I perceive is against your opinion; you must also own religion in his rags, as well as when in his silver slippers, and stand by him too when bound in irons, as well as when he walks the streets with applause.

By Ends. You must not impose, nor lord it over my faith; leave me to my liberty, and let me go with you.

Christian. Not a step further, unless you will do in what I propound, as we.

Then said By Ends, "I shall never desert my old principles, since they are harmless and profitable. If I may not go with you, I must do as I did before you overtook me, even go by myself, until some overtake me that will be glad of my company."

Now I saw in my dream, that Christian and Hopeful forsook him, and kept their distance before him, but one of them looking back saw three men following Mr By Ends, and behold, as they came up with him, he made them a very low bow, and they also gave him a compliment. The men's names were Mr Hold the World, Mr Moneylove, and Mr Save All; men that Mr By Ends had formerly been acquainted with; for in their minority they were schoolfellows, and were taught by one Mr Gripeman, a schoolmaster in Lovegain, which is a market town in the country of Coveting in the north. This schoolmaster taught them the art of getting, either by violence, cozenage, flattery, lying or by putting on a guise of religion, and these four gentlemen had attained much of the art of their master, so that they could each of them have kept such a school themselves.

Well, when they had, as I said, thus saluted each other, Mr Moneylove said to Mr By Ends, "Who are they upon the road before us?" For Christian and Hopeful were yet within view.

By Ends. They are a couple of far countrymen, that, after their mode, are going on pilgrimage.

Mr Moneylove. Alas, why did they not stay, that we might have had their good company? For they, and we, and you sir, I hope, are all going on pilgrimage.

By Ends. We are so indeed, but the men before us are so rigid, and love so much their own notions, and do also so lightly esteem the opinions of others, that let a men be never so godly, yet if he jumps not with them in all things they thrust him quite out of their company.

Mr Save All. That's bad; but we read of some, that are righteous over-much, and such men's rigidness prevails with them to judge and condemn all but themselves. But I pray what and how many, were the things wherein you differed?

By Ends. Why, they after their headstrong manner conclude that it is duty to rush on their journey all weathers, and I am for waiting for wind and tide. They are for hazarding all for God at a clap, and I am for taking all advantages to secure my life and estate. They are for holding their notions, though all other men are against them, but I am for religion in what and so far as the times and my safety will bear it. They are for religion, when in rags and contempt, but I am for him when he walks in his golden slippers in the sunshine, and with applause.

Mr Hold the World. Ay, and hold you there still, good Mr By Ends, for, for my part, I can count him but a fool that having the liberty to keep what he has, shall be so unwise as to lose it. Let us be wise as serpents, 'tis best to make hay when the sun shines; you see how the bee lies still all winter and bestirs her then only when she can have profit with pleasure. God sends sometimes rain and sometimes sunshine; if they be such fools to go through the first, yet let us be content to take fair weather along with us. For my part I like that religion best that will stand with the security of God's good blessings unto us; for who can imagine, that is ruled by his reason, since God has bestowed upon us the good things of this life, but that He would have us keep them for His sake. Abraham and Solomon grew rich in religion. And Job says that a good man, "shall lay up gold as dust". He must not be such as the men before us, if they be as you have described them.

Mr Save All. I think that we are all agreed in this matter, and therefore there needs no more words about it.

Mr Moneylove. No, there needs no more words about this matter indeed, for he that believes neither Scripture nor reason (and you see we have both on our side) neither knows his own liberty, nor seeks his own safety.

Mr By Ends. My brethren, we are, as you see, going all on pilgrimage, and for our better diversion from things that are bad, give me leave to propound unto you this question:

Suppose a man, a minister, or a tradesman, should have an advantage lie before him to get the good blessings of this life, yet so that he can by no means come by them except, in appearance at least, he becomes extraordinary zealous in some points of religion that he meddled not with before: may he not use this means to attain his end, and yet be a right honest man?

Mr Moneylove. I see the bottom of your question, and with these gentlemen's good leave I will endeavour to shape you an answer. And first to speak to your question, as it concerns a minister himself. Suppose a minister, a worthy man, possessed but of a very small benefice, and has in his eye a greater, more fat and plump by far; he has also now an opportunity of getting of it; yet so as by being more studious, by preaching more frequently and zealously, and because the temper of the people requires it, by altering of some of his principles, for my part I see no reason but a man may do this (provided he has a call). Ay, and more a great deal besides, and yet be an honest man. Because:

1 His desire of a greater benefice is lawful (this cannot be contradicted) since 'tis set before him by providence; so then, he may get it if he can, making no question for conscience sake.

2 Besides, his desire after that benefice makes him more studious, a more zealous preacher, and so makes him a better man. Yea, makes him better improve his parts, which is according to the mind of God.

3 Now as for his complying with the temper of his people, by deserting, to serve them, some of his principles, this argues:
(1) That he is of a self-denying temper.
(2) Of a sweet and winning deportment.
(3) And so more fit for the ministerial function.

4 I conclude then that a minister that changes a small for a great, should not for so doing be judged as covetous, but rather, since he is improved in his parts and industry thereby, be counted as one that pursues his call and the opportunity put into his hand to do good.

And now to the second part of the question, which concerns the tradesman you mentioned: suppose such a one to have but a poor employ in the world, but by becoming religious he may mend his market, perhaps get a rich wife or more and far better customers to his shop, for my part I see no reason but that this may be lawfully done. Because:

1 To become religious is a virtue, by whatsoever means a man becomes so.

2 Nor is it unlawful to get a rich wife or more custom to one's shop.

3 Besides, the man that gets these by becoming religious, gets that which is good, of them that are good, by becoming good himself, so then here is a good wife and good customers, and good gain, and all these by becoming religious, which is good. Therefore to become religious to get all these is a good and profitable design.

This answer, thus made by this Mr Moneylove, to Mr By Ends' question, was highly applauded by them all; wherefore they concluded upon the whole, that it was most wholesome and advantageous. And because, as they thought, no man was able to contradict it, and because Christian and Hopeful were yet within call they joyfully agreed to assault them with the question as soon as they overtook them and the rather because they had opposed Mr By Ends before. So they called after them, and they stopped and stood still till they came up to them, but they concluded as they went that not By Ends, but old Mr Hold the World should propound the question to them, because, as they supposed, their answer to him would be without the remainder of that heat that was kindled betwixt Mr By Ends and them at their parting a little before.

So they came up to each other and after a short salutation Mr Hold the World propounded the question to Christian and his fellow, and bid them to answer it if they could.

Christian. Even a babe in religion may answer ten thousand such questions. For if it be unlawful to follow Christ for loaves, as it is, how much more abominable is it to make of Him and religion a stalking horse to get and enjoy the world. Nor do we find any other than heathens, hypocrites, devils and witches that are of this opinion.

1 Heathens, for when Hamor and Shechem had a mind to the daughter and cattle of Jacob, and saw that there was no way for them to come at them but by becoming circumcised, they say to their companions: "If every male of us be circumcised, as they are circumcised, shall not their cattle, and their substance, and every beast of theirs be ours?" Their daughters and their cattle were that which they

sought to obtain, and their religion the stalking horse they made use of to come at them. Read the whole story.

2 The hypocritical Pharisees were also of this religion, long prayers were their pretence, but to get widows' houses was their intent, and greater damnation was from God their judgment.

3 Judas the devil was also of this religion, he was religious for the bag, that he might be possessed of what was therein, but he was lost, cast away, and the very son of perdition.

4 Simon the witch was of this religion too, for he would have had the Holy Ghost that he might have got money therewith, and his sentence from Peter's mouth was according.

5 Neither will it out of my mind but that that man who takes up religion for the world will throw away religion for the world; for so surely as Judas designed the world in becoming religious, so surely did he also sell religion and his master for the same. To answer the question therefore affirmatively as I perceive you have done, and to accept as authentic such answer, is both heathenish, hypocritical and devilish, and your reward will be according to your works.

Then they stood staring one upon another, but had not wherewith to answer Christian. Hopeful also approved of the soundness of Christian's answer, so there was a great silence among them. Mr By Ends and his company also staggered, and kept behind, that Christian and Hopeful might outgo them.

Then said Christian to his fellow, If these men cannot stand before the sentence of men, what will they do with the sentence of God? And if they are mute when dealt with by vessels of clay, what will they do when they shall be rebuked by the flames of a devouring fire?"

Then Christian and Hopeful outwent them again, and went till they came at a delicate plain, called Ease, where they went with much content; but that plain was but narrow, so they were quickly got over it. Now at the further side of that plain was a little hill called Lucre, and in that hill a silver mine, which some of them that had formerly gone that way because of the rarity of it had turned aside to see; but going too near the brink of the pit, the ground being deceitful under them broke, and they were slain; some also had been maimed there, and could not to their dying day be their own men again.

Then I saw in my dream that a little off the road, over against the silver mine, stood Demas (gentleman-like), to call to passengers to come and see; who said to Christian and his fellow, "Ho, turn aside hither, and I will show you a thing."

Christian. What thing so deserving as to turn us out of the way?

Demas. Here is a silver mine, and some digging in it for treasure; if you will come, with a little pains you may richly provide for yourselves.

Hopeful. Let us go see.

Christian. Not I, I have heard of this place before now, and how many have there been slain; and besides, that treasure is a snare to those that seek it, for it hinders them in their pilgrimage.

Then Christian called to Demas saying, "Is not the place dangerous? Has it not hindered many in their pilgrimage?"

Demas. Not very dangerous, except to those that are careless.

But withal, he blushed as he spoke.

Then said Christian to Hopeful, Let us not stir a step, but still keep on our way.

Hopeful. I will warrant you, when By Ends come up, if he has the same invitations as we, he will turn in thither to see.

Christian. No doubt thereof, for his principles lead him that way, and a hundred to one but he dies there.

Then Demas called again, saying, "But will you not come over and see?"

Then Christian roundly answered, saying, "Demas, you are an enemy to the right ways of the Lord of this way, and have been already condemned for your own turning aside, by one of His Majesty's judges; and why seek you to bring us into the like condemnation? Besides, if we at all turn aside our Lord the King will certainly hear thereof; and will there put us to shame where we would stand with boldness before Him."

Demas cried again that he also was one of their fraternity and that if they would tarry a little, he also himself would walk with them.

Christian. What is your name? Is it not the same by which I have called you?

Demas. Yes, my name is Demas, I am the son of Abraham.

Christian. I know you, Gehazi was your great-grandfather, and Judas your father, and you have trod their steps. It is but a devilish prank that you use: your father was hanged for a traitor and you deserve no better reward. Assure yourself, that when we come to the king we will give Him word of this your behaviour.

Thus they went their way.

By this time By Ends and his companions were come again within sight, and they at the first beck went over to Demas. Now whether they fell into the pit by looking over the brink thereof, or whether they went down to dig, or whether they were smothered in the bottom by the damps that commonly arise, of these things I am not certain: but this I observed, that they never were seen again in the way.

Then sang Christian,

By Ends, and Silver Demas, both agree;
One calls, the other runs, that he may be
A sharer in his lucre: so these two
Take up in this world, and no further go.

Now I saw that just on the other side of this plain, the pilgrims came to a place where stood an old monument, hard by the highwayside, at the sight of which they were both concerned because of the strangeness of the form thereof; for it seemed to them as if it had been a woman transformed into the shape of a pillar. Here therefore, they stood looking and looking upon it, but could not for a time tell what they should make thereof. At last Hopeful espied written above upon the head thereof a writing in an unusual hand; but he being no scholar called to Christian (for he was learned) to see if he could pick out the meaning. So he came, and after a little laying of letters together he found the same to be thus, "Remember Lot's wife." So he read it to his fellow, after which they both concluded that that was the pillar of salt into which Lot's wife was turned for her looking back with a covetous heart when she was going from Sodom for safety. Which sudden and amazing sight gave them occasion of this discourse.

Christian. Ah, my brother, this is a seasonable sight, it came opportunely to us after the invitation which Demas gave us to come over to view the hill Lucre: and had we gone over as he desired us, and as you were inclining to do (my brother) we had, for aught I know, been made ourselves a spectacle for those that shall come after to behold.

Hopeful. I am sorry that I was so foolish, and am made to wonder that I am not now as Lot's wife; for wherein was the difference 'twixt her sin and mine? She only looked back, and I had a desire to go see. Let grace be adored, and let me be ashamed, that ever such a thing should be in my heart.

Christian. Let us take notice of what we see here for our help for time to come. This woman escaped one judgment; for she fell not by the destruction of Sodom, yet she was destroyed by another; as we see, she is turned into a pillar of salt.

Hopeful. True, and she may be to us both caution, and example; caution that we should shun her sin, or a sign of what judgment will overtake such as shall not be prevented by this caution. So Korah, Dathan, and Abiram, with two hundred and fifty men that perished in their sin, did also become a sign or example to others to beware. But above all I muse at one thing, to wit, how Demas and his fellows can stand so confidently yonder to look for that treasure, which this woman, but for looking behind her (for we read not that she stepped one foot out of the way), after was turned into a pillar of salt; specially since the judgement which overtook her did make her an example within sight of where they are, for they cannot choose but see her, did they but lift up their eyes.

Christian. It is a thing to be wondered at, and it argues that their heart is grown desperate in the case; and I cannot tell who to compare them to so fitly, as to them that pick pockets in the presence of the judge, or that will cut purses under the gallows. It is said of the men of Sodom that they were sinners exceedingly, because they were sinners before the Lord, that is, in His eyesight; and notwithstanding the kindnesses that He had showed them, for the land of Sodom was now like the Garden of Eden heretofore. This therefore provoked Him the more to jealousy, and made their plague as hot as the fire of the Lord out of Heaven could make it. And it is most rationally to be concluded that such, even such as these are, that shall sin in the sight, yea, and that too in spite of such examples that are set continually before them to caution them to the contrary, must be partakers of severest judgments.

Hopeful. Doubtless you have said the truth, but what a mercy is it, that neither you, but especially I, am not made myself this example: this ministers occasion to us to thank God, to fear before Him, and always to remember Lot's wife.

I saw then that they went on their way to a pleasant river, which David the King called the "River of God"; but, John, "The River of the Water of Life". Now their way lay just upon the bank of the river. Here therefore Christian and his companion walked with great delight; they drank also of the water of the river which was pleasant and enlivening to their weary spirits. Besides, on the banks of the river, on either side, were green trees that bore all manner of fruit; and the leaves of the trees were good for medicine. With the fruit of these trees they were also much delighted, and the leaves they ate to prevent surfeits, and other diseases that are incident to those that heat their blood by travels. On either side of the river was also a meadow, curiously beautified with lilies and it was green all the year long. In this meadow they lay down and slept, for here they might lie down safely. When they awoke, they gathered again of the fruit of the trees, and drank again of the water of the river, and then lay down again to sleep. Thus they did several days and nights. Then they sang,

Behold how these crystal streams do glide
To comfort pilgrims by the highway side;
The meadows green besides their fragrant smell,
Yield dainties for them; and he that can tell
What pleasant fruit, yea leaves, these trees do yield,
Will soon sell all, that he may buy this field.

So when they were disposed to go on (for they were not as yet at their journey's end) they ate and drank and departed.

Now I beheld in my dream that they had not journeyed far but the river and the way for a time parted. At which they were not a little sorry, yet they dared not go out of the way. Now the way from the river was rough, and their feet tender by reason of their travels; so the soul of the pilgrims was much discouraged, because of the way. Wherefore still as they went on they wished for better way. Now a little before them there was on the left hand of the road, a meadow, and a stile to go over into it, and that meadow is called By Path Meadow. Then said Christian to his fellow, "If this meadow lies along by our wayside, let's go over into it." Then he went to the stile to see, and behold, a path lay along by the way on the other side of the fence. "'Tis according to my wish," said Christian, "here is the easiest going. Come, good Hopeful, and let us go over."

Hopeful. But how if this path should lead us out of the way?

Christian. That's not like, look, does it not go along by the wayside?

So Hopeful, being persuaded by his fellow went after him over the stile. When they were gone over and were got into the path, they found it very easy for their feet; and withal, they, looking before them, espied a man walking as they did (and his name was Vainconfidence); so they called after him, and asked him whither that way led. He said, "To the Celestial Gate." "Look, said Christian", did not I tell you so? By this you may see we are right." So they followed, and he went before them. But behold the night came on, and it grew very dark; so that they that were behind lost the sight of him that went before.

He therefore that went before (Vainconfidence by name) not seeing the way before him, fell into a deep pit, which was on purpose there made by the prince of those grounds to catch vainglorious fools withal, and was dashed in pieces with his fall.

Now Christian and his fellow heard him fall. So they called to know the matter but there was none to answer, only they heard a groaning. Then said Hopeful, "Where are we now?" Then was his fellow silent, as mistrusting that he had led him out of the way. And now it began to rain, and thunder, and lighten in a very dreadful manner, and the water rose fast.

Then Hopeful groaned in himself, saying, "Oh that I had kept on my way!"

Christian. Who could have thought that this path should have led us out of the way?

Hopeful. I was afraid on't at very first, and therefore gave you that gentle caution.

I would have spoke plainer, but that you are older than I.

Christian. Good brother, be not offended, I am sorry I have brought you out of the way, and that I have put you into such eminent danger; pray, my brother, forgive me, I did not do it of an evil intent.

Hopeful. Be comforted my brother, for I forgive you; and believe too, that this shall be for our good.

Christian. I am glad I have with me a merciful brother; but we must not stand thus, let's try to go back again.

Hopeful. But, good brother, let me go before.

Christian. No, if you please let me go first; that if there be any danger I may be first therein, because by my means we are both gone out of the way.

Hopeful. No, you shall not go first, for your mind being troubled may lead you out of the way again.

Then for their encouragement, they heard the voice of one, saying, "Let your heart be towards the highway, even the way that you went turn again." But by this time the waters were greatly risen, by reason of which the way of going back was very dangerous. (Then I thought that it is easier going out of the way when we are in, than going in when we are out.) Yet they adventured to go back; but it was so dark, and the flood was so high, that in their going back, they had like to have been drowned nine or ten times.

Neither could they, with all the skill they had, get again to the stile that night. Wherefore at last, lighting under a little shelter, they sat down there till the day broke; but being weary, they fell asleep. Now there was not far from the place where they lay, a castle called Doubting Castle, the owner whereof was Giant Despair, and it was in his gounds they now were sleeping. Wherefore he getting up in the morning early and walking up and down in his fields, caught Christian and Hopeful asleep in his grounds. Then with a grim and surly voice he bade them awake, and asked them whence they were and what they did in his grounds. They told him they were pilgrims, and that they had lost their way. Then said the giant, "You have this night trespassed on me, by trampling in, and lying on my grounds, and therefore you must go along with me." So they were forced to go, because he was stronger than they. They also had but little to say, for they knew themselves at fault. The giant therefore drove them before him and put them into his castle, into a very dark dungeon, nasty and stinking to the spirit of these two men. Here then they lay from Wednesday morning till Saturday night, without one bit of bread or drop of drink, or any light, or any to ask how they did. They were therefore here in evil case, and were far from friends and acquaintance. Now in this place, Christian had double sorrow, because 'twas through his unadvised haste that they were brought into this distress.

Now Giant Despair had a wife, and her name was Diffidence. So when he was gone to bed, he told his wife what he had done; to wit, that he had taken a couple of prisoners, and cast them into his dungeon, for trespassing on his grounds. Then he asked her also what he had best to do further to them. so she asked him what they were, whence they came, and whither they were bound; and he told her. Then she counselled him that when he arose in the morning, he should beat them without any mercy. So when he arose, he took him a grievous crab-tree cudgel and went down into the dungeon to them; and there, first fell to rating of them as if they were dogs, although they gave him never a word of distaste; then he fell upon them, and beat them fearfully, in such sort, that they were not able to help themselves, or to turn them upon the floor. This done, he withdrew and left them there to condole their misery, and to mourn under their distress, so all that day they spent the time in nothing but sighs and bitter lamentations. The next night she, talking with her husband about them further, and understanding that they were yet alive, did advise him to counsel them to make away themselves. So when morning was come, he went to them in a surly manner, as before, and perceiving them to be very sore with the stripes that he had given them the day before, he told them that since they were never like to come out of that place their only way would be forthwith to make an end of themselves, either with knife, halter or poison. "For why", said he, "should you choose life, seeing it is attended with so much bitterness?" But they desired him to let them go; with that he looked ugly upon them and rushing to them had doubtless made an end of them himself, but that he fell into one of his fits (for he sometimes in sunshine weather fell into fits) and lost (for a time) the use of his hand. Wherefore he withdrew, and left them (as before) to consider what to do. Then did the prisoners consult between themselves, whether 'twas best to take his counsel or no: and thus they began to discourse.

Christian. Brother, what shall we do? The life that we now live is miserable; for my part, I know not whether it is best to live thus or to die out of hand? "My soul chooseth strangling rather than life"; and the grave is more easy for me than this dungeon: shall we be ruled by the giant?

Hopeful. Indeed our present condition is dreadful, and death would be far more welcome to me than thus for ever to abide: but yet let us consider, the lord of the country to which we are going has said, "You shall do no murder", no not to another man's person; much more then are we forbidden to take his counsel to kill ourselves. Besides, he that kills another can but commit murder upon his body; but for one to kill himself is to kill body and soul at once. And moreover, my brother, you talk of ease in the grave; but have you forgotten the Hell whither, for certain, the murderers go? For no murderer has eternal life. And, let us consider again, that all the law is not in the hand of Giant Despair: others, so far as I can understand, have been taken by him, as well as we, and yet have escaped out of his hand: who knows, but that God that made the world may cause that Giant Despair may die; or that, at some time or other he may forget to lock us in; or but he may in short time have another of his fits before us, and may lose the use of his limbs? And if ever that should come to pass again, for my part I am resolved to pluck up the heart of a man and to try my utmost to get from under his hand. I was a fool that I did not try to do it before. But however, my brother, let's be patient, and endure a while; the time may come that may give us a happy release: but let us not be our own murderers.

With these words, Hopeful at present did moderate the mind of his brother; so they continued together (in the dark) that day, in their said and doleful condition.

Well, towards evening the giant went down into the dungeon again, to see if his prisoners had taken his counsel; but when he came there he found them alive, and truly, alive was all: for now, what for want of bread and water, and by reason of the wounds they received when he beat them, they could do little but breathe. But, I say, he found them alive, at which he fell into a grievous rage, and told them that seeing they had disobeyed his counsel, it should be worse with them than if they had never been born.

At this they trembled greatly, and I think that Christian fell into a swoon; but coming a little to himself again, they renewed their discourse about the giant's counsel; and whether yet they had best to take it or no. Now Christian again seemed to be for doing it, but Hopeful made his second reply as follows:

Hopeful. My brother, rememberest you now how valiant you have been heretofore. Apollyon could not crush you, nor could all that you did hear, or see, or feel in the Valley of the Shadow of Death; what hardship, terror, and amazement have you already gone through, and are you now nothing but fear? You see that I am in the dungeon with you, a far weaker man by nature than you are: also this giant has wounded me as well as you; and has also cut off the bread and water from my mouth; and with you I mourn without the light: but let's exercise a little more patience. Remember how you played the man at Vanity Fair, and were neither afraid of the chain nor cage, nor yet of bloody death. Wherefore let us (at least to avoid the shame that becomes not a Christian to be found in) bear up with patience as well as we can.

Now night being come again, and the giant and his wife being in bed, she asked him concerning the prisoners, and if they had taken his counsel: to which he replied, "They are sturdy rogues, they choose rather to bear all hardship, than to make away with themselves." Then said she, "Take them into the castle-yard tomorrow, and show them the bones and skulls of those that you have already dispatched; and make them believe ere a week comes to an end you also will tear them in pieces as you have done their fellows before them.

So when the morning was come the giant went to them again, and took them into the castle-yard, and showed them as his wife had bidden him. "These", said he, "were pilgrims as you are, once, and they trespassed in my grounds as you have done; and when I thought fit, I tore them in pieces; and so within ten days I will do you. Go, get you down to your den again." And with that he beat them all the way thither. They lay therefore all day on Saturday in a lamentable case, as before. Now when night was come, and when Mrs Diffidence and her husband the Giant were got to bed, they began to renew their discourse of their prisoners, and withal, the old giant wondered that he could neither by his blows nor counsel bring them to an end. And with that his wife replied, "I fear", said she, "that they live in hope that some will come to relieve them, or that they have pick-locks about them by the means of which they hope to escape." "And sayest thou so, my dear," said the giant, "I will therefore search them in the morning."

Well, on Saturday about midnight they began to pray, and continued in prayer till almost break of day.

Now a little before it was day, good Christian, as one half amazed, broke out in this passionate speech, "What a fool", said he, "am I, thus to lie in a stinking dungeon, when I may as well walk at liberty. I have a key in my bosom, called Promise, that will (I am persuaded) open any lock in Doubting Castle." Then said Hopeful, "That's good news, good brother, pluck it out of thy bosom, and try." Then Christian pulled it out of his bosom and began to try at the dungeon door, whose bolt (as he turned the key) gave back, and the door flew open with ease, and Christian and Hopeful both came out. Then he went to the outward door that leads into the castle-yard and with his key opened the door also. After he went to the iron gate, for that must be opened too, but that lock went damnable hard, yet the key did open it; then they thrust open the gate to make their escape with speed, but that gate, as it opened, made such a creaking that it waked Giant Despair, who hastily rising to pursue his prisoners felt his limbs to fail, for his fits took him again, so that he could by no means go after them. Then they went on, and came to the king's highway again, and so were safe, because they were out of his jurisdiction.

Now when they were gone over the stile, they began to contrive with themselves what they should do at that stile to prevent those that should come after from falling into the hands of Giant Despair. So they consented to erect there a pillar, and to engrave upon the side thereof: "Over the stile is the way to Doubting Castle, which is kept by Giant Despair, who despises the king of the Celestial Country, and seeks to destroy His holy pilgrims." Many therefore that followed after read what was written, and escaped the danger. This done, they sang as follows:

> Out of the way we went, and then we found
> What 'twas to tread upon forbidden ground;
> And let them that come after have a care,
> Lest heedlessness makes them as we to fare,
> Lest they for trespassing his prisoners are,
> Whose castle's Doubting, and whose name's Despair.

They went then till they came to the Delectable Mountains, which mountains belong to the lord of that hill of which we have spoken before; so they went up to the mountains to behold the gardens, and orchards, the vineyards, and fountains of water, where also they drank, and washed themselves, and did freely eat of the vineyards. Now there were on the tops of these mountains shepherds feeding their flocks, and they stood by the highway side. The pilgrims therefore went to them, and leaning upon their staves (as is common with weary pilgrims, when they stand to talk with any by the way), they asked, "Whose delectable mountains are these? And whose be the sheep that feed upon them?"

Shepherds. These mountains are Immanuel's land, and they are within sight of his city, and the sheep also are His, and He laid down His life for them.

Christian. Is this the way to the Celestial City?

Shepherds. You are just in your way.

Christian. How far is it thither?

Shepherds. Too far for any but those that shall get thither indeed.

Christian. Is the way safe or dangerous?

Shepherds. Safe for those whom it is

to be safe, "but transgressors shall fall therein".

Christian. Is there in this place any relief for pilgrims that are weary and faint in this way?

Shepherds. The lord of these mountains has given us a charge, "Not to be forgetful to entertain strangers": therefore the good of the place is before you.

I saw also in my dream that when the shepherds perceived that they were wayfaring men they also put questions to them to which they made answer as in other places, as, "Whence come you?" and, "How got you into the way?" and, "By what means have you so persevered therein? For but few of them that begin to come hither, do show their face on these mountains." But when the shepherds heard their answers, being pleased therewith, they looked very lovingly upon them, and said, "Welcome to the Delectable Mountains."

The shepherds, I say, whose names were Knowledge, Experience, Watchful, and Sincere, took them by the hand, and had them to their tents, and made them partake of that which was ready at present. They said moreover, "We would that you should stay here a while, to acquaint with us, and yet more to solace yourselves with the good of these delectable mountains." They then told them that they were content to stay; and so they went to their rest that night, because it was very late.

Then I saw in my dream that in the morning the shepherds called up Christian and Hopeful to walk with them upon the mountains. So they went forth with them, and walked a while, having a pleasant prospect on every side. Then said the shepherds one to another, "Shall we show these pilgrims some wonders?" So when they had concluded to do it, they had them first to the top of a hill called Error, which was very steep on the furthest side, and bid them look down to the bottom. So Christian and Hopeful looked down and saw at the bottom several men dashed all to pieces by a fall that they had from the top. Then said Christian, "What means this?" The shepherds answered, "Have you not heard of them that were made to err by hearkening to Hymeneus and Philetus, as concerning the faith of the resurrection of the body?" They answered, "Yes". Then said the shepherds, "Those that you see lying dashed in pieces at the bottom of this mountain are they; and they have continued to this day unburied (as you see) for an example to others to take heed how they clamber too high, or how they come too near the brink of this mountain."

Then I saw that they had them to the top of another mountain, and the name of that is Caution, and bid them look afar off; which when they did, they perceived, as they thought, several men walking up and down among the tombs that were there. And they perceived that the men were blind, because they stumbled sometimes upon the tombs, and because they could not get out from among them. Then said Christian, "What means this?"

The shepherds then answered, "Did you not see a little below these mountains a stile that led into a meadow on the left hand of this way? They answered, "Yes". Then said the shepherds, "From that stile there goes a path that leads directly to Doubting Castle, which is kept by Giant Despair; and these men (pointing to them among the tombs) came once on pilgrimage, as you do now, even till they came to that same stile. And because the right way was rough in that place, they chose to go out of it into that meadow, and there were taken by Giant Despair, and cast into Doubting Castle; where, after they had a while been kept in the dungeon, he at last did put out their eyes, and led them among those tombs, where he has left them to wander to this very day, that the saying of the wise man might be fulfilled, "He that wanders out of the way of understanding, shall remain in the congregation of the dead." Then Christian and Hopeful looked one upon another, with tears gushing out, but yet said nothing to the shepherds.

Then I saw in my dream that the shepherds had them to another place, in a valley, where was a door in the side of an hill; and they opened the door, and bid them look in. They looked in therefore, and saw that within it was very dark and smoky; they also thought that they heard there a lumbering noise as of fire and a cry of some tormented, and that they smelt the scent of brimstone. Then said Christian, "What means this?" The shepherds told them, saying, "This is a byway to Hell, a way that hypocrites go in at, namely, such as sell their birthright with Esau, such as sell their master with Judas, such as blaspheme the gospel with Alexander, and that lie and dissemble with Ananias and Sapphira his wife.

Then said Hopeful to the shepherds, "I perceive that these had on them, even every one, a show of pilgrimage as we have now, had they not?"

Shepherd. Yes, and held it a long time too.

Hopeful. How far might they go on pilgrimage in their day, since they notwithstanding were thus miserably cast away?

Shepherd. Some further, and some not so far as these mountains.

Then said the pilgrims one to another, "We had need cry to the strong for strength."

Shepherd. Ay, and you will have need to use it when you have it, too.

By this time the pilgrims had a desire to go forwards, and the shepherds a desire they should; so they walked together towards the end of the mountains. Then said the shepherds one to another, "Let us here show to the pilgrims the gates of the Celestial City, if they have skill to look through our perspective glass." The pilgrims then lovingly accepted the motion: so they had them to the top of a high hill called Clear, and gave them their glass to look. Then they essayed to look, but the remembrance of that last thing that the shepherds had showed them made their hands shake; by means of which impediment they could not look steadily through the glass; yet they thought they saw something like the gate, and also some of the glory of the place. Then they went away and sang.

Thus by the shepherds, secrets are
revealed,
Which from all other men are kept
concealed:
Come to the shepherds then, if you
would see
Things deep, things hid, and that
mysterious be.

When they were about to depart, one of the shepherds gave them a note of the way. Another of them bade them, "Beware of the flatterer." The third bade them, "Take heed that they sleep not upon the enchanted ground." And the fourth bade them "Godspeed." So I awoke from my dream.

And I slept and dreamed again, and saw the same two pilgrims going down the mountains along the highway towards the city. Now a little below these mountains, on the left hand, lies the country of Conceit; from which country there comes into the way in which the pilgrims walked a little crooked lane. Here therefore they met with a very brisk lad, that came out of that country; and his name was Ignorance. So Christian asked him from what parts he came and whither he was going.

Ignorance. Sir, I was born in the country that lies off there, a little on the left hand; and I am going to the Celestial City.

Christian. But how do you think to get in at the gate, for you may find some difficulty there?

Ignorance. As other good people do.

Christian. But what have you to show at that gate, that may cause that the gate should be opened unto you?

Ignorance. I know my Lord's will, and I have been a good liver. I pray every man his own; I pray, fast, pay tithes, and give alms, and have left my country, for whither I am going.

Christian. But you came not in at the Wicket Gate that is at the head of this way: you came in hither through that same crooked lane, and therefore I fear, however you may think of yourself, when the reckoning day shall come you will have laid to your charge that you are a thief and a robber instead of getting admittance into the city.

Ignorance. Gentleman, you are utter strangers to me, I know you not, be content to follow the religion of your country, and I will follow the religion of mine. I hope all will be well. And as for the gate that you talk of, all the world knows that that is a great way from our country. I cannot think that any man in all our parts so much as knows the way of it; nor need it matter whether they do or no, since we have, as you see, a fine, pleasant, green lane, that comes down from our country the next way into it.

When Christian saw that the man was wise in his own conceit, he said to Hopeful, whisperingly, "There is more hope of a fool than of him." And said moreover, "When he that is a fool walks by the way, his wisdom fails him, and he says to everyone that he is a fool. What, shall we talk further with him? Or outgo him at present, and so leave him to think of what he has heard already, and then stop again for him afterwards, and see if by degrees we can do any good of him?" Then said Hopeful,

Let Ignorance a little while now muse
On what is said, and let him not refuse
Good counsel to embrace, lest he remain
Still ignorant of what's the chiefest gain.
God says those that no understanding have,
Although He made them, them He will not save.

He further added "It is not good, I think, to say all to him at once; let us pass him by, if you will, and talk to him anon, even as he is able to bear it."

So they both went on, and Ignorance he came after. Now when they had passed him a little way, they entered into a very dark lane where they met a man whom seven devils had bound with seven strong cords, and were carrying him back to the door that they saw in the side of the hill. Now good Christian began to tremble, and so did Hopeful his companion. Yet as the devils led away the man, Christian looked to see if he knew him, and he thought it might be one Turnaway that dwelt in the town of Apostasy. But he did not perfectly see his face, for he did hang his head like a thief that is found: but being gone past, Hopeful looked at him, and espied on his back a paper with this inscription, "Wanton professor, and damnable apostate". Then said Christian to his fellow, "Now I call to remembrance that which was told me of a thing that happened to a good man hereabout. The name of the man was Little Faith, but a good man, and he dwelt in the town of Sincere. The thing was this: at the entering in of this passage there comes down from Broadway Gate a lane, called Deadman's Lane; so called because of the murders that are commonly done there. And this Little Faith, going on pilgrimage as we do now, chanced to sit down there and slept. Now there happened at that time to come down that lane from Broadway-gate, three sturdy rogues, and their names were Faintheart, Mistrust and Guilt (three brothers), and they, espying Little Faith where he was, came galloping up with speed. Now the good man was just awakened from his sleep, and was getting up to go on his journey. So they came all up to him, and with threatening language bade him stand. At this Little Faith looked as white as a clout, and had neither power to fight, nor fly. Then said Faintheart, "Deliver your purse," but he making no haste to do it (for he was loth to lose his money), Mistrust ran up to him, and thrusting his hand into his pocket, pulled out thence a bag of silver. Then he cried out, "Thieves, thieves." With that Guilt with a great club that was in his hand struck Little Faith on the head, and with that blow felled him flat to the ground where he lay bleeding as one that would bleed to death. All this while the thieves stood by. But at last, they hearing that some were upon the road, and fearing lest it should be one Greatgrace that dwells in the city of Good Confidence, they betook themselves to their heels, and left this good man to shift for himself. Now after a while Little Faith came to himself, and getting up, made shift to scrabble on his way. This was the story."

Hopeful. But did they take from him all that ever he had?

Christian. No: the place where his jewels were, they never ransacked, so those he kept still; but as I was told, the good man was much afflicted for his loss. For the thieves got most of his spending money. That which they got not (as I said) were jewels, also he had a little odd money left, but scarce enough to bring him to his journey's end; nay (if I was not misinformed), he was forced to beg as he went, to keep himself alive (for his jewels he might not sell). But beg and do what he could, he went (as we say) with many a hungry belly the most part of the rest of the way.

Hopeful. But is it not a wonder they got not from him his certificate, by which he was to receive his admittance at the Celestial Gate?

Christian. 'Tis a wonder, but they got not that; though they missed it not through any good cunning of his, for he being dismayed with their coming upon him, had neither power nor skill to hide anything, so 'twas more by good providence than by his endeavour that they missed of that good thing.

Hopeful. But it must needs be a comfort to him that they got not this jewel from him.

Christian. It might have been great comfort to him, had he used it as he should; but they that told me the story said that he made but little use of it all the rest of the way; and that because of the dismay that he had in their taking away his money, indeed he forgot it a great part of the rest of the journey; and besides, when at any time it came into his mind, and he began to be comforted therewith, then would fresh thoughts of his loss come again upon him, and those thoughts would swallow up all.

Hopeful. Alas poor man! This could not but be a great grief unto him.

Christian. Grief! Ay, a grief indeed! Would it not have been so to any of us, had we been used as he, to be robbed and wounded too, and that in a strange place as he was? 'Tis a wonder he did not die with grief, poor heart! I was told that he scattered almost all the rest of the way with nothing but doleful and bitter complaints, telling also to all that overtook him, or that he overtook in the way as he went, where he was robbed, and how, who they were that did it, and what he lost, how he was wounded, and that he hardly escaped with life.

Hopeful. But 'tis a wonder that his necessities did not put him upon selling or pawning some of his jewels, that he might have wherewith to relieve himself in his journey.

Christian. You talk like one upon whose head is the shell to this very day: for what should he pawn them? Or to whom should he sell them? In all that country where he was robbed his jewels were not accounted of, nor did he want that relief which could from thence be administered to him. Besides, had his jewels been missing at the gate of the Celestial City, he had (and that he knew well enough) been excluded from an inheritance there; and that would have been worse to him than the appearance and villainy of ten thousand thieves.

Hopeful. Why are you so tart, my brother? Esau sold his birthright, and that for a mess of potage, and that birthright was his greatest jewel; and if he, why might not Little Faith do so too?

Christian. Esau did sell his birthright indeed, and so do many besides; and by so doing exclude themselves from the chief blessing, as also that coward did. But you must put a difference betwixt Esau and Little Faith, and also betwixt their estates. Esau's birthright was typical, but Little Faith's jewels were not so. Esau's belly was his god, but Little Faith's belly was not so. Esau's want lay in his fleshly appetite, Little Faith's did not so. Besides, Esau could see no further than to the fulfilling of his lusts. "For I am at the point to die," said he, "and what good will this birthright do me?" But Little Faith, though it was his lot to have but a little faith, was by his little faith kept from such extravagancies; and made to see and prize his jewels more than to sell them, as Esau did his birthright. You read not anywhere that Esau had faith, no not so much as a little: therefore no marvel if where the flesh alone bears sway (as it will in that man where no faith is to resist) if he sells his birthright, and his soul and all, and that to the Devil of Hell. For it is with such, as it is with the ass, "Who in her occasions cannot be turned away". When their minds are set upon their lusts, they will have them whatever they cost. But Little Faith was of another temper, his mind was on things divine; his livelihood was upon things that were spiritual and from above; therefore to what end should he that is of such a temper sell his jewels (had there been any that would have bought them) to fill his mind with empty things? Will a man give a penny to fill his belly with hay? Or can you persuade the turtle dove to live upon carrion like the crow? Though faithless ones can for carnal lusts pawn, or mortgage, or sell what they have, and themselves outright to boot; yet they that have faith, saving faith, though but a little of it, cannot do so. Here therefore, my brother, is your mistake.

Hopeful. I acknowledge it; but yet your severe reflection had almost made me angry.

Christian. Why, I did but compare you to some of the birds that are of the brisker sort, who will run to and fro in untrodden paths with the shell upon their heads: but pass by that and consider the matter under debate, and all shall be well betwixt you and me.

Hopeful. But Christian, these three fellows, I am persuaded in my heart, are but a company of cowards: would they have run else, think you, as they did, at the noise of one that was coming on the road? Why did not Little Faith pluck up a greater heart? He might, methinks, have stood one brush with them, and have yielded when there had been no remedy.

Christian. That they are cowards many have said, but few have found it so in the time of trial. As for a great heart, Little Faith had none; and I perceive by you, my brother, had you been the man concerned, you are but for a brush and then to yield. And verily, since this is the height of your stomach now they are at a distance from us, should they appear to you as they did to him, they might put you to second thoughts.

But consider again, they are but journeymen thieves, they serve under the King of the Bottomless Pit; who if need be will come in to their aid himself and his voice is as the roaring of a lion. I myself have been engaged as this Little Faith was, and I found it a terrible thing. These three villains set upon me, and I beginning like a Christian to resist, they gave but a call and in came their master. I would, as the saying is, have given my life for a penny; but that, as God would have it, I was clothed with armour of proof. Ay, and yet, though I was so harnessed, I found it hard work to acquit myself like a man; no man can tell what in that combat attends us but he that has been in the battle himself.

Hopeful. Well, but they ran, you see, when they did but suppose that one Greatgrace was on the way.

Christian. True, they often fled, both they and their master, when Greatgrace had but appeared; and no marvel, for he is the king's champion: but I think you will put some difference between Little Faith and the king's champion; all the king's subjects are not his champions: nor can they, when tried, do such feats of war as he. Is it meet to think that a little child should handle Goliath as David did? Or that there should be the strength of an ox in a wren? Some are strong, some are weak, some have great faith, some have little. This man was one of the weak, and therefore he went to the walls.

Hopeful. I would it had been Greatgrace for their sakes.

Christian. If it had been he, he might have had his hands full: for I must tell you, that though Greatgrace is excellent good at his weapons, and has and can, so long as he keeps them at sword's point, do well enough with them: yet if they get within him, even Faintheart, Mistrust, or the other, it shall go hard but they will throw up his heels. And when a man is down, you know, what can he do?

Whoso looks well upon Greatgrace's face, shall see those scars and cuts there that shall easily give demonstration of what I say. Yea, once I heard he should say (and that when he was in the combat), "We despaired even of life." How did these sturdy rogues and their fellows make David groan, mourn and roar? Yea, Heman and Hezekiah too, though champions in their day, were forced to bestir them when by these assaulted; and yet that notwithstanding they had their coats soundly brushed by them. Peter upon a time would go try what he could do; but though some do say of him that he is the prince of the apostles, they handled him so that they made him at last afraid of a sorry girl.

Besides, their king is at their whistle, he is never out of hearing; and if at any time they be put to the worst, he, if possible, comes in to help them: and of him it is said, "The sword of him that lays at him cannot hold: the spear, the dart, nor the habergeon; he esteems iron as straw, and brass as rotten wood. The arrow cannot make him fly, sling-stones are turned with him into stubble, darts are counted as stubble, he laughs at the shaking of a spear. "What can a man do in this case? 'Tis true, if a man could at every turn have Job's horse, and had skill and courage to ride him, he might do notable things. "For his neck is clothed with thunder, he will not be afraid as the grasshopper, the glory of his nostrils is terrible, he paws in the valley, rejoices in his strength, and goes out to meet the armed men. He mocks at fear, and is not affrighted, neither turns back from the sword. The quiver rattles against him, the glittering spear, and the shield. He swallows the ground with fierceness and rage, neither believes he that it is the sound of the trumpet. He says among the trumpets, 'Ha, ha'; and he smells the battle afar off, the thundering of the captains, and the shoutings."

But for such footmen as you and I are, let us never desire to meet with an enemy, nor vaunt as if we could do better, when we hear of others that they have been foiled, nor be tickled at the thoughts of our own manhood, for such commonly come by the worst when tried. Witness Peter, of whom I made mention before. He would swagger, ay he would. He would, as his vain mind prompted him to say, do better, and stand more for his master, than all men. But who so foiled, and run down with these villians as he?

When therefore we hear that such robberies are done on the king's highway, two things become us to do: first to go out harnessed, and to be sure to take a shield with us, for it was for want of that, that he that laid so lustily at Leviathan could not make him yield. For indeed, if that be wanting, he fears us not at all. Therefore he that had skill has said, "Above all take the shield of faith, wherewith you shall be able to quench all the fiery darts of the wicked."

'Tis good also that we desire of the king a convoy, yea, that he will go with us himself. This made David rejoice when in the Valley of the Shadow of Death; and Moses was rather for dying where he stood, than to go one step without his God. O my brother, if he will but go along with us, what need we be afraid of ten thousand that shall set themselves against us, but without him, "the proud helpers fall under the slain".

I for my part have been in the fray before now, and though (through the goodness of Him that is best) I am as you see alive, yet I cannot boast of my manhood. Glad shall I be if I meet with no more such brunts, though I fear we are not beyond all danger. However, since the lion and the bear have not as yet devoured me, I hope God will also deliver us from the next uncircumcised Philistine. Then sang Christian:

> Poor Little Faith! Have you been among
> the thieves?
> Were you robbed? Remember this,
> whoso believes
> And gets more faith shall then a victor be
> Over ten thousand, else scarce over
> three.

So they went on, and Ignorance followed. They went then till they came to a place where they saw a way put itself into their way, and seemed withal to lie as straight as the way which they should go; and here they knew not which of the two to take, for both seemed straight before them, therefore here they stood still to consider. And as they were thinking about the way, behold, a man black of flesh, but covered with a very light robe, came to them, and asked them why they stood there. They answered they were going to the Celestial City, but knew not which of these ways to take. "Follow me", said the man, "it is thither that I am going." So they followed him in the way that but now came into the road, which by degrees turned, and turned them so from the city that they desired to go to, that in little time their faces were turned away from it; yet they followed him. But by and by, before they were aware, he let them both within the compass of a net, in whch they were both so entangled that they knew not what to do; and with that, the white robe fell off the black man's back: then they saw where they were. Wherefore there they lay crying some time, for they could not get themselves out.

Then said Christian to his fellow, "Now do I see myself in an error; did not the shepherds bid us beware of the flatterers? As is the saying of the wise man, so we have found it this day: 'A man that flatters his neighbour spreads a net for his feet.'"

Hopeful. They also gave us a note of directions about the way for our more sure finding thereof: but therein we have also forgotten to read, and have not kept ourselves from the paths of the destroyer. Here David was wiser than we; for said he, "Concerning the works of men, by the word of thy lips, I have kept me from the paths of the destroyer."

Thus they lay bewailing themselves in the net. At last they espied a shining one coming towards them with a whip of small cord in his hand. When he was come to the place where they were, he asked them whence they came and what they did there. They told him that they were poor pilgrims going to Zion, but were led out of their way by a black man, clothed in white, "who bade us", said they, "follow him; for he was going thither too." Then said he with a whip, "It is Flatterer, a false apostle, that has transformed himself into an angel of light." So he rent the net and let the men out. Then said he to them, "Follow me, that I may set you in your way again". So he led them back to the way, which they had left to follow the Flatterer. Then he asked them, saying, "Where did you lie the last night?" They said, "With the shepherd upon the Delectable Mountains." He asked them then if they had not of the shepherds a note of direction for the way. They answered, "Yes". "But did you", said he, "when you were at a stand, pluck out and read your note?" They aswered, "No". He asked them why. They said they forgot. He asked moreover if the shepherds did not bid them beware of the Flatterer. They answered, "Yes. But we did not imagine", said they, "that this fine-spoken man had been he."

Then I saw in my dream, that he commanded them to lie down, which when they did, he chastised them sore, to teach them the good way wherein they should walk, and as he chastised them, he said, "As many as I love, I rebuke and chasten; be zealous therefore and repent." This done, he bade them go on their way and take good heed to the other directions of the shepherds. So they thanked him for all his kindness and went softly along the right way, singing,

Come hither, you that walk along the way,
See how the pilgrims fare, that go astray!
They caught are in an entangling net,
'Cause they good counsel lightly did forget.
'Tis true, they rescued were, but yet you see
They're scourged to boot, let this your caution be.

Now after a while they perceived afar off, one coming softly and alone all along the highway to meet them. Then said Christian to his fellow, "Yonder is a man with his back toward Zion, and he is coming to meet us."

Hopeful. I see him, let us take heed to ourselves now, lest he should prove a Flatterer also.

So he drew nearer and nearer, and at last came up unto them. His name was Atheist, and he asked them whither they were going.

Christian. We are going to the Mount Zion.

Then Atheist fell into a very great laughter.

Christian. What is the meaning of your laughter?

Atheist. I laugh to see what ignorant persons you are, to take upon you so tedious a journey and yet are like to have nothing but your travel for your pains.

Christian. Why man? Do you think we shall not be received?

Atheist. Received! There is no such place as you dream of in all this world.

Christian. But there is in the world to come.

Atheist. When I was at home in mine own country, I heard as you now affirm and from that hearing went out to see, and have been seeking this City this twenty years, but find no more of it than I did the first day I set out.

Christian. We have both heard and believe that there is such a place to be found.

Atheist. Had not I, when at home, believed, I would not come thus far to seek; but finding none (and yet I should, had there been such a place to be found, for I have gone to seek it further than you), I am going back again, and will seek to refresh myself with the things that I then cast away for hopes of that which I now see is not.

Then said Christian to Hopeful his fellow, "Is it true what this man has said?"

Hopeful. Take heed, he is one of the Flatterers; remember what it hath cost us once already for your hearkening to such kind of fellows. What! No Mount Zion? Did we not see from the Delectable Mountains the gate of the city? Also, are we not now to walk by faith? Let us go on, lest the man with the whip overtakes us again. You should have taught me that lesson, which I will round you in the ears withal; "Cease, my son, to hear the instruction that causes to err from the words of knowledge." I say my brother, cease to hear him, and let us believe to the saving of the soul.

Christian. My brother, I did not put the question to you, for that I doubted of the truth of our belief myself but to prove you, and to fetch from you a fruit of the honesty of your heart. As for this man, I know that he is blinded by the god of this world. Let you and I go on knowing that we have belief of the truth, and no lie is of the truth.

Hopeful. Now do I rejoice in hope of the glory of God.

So they turned away from the man, and he, laughing at them, went his way.

I saw then in my dream that they went on till they came into a certain country, whose air naturally tended to make one drowsy, if he came a stranger into it. And here Hopeful began to be very dull and heavy of sleep, wherefore he said unto Christian, "I do now begin to grow so drowsy that I can scarcely hold up my eyes; let us lie down here and take one nap."

Christian. By no means, lest sleeping, we never awake more.

Hopeful. Why my brother? Sleep is sweet to the labouring man; we may be refreshed if we take a nap.

Christian. Do you not remember, that one of the shepherds bid us beware of the Enchanted Ground? He meant by that that we should beware of sleeping; wherefore let us not sleep as do others, but let us watch and be sober.

Hopeful. I acknowledge myself in a fault, and had I been here alone, I had by sleeping run the danger of death. I see it is true that the wise man says, "Two are better than one." Hitherto has your company been my mercy; and you shall have a good reward for your labour.

Christian. Now then, to prevent drowsiness in this place, let us fall into good discourse.

Hopeful. With all my heart.

Christian. Where shall we begin?

Hopeful. Where God began with us. But do you begin if you please.

When saints do sleepy grow, let them
come hither,
And hear how these two pilgrims talk
together:
Yea, let them learn of them, in any wise
Thus to keep open their drowsy
slumbering eyes.
Saints' fellowship, if it be managed well,
Keeps them awake, and that in spite of
Hell.

Then Christian began and said, "I will ask you a question. How came you to think at first of doing as you do now?"

Hopeful. Do you mean, How came I at first to look after the good of my soul?

Christian. Yes, that is my meaning.

Hopeful. I continued a great while in the delight of those things which were seen and sold at our fair; things which, as I believe now, would have (had I continued in them still) drowned me in perdition and destruction.

Christian. What things were they?

Hopeful. All the treasures and riches of the world. Also I delighted much in rioting, revelling, drinking, swearing, lying, uncleanness, sabbath-breaking, and what not, that tended to destroy the soul. But I found at last, by hearing and considering of things that are divine, which indeed I heard of you, as also of beloved Faithful that was put to death for his faith and good living in Vanity Fair, "That the end of these things is death". And that for these things' sake the wrath of God comes upon the children of disobedience.

Christian. And did you presently fall under the power of this conviction?

Hopeful. No, I was not willing presently to know the evil of sin, nor the damnation that follows upoon the commission of it, but endeavoured, when my mind at first began to be shaken with the Word, to shut my eyes against the light thereof.

Christian. But what was the cause of your carrying of it thus to the first workings of God's blessed spirit upon you?

Hopeful. The causes were:

1 I was ignorant that this was the work of God upon me. I never thought that by awakenings for sin, God at first begins the conversion of a sinner.

2 Sin was yet very sweet to my flesh, and I was loath to leave it.

3 I could not tell how to part with my old companions, their presence and actions were so desirable unto me.

4 The hours in which convictions were upon me were such troublesome and such heart-affrighting hours that I could not bear no not so much as the remembrance of them upon my heart.

Christian. Then as it seems, sometimes you got rid of your trouble.

Hopeful. Yes, verily, but it would come into my mind again; and then I should be as bad, nay, worse than I was before.

Christian. Why, what was it that brought your sins to mind again?

Hopeful. Many things as:

1 If I did but meet a good man in the streets, or,

2 If I have heard any read in the Bible, or,

3 If mine head did begin to ache, or,

4 If I were told that some of my neighbours were sick, or,

5 If I heard the bell toll for some that were dead, or,

6 If I thought of dying myself, or,

7 If I heard that sudden death happened to others.

8 But especially, when I thought of myself that I must quickly come to judgement.

Christian. And could you at any time with ease get off the guilt of sin when by any of these ways it came upon you?

Hopeful. No, not latterly, for then they got faster hold of my conscience. And then, if I did but think of going back to sin (though my mind was turned against it) it would be double torment to me.

Christian. And how did you do then?

Hopeful. I thought I must endeavour to mend my life, or else, thought I, I am sure to be damned.

Christian. And did you endeavour to mend?

Hopeful. Yes, and fled from, not only my sins, but sinful company too; and betook me to religious duties, as praying, reading, weeping for sin, speaking truth to my neighbours, and so on. These things I did, with many others, too much here to relate.

Christian. And did you think yourself well then?

Hopeful. Yes, for a while; but at the last my trouble came tumbling upon me again, and that over the neck of all my reformations.

Christian. How came that about, since you were now reformed?

Hopeful. There were several things brought it upon me, especially such sayings as these: "All our righteousnesses are as filthy rags". "By the works of the law no man shall be justified". "When you have done all things, say, 'We are unprofitable'," with many more the like: from whence I began to reason with myself thus: if all my righteousnesses are filthy rags, if by the deeds of the law no man can be justified, and if when we have done all, we are yet unprofitable, then 'tis but a folly to think of Heaven by the law. I further thought thus: if a man runs a hundred pounds into the shop-keeper's debt, and after that shall pay for all that he shall fetch, yet his old debt stands still in the book uncrossed for the which the shop-keeper may sue him, and cast him into prison till he shall pay the debt.

Christian. Well, and how did you apply this to yourself?

Hopeful. Why, I thought thus with myself: I have by my sins run a great way into God's book, and that my now reforming will not pay off that score; therefore I should think still under all my present amendments. But how shall I be freed from that damnation that I have brought myself in danger of by my former transgressions?

Christian. A very good application: but pray go on.

Hopeful. Another thing that has troubled me, ever since my late amendments, is, that if I look narrowly into the best of what I do now, I still see sin, new sin, mixing itself with the best of that I do. So that now I am forced to conclude that notwithstanding my former fond conceits of myself and duties, I have committed sin enough in one duty to send me to Hell though my former life had been faultless.

Christian. And what did you do then?

Hopeful. Do! I could not tell what to do till I spoke my mind to Faithful; for he and I were well acquainted. And he told me that unless I could obtain the righteousness of a man that never had sinned, neither mine nor all the righteousness of the world could save me.

Christian. And did you think he spoke true?

Hopeful. Had he told me so when I was pleased and satisfied with mine own amendments, I had called him fool for his pains, but now, since I see my own infirmity, and the sin that cleaves to my best performance, I have been forced to be of his opinion.

Christian. But did you think, when at first he suggested it to you, that there was such a man to be found of whom it might justly be said that he never committed sin?

Hopeful. I must confess the words at first sounded strangely, but after a little more talk and company with him I had full conviction about it.

Christian. And did you ask him what man this was and how you must be justified by him?

Hopeful. Yes, and he told me it was the Lord Jesus, that dwells on the right hand of the Most High: "and thus", said he, "you must be justified by Him, even by trusting to what He has done by Himself in the days of His flesh, and suffered when He did hang on the tree." I asked him further, how that man's righteousness could be of that efficacy to justify another before God. And he told me He was the mighty God, and did what He did, and died the death also, not for Himself, but for me; to whom His doings, and the worthiness of them should be imputed, if I believed in Him.

Christian. And what did you do then?

Hopeful. I made my objections against my believing, for that I thought He was not willing to save me.

Christian. And what said Faithful to you then?

Hopeful. He bade me to go to him and see. Then I said it was presumption; but he said, "No, for I was invited to come". Then he gave a book of Jesus, of His inditing, to encourage me the more freely to come. And he said, concerning that book, that every jot and tittle thereof stood firmer than Heaven and earth. Then I asked him what I must do when I came and he told me I must entreat upon my knees with all my heart and soul, the Father to reveal Him to me. Then I asked him further, how I must make my supplication to him? And he said, "Go, and you shall find him upon a mercy-seat, where he sits all the year long to give pardon and forgiveness to them that come. I told him that I knew not what to say when I came: and he bid me say to this effect, God be merciful to me a sinner, and make me to know and believe in Jesus Christ; for I sec that is His righteousness had not been, or I have not faith in that righteousness, I am utterly cast away: Lord, I have heard that you are a merciful God, and have ordained that your Son Jesus Christ should be the saviour of the world; and moreover, You are willing to bestow Him upon such a poor sinner as I am (and I am a sinner indeed), Lord take therefore this opportunity, and magnify Your grace in the salvation of my soul, through Your Son Jesus Christ. Amen.

Christian. And did you do as you were bidden?

Hopeful. Yes, over and over and over.

Christian. And did the Father reveal His Son to you?

Hopeful. Not at the first, nor second, nor third, nor fourth, nor fifth, no, nor at the sixth time neither.

Christian. What did you do then?

Hopeful. What! Why I could not tell what to do.

Christian. Had you not thoughts of leaving off praying?

Hopeful. Yes, an hundred times, twice told.

Christian. And what was the reason you did not?

Hopeful. I believed that that was true which had been told me, to wit, that without the righteousness of this Christ, all the world could not save me; and therefore thought I with myself, if I leave off, I die, and I can but die at the throne of grace. And withal, this came into my mind, "If it tarry, wait for it, because it will surely come, and will not tarry". So I continued praying until the Father showed me His Son.

Christian. And how was He revealed unto you?

Hopeful. I did not see Him with my bodily eyes, but with the eyes of my understanding; and thus it was. One day I was very sad, I think sadder than at any one time in my life; and this sadness was through a fresh sight of the greatness and vileness of my sins: and as I was then looking for nothing but Hell, and the everlasting damnation of my soul, suddenly as I thought, I saw the Lord Jesus look down from Heaven upon me, and saying, "Believe on the Lord Jesus Christ, and you shall be saved."

But I replied, "Lord, I am a great, a very great sinner", and he answered, "My grace is sufficient for you." Then I said, "But Lord, what is believing?" And then I saw from that saying "He that comes to me shall never hunger, and he that believes on me shall never thirst", that believing and coming was all one, and that he that came, that is, ran out in his heart and affections after salvation by Christ, he indeed believed in Christ. Then the water stood in my eyes, and I asked further, "But Lord, may such a great sinner as I am be indeed accepted of You, and be saved by You?" And I heard Him say, "And him that comes to me, I will in no wise cast out." Then I said, "But how, Lord, must I consider of You in my coming to You, that my faith may be placed aright upon You?" Then He said, "Christ Jesus came into the world to save sinners. He is the end of the law for righteousness to everyone that believes. He died for our sins, and rose again for our justification. He loved us, and washed us from our sins in His own blood. He is mediator between God and us. He ever lives to make intercession for us." From all which I gathered that I must look for righteousness in His person, and for satisfaction for my sins by His blood; that what He did in obedience to His Father's law, and in submitting to the penalty thereof, was not for Himself, but for him that will accept it for his salvation, and be thankful. And now was my heart full of joy, my eyes full of tears, and my affections running over with love, to the name, people, and ways of Jesus Christ.

Christian. This was a revelation of Christ to your soul indeed: but tell me particularly what effect this had upon your spirit?

Hopeful. It made me see that all the world, notwithstanding all the righteousness thereof, is in a state of condemnation. It made me see that God the Father, though He be just, can justly justify the coming sinner. It made me greatly ashamed of the vileness of my former life, and confounded me with the sense of my own ignorance; for there never came thought into my heart before now that showed me so the beauty of Jesus Christ. It made me love a holy life, and long to do something for the honour and glory of the name of the Lord Jesus. Yea, I thought that had I now a thousand gallons of blood in my body, I could spill it all for the sake of the Lord Jesus.

I then saw in my dream that Hopeful looked back and saw Ignorance, whom they had left behind, coming after. "Look," said he to Christian, "how far yonder youngster loiters behind."

Christian. Ay, ay, I see him; he cares not for our company.

Hopeful. But I think, it would not have hurt him had he kept peace with us hitherto.

Christian. That's true, but I warrant you he thinks otherwise.

Hopeful. That I think he does, but however let us tarry for him.

So they did. Then Christian said to him, "Come away man, why do you stay so behind?"

Ignorance. I take my pleasure in walking alone, even more a great deal than in company, unless I like it the better.

Then said Christian to Hopeful (but softly), "Did I not tell you he cared not for our company? But however, come up and let us talk away the time in this solitary place." Then directing his speech to Ignorance, he said, "Come, how do you? How stands it between God and your soul now?"

Ignorance. I hope well for I am always full of good notions, that come into my mind to comfort me as I walk.

Christian. What good notions? Pray tell us.

Ignorance. Why, I think of God and Heaven.

Christian. So do the devils and damned souls.

Ignorance. But I think of them and desire them.

Christian. So do many that are never like to come there: "The soul of the sluggard desires and has nothing."

Ignorance. But I think of them, and leave all for them.

Christian. That I doubt, for leaving of all is a hard matter, yea, a harder matter than many are aware of. But why or by what are you persuaded that you have left all for God and Heaven?

Ignorance. My heart tells me so.

Christian. The wise man says, "He that trusts his own heart is a fool."

Ignorance. That is spoken of an evil heart, but mine is a good one.

Christian. But how do you prove that?

Ignorance. It comforts me in the hopes of Heaven.

Christian. That may be through its deceitfulness, for a man's heart may minister comfort to him in the hopes of that thing for which he yet has no grounds to hope.

Ignorance. But my heart and life agree together, and therefore my hope is well grounded.

Christian. Who told you that your heart and life agree together?

Ignorance. My heart tells me so.

Christian. Ask my fellow if I be a thief; your heart tells you so! Except the Word of God bears witness in this matter, other testimony is of no value.

Ignorance. But is it not a good heart that has good thoughts? And is not that a good life that is according to God's commandments?

Christian. Yes, that is a good heart that has good thoughts and that is a good life that is according to God's commandments. But it is one thing indeed to have these, and another thing only to think so.

Ignorance. Pray, what count you good thoughts and a life according to God's commandments?

Christian. There are good thoughts of divers kinds, some respecting ourselves, some God, some Christ and some other things.

Ignorance. What be good thoughts respecting ourselves?

Christian. Such as agree with the Word of God.

Ignorance. When do our thoughts of ourselves agree with the Word of God?

Christian. When we pass the same judgement upon ourselves which the Word passes. To explain myself, the Word of God says of persons in a natural condition, "There is none righteous, there is none that does good". It says also, "That every imagination of the heart of man is only evil, and that continually". And again, "The imagination of man's heart is evil from his youth". Now then, when we think thus of ourselves, having sense thereof, then are our thoughts good ones, because according to the Word of God.

Ignorance. I will never believe that my heart is thus bad.

Christian. Therefore you never had one good thought concerning yourself in your life. But let me go on: as the Word passes a judgment upon our heart, so it passes a judgment upon our ways; and when our thoughts of our hearts and ways agree with the judgment which the Word gives of both, then are both good because agreeing thereto.

Ignorance. Make out your meaning.

Christian. Why, the Word of God says that man's ways are crooked ways, not good, but perverse: it says, "They are naturally out of the good way", they that have not known it. Now when a man thus thinks of his ways, I say when he does sensibly, and with heart-humiliation thus think, then has he good thoughts of his own ways, because his thoughts now agree with the judgment of the Word of God.

Ignorance. What are good thoughts concerning God?

Christian. Even (as I have said concerning ourselves) when our thoughts of God do agree with what the Word says of Him. And that is when we think of his being and attributes as the Word has taught: of which I cannot now discourse at large. But to speak of Him with reference to us, then we have the right thoughts of God, when we think that He knows us better than we know ourselves, and can see sin in us when and where we can see none in ourselves; when we think He knows our inmost thoughts, and that our heart, with all its depths, is always open unto His eyes: also when we think that all our righteousness stinks in His nostrils, and that therefore he cannot abide to see us stand before Him in any confidence, even of all our best performances.

Ignorance. Do you think that I am such a fool as to think God can see no further than I? Or that I would come to God in the best of my performances?

Christian. Why, how do you think in this matter?

Ignorance. Why, to be short, I think I must believe in Christ for justification.

Christian. How! Think you must believe in Christ, when you see not your need of Him! You neither see your original, nor actual infirmities, but have such an opinion of yourself, and of what you do as plainly renders you to be one that did never see a necessity of Christ's personal righteousness to justify you before God. How then do you say, "I believe in Christ?"

Ignorance. I believe well enough for all that.

Christian. How do you believe?

Ignorance. I believe that Christ died for sinners, and that I shall be justified before God from the curse through His gracious acceptance of my obedience to His law: or thus, Christ makes my duties that are religious, acceptable to His Father by virtue of His merits; and so shall I be justified.

Christian. Let me give an answer to this confession of your faith.

1 You believe with a fantastical faith, for this faith is nowhere described in the word.

2 You believe with a false faith, because it takes justification from the personal righteousness of Christ and applies it to your own.

3 This faith makes not Christ a justifier of your person, but of your actions; and of your person for your actions' sake, which is false.

4 Therefore this faith is deceitful, even such as will leave you under wrath, in the day of God Almighty. For true justifying faith puts the soul (as sensible of its lost condition by the law) upon flying for refuge unto Christ's righteousness (which

righteousness of His is not an act of grace by which He makes for justification your obedience accepted with God, but His personal obedience to the law in doing and suffering for us what that required at our hands). This righteousness I say true faith accepts, under the skirt of which the soul being shrouded, and by it presented as spotless before God, it is accepted, and acquited from condemnation.

Ignorance. What! Would you have us trust to what Christ in His own person has done without us? This conceit would loosen the reins of our lust, and tolerate us to live as we list: for what matter how we live if we may be justified by Christ's personal righteousness from all, when we believe it?

Christian. Ignorance is your name and as your name is, so are you; even this your answer demonstrates what I say. Ignorant you are of what justifying righteousness is, and as ignorant of how to secure your soul through the faith of it from the heavy wrath of God. Yea, you also are ignorant of the true effects of saving faith in this righteousness of Christ, which is to bow and win over the heart to God in Christ to love His name, His word, ways and people, and not as you ignorantly imagine.

Hopeful. Ask him if ever he had Christ revealed to him from Heaven?

Ignorance. What! You are a man for revelations! I believe that what both you, and all the rest of you say about that matter, is but the fruit of distracted brains.

Hopeful. Why man! Christ is so hid in God from the natural apprehensions of all flesh, that He cannot by any man be savingly known, unless God the Father reveals Him to them.

Ignorance. That is your faith, but not mine; yet, mine I doubt not, is as good as yours, though I have not in my head so many whimsies as you.

Christian. Give me leave to put in a word: you ought not so slightly to speak of this matter: for this I will boldly affirm (even as my good companion has done), that no man can know Jesus Christ but by the revelation of the Father: yea, and faith too, by which the soul lays hold upon Christ (if it be right) must be wrought by the exceeding greatness of His mighty power, the working of which faith, I perceive, poor Ignorance, you are ignorant of. Be awakened then, see your own wretchedness, and fly to the Lord Jesus, and by His righteousness, which is the righteousness of God (for He himself is God), you shall be delivered from condemnation.

Ignorance. You go so fast, I cannot keep pace with you; do you go on before, I must stay a while behind.

Then they said,

Well, Ignorance, will you yet foolish be,
To slight good counsel ten times given thee?
And if you yet refuse it, you shall know
Ere long the evil of your doing so:
Remember man in time, stoop, do not fear,
Good counsel taken well, saves; therefore hear:
But if you yet shall slight it, you will be
The loser, Ignorance, I'll warrant thee.

Then Christian addressed thus himself to his fellow.

Christian. Well, come my good Hopeful, I perceive that you and I must walk by ourselves again.

So I saw in my dream, that they went on a pace before, and Ignorance he came hobbling after. Then said Christian to his companion, "It pities me much for this poor man, it will certainly go ill with him at last."

Hopeful. Alas, there are in abundance, in our towns in his condition, whole families, yea, whole streets (and that of pilgrims too), and if there be so many in our parts, how many, think you, must there be in the place where he was born?

Christian. Indeed the word says, "He has blinded their eyes, lest they should see". But now we are by ourselves, what do you think of such men? Have they at no time, think you, convictions of sin, and so consequently fear that their state is dangerous?

Hopeful. Nay, do you answer that question yourself, for you are the elder man.

Christian. Then, I say, sometimes (as I think) they may, but they being naturally ignorant, understand not that such convictions tend to their good; and therefore they do desperately seek to stifle them, and presumptuously continue to flatter themselves in the way of their own hearts.

Hopeful. I do believe as you say that fear tends much to men's good, and to make them right at their beginning to go on pilgrimage.

Christian. Without all doubt it does, if it be right: for so says the Word, "The fear of the Lord is the beginning of wisdom."

Hopeful. How will you describe right fear?

Christian. True, or right, fear is discovered by three things:

1 By its rise, it is caused by saving convictions for sin.

2 It drives the soul to lay fast hold of Christ for salvation.

3 It begets and continues in the soul a great reverence of God, His Word, and ways, keeping it tender and making it afraid to turn from them, to the right hand, or to the left, to any thing that may dishonour God, break its peace, grieve the Spirit, or cause the enemy to speak reproachfully.

Hopeful. Well said, I believe you have said the truth. Are we now almost got past the Enchanted Ground?

Christian. Why, are you weary of this discourse?

Hopeful. No, verily, but that I would know where we are.

Christian. We have not now above two miles further to go thereon. But let us return to our matter. Now the ignorant know not that such convictions that tend to put them in fear are for their good, and therefore they seek to stifle them.

Hopeful. How do they seek to stifle them?

Christian. 1 They think that those fears are wrought by the Devil (though indeed they are wrought of God) and thinking so, they resist them, as things that directly tend to their overthrow.

2 They also think that these fears tend to the spoiling of their faith when, alas for them, poor men that they are! they have none at all, and therefore they harden their hearts against them.

3 They presume they ought not to fear, and therefore, in despite of them, wax presumptuously confident.

4 They see that these fears tend to take away from them their pitful old self-holiness, and therefore they resist them with all their might.

Hopeful. I know something of this myself; for before I knew myself it was so with me.

Christian. Well, we will leave at this time our neighbour Ignorance by himself, and fall upon another profitable question.

Hopeful. With all my heart, but you shall still begin.

Christian. Well then, did you not know about ten years ago, one Temporary in your parts, who was a forward man in religion then?

Hopeful. Know him! Yes, he dwelt in Graceless, a town about two miles off of Honesty, and he dwelt next door to one Turnback.

Christian. Right, he dwelt under the same roof with him. Well, that man was much awakened once; I believe that when he had some sight of his sins, and of the wages that was due thereto.

Hopeful. I am of your mind, for (my house not being above three miles from him) he would oft-times come to me, and that with many tears. Truly I pitied the man, and was not altogether without hope of him; but one may see, "It is not every one that cries, Lord, Lord".

Christian. He told me once that he was resolved to go on pilgrimage, as we do now; but all of a sudden he grew acquainted with one Saveself, and then he became a stranger to me.

Hopeful. Now since we are talking about him, let us a little inquire into the reason of the sudden backsliding of him and such others.

Christian. It may be very profitable, but do you begin.

Hopeful. Well then, there are in my judgment four reasons for it.

1 Though the consciences of such men are awakened, yet their minds are not changed: therefore when the power of guilt wears away, that which provoked them to be religious ceases. Wherefore they naturally turn to their own course again; even as we see the dog that is sick of what he has eaten, so long as his sickness prevails, he vomits and casts up all; not that he does this of a free mind (if we may say a dog has a mind) but because it troubles his stomach; but now when his sickness is over, and so his stomach eased, his desires being not at all alienate from his vomit, he turns him about, and licks up all. And so it is true which is written, "The dog is turned to his own vomit again." Thus, I say, being hot for Heaven, by virtue only of the sense and

fear of the torments of Hell, as their sense of Hell, and the fears of damnation chills and cools, so their desires for Heaven and salvation cool also. So then it comes to pass, that when their guilt and fear is gone, their desires for Heaven and happiness die; and they return to their course again.

2 Another reason is, they have slavish fears that do overmaster them. I speak now of the fears that they have of men: "For the fear of men brings a snare." So then, though they seem to be hot for Heaven so long as the flames of Hell are about their ears yet when that terror is a little over, they betake themselves to second thoughts, namely that 'tis good to be wise, and not to run (for they know not what) the hazard of losing all; or at least, of bringing themselves into unavoidable and unnecessary troubles: and so they fall in with the world again.

3 The shame that attends religion lies also as a block in their way; they are proud and haughty, and religion in their eye is low and contemptible: therefore when they have lost their sense of Hell and wrath to come, they return again to their former course.

4 Guilt, and to meditate on terror, are grievous to them, they like not to see their misery before they come into it, though perhaps the sight of it first, if they love that sight, might make them fly whither the righteous fly and are safe. But because they do as I hinted before, even shun the thoughts of guilt and terror therefore, when once they are rid of their awakenings about the terrors and wrath of God they harden their hearts gladly, and choose such ways as will harden them more and more.

Christian. You are pretty near the business, for the bottom of all is for want of a change in their mind and will. And therefore they are but like the felon that stands before the judge; he quakes and trembles, and seems to repent most heartily; but the bottom of all is the fear of the halter, not of any detestation of the offence, as is evident, because, let but this man have his liberty, and he will be a thief, and so a rogue still, whereas, if his mind was changed, he would be otherwise.

Hopeful. Now I have showed you the reasons of their going back, do you show me the manner thereof.

Christian. So I will willingly

1 They draw off their thoughts all that they may from the remembrance of God, death, and judgment to come.

2 Then they cast off by degrees private duties, as closet-prayer, curbing their lusts, watching, sorrow for sin and the like.

3 Then they shun the company of lively and warm Christians.

4 After that, they grow cold to public duty, as hearing, reading, godly conference, and the like.

5 Then they begin to pick holes, as we say, in the coats of some of the godly, and that devilishly, that they may have a seeming colour to throw religion (for the sake of some infirmity they have spied in them) behind their backs.

6 Then they begin to adhere to and associate themselves with carnal, loose, and wanton men.

7 Then they give way to carnal and wanton discourses in secret; and glad are they if they can see such things in any that are counted honest, that they may the more boldly do it through their example.

8 After this, they begin to play with little sins openly.

9 And then, being hardened, they show themselves as they are. Thus being launched again into the gulf of misery, unless a miracle of grace prevent it they everlastingly perish in their own deceivings.

Now I saw in my dream that by this time the pilgrims were got over the Enchanted Ground, and entering into the country of Beulah, whose air was very sweet and pleasant; the way lying directly through it, they solaced themselves there for a season. Yea, here they heard continually the singing of birds, and saw every day the flowers appear in the earth and heard the voice of the turtle in the land. In this country the sun shines night and day; wherefore this was beyond the Valley of the Shadow of Death, and also out of the reach of Giant Despair; neither could they from this place so much as see Doubting Castle. Here they were within sight of the city they were going to, also here met them some of the inhabitants thereof. For in this land the shining ones commonly walked, because it was upon the borders of Heaven. In this land also the contract between the bride and the bridegroom was renewed. Yea here, as the bridgroom rejoices over the bride, so did their God rejoice over them. Here they had no want of corn and wine; for in this place they met with abundance of what they had sought for in all their pilgrimage. Here they heard voices from out of the city, loud voices, saying, "Say ye to the daughter of Zion, behold your salvation comes, behold His reward is with Him." Here all the inhabitants of the country called them, "The holy people, the redeemed of the Lord, sought out".

Now as they walked in this land they had more rejoicing than in parts more remote from the kingdom to which they were bound; and drawing near to the city, they had yet a more perfect view thereof. It was built of pearls and precious stones, also the street thereof was paved with gold, so that by reason of the natural glory of the city, and the reflection of the sunbeams upon it, Christian fell sick with desire, Hopeful also had a fit or two of the same disease: wherefore here they lay by it a while, crying out because of their pangs, "If you see my beloved, tell him that I am sick of love."

But being a little strengthened, and better able to bear their sickness, they walked on their way, and came yet nearer and nearer, where were orchards, vineyards, and gardens, and their gates opened into the highway. Now as they came up to these places, behold the gardener stood in the way; to whom the pilgrims said, "Whose goodly vineyards and gardens are these?" He answered, "They are the king's, and are planted here for his own delights, and also for the solace of pilgrims." So the gardener had them into the vineyards and bade them refresh themselves with the dainties; he also showed them there the king's walks and the arbours where he delighted to be. And here they tarried and slept.

Now I beheld in my dream, that they talked more in their sleep at this time, than ever they did in all their journey; and being in a muse thereabout, the gardener said even to me, "Wherefore muse you at the matter? It is the nature of the fruit of the grapes of these vineyards to go down so sweetly as to cause the lips of them that are asleep to speak."

So I saw that when they awoke, they addressed themselves to go up to the city. But, as I said, the reflections of the sun upon the city (for the city was pure gold) was so extremely glorious that they could not, as yet, with open face behold it, but through an instrument made for that purpose. So I saw that as they went on, there met them two men in raiment that shone like gold, also their faces shone as the light.

These men asked the pilgrims whence they came, and they told them; they also asked them where they had lodged, what difficulties and dangers, what comforts and pleasures they had met in the way, and they told them. Then said the men that met them, "You have but two difficulties more to meet with, and then you are in the city."

Christian then and his companion asked the men to go along with them, so they told them they would: "But", said they, "you must obtain it by your own faith." So I saw in my dream that they went on together till they came within sight of the gate.

Now I further saw that betwixt them and the gate was a river, but there was no bridge to go over; the river was very deep; at the sight therefore of this river, the pilgrims were much astounded, but the men that went with them said, "You must go through, or you cannot come at the gate."

The pilgrims then began to inquire if there was no other way to the gate; to which they answered, "Yes, but there have not any, save two, to wit, Enoch and Elijah, been permitted to tread the path, since the foundation of the world, nor shall, until the last trumpet shall sound." The pilgrims then, especially Christian, began to despond in their minds, and looked this way and that, but no way could be found by them by which they might escape the river. They they asked the men if the waters were all of a depth. They said no; yet they could not help them in that case; for said they, "You shall find it deeper or shallower, as you believe in the king of the place."

They then addressed themselves to the water; and entering, Christian began to sink, and crying out to his good friend Hopeful, he said, "I sink in deep waters, the billows go over my head, all His waves go over me."

Then said the other, "Be of good cheer, my brother, I feel the bottom, and it is good." Then said Christian, "Ah my friend, the sorrows of death have compassed me about, I shall not see the land that flows with milk and honey." And with that, a great darkness and horror fell upon

Christian, so that he could not see before him; also here he in great measure lost his senses, so that he could neither remember nor orderly talk of any of those sweet refreshments that he had met with in the way of his pilgrimage. But all the words that he spoke still tended to discover that he had horror of mind and hearty fears that he should die in that river, and never obtain entrance in at the gate. Here also, as they that stood by perceived, he was much in the troublesome thoughts of the sins that he had committed both since and before he began to be a pilgrim. 'Twas also observed that he was troubled with apparitions of hobgoblins and evil spirits, for ever and anon he would intimate so much by words. Hopeful therefore here had much ado to keep his brother's head above water, yea, sometimes he would be quite gone down, and then ere a while he would rise up again half dead. Hopeful also would endeavour to comfort him, saying, "Brother, I see the gate, and men standing by it to receive us." But Christian would answer, "'Tis you, 'tis you they wait for, you have been Hopeful ever since I knew you." "And so have you," said he to Christian. "Ah brother," said he, "surely if I was right, He would now arise to help me; but for my sins He has brought me into the snare and has left me." Then said Hopeful, "My brother, you have quite forgot the text where it's said of the wicked, 'There is no band in their death, but their strength is firm, they are not troubled as other men, neither are they plagued like other men.' These troubles and distresses that you go through in these waters are no sign that God has forsaken you, but are sent to try you whether you will bring to mind that which heretofore you have received of His goodness, and live upon Him in your distresses."

Then I saw in my dream that Christian was as in a muse a while; to whom also Hopeful added this word, "Be of good cheer, Jesus Christ makes you whole." And with that, Christian broke out with a loud voice, "Oh I see Him again! And he tells me, 'When you pass through the waters, I will be with you, and through the rivers, they shall not overflow you'."

Then they both took courage, and the enemy was after that as still as a stone, until they were gone over. Christian therefore presently found ground to stand upon; and so it followed that the rest of the river was but shallow. Thus they got over. Now upon the bank of the river, on the other side, they saw the two shining men again who there waited for them. Wherefore being come up out of the river they saluted them, saying, "We are ministering spirits, sent forth to minister to those that shall be heirs of salvation." Thus they went along towards the gate; now you must note that the city stood upon a mighty hill, but the pilgrims went up that hill with ease, because they had these two men to lead them up by the arms; also they had left their mortal garments behind them in the river: for though they went in with them, they came out without them. They therefore went up through the regions of the air, sweetly talking as they went, being comforted because they safely got over the river, and had such glorious companions to attend them.

The talk that they had with the shining ones, was about the glory of the place, who told them, that the beauty, and glory of it was inexpressible. "There", said they, "is the Mount Zion, the heavenly Jerusalem, the innumerable company of angels, and the spirits of just men made perfect; you are going now", said they, "to the Paradise of God, wherein you shall see the tree of life, and eat of the never-fading fruits thereof; and when you come there you shall have white robes given you, and your walk and talk shall be every day with the king, even all the days of eternity. There you shall not see again such things as you saw when you were in the lower region upon the earth, to wit, sorrow, sickness, affliction, and death, for the former things are passed away. You are going now to Abraham, to Isaac, and Jacob, and to the prophets, men that God has taken away from the evil to come, and that are now resting upon their beds, each one walking in his righteousness." The men then asked, "What must we do in the holy place?" To whom it was answered, "You must there receive the comfort of all your toil, and have joy for all your sorrow; you must reap what you have sown, even the fruit of all your prayers and tears, and sufferings for the king by the way. In that place you must wear crowns of gold, and enjoy the perpetual sight and visions of the Holy One, 'for there you shall see Him as He is'.

There also you shall serve Him continually with praise, with shouting and thanksgiving, whom you desired to serve in the world, though with much difficulty, because of the infirmity of your flesh. There your eyes shall be delighted with seeing and your ears with hearing the pleasant voice of the Mighty One. There you shall enjoy your friends again that are got thither before you; and there you shall with joy receive even every one that follows into the holy place after you. There also you shall be clothed with glory and majesty, and put into an equipage fit to ride out with the King of Glory. When He shall come with sound of trumpet in the clouds as upon the wings of the wind, you shall come with Him; and when He shall sit upon the throne of judgment, you shall sit by Him; yea, and when He shall pass sentence upon all the workers of iniquity, let them be angels or men, you also shall have a voice in that judgment, because they were His and your enemies. Also when He shall again return to the city, you shall go too, with sound of trumpet, and be ever with Him."

Now while they were thus drawing towards the gate, behold a company of the heavenly host came out to meet them, to whom it was said, by the other two shining ones, "These are the men that have loved our Lord, when they were in the world, and that have left all for His holy name, and He has sent us to fetch them, and we have brought them thus far on their desired journey, that they may go in and look their redeemer in the face with joy." Then the heavenly host gave a great shout, saying, "Blessed are they that are called to the marriage supper of the Lamb."

There came out also at this time to meet them several of the king's trumpeters, clothed in white and shining raiment, who with melodious noises and loud, made even the heavens to echo with their sound. These trumpeters saluted Christian and his fellow with ten thousand welcomes from the world: and this they did with shouting and sound of trumpet.

This done, they compassed them round on every side; some went before, some behind, and some on the right hand, some on the left (as 'twere to guard them through the upper regions) continually sounding as they went with melodious noise in notes on high; so that the very sight was to them that could behold it as if Heaven itself was come down to meet them. Thus therefore they walked on together and as they walked, ever and anon these trumpeters, even with joyful sound would, by mixing their music, with looks and gestures, still signify to Christian and his brother how welcome they were into their company and with what gladness they came to meet them. And now were these two men, as 'twere, in Heaven, before they came at it; being swallowed up with the sight of angels, and with hearing of their melodious notes. Here also they had the city itself in view, and they thought they heard all the bells therein to ring, to welcome them thereto; but above all the warm and joyful thoughts that they had about their own dwelling there with such company, and that for ever and ever. Oh, by what tongue or pen can their glorious joy be expressed! And thus they came up to the gate.

Now when they were come up to the gate, there was written over it, in letters of gold, "Blessed are they that do His commandments, that they may have right to the tree of life; and may enter in through the gates into the city."

Then I saw in my dream that the shining men bid them call at the gate, the which when they did, some from above looked over the gate; to wit, Enoch, Moses and Elijah, to whom it was said, "These pilgrims are come from the City of Destruction, for the love that they bear to the king of this place". And then the pilgrims gave in unto them each man his certificate, which they had received in the beginning; those therefore were carried into the king, who, when He had read them, said, "Where are the men?" to whom it was answered, "They are standing without the gate." The king then commanded to open the gate; "That the righteous nation", said he, "that keeps truth may enter in."

Now I saw in my dream, that these two men went in at the gate; and lo, as they entered they were transfigured, and they had raiment put on that shone like gold. There were also some that met them with harps and crowns, and gave them to them the harp to praise withal, and the crowns in token of honour. Then I heard in my dream, that all the bells in the city rang again for joy; and that it was said unto them, "Enter ye into the joy of your Lord." I also heard the men themselves, that they sang with a loud voice, saying, "Blessing, honour, glory and power, be to Him that sits upon the throne, and to the Lamb for ever and ever."

Now just as the gates were opened to let in the men, I looked in after them; and behold, the city shone like the sun, the streets also were paved with gold, and in them walked many men with crowns on their heads, palms in their hands, and golden harps to sing praises withal.

There were also of them that had wings, and they answered one another without intermission, saying, "Holy, holy, holy, is the Lord." And after that, they shut up the gates: which when I had seen, I wished myself among them.

Now while I was gazing upon all these things, I turned my head to look back and saw Ignorance come up to the Riverside: but he soon got over, and that without half that difficulty which the other two men met with. For it happened, that there was then in that place one Vainhope a ferryman, that with his boat helped him over. So he, as the other I saw, did ascend the hill to come up to the gate, only he came alone, neither did any man meet him with the least encouragement. When he was come up to the gate he looked up to the writing that was above, and then began to knock, supposing that entrance should have been quickly administered to him. But he was asked by the men that looked over the top of the gate, "Whence came you, and what would you have?" He answered, "I have eaten and drunk in the presence of the king, and He has taught in our streets." Then they asked him for his certificate, that they might go in and show it to the king. So he fumbled in his bosom for one and found none.

Then said they, "Have you none?" But the man answered never a word. So they told the king, but He would not come down to see him; but commanded the two shining ones that conducted Christian and Hopeful to the city to go out and take Ignorance and bind him hand and foot, and have him away. Then they took him up, and carried him through the air to the door that I saw in the side of the hill, and put him in there. Then I saw that there was a way to Hell, even from the gates of Heaven, as well as from the City of Destruction. So I awoke, and behold it was a dream.

RICHARD BAXTER: Warning to the Born Again

Be acquainted with the root and remnant of your sins: with your particular inclinations and corrupt affections; with their quality, their degree and strength: with the weaknesses of every grace: with your disability to duty; and with the omissions or sinful practices of your lives. Search diligently and deeply; frequently and accurately peruse your hearts and ways, till you certainly and thoroughly know yourselves.

And I beseech you, let it not suffice you that you know your states, and have found yourselves in the love of God, in the faith of Christ, and possessed by His Spirit. Though this be mercy worth many worlds, yet this is not all concerning yourselves that you have to know. If yet you say that you have no sin, you deceive yourselves. If yet you think you are past all danger, your danger is the greater for this mistake. As much as you have been humbled for sin: as much as you have loathed it; as often as you have confessed it, lamented it, and complained and prayed against it, yet it is alive: though it be mortified, it is alive.

O that God would but open these too-close hearts unto us, and anatomise the relics of the old man, and show us all the recesses of our self-deceit, and the filth of worldliness, and carnal inclinations that lurk within us, and read us a lecture upon every part; what prayers would it teach us to indite! That you may not be proud of your holiness, let me tell you, Christians, that a full display of the corruptions that the best of you carry about you, would not only take down self-exalting thoughts, that you be not lifted up above measure, but would also teach you to pray with fervour and importunity, and waken you out of your sleepy indifference, and make you cry, "O wretched man that I am, who shall deliver me?"

It is for want of a fuller knowledge of yourselves that you are so negligent in your Christian watch; that you do not better guard your senses; that you make no stricter covenant with your eyes, your appetites, your tongues: that you no more examine what you think, affect and say: what passes in your heart and out of it: that you call not yourselves more frequently to account; but days run on, and duties are carelessly performed as a matter of course, and no daily or weekly reckoning made of the conscience of all. The knowledge of your weaknesses, and readiness to yield, and of your treacherous corruptions that comply with the enemy, would make you more suspicious of yourselves, and to walk more "circumspectly, not as fools, but as wise," (Ephesians 5:15) and to look under your feet, and consider your ways before you were too bold and venturous. It was the consciousness of their own infirmity, that should have moved the disciples to watch and pray. "Watch and pray that ye enter not into temptation: the spirit indeed is willing, but the flesh is weak." (Matthew 26:41.)

The knowledge of ourselves does show us all the advantages of the tempter: what he has to work upon, and what there is in us to take his part, and consequently where he is most likely to assault us: and so puts us into so prepared a posture for defence, as very much hinders his success. But so far as we do not know ourselves, we are like blind men in fencing, that the adversary may hit what part he please: we have so many hidden enemies in our houses, as will quickly open the door to more. What sin may not Satan tempt a man into, that is not acquainted with the corruptions and frailties of his own heart!

There are few of us, I think, that observe our hearts at all, but find both upon any special illumination, and in the hour of discovering trials, that there were many distempers in our hearts, and many miscarriages in our lives, that we never took notice of before. The heart has such secret corners of uncleanness, such mysteries of iniquity, and depths of deceitfulness, that many, fearing God, are strangely unacquainted with themselves as to the particular motions and degrees of sin, until some notable providence or gracious light assists them in the discovery.

The secret habits of sin, being discernible only by certain acts, are many times unknown to us, because we are under no strong temptation to commit those sins. And it is a wonderful hard thing for a man that has little or no temptation to know himself and to know what he should do if he had the temptations of other men. And O, what sad discoveries are made in the hour of temptation! What swarms of vice break out in some, like vermin, that lay hid in the cold of winter, and crawl about when they feel the summer's heat! What horrid corruptions which we never observed in ourselves before, do show themselves in the hour of temptation! Who would have thought that righteous Noah had in the ark such a heart as would by carelessness fall into the sin of drunkenness! Or that righteous Lot had carried from Sodom the seed of drunkenness and incest in him! Or that David a man so eminent in holiness, and a man after God's own heart, had a heart that had in it the seeds of adultery and murder!

And as the sinful inclinations are hardly discerned, and long lie hid until some temptation draw them out; so the act itself is hardly discerned in any of its malignity, till it be done and past, and the soul is brought to a deliberate review. For while a man is in the act of sin, either his understanding is so far deluded as to think it is no sin in its kind, or none to him that then commits it; or that it is better to venture on it than not, for the attaining of some seeming good, or the avoiding of some evil: or else the restraining act of the understanding is suspended and withdrawn; or it discerns not practically the pernicious evil of the sin, and forbids not the committing of it, or forbids it so remissly and with so low a voice, that it is drowned by the clamour of contradicting passion: so that the prohibition is not heard. And how can it be then expected, that when a man has not wit enough in use, to see his sin let alone to forbear it, he should even then see it clearly enough to judge of himself and it? And that when reason is low, and sensuality prevails, we should then have the right use of reason for self-discerning? When a storm of passion has blown out the light, and error has extinguished it we are unlikely then to know ourselves. When the sensual part is pleasing itself with its forbidden objects, that pleasure corrupts the judgment so much that men will easily believe that is is lawful or that it is not very bad: so that sin is usually least known and felt when it is greatest and in exercise and, one would think, should then be most perceptible. Like a frenzy or madness or other delirium, that is least known when it is greatest and most active, because its nature is destructive to the reason that should know it: like a spot in the eye, that is itself unseen, and hinders the sight of all things else. Or as the deeper a man's sleep is, the less he knows that he is asleep.

Little do we think what odious and dangerous errors may befall a person that now is orthodox! What a slippery mutability the mind of man is liable to! How variety of representations causes variety of apprehensions: like some pictures that seem one thing when you look on them on one side, and another thing when on another side; if you change your place, or change your light, they seem to change. Indeed God's word has nothing in it thus fitted to deceive: but our weakness has that which disposes us to mistakes. We are like an unlearned judge that thinks the cause is good which he first hears pleaded for, till he hear the confutation by the other party, and then he thinks the other has the best cause, till perhaps he hear both so long, he knows not whose cause is the best. The person that now is a zealous lover of the truth, (when it has procured entertainment by the happy advantage of friends, acquaintance, ministers, magistrates, or common consent being on its side) may possibly turn a zealous adversary to it, when it loses those advantages. When a minister shall change his mind, how many of the flock may he mislead!

When you marry, or contract any intimate friendship with a person of unsound and dangerous principles, how easily are they received!

When the stream of the times and authority shall change, and put the name of truth on falsehood, how many may be carried down the stream!

Little do many think in their adversity, or low estate, what seeds are in their hearts, which prosperity would turn into very odious, scandalous sins, unless their vigilance, and a special preservation, prevent it. Many a man that in his shop, or at his plough, is censuring the great miscarriages of his superiors, little thinks how bad he might prove, if he were in the place of those he censures. Many a poor man that freely talks against the luxury, pride, and cruelty of the rich, little thinks how like them he should be, if he had their temptations and estates. How many persons that lived in good repute for humility, temperance, and piety, have we seen turn proud and sensual and ungodly, when they have been exalted! I would mention no man's case by way of insult or reproach, but by way of compassion, and in order for the repentance of those that survive. I must say that this age has given us such lamentable instances, as should make all our hearts ache and fear, when we consider the crimes and their effects. Would the person that once walked with us in the ways of peace and concord, and obedience, have believed that man that should have foretold them twenty years ago, how many should be puffed up and deluded by success, and make themselves believe, by the ebullience of pride, that victories authorised them to deny subjection to the higher powers, and by right or wrong to take down all that stood in their way, and to take the government into their own hands, and to depose their rightful governors, never once vouchsafing to ask themselves the question that Christ asked (Luke 12:14), "Man, who made me a judge, or a divider over you?"

A man who in adversity is touched with penitent and mortifying considerations, and strongly resolves how holily and diligently he will live hereafter, if he is recovered or delivered from his suffering, does oft-times little think what a treacherous heart he has and how little he may retain of all this sense of sin or duty when he is delivered and that he will be so much worse than he seemed or promised, as that he may have cause to wish he had been afflicted still. O how many sick-bed promises are as pious as we can desire, that wither away and come to almost nothing, when health has scattered the fears that caused them! How many with the great imprisoned Lord, do as it were, write the story of Christ upon their prison walls, that forget him when they are set at liberty!

How many are tender-conscienced in a low estate, that when they are exalted and converse with great ones, think that they may waste their time in idleness and needless scandalous recreations, and be silent witnesses of the most odious sins from day to day! O what a preservative would it be to us in prosperity, to know the corruption of our hearts, and foresee in adversity what we are in danger of!

Alas, how quickly and insensibly do we slide into our former insensibility, and into our dull and heavy fruitless course, when one adversity is gone! And then when the next affliction comes, we are confounded and covered with shame, and have not the confidence with God in our prayers and cries as we had before, because we are conscious of our covenant-breaking and backsliding; and at last we grow so distrustful of our hearts, that we know not how to believe any promises which they make, or how to be confident of any evidence of grace that is in them; and so we lose the comfort of our sincerity, and are cast into a state of too much heaviness and unthankful denial of our dearest mercies. And all this comes from the foul, unexpected relapses, coolings and declinings of the heart that comes not up to the promises we made to God in our distress.

O what pillars have been shaken by prosperity! What promises broken! What sad eruptions of pride and worldliness! What revealing and sad discoveries of heart, does this alluring, charming trial make! And why is it that men know not themselves when they are exalted? Is it not because they did not sufficiently know themselves when they were brought low, nor suspected enough the purposes and promises of their hearts, in the day of their distress!

We would little think, when the heart is warmed and raised even to Heaven, in holy ordinances, how cold it will grow again, and how low it will fall! And when we have attained the clearest sight of our sincerity, we little think how quickly all such apprehensions may be lost; and the misjudging soul, that reckons upon nothing but what it sees, or feels at present, may be at a great a loss as if it had never perceived any fruits of the Spirit, or lineaments of the image of God upon itself. How confident, upon good grounds, is many an honest heart of its sincerity! How certain that it desires to be perfectly holy! How clearly may the heart perceive all these, and write them down; and yet before long have lost the sight and sense of them all, and find itself in darkness and confusion, and perhaps be persuaded that all is contrary with them!

Now, no joy, no assurace, no boldness, or confidence, or sense of love and pardon appear; but the soul seems dead, and carnal, and unrenewed. As the same trees that in summer are beautified with pleasant fruits and flowers, in winter are deprived of their natural ornaments and seem as if dead when the life is retired to the root. The soul that once would have defied the accuser, if he had told him that he did not love the brethren, nor love the sanctifying word and means, nor desire to be holy, and to be free from sin, is now as ready to believe the tempter than the minister that watches for them, as one that must give account. Yea, now it will turn the accuser, and say as Satan, and falsely charge itself with that which Christ will acquit it of.

And there is not a soul so high in joy and sweet assurance, but is liable to fall as low as this. And it makes our case to be much more grievous than otherwise it would be, because we know not ourselves in the hour of our consolations, and think not how apt we are to lose all our joy, and what seeds of doubts, and fears, and grief, are still within us, and what cause we have to expect a change. And therefore when so sad a change befalls us, so contrary to our expectations, it surprises us with terror, and casts the poor soul almost into despair. Then cries the distressed sinner, "Did I ever think to see this day! Are my hopes and comforts come to this! Did I think so long that I was a child of God and must I now perceive that He disowns me! Did I draw near Him as my father, and place my hope in His relief; and now must my mouth be stopped with unbelief, and must I look at Him afar off, and pass by the doors of mercy with despair! Is all my sweet familiarity with the godly, and all my comfortable hours under the precious means of grace, now come to this!" O how the poor soul here calls itself "O vile apostate, miserable sinner! O that I had never lived to see this gloomy day! It had been better for me never to have known the way of righteousness, than thus to have relapsed; and have all the prayers that I have put up, and all the sermons I have heard, and the books that I have read, to aggravate my sin and misery."

Take warning, therefore, dear Christians, you that are yet in the sunshine of mercy and have never been at so sad a loss, nor put to grope in the darkness of mistake and terror. No man is so well in health, but must reckon on it that he may be sick. When you feel nothing but peace and quietness of mind, expect a stormy night of fears, that may disquiet you. When you are feasting upon the sweet entertainments of your Father's love, consider that harder fare is likely to be your ordinary diet.

So when you are clear and vigorous in the life of faith, and can abhor all temptations to unbelief, and the beams of sacred verity in the Scriptures, have showed you that it is the undoubted word of God, and you have quietly founded your soul on Chist, and built your hopes upon His promises, and can with a cheerful contempt let go the world for the accomplishment of your hopes; remember yet that there is a secret root of unbelief remaining in you, and that this odious sin is but imperfectly mortified at best: and that it is more than possible that you may see the day when the tempter will assault you with questionings of the word of God, and trouble you with the injections of blasphemous thoughts and doubts about whether it be true or not! And that you that have thought of God, of Christ, of Heaven, of the immortal state of souls, with joy and satisfied confidence; you may be in the dark about them, affrighted with ugly suggestions of the enemy, and may think of them all with troublesome distracting doubts, and be forced to cry with the disciples: "Lord, increase our faith."

You see then how often and dangerously we are decieved by unacquaintedness with ourselves; and how selfish, carnal principles, ends and motives, are often mixed in the actions which we think are the most excellent for wisdom, zeal and piety, that ever we did perform. O therefore, what cause have we to study, and search, and watch such hearts, and not too boldly or carelessly to trust them!

GEORGE FOX: Epistles to the New World and to Friends Everywhere

Dear brethren, in the mighty power of God go on preaching the gospel to every creature, and making disciples of them in the name of the Father, Son and Holy Spirit. In the name of Christ, preach the mighty day of the Lord to all the consciences of them who have lain long in darkness and under its chain, where the light shined, but the darkness could not comprehend it. Go on to plant a vineyard, and to plough, that you may eat the fruit thereof; and to plant in hope, and to thresh in hope, that you may be made partakers of your hope, and to thresh out the corn, that the wind may scatter the chaff, that the corn may be gathered into the barn. So, in the power of the Lord Jesus Christ, preach the everlasting gospel, that by His power the sick may be healed, the leprous cleansed, the dead raised, the blind eyes opened, and the devils cast out. In the name of the Lord Jesus Christ go on, that what is of God in all consciences may witness that you are sent of God, and are of God: and so according to that speak, to bring up all unto the head, Christ, and into the life, which gave forth the Scriptures; for there is the unity, and apart from it is confusion.

Sound, sound the trumpet abroad, you valiant soldiers of Christ's kingdom, of which there is no end! All the Antichrists in the kingdom of fallen men are up in arms against Christ.

Dear friends, I am moved to write these things to you in all the plantations. God that made the world, and all things therein, and gives life and breath to all, is the God of the spirits of all flesh, and is "no respecter of persons", but whosoever fears Him, and works righteousness, is accepted of Him. And He has made all nations of one blood to dwell upon the face of the earth and His eyes are over all the works of His hands and see everything that is done under the whole heavens; and the earth is the Lord's and the fullness thereof. And He causes the rain to fall upon the just and upon the unjust, and also He causes the sun to shine upon the just and the unjust; and He commands us to love all men; for Christ so loved all, that He died for sinners. And this is God's love to the world, in giving His Son into the world; that whosoever believes in Him, should not perish. And He does enlighten every man that comes into the world, that they might believe in the Son. And the gospel is preached to every creature under Heaven; which is the power that gives liberty and freedom, and is glad tidings to every captive creature under the whole heavens. And the word of God is in the heart and mouth. For Christ is given for a covenant to the people, and a light to the Gentiles, and to enlighten them; who is the glory of Israel, and God's salvation to the ends of the earth. And so you are to have the mind of Christ, and so be merciful, as your heavenly Father is merciful.

Friends, keep out of the vain fashions of the world; let not your eyes, and minds, and spirits run after every fashion in apparel; for that will lead you from the solid life into unity with that spirit that leads to follow the fashions of the nations. But mind that which is sober and modest, and keep plain fashions, that therein you may judge the world, whose minds and eyes are in what they shall put on, and what they shall eat. But keep all in modesty, and plainness, and fervency, and sincerity, and be circumspect; for they that follow those things that the world's spirit invents daily, cannot be solid. Therefore all must keep down that spirit of the world that runs into so many fashions to please the lust of the eye, the lust of the flesh, and the pride of life. And fashion not yourselves according to your former lust of ignorance; and let the time past, in which you have lived according to the lusts of men, and the course of the world be sufficient; that the rest of your time you may live to the will of God; taking no thought what you shall eat, what you shall drink, or what you shall put on. Therefore take heed of the world's vanity, and trust not in uncertain riches, neither covet the riches of this world; but seek the kingdom of God, and the righteousness thereof, and all other things will follow. And let your minds rise above the costly and vain fashions of attire, but mind the hidden man of the heart, which is a meek and a quiet spirit, which is of great price with the Lord. And keep to justice and truth in all your dealings and tradings, and to the form of sound words, in the power of the Lord and in equity, in yea and nay in all your dealings, that your lives and conversations may be in Heaven, and above the earth; that they may preach to all that you have to deal with; so that you may be as a city set on a hill, that cannot be hid, as as lights of the world, answering the equal principle in all; that God may in all things be glorified. Then you may pass your time here with fear, as pilgrims, and strangers, and sojourners, having an eye over all things that are uncertain, as cities, houses, lands, goods, and all things below; possessing them as if you did not; and as having a city whose maker and builder is God, and an inheritance that will never fade away, in which you have riches that will abide with you eternally.

Friends, dwell in the Living Spirit, and quench not the motions of it in yourselves, nor the movings of it in others. Though many have run out, and gone beyond their measures, yet many more have quenched the measure of the Spirit of God, and have become dead and dull, and have questioned through a false fear; so they have been hurt both ways. Therefore be obedient to the power of the Lord, and his Spirit; war with that Philistine that would stop up your wells and springs. The belief in the power keeps the spring open, none are to despise prophecy, neither to quench the Spirit; so that all may be kept open to the spring, that everyone's cup may run over. For you may all prophesy one by one, and the spirit of the prophets is subject to the prophets: "would that all the Lord's people were prophets", said Moses in his time, when some found fault; but the last time is the Christian's time, who enjoys the substance, Christ Jesus; and His church is called a royal priesthood, offering up spiritual sacrifices; and His church are His believers in the Light. And so in the Light everyone should have something to offer; and to offer an offering in righteousness to the living God, else they are not priests and such as quench the Spirit cannot offer, but become dull. "I will pour out my Spirit upon all flesh, in the last time", says the Lord. This is the true Christian time: "God's sons and daughters shall prophesy, and your young men shall see visions, and old men shall dream dreams; and on my servants and handmaids I will pour out my Spirit in those days, and they shall prophesy." Now, friends, if this be fulfilled, servants, handmaids, sons, daughters, old men, young men, everyone is to feel the Spirit of God, by which you may see the things of God, and declare them to His praise; for with the heart man does believe, and with the mouth confession is made unto salvation.

So, with the Holy Ghost, and with the light and power of God, build upon Christ, the Foundation and Life; and by the same heavenly Light, and Power, and Spirit, labour in the vineyard, and minister and speak forth the things of God, and dig for your pearls; therefore bring them forth, and let it be seen how they glisten. Friends, you see how men and women can speak enough for the world, for merchandise, for husbandry, the ploughman for his plough; but when they should come to speak for God, they quench the Spirit, and do not obey God's will.

So none is to quench the Spirit, nor to despise prophecy, lest you limit the Holy One; and everyone is to minister as he has received the grace, which has appeared to all men, and which brings salvation; so that the Lord's grace, His light, and truth, and Spirit, and power, may have the passage and the rule in all men and women; that by it and from it in all, He may have the glory, who is blessed for ever and for ever. The Lord has said: "From the rising of the sun to the going down of the same, my name shall be great among the Gentiles." Now mark, friends, this is a large space wherein God's name shall be great; and the Lord further says: "In every place, incense shall be offered unto my name, and a pure offering; for my name shall be great among the heathen", said the Lord of Hosts. Now mark, friends, this heavenly incense, and pure offering, is a spiritual offering, which is to be offered by the spirit of God, who is a spirit; then here none must quench the Spirit of God in his own heart; and all such come under the title of the royal priesthood, offering up spiritual sacrifices; which royal priesthood has a priest that lives for ever, Christ Jesus.

And, friends, do not quench the Spirit, nor abuse the Power. When it moves and stirs in you, be obedient; but do not go beyond, nor add to it, nor take from it; for if you do, you are reproved, either for going beyond, or taking from it. And when any have spoken forth the things of the Lord, by His Power and Spirit, let them keep in the Power and Spirit that keeps them in humility, that when they have spoken forth the things of God, they are neither higher nor lower, but still keep in the Power, before and after. Being obedient to the Spirit and Power of God, keeps them from deadness, and alive to God, and keeps them in a sense that they do not go beyond and run out, as some you know have done: and all that has happened for want of living in the Power of God, and in His Spirit, which keeps all things in subjection and in order that in the fear of the Lord, always to feel the presence of the Lord with you.

Come, fishermen, what have you caught with your nets? What can you say for God? Your brethren Peter and John, fishermen, could say much for God. Read in the Acts and you may see it; I would not have you degenerate from their spirit.

Shepherds and herdsmen, who are you? What can you say now for God, who abides much in the fields? David, Jacob, and Amos, your fellow shepherds and herdsmen, (do not you see?) they could say much for God; I would have you be like them, and not to degenerate from their spirit.

Come, tradesmen, tent-makers, physicians and custom-men, what can you say for God? Do not you read that your fellow tradesmen in ages past could say much for God? Do not degenerate from their spirit. Do you not remember the accusations of the wise and learned Greeks, when the apostles preached Christ among them, that they were called poor tradesmen and fishermen? Therefore be faithful. The preachers of Jesus Christ now are the same to the wise of the world as then.

TO ALL WOMEN'S MEETINGS

Friends, keep your women's meetings in the power of God, and take your possession of that which you are heirs of, and keep the gospel order. For man and woman were helpmates in the image of God, and in righteousness and holiness, in the dominion, before they fell; but after the fall, in the transgression, the man was to rule over his wife; but in the restoration by Christ, they will be made in the image of God, and his righteousness and holiness again, in that they will be helpmates, man and woman, as they were before the fall. Sarah obeyed Abraham, and called him lord. Abraham did also obey the voice of his wife Sarah, in casting out the bondwoman and her son. Dorcas, a woman, was a disciple. So there was a woman disciple, as well as men disciples; and remember the women that accompanied her. And women are to take up the cross daily, and follow Christ daily, as well as the men; and so to be taught of Him their Shepherd, and counselled of Him their Counsellor, and sanctified by Him who offered Himself once for all. And there were elder women in the truth as well as elder men in the truth; so they have an office as well as the men, for they have a stewardship, and must give account of their stewardship to the Lord, as well as the men.

Deborah was a judge; Miriam and Huldah were prophetesses; old Anna was a prophetess, and a preacher of Christ. To all them that looked for redemption in Jerusalem, Mary Magdalene, and the other Mary, were the first preachers of Christ's resurrection to the disciples, and the disciples could not believe their message and testimony that they had from Jesus, as some nowadays cannot; but they received the command and, being sent, preached it. So is every woman and man to do, that sees Him risen, and has the command and message; daughters shall prophesy as well as sons. So they are to be obedient that have the Spirit poured upon them. Women are to prophesy; and prophecy is not to be quenched. They that have the testimony of Jesus are commanded to keep it, whether men or women. Priscilla and Aquila were both exhorters and expounders, or instructers to Apollos. So in the church there were women instructors, and prophetesses, and daughters were prophetesses in the church; for Philip had four virgins that were prophetesses; and there were women disciples in the church, and women elders in the church, as well as men. So women are to keep in the government of Christ, and to be obeyers of Christ; and women are to keep the comely order of the gospel, as well as men; and to see that all that have received Christ Jesus, do walk in Christ Jesus; and to see that all have received the gospel, do walk in the gospel, the power of God which they are heirs of. I say, they are heirs of the comely order of the gospel; and therefore, I say your posession of it, and walk as becomes the gospel; and keep the comely order of it, and in it keep your meetings. And here is the ground and foundation of our women's meetings.

Now mothers of families, that have the ordering of children, maids and servants, may do a great deal of good or harm in their families, to the making or spoiling of children, maids and servants; and many things women may do and speak of among women, which are not men's business. So men and women become helpmates in the image of God.

And the elder women in the truth were not only called elders, but mothers. Now a mother in the church of Christ, and a mother in Israel, is one that nourishes, and feeds, and washes, and rules, and is a teacher in the church, and in the Israel of God, and an admonisher, an instructor, an exhorter. So the elder women and mothers are to be teachers of good things, and to be teachers of the young and trainers of them in virtue, in holiness, in godliness and righteousness, in wisdom, and in the fear of the Lord, in the church of Christ. And if the unbelieving husband is sanctified by the believing wife, then who is the speaker, and who is the hearer? Surely such a woman is permitted to speak, and to work the works of God, and to make a member in the church; and then as an elder, to oversee that they walk according to the order of the gospel.

TO FRIENDS IN AMERICA, 1680

Dear friends, my love is to you all in the holy, peaceable truth; and my desires are, that whatsoever you do may be done in the name of Jesus, to the glory of God and the Father: and all be subject one to another in the fear of the Lord God, so that you may all come to dwell in the love of God, which edifies the body of Christ, who is the heavenly man. And let all strifes, and divisions, and backbitings, or whisperings, or prejudices, cease and be buried; and so whatsoever is amiss, or has been amiss, let it be put down by the truth and Spirit of God, that it may be uppermost, which is a strong bond to unite your hearts, and minds, and souls together, and to the Lord; and be kind and courteous one towards another, all studying to be quiet, and to excel one another in virtue, purity, holiness, righteousness, and godliness, in all your words, lives, and conversations; so that you may all walk as becomes saints and Christians, every one esteeming and preferring one another above himself in the truth in meekness, and lowliness of mind and humility: for He that inhabits eternity, dwells with the humble heart. And therefore do not quench the least motion of God's good Spirit in yourselves, nor in any other; but let truth and goodness be cherished in all; and let all harshness, and bitterness, and revilings be kept down by truth, that in it you may bear one another's weakness and infirmities, and so fulful the law of Christ; keeping down revenge, hastiness, or passion; knowing vengeance is the Lord's, and He will repay it on everyone that does wrong.

For if, friends, you should be as lights, or as a city that cannot be hid, and as the salt of the earth, to be a good savour: take heed of losing the salt's savour, either in word or conversation; for if you do, you will come under the foot of men, they will trample upon you; therefore be careful, fervent, circumspect, and faithful in the truth, and let your moderation, temperance, and sobriety appear to all men, showing forth the work of the Lord, and your honesty and justness in all your words and dealing between man and man; and owe nothing to any man but love, that every one of you may be adorned with a meek and quiet spirit, which is with the Lord of great price: and be endued with wisdom for on high, which is pure and peaceable, gentle and easy to be entreated, and full of mercy and good works; let the fruits of this wisdom appear among you all, and then you will be able to be gentle and easily entreated one of another.

And keep in the unity of the Spirit, which is the bond of the heavenly peace; and all walk as becomes the glorious, joyful, peaceable gospel of Christ, which is the power of God. And therefore, all you who know this glorious gospel of peace, live and walk in it, keeping your glorious, heavenly, comfortable fellowship in this glorious gospel of peace, in which enmity cannot come; and in this everlasting gospel, the everlasting God, who is over all, from everlasting to everlasting, will have the praise, glory and thanks, who is worthy of all, for ever and evermore.

JOHN WESLEY: The Almost Christian

"Almost you persuade me to be a Christian" (Acts 26:28)

And many there are who go thus far: ever since the Christian religion was in the world, there have been many, in every age and nation, who were almost persuaded to be Christians. But seeing it avails nothing before God to go only thus far, it highly imports us to consider first, what is implied in being *almost*, and secondly, what is being *altogether*, a Christian. Now in the being *almost* a Christian is implied, first, heathen honesty. No one, I suppose, will make any question of this; especially since, by heathen honesty, I mean not that which is recommended in the writings of their philosophers only, but such as the common heathens expected one of another, and many of them actually practised. By the rules of this they were taught that they ought not be unjust; not to take away their neighbour's goods, either by robbery or theft; not to oppress the poor, neither to use extortion toward any; not to cheat, or over-reach either the poor or rich, in whatsoever commerce they had with them; to defraud no man of his right; and, if it were possible, to owe no man anything.

Again, the common heathens allowed that some regard was to be paid to truth, as well as to justice. And accordingly, they not only held him in abomination who was forsworn, who called God to witness a lie; but also him who was known to be a slanderer of his neighbour, who falsely accused any man, and, indeed, little better did they esteem wilful liars of any sort, accounting them the disgrace of human kind, and the pests of society.

Yet again, there was a sort of love and assistance which they expected one from another. They expected whatever assistance any one could give another without prejudice to himself. And this they extended not only to those little offices of humanity which are performed without any expense or labour, but likewise to feeding the hungry, if they had food to spare; clothing the naked with their own superfluous raiment; and, in general, giving, to any that needed, such things as they needed not themselves. Thus far, in the lowest account of it, heathen honesty went; the first thing implied in being *almost* Christian.

A second thing implied in being *almost* a Christian, is, having a form of godliness, of that godliness which is prescribed in the gospel of Christ; having the outside of a real Christian. Accordingly, the *almost* Christian does nothing which the gospel forbids. He takes not the name of God in vain; he blesses and curses not; he swears not at all, but his communication is, yea, yea; nay, nay. He profanes not the day of the Lord, nor suffers it to be profaned, even by the stranger that is within his gates. He not only avoids all actual adultery, fornication, and uncleanness, but every word or look that either directly or indirectly tends thereto; nay, and all idle words, abstaining both from detraction, backbiting, tale-bearing, evil speaking, and from "all foolish talking and jesting", briefly, from all coversation that is not "good for the use of edifying" and that, consequently, "grieves the Holy Spirit of God, whereby we are sealed to the day of redemption".

He abstains from "wine wherein is excess", from revelling and gluttony. He avoids, as much as in him lies, all strife and contention, continually endeavouring to live peaceably with all men. And, if he suffer wrong, he avenges not himself, neither returns evil for evil. He is no railer, no brawler, no scoffer, either at the faults of infirmities of his neighbours. He does not willingly wrong, hurt, or grieve any man; but in all things acts and speaks by the plain rule: "Whatsoever you would not he should do unto you, that do not you to another."

And in doing good, he does not confine himself to cheap and easy offices of kindness, but labours and suffers for the profit of many, that by all means he may help some. In spite of toil or pain, "whatsoever his hand finds to do, he does with his might", whether it be for his friends or for his enemies, for the evil or for the good. For, being "not slothful" in this or in any "business", as he "has opportunity" he does "good", all manner of good, "to all men"; and to their souls as well as their bodies. He reproves the wicked, instructs the ignorant, confirms the wavering, quickens the good and comforts the afflicted. He labours to awaken those that sleep; to lead those whom God has already awakened to the "fountain opened for sin and for uncleanness", that they may wash therein and be clean; and to stir up those who are saved, through faith, to adorn the gospel of Christ in all things.

He that has the form of godliness uses also the means of grace; yea, all of them, and at all opportunities. He constantly frequents the house of God; and that, not as the manner of some is, who come into the presence of the Most High, either loaded with gold and costly apparel, or in all the gaudy vanity of dress, and either by their unseasonable civilities to each other, or the impertinent gaiety of their behaviour, disclaim all pretensions to the form as well as to the power of godliness. Would to God there were none even among ourselves who fall under the same condemnation; who come into this house, it may be, gazing about, or with all the signs of the most listless, careless indifference, though sometimes they may seem to use a prayer to God for His blessing on what they are entering upon; who, during that awful service, are either asleep, or reclined in the most convenient posture for it; or, as though they supposed God was asleep, talking with one another, or looking round, as utterly void of employment. Neither let these be accused of the form of godliness. No, he who has even this behaves with seriousness and attention in every part of that solemn service. More especially when he approaches the table of the Lord, it is not with light or careless behaviour, but with an air, gesture and deportment which speaks nothing else but, "God be merciful to me, a sinner!"

To this, if we add the constant use of family prayer, by those who are masters of families, and the setting times apart for private addresses to God, with a daily seriousness of behaviour; he who uniformly practises this outward religion, has the form of godliness. There needs but one thing more in order to his being *almost* a Christian, and that is sincerity.

By sincerity I mean a real, inward principle of religion, from whence these outward actions flow. And, indeed, if we have not this, we have not heathen honesty. If any man, to avoid punishment, to avoid the loss of his friends, for his gain, for his reputation, should not only abstain from doing evil, but also do ever so much good; yea, and use all the means of grace; yet we could not, with any propriety, say, this man is even *almost* a Christian. If he has no better principle in his heart, he is only a hypocrite altogether.

Sincerity, therefore, is necessarily implied in being *almost* a Christian; a real design to serve God, a hearty desire to do His will. It is necessarily implied by this, that a man has a sincere view of pleasing God in all things; in all his conversation; in all his actions; in all he does, or leaves undone. This design, if any man be *almost* a Christian, runs through the whole tenor of his life. This is the moving principle, both in his doing good, his abstaining from evil, and his using the ordinances of God.

But here it will probably be inquired: "Is it possible that any man living should go so far as this, and, nevertheless, be only *almost* a Christian? What more than this can be implied in the being a Christian *altogether*?" I answer, first, that it is possible to go thus far, and yet be but *almost* a Christian, I learn, not only from the oracles of God, but also from the sure testimony of experience.

Brethren, great is "my boldness towards you in this behalf". And "forgive me this wrong", if I declare my own folly upon the house-top, for yours and the gospel's sake. Suffer me, then, to speak freely of myself, even as of another man, I am content to be abased so that you may be exalted, and to be yet more vile for the glory of my Lord.

I did go thus far for many years, as many of this place can testify; using diligence to eschew all evil, and to have a conscience void of offence; redeeming the time; buying up every opportunity of doing all good to all men; constantly and carefully using all the public and all the private means of grace; endeavouring after a steady seriousness of behaviour, at all times, and in all places; and, God is my record, before whom I stand, doing all this in sincerity; having a real design to serve God; a hearty desire to do His will in all things; to please Him who had called me to "fight the good fight", and to "lay hold of eternal life". Yet my own conscience bears me witness in the Holy Ghost, that all this time I was but *almost* a Christian.

If it be inquired: "What more than this is implied in being *altogether* a Christian?", I answer thus.

First, the love of God. For thus says His word: "You shall love the Lord your God, with all your heart, and with all your soul, and with all your mind, and with all your strength." Such a love is this, as engrosses the whole heart, as takes up all the affections, as fills the entire capacity of the soul and employs the utmost extent of all its faculties. He that thus loves the Lord his God, his spirit continually "rejoices in God his saviour". His delight is in the Lord, his Lord and his all, to whom "in everything he gives thanks". All his desire is unto God and to the remembrance of His name. His heart is ever crying out: "Whom have I in Heaven but you? And there is none upon earth that I desire beside you." Indeed, what can he desire beside God? Not the world, nor the things of the world: for he is "crucified to the world, and the world crucified to him". He is crucified to "the desire of the flesh, the desire of the eye, and the pride of life". Yea, he is dead to pride of every kind: for "love is not puffed up" but "he that dwelling in love dwells in God, and God in him," is less than nothing in his own eyes.

The second thing implied in the being *altogether* a Christian, is the love of our neighbour. For thus said our Lord, in the following words: "You shall love your neighbour as yourself." If any man ask: "Who is my neighbour?" we reply, every man in the world; every child of His who is the Father of the spirits of all flesh. Nor may we in anywise except our enemies, or the enemies of God and their own souls. But every Christian loves these also as himself, yea, "as Christ loved us". He that would more fully understand what manner of love this is, may consider St Paul's description of it. It is "long-suffering and kind". It "envies not". It is not rash or hasty in judging. It "is not puffed up" but makes him that loves, the least, the servant of all. Love "does not behave itself unseemly" but becomes "all things to all men". She "seeks not her own" but only the good of others, that they may be saved. "Love is not provoked." It casts out wrath, which he has who is wanting in love. "It thinks no evil. It rejoices not in iniquity, but rejoices in the truth. It covers all things, believes all things, hopes all things, endures all things."

There is yet one thing more that may be separately considered, though it cannot actually be separate from the preceding, *altogether* which is implied in the being a Christian, and that is the ground of all, even faith. Very excellent things are spoken of this throughout the oracles of God. "Everyone", says the beloved diciple, "that believes, is born of God." "To as many as received Him, gave He power to become the sons of God, even to them that believe on his name." And, "this is the victory that overcomes the world, even our faith." Yea, our Lord himself declares: "He that believes in the Son has everlasting life; and comes not into condemnation, but is passed from death unto life."

But here let no man deceive his own soul. "It is diligently to be noted, the faith which brings not forth repentance, and love, and all good works, is not that right living faith, but a dead and devilish one. For, even the devils believe that Christ was born of a virgin; that he wrought all kinds of miracles, declaring himself very God; that, for our sakes, He suffered a most painful death, to redeem us from death everlasting; that He rose again the third day; that He ascended into Heaven; and sits at the right hand of the Father, and at the end of the world shall come again to judge both the quick and dead. These articles of our faith the devils believe, and so they believe all that is written in the Old and New Testament. And yet for all this faith, they be but devils. They remain still in their damnable estate, lacking the very true Christian faith."

"The right and true Christian faith is" (to go on in the words of our own Church) "not only to believe that holy Scripture and the articles of our faith are true, but also to have a sure trust and confidence to be saved from everlasting damnation by Christ. It is a sure trust and confidence which a man has in God, that, by the merits of Christ, his sins are forgiven, and he is reconciled to the favour of God; whereof does follow a loving heart, to obey His commandments."

Now, whosoever has this faith, which "purifies the heart" (by the power of God, who dwells therein) from pride, anger, desire, "From all unrighteousness", from "all filthiness of flesh and spirit"; which fills it with love stronger than death, both to God and to mankind; love that does the works of God, glorying to spend and to be spent for all men, and that endures with joy, not only the reproach of Christ, the being mocked, despised and hated of all men, but whatsoever the wisdom of God permits the malice of men or devils to inflict; whosoever has this faith, his working by love, is not only *almost,* but *altogether,* a Christian.

But who are the living witnesses of these things? I beseech you, brethren, as in the presence of that God before whom "hell and destruction are without a covering", that each of you would ask his own heart: "Am I of that number? Do I so far practise justice, mercy, and truth, as even the rules of heathen honesty require? If so, have I the very outside of a Christian? The form of godliness? Do I abstain from evil, from whatsoever is forbidden in the written word of God? Do I, whatever good my hand finds to do, do it with all my might? Do I seriously use all the ordinances of God at all opportunities? And, is all this done with a sincere design and desire to please God in all things?"

Are not many of you conscious that you never came thus far; that you have not been even *almost* a Christian; that you have not come up to the standard of heathen honesty; at least, not to the form of Christian godliness? Much less has God seen sincerity in you, a real design of pleasing Him in all things. You never so much as intended to devote all your words and works, your business, studies, diversions, to His glory. You never even designed or desired that whatsoever you did should be done "in the name of the Lord Jesus", and as such should be a "spiritual sacrifice, acceptable to God through Christ".

But, supposing you had, do good designs and good desires make a Christian? By no means, unless they are brought to good effect. "Hell is paved", says one, "with good intentions." The great question of all, then, still remains. Is the love of God shed abroad in your heart? Can you cry out:

"My God, and my all?" Do you desire nothing but him? Are you happy in God? Is He your glory, your delight, your crown of rejoicing? And is this commandment written in your heart: "That he who loves God love his brother also?" Do you then love your neighbour as yourself? Do you love every man, even your enemies, even the enemies of God, as your own soul? As Christ loved you? Yea, do you believe that Christ loved you, and gave Himself for you? Have you faith in His blood? Do you believe the Lamb of God has taken away your sins, and cast them as a stone into the depths of the sea? That He has blotted out the handwriting that was against you, taking it out of the way, nailing it to His cross? Have you indeed redemption through his blood, even the remission of your sins? And does His Spirit bear witness with your spirit, that you are a child of God?

The God and Father of our Lord Jesus Christ, who now stands in the midst of us, knows that if any man die without this faith and this love, good it were for him that he had never been born. Awake, then, you that sleep, and call upon your God: call in the day when He may be found. Let him not rest, till he make "his goodness to pass before you", till he proclaim unto you the name of the Lord: "The Lord, the Lord God, merciful and gracious, long-suffering, and abundant in goodness and truth, keeping mercy for thousands, forgiving iniquity, and transgression, and sin." Let no man persuade you, by vain words, to rest short of this prize of high callng. But cry unto Him day and night, who, "while we were without strength died for the ungodly", until you know in whom you have believed, and can say: "My Lord, and my God!" Remember, "always to pray, and not to faint", till you also can lift up your hand to Heaven, declaring: "Lord, You know all things, You know that I love You."

May we all thus experience what it is to be, not only *almost*, but *altogether* Christians; being justified freely by His grace, through the redemption that is in Jesus; knowing we have peace with God through Jesus Christ; rejoicing in hope of the glory of God; and having the love of God shed abroad in our hearts, by the Holy Ghost given unto us!

CHARLES WESLEY: Hymns

O THOU WHO CAMEST FROM ABOVE

O Thou who camest from above,
The pure celestial fire to impart,
Kindle a flame of sacred love
On the low altar of my heart.

Jesus, confirm my heart's desire
To work, and speak, and think for Thee;
Still let me guard the holy fire,
And still stir up Thy gift in me.

Ready for all Thy perfect will,
My acts of faith and love repeat,
Till death Thy endless mercies seal,
And make my sacrifice complete.

LOVE DIVINE, ALL LOVES EXCELLING

Love Divine, all loves excelling,
Joy of Heav'n, to earth come down,
Fix in us Thy humble dwelling,
All Thy faithful mercies crown.

Jesu, Thou art all compassion,
Pure unbounded love Thou art;
Visit us with Thy salvation,
Enter every trembling heart,

Come, Almighty to deliver,
Let us all Thy grace receive;
Suddenly return, and never,
Never more Thy temples leave.

Thee we would be always blessing,
Serve Thee as Thy Hosts above;
Pray, and praise Thee, without ceasing,
Glory in Thy perfect love.

Finish then Thy new creation,
Pure and spotless let us be;
Let us see Thy great salvation,
Perfectly restored in Thee.

Changed from glory into glory,
Till in Heav'n we take our place,
Till we cast our crowns before Thee,
Lost in wonder, love, and praise.

JESU, LOVER OF MY SOUL

Jesu, lover of my soul,
Let me to Thy bosom fly,
While the gathering waters roll,
While the tempest still is high:
Hide me, O my Saviour, hide,
Till the storm of life is past;
Safe into the haven guide,
O receive my soul at last.

Other refuge have I none;
Hangs my helpless soul on Thee;
Leave, ah! leave me not alone,
Still support and comfort me.
All my trust on Thee is stay'd,
All my help from Thee I bring;
Cover my defenceless head
With the shadow of Thy wing.

Plenteous grace with Thee is found,
Grace to cleanse from every sin;
Let the healing streams abound;
Wake and keep me pure within;
Thou of life the fountain art;
Freely let me take of Thee;
Spring Thou up within my heart,
Rise to all eternity.

HARK! THE HERALD ANGELS SING

Hark! the herald angels sing
Glory to the new-born King,
Peace on earth, and mercy mild.
God and sinners reconciled.
Joyful, all ye nations, rise,
Join the triumph of the skies;
With the angelic host proclaim,
"Christ is born in Bethlehem."
Hark! the herald angels sing
Glory to the new-born King.

Christ, by highest Heav'n adored,
Christ, the Everlasting Lord,
Late in time behold Him come,
Offspring of a virgin's womb.
Veil'd in flesh the Godhead see!
Hail, the Incarnate Deity!
Pleased as man with man to dwell,
Jesus, our Emmanuel.
Hark! the herald angels sing
Glory to the new-born King.

Hail, the Heaven-born Prince of Peace!
Hail, the Sun of righteousness!
Light and life to all He brings,
Risen with healing in His wings,
Mild He lays His glory by.
Born that man no more may die,
Born to raise the sons of earth,
Born to give them second birth.
Hark! the herald angels sing
Glory to the new-born King.

REJOICE! THE LORD IS KING

Rejoice! The Lord is King,
Your Lord and King adore;
Mortals, give thanks and sing,
And triumph evermore:
Lift up your heart, lift up your voice;
Rejoice, again I say, rejoice.

Jesus, the Saviour, reigns,
The God of truth and love;
When He had purged our stains,
He took His seat above;

His kingdom cannot fail;
He rules o'er earth and Heaven;
The keys of death and Hell
Are to our Jesus given:

He sits at God's right hand
Till all His foes submit,
And bow to His command,
And fall beneath His feet:

LO! HE COMES WITH CLOUDS DESCENDING

Lo! He comes with clouds descending,
Once for favour'd sinners slain;
Thousand thousand saints attending
Swell the triumph of His train;
 Alleluia!
Christ appears on earth again.

Every eye shall now behold Him
Robed in dreadful majesty;
Those who set at nought and sold Him
Pierced and nail'd Him to the tree
 Deeply wailing,
Shall the true Messiah see.

The dear tokens of his Passion
Still His dazzling body bears,
Cause of endless exultation
To His ransom's worshippers:
With what rapture
Gaze we on those glorious scars.

Yea, Amen, let all adore Thee,
High on Thine eternal throne:
Saviour, take the power and glory;
Claim the Kingdom for Thine own:
Alleluia!
Thou shalt reign, and Thou alone.

ISAAC WATTS: Hymns

WHEN I SURVEY THE WONDROUS CROSS

When I survey the wondrous cross,
On which the Prince of Glory died,
My richest gain I count but loss,
And pour contempt on all my pride.

Forbid it, Lord, that I should boast
Save in the death of Christ my God;
All the vain things that charm me most,
I sacrifice them to His blood.

See from His head, His hands, His feet,
Sorrow and love flow mingled down;
Did e'er such love and sorrow meet,
Or thorns compose so rich a crown?

His dying crimson, like a robe,
Spreads o'er His body on the tree;
Then am I dead to all the globe,
And all the globe is dead to me.

Were the whole realm of nature mine,
That were a present far too small;
Love so amazing, so divine,
Demands my soul, my life, my all.

JESUS SHALL REIGN WHERE'ER THE SUN

Jesus shall reign where'er the sun
Doth his successive journeys run;
His kingdom stretch from shore to shore,
'Till moons shall wax and wane no more.

People and realms of every tongue
Dwell on His love with sweetest song,
And infant voices shall proclaim
Their early blessings on His name.

Blessings abound where'er He reigns;
The prisoner leaps to loose his chains;
The weary find eternal rest,
And all the sons of want are blest.

Let every creature rise and bring
Peculiar honours to our King;
Angels descend with songs again,
And earth repeat the loud Amen.

O GOD, OUR HELP IN AGES PAST

O God, our help in ages past,
Our hope for years to come,
Our shelter from the stormy blast,
And our eternal home;

Beneath the shadow of Thy throne
Thy saints have dwelt secure;
Sufficient is Thine arm alone,
And our defence is sure.

Before the hills in order stood,
Or earth received her frame,
From everlasting Thou art God,
To endless years the same.

A thousand ages in Thy sight
Are like an evening gone;
Short as the watch that ends the night
Before the rising sun.

Time, like an ever-rolling stream,
Bears all its sons away;
They fly forgotten, as a dream
Dies at the opening day.

O God, our help in ages past,
Our hope for years to come,
Be thou our guard while troubles last,
And our eternal home.

SAMUEL DAVIES: Hymn

GREAT GOD OF WONDERS! ALL THY WAYS

Great God of wonders! all Thy ways
Are worthy of Thyself divine;
And the bright glories of Thy grace
Among Thine other wonders shine:
Who is a pard'ning God like Thee?
Or who has grace so rich and free?

Pardon from an offended God!
Pardon for sins of deepest dye!
Pardon bestowed through Jesus' blood!
Pardon that brings the rebel nigh!
Who is a pard'ning God like Thee?
Or who has grace so rich and free?

O may this glorious, matchless love,
This God-like miracle of grace,
Teach mortal tongues, like those above,
To raise this song of lofty praise:
Who is a pard'ning God like Thee?
Or who has grace so rich and free?

JONATHAN EDWARDS: Sinners in the Hands of an Angry God

"Their foot shall slide in due time" (Deuteronomy 32:35)

In this verse is threatened the vengeance of God on the wicked, unbelieving Israelites, who were God's visible people, and who lived under the means of grace; but who, notwithstanding all God's wonderful works towards them, remained void of counsel, having no understanding in them. Under all the cultivations of Heaven, they brought forth bitter and poisonous fruit.

The expression I have chosen for my text, "their foot shall slide in due time", seems to imply the following things, relating to the punishment and destruction to which these wicked Israelites were exposed.

1 That they were always exposed to destruction; as one that stands or walks in slippery places is always exposed to fall. This is implied in the manner of their destruction coming upon them, being represented by their foot sliding. The same is expressed (Psalm 73:18) "Surely, You did set them in slippery places; You cast them down into destruction".

2 It implies that they were always exposed to sudden unexpected destruction. As he that walks in slippery places is every moment liable to fall, he cannot foresee one moment whether he shall stand or fall the next; and when he does fall, he falls at once without warning. Which is also expressed (in Psalm 73:18, 19), "Surely You did set them in slippery places; You cast them down into destruction: How are they brought into desolation as in a moment!"

3 Another thing implied is that they are liable to fall of themselves, without being thrown down by the hand of another; as he that stands or walks on slippery ground needs nothing but his own weight to throw him down.

4 That the reason why they are not fallen already, and do not fall now, is only that God's appointed time is not come. For it is said, that when that due time, or appointed time comes, their foot shall slide. Then they shall be left to fall, as they are inclined by their own weight. God will not hold them up in these slippery places any longer, but will let them go; and then, at that very instant, they shall fall into destruction; as he that stands on such slippery declining ground, on the edge of a pit, he cannot stand alone; when he is let go he immediately falls and is lost.

The observation from the words that I would now insist upon is this. "There is nothing that keeps wicked men at any one moment out of Hell, but the mere pleasure of God." By the mere pleasure of God, I mean His sovereign pleasure, His arbitrary will, restrained by no obligation, hindered by no manner of difficulty, any more than if nothing else but God's mere will had in the least degree, or in any respect whatsoever, any hand in the preservation of wicked men one moment. The truth of this observation may appear by the following considerations.

1 There is no want of power in God to cast wicked men into Hell at any moment. Men's hands cannot be strong when God rises up: the strongest have no power to resist Him, nor can any deliver out of His hands. He is not only able to cast wicked men into Hell, but He can most easily do it. Sometimes an earthly prince meets with a great deal of difficulty to subdue a rebel, who has found means to fortify himself and has made himself strong by the numbers of his followers. But it is not so with God. There is no fortress that is any defence from the power of God. Though hand join in hand, the vast multitudes of God's enemies combine and associate themselves, they are easily broken in pieces. They are as great heaps of light chaff before the whirlwind; or large quantities of dry stubble before devouring flames. We find it easy to tread on and crush a worm that we see crawling on the earth; so it is easy for us to cut or singe a slender thread that any thing hangs by: thus easy is it for God, when He pleases, to cast His enemies down to Hell. What are we, that we should think to stand before Him, at whose rebuke the earth trembles, and before whom the rocks are thrown down?

2 The wicked deserve to be cast into Hell; so that divine justice never stands in the way, it makes no objection against God's using His power at any moment to destroy them. Yea, on the contrary, justice calls aloud for an infinite punishment of their sins. Divine justice says of the tree that brings forth such grapes of Sodom, "Cut it down, why cumbers it the ground?" (Luke 13:7). The sword of divine justice is every moment brandished over their heads, and it is nothing but the hand of arbitrary mercy, and God's mere will, that holds it back.

3 They are already under a sentence of condemnation to Hell. They do not only justly deserve to be cast down there, but the sentence of the law of God, that eternal and immutable rule of righteousness that God has fixed between Him and mankind, has gone out against them, and stands against them; so that they are bound over already to Hell (John 3:18): "He that does not believe is condemned already." So that every unconverted man properly belongs to Hell; that is his place, for thence he is. (John 8:23): "You are from beneath." And there he is bound; it is the place that justice, and God's word, and the sentence of his unchangeable law, assign to him.

4 They are now the objects of that very same anger and wrath of God, that is expressed in the torments of Hell. And the reason why they do not go down to Hell at each moment, is not because God, in whose power they are, is not then very angry with them; as He is with many miserable creatures now tormented in Hell, who there feel and bear the fierceness of His wrath. Yea, God is a great deal more angry with great numbers that are now on earth; yea, doubtless, with many that are now in this congregation, who it may be are at ease, than He is with many of those who are now in the flames of Hell.

So that it is not because God is unmindful of their wickedness, and does not resent it, that He does not let loose His hand and cut them off. God is not altogether such a one as themselves, though they may imagine him to be so. The wrath of God burns against them, their damnation does not slumber; the pit is prepared, the fire is made ready, the furnace is now hot, ready to receive them; the flames do now rage and glow. The glittering sword is whetted, and held over them, and the pit has opened its mouth under them.

5 The Devil stands ready to fall upon them, and seize them as his own, at what moment God shall permit him. They belong to him, he has their souls in his possession, and under his dominion. The scripture represents them as his goods, (Luke 11:21). The devils watch them; they are ever by them, like greedy hungry lions that see their prey, and expect to have it, but are for the present kept back. If God should withdraw His hand, by which they are restrained, they would in one moment fly upon their poor souls. The old serpent is gaping for them; Hell opens its mouth wide to receive them; and if God should permit it, they would be hastily swallowed up and lost.

6 There are in the souls of wicked men those hellish principles reigning, that would presently kindle and flame out into hell-fire, if it were not for God's restraints.

There is laid in the very nature of carnal men, a foundation for the torments of Hell. There are those corrupt principles reigning in them, and in full possession of them that are seeds of hell-fire. These principles are active and powerful, exceeding violent in their nature, and if it were not for the restraining hand of God upon them, they would soon break out, they would flame out after the same manner as the same corruptions, the same enmity does in the hearts of damned souls, and would beget the same torments as they do in them. The souls of the wicked are in scripture compared to the troubled sea, (Isaiah 57:20). For the present, God restrains their wickedness by His mighty power, as He does the raging waves of the troubled sea, saying, "You will come thus far, but no further", but if God should withdraw that restraining power, it would soon carry all before it. Sin is the ruin and misery of the soul; it is destructive in its nature; and if God should leave it without restraint, there would be need of nothing else to make the soul perfectly miserable. The corruption of the heart of man is immoderate and boundless in its fury; and while wicked men live here, it is like fire pent up by God's restraints, whereas if it were let loose, it would set on fire the course of nature; and as the heart is now a sink of sin so, if sin was not restrained, it would immediately turn the soul into a fiery oven, or a furnace of fire and brimstone.

7 It is no security to wicked men even for one moment, that there are no visible means of death at hand. It is no security to a natural man that he is now in health, and that he does not see which way he should now immediately go out of the world by any accident, and that there is no visible danger in any respect in his circumstances. The manifold and continual experience of the world in all ages, shows this is no evidence, that a man is not on the very brink of eternity, and that the next step will not be into another world. The unseen, unthought of ways and means of persons going suddenly out of the world are innumerable and inconceivable. Unconverted men walk over the pit of Hell on a rotten covering, and there are innumerable places in this covering so weak that they will not bear their weight, and these places are not seen. The arrows of death fly unseen at noonday; the sharpest sight cannot discern them. God has so many different unsearchable ways of taking wicked men out of the world and sending them to Hell, that there is nothing to make it appear that God had need to be at the expense of a miracle, or to go out of the ordinary course of His providence, to destroy any wicked man, at any moment. All the means that there are of sinners going out of the world, are so in God's hands, and so universally and absolutely subject to His power and determination, that it does not depend at all the less on the mere will of God, whether sinners shall at any moment go to Hell, than if means were never made use of, or at all concerned in the case.

8 Natural men's prudence and care to preserve their own lives, or the care of others to preserve them, do not secure them a moment. To this, divine providence and universal experience do also bear testimony. There is this clear evidence that men's own wisdom is no security to them from death; that if it were otherwise we should see some difference between the wise and politic men of the world, and others, with regard to their liableness to early and unexpected death; but how is it in fact? (Ecclesiastes 2:16): "How does the wise man die? In the same way as the fool."

9 All wicked men's pains and contrivances which they use to escape Hell, while they continue to reject Christ, and so remain wicked men, do not secure them from Hell one moment. Almost every natural man that hears of Hell flatters himself that he shall escape it; he depends upon himself for his own security; he flatters himself in what he has done, in what he is now doing, or in what he intends to do. Everyone lays out matters in his own mind how he shall avoid damnation, and flatters himself that he contrives well for himself, and that his schemes will not fail. They hear indeed that there are but few saved, and that the greater part of men that have died before are gone to Hell; but each one imagines that he lays out matters better for his own escape than others have done. He does not intend to come to that place of torment; he says within himself that he intends to take effectual care, and to order matters so for himself as not to fail.

But the foolish children of men miserably delude themselves in their own schemes, and in confidence in their own strength and wisdom: they trust to nothing but a shadow. The greater part of those who before now have lived under the same means of grace, and are now dead, are undoubtedly gone to Hell; and it was not because they were not as wise as those who are now alive: it was not because they did not lay out matters as well for themselves to secure their own escape. If we could speak with them and inquire of them, one by one, whether they expected when they used to hear about Hell, ever to be the subjects of that misery; we doubtless should hear one and another reply, "No, I never intended to come here: I had laid out matters otherwise in my mind; I thought I should contrive well for myself: I thought my scheme good. I intended to take effectual care; but it came upon me unexpected; I did not look for it at that time, and in that manner; it came as a quick thief. Death outwitted me. God's wrath was too quick for me. Oh, my cursed foolishness! I was flattering myself, and pleasing myself with vain dreams of what I would do hereafter; and when I was saying, 'peace and safety', then sudden destruction came upon me."

10 God has laid Himself under no obligation by any promise, to keep any natural man out of Hell one moment. God certainly has made no promises either of eternal life, or of any deliverance or preservation from eternal death, but only those contained in the covenant of grace, the promises that are given in Christ, in whom all the promises are yea and Amen. But surely they have no interest in the promises of the covenant of grace who are not the children of the covenant, who do not believe in any of the promises, and have no interest in the mediator of the covenant. So that, whatever some have imagined and pretended about promises made to natural men's earnest seeking and knocking, it is plain and manifest that whatever pains a natural men takes in religion, whatever prayers he makes; till he believes in Christ, God is under no manner of obligation to keep him a moment from eternal destruction.

So thus it is that natural men are held in the hand of God, over the pit of Hell; they have deserved the fiery pit, and are already sentenced to it, and God is dreadfully provoked, His anger is as great towards them as to those that are actually suffering the executions of the fierceness of His wrath in Hell, and they have done nothing in the least to appease or abate that anger. Neither is God in the least bound by any promise to hold them up one moment; the devil is waiting for them, Hell is gaping for them, the flames gather and flash about them, and would fain lay hold on them, and swallow them up; the fire pent up in their own hearts is struggling to break out; and they have no interest in any mediator, there are no means within reach that can be any security to them. In short, they have no refuge, nothing to take hold of; all that preserves them every moment is the mere arbitrary will, and uncovenanted, unobliged forbearance of an incensed God.

The use of this awful subject is awakening unconverted persons in this congregation. This that you have heard is the case of every one of you that are out of Christ. That world of misery, that lake of burning brimstone, is extended abroad under you. There is the dreadful pit of the glowing flames of the wrath of God; there is Hell's wide gaping mouth open; and you have nothing to stand upon, nor anything to take hold of; there is nothing between you and Hell but the air; it is only the power and mere pleasure of God that holds you up.

You probably are not sensible of this; you find you are kept out of Hell, you do not see the hand of God in it, but look at other things, as the good state of your bodily constitution, your care of your own life, and the means you use for your own preservation. But indeed these things are nothing; if God should withdraw His hand, they would avail no more to keep you from falling, than the thin air to hold up a person that is suspended in it.

Your wickedness makes you as it were heavy as lead, and to tend downwards with great weight and pressure towards Hell; and if God should let you go, you would immediately sink and swiftly descend and plunge into the bottomless gulf, and your healthy constitution, and your own care and prudence, and best contrivance, and all your righteousness, would have no more influence to uphold you and keep you out of Hell than a spider's web would have to stop a falling rock. Were it not for the sovereign pleasure of God, the earth would not bear you one moment; for you are a burden to it; the creation groans with you; the creature is made subject to the bondage of our corruption, not willingly; the sun does not willingly shine upon you to give you light to serve sin and Satan; the earth does not willingly yield her increase to satisfy your lusts; nor is it willingly a stage for your wickedness to be acted upon; the air does not willingly serve you for breath to maintain the flame of life in the service of God's enemies. God's creatures are good, and were made for men to serve God with, and do not willingly subserve to any other purpose, and groan when they are abused to purposes so directly contrary to their nature and end. And the world would spew you out, were it not for the sovereign hand of Him who has subjected it in hope. There are the black clouds of God's wrath now hanging directly over your heads, full of the dreadful storm, and big with thunder; and were it not for the restraining hand of God, it would immediately burst forth upon you. The sovereign pleasure of God, for the present, stays His rough wind; otherwise it would come with fury, and your destruction would come like a whirlwind, and you would be like the chaff of the summer threshing floor.

The wrath of God is like great waters that are dammed for the present; they increase more and more, and rise higher and higher, till an outlet is given; and the longer the stream is stopped, the more rapid and mighty is its course when once it is let loose. It is true that judgment against your evil works has not been executed hithero; the floods of God's vengeance have been withheld; but your guilt in the meantime is constantly increasing, and you are every day treasuring up more wrath; the waters are constantly rising, and waxing more and more mighty; and there is nothing but the mere pleasure of God that holds the waters back, that are unwilling to be stopped and press hard to go forward. If God should only withdraw His hand from the flood-gate, it would immediately fly open, and the fiery floods of the fierceness and wrath of God, would rush forth with inconceivable fury, and would come upon you with omnipotent power; and if your strength were ten thousand times greater than it is, yea, ten thousand times greater than the strength of the stoutest, sturdiest devil in Hell, it would be nothing to withstand or endure it.

The bow of God's wrath is bent, and the arrow made ready on the string, and justice bends the arrow at your heart, and strains the bow, and it is nothing but the mere pleasure of God, and that of an angry God, without any promise or obligation at all that keeps the arrow one moment from being made drunk with your blood. Thus all you that never passed under a great change of heart, by the mighty power of the Spirit of God upon your souls; all you that were never born again, and made new creatures, and raised from being dead in sin, to a state of new, and before altogether unexperienced light and life, are in the hands of an angry God. However you may have reformed your life in many things, and may have had religious affections, and may keep up a form of religion in your families and closets, and in the house of God, it is nothing but His mere pleasure that keeps you from being this moment swallowed up in everlasting destruction. However unconvinced you may now be of the truth if what you hear, by and by you will be fully convinced of it. Those that are gone from being in the like circumstances with you, see that it was so with them; for destruction came suddenly upon most of them, when they expected nothing of it, and while they were saying,"peace and safety". Now they see that those things on which they depended for peace and safety, were nothing but thin air and empty shadows.

The God that holds you over the pit of hell, much as one holds a spider, or some loathsome insect over the fire, abhors you, and is dreadfully provoked: His wrath towards you burns like fire: He looks upon you as worthy of nothing but to be cast into the fire; He is of purer eyes than to bear to have you in His sight; you are ten thousand times more abominable in His eyes than the most hateful venomous serpent is in ours. You have offended Him infinitely more than ever a stubborn rebel did his prince; and yet it is nothing but His hand that holds you from falling into the fire every moment. It is to be ascribed to nothing else, that you did not go to Hell last night; that you were suffered to awake again in this world, after you closed your eyes to sleep. And there is no other reason to be given, why you have not dropped into Hell since you arose in the morning, but that God's hand has held you up. There is no other reason to be given why you have not gone to Hell since you have sat here in the house of God, provoking His pure eyes by your sinful wicked manner of attending His solemn worship. Yea, there is nothing else that is to be given as a reason why you do not this very moment drop down into Hell.

O sinner! Consider the fearful danger you are in: it is a great furnace of wrath, a wide and bottomless pit, full of the fire of wrath, that you are held over in the hand of that God whose wrath is provoked and incensed as much against you, as against any of the damned in Hell. You hang by a slender thread, with the flames of divine wrath flashing about it, and ready every moment to singe it, and burn it asunder; and you have no interest in any mediator, and nothing to lay hold of to save yourself, nothing of your own, nothing that you ever have done, nothing you can do, to induce God to spare you one moment. And consider here more particularly:

1 Whose wrath it is: it is the wrath of the infinite God. If it were only the wrath of man, though it were of the most potent prince, it would be comparatively little to be regarded. The wrath of kings is very much dreaded, especially of absolute monarchs, who have the possessions and lives of their subjects wholly in their power, to be disposed of at their mere will. (Proverbs 20:2) "The fear of a king is as the roaring of a lion: whoever provokes him to anger, sins against his own soul." The subject that very much enrages an arbitrary prince is liable to suffer the most extreme torments that human art can invent, or human power can inflict. But the greatest earthly potentates in their greatest majesty and strength, and when clothed in their greatest terrors, are but feeble, despicable worms of the dust, in comparison with the great and almighty Creator and King of Heaven and earth. It is but little that they can do, when most enraged, and when they have exerted the utmost of their fury. All the kings of the earth, before God, are as grasshoppers; they are nothing, and less than nothing: both their love and their hatred is to be despised. The wrath of the great King of kings is as much more terrible than theirs, as his majesty is greater. (Luke 12:4, 5): "And I say unto you, my friends, be not afraid of them that kill the body, and after that, have no more that they can do. But I will forewarn you whom you shall fear: fear Him, which after He has killed has power to cast into Hell; yea, I say unto you, fear Him."

2 It is the fierceness of His wrath that you are exposed to. We often read of the fury of God; as in Isaiah 59:18: "According to their deeds, accordingly He will repay fury to his adversaries." So, (Isaiah 66:15): "For behold, the Lord will come with fire, and with His chariots like a whirlwind, to render His anger with fury, and His rebuke with flames of fire." And in many other places. So, (Revelation 19:15): we read of "the wine-press of the fierceness and wrath of Almighty God." The words are exceedingly terrible. If it had only been said, "the wrath of God", the words would have implied that which is infinitely dreadful: but it is "the fierceness and wrath of God". The fury of God! The fierceness of Jehovah! Oh, how dreadful must that be! Who can utter or conceive what such expressions carry in them! But it is also "the fierceness and wrath of Almighty God". As though there would be a very great manifestation of His almighty power in what fierceness of His wrath should inflict, as though omnipotence should be as it were enraged, and exerted, as men are wont to exert their strength in the fierceness of their wrath. Oh! then, what will be the consequence! What will become of the poor worm that shall suffer it! Whose hands can be strong? And whose heart can endure? To what a dreadful, inexpressible, inconceivable depth of misery must the poor creature be sunk who shall be the subject of this!

Consider this, you that are here present that yet remain in an unregenerate state. That God will execute the fierceness of His anger, implies that He will inflict wrath without any pity. When God beholds the ineffable extremity of your case, and sees your torment to be so vastly disproportionate to your strength, and sees how your poor soul is crushed, and sinks down, as it were, into an infinite gloom; He will have no compassion upon you, He will not forbear the executions of His wrath, or in the last lighten His hand; there shall be no moderation or mercy, nor will God then at all stay His rough wind; He will have no regard to your welfare, nor be at all careful lest you should suffer too much in any other sense, except that you shall not suffer beyond what astrict justice requires. Nothing shall be withheld, because it is too hard for you to bear. (Ezekiel 8:18): "Therefore will I also deal in fury; mine eye shall not spare, neither will I have pity; and though they cry in mine ears with a loud voice, yet I will not hear them." Now God stands ready to pity you; this is a day of mercy; you may cry now with some encouragement of obtaining mercy. But when once the day of mercy is past your most lamentable and dolorous cries and shrieks will be in vain; you will be wholly lost and thrown away by God, as to any regard to your welfare. God will have no other use to put you to, but to suffer misery; you shall be continued in being to no other end; for you will be a vessel of wrath fitted to destruction; and there will be no other use of His vessel, but to be filled full of wrath. God will be so far from pitying you when you cry to Him, that it is said He will only "laugh and mock," (Proverbs 1:25, 26).

How awful are those words, (Isaiah 63:3) which are the words of the great God, "I will tread them in mine anger, and will trample them in my fury, and their blood will be sprinkled on my garments, and I will stain all my raiment." It is perhaps impossible to conceive of words that carry in them greater manifestations of these three things: contempt, and hatred, and fierceness of indignation. If you cry to God to pity you, He will be so far from pitying you in your doleful case, or showing you the least regard or favour, that instead of that, He will only tread you underfoot. And though He will know that you cannot bear the weight of omnipotence treading upon you, yet He will not regard that, but He will crush you under his feet without mercy; he will crush out your blood, and make it fly, and it shall be sprinkled on His garments, so as to stain all His raiment. He will not only hate you, but He will have you in the utmost contempt; no place shall be thought fit for you, but under His feet to be trodden down as the mire of the streets.

3 The misery you are exposed to is that which God will inflict to the purpose, that He might show what that wrath of Jehovah is. God has had it in His heart to show to angels and men, both how excellent His love is, and also how terrible His wrath is. Sometimes earthly kings have a mind to show how terrible their wrath is, by the extreme punishments they would execute on those that provoke them. Nebuchadnezzar, that mighty and haughty monarch of the Chaldean empire, was willing to show his wrath when enraged with Shadrach, Meshech, and Abednego; and accordingly gave orders that the burning fiery furnace should be heated seven times hotter than it was before; doubtless, it was raised to the utmost degree of fierceness that human art could raise it. But the great magnify His awful majesty and mighty power in the extreme sufferings of His enemies. (Romans 9:22): "What if God, willing to show His wrath, and to make His power known, endured with much longsuffering the vessels of wrath fitted to destruction?" And seeing this is His design, and what He has determined, even to show how terrible the unrestrained wrath, the fury and fierceness of Jehovah is, He will do it to effect. There will be something accomplished and brought to pass that will be dreadful to witness. When the great and angry God has risen up and executed His awful vengeance on the poor sinner, and the wretch is actually suffering the infinite weight and power of His indignation, then will God call upon the whole universe to behold that awful majesty and mighty power that is to be seen in it. (Isaiah 33:12–14): "And the people shall be like the burnings of lime, like thorns cut up shall they be burnt in the fire. Hear, you who are far off, what I have done; and you who are near, acknowledge my might. The sinners in Zion are afraid; fearfulness has surprised the hypocrites."

Thus it will be with you that are in an unconverted state, if you continue in it; the infinite might, and majesty, and terribleness of the omnipotent God shall be magnified upon you, in the ineffable strength of your torments. You shall be tormented in the presence of the holy angels,and in the presence of the Lamb; and when you shall be in this state of suffering, the glorious inhabitants of Heaven shall go forth and look on the awful spectacle, that they may see what the wrath and fierceness of the Almighty is; and when they have seen it, they will fall down and adore that great power and majesty. (Isaiah 66: 23,24): "And it shall come to pass that from one new moon to another, and from one sabbath to another, all flesh will come to worship before me, says the Lord. And they shall go forth and look upon the corpses of the men that have transgressed against me; for their worm shall not die, and their fire is not quenched, and they shall be an abhorrence to all flesh."

4 It is everlasting wrath. It would be dreadful to suffer this fierceness and wrath of Almighty God one moment; but you must suffer it to all eternity. There will be no end to this exquisite horrible misery. When you look forward, you shall see a long forever, a boundless duration before you, which will swallow up your thoughts, and amaze your soul; and you will absolutely despair of ever having any deliverance, any end, any mitigation, any rest at all. You will know certainly that you must wear out long ages, millions of millions of ages, in wrestling and conflict with this almighty merciless vengeance; and then when you have so done, when so many ages have actually been spent by you in this manner, you will know that all is but a dot to what remains. So that your punishment will indeed be infinite. Oh, who can express what the state of a soul in such circumstances is! All that we can possibly say about it, gives but a very feeble, faint representation of it; it is inexpressible and inconceivable: for "who knows the power of God's anger?"

How dreadful is the state of those that are daily and hourly in danger of this great wrath and infinite misery! But this is the dismal case of every soul in this congregation that has not been born again, however moral and strict, sober and religious, they may otherwise be. Oh that you would consider it, whether you be young or old! There is reason to think that there are many in this congregation now hearing this discourse, that will actually be the subjects of this very misery to all eternity. We know not who they are, or what seats they now have. It may be they are now at ease, and hear all these things without much disturbance, and are now flattering themselves that they are not the persons, promising themselves that they shall escape. If we knew that there was one person, and only one, in the whole congregation, that was to be the subject of this misery, what an awful thing would it be to think of! If we knew who it was, what an awful sight would it be to see such a person! How might all the rest of the congregation lift up a lamentable and bitter cry over him! But, alas! instead of one, how many is it likely will remember this discourse in Hell? And it would be no wonder if some persons that now sit here, in some seats of this meeting-house, in health, quiet and secure, should be there before tomorrow morning. Those of you that finally keep out of Hell longest, will be there in a little time! Your damnation does not slumber; it will come swiftly, and, in all probability, very suddenly upon many of you. You have reason to wonder that you are not already in Hell. It is doubtless the case of some whom you have seen and known, that never deserved Hell more than you, and that heretofore appeared as likely to have been now alive as you. Their case is past all hope; they are crying in extreme misery and perfect despair; but here you are in the land of the living and in the house of God, and have an opportunity to obtain salvation. What would not those poor damned hopeless souls give for one day's opportunity such as you now enjoy!

And now you have an extraordinary opportunity, a day wherein Christ has thrown the door of mercy wide open, and stands in calling and crying with a loud voice to poor sinners; a day wherein many are flocking to him, and pressing into the kingdom of God. Many are daily coming from the east, west, north and south; many that were very lately in the same miserable condition that you are in, are now in a happy state, with their hearts filled with love of Him who has loved them, and washed them from their sins in His own blood, and rejoicing in hope of the glory of God. How awful is it to be left behind at such a day! To see so many others feasting, while you are pining and perishing! To see so many rejoicing and singing for joy of heart, while you have cause to mourn for sorrow of heart, and howl for vexation of spirit! How can you rest one moment in such a condition? Are not your souls as precious as the souls of the people at Suffield, where they are flocking from day to day to Christ?

Are there not many here who have lived long in the world, and are not to this day born again? And so are aliens from the commonwealth of Israel, and have done nothing ever since they have lived, but treasure up wrath against the day of wrath? Oh, sirs, your case, in an especial manner, is extremely dangerous. Your guilt and hardness of heart is extremely great. Do you not see how generally persons of your years are passed over and left, in the present remarkable and wonderful dispensation of God's mercy? You need to consider yourselves, and awake thoroughly out of sleep.

You cannot bear the fierceness and wrath of the infinite God. And you, young men and young women, will you neglect this precious season which you now enjoy, when so many others of your age are renouncing all youthful vanities, and flocking to Christ? You especially have now an extraordinary opportunity; but if you neglect it, it will soon be with you as with those persons who spent all the precious days of youth in sin, and are now come to such a dreadful pass in blindness and hardness. And you, children, who are unconverted, do not you know that you are going down to Hell, to bear the dreadful wrath of that God, who is now angry with you every day and every night? Will you be content to be the children of the Devil, when so many other children in the land are converted, and are become the holy and happy children of the King of kings?

And let everyone that is yet out of Christ, and hanging over the pit of Hell, whether they be old men and women, or middle aged, or young people, or little children, now hearken to the loud calls of God's word and providence. This acceptable year of the Lord, a day of such great favour to some, will doubtless be a day of as remarkable vengeance to others. Men's hearts harden, and their guilt increases apace at such a day as this, if they neglect their souls; and never was there so great danger of such persons being given up to hardness of heart and blindness of mind.

God seems now to be hastily gathering in His elect all over the land; and probably the greater part of adult persons that ever shall be saved, will be brought in now in a little time, and it will be as it was on the great out-pouring of the Spirit upon the Jews in the apostles' days; the elected will obtain, and the rest will be blinded. If this should be the case with you, you will eternally curse this day, and will curse the season of the pouring out of God's Spirit, and will wish that you had died and gone to Hell before you had seen it. Now undoubtedly it is, as it was in the days of John the Baptist, the axe is in an extraordinary manner laid at the root of the trees, that every tree which brings not forth good fruit, may be hewn down and cast into the fire.

Therefore, let everyone that is out of Christ, now awake and fly from the wrath to come. The wrath of Almighty God is now undoubtedly hanging over a great part of this congregation. Let every one fly out of Sodom: "Haste and escape for your lives, do not look behind you, escape to the mountain, lest you be consumed."

CHARLES FINNEY: How to Win Souls

"Take heed unto yourself, and the doctrine; continue in them: for in doing this you shall both save yourself, and them that hear you". (I Timothy 4:16).

I beg leave in this article to suggest to my younger brethren in the ministry some thoughts on the philosophy of so preaching the gospel as to secure the salvation of souls. They are the result of much study, much prayer for divine teaching, and a practical experience of many years.

I understand the admonition at the head of this article to relate to the matter, order and manner of preaching.

The problem is: How shall we win souls wholly to Christ? Certainly we must win them away from themselves.

1 They are free moral agents, of course – rational, accountable.

2 They are in rebellion against God, wholly alienated, intensely prejudiced, and committed against Him.

3 They are committed to self-gratification as the end of their being.

4 This committed state is moral depravity, the fountain of sin within them, from which flows by a natural law all their sinful ways. This committed voluntary state is their "wicked heart". That it is that needs a radical change.

5 God is infinitely benevolent, and unconverted sinners are supremely selfish, so that they are radically opposed to God. Their committal to the gratification of their appetites and propensities is known in Bible language as the "carnal mind"; or, as in the margin, "the minding of the flesh", which is enmity against God.

6 This enmity is voluntary, and must be overcome, if at all, by the Word of God, made effectual by the teaching of the Holy Spirit.

7 The gospel is adapted to this end, and when wisely presented we may confidently expect the effectual co-operation of the Holy Spirit. This is implied in our commission: "Go and make disciples of all nations", and "Lo! I am with you always, even to the end of the world".

8 If we are unwise, illogical, unphilosophical, and out of all natural order in presenting the gospel, we have no warrant for expecting divine co-operation.

9 In winning souls, as in everything else, God works through and in accordance with natural laws. Hence, if we would win souls we must wisely adapt means to this end. We must present those truths and in that order which is adapted to the natural laws of mind, of thought and mental action. A false mental philosophy will greatly mislead us, and we shall often be found ignorantly working against the agency of the Holy Spirit.

10 Sinners must be convinced of their enmity. They do not know God, and consequently are often ignorant of the opposition of their hearts to Him."By the law is the knowledge of sin", because by the law the sinner gets his first true idea of God. By the law he first learns that God is perfectly benevolent, and infinitely opposed to all selfishness. This law, then, should be arrayed in all its majesty against the selfishness and enmity of the sinner.

11 This law carries irresistible conviction of its righteousness, and no moral agent can doubt it.

12 All men know that they have sinned but all are not convinced of the guilt and ill desert of sin. Many are careless and do not feel the burden of sin, the horrors and terrors of remorse, and have not a sense of condemnation and of being lost.

13 But without this they cannot understand or appreciate the gospel method of salvation. One cannot intelligently and heartily ask or accept pardon until he sees and feels the fact and justice of his condemnation.

14 It is absurd to suppose that a careless, unconvinced sinner can intelligently and thankfully accept the gospel offer of pardon until he accepts the righteousness of God in his condemnation. Conversion to Christ is an intelligent change. Hence the conviction of ill desert must precede the acceptance of mercy; for without this conviction the soul does not understand its need of mercy. Of course, the offer is rejected. The gospel is no glad tidings to the careless, unconvinced sinner.

15 The spirituality of the law should be unsparingly applied to the conscience until the sinner's self-rightousness is annihilated, and he stands speechless and selfcondemned before a holy God.

16 In some men this conviction is already ripe, and the preacher may at once present Christ, with the hope of His being accepted; but at ordinary times such cases are exceptional. The great mass of sinners are careless, unconvinced, and to assume their conviction and preparedness to receive Christ, and, hence, to urge sinners immediately to accept Him, is to begin at the wrong end of our work – to render our teaching unintelligible. And such a course will be found to have been a mistaken one, whatever present appearances and professions may indicate. The sinner may obtain a hope under such teaching; but, unless the Holy Spirit supplies something which the preacher has failed to do, it will be found to be a false one. All the essential links of truth must be supplied.

17 When the law has done its work, annihilated self-righteousness, and shut the sinner up to the acceptance of mercy, he should be made to understand the delicacy and danger of dispensing with the execution of the penalty when the precept of law has been violated.

18 Right here the sinner should be

made to understand that from the benevolence of God he cannot justly infer that God can consistently forgive him. For unless public justice can be satisfied, the law of universal benevolence forbids the forgiveness of sin. If public justice is not regarded in the exercise of mercy, the good of the public is sacrificed to that of the individual. God will never do this.

19 This teaching will shut the sinner up to look for some offering to public justice.

20 Now give him the atonement as a revealed fact, and shut him up with Christ as his own sin offering. Press the revealed fact that God has accepted the death of Christ as a substitute for the sinner's death, and that this is to be received upon the testimony of God.

21 Being already crushed into contrition by the convincing power of the law, the revelation of the love of God manifested in the death of Christ will naturally beget great self-loathing, and the godly sorrow that needs not to be repented of. Under this showing the sinner can never forgive himself. God is holy and glorious; and he a sinner, saved by sovereign grace. This teaching may be more or less formal as the souls you address are more or less thoughtful, intelligent, and careful to understand.

22 It was not by accident that the dispensation of law precedes the dispensation of grace; but it is in the natural order of things, in accordance with established mental laws, and evermore the law must prepare the way for the gospel. To overlook this in instructing souls is almost certain to result in false hope, the introduction of a false standard of Christian experience, and to fill the Church with spurious converts. Time will make this plain.

23 The truth should be preached to the persons present, and so personally applied as to compel everyone to feel that you mean him or her. As has been often said of a certain preacher: "He does not preach, but explains what other people preach, and seems to be talking directly to me."

24 This course will rivet attention, and cause your hearers to lose sight of the length of your sermon. They will tire if they feel no personal interest in what you say. To secure their individual interest in what you saying is an indispensable condition of their being converted. And, while their individual interest is thus awakened, and held fast to your subject, they will seldom complain of the length of your sermon. In nearly all cases, if the people complain of the length of our sermons, it is because we fail to interest them personally in what we say.

25 If we fail to interest them personally, it is either because we do not address them personally, or because we lack unction and earnestness, or because we lack clearness and force, or certainly because we lack something that we ought to possess. To make them feel that we and that God means *them* is indispensable.

26 Do not think that earnest piety alone can make you successful in winning souls. This is only one condition of success. There must be common sense, there must be spititual wisdom in adapting the means to the end. Matter and manner and order and time and place all need to be wisely adjusted to the end we have in view.

27 God may sometimes convert souls by men who are not spiritually minded, when they possess that natural sagacity which enables them to adapt means to that end; but the Bible warrants us in affirming that these are exceptional cases. Without this sagacity and adaptation of means to this end a spiritual mind will fail to win souls to Christ.

28 Souls need instruction in accordance with the measure of their intelligence. A few simple truths, when wisely applied and illuminated by the Holy Ghost, will convert children to Christ. I say wisely applied, for they too are sinners, and need the application of the law as a schoolmaster, to bring them to Christ, that they may be justified by faith. It will sooner or later appear that supposed conversions to Christ are spurious where the preparatory law work has been omitted, and Christ has not been embraced as a saviour from sin and condemnation.

29 Sinners of education and culture, who are, after all, unconvinced and sceptical in their hearts, need a vastly more extended and thorough application of truth. Professional men need the gospel net to be thrown quite around them, with no break through which they can escape; and, when thus dealt with, they are all the more sure to be converted in proportion to their real intelligence. I have found that a

course of lectures addressed to lawyers and adapted to their habits of thought and reasoning, is most sure to convert them.

30 To be successful in winning souls, we need to be observant – to study individual character, to rest the facts of experience, observation, and revelation upon the consciences of all classes.

31 Be sure to explain the terms you use. Before I was converted, I failed to hear the terms repentance, faith, regeneration, and conversion intelligibly explained. Repentance was described as a feeling. Faith was represented as an intellectual act or state, and not as a voluntary act of trust. Regeneration was represented as some physical change in the nature, produced by the direct power of the Holy Ghost, instead of a voluntary change of the ultimate preference of the soul, produced by the spiritual illumination of the Holy Ghost. Even conversion was represented as being the work of the Holy Ghost in such a sense as to cover up the fact that it is the sinner's own act, under the persuasions of the Holy Ghost.

32 Urge the fact that repentance involves the voluntary and actual renunciation of all sin; that it is a radical change of mind toward God.

33 Also the fact that saving faith is the heart's trust in Christ; that it works by love, it purifies the heart, and overcomes the world; that no faith is saving that has not these attributes.

34 The sinner is required to put forth certain mental acts; what these are he needs to understand. Error in mental philosophy merely embarrasses, and may fatally deceive the inquiring soul. Sinners are often put upon a wrong track. They are put upon a strain to feel, instead of putting forth the recquired acts of will. Before my conversion I never received from man any intelligible idea of the mental acts that God required of me.

35 The deceitfulness of sin renders the inquiring soul exceedingly exposed to delusion; therefore it behoves teachers to beat about every bush, and to search out every nook and corner where a soul can find a false refuge. Be so thorough and discriminating as to render it as nearly impossible as the nature of the case will admit that the inquirer should entertain a false hope.

36 Do not fear to be thorough. Do not through false pity put on a plaster where the probe is needed. Do not fear that you shall discourage the convicted sinner, and turn him back, by searching him out to the bottom. If the Holy Spirit is dealing with him, the more you search and probe, the more impossible it will be for the soul to turn back or rest in sin.

37 If you would save the soul, do not spare a right hand, or right eye, or any darling idol; but see to it that every form of sin is given up. Insist upon full restitution, so far as is possible, to all injured parties. Do not fall short of the express teachings of Christ on this subject. Whoever the sinner may be, let him distinctly understand that unless he forsakes all that he has he cannot be the disciple of Christ. Insist upon entire and universal consecration of all the powers of body and mind, and of all property, possessions, character, and influence to God. Insist upon the total abandonment to God of all ownership of self, or anything else, as a condition of being accepted.

38 Understand yourself, and, if possible, make the sinner understand, that nothing short of this is involved in true faith or true repentance, and that true consecration involves them all.

39 Keep constantly before the sinner's mind that it is the personal Christ with whom he is dealing, that God in Christ is seeking his reconciliation to Himself, and that the condition of his reconciliation is that he gives up his will and his whole being to God – that he "leave not a hoof behind".

40 Assure him that "God has given to him eternal life, and this life is in His Son"; that "Christ is made unto him wisdom, righteousness, sanctification, and redemption"; and that from first to last he is to find his whole salvation in Christ.

41 When satisfied that the soul intelligently receives all this doctrine, and the Christ herein revealed, then remember that he must persevere to the end, as the further condition of his salvation. Here you have before you the great work of preventing the soul from backsliding, of securing its permanent sanctification and sealing for eternal glory.

42 Does not the very common backsliding in heart of converts indicate some grave defect in the teachings of the pulpit on the subject? What does it mean that so

many hopeful converts, within a few months of their apparent conversion, lose their first love, lose all their fervency in religion, neglect their duty, and live on in name Christians, but in spirit and life worldlings?

43 A truly successful preacher must not only win souls to Christ, but must keep them won. He must not only secure their conversion, but their permanent santification.

44 Nothing in the Bible is more expressly promised in this life than permanent sanctification (I Thessalonians 5:23, 24): "The very God of peace sanctify you wholly; and I pray God your whole spirit, soul, and body be preserved blameless until the coming of our Lord Jesus Christ. Faithful is He that calls you, who also will do it." This is unquestionably a prayer of the apostle for permanent sanctification in this life, with an express promise that He who has called us will do it.

45 We learn from the Scriptures that "after we believe" we are, or may be, sealed with the Holy Spirit of promise, and that this sealing is the earnest of our salvation. (Ephesians 1:13, 14): "In whom you also trusted after you heard the word of truth, the gospel of your salvation; in whom also after that you believed, you were sealed with the Holy Spirit of promise, which is the earnest of our inheritance until the redemption of the purchased possession, unto the praise of His glory." This sealing, this earnest of our inheritance, is that which renders our salvation sure. Hence, (in Ephesians 4:30) the apostle says: "Greive not the Holy Spirit of God, whereby you are sealed unto the day of redemption." And (in II Corinthians 1: 21, 22) the apostle says: "Now He which esablishes us with you in Christ, and has anointed us, is God, who has also sealed us and given the earnest of the Spirit in our hearts." Thus we are established in Christ and anointed by the Spirit, and also sealed by the Spirit, and also sealed by the earnest of the Spirit in our hearts. And this, remember, is a blessing that we receive after we believe, as Paul has informed us in his epistle to Ephesians, above quoted. Now, it is of the first importance that converts should be taught not to rest short of this permanent sanctification, this sealing, this being established in Christ by the special anointing of the Holy Ghost.

46 Now, brethren, unless we know what this means by our own experience, and lead converts to this experience, we fail most lamentably and essentially in our teaching. We leave out the very cream and fullness of the gospel.

47 It should be understood that while this experience is rare amongst ministers it will be descredited by the churches, and it will be next to impossible for an isolated preacher of this doctrine to overcome the unbelief of his Church. They will feel doubtful about it, because so few preach it or believe in it; and will account for their pastor's insisting upon it by saying that his experience is owing to his peculiar temperament, and thus they will fail to receive this anointing because of their unbelief. Under such circumstances it is all the more necessary to insist much upon the importance and privilege of permanent sanctification.

48 Sin consists in carnal-mindedness, in "obeying the desires of the flesh and of the mind". Permanent sanctification consists in entire and permanent consecration to God. It implies the refusal to obey the desire of the flesh or of the mind. The baptism or sealing of the Holy Spirit subdues the power of the desires, and strengthens and confirms the will in resisting the impules of desire, and in abiding permanently in a state of making the whole being an offering to God.

49 If we are silent upon this subject, the natural inference will be that we do not believe in it, and, of course, that we know nothing about in experience. This will inevitably be a stumbling-block to the Church.

50 Since this is undeniably an important doctrine, and plainly taught in the gospel, and is, indeed, the marrow and fatness of the gospel, to fail in teaching this is to rob the Church of its richest inheritance.

51 The testimony of the Church, and to a great extent of the ministry, on the subject has been lamentably defective. This legacy has been withheld from the Church, and is it any wonder that she so disgracefully backslides? The testimony of the comparatively few, here and there, that insist upon this doctrine is almost nullified by the counter-testimony or culpable silence of the great mass of Christ's witnesses.

52 My dear brethren, my convictions are so ripe and my feelings so deep upon

this subject that I must not conceal from you my fears that lack of personal experience, in many cases, is the reason for this great defect in preaching the gospel. I do not say this to reproach you; it is not in my heart to do so. It is not surprising that many of you, at least, have not this experience. Your religious training has been defective. You have been led to take a different view of this subject. Various causes have operated to prejudice you against this blessed doctrine which to you has been a stumbling block and a rock of offence; but I pray you let not prejudice prevail, but venture upon Christ by a present acceptance of Him as your wisdom, righteousness, sanctification, and redemption, and see if He will not do for you exceeding abundantly above all that you asked or thought.

53 No man, saint or sinner, should be left by us to rest or be quiet in the indulgence of any sin. No one should be allowed to entertain the hope of Heaven, if we can prevent it, who lives in the indulgence of known sin in any form. Our constant demand and persuasion should be: "Be holy, for God is holy." "Be perfect, even as your Father in Heaven is perfect." Let us remember the manner in which Christ concludes His memorable Sermon on the Mount. After spreading out those awfully searching truths before His hearers, and demanding that they should be perfect, as their Father in Heaven is perfect, He concludes by assuring them that no one could be saved who did not receive and obey His teachings. Instead of attempting to please our people in their sins, we should continually endeavour to hunt and persuade them out of their sins. Brethren, let us do it, as we would not have our skirts defiled with their blood. If we pursue this course and constantly preach with unction and power, and abide in the fullness of the doctrine of Christ, we may joyfully expect to save ourselves and them that hear us.

VICTORIAN HYMNODY

NEW EVERY MORNING IS THE LOVE

New every morning is the love
Our wakening and uprising prove;
Through sleep and darkness safely
  brought,
Restored to life, and power, and
  thought.

New mercies, each returning day,
Hover around us while we pray;
New perils past, new sins forgiven,
New thoughts of God, new hopes of
  Heaven.

If on our daily course our mind
Be set to hallow all we find,
New treasures still, of countless price,
God will provide for sacrifice.

Old friends, old scenes, will lovelier be,
As more of Heaven in each we see;
Some softening gleam of love and
  prayer
Shall dawn on every cross and care.

We need not bid, for cloistered cell,
Our neighbour and our work farewell,
Nor strive to wind ourselves too high
For sinful man beneath the sky:

The trivial round, the common task,
Would furnish all we ought to ask,
Room to deny ourselves, a road
To bring us daily nearer God.

Only, O Lord, in Thy dear love
Fit us for perfect rest above;
And help us this and every day
To live more nearly as we pray.

John Keble

LEAD, KINDLY LIGHT, AMID THE ENCIRCLING GLOOM

Lead, kindly Light, amid the encircling
  gloom,
Lead Thou me on;
The night is dark, and I am far from
  home,
Lead Thou me on.

Keep Thou my feet; I do not ask to see
The distant scene; one step enough
for me.

I was not ever thus, nor prayed that
Thou
Should'st lead me on;
I loved to choose and see my path;
but now
Lead Thou me on.
I loved the garish day, and, spite of
fears,
Pride ruled my will: remember not
past years.

So long Thy power hath blest me, sure
it still
Will lead me on
O'er moor and fen, o'er crag and
torrent, till
The night is gone,
And with the morn those angel faces
smile,
Which I have loved long since, and lost
awhile.

Cardinal John Newman

FIRMLY I BELIEVE AND TRULY

Firmly I believe and truly
God is Three and God is One;
And I next acknowledge duly
Manhood taken by the Son.

And I trust and hope most fully
In that Manhood crucified;
And each thought and deed unruly
Do to death, as He has died.

Simply to His grace and wholly
Light and life and strength belong,
And I love supremely, solely,
Him the holy, Him the strong.

Adoration ay be given,
With and through the angelic host,
To the God of earth and Heaven,
Father, Son, and Holy Ghost.

Cardinal John Newman

PRAISE TO THE HOLIEST IN THE HEIGHT

Praise to the Holiest in the height,
And in the depth be praise,
In all His words most wonderful,
Most sure in all His ways.

O living wisdom of our God!
When all was sin and shame,
A second Adam to the fight
And to the rescue came.

O wisest love! that flesh and blood,
Which did in Adam fail,
Should strive afresh against their foe,
Should strive and should prevail;

And that a higher gift than grace
Should flesh and blood refine,
God's presence and His very self,
And essence all-divine.

O generous love! that He who smote
In man for man the foe,
The double agony in man
For man should undergo;

And in the garden secretly,
And on the cross on high,
Should teach His brethren, and inspire
To suffer and to die.

Praise to the Holiest in the height,
And in the depth be praise,
In all His words most wonderful,
Most sure in all His ways.

Cardinal John Newman

RIDE ON! RIDE ON IN MAJESTY

Ride on! ride on in majesty!
Hark, all the tribes hosanna cry;
Thine humble beast pursues His road
With palms and scattered garments
strowed.

Ride on! ride on in majesty!
In lowly pomp ride on to die:
O Christ, Thy triumphs now begin
O'er captive death and conquered sin.

Ride on! ride on in majesty!
The winged squadrons of the sky
Look down with sad and wondering
eyes
To see the approaching sacrifice.

Ride on! ride on in majesty!
Thy last and fiercest strife is nigh;
The Father, on his sapphire throne,
Expects His own anointed Son.

Ride on! ride on in majesty!
In lowly pomp ride on to die;
Bow Thy meek head to mortal pain,
Then take, O God, Thy power, and
reign.

H. H. Milman

ABIDE WITH ME; FAST FALLS THE EVENTIDE

Abide with me; fast falls the eventide:
The darkness deepens; Lord, with me
abide!
When other helpers fail, and comforts
flee,
Help of the helpless, O abide with me.

Swift to its close ebbs out life's little day;
Earth's joys grow dim, its glories pass
away;
Change and decay in all around I see;
O Thou who changest not, abide with
me.

I need Thy presence every passing
hour;
What but Thy grace can foil the
tempter's power?
Who like Thyself my guide and stay can
be?
Through cloud and sunshine, O abide
with me.

I fear no foe with Thee at hand to bless;
Ills have no weight, and tears no
bitterness.
Where is death's sting? Where, grave,
thy victory?
I triumph still, if Thou abide with me.

Hold Thou Thy cross before my closing
eyes;
Shine through the gloom, and point
me to the skies:
Heaven's morning breaks, and earth's
vain shadows flee;
In life, in death, O Lord, abide with
me!

H. F. Lyte

DEAR LORD AND FATHER OF MANKIND

Dear Lord and Father of mankind,
Forgive our foolish ways!
Re-clothe us in our rightful mind,
In purer lives Thy service find,
In deeper reverence praise.

In simple trust like theirs who heard,
Beside the Syrian sea,
The gracious calling of the Lord,
Let us, like them, without a word
Rise up and follow Thee.

O sabbath rest by Galilee!
O calm of hills above,
When Jesus knelt to share with Thee
The silence of eternity,
Interpreted by love!

Drop Thy still dews of quietness,
Till all our strivings cease;
Take from our souls the strain and
stress,
And let our ordered lives confess
The beauty of Thy peace.

Breathe through the heats of our desire
Thy coolness and Thy balm;
Let sense be dumb, let flesh retire;
Speak through the earthquake, wind,
and fire,
O still small voice of calm!

J. G. Whittier

FIGHT THE GOOD FIGHT WITH ALL THY MIGHT

Fight the good fight with all thy might,
Christ is thy strength, and Christ thy
right;
Lay hold on life, and it shall be
Thy joy and crown eternally.

Run the straight race through God's
good grace,
Life up thine eyes, and seek His face;
Life with its way before us lies,
Christ is the path, and Christ the prize.

Cast care aside, upon the guide
Lean, and His mercy will provide;
Lean, and the trusting soul shall prove
Christ is its life, and Christ its love.

Faint not nor fear, His arms are near,
He changeth not, and thou art dear;
Only believe, and thou shalt see
That Christ is all in all to thee.

J. S. B. Mansell

AT THE NAME OF JESUS

At the name of Jesus
Every knee shall bow,
Every tongue confess Him
King of glory now;
'Tis the Father's pleasure
We should call Him Lord,
Who from the beginning
Was the mighty Word.

Humbled for a season
To receive a name
From the lips of sinners
Unto whom He came,
Faithfully He bore it,
Spotless to the last,
Brought it back victorious
When through death He passed.

Bore it up triumphant
With its human light,
Through all ranks of creatures,
To the central height,
To the throne of Godhead,
To the Father's breast;
Filled it with the glory
Of that perfect rest.

Name Him, brothers, name Him
Strong your love as death
But with awe and wonder,
And with bated breath;
He is God the Saviour,
His is Christ the Lord,
Ever to be worshipped,
Evermore adored.

In your hearts enthrone Him;
There let Him subdue
All that is not holy,
All that is not true:
Crown Him as your captain
In temptation's hour;
Let His will enfold you
In its light and power.

Brothers, this Lord Jesus
Dwells with us again,
In His Father's wisdom
O'er the earth to reign;
For all wreaths of empire
Meet upon His brow,
And our hearts confess Him
King of glory now.

Glory then to Jesus,
Who, the Prince of Light,
To a world in darkness
Brought the gift of sight;
Praise to God the Father;
In the Spirit's love
Praise we all together
Him who reigns above.

Caroline M. Noel

STAND UP, STAND UP FOR JESUS

Stand up, stand up for Jesus,
Ye soldiers of the cross!
Lift high His royal banner;
It must not suffer loss.
From victory unto victory
His army he shall lead,
Till every foe is vanquished,
And Christ is Lord indeed.

Stand up, stand up for Jesus!
The solemn watchword hear:
If while ye sleep He suffers,
Away with shame and fear;
Where'er ye meet with evil,
Within you or without,
Charge for the God of freedom,
And put the foe to rout.

Stand up, stand up for Jesus!
The trumpet call obey:
Forth to the mighty conflict
In this His glorious day.
Ye that are men now serve Him
Against unnumbered foes;
Let courage rise with danger,
And strength to strength oppose.

Stand up, stand up for Jesus!
Stand in His strength alone;
The arm of flesh will fail you,
Ye dare not trust your own.
Put on the Gospel armour,
Each piece put on with prayer;
Where duty calls or danger,
Be never wanting there!

Stand up, stand up for Jesus!
The strife will not be long;
This day the noise of battle,
The next the victor's song.
To him that overcometh
A crown of life shall be;
He with the King of Glory
Shall reign eternally.

G. Driffield

ONCE IN ROYAL DAVID'S CITY

Once in royal David's city
Stood a lowly cattle shed,
Where a mother laid her baby
In a manger for His bed:
Mary was that mother mild,
Jesus Christ her little child.

He came down to earth from Heaven
Who is God and Lord of all,
And His shelter was a stable,
And His cradle was a stall;
With the poor, and mean, and lowly
Lived on earth our Saviour holy,

And through all His wondrous
  childhood
He would honour and obey,
Love and watch the lowly maiden,
In whose gentle arms He lay:
Christian children all must be
Mild, obedient, good as He.

For He is our childhood's pattern;
Day by day like us He grew,
He was little, weak, and helpless,
Tears and smiles like us He knew;
And He feeleth for our sadness,
And He shareth in our gladness.

And our eyes at last shall see Him,
Through His own redeeming love,
For that child so dear and gentle
Is our Lord in Heaven above;
And He leads His children on
To the place where He is gone.

Mrs. C. F. Alexander

THERE IS A GREEN HILL FAR AWAY

There is a green hill far away,
Without a city wall,
Where the dear Lord was crucified
Who died to save us all.

We may not know, we cannot tell,
What pains He had to bear,
But we believe it was for us
He hung and suffered there.

He died that we might be forgiven,
He died to make us good;
That we might go at last to Heaven,
Saved by His precious blood.

O, dearly, dearly has He loved,
And we must love Him too,
And trust in His redeeming blood
And try His works to do.

Mrs C. F. Alexander

ALL THINGS BRIGHT AND BEAUTIFUL

All things bright and beautiful,
All creatures great and small,
All things wise and wonderful,
The Lord God made them all.

Each little flower that opens,
Each little bird that sings,
He made their glowing colours,
He made their tiny wings:

The purple-headed mountain,
The river running by,
The sunset and the morning,
That brightens up the sky:

The cold wind in the winter,
The pleasant summer sun,
The ripe fruit in the garden,
He made them every one:

The tall trees in the greenwood,
The meadows for our play,
The rushes by the water
To gather every day:

He gave us eyes to see them,
And lips that we might tell
How great is God Almighty,
Who has made all things well.

Mrs C. F. Alexander

MINE EYES HAVE SEEN THE GLORY OF THE COMING OF THE LORD

Mine eyes have seen the glory of the
coming of the Lord:
He is trampling out the vintage where
the grapes of wrath are stored;
He hath loosed the fateful lightning of
his terrible swift sword:
His truth is marching on.

He has sounded forth the trumpet
that shall never call retreat;
He is sifting out the hearts of men
before His judgment-seat;
O, be swift, my soul, to answer Him;
be jubilant, my feet!
Our God is marching on.

In the beauty of the lilies Christ was
born across the sea,
With a glory in His bosom that
transfigures you and me:
As He died to make men holy, let us die
to make men free,
While God is marching on.

He is coming like the glory of the
morning on the wave;
He is wisdom to the mighty, He is
succour to the brave;
So the world shall be His footstool, and
the soul of time His slave:
Our God is marching on.

J. W. Howe

O PRAISE YE THE LORD!

O Praise ye the Lord!
Praise Him in the height;
Rejoice in His word,
Ye angels of light;
Ye heavens, adore Him
By whom ye were made,
And worship before Him,
In brightness arrayed.

O praise ye the Lord!
Praise Him upon earth,
In tuneful accord,
Ye sons of new birth;
Praise Him who hath brought you
His grace from above,
Praise Him who hath taught you
To sing of His love.

O praise ye the Lord,
All things that give sound;
Each jubilant chord,
Re-echo around;
Loud organs, His glory
Forth tell in deep tone,
And sweet harp, the story
Of what He hath done.

O praise ye the Lord!
Thanksgiving and song
To Him be outpoured
All ages along:
For love in creation,
For Heaven restored,
For grace of salvation,
O praise ye the Lord!

Sir H. W. Barker

IMMORTAL, INVISIBLE, GOD ONLY WISE

Immortal, invisible, God only wise,
In light inaccessible hid from our eyes,
Most blessèd, most glorious,
the ancient of days,
Almighty, victorious, Thy great
name we praise.

Unresting, unhasting, and silent
as light,
Nor wanting, nor wasting, Thou
rulest in might;
Thy justice like mountains high
soaring above,
Thy clouds which are fountains of
goodness and love.

To all life Thou givest, to both
great and small;
In all life Thou livest, the true life
of all;
We blossom and flourish as leaves
on the tree,
And wither and perish; but
nought changeth Thee.

Great Father of glory, pure Father
of light,
Thine angels adore Thee, all
veiling their sight;
All laud we would render: O help
us to see
'Tis only the splendour of light
hideth thee.

W. Chalmers Smith

ETERNAL FATHER, STRONG TO SAVE

Eternal Father, strong to save,
Whose arm doth bind the restless wave,
Who bid'st the mighty ocean deep
Its own appointed limited keep:
O hear us when we cry to Thee
For those in peril on the sea.

O Saviour, whose almighty word
The winds and waves submissive heard,
Who walkedst on the foaming deep,
And calm amid its rage didst sleep:
O hear us when we cry to Thee
For those in peril on the sea.

O sacred Spirit, who didst brood
Upon the chaos dark and rude,
Who bad'st its angry tumult cease,
And gavest light and life and peace;
O hear us when we cry to Thee
For those in peril on the sea.

O Trinity of love and power,
Our brethren shield in danger's hour;
From rock and tempest, fire and foe,
Protect them whereso'er they go:
And ever let there rise to Thee
Glad hymns of praise from land and sea.

W. Whiting

IN THE BLEAK MID-WINTER

In the bleak mid-winter
Frosty wind made moan;
Earth stood hard as iron,
Water like a stone;
Snow had fallen, snow on snow,
Snow on snow,
In the bleak mid-winter,
Long ago.

Our God, heaven cannot hold Him
Nor earth sustain;
Heaven and earth shall flee away
When He comes to reign:
In the bleak mid-winter
A stable-place sufficed
The Lord God almighty,
Jesus Christ.

Enough for Him, whom cherubim
Worship night and day,
A breastful of milk,
And a mangerful of hay;
Enough for Him, whom angels
Fall down before,
The ox and ass and camel
Which adore.

Angels and archangels
May have gathered there,
Cherubim and seraphim
Thronged the air:
But only His mother
In her maiden bliss
Worshipped the Belovèd
With a kiss.

What can I give Him,
Poor as I am?
If I were a shepherd
I would bring a lamb;
If I were a wise man
I would do my part;
Yet what I can I give Him
Give my heart.

Christina Rossetti

LIFT UP YOUR HEARTS! WE LIFT THEM, LORD, TO THEE

"Lift up your hearts!" We lift them, Lord, to Thee;
Here at Thy feet none other may we see:
"Lift up your hearts!" E'en so, with one accord,
We lift them up, we lift them to the Lord.

Above the level of the former years,
The mire of sin, the slough of guilty fears,
The mist of doubt, the blight of love's decay,
O Lord of Light, lift all our hearts today!

Above the swamps of subterfuge and shame,
The deeds, the thoughts, that honour may not name,

The halting tongue that dares not tell
the whole,
O Lord of Truth, lift every Christian
soul!

Lift every gift that Thou Thyself hast
given;
Low lies the best till lifted up to
heaven:
Low lie the bounding heart, the
teeming brain,
Till, sent from God, they mount to
God again.

Then, as the trumpet-call in after years,
"Lift up your hearts!", rings pealing
in our ears,
Still shall those hearts respond with
full accord,
"We lift them up, we lift them to the
Lord!"

H. Montagu Butler

ONWARD, CHRISTIAN SOLDIERS!

Onward, Christian soldiers!
Marching as to war,
With the cross of Jesus
Going on before.
Christ the royal Master
Leads against the foe;
Forward into battle,
See, His banners go:
Onward, Christian soldiers,
Marching as to war,
With the cross of Jesus
Going on before.

At the sign of triumph
Satan's legions flee;
Christian soldiers, on then,
On to victory!
Hell's foundations quiver
At the shout of praise;
Brothers, lift your voices,
Loud your anthems raise:

Like a mighty army
Moves the Church of God;
Brothers, we are treading
Where the saints have trod;
We are not divided,
All one body we,
One in hope and doctrine,
One in charity:

Crowns and thrones may perish,
Kingdoms rise and wane,
But the Church of Jesus
Constant will remain;
Gates of Hell can never
'Gainst that Church prevail;
We have Christ's own promise,
And that cannot fail:

Onward, then, ye people,
Join our happy throng,
Blend with ours your voices
In the triumphant song;
Glory, laud, and honour
Unto Christ the King;
This through countless ages
Men and angels sing:

S. Baring Gould

O LITTLE TOWN OF BETHLEHEM

O little town of Bethlehem,
How still we see thee lie!
Above thy deep and dreamless sleep
The silent stars go by.
Yet in thy dark streets shineth
The everlasting light;
The hopes and fears of all the years
Are met in thee tonight.

O morning stars, together
Proclaim the holy birth,
And praises sing to God the King,
And peace to men on earth;
For Christ is born of Mary;
And, gathered all above,
While mortals sleep, the angels keep
Their watch of wondering love.

How silently, how silently,
The wondrous gift is given!
So God imparts to human hearts
The blessings of His Heaven.
No ear may hear His coming;
But in this world of sin,
Where meek souls will receive Him, still
The dear Christ enters in.

Bishop Phillips Brooks

SØREN KIERKEGAARD: Blessed Moments

As one goes from the inn through Sortebro across the bare fields that run along the coast, about a mile and a quarter to the north one comes to the highest point in the district, to Gilbjerg. It has always been one of my favourite places. And as I stood there one quiet evening as the sea struck up its song with a deep and calm solemnity, whilst my eye met not a single sail on the vast expanse of water, and the sea set bounds to the heavens, and the heavens to the sea; whilst on the other side the busy noise of life subsided and the birds sang their evening prayer – the few that are dear to me came forth from their graves, or rather it seemed to me as though they had not died. I felt so content in their midst, I rested in their embrace, and it was as though I were out of the body, wafted with them into the ether above – and the hoarse screech of the gulls reminded me that I stood alone, and everything vanished before my eyes, and I turned back with a heavy heart to mix in the busy world, yet without forgetting such blessed moments. I have often stood there and looked out upon my past life and upon the different surroundings which have exercised their power upon me; and the pettiness which so often gives offence in life, the numerous misunderstandings too often separating minds which, if they properly understood one another, would be bound together by indissoluble ties, vanished before my gaze. Seen thus in perspective only the broad and powerful outline showed, and I did not, as so frequently happens to me, lose myself in the moment, but saw everything as a whole and was strengthened to understand things differently, to admit how often I had blundered, and to forgive others.

As I stood there, without that feeling of dejection and despondency which makes me look upon myself as the misfit among the men who usually surround me, and without that feeling of pride which makes me into the formative principle of a small circle – as I stood there alone and forsaken, and the power of the sea and the battle of the elements reminded me of my own nothingness, and on the other hand the sure flight of the birds recalled the words spoken by Christ: "Not a sparrow shall fall on the ground without your Father": then all at once I felt how great and how small I was; then did those two mighty forces, pride and humility, happily unite in friendship. Lucky is the man to whom that is possible at every moment of his life; in whose breast those two factors have not only come to an agreement but have joined hands and been wedded – a marriage which is neither a *mariage de convenance* nor a *mèsalliance,* but a tranquil marriage of love held in the most secret chamber of a man's heart, in the holy of holies, where there are few witnesses, but where everything proceeds before the eyes of Him who alone witnessed the marriage in the Garden of Eden – a marriage which will not remain unfruitful but bears blessed fruits, as may be seen in the world by an experienced observer; for like cryptogams among plants, they withdraw from the notice of the masses and only the solitary inquirer discovers them and rejoices over his find. His life will flow on peacefully and quietly, and he will neither drain the intoxicating cup of pride nor the bitter chalice of despair. He has found what the great philosopher desired, but did not find: that Archimedian point from which he could lift the whole world, the point which for that very reason must lie outside the world, outside the limitations of time and space.

The Way of THE PILGRIM

By the grace of God I am a Christian man, by my actions a great sinner, and by calling a homeless wanderer of the humblest birth who roams from place to place. My wordly goods are a knapsack with some dried bread in it on my back, and in my breast pocket a Bible. And that is all.

On the twenty-fourth Sunday after Pentecost I went to church to say my prayers there during the liturgy. The first epistle of St Paul to the Thessalonians was being read, and among other words I heard these – "Pray without ceasing." It was this text, more than any other, which forced itself upon my mind, and I began to think how it was possible to pray without ceasing, since a man has to concern himself with other things also in order to make a living. I looked at my Bible, and with my own eyes read the words which I had heard, that we ought always, at all times and in all places, to pray with uplifted hands. I thought and thought, but knew not what to make of it. "What ought I to do?" I thought. "Where shall I find someone to explain it to me? I will go the the churches where famous preachers are to be heard; perhaps there I shall hear something which will thow light on it for me." I did so. I heard a number of very fine sermons on prayer; what prayer is, how much we need it, and what its fruits are; but no one said how one could succeed in prayer. I heard a sermon on spiritual prayer, and unceasing prayer, but how it was to be done was not pointed out.

Thus, listening to sermons failed to give me what I wanted, and having had my fill of them without gaining understanding I gave up going to hear public sermons. I settled on another plan – by God's help to look for some experienced and skilled person who would give me in conversation that teaching about unceasing prayer which drew me so urgently.

For a long time I wandered through many places, I read my Bible always, and everywhere I asked whether there was not in the neighbourhood a spiritual teacher, a devout and experienced guide, to be found. One day I was told that in a certain village a gentleman had long been living and seeking the salvation of his soul. He had a chapel in his house. He never left his estate, and he spent his time in prayer and reading devotional books. Hearing this, I ran rather than walked to the village named. I got there and found him.

"What do you want of me?" he asked.

"I have heard that you are a devout and clever person," said I. "In God's name please explain to me the meaning of the apostle's words, 'Pray without ceasing.' How is it possible to pray without ceasing? I want to know so much, but I cannot understand it at all."

He was silent for a while and looked at me closely. Then he said, "Ceaseless interior prayer is a continual yearning of the human spirit towards God. To succeed in this consoling exercise we must pray more often to God to teach us to pray without ceasing. Pray more and pray more fervently. It is prayer itself which will reveal to you how it can be achieved unceasingly; but it will take some time."

So saying, he had food brought to me, gave me money for my journey, and let me go.

He did not explain the matter.

Again I set off. I thought and thought, I read and read, I dwelt over and over again upon what this man had said to me, but I could not get to the bottom of it. Yet so greatly did I wish to understand that I could not sleep at night.

I walked at least a hundred and twenty-five miles, and then I came to a large town, a provincial capital, where I saw a monastery. At the inn where I stopped I heard it said that the abbot was a man of great kindness, devout and hospitable. I went to see him. He met me in a very friendly manner, asked me to sit down, and offered me refreshment.

"I do not need refreshment, holy father," I said, "but I beg you to give me some spiritual teaching. How can I save my soul?"

"What? Save your soul? Well, live according to the commandments, say your prayers, and you will be saved."

"But I hear it said that we should pray without ceasing, and I don't know how to pray without ceasing. I cannot even understand what unceasing prayer means. I beg you, father, explain this to me."

"I don't know how to explain further, dear brother. But, stop a moment, I have a little book, and it is explained there." And he handed me St Dmitri's book on *The Spiritual Education of the Inner Man,* saying, "Look, read this page."

I began to read as follows: "The words of the apostle, 'Pray without ceasing' should be understood as referring to the creative prayer of the understanding. The understanding can always be reaching out towards God, and praying to Him unceasingly."

"But", I asked, "what is the method by which the understanding can always be turned towards God, never be disturbed, and pray without ceasing?"

"It is very difficult, even for one to whom God Himself gives such a gift," replied the abbot.

He did not give me the explanation.

I spent the night at his house, and in the morning, thanking him for his kindly hospitality, I went on my way; where to, I did not know myself. My failure to understand made me sad, and by way of comforting myself I read my Bible. In this way I followed the main road for five days.

At last towards evening I was overtaken by an old man who looked like a cleric of some sort. In answer to my question he told me that he was a monk belonging to a monastery some six miles off the main road. He asked me to go there with him. "We take in pilgrims", said he, "and give them rest and food with devout persons in the guest house." I did not feel like going. So in reply I said that my peace of mind in no way depended upon my finding a resting place, but upon finding spiritual teaching. Neither was I running after food, for I had plenty of dried bread in my knapsack.

"What sort of spiritual teaching are you wanting to get?" he asked me. "What is it puzzling you? Come now! Do come to our house, dear brother. We have holy teachers of ripe experience well able to give guidance to your soul and to set it upon the true path, in the light of the word of God and the writings of the holy fathers."

"Well, it's like this, father," said I. "About a year ago, while I was at the liturgy, I heard a passage from the epistles which bade men pray without ceasing. Failing to understand, I began to read my Bible, and there also in many places I found the divine command that we ought to pray at all times, in all places; not only while about our business, not only while awake but even during sleep: 'I sleep, but my heart waketh.' This surprised me very much, and I was at a loss to understand how it could be carried out and in what way it was to be done. A burning desire and thirst for knowledge awoke in me. Day and night the matter was never out of my mind. So I began to go to churches and to listen to sermons. But however many I heard, from not one of them did I get any teaching about how to pray without ceasing. They always talked about getting ready for prayer, or about its fruits and the like, without teaching one how to pray without ceasing, or what such prayer means. I have often read the Bible and there made sure of what I have heard. But meanwhile I have not reached the understanding that I long for, and so to this hour I am still uneasy and in doubt."

Then the old man crossed himself and spoke. "Thank God, my dear brother, for having revealed to you this unappeasable desire for unceasing interior prayer. Recognise in it the call of God, and calm yourself. Rest assured that what has hitherto been accomplished in you is the testing of the harmony of your own will with the voice of God. It has been granted to you to understand that the heavenly light of unceasing interior prayer is attained neither by the wisdom of this world, nor by the mere outward desire for knowledge, but that on the contrary it is found in poverty of spirit and in active experience in simplicity of heart. That is why it is not surprising that you have been unable to hear anything about the essential work of prayer, and to acquire the knowledge by which ceaseless activity in it is attained. Doubtless a great deal has been preached about prayer, and there is much about it in the teaching of various writers. But since for the most part all their reasonings are based upon speculation and the working of natural wisdom, and not upon active experience, they sermonise about the qualities of prayer, rather than about the nature of the thing itself. One argues beautifully about the necessity of prayer, another about its power and the blessings which attend it, a third again about the things which lead to perfection in prayer, that is, about the absolute necessity of zeal, an attentive mind, warmth of heart, purity of thought, reconciliation with one's enemies, humility, contrition, and so on. But what is prayer? And how does one learn to pray? Upon these questions, primary and essential as they are, one very rarely gets any precise enlightenment from present-day preachers. For these questions are more difficult to understand than all their arguments that I have just spoken of, and require mystical knowledge, not simply the learning of the schools. And the most deplorable thing of all is that the vain wisdom of the world compels them to apply the human standard to the divine. Many people reason quite the wrong way round about prayer, thinking that good actions and all sorts of preliminary measures render us capable of prayer. But quite the reverse is the case, it is prayer which bears fruit in good works and all the virtues. Those who reason so take, incorrectly, the fruits and the results of prayer for the means of attaining it, and this is to depreciate the power of prayer. And it is quite contrary to holy Scripture, for the apostle Paul says: 'I exhort therefore that first of all supplications be made' (I Timothy 2:l). The first thing laid down in the apostle's words about prayer is that the work of prayer comes before everything else: 'I exhort therefore that first of all . . .' The Christian is bound to perform many good works, but before all else, what he ought to do is to pray, for without prayer no other good work whatever can be accomplished. Without prayer he cannot find the way to the Lord, he cannot understand the truth, he cannot crucify the flesh with its passions and lusts, his heart cannot be enlightened with the light of Christ, he cannot be savingly united to God. None of those things can be effected unless they are preceded by constant prayer. I say 'constant,' for the perfection of prayer does not lie within our power; as the apostle Paul says: 'For we know not what we should pray for as we ought' (Romans 8:26). Consequently it is just to pray often, to pray always, which falls within our power as the means of attaining purity of prayer, which is the mother of all spiritual blessings. 'Capture the mother, and she will bring you the children' said St Isaac the Syrian. Learn first to acquire the power of prayer and you will easily practise all the other virtues. But those who know little of this from practical experience and the profoundest teaching of the holy fathers, have no clear knowledge of it and speak of it but little."

During this talk, we had almost reached the monastery. And so as not to lose touch with this wise old man, and to get what I wanted more quickly, I hastened to say, "Be so kind, Reverend Father, as to show me what prayer without ceasing means and how it is learnt. I see you know all about these things."

He took my request kindly and asked me into his cell. "Come in," said he, "I will give you a volume of the holy fathers from which with God's help you can learn about prayer clearly and in detail."

We went into his cell and he began to speak as follows. "The continuous interior Prayer of Jesus is a constant uninterrupted calling upon the divine name of Jesus with the lips, in the spirit, in the heart; while forming a mental picture of His constant presence, and imploring His grace, during every occupation, at all times, in all places, even during sleep. The appeal is couched in these terms, 'Lord Jesus Christ, have mercy on me.' One who accustoms himself to this appeal experiences as a result so deep a consolation and so great a need to offer the prayer always, that he can no longer live without it, and it will continue to voice itself within him of its own accord. Now do you understand what prayer without ceasing is?"

"Yes indeed, father, and in God's name teach me how to gain the habit of it," I cried, filled with joy.

"Read this book," he said. "It is called the *Philokalia*, and it contains the full and detailed science of constant interor prayer, set forth by twenty-five holy fathers. The book is marked by a lofty wisdom and is so profitable to use that it is considered the foremost and best manual of the contemplative spiritual life. As the revered Nicephorus said, 'It leads one to salvation without labour and sweat.'"

"Is it then more sublime and holy than the Bible?" I asked.

"No, it is not that. But it contains clear explanations of what the Bible holds in secret and which cannot be easily grasped by our short-sighted understanding. I will give you an illustration. The sun is the greatest, the most resplendent and the most wonderful of heavenly luminaries, but you cannot contemplate and examine it simply with unprotected eyes. You have to use a piece of artificial glass which is many millions of times smaller and darker than the sun. But through this little piece of glass you can examine the magnificent monarch of stars, delight in it, and endure its fiery rays. Holy Scripture also is a dazzling sun, and this book, the *Philokalia*, is the piece of glass which we use to enable us to contemplate the sun in its imperial splendour. listen now, I am going to read you the sort of instruction it gives on unceasing interior prayer."

He opened the book, found the instruction by St Simeon the New Theologian, and read: "Sit down alone and in silence. Lower your head, shut your eyes, breathe out gently and imagine yourself looking into your own heart. Carry your mind, your thoughts, from your head to your heart. As you breathe out, say 'Lord Jesus Christ, have mercy on me.' Say it moving your lips gently, or simply say it in your mind. Try to put all other thoughts aside. Be calm, be patient, and repeat the process very frequently."

The old man explained all this to me and illustrated its meaning. We went on reading from the *Philokalia* passages of St Gregory of Sinai, St Callistus and St Ignatius, and what we read from the book the holy man explained in his own words. I listened closely and with great delight, fixed it in my memory, and tried as far as possible to remember every detail. In this way we spent the whole night together and went to matins without having slept at all.

The holy man sent me away with his blessing and told me that while learning the prayer I must always come back to him and tell him everything, making a very frank confession and report; for the inward process could not go on properly and successfully without the guidance of a teacher.

In church I felt a glowing eagerness to take all the pains I could to learn unceasing interior prayer, and I prayed to God to come to my help. Then I began to wonder how I should manage to see my holy man again for counsel or confession, since leave was not given to remain for more than three days in the monastery guesthouse, and there were no houses near.

However, I learned that there was a village between two and three miles from the monastery. I went there to look for a place to live, and to my great happiness God showed me the thing I needed. A peasant hired me for the whole summer to look after his kitchen garden, and what is more gave me the use of a little thatched hut in it where I could live alone. God be praised! I had found a quiet place. And in this manner I took up my abode and began to learn interior prayer in the way I had been shown, and to go to see my confessor from time to time.

For a week, alone in my garden, I steadily set myself to learn to pray without ceasing exactly as the teacher had explained. At first things seemed to go very well. But then it tired me very much. I felt lazy and bored and overwhelmingly sleepy, and a cloud of all sorts of other thoughts closed round me. I went in distress to my confessor and told him the state I was in.

He greeted me in a friendly way and said, "My dear brother, it is the attack of the world of darkness upon you. To that world, nothing is worse than heartfelt prayer on our part. And it is trying by every means to hinder you and to turn you aside from learning the prayer. But all the same, the enemy only does what God sees fit to allow, and no more than is necessary for us. It would appear that you need a further testing of your humility, and that it is too soon, therefore, for your unmeasured zeal to approach the loftiest entrance to the heart. You might fall into spiritual covetousness. I will read you a little instruction from the *Philokalia* upon such cases."

He turned to the teaching of Nicephorus and read: "If after a few attempts you do not succeed in reaching the realm of your heart in the way you have been taught, do what I am about to say, and by God's help you will find what you seek. The faculty of pronouncing words lies in the throat. Reject all other thoughts (you can do this if you will) and allow that faculty to repeat only the following words constantly: 'Lord Jesus Christ, have mercy on me.' Compel yourself to do it always. If you succeed for a time, then without a doubt your heart also will open to prayer. We know it from experience."

"There you have the teaching of the holy Fathers on such cases," said my teacher, "and therefore you ought from today onwards to carry out my directions with confidence, and repeat the Prayer of Jesus as often as possible. Here is a rosary. Take it, and to start with say the prayer three thousand times a day. Whether you are standing or sitting, walking or lying down, continually repeat, 'Lord Jesus Christ, have mercy on me.' Say it quietly and without hurry, but without fail exactly three thousand times a day without deliberately increasing or diminishing the number. God will help you and by this means you will reach also the unceasing activity of the heart."

I gladly accepted this guidance and went home and began to carry out faithfully and exactly what my teacher had bidden. For two days I found it rather difficult, but after that it became so easy and likeable, that as soon as I stopped, I felt a sort of need to go on saying the Prayer of Jesus and I did it freely and willingly, not forcing myself to it as before.

I reported to my teacher, and he bade me say the prayer six thousand times a day, saying, "Be calm, just try as faithfully as possible to carry out the set number of prayers. God will vouchsafe you His grace."

In my lonely hut I said the Prayer of Jesus six thousand times a day for a whole week. I felt no anxiety. Taking no notice of any other thoughts however much they assailed me, I had but one object, to carry out my teacher's bidding exactly. And what happened? I grew so used to my prayer that when I stopped for a single moment, I felt, so to speak, as though something were missing, as though I had lost something. The very moment I started the prayer again, it went on easily and joyously. If I met anyone I had no wish to talk to him. All I wanted was to be alone and to say my prayer, so used to it had I become in a week.

My teacher had not seen me for ten days. On the eleventh day he came to see me himself, and I told him how things were going. He listened and said, "Now you have got used to the prayer. See that you preserve the habit and strengthen it. Waste no time, therefore, but make up your mind by God's help from today to say the Prayer of Jesus twelve thousand times a day. Remain in your solitude, get up early, go to bed late, and come and ask advice of me every fortnight."

I did as he bade me. The first day I scarcely succeeded in finishing my task of saying twelve thousand prayers by late evening. The second day I did it easily and contentedly. To begin with, this ceaseless saying of the prayer brought a certain amount of weariness, my tongue felt numbed, I had a stiff sort of feeling in my jaws, I had a feeling at first pleasant but afterwards slightly painful in the roof of my mouth. The thumb of my left hand, with which I counted my beads, hurt a little. I felt a slight inflammation in the whole of that wrist, and even up to the elbow, which was not unpleasant. Moreover, all this aroused me, as it were, and urged me on to frequent saying of the prayer. For five days I did my set number of twelve thousand prayers, and as I formed the habit I found at the same time pleasure and satisfaction in it.

Early one morning the prayer as it were woke me up. I started to say my usual morning prayers, but my tongue refused to say them easily or exactly. My whole desire was fixed upon one thing only – to say the Prayer of Jesus, and as soon as I went on with it I was filled with joy and relief. It was as though my lips and my tongue pronounced the words entirely of themselves without any urging from me. I spent the whole day in a state of the greatest contentment, I felt as though I was cut off from everything else. I lived as though in another world, and I easily finished my twelve thousand prayers by the early evening. I felt very much like still going on with them, but I did not dare to go beyond the number my teacher had set me. Every day following I went on in the same way with my calling on the name of Jesus Christ, and that with great readiness and liking. Then I went to see my teacher and told him everything frankly and in detail.

He heard me out and then said, "Be thankful to God that this desire for the prayer and this facility in it have been manifested in you. It is a natural conseqence which follows constant effort and spiritual achievement. So a machine to the principal wheel of which one gives a drive, works for a long while afterwards by itself; but if it is to go on working still longer, one must oil it and give it another drive. Now you see with what admirable gifts God in His love for mankind has endowed even the bodily nature of man. You see what feelings can be produced even outside a state of grace in a soul which is sinful and with passions unsubdued, as you yourself have experienced. But how wonderful, how delightful and how consoling a thing it is when God is pleased to grant the gift of self-acting spiritual prayer, and to cleanse the soul from all sensuality! It is a condition which is impossible to describe, and the discovery of this mystery of prayer is a foretaste on earth of the bliss of Heaven. Such happiness is reserved for those who seek after God in the simplicity of a loving heart. Now I give you my permission to say your prayer as often as you wish and as often as you can. Try to devote every moment you are awake to the prayer, call on the name of Jesus Christ without counting the number of times, and submit yourself humbly to the will of God, looking to Him for help. I am sure He will not forsake you, and that He will lead you into the right path.

Under this guidance I spent the whole summer in ceaseless oral prayer to Jesus Christ, and I felt absolute peace in my soul. During sleep I often dreamed that I was saying the prayer. And during the day if I happened to meet anyone, all men without exception were as dear to me as if they had been my nearest relations. But I did not concern myself with them much. All my ideas were quite calmed of their own accord. I thought of nothing whatever but my prayer, my mind tended to listen to it, and my heart began of itself to feel at times a certain warmth and pleasure. If I happened to go to church, the lengthy service of the monastery seemed short to me, and no longer wearied me as it had in time past. My lonely hut seemed like a splendid palace, and I knew not how to thank God for having sent to me, a lost sinner, so wholesome a guide and master.

But I was not long to enjoy the teaching of my dear teacher, who was so full of divine wisdom. He died at the end of the summer. Weeping freely I bade him farewell, and thanked him for the fatherly teaching he had given my wretched self, and as a blessing and a keepsake I begged for the rosary with which he said his prayers.

And so I was left alone. Summer came to an end and the kitchen-garden was cleared. I had no longer anywhere to live. My peasant sent me away, giving me by way of wages two roubles, and filling up my bag with dried bread for my journey. Again I started off on my wanderings. But now I did not walk along as before, filled with care. The calling upon the name of Jesus Christ gladdened my way. Everybody was kind to me, it was as though everyone loved me.

Then it occurred to me to wonder what I was to do with the money I had earned by my care of the kitchen-garden. What good was it to me? Yet stay! I no longer had a guide, there was no one to go on teaching me. Why not buy the *Philokalia* and continue to learn from it more about interior prayer?

I crossed myself and set off with my prayer. I came to a large town, where I asked for the book in all the shops. In the end I found it, but they asked me three roubles for it, and I had only two. I bargained for a long time but the shopkeeper would not budge an inch. Finally he said, "Go to this church near by, and speak to the churchwarden. He has a book like that, but it's a very old copy. Perhaps he will let you have it for two roubles." I went, and sure enough I found and bought for my two roubles a worn and old copy of the *Philokalia*. I was delighted with it. I mended my book as much as I could, I made a cover for it with a piece of cloth, and put it into my breast pocket with my Bible.

And that is how I go about now, and ceaselessly repeat the Prayer of Jesus, which is more precious and sweet to me than anything in the world. At times I do as much as forty-three or four miles a day, and do not feel that I am walking at all, I am aware only of the fact that I am saying my prayer. When the bitter cold pierces me, I begin to say my Prayer more earnestly and I quickly get warm all over. When hunger begins to overcome me, I call more often on the name of Jesus, and I forget my wish for food. When I fall ill and get rheumatism in my back and legs, I fix my thoughts on the prayer and do not notice the pain. If anyone harms me I have only to think, "How sweet is the Prayer of Jesus!" and the injury and the anger alike pass away and I forget it all. I have become a sort of half-conscious person. I have no cares and no interests. The fussy business of the world I would not give a glance to. The only thing I wish for is to be alone, and all by myself to pray, to pray without ceasing; and doing this, I am filled with joy. God knows what is happening to me! Of course, all this is sensuous, or as my departed teacher said, an artificial state which follows naturally upon routine. But because of my unworthiness and stupidity I dare not venture yet to go on further, and learn and make my own spiritual prayer within the depths of my heart. I await God's time. And in the meanwhile I rest my hope on the prayers of my departed teacher. Thus, although I have not yet reached the ceaseless spiritual prayer which is self-acting in the heart, yet I thank God I do now understand the meaning of those words I heard in the epistle: "Pray without ceasing."

The Little Way of Saint THERESE OF LISIEUX: Letter to Sister Maria

Dear Sister, you want me to give you a keepsake of my retreat, perhaps the last retreat I shall ever make. I have Reverend Mother's leave, and I welcome this chance of conversing with you. You are my sister by a double title, and it was you who lent me your voice long ago, promising in my name that I would serve our Lord faithfully, when I was not yet capable of speech. Here then, dear godmother, is the child you offered to God, speaking to you this evening with all the love a child can feel for its mother, with a gratitude which you'll only be able to realise in Heaven. But why should you, Sister, of all people want to know about the secrets our Lord reveals to your god-daughter? I feel sure that He reveals them equally to you; wasn't it you who taught me how to gather up the threads of the divine teaching? Anyhow I'll try to put a few words together in a childish way, though always with the feeling that human speech itself is incapable of reproducing those experiences which the human heart only perceives confusedly.

Don't think of me as buoyed up on a tide of spiritual consolation; my only consolation is to have none on this side of the grave. As for the instruction I get, our Lord bestows that on me in some hidden way, without ever making His voice heard. I don't get it from books, because I can't follow what I read nowadays; only now and again, after a long interval of stupidity and dryness, a sentence I've read at the end of my prayer will stay with me; this for example: "You want a guide to dictate your actions to you? Then you must read in the book of life, which contains the whole science of loving." The science of loving, yes, that phrase wakes a gracious echo in my soul; that's the only kind of science I want – I'd barter away everything I possess to win it, and then, like the bride in the Canticles, think nothing of my loss. It's only love that makes us what God wants us to be, and for that reason it's the only possession I covet. But how to come by it? Our Lord has seen fit to show me the only way which leads to it, and that is the unconcern with which a child goes to sleep in its father's arms. "Simple hearts, draw near me," says the Holy Spirit in the book of Proverbs, and elsewhere He tells us that it is the insignificant who are treated with mercy. In His name the prophet Isaiah has revealed to us that at the last day He will "tend his flock like a shepherd, gather up the lambs and carry them in His bosom." And as if all this were not enough, the same prophet, penetrating with his inspired gaze the depths of eternity, cries out to us in God's name: "I will console you then, like a mother caressing her son: you shall be like children carried at the breast, fondled on a mother's lap."

When God makes promises like that, what's left for us except to keep silence before Him with tears of gratitude and love? Oh dear, if all the weak, imperfect souls in the world could only feel as I do about it – I, who am really the least considerable of them all – there'd be no reason why a single one of them should despair of scaling the hill of charity and reaching the very top. Our Lord doesn't ask for great achievements, only for self-surrender and for gratitude. Listen to what he says: "The gifts I accept are not buck-goats from your folds; I own already every wild beast in the forest, the hills are mine, and the herds that people them; there is no bird flies in heaven but I know of it. If I am hungry, I am master of earth and all that earth contains. Would you have me eat bull's flesh, and drink the blood of goats? The sacrifice you must offer to God is a sacrifice of praise; so will you perform your vows to the Most High." You see what it is that our Lord claims; it isn't that he wants us to do this or that, He wants us to love Him. The same God who tells us that He has no need of us when He is hungry wasn't ashamed to beg for a drop of water from the Samaritan woman – but then, He was thirsty, and thirsty for what? It was the love of this one despised creature that the Maker of Heaven and earth asked for, when he said: "Give me some to drink", He was thirsty for love.

I feel continually more conscious of it, this deep longing our Lord has. Among those who follow the call of the world, He meets with nothing but ingratitude and indifference; and even among His own disciples how few hearts there are that give themselves to Him without reserve, that really understand the tenderness of His infinite love. Dear Sister, you and I are privileged to share the intimate secrets of our heavenly bridegroom; and if only you would write down all you know about them, we should have some splendid pages to read. But no, you hold for yourself that "Kings have their counsel that must be kept secret", it's only to me that you say: "He honours God's ways best that proclaims them openly." I'm sure you're right to keep silence as you do; and it's only for your pleasure that I'm writing these lines. How am I to express heavenly mysteries in the language of earth? And besides, do what I could, I should find that I'd written pages and pages without ever really getting down to the subject. There are so many wide horizons, so many effects of light and shade, infinitely varied, that I shall have to wait till this earthly night has passed away before He, the divine artist, lends me the colours to portray the wonderful vistas which He opens up, even now, to the eye of my soul.

Still, you've asked me to give some account of that dream I had, and of what you call the "little doctrine" which I try to hand on. I've done it in these pages which follow, but so badly that I can't imagine how you will take in what I've written. It may be that you'll find some of my expressions overstrained; if so, you must make allowances and put it down to my wretched style. I assure you that there is nothing overstrained about the attitude of my soul; that is all calm and peace. In what follows, I mean to address our Lord Himself; I find it easier to express my thoughts that way. I'm afraid they'll be very badly expressed even so.

Jesus, my well-beloved, how considerate You are in Your treatment of my worthless soul; storms all around me, and suddenly the sunshine of Your grace peeps out! Easter Day had come and gone, the day of Your splendid triumph, and it was a Saturday in May; my soul was still storm-tossed. I remember thinking about the wonderful dreams which certain souls have been privileged to experience, and how consoling an experience it would be; but I didn't pray for anything of the kind. When I went to bed, my sky was still overcast, and I told myself that dreams weren't for unimprtant souls like mine; it was a storm that rocked me to sleep. Next day was Sunday, the second Sunday of May, and I'm not sure it wasn't actually the anniversary of the day when our Lady did me the grace to come, I went to sleep again, and dreamed.

I was standing in a sort of gallery where several other people were present, but our Mother was the only person near me. Suddenly, without seeing how they got there, I was conscious of the presence of three Carmelite sisters. I had the impression that they'd come there to see our Mother; what was borne in upon me with certainty was that they came from Heaven. I found myself crying out (but or course it was only in the silence of my heart): "Oh, how I would love to see the face of one of these Carmelites!" Upon which, as if granting my request, the tallest of the three saintly figures moved towards me, and, as I sank to my knees, lifted her veil, lifted it right up, I mean, and threw it over me. I recognised here without the slightest difficulty; the face was that of our Venerable Mother Anne of Jesus, who brought the reformed Carmelite order into France. There was a kind of ethereal beauty about her features, which were not radiant but transfused with light – the light seemed to come from her without being communicated to her, so that the heavenly face was fully visible to me in spite of the veil which surrounded both of us.

I can't describe what a weight was taken off my mind; an experience like that can't be put down on paper. Months have passed by now since I had this reassuring dream, but the memory of it is as fresh as ever, as delightful as ever. I can still see the look on Mother Anne's face, her loving smile; I can still feel the touch of the kisses she gave me. And now, treated with all this tenderness, I plucked up my courage: "Please, Mother," I said, "tell me whether God means to leave me much longer on earth? Or will He come and fetch me soon?" And she, with a most gracious smile, answered: "Yes, soon; very soon, I promise you." Then I added: "Mother, answer me one other question; does God really ask no more of me than these unimportant little sacrifices I offer him, these desires to do something better? Is He really content with me as I am?" That brought into the saint's face an expression far more loving that I'd seen there yet; and the embrace she gave me was all the answer I needed. But she did speak too: "God asks no more," she said. "He is content with you, well content." And so she embraced me as lovingly as ever mother embraced her child, and then I saw her withdraw. In the midst of all that happiness, I remembered my sisters, and some favours I wanted to ask for them; but it was too late, I'd woken up. And now the storm no longer raged, all my sky was calm and serene. I didn't merely believe, I felt certain that there was a Heaven, and that the souls who were its citizens looked after me, thought of me as their child. What gave more strength to this impression was the fact that, up till then, Mother Anne of Jesus meant nothing to me; I'd never asked for her prayers or even though about her except on the rare occasions when her name came up in conversation. So when I realised how she loved me, and how much I meant to her, my heart melted towards her in love and gratitude; and for that matter towards all the blessed in Heaven.

Jesus, my beloved, this was only a prelude to greater graces still with which You'd determined to enrich me. Forgive me if I recall them to memory today; its the sixth anniversary of the day when you took me for Your bride. Forgive me Jesus, if I overstep the bounds of right reason in telling You about these longings and hopes of mine, which oversteps all bounds; and heal the hurt of my soul by granting these wishes fulfilment.

To be betrothed to You, Jesus, to be a Carmelite, to become, through my union with You, a mother of souls – surely that ought to be enough for anybody? But, somehow not for me; those privileges I've mentioned are the stuff of my vocations as well! I feel as if I were called to be a fighter, a priest, an apostle, a doctor, a martyr; as if I could never satisfy the needs of my nature without performing, for Your sake, every kind of heroic action at once. I feel as if I'd got the courage to be a crusader, a pontifical zouave, dying on the battlefield in defence of the Church. And at the same time I want to be a priest; how lovingly I'd carry You upon men's souls! And yet, with all this desire to be a priest, I've nothing but admiration and envy for the humility of St, Francis; I'd willingly imitate him in refusing the honour of the priesthood. Dear Jesus, how am I to reconcile these conflicting ambitions, how am I to give substance to the dreams of one insignificant soul? Insignificant as I am, I long to enlighten men's minds as the prophets and doctors did; I feel the call of an apostle. I'd like to travel all over the world, making Your name known and planting Your cross on heathen soil; only I shouldn't be content with one particular mission, I should want to be preaching the gospel on all five continents and in the most distant islands, all at once. And even then it wouldn't do, carrying on my mission for a limited number of years; I should want to have been a missionary ever since the creation, and go on being a missionary till the world came to an end.

But above all I long to shed my blood for You, my Saviour, to the last drop. Martyrdom was the dream of my youth, has been my dream in the sheltered world of Carmel; and yet here too I realise that the dream I cherish is an extravagant one – a single form of martyrdom would never be enough for me, I should want to experience them all. I should want to be scourged and crucified as you were; to be flayed alive like St Bartholomew, to be dipped in boiling oil like St John, to undergo all that a martyr ever underwent; offering my neck to the executioner like St Agnes and St Cecily, and, like my favourite St Joan of Arc, whispering your name as I was tied to the stake. When I think of what Christians will have to go through in the days of Antichrist, my heart beats fast, and I could wish that all these torments were being kept in store for me. Dear Jesus, I couldn't put down all these longings of mine without borrowing from You the book of life, and copying out the exploits of the saints; I do so want them to be mine! What are You going to say to all these fond imaginations of mine, of a soul so unimportant, so ineffective? Why, in consideration of my weakness, You found a way to fulfil my childhood's ambitions, and You've found a way now to fulfil these other ambitions of mine, world-wide in their compass.

I was still being tormented by this question of unfulfilled longings and it was a distraction in my prayer, when I decided to consult St Paul's epistles in the hopes of getting an answer. It was the twelfth and thirteenth chapters of Corinthians I that claimed my attention. The first of these told me that we can't all of us be apostles, all of us be prophets, all of us doctors, and so on; the eye is one thing and the hand is another. It was a clear enough answer, but it didn't satisfy my aspirations, didn't set my heart at rest. The Magdalene, by stooping now and again into the empty tomb, was at last rewarded for her search; and I, by sinking down into the depths of my own nothingness, rose high enough to find what I wanted! Reading on to the end of the chapter, I met this comforting phrase: "Prize the best gifts of Heaven. Meanwhile, I can show you a way which is better than any other."

What was it? The apostle goes on to explain that all the gifts of Heaven, even the most perfect of them, without love, are absolutely nothing; charity is the best way of all, because it leads straight to God. Now I was at peace; when St Paul was talking about the different members of the mystical body I couldn't recognise myself in all of them; or rather I could recognise myself in all of them. But charity – that was the key to my vocation. If the Church was a body composed of different members, it couldn't lack the noblest of all; it must have a heart, and a heart burning with love. And I realised that this love was the true motive force which enabled the other members of the Church to act; if it ceased to function the apostles would forget to preach the gospel, the martyrs would refuse to shed their blood. Love, in fact, is the vocation which includes all others; it's a universe of its own, comprising all time and space – it's eternal. Beside myself with joy, I cried out: "Jesus, my love! I've found my vocation, and my vocation is love." I had discovered where it is that I belong in the Church, the niche God has appointed for me. To be nothing else than love, deep down in the heart of mother Church; that's to be everything at once – my dream wasn't a dream after all.

Beside myself with joy? No, that's the wrong expression; my feeling was rather the calm, restful feeling which comes when you see the lighthouse which is going to guide you into harbour. The beacon of love now shone bright before me; I could reflect its beams. Oh, I know quite well that I am only a child, with all a child's weaknesses; but that's precisely what emboldens me to offer myself as a victim to Your love. Under the old law the Lord of Hosts, the great king, would only accept in sacrifice such beasts as were pure and without spot; only perfect victims could satisfy the divine justice. But now, the law of fear has been replaced by the law of love. And love has chosen me, weak and imperfect creature that I am, for its burnt offering; that is the gesture we might have expected. Love cannot be content without condescending – condescending to mere nothingness, and making this nothingness the fuel for its flame.

I know well, Jesus, that love can only be repaid by love; what I've always looked for and have found at last is some way of satisfying my feelings by returning love for Your love. "Make use of your base wealth to win yourselves friends who will welcome you into eternal habitations", that was the advice You gave to Your disciples, after warning them that "the children of this world are more prudent after their own fashion than the children of the light." Well, here was I with this restless ambition to be everything at once, to combine all the vocations which might easily prove to be base wealth, harmful to my soul; as a child of the light, then, I'd better use it to make myself friends in eternity. I thought of the prayer Elisha made to our father Elijah when he asked him for a double portion of his spirit, and in that sense I prayed to all the angels and saints in Heaven. "I'm the most insignificant of all creatures," I told them, "and I couldn't be more conscious of my own wretched failings. But I know how generous hearts like yours love to do good to those around them, and I want you, the blessed citizens of Heaven, to adopt me as your child. Whatever credit I win by such means will belong to you entirely, but don't despise the rash request I make of you when I ask you to obtain for me a double portion of your love."

Jesus, I don't know how to express it accurately, this petition of mine; if I tried to, I might find myself sinking under the weight of my own presumption. My excuse is that I'm just a child, and children don't always weigh their words. But a parent who has great resources at his disposal is ready to humour the caprices of the child he loves, even to the point of foolishness, even to the point of weakness. And here am I, a child, the child of holy Church, that mother who is also a queen because she is a king's bride. Childlike, I'm not concerned with riches or honour, or even with the glory of Heaven; I quite realise that that belongs to my elder brothers, the angels and the saints. The reflection of the jewels in my mother's crown will be glory enough for me; it's love I ask for, love is all the skill I have. Sensational acts of piety are not for me; not for me to preach the gospel, or to shed my blood as a martyr, but I see now that all that doesn't matter; my elder brothers will do the world for me, while I, as the baby of the family, stay close to the king's throne, the queen's throne, and go on loving on behalf of my brothers, out on the battlefield.

But this love of mine, how to show it? Love needs to be proved by action. Well, even a little child can scatter flowers, to scent the throne-room with their fragrance; even a little child can sing, in its shrill treble, the great canticle of love. That shall be my life, to scatter flowers – to miss no single opportunity of making some small sacrifice, here by a smiling look, there by a kindly word, always doing the tiniest things right, and doing it for love. I shall suffer all that I have to suffer – yes, and enjoy all my enjoyments too – in the spirit of love, so that I shall always be scattering flowers before Your throne; nothing that comes my way but shall yield up its petals in Your honour. And, as I scatter my flowers, I shall be singing; how could one be sad when occupied so pleasantly? I shall be singing even when I have to pluck my flowers from a thorn-bush; never in better voice than when the thorns are longest and sharpest. I don't ask what use they will be to You, Jesus, these flowers, this music of mine; I know that You will take pleasure in this fragrant shower of worthless petals, in these songs of love in which a worthless heart like mine sings itself out. And because they give pleasure to You, the Church triumphant in Heaven will smile upon them too; and will take these flowers so bruised by love and pass them on into Your divine hands. And so the Church in Heaven, ready to take part in the childish game I am playing will begin scattering these flowers now hallowed by Your touch beyond all recognition; will scatter them on the souls in purgatory, to abate their sufferings, scatter them on the Church militant, and give her the strength for fresh conquests.

Yes, Jesus I do love you; I do love the Church, my mother. And it sticks in my mind that "the slightest movement of disinterested love has more value than all the other acts of a human soul put together." But is mine a disinterested love? Or are these wide-ranging aspirations of mine no better than a dream, a fond illusion? If so, Jesus, make it known to me; I only want to be told the truth. If my longings are presumptuous, make them fade away; why should I suffer needless torment? And yet, I don't think I shall really regret having aspired to the highest levels of love, even if it doesn't mean attaining them hereafter; unless, after death, the memory of all my earthly hopes disappears by some miracle, that memory will always be my consolation; to have suffered like that, to have been a fool for Your sake like that, will be something dearer to me than any reward I could have expected in Heaven. Let me go on, during my exile, relishing the bittersweet experience of this ordeal. Jesus, if the mere desire to love You can yield such happiness, what must it be like to possess, to enjoy Your love?

But then, how can a soul so imperfect as mine ever hope to possess love in its fullness? It is to you, Jesus, my first and only love, that I must come for the answer to such a question. Surely it would have been better to reserve these vaulting ambitions for the really great souls, that can take their eagle flight close to the summits! Whereas I think of myself as a chick not yet fledged, and no eagle in any case; only somehow, feeble as I am, the eyes of my heart have caught the eagle's trick of staring at the sun, the sun of divine love. The poor fledgling can't hope to imitate those eagles, the great souls who make straight for the throne of the blessed Trinity; it can only flap its wings in a pathetic attempt to fly. Nothing left for it, you'd think, but to die of disappointment when it finds itself so handicapped. But no, I don't even worry about that; by a bold act of self-committal, I stay where I am, keeping my eyes fixed on the sun, deterred by no obstacle; storm and rain and cloud-wrack may conceal its heavenly radiance, but I don't shift my view – I know that it is there all the time behind the clouds, its brightness never dimmed. Sometimes, to be sure, the storm thunders at my heart; I find it difficult to believe in the existence of anything except the clouds which limit my horizon. It's only then that I realise the possibilities of my weakness; and find consolation in staying at my post, and directing my gaze towards one invisible light which communicates itself, now, only to the eye of faith.

Jesus, you've been very patient with me up to now, and it's true that I haven't ever strayed far from You; but I know, and You know, how often in my wretched imperfection I allow myself to be distracted, when I ought to be looking steadily all the time at this sun which claims all my attention. I must look like a bird, picking up a bit of grain now on this side, now on that, running off to catch a worm, coming across a bird-bath and wetting its half-fledged wings there, even having a look at some attractive flower it comes across. Finding that I can't compete with the eagles, I am the more ready to occupy my mind with the trifles of earth. But after all these infidelities I don't rush away into a corner and try to weep myself to death. I turn back to that sun which is the centre of my love, and dry my bedabbled wings in its rays. I tell God all about my faults, in soft swallow-notes, down to that last detail; I throw myself recklessly on Him, as the best way to gain control over myself, and to win a greater measure of Your love – haven't You told us that You came to call sinners, not the just?

And what if God gives no sign of listening to these twitterings of mine; what if the sun seems hidden away as much as ever? Well, I have to put up with the discomfort of those wet wings; I stay out in the cold, and derive satisfaction from being allowed to suffer, even though I know that this time it's my own fault. How lucky I count myself, Jesus, in being the frail, weak thing I am! If I were one of the great souls, I'd be ashamed to present myself before You in prayer, and go to sleep over it. That's what I do; when I want to fasten my eyes on the heavenly sun, and find that the clouds won't let me see a single ray of it, I go to sleep without meaning to. I'm like a bird that shuts its eyes and puts its head under its wing when darkness comes on; does it dream, perhaps, that it is still in the sunshine? Anyhow, when I recollect myself, I don't get distressed over it; with my heart still at rest, I take up again my task of love. I call upon the angels and saints, who fly like eagles straight towards their fiery goal; their protection will defend me against the birds of prey which threaten to devour me. The spirits of evil cannot claim me for their own; I belong only to You, Jesus, You who have your eyrie up there in the sun of love.

Divine Word, worthy of all admiration and all love, You draw me continually towards Yourself. You came down into this world of exile ready to suffer and die, so as to bring souls within their true orbit, the bosom of the blessed Trinity; and now, reascended into that inaccessible light which is evermore Your dwelling-place, You still frequent this valley of tears, hidden under the appearance of the sacred Host. You are still ready to feed my soul with Your own divinity, my wretched soul, that would sink back into nothingness at any moment if You did not give it life with a look! Jesus, my gratitude bids me say that You love me fondly; and when I meet with such fondness from You, how can my heart fail to go out to You, how can my trust in You have any limits? The great saints, in their eagle strength, have gone close to the verge of folly in the wonderful things they did for You; I am too poor a creature to do anything wonderful, but I must be allowed the folly of hoping that Your love will accept me as its victim. I must be allowed the folly of entreating these eagles of Yours, my elder brothers, to win me the grace I need, that of flying upwards towards the sun of love on the eagle-wings You, and You only, can lend me. As long as it is Your will, my beloved, I am ready to remain without any power to fly, as long as I may keep my eyes fixed on You, fascinated by Your gracious regard, the prey of Your love. And one day, I hope, You will come down from Your eyrie to carry off this poor creature of Yours, to be consumed in the furnace of love.

Dear Jesus, how I wish I could explain to all the souls that are conscious of their own littleness, how great Your condescension is! I am certain that if, by some impossible chance, You could find a soul more feeble, more insignificant than mine, You would overwhelm it with graces still more extraordinary, provided that it would give itself up in entire confidence to Your infinite mercy. But why should I feel any need to tell others about the secrets of Your love? You, nobody else, have taught them to me, and can I doubt that You Yourself will reveal them to others as well? I implore You to look down in mercy on a whole multitude of souls that share my littleness; to choose out for Yourself a whole legion of victims, so little as to be worthy of Your love.

KARL BARTH: Saved by Grace

O Lord, our God! Through Your Son, our Lord Jesus Christ, You have made us Your children. We have heard Your voice and have gathered here to give You praise, to listen to Your word, to call upon You and to entrust our burdens and our needs to your care. Be with us and be our teacher so that all anxiety and despair, all vanity and defiance within us, all our unbelief and superstition may diminish and Your greatness and goodness may show forth:

– that our hearts may be open to one another, that we may understand each other, and help one another;

– that this hour may be an hour of light in which we may catch sight of the open sky and thus of the dawn on this dark earth.

The old has passed away, look, the new has come. This is true, and it is true for us, as certainly as You are in Jesus Christ the saviour of us all. But only You can truly tell us and show us that this is so. Speak and show the truth to us and to all those who pray with us this Sunday morning. They pray for us. And we are praying for them. Grant their requests and ours! Amen.

My dear brothers and sisters, I now read a passage from the letter of the apostle Paul to the Ephesians (2:5): "By grace have you been saved." This, I think, is brief enough for it to be remembered by all, for it to impress itself upon you and, if it be God's will, to be understood.

We are gathered here this Sunday morning to hear this word: "By grace you have been saved"! Whatever else we do, praying and singing, is but an answer to this word spoken to us by God Himself. The prophets and apostles wrote a strange book, called the Bible, for the very purpose of testifying to this fact before mankind. The Bible alone contains this sentence. We do not read it in Kant or in Schopenhauer, or in any book of natural or secular history, and certainly not in any novel, but in the Bible alone. In order to hear this word, we need what is called the Church – the company of Christians, of human beings called and willing to listen together to the Bible and through it to the word of God. This is the word of God: "By grace you have been saved"!

Someone once said to me: "I need not go to church. I need not read the Bible. I know already what the Church teaches and what the Bible says: 'Do what is right and fear no one!'" Let me say this at this point: If this were the message at stake, I would most certainly not have come here. My time is too precious and so is yours. To say that neither prophets nor apostles, neither Bible, Jesus Christ, nor God are needed. Anybody is at liberty to say this to himself. By the same token this saying is void of any new, of any very special and exciting message. It does not help anyone. I have never seen a smile on the face of a person reassuring himself with this kind of talk. As a rule, those who use it are a sad-looking lot, revealing all too easily that this word does not help them, does not comfort them, does not bring them joy.

Let us hear therefore what the Bible says and what we as Christians are called to hear together: "By grace you have been saved"! No man can say this to himself. Neither can he say it to someone else. This can only be said by God to each one of us. It takes Jesus Christ to make this saying true. It takes the apostles to communicate it. And our gathering here as Christians is needed to spread it among us. This is why it is truly news, and very special news, the most exciting news of all, the most helpful thing also, indeed the only helpful thing.

"By grace you have been saved"! How strange to have this message addressed to us! Who are we, anyway? Let me tell you quite frankly: we are all together great sinners. Please understand me: I include myself. I stand ready to confess being the greatest sinner among you all; yet you may then not exclude yourself from the group! Sinners are people who, in the judgment of God, and perhaps of their own consciences, missed and lost their way, who are not just a little, but totally guilty, hopelessly indebted and lost not only in time, but in eternity. We are such sinners. And we are prisoners. Believe me, there is a captivity much worse than the captivity in this house. There are walls much thicker and doors much heavier than those closed upon you. All of us, the people without and you within, are prisoners of our own obstinacy, of our many greeds, of our various anxieties, of our mistrust and in the last analysis of our unbelief. We are all sufferers. Most of all we suffer from ourselves. We each make life difficult for ourselves and in so doing for our fellow men. We suffer from life's lack of meaning. We suffer in the shadow of death and of eternal judgment towards which we are moving. We spend our life in the midst of a whole world of sin and captivity and suffering.

But now listen. Into the depth of our predicament the word is spoken from on high: "By grace you have been saved"! To be saved does not just mean to be a little encouraged, a little comforted, a little relieved. It means to be pulled out like a log from a burning fire. You have been saved! We are not told: you may be saved sometimes, or a little bit. No, you have been saved, totally and for all times. You? Yes, we! Not just any other people, more pious and better than we are, no, we, each one of us.

This is so because Jesus Christ is our brother and, through His life and death, has become our saviour who has wrought our salvation. He is the word of God for us. And this word is: "By grace you have been saved"!

You probably all know the legend of the rider who crossed the frozen Lake of Constance by night without knowing it. When he reached the opposite shore and was told whence he came, he broke down, horrified. This is the human situation when the sky opens and the earth is bright, when we may hear: "By grace you have been saved"! In such a moment we are like that terrified rider. When we hear this word we involuntarily look back, do we not, asking ourselves: where have I been? Over an abyss, in mortal danger! What did I do? The most foolish thing I ever attempted! What happened? I was doomed and miraculously escaped and now I am safe! You ask: "Do we really live in such danger?" Yes, we live on the brink of death. But we have been saved. Look at our saviour and at our salvation! Look at Jesus Christ on the cross, accused, sentenced and punished instead of us! Do you know for whose sake he is hanging there? For our sake – because of our sin – sharing our captivity – burdened with our suffering! He nails our life to the cross. This is how God had to deal with us. From this darkness He has saved us. He who is not shattered after hearing this news may not yet have grasped the word of God: "By grace you have been saved"!

But more important than the fear of sudden death is the knowledge of life imparted to us: "By grace you have been saved"! Therefore, we have reached the shore, the Lake of Constance is behind us, we may breathe freely, even though we still are in the grip of panic, and rightly so. This panic is but an aftermath. By virtue of the good news the sky truly opens and the earth is bright. What a glorious relief to be told that there I was, in that darkness, over that abyss, on the brink of death, but there I am no longer. Through this folly I lived, but I cannot and I will not do it again, never again. This happened, but it must not and it will not happen again. My sin, my captivity, my suffering are yesterday's reality, nor today's. They are things of my past, not of the present not of the future. I have been saved! Is this really so, is this the truth? Look once again to Jesus Christ in his death upon the cross. Look, and try to understand that what He did and suffered, He did and suffered, for you, for me, for us all. He carried our sin, our captivity and our suffering, and did not carry it in vain. He carried it away. He acted as the captain of us all. He broke through the ranks of our enemies. He has already won the battle, our battle. All we have to do is to follow Him, to be victorious with Him. Through Him, in Him, we are saved. Our sin has no longer any power over us. Our prison door is open. Our suffering has come to an end. This is a great word indeed. The word of God is indeed a great word. And w would deny Him, we would deny the Lord Jesus Christ, were we to deny the greatness of this word: He sets us free. When He, the

Son of God, sets us free, we are truly fee.

Because we are saved by no other than Jesus Christ, we are saved by grace. This means that we did not deserve to be saved. What we deserved would be quite different. We cannot secure salvation for ourselves. Did you read in the newspapers the other day that man will soon be able to produce an artificial moon? But we cannot produce our salvation. No one can be proud of being saved. Each one can only fold his hands in great lowliness of heart and be thankful like a child. Consequently we shall never possess salvation as our property. We may only receive it as a gift over and over again, with hands outstretched. "By grace you have been saved"! This means constantly to look away from ourselves to God and to the man on the cross where this truth is revealed. This truth is ever anew to be believed and to be grasped by faith. To believe means to look to Jesus Christ and to God and to trust that there is the truth for us, for our lives, for the life of all men.

Is it not a pity that we rebel against this very truth in the depth of our hearts? Indeed, we dislike hearing that we are saved by grace, and by grace alone. We do not appreciate that God does not owe us anything, that we are bound to live from His goodness alone, that we are left with nothing but the great humility, the thankfulness of a child presented with many gifts. For we do not like at all to look away from ourselves. We would much prefer to withdraw into our own inner circle, not unlike the snail into its shell, and to be with ourselves. To put it bluntly: we do not like to believe. And yet grace and therefore faith as I just described it is the beginning of the true life of freedom, of a carefree heart, of joy deep within, of love of God and neighbour, of great and assured hope! And yet grace and faith would make things so very simple in our lives!

Dear brothers and sisters, where do we stand now? One thing is certain: the bright day has dawned, the sun of God does shine into our dark lives, even though we may close our eyes to its radiance. His voice does call us from Heaven, even though we may obstruct our ears. The bread of life is offered to us, even though we are inclined to clench our fists instead of opening our hands to take the bread and eat it. The door of our prison is open, even though, strangely enough, we prefer to remain within. God has put the house in order, even though we like to mess it up all over again. "By grace you have been saved"! – this is true, even though we may not believe it, may not accept it as valid for ourselves and unfortunately in so doing may forgo its benefits. Why should we want to forgo the benefits? Why should we not want to believe? Why do we not go out through the open door? Why do we not open our clenched fists? Why do we obstruct our ears? Why are we blindfolded? Honestly, why?

One remark in reply must suffice. All this is so because perhaps we failed to pray fervently enough for a change within ourselves, on our part. That God is God, not only almighty, but merciful and good, that He wills and does what is best for us, that Jesus Christ died for us to set us free, that by grace, in Him, we have been saved – all this need not be a concern for our prayers. All these things are true apart from our own deeds and prayers. But to believe, to accept, to let it be true for us, to begin to live with this truth, to believe it not only with our minds and with our lips, but also with our hearts and with all our life, so that our fellow men may sense it, and finally to let our total existence be immersed in the great divine truth, "by grace you have been saved", this is to be the concern for our prayers. No human being has ever prayed for this in vain. If anyone asks for this, the answer is already being given and faith begins. And because no one has ever asked for this in vain, no one may omit praying like a little child for the assurance that God's truth, this terrible, this glorious truth, is shining even today, a small, yet increasingly bright light. "By grace you have been saved." Ask that you may believe this and it will be given you; seek this, and you will find it; knock on this door, and it will be opened to you.

This, my dear friends, is what I have been privileged and empowered to tell you of the good news as the word of God today. Amen.

O Lord, our God! You see and hear us. You know each one of us far better than we know ourselves. You love us without our deserving it. You have helped us and do help us still, although we are ever again inclined to spoil your work by wanting to help ourselves. You are the judge, but You are also the saviour of the poor and perplexed human race. For this we give You thanks. For this we praise You. We rejoice in the prospect of seeing with our own eyes on Your great day what we already now may believe.

Make us free to believe! Give us the true, honest and active faith in You and in Your truth! Give it to many! Give it to all men! Give it to the peoples and their governments, to the rich and to the poor, to the healthy and to the sick, to the prisoners and to those who think they are free, to the old and to the young, to the joyful and to the sorrowful, to the heavy-laden and to the light-minded! There is no one who does not stand in need of faith, no one to whom the promise of faith is denied. Tell all our people, ourselves included, that You are their merciful God and Father and ours! This we ask You in the name of Jesus Christ who commanded us to pray.

C. S. LEWIS: The Weight of Glory

If you asked twenty good men today what they thought the highest of the virtues, nineteen of them would reply, "unselfishness". But if you had asked almost any of the great Christians of old he would have replied, "love". You see what has happened? A negative term has been substituted for a positive, and this is of more than philological importance. The negative idea of unselfishness carries with it the suggestion not primarily of securing good things for others, but of going without them ourselves, as if our abstinence and not their happiness was the important point. I do not think this is the Christian virtue of love. The New Testament has lots to say about self-denial but not about self-denial as an end in itself. We are told to deny ourselves and to take up our crosses in order that we may follow Christ; and nearly every description of what we shall ultimately find if we do so contains an appeal to desire. If there lurks in most modern minds the notion that to desire our own good and earnestly to hope for the enjoyment of it is a bad thing, I submit that this notion has crept in from Kant and the Stoics and is no part of the Christian faith. Indeed, if we consider the unblushing promises of reward and the staggering nature of the rewards promised in the gospels, it would seem that our Lord finds our desires not too strong, but too weak. We are half-hearted creatures, fooling about with drink and sex and ambition when infinite joy is offered us, like an ignorant child who wants to go on making mud pies in a slum because he cannot imagine what is meant by the offer of a holiday at the sea. We are far too easily pleased.

We must not be troubled by unbelievers when they say that this promise of reward makes the Christian life a mercenary affair. There are different kinds of reward. There is the reward which has no natural connection with the things you do to earn it, and is quite foreign to the desires that ought to accompany those things. Money is not the natural reward of love, that is why we call a man mercenary if he marries a woman for the sake of her money. But marriage is the proper reward for a real lover, and he is not mercenary for desiring it. A general who fights well in order to get a peerage is mercenary; a general who fights for victory is not, victory being the proper reward of battle as marriage is the proper reward of love. The proper rewards are not simply tacked on to the activity for which they are given, but are the activity itself in consummation. There is also a third case, which is more complicated. An enjoyment of Greek poetry is certainly a proper, and not a mercenary, reward for learning Greek; but only those who have reached the stage of enjoying Greek poetry can tell from their own experience that this is so. The schoolboy beginning Greek grammar cannot look forward to his adult enjoyment of Sophocles as a lover looks forward to marriage or a general victory. He has to begin by working for marks, or to escape punishment, or to please his parents, or, at best, in the hope of a future good which he cannot at present imagine or desire. His position, therefore, bears a certain resemblance to that of the mercenary; the reward he is going to get will, in actual fact, be a natural or proper reward, but he will not know that till he has got it. Of course, he gets it gradually; enjoyment creeps in upon the mere drudgery, and nobody could point to a day or an hour when the one ceased and the other began. But it is just in so far as he approaches the reward that he becomes able to desire it for its own sake; indeed, the power of so desiring it is itself a preliminary reward.

The Christian, in relation to Heaven, is in much the same position as this schoolboy. Those who have attained everlasting life in the vision of God doubtless know very well that it is no mere bribe, but the very consummation of their earthly discipleship; but we who have not yet attained it cannot know this in the same way, and cannot even begin to know it at all except by continuing to obey and finding the first reward of our obedience in our increasing power to desire the ultimate reward. Just in proportion as the desire grows, our fear lest it should be mercenary desire will die away and finally be recognised as an absurdity. But probably this will not, for most us, happen in a day; poetry replaces grammar, gospel replaces law, longing transforms obedience, as gradually as the tide lifts a grounded ship.

But there is one other important similarity between the schoolboy and ourselves. If he is an imaginative boy he will, quite probably, be revelling in the English poets and romancers suitable to his age some time before he begins to suspect that Greek grammar is going to lead him to more and more enjoyments of this same sort. He may even be neglecting his Greek to read Shelley and Swinburne in secret. In other words, the desire which Greek is really going to gratify already exists in him and is attached to objects which seem to him quite unconnected with Xenophon and the verbs in μι. Now, if we are made for Heaven, the desire for our proper place will be already in us, but not yet attached to the true object, and will even appear as the rival of that object. And this, I think, is just what we find. No doubt there is one point in which my analogy of the schoolboy breaks down. The English poetry which he reads when he ought to be doing Greek exercises may be just as good as the Greek poetry to which the exercises are leading him, so that in fixing on Milton instead of journeying on to Aeschylus his desire is not embracing a false object. But our case is very different. If a transtemporal, transfinite good is our real destiny, then any other good on which our desire fixes must be in some degree fallacious, must bear at best only a symbolical relation to what will truly satisfy.

In speaking of this desire for our own far-off country, which we find in ourselves even now, I feel a certain shyness. I am almost committing an indecency. I am trying to rip open the inconsolable secret in each one of you – the secret which hurts so much that you take your revenge on it by calling it names like nostalgia and romanticism and adolescence; the secret also which pierces with such sweetness that when, in very intimate conversation, the mention of it becomes imminent, we grow awkward and affect to laugh at ourselves; the secret we cannot hide and cannot tell, though we desire to do both. We cannot tell it because it is a desire for something that has never actually appeared in our experience. We cannot hide it because our experience is constantly suggesting it, and we betray ourselves like lovers at the mention of a name. Our commonest expedient is to call it beauty and behave as if it had settled the matter. Wordworth's expedient was to identify it with certain moments in his own past. But all this is a cheat. If Wordsworth had gone back to those moments in the past, he would not have found the thing itself, but only the reminder of it; what he remembered would turn out to be itself a remembering. The books or the music in which we thought the beauty was located will betray us if we trust to them; it was not in them, it only came through them, and what came through them was longing. These things – the beauty, the memory of our own past – are good images of what we really desire; but if they are mistaken for the thing itself they turn into dumb idols, breaking the hearts of their worshippers. For they are not the thing itself; they are only the scent of a flower we have not found, the echo of a tune we have not heard, news from a country we have never yet visited. Do you think I am trying to weave a spell? Perhaps I am; but remember your fairy tales. Spells are used for breaking enchantments as well as for inducing them. And you and I have need of the strongest spell that can be found to wake us from the evil enchantment of worldliness which has been laid upon us for nearly a hundred years. Almost our whole education has been directed to silencing this shy, persistent, inner voice; almost all our modern philosophies have been devised to convince us that the good of man is to be found on this earth. And yet it is a remarkable thing that such philosophies of progress or creative evolution themselves bear reluctant witness to the truth that our real goal is elsewhere. When they want to convince you that earth is your home, notice how they set about it. They begin by trying to persuade you that earth can be made into Heaven, thus giving a sop to your sense of exile in earth as it is. Next, they tell you that this fortunate event is still a good way off in the future, thus giving a sop to your knowledge that the fatherland is not here and now. Finally, lest your longing for the transtemporal should awake and spoil the whole affair, they use any rhetoric that comes to hand to keep out of your mind the recollection that even if all the happiness they promised could come to man on earth, yet still each generation would lose it by death, including the last generation of all, and the whole story would be nothing, not even a story, for ever and ever. Hence all the nonsense that Mr Shaw puts into the final speech of Lilith, and Bergson's remark that the flame of life is capable of surmounting all obstacles, perhaps even death – as if we could believe that any social or biological development on this planet will delay the senility of the sun or reverse the second law of thermodynamics.

Do what they will, then, we remain conscious of a desire which no natural happiness will satisfy. But is there any reason to suppose that reality offers any satisfaction to it? "Nor does the being hungry prove that we have bread." But I think it may be urged that this misses the point. A man's physical hunger does not prove that that man will get any bread; he may die of starvation on a raft in the Atlantic. But surely a man's hunger does prove that he comes of a race which repairs its body by eating and inhabits a world where eatable substances exist. In the same way, though I do not believe (I wish I did) that my desire for Paradise proves that I shall enjoy it, I think it a pretty good indication that such a thing exists and that some men will. A man may love a woman and not win her; but it would be very odd if the phenomenon called "falling in love" occurred in a sexless world.

Here, then, is the desire, still wandering and uncertain of its object and still largely unable to see that object in the direction where it really lies. Our sacred books give us some account of the object. It is, of course, a symbolical account. Heaven is, by definition, outside our experience, but all intelligible descriptions must be of things within our experience. The scriptural picture of Heaven is therefore just as symbolical as the picture which our desire, unaided, invents for itself; Heaven is not really full of jewellery any more than it is really the beauty of nature, or a fine piece of music. The difference is that the scriptural imagery has authority. It comes to us from writers who were closer to God than we, and it has stood the test of Christian experience down the centuries. The natural appeal of this authoritative imagery is to me, at first, very small. At first sight it chills, rather than awakes, my desire. And that is just what I ought to expect. If Christianity could tell me no more of the far-off land than my own temperament led me to surmise already, then Christianity would be no higher than myself. If it has more to give me I must expect it to be less immediately attractive than "my own stuff". Sophocles at first seems dull and cold to the boy who has only reached Shelley. If our religion is something objective, then we must never avert our eyes from those elements in it which seem puzzling or repellent; for it will be precisely the puzzling or the repellent which conceals what we do not yet know and need to know.

The promises of Scripture may very roughly be reduced to five heads. It is promised, firstly, that we shall be with Christ; secondly, that we shall be like Him; thirdly, with an enormous wealth of imagery, that we shall have "glory"; fourthly, that we shall, in some sense, be fed or feasted or entertained; and, finally, that we shall have some sort of official position in the universe – ruling cities, judging angels, being pillars of God's temple. The first question I ask about these promises is: "Why any of them except the first?" Can anything be added to the conception of being with Christ? For it must be true, as an old writer says, that he who has God and everything else has no more than he who has God only. I think the answer turns again on the nature of symbols. For though it may escape our notice at first glance, yet it is true that any conception of being with Christ which most of us can now form will be not very much less symbolical than the other promises; for it will smuggle in ideas of proximity in space and loving conversation as we now understand conversation, and it will probably concentrate on the humanity of Christ to the exclusion of His divinity. And, in fact, we find that those Christians who attend solely to this first promise always do fill it up with very earthly imagery indeed – in fact with hymeneal or erotic imagery. I am not for a moment condemning such imagery. I heartily wish I could enter into it more deeply than I do, and pray that I yet shall. But my point is that this also is only a symbol, like the reality in some respects but unlike it in others, and therefore needs correction from the different symbols in the other promises. The variation of the promises does not mean that anything other than God will be our ultimate bliss; but because God is more than a person, and lest we should imagine the joy of His presence too exclusively in terms of our present poor experience of personal love, with all its narrowness and strain and monotony, a dozen changing images correcting and relieving each other are supplied.

I turn next to the idea of glory. There is no getting away from the fact that this idea is very prominent in the New Testament and in early Christian writings. Salvation is constantly associated with palms, crowns, white robes, thrones, and splendour like the sun and stars. All this makes no immediate appeal to me at all, and in that respect I fancy I am a typical modern. Glory suggests two ideas to me, of which one seems wicked and the other ridiculous. Either glory means to me fame, or it means luminosity. As for the first, since to be famous means to be better known than other people, the desire for fame appears to me as a competitive passion and therefore of Hell rather than Heaven. As for the second, who wishes to become a kind of living electric light bulb?

When I began to look into this matter I was shocked to find such different Christians as Milton, Johnson and Thomas Aquinas taking heavenly glory quite frankly in the sense of fame or good report. But not fame conferred by our fellow creatures – fame with God, approval or (I might say) "appreciation" by God. And then, when I had thought it over, I saw that this view was scriptural; nothing can eliminate from the parable the divine accolade, "Well done, you good and faithful servant". With that, a good deal of what I had been thinking all my life fell down like a house of cards. I suddenly remembered that no one can enter Heaven except as a child; and nothing is so obvious in a child – not in a conceited child, but in a good child – as its great and undisguised pleasure in being praised. Not only in a child, either, but even in a dog or a horse. Apparently what I had mistaken for humility had, all these years, prevented me from understanding what is in fact the humblest, the most childlike, the most creaturely of pleasures – nay, the specific pleasure of the inferior; the pleasure of a beast before men, a child before its father, a pupil before his teacher, a creature before its Creator. I am not forgetting how horribly this most innocent desire is parodied in our human ambitions, nor how very quickly, in my own experience, the lawful pleasure of praise from those whom it was my duty to please turns into the deadly poison of self-admiration. But I thought I could detect a moment – a very, very short moment – before this happened, during which the satisfaction of having pleased those whom I rightly loved and rightly feared was pure. And that is enough to raise our thoughts to what may happen when the redeemed soul, beyond all hope and nearly beyond belief, learns at last that she has pleased Him whom she was created to please. There will be no room for vanity then. She will be free from the miserable illusion that it is her doing. With no taint of what we should now call self-appoval she will most innocently rejoice in the thing that God has made her to be, and the moment which heals her old inferiority complex for ever will also drown her pride deeper than Prospero's book. Perfect humility dispenses with modesty. If God is satisfied with the work, the work may be satisfied with itself; "it is not for her to bandy compliments with her sovereign". I can imagine someone saying that he disliked my idea of Heaven as a place where we are patted on the back. But proud misunderstanding is behind that dislike. In the end that face which is the delight or the terror of the universe must be turned upon each of us either with one expression or with the other, either conferring glory inexpressible or inflicting shame that can never be cured or disguised. I read in a periodical the other day that the fundamental thing is how we think of God. By God Himself, it is not! How God thinks of us is not only more important, but infinitely more important. Indeed, how we think of Him is of no importance except in so far as it is related to how He thinks of us. It is written that we shall "stand before" Him, shall appear, shall be inspected. The promise of glory is the promise, almost incredible and only possible by the work of Christ, that some of us, that any of us who really chooses, shall actually survive that examination, shall find approval, shall please God. To please God . . . to be a real ingredient in the divine happiness . . . to be loved by God, not merely pitied, but delighted in as an artist delights in his work or a father in a son – it seems impossible, a weight or burden of glory which our thoughts can hardly sustain. But so it is.

And now notice what is happening. If I had rejected the authoritative and scriptural image of glory and stuck obstinately to the vague desire which was, at the outset, my only pointer to Heaven, I could have seen no connection at all between that desire and the Christian promise. But now, having followed up what seemed puzzling and repellent in the sacred books, I find, to my great surprise, looking back, that the connection is perfectly clear. Glory, as Christianity teaches me to hope for it, turns out to satisfy my original desire and indeed to reveal an element in that desire which I had not noticed. By ceasing for a moment to consider my own wants I have begun to learn better what I really wanted. When I attempted, a few minutes ago, to describe our spiritual longings, I was omitting one of their most curious characteristics. We usually notice it just as the moment of vision dies away, as the music ends or as the landscape loses the celestial light. What we feel then has been well described by Keats as, "the journey homeward to habitual self". You know what I mean. For a few minutes we have had the illusion of belonging to that world. Now we wake to find that it is no such thing. We have been mere spectators. Beauty has smiled, but not to welcome us; her face was turned in our direction, but not to see us. We have not been accepted, welcomed, or taken into the dance. We may go when we please, we may stay if we can: "Nobody marks us." A scientist may reply that since most of the things we call beautiful are inanimate, it is not very surprising that they take no notice of us. That, of course, is true. It is not the physical objects that I am speaking of, but that indescribable something of which they become for a moment the messengers. And part of the bitterness which mixes with the sweetness of that message is due to the fact that it so seldom seems to be a message intended for us, but rather something we have overheard. By bitterness I mean pain, not resentment. We should hardly dare to ask that any notice be taken of ourselves. But we pine. The sense that in this universe we are treated as strangers, the longing to be acknowledged, to meet with some response, to bridge some chasm that yawns between us and reality, is part of our inconsolable secret. And surely, from this point of view, the promise of glory, in the sense described, becomes highly relevant to our deep desire. For glory means good report with God, acceptance by God, response, acknowledgement, and welcome into the heart of things. The door on which we have been knocking all our lives will open at last.

Perhaps it seems rather crude to describe glory as the fact of being "noticed" by God. But this is almost the language of the New Testament. St Paul promises to those who love God not, as we should expect, that they will knew Him, but that they will be known by Him (I Corinthians 8:3). It is a strange promise. Does not God know all things at all times? But it is dreadfully re-echoed in another passage of the New Testament. There we are warned that it may happen to anyone of us to appear at last before the face of God and hear only the appalling words:"I never knew you. Depart from me." In some sense, as dark to the intellect as it is unendurable to the feelings, we can be both banished from the presence of Him who is present everywhere and erased from the knowledge of Him who knows all. We can be left utterly and absolutely outside – repelled, exiled, estranged, finally and unspeakably ignored. On the other hand, we can be called in, welcomed, received, acknowledged. We walk every day on the razor edge between these two incredible possibilities. Apparently, then, our lifelong nostalgia, our longing to be reunited with something in the universe from which we now feel cut off, to be on the inside of some door which we have always seen from the outside, is no mere neurotic fancy, but the truest index of our real situation. And to be at last summoned inside would be both glory and honour beyond all our merits, and also the healing of that old ache.

And this brings me to the other sense of glory – glory as brightness, splendour, luminosity. We are to shine as the sun; we are to be given the morning star. I think I begin to see what it means. In one way, of course, God has given us the morning star already: you can go and enjoy the gift on many fine mornings if you get up early enough. What more, you may ask, do we want? Ah, but we want so much more – something the books on aesthetics take little notice of. But the poets and the mythologies know all about it. We do not want merely to see beauty, though, God knows, even that is bounty enough. We want something else which can hardly be put into words – to be united with the beauty we see, to pass into it, to receive it into ourselves, to bathe in it, to become part of it. That is why we have peopled air and earth and water with gods and goddesses and nymphs and elves – that, though we cannot, yet these projections can, enjoy in themselves that beauty, grace and power of which nature is the image. That is why the poets tell us such lovely falsehoods. They talk as if the west wind could really sweep into a human soul; but it can't. They tell us that "beauty born of murmuring sound" will pass into a human face; but it won't. Or not yet. For if we take the imagery of Scripure seriously, if we believe that God will one day give us the morning star and cause us to put on the splendour of the sun, then we may surmise that both the ancient myths and the modern poetry, so false as history, may be very near the truth, as prophecy. At present we are on the outside of the world, the wrong side of the door. We discern the freshness and purity of morning, but they do not make us fresh and pure. We cannot mingle with the splendours we see. But all the leaves of the New Testament are rustling with the rumour that it will not always be so. Some day, God willing, we shall get in. When human souls have become as perfect in voluntary obedience as the inanimate creation is in its lifeless obedience, then they will put on its glory, or rather that greater glory of which nature is only the first sketch. For you must not think that I am putting forward any heathen fancy of being absorbed into nature. Nature is mortal; we shall outlive her. When all the suns and nebulae have passed away, each one of you will still be alive. Nature is only the image, the symbol; but it is the symbol Scripture invites me to use. We are summoned to pass in through nature, beyond her, into that splendour which she fitfully reflects.

And in there, in beyond nature, we shall eat of the tree of life. At present, if we are reborn in Christ, the spirit in us lives directly in God; but the mind, and still more the body, receives life from Him at a thousand removes – through our ancestors, through our food, through the elements. The faint, far-off results of those energies which God's creative rapture implanted in matter when He made the worlds are what we now call physical pleasures; and even thus filtered, they are too much for our present management. What would it be to taste at the fountain-head the stream of which even these lower reaches prove so intoxicating? Yet that, I believe, is what lies before us. The whole man is to drink joy from the fountain of joy. As St Augustine said, the rapture of the saved soul will "flow over" into the glorified body. In the light of our present specialised and depraved appetites we cannot imagine this torrent of beauty, and I warn everyone most seriously not to try. But it must be mentioned, to drive out thoughts even more misleading – thoughts that what is saved is mere ghost, or that the risen body lives in numb insensibility. The body was made for the Lord, and these dismal fancies are wide of the mark.

Meanwhile the cross comes before the crown and tomorrow is a Monday morning. A cleft has opened in the pitiless walls of the world, and we are invited to follow our great captain inside. The following Him is, of course, the essential point. That being so, it may be asked what practical use there is in the speculations which I have been indulging. I can think of at least one such use. It may be possible for each to think too much of his own potential glory hereafter; it is hardly possible for him to think too often or too deeply about that of his neighbour. The load, or weight, or burden of my neighbour's glory should be laid daily on my back, a load so heavy that only humility can carry it, and the backs of the proud will be broken. It is a serious thing to live in a society of possible gods and goddesses, to remember that the dullest and most uninteresting person you can talk to may one day be a creature which, if you saw it now, you would be strongly tempted to worship, or else a horror and a corruption such as you now meet, if at all, only in a nightmare.

All day long we are, in some degree, helping each other to one or other of these destinations. It is in the light of these overwhelming possibilities, it is with the awe and the circumspection proper to them that we should conduct all our dealing with one another, all friendships, all loves, all play, all politics. There are no ordinary people. You have never talked to a mere mortal. Nations, cultures, arts, civilisations – these are mortal, and their life is to ours as the life of a gnat. But it is immortals whom we joke with, work with, marry, snub, and exploit – immortal horrors or everlasting splendours.

This does not mean that we are to be perpetually solemn. We must play. But our merriment must be of that kind (and it is, in fact, the merriest kind) which exists between people who have, from the outset, taken each other seriously – no flippancy, no superiority, no presumption. And our charity must be a real and costly love, with deep feeling for the sins in spite of which we love the sinner – no mere tolerance, or indulgence which parodies love as flippancy parodies merriment. Next to the Blessed Sacrament itself, your neighbour is the holiest object presented to your senses. If he is your Christian neighbour he is holy in almost the same way, for in him Christ – the glorifier and the glorified, Glory Himself – is truly hidden.

MARTIN LUTHER KING: I've been to the Mountain Top

I'm delighted to see each of you here tonight in spite of a storm warning. You reveal that you are determined to go on anyhow. Something is happening in Memphis, something is happening in our world.

As you know, if I were standing at the beginning of time, with the possibility of a general and panoramic view of the whole human history up to now, and the Almighty said to me, "Martin Luther King, which age would you like to live in?" – I would take my mental flight by Egypt through, or rather across, the Red Sea, through the wilderness on toward the promised land. And, in spite of its magnificence, I wouldn't stop there. I would move on by Greece, and take my mind to Mount Olympus. And I would see Plato, Aristotle, Socrates, Euripides and Aristophanes assembled around the Parthenon as they discussed the great and eternal issues of reality.

But I wouldn't stop there. I would go on, even to the great heyday of the Roman Empire. And I would see developments around there, through various emperors and leaders. But I wouldn't stop there. I would even come up to the day of the Renaissance, and get a quick picture of all that the Renaissance did for the cultural and aesthetic life of man. But I wouldn't stop there. I would even go by the way that the man for whom I'm named had his habitat. And I would watch Martin Luther as he tacked his ninety-five theses on the door at the church in Wittenberg.

But I wouldn't stop there. I would come on up even to 1863, and watch a vacillating president by the name of Abraham Lincoln finally come to the conclusion that he had to sign the emancipation proclamation. But I wouldn't stop there. I would even come up to the early thirties, and see a man grappling with the problems of the bankruptcy of his nation. And come with an eloquent cry that we have nothing to fear but fear itself.

But I wouldn't stop there. Strangely

enough, I would turn to the Almighty, and say, "If you allow me to live just a few years in the second half of the twentieth century, I will be happy." Now that's a strange statement to make, because the world is all messed up. The nation is sick. Trouble is in the land. Confusion all around. That's a strange statement. But I know, somehow, that only when it is dark enough can you see the stars. And I see God working in this period of the twentieth century in a way that men, in some strange way, are responding to – something is happening in our world. The masses of people are rising up. And wherever they are assembled today, whether they are in Johannesburg, South Africa; Nairobi, Kenya; Accra, Ghana; New York City; Atlanta, Georgia; Jackson, Mississippi; or Memphis, Tennessee – the cry is always the same – "We want to be free."

And another reason that I'm happy to live in this period is that we have been forced to a point where we're going to have to grapple with the problems that men have been trying to grapple with through history, but the demands didn't force them to do it. Survival demands that we grapple with them. Men, for years now, have been talking about war and peace. But now, no longer can they just talk about it. It is no longer a choice between violence and non-violence in this world, it's non-violence or non-existence.

That is where we are are today. And also in the human rights revolution, if something isn't done, and in a hurry, to bring the coloured peoples of the world out of their long years of poverty, their long years of hurt and neglect, the whole world is doomed. Now, I'm just happy that God has allowed me to live in this period, to see what is unfolding. And I'm happy that He's allowed me to be in Memphis.

I can remember, I can remember when Negroes were just going around, as Ralph has said so often, scratching where they didn't itch, and laughing when they were not tickled. But that day is all over. We mean business now, and we are determined to gain our rightful place in God's world.

And that's all this whole thing is about. We aren't engaged in any negative protest and in any negative arguments with anybody. We are saying that we are determined to be men. We are determined to be people. We are saying that we are God's children. And that we don't have to live like we are forced to live.

Now, what does all of this mean in this great period of history? It means that we've got to stay together. We've got to stay together and maintain unity. You know, whenever Pharaoh wanted to prolong the period of slavery in Egypt, he had a favourite, favourite formula for doing it. What was that? He kept the slaves fighting among themselves. But whenever the slaves get together, something happens in Pharaoh's court, and he cannot hold the slaves in slavery. When the slaves get together, that's the beginning of getting out of slavery. Now let us maintain unity.

Secondly, let us keep the issues where they are. The issue is injustice. The issue is the refusal of Memphis to be fair and honest in its dealings with its public servants, who happen to be sanitation workers. Now, we've got to keep attention on that. That's always the problem with a little violence. You know what happened the other day, and the press dealt only with the window breaking. I read the articles. They very seldom got around to mentioning the fact that one thousand three hundred sanitation workers were on strike, and that Memphis is not being fair to them, and that Mayor Loeb is in dire need of a doctor. They didn't get around to that.

Now we're going on to march again, and we've got to march again, in order to put the issue where it is supposed to be. And force everybody to see that there are one thousand three hundred of God's children here suffering, sometimes going hungry, going through dark and dreary nights wondering how this thing is going to come out. That's the issue. And we've got to say to the nation: we know it's coming out. For when people get caught up with that which is right and they are willing to sacrifice for it, there is no stopping point short of victory.

We aren't going to let any Mace stop us. We are masters in our non-violent movement in disarming police forces. They don't know what to do. I've seen them so often. I remember in Birmingham, Alabama, when we were in that majestic struggle there. We would move out of the 16th Street Baptist Church day after day;

by the hundreds we would move out. And Bull Connor would tell them to send the dogs forth and they did come; but we just went before the dogs singing, "Ain't gonna let nobody turn me round". Bull Connor next would say, "turn the fire hoses on." And as I said to you the other night, Bull Connor didn't know history. He knew a kind of physics that somehow didn't relate to the transphysics that we knew about. And that was the fact that there was a certain kind of fire that no water could put out. And we went before the fire hoses; we had known water. If we were Baptist or some other denomination, we had been immersed. If we were Methodist, and some others, we had been sprinkled, but we knew water.

That couldn't stop us. And we just went on before the dogs and we would look at them; and we'd go on before the water hoses and we would look at them, and we'd just go on singing, "Over my head I see freedom in the air". And then we would be thrown in the paddy wagons, and sometimes we were stacked in there like sardines in a can. And they would throw us in, and old Bull would say, "take them off," and they did; and we would just go in the paddy wagon singing, "We Shall Overcome". And every now and then we'd get in the jail, and we'd see the jailers looking through the windows being moved by our prayers, and being moved by our words and our songs. And there was a power there which Bull Connor couldn't adjust to; and so we ended up transforming Bull into a steer, and we won our struggle in Birmingham.

Now we've got to go on to Memphis just like that. I call upon you to be with us Monday. Now, about injunctions, We have an injunction and we're going into court tomorrow to fight this illegal, unconstitutional injunction. All we say to America is: "Be true to what you said on paper." If I lived in China or even Russia, or any totalitarian country, maybe I could understand the denial of certain basic First Amendment privileges because they hadn't committed themselves to that over there. But somewhere I read of the freedom of assembly. Somewhere I read of the freedom of speech. Somewhere I read of the freedom of the press. Somewhere I read that the greatness of America is the right to protest for right. And so, just as I say, we aren't going to let any injunction turn us around. We are going on.

We need all of you. And you know what's beautiful to me is to see all of these ministers of the gospel. It's a marvellous picture. Who is it that is supposed to articulate the longings and aspirations of the people more than the preacher? Somehow the preacher must be an Amos, and say: "Let justice roll down like waters and righteousness like a mighty stream." Somehow the preacher must say with Jesus: "The spirit of the Lord is upon me, because he has annointed me to deal with the problems of the poor."

And I want to commend the preachers under the leadership of these noble men. James Lawson, one who has been in this struggle for many years; he's been to jail for struggling; but he's still going on, fighting for the rights of his people. Reverend Ralph Jackson, Billy Kyles, I could just go right on down the list, but time will not permit. But I want to thank them all. And I want you to thank them, because, so often, preachers aren't concerned about anything but themselves. And I'm always happy to see a relevant ministry.

It's all right to talk about "long white robes over yonder" in all of its symbolism. But ultimately people want some suits and dresses and shoes to wear down here. It's all right to talk about "streets flowing with milk and honey", but God has commanded us to be concerned about the slums down here, and His children who can't eat three square meals a day. It's all right to talk about the new Jerusalem, but one day God's preacher must talk about the new New York, the new Atlanta, the new Philadelphia, the new Los Angeles, the new Memphis, Tennessee. This is what we have to do.

Now the other thing we'll have to do is this: always anchor our external direct action with the power of economic withdrawal. Now we are poor people, individually; we are poor when you compare us with white society in America. We are poor. Never stop and forget that collectively – that means all of us together – collectively, we are richer than all the nations in the world, with the exception of nine. Did you ever think about that? After you leave the

United States, Russia, Great Britain, West Germany, France, and I could name the others, the Negro collectively is richer than most nations of the world. We have an annual income of more than thirty billion dollars a year, which is more than all of the exports of the United States, and more than the national budget of Canada. Did you know that? That's power right there, if we know how to pool it.

We don't have to argue with anybody. We don't have to curse and go around acting bad with our words. We don't need any bricks and bottles, we don't need any Molotov cocktails. We just need to go around to these stores, and to these massive industries in our country, and say: "God sent us by here to say to you that you're not treating his children right. And we've come by here to ask you to make the first item on your agenda 'fair treatment, where God's children are concerned'. Now, if you are not prepared to do that, we do have an agenda that we must follow. And our agenda calls for withdrawing economic support from you."

And so, as a result of this, we are asking you tonight to go out and tell your neighbours not to buy Coca-Cola in Memphis. Go by and tell them not to buy Sealtest Milk. Tell them not to buy – what is the other bread? – Wonder Bread. And what is the other bread company, Jesse? Tell them not to buy Hart's Bread. As Jesse Jackson has said, up to now only the garbage men have been feeling pain; now we must kind of redistribute the pain. We are choosing these companies because they haven't been fair in their hiring policies. We are choosing them because they can begin the process of saying that they are going to support the needs and the rights of these men, who are on strike. And then they can move on downtown and tell Mayor Loeb to do what is right.

But not only that, we've got to strengthen black institutions. I call upon you to take your money out of the banks downtown and deposit your money in Tri-State bank – we want a "bank-in" movement in Memphis. So go by the Savings and Loan Association. I'm not asking you something that we don't do ourselves at SCLC. Judge Hooks and others will tell you that we have an account here in the savings and loan associations from the Southern Christian Leadership Conference. We're just telling you to follow what we're doing. Put your money there. You have six or seven black insurance companies in Memphis. Take out your insurance there. We want to have an "insurance- in."

Now these are some practical things we can do. We begin the process of building a greater economic base. And at the same time, we are putting pressure where it really hurts. I ask you to follow through here.

Now let me say, as I move to my conclusion, that we've got to give ourselves to this struggle until the end. Nothing would be more tragic than to stop at this point in Memphis. We've got to see it through. And when we have our march, you need to be there. Be concerned about your brother. You may not be on strike. But either we go up together, or we go down together.

Let us develop a kind of dangerous unselfishness. One day a man came to Jesus and he wanted to raise some questions about some vital matters in life. At points he wanted to trick Jesus and show him that he knew a little more than Jesus knew, and through this throw him off base. Now that question could have easily ended up in a philosophical and theological debate. But Jesus immediately pulled that question from mid-air and placed it on a dangerous curve between Jerusalem and Jericho. And He talked about a certain man who fell among thieves. You remember that a Levite and a priest passed by on the other side. They didn't stop to help him. And finally a man of another race came by. He got down from his beast and decided not to be compassionate by proxy, but he got down with him, administered first aid, and helped the man in need. Jesus ended up saying that this was the good man, this was the great man, because he had the capacity to project the "I" into the "you", and to be concerned about his brother. Now you know we use our imagination a great deal to try to determine why the priest and the Levite didn't stop. At times we say they were busy going to church meetings – an ecclesiastical gathering – and they had to get on down to Jerusalem so they wouldn't be late for their meeting. At other times we would speculate that there was a religious law that "one who was engaged in religious ceremonials was not to touch a human body twenty-four hours before the ceremony". And every now and then we begin to wonder whether maybe they were not going down to Jerusalem, or down to Jericho, rather to organize a "Jericho Road Improvement Association". That's a possibility. Maybe they felt that it was better to deal with the problem from the causal root, rather than to get bogged down with an individual effort.

But I'm going to tell you what my imagination tells me. It's possible that those men were afraid. You see, the Jericho road is a dangerous road. I remember when Mrs King and I were first in Jerusalem. We rented a car and drove from Jerusalem down to Jericho. And as soon as we got on that road I said to my wife: "I can see why Jesus used this as a setting for his parable." It's a winding, meandering road. It's really conducive to ambushing. You start out in Jerusalem, which is about 1,200 feet above sea level. And by the time you get down to Jericho, fifteen or twenty minutes later, you're about 2,200 feet below sea level. That's a dangerous road. In the days of Jesus it came to be known as the "Bloody Pass."

And you know, it's possible that the priest and the Levite looked over that man on the ground and wondered if the robbers were still around. Or it's possible that they felt that the man on the ground was merely faking, and he was acting like he had been robbed and hurt, in order to seize them over there, lure them there, for quick and easy seizure. And so the first question that the Levite asked was: "If I stop to help this man, what will happen to me?" But then the good Samaritan came by, and he reversed the question: "If I do not stop to help this man, what will happen to him?"

That's the question before you tonight. Not: "If I stop to help the sanitation workers, what will happen to all of the hours that I usually spend in my office every day and every week as a pastor?" The question is not: "If I stop to help this man in need, what will happen to me?"

"If I do not stop to help the sanitation workers, what will happen to them?" "If I do not stop to help the sanitation workers, what will happen to them?" That's the question.

Let us rise up tonight with a greater readiness. Let us stand with a greater determination. And let us move on in these powerful days, these days of challenge to make America what it ought to be. We have an opportunity to make America a better nation. And I want to thank God, once more, for allowing me to be here with you.

You know, several years ago, I was in New York City autographing the first book that I had written. And while I was sitting there autographing books, a demented black woman came up. The only question I heard from her was: "Are you Martin Luther King?" And I was looking down writing, and I said yes. And the next minute I felt something beating on my chest. Before I knew it I had been stabbed by this demented woman. I was rushed to Harlem Hospital. It was a dark Saturday afternoon. And that blade had gone through and the X-rays revealed that the tip of the blade was on the edge of my aorta, the main artery. And once that's punctured, you drown in your blood – that's the end of you.

It came out in the *New York Times* the next morning that if I had sneezed I would have died. Well, about four days later, they allowed me, after the operation, after my chest had been opened and the blade had been taken out, to move around in the wheelchair in the hospital. They allowed me to read some of the mail that came in; and from all over the States and the world, kind letters came in. I read a few, but one of them I will never forget. I had received one from the President and the Vice-President. I've forgotten what those telegrams said. I'd received a visit from the Governor of New York, but I've forgotten what the letter said. But there was another letter that came from a little girl, a young girl who was student at the White Plains High School. And I looked at that letter and I'll never forget it. It said simply: "Dear Dr King: I am a ninth-grade student at the White Plains High School." She said: "While it should not matter, I would like to mention that I'm a white girl. I read in the paper of your misfortune, and of your suffering. And I read that if you had sneezed, you would have died. And I'm simply writing you to say that I'm so happy that you didn't sneeze."

And I want to say tonight, I want to say that I am happy that I didn't sneeze. Because if I had sneezed, I wouldn't have been around here in 1960, when students all over the South started sitting-in at lunch counters. And I knew that as they were sitting in, they were really standing up for the best in the American dream; and taking the whole nation back to those great walls of democracy which were dug deep by the founding fathers in the Declaration of Independence and the Constitution. If I had sneezed, I wouldn't have been around here in 1961, when we decided to take a ride for freedom, and ended segregation in the interstate travel. If I had sneezed, I wouldn't have been around in 1962, when Negroes in Albany, Georgia, decided to straighten their backs up. And whenever men and women straighten their backs up, they are doing something, because a man can't ride your back unless it is bent. If I had sneezed, I wouldn't have been here in 1963 when the black people in Birmingham, Alabama, aroused the conscience of this nation, and brought into being the Civil Rights Bill. If I had sneezed, I wouldn't have had a chance later that year, in August, to try to tell America about a dream that I had had. If I had sneezed, I wouldn't have been down in Selma, Alabama, to see the great movement there. If I had sneezed, I wouldn't have been in Memphis to see a community rally around those brothers and sisters who are suffering. I'm so happy that I didn't sneeze.

And they were telling me, now, it doesn't matter now. It really doesn't matter what happens now. I left Atlanta this morning, and as we got started on the plane, there were six of us, the pilot said over the public address system: "We are sorry for the delay, but we have Dr Martin Luther King on the plane. And to be sure that all of the bags were checked, and to be sure that nothing would be wrong with the plane, we had to check out everything carefully. And we've had the plane protected and guarded all night."

And then I got into Memphis. And some began to say the threats, or talk about the the threats that were out. What would happen to me from some of our sick white brothers?

Well, I don't know what will happen now. We've got some difficult days ahead. But it doesn't matter with me now. Because I've been to the mountain top. And I don't mind. Like anybody, I would like to live a long life. Longevity has its place. But I'm not concerned about that now. I just want to do God's will. And He's allowed me to go up to the mountain. And I've looked over. And I've seen the promised land. I may not get there with you. But I want you to know tonight, that we, as a people, will get to the promised land. And I'm happy tonight. I'm not worried about anything. I'm not fearing any man. Mine eyes have seen the glory of the coming of the Lord.

MOTHER TERESA of Calcutta: Poverty

God has identified himself with the hungry, the sick, the naked, the homeless; hunger, not only for bread, but for love, for care, to be somebody to someone; nakedness, not of clothing only, but nakedness of that compassion that very few people give to the unknown; homelessness, not only just for a shelter made of stone but that homelessness that comes from having no one to call your own.

Let each of us, as we have resolved to become a true child of God, a carrier of God's love, let us love others as God has loved each one of us, for Jesus has said, "Love one another as I have loved you."

The spiritual poverty of the western world is much greater than the physical poverty of our people. You in the West have milions of people who suffer such terrible loneliness and emptiness. They feel unloved and unwanted.

These people are not hungry in the physical sense but they are in another way. They know they need something more than money, yet they don't know what it is. What they are missing really is a living relationship with God.

Today, the poor are hungry for bread
and rice – and for love and the living
word of God.
The poor are thirsty – for water and for
peace, truth and justice.
The poor are homeless – for a shelter

made of bricks, and for a joyful heart
that understands, covers, loves.
The poor are naked – for clothes, for
human dignity and compassion for the
naked sinner.
They are sick – for medical care, and for
that gentle touch and a warm smile.

The "shut-in", the unwanted, the unloved, the alcoholics, the dying destitutes, the abandoned and the lonely, the outcasts and the untouchables, the leprosy sufferers – all those who are a burden to human society, who have lost all hope and faith in life, who have forgotten how to smile, who have lost the sensibility of the warm hand-touch of love and friendship – they look to us for comfort. If we turn our back on them, we turn it on Christ, and at the hour of our death we shall be judged if we have recognised Christ in them, and on what we have done for and to them. There will only be two ways, "come" or "go".

Therefore, I appeal to every one of you – poor and rich young and old – to give your own hands to serve Christ in His poor and your hearts to love Him in them. They may be far or near, materially poor or spiritually poor, hungry for love and friendship, ignorant of the riches of the love of God for them, homeless for want of a home made of love in your heart; and since love begins at home, maybe Christ is hungry, naked, sick or homeless in your own heart, in your family, in your neighbours, in your country, in the world.

BILLY GRAHAM: Open Your Heart Today

As I read the Bible, I find love to be the supreme and dominant attribute of God. The promises of God's love and forgiveness are as real, as sure, as positive as human words can make them.

But the total beauty of the ocean cannot be understood until it is seen, and it is the same with God's love. Until you actually experience it, until you actually possess it, no one can describe its wonders to you.

Some of our modern experts in theology have made attempts to rob God of His warmth, His personal affection for mankind and His sympathy for His creatures.

Never question God's great love, for it is as unchangeable a part of God as His holiness. Were it not for the love of God, none of us would ever have a chance in the future life. But God is love! And His love for us is everlasting!

Because of His holiness, God cannot condone or countenance sin, but He loves the sinner. A just God cannot excuse sin. Yet since the heavenly Father's love goes hand in hand with His justice, He has made provision to forgive sin through the atonement of His Son. "God commends His love towards us, in that, while we were yet sinners, Christ died for us" (Romans 5:8).

Ours is the God of law who, loving the earth's people, and realising that we had offended in every point, sent His only Son to redeem us to Himself and to instil the law of the spirit of life within us. His eyes of compassion have been following man as he has stumbled through history under the burden of his own wretchedness.

Yet Calvary should prove even to the most sceptical that God is not blind to man's plight, but that He was willing to suffer with him. Compassion comes from two Latin words meaning "to suffer with". God's all-consuming love for mankind was best demonstrated at the cross, where His compassion was embodied in Jesus Christ. "God was in Christ, reconciling the world unto himself" (II Corinthians 5:19).

Never question God's great love. Jeremiah the prophet wrote, "The Lord has appeared of old unto me, saying, Yea, I have loved you with an everlasting love: therefore with loving kindness have I drawn you" (Jeremiah 31:3).

Paul speaks of God as one "who is rich in mercy, for His great love wherewith He loved us" (Ephesians 2:4). It was the love of God that sent Jesus Christ to the cross.

But God's love did not begin at Calvary. Before the morning stars of the pre-Edenic world sang together, before the world was baptised with the first light, before the first blades of tender grass peeped out, God was love.

Turn back, if you will, to the unwritten pages of countless aeons and centuries before God spoke this present earth into existence, when the earth was "without form and void" and the deep, silent darkness of outer space formed a vast gulf between the brilliance of God's throne and the dark vacuum where our present solar system now is.

Behold God's dazzling, scintillating glory as cherubim and seraphim cover their faces with their wings in awe and reverence toward Him who is high and holy!

Yet lofty as the vaults of Heaven may be, and pure as God's holiness glistens, there comes to our ears the word that the majesty of His love was moved for us, and the Lamb was slain from the foundation of the world.

It was love that prompted God to fashion a creature in His own image and likeness, and to place him in a paradise of enchanting loveliness.

It was love that moved God to speak the stars into being to adorn the night, and to place the sun in the heaven to provide us with heat and light by day.

It was love that inspired God to fashion rivers teeming with fish, and forests abounding with rich fruit.

Yes, it was love, the love of God, which granted to man the privilege of preference when He said: "Of every tree of the garden you may freely eat: but of the tree of the knowledge of good and evil, you shall not eat of it: for in the day that you eat thereof you shall surely die" (Genesis 2: 16–17).

It was love, the love of God, which was so concerned for man's welfare that He carefully marked the only danger spot in this exquisite garden of God. "Eat of every other tree," said God, "but not of this one. There is death in this one."

It was love which moved God to seek out man after he had made that fatal blunder and had, in spite of God's warning, eaten of that tree.

It was love which made God call out, "Where are you, Adam?" It was love which initiated God's preparation for man to return to Himself.

It was love, the love of God, which stood low over Sinai, and put into Moses's hands the ten commandments.

It was love which caused God to engrave these statutes upon the hearts of all people of all times and make them the basis of all civil, statutory and moral law.

It was love, seeing through the centuries that men were incapable of being what they ought to be without the help of God, which promised a redeemer, our saviour, who should save His people from their sins.

It was love, the love of God, which put words such as these into the mouths and hearts of the prophets: "All we like sheep have gone astray; we have turned every one to his own way; and the Lord has laid on him the iniquity of us all" (Isaiah 53:6).

It was love, the unerring love of God, which brought these prophecies into precise fulfilment. On a specific day marked on earth's calendar and in a specific place marked on earth's map, the Son of God came to this planet.

It was love that prompted the Son of God to reflect the same affection for the world as did God the Father and to show a selfless compassion to the sick, the distressed and the sin-burdened.

It was love that enabled Jesus Christ to become poor that we through His poverty might be made rich.

It was love, divine love, that made Him endure the cross, despising the shame, and made Him endure the contradictions of sinners against Himself.

It was love that restrained Him when He was falsely accused of blasphemy and was led to Golgotha to die with common thieves; He raised not a hand against His enemies.

It was nothing but love that kept Him from calling twelve legions of angels to come to His defence.

It was love which made Him, in a moment of agonising pain, pause and give life to a repentant sinner who cried, "Lord, remember me when You come into Your kingdom!"

It was love that, after every known torture devised by degenerate man had been heaped up Him, caused Him to lift His voice and pray, "Father, forgive them; for they know not what they do" (Luke 23:34).

From Genesis to Revelation, from earth's greatest tragedy to earth's greatest triumph, the dramatic story of man's lowest depths and God's highest heights can be couched in twenty-five beautiful words: "For God so loved the world, that he gave his only begotten Son, that whosoever believe in him should not perish, but have everlasting life" (John 3:16).

Many people misunderstand the attribute of God's nature which is love. "God is love" does not mean that everything is sweet, beautiful and happy, and that God's love could not possibly allow punishment for sin.

God's holiness demands that all sin be punished, but God's love provided a plan of redemption and salvation for sinful man. God's love provided the cross of Jesus Christ by which man can have forgiveness and cleansing. It was the love of God that sent Jesus Christ to that cross.

Who can describe or measure the love of God? The Bible is a revelation of the fact that God is love. When we preach justice, it is justice tempered with love. When we preach righteousness, it is righteousness founded on love.

When we preach atonement, it is atonement planned by love, provided by love, given by love, finished by love, necessitated because of love. When we preach the resurrection of Christ, we are preaching the miracle of love. When we preach the return of Christ, we are preaching the fulfilment of love.

No matter what sin you have committed, or how black, dirty, shameful or terrible it may be, God loves you. You may be at the very gate of Hell itself, but God loves you with eternal love.

Because He is a holy God, our sins have separated us from Him.

But thanks be unto God; because of His love there is a way of salvation, a way back to God through Jesus Christ, His Son.

This love of God that is immeasurable, unmistakable and unending, this love of God that reaches to wherever a man is, can be entirely rejected. God will not force Himself upon any man against his will.

You can hear a message about the love of God and say: "No, I will not have it", and God will let you go on without His love.

But if you really want it, you must believe – you must receive the love of God, you must take it.

There must be a definite, positive act of commitment and surrender to the love of God. Nobody else can do it for you. You can sit all the days of your life under the preaching of the love of God and go out and die without Christ.

Or you can open your heart today and say: "Yes, my heart is open, I receive Christ."

Now, as in the first dawn of creation, He beckons you to a fellowship with Him, and His great heart yearns for companionship with those for whom His Son died.

Could we with ink the ocean fill,
And were the skies of parchment made,
Were every blade of grass a quill,
And every man a scribe by trade,
To write the love of God above
Would drain the ocean dry,
Nor could the scroll contain the whole
Though stretched from sky to sky.

Over nine hundred years ago those words were penned as a confession of faith by a Hebrew rabbi, Meir ben Isaac Nehorai. Today they form part of a beautiful song written by F. L. Lehman while working as a fruit packer in Pasadena, California, in 1917. The song is entitled, "The Love of God".

You, too, can join in this glad song of the redeemed. You, too, can sing:

The dying thief rejoiced to see
That fountain in his day,
And there may I, though vile as he,
Wash all my sins away.

Respond to the love of God, and receive Jesus Christ as your personal saviour, master and Lord; and become transformed by surrendering your life to Him.

KEY

1 The Apostles' Creed

The *Apostles' Creed* is an elaboration of an early baptismal creed used in Rome, late in the second century: candidates for baptism were required to make a simple confession of faith. It continues to occupy a prominent position in the liturgy of the Western Church as a succinct and authoritative statement of religious belief.

2 The Teaching of the Twelve Apostles to the Heathen

The Teaching of the Twelve Apostles to the Heathen is a short manual on morals and church practice, some of which certainly dates from the first century AD. It gives a crucial picture of Church life between the New Testament and the more developed theology of the second century, offering an impression, among other matters, of the celebration of baptism and the eucharist in an early Church community.

3 The Epistle of Saint Clement to the Corinthians

Clement was probably the third bishop of Rome after Saint Peter. This epistle to the Corinthians is the only surviving work generally thought to have been written by him. Dating from about 96, and written in response to a schism in the Corinthian church, it illustrates the developing organisation of the early Church, and shows the foundations of a central authority that was eventually to become the papal primacy. In subject-matter and style it provides an interesting continuity with the letters of the New Testament, notably with St Paul's own letters to the Corinthians. Moving from the observation of notorious sins to the need for repentance and the example of Christ and the saints, the epistle contains notable passages on the futility of doubting the resurrection in chs. 23–25, on the vision of God in ch. 36, and on the true beatitude of Christian love in chs. 48–50.

4 The Epistle of Saint Ignatius to the Ephesians

Ignatius (*c.* 35–107) was bishop of Antioch and the author of letters which have been greatly treasured in the Church for their doctrine and their strong Christian commitment. Taken under a guard of ten soldiers from Antioch to Rome to suffer martyrdom, he received visitors from various churches, and to some he sent letters in reply, the first of which is this letter to the church at Ephesus. A forceful, vivid writer, the compressed style of the letter reflects the terrible conditions under which it was written. It is interesting to note that Ignatius was the first writer to outline the threefold ministry: bishop, presbyters and deacons. A bishop is a clergyman consecrated as governor of a diocese; a presbyter is a minister of the second order; a deacon is a minister of the third order. Ignatius also has a fascinating passage in ch. 19 on the "trumpet-tongued secrets which were wrought deep in the silence of God". The idea of the silence of God is important for later mystical writers, notably St John of the Cross.

5 The Epistle of Saint Ignatius to the Romans

This personal, turbulent letter takes the form of an impassioned plea to the church at Rome not to prevent his martyrdom by interceding with the Roman authorities. Ignatius sees martyrdom as the goal and crown of Christian life. The vehement tone of the letter makes disturbing reading, but it adds a rarely equalled intensity to the cry of Saint Paul: "For me to live is Christ and to die is gain" (Philippians 1:21).

6 The Martyrdom of Saint Polycarp, Bishop of Smyrna

This letter from the church at Smyrna is generally agreed to be the earliest genuine account of the death of a Christian martyr after the New Testament, and was written in 156. Polycarp was martyred probably in 155 at about the age of eighty-six. The work, compiled from eye-witness reports by Marcion, is a classic of Christian history, conveying throughout a profound sense of the drama of Polycarp's arrest, condemnation and execution, and emphasising his abandonment to the will of the Lord and his complete trust in His saving power. It contains many passages of great pathos, and a recurrent theme is the resemblance of Polycarp's martyrdom to the passion of Christ.

7 The Passion of Saints Perpetua and Felicity

This account relates the martyrdom of three men, and of Perpetua, a young married woman of twenty-two, and her slave Felicity, on 7 March 202 at Carthage. A large part of the account (chs. 1–4) comprises Perpetua's own diary, giving the work a particular value. The diary is the account of a recent convert, with a gentle feminine tone that gives this work a unique beauty. It was so highly thought of in the early Church that Saint Augustine had to warn his audience not to put it on the same level as the Scriptures.

8 The Sanctus

The *Sanctus* is the anthem sung or said today as the conclusion of the preface to the Eucharistic Prayer. A wonderful hymn of adoration, of a profound and impressive solemnity, it provides a valuable opportunity for the whole congregation to join in at a climactic stage of the thanksgiving. Included in most of the ancient liturgies, it is based upon the cry of the cherubim in Isaiah 6:3. Clement seems to be mentioning it in 34:6 of his epistle to the Corinthians, and it has certainly been part of Christian worship since the earliest times.

9 The Odes of Solomon

The *Odes* are a collection of psalms showing definite Christian influence which may come from either the first or second century. They show the way early Christians were adapting non-Christian forms, and so give a fascinating insight into the origins of Christian worship. Echoing the exalted language of St John's gospel, they offer fruitful material for meditation on the mysteries of the Christian message, and are among the earliest writings to place an emphasis on Mariology.

10 The Prophecies of the Christian Sibylline

These prophecies, dating from the late second century, again show Christian literature growing out of pre-Church forms. Their fearsome imagery recalls the tirades of the Old Testament prophets. These writings had a particular influence in the Middle Ages and on such various figures as Thomas Aquinas, Dante, Raphael and Michelangelo (in his painting of the Sistine Chapel). There are interesting passages on the cross of Christ: "among the faithful a distinguished seal . . . the world's stumbling block", a theme which has remained popular in Christian traditions.

11 Origen: The Scriptures are Divinely Inspired

Origen (*c.* 185–254) was the greatest and most original of the theologians of his day and the single most influential father of the early Church. Here he offers some fascinating personal "proofs" for the truth of Christianity and the inspiration of holy Scripture. This piece was a decisive development of the idea that New Testament texts are revelatory, representing God speaking directly to the people.

12 Saint Athanasius: The Incarnation of the Word

Saint Athanasius (*c.* 296–373), bishop of Alexandria, was the Church's champion of the divinity of Christ. Here, Athanasius sets out his beliefs about creation and the fall of man, and the necessity of the incarnation. He presents an eloquent account of the desperate need of humanity for a divine saviour, a testimony to the great "good news" that Jesus is Himself this saviour, and he explores some of the questions that must be answered in the face of so dramatic and extraordinary a belief. He also includes a section on the reasons for believing in the resurrection, which remains of enduring importance for Christians.

13 Saint Basil the Great: Prayer Must Come First

Saint Basil (*c.* 330–379), bishop of Caesarea, played a crucial role in the settlement of Christian doctrine as we understand it today. In this sermon on prayer he appears as the "physician of souls", appealing to the conscience of the listener. He gives an exposition of the story of Mary and Martha (Luke 10: 38–42), which was to become a favourite text for writers on the spiritual life. Basil's treatment is very balanced. He distinguishes between praise, petition and confession, and it is interesting to note that he stresses that Scripture should be the source of prayer. He extols steadfastness in prayer, and explains why, in his understanding, petition is not always answered.

14 Saint Basil the Great: The Spirit

Saint Basil above all others established the divinity of the Holy Spirit. In about 375 he wrote his treatise on the Holy Spirit dealing with the consubstantiality of two divine persons, the Son and the Holy Spirit, with the Father. He explores the titles and powers of the Holy Spirit, and the effects that the Spirit works on the Christian soul. Basil sees that the Christian's goal is in God, and since this goal is reached by the operation of the Son and the Spirit on the Christian, both the Son and the Spirit must be one with God.

15 Saint Gregory of Nazianzus: The Necessity of the Trinity

Saint Gregory (329–389) was a friend of Saint Basil, and he also played a formative role in outlining Christian belief. He was the outstanding orator on the subject of the Trinity and here he expounds the great mystery and paradox of the Christian conception of God as it emerged in the study and prayer of the first Christian centuries: "They are not so separate from each other that they are divided in nature; neither are they so confined in their nature as to be restricted to one person." It is important to notice that Saint Gregory stresses that the doctrine of the Trinity is not simply a piece of speculative thought, but affects the life and worship of the Church.

16 Saint Gregory of Nyssa: Purgatory and the Resurrection

Saint Gregory (330–*c.* 395) was the younger brother of Saint Basil. As a speculative theologian and mystic Gregory was the most talented of the three Cappadocian fathers (the others being Basil the Great and Gregory of Nazianzus). He taught that fallen man must go through a process of purgation before his soul can enter upon the mystical ascent towards God, and he believed that ultimately the whole of creation (including the Devil) would be restored to union with God. A man of great originality, Gregory writes in a lively, energetic style with a fondness for rich rhetorical ornament.

17 The Sayings of Saint Anthony the Great

Known as the "Father of Monks", Saint Anthony (*c.* 251–356) abandoned his possessions and gave himself to a life of asceticism. He retired to the desert to become the most famous of the early hermits. His great holiness and deep spirituality strongly influenced the Christians of his time, and in many ways the development of monasticism, in which Anthony and his followers played a crucial role, provided an outlet for Christian heroism in an age when persecution and martyrdom had generally passed away. His sayings represent the sublime wisdom of this desert monasticism.

18 The Epistle of Saint Jerome to Heliodorus

Saint Jerome (*c.* 342–420) was the greatest scholar of the early Church, famous for his translation of the Scriptures into Latin (the Vulgate). Mostly he lived as a hermit or in religious communities, latterly in Bethlehem. He had a strict and uncompromising view of the call of Christian asceticism, as this letter to Heliodorus illustrates. He put great emphasis on the command to the Christian disciple who would be a monk to give up all that he has: "a monk cannot be perfect in his own country"; which is complemented by a rich view of the heavenly goal which awaits the faithful.

19 Saint John Chrysostom: The Joys of Christmas

Saint John Chrysostom (*c.* 347–407), bishop of Constantinople, has been called the greatest of all Christian preachers: Chrysostom in fact means "the golden-mouthed". In this great sermon Chrysostom proclaims the mystery of the incarnation with sustained and enthusiastic rhetoric. He is aware of great wonder: "Bethlehem this day resembles Heaven", and fully realises that human reason will never fully grasp it: "Ask not how, for where God wills the order of nature yields". It is quite probable that John was responsible for introducing the Western date of Christmas (25 December) into the East.

20 Saint John Chrysostom: The Happiness of Acting out Our Love

Saint John Chrysostom preached vehemently against lax morals in monasteries, at court and among the people. His preaching was not, however, a killjoy list of do-nots, and it was never more positive than in this piece, where he succeeds in filling the reader with a strong desire to be good. In his world view goodness is not a matter of dreary duty, but the stuff of dreams.

21 Saint Ambrose: The Hymns of the Little Hours

Saint Ambrose (*c.* 339–397), bishop of Milan, was an outstanding preacher and defender of orthodoxy, and the most influential of all the Latin hymn writers. He was the first to introduce congregational hymn-singing in the West, and it was largely as a result of his work that hymns became a recognised part of public worship. It is interesting to note the development between the hymns of Saint Ambrose and the earlier Odes of Solomon. Ambrose's hymns are designed for use in prayer at different times of the day as well as on the special occasions of the Christian year. They are full of the teaching of the early Church, devotional without sentimentality, providing a rich source for worship and meditation. Since the time of Ambrose, hymns have played a vital part in forging bonds of unity between Christians, encouraging praise and offering consolation.

22 Te Deum and Gloria in Excelsis

These two great hymns of praise, written in the fourth century, remain an integral part of many modern liturgies, expressing some of the central convictions of the Christian faith. The *Te Deum* is a hymn to the Father and the Son, which has traditionally been assigned to the authorship of Saints Ambrose and Augustine. The *Gloria in Excelsis* is a hymn of unknown date consciously composed on the model of the Psalms; it is sometimes known as the Angelic Hymn, since it begins with the song of the angels at Christ's Nativity (Luke 2:14). Both hymns are of magnificent grandeur and dignity.

23 Hymns from the Liturgy of Saint James

The liturgy of Saint James comes from Syria, and has a close connection with the fourth-century form of the liturgy celebrated at Jerusalem. These two hymns, especially "Let all mortal flesh keep silence", are full of the unspeakable awe and mystery of the eucharistic celebration, which remain notable features of the Orthodox liturgy to the present day.

24 The Conversion of Saint Augustine

Saint Augustine (354–430) has been called "the greatest Christian theologian since the apostle Paul". Certainly he was the most influential of the fathers of the Western Church. It is not surprising, therefore, that this vivid and moving account of his conversion should be of abiding interest to all Christians. It takes the form of a prayer written in fervent praise of God's goodness and truth, and it takes us, with unmatched sensitivity, step by step on the spiritual path to self-knowledge and consequent conversion.

25 Saint Augustine: On Anger

Saint Augustine is of crucial importance in the development of Western theology, and he has had incalculable influence on both Catholic and Protestant traditions. In this sermon he uses the story of Jesus's stilling of the storm from Matthew 8:23–27 as the basis for advice on how to deal with anger and other sins. His compelling message is that we must awaken Christ in our souls just as the disciples had to awaken him in the boat.

26 Saint Augustine: The Love of God

In this very short sermon Augustine compares Bartimaeus, the blind beggar of Mark 10: 46–52, who insisted on shouting after the Lord, to the Christian who must cry out to the Lord not with words but with virtuous living. This sermon provides a fascinating glimpse of the allegorical method of the fathers; Augustine sees Christ's passing by as a figure for the passing of His historical life, and the fact that He stood still as a figure for His sitting down at the right hand of God the Father.

27 Saint Leo the Great: The Mystery of the Nativity

Saint Leo (d. 461) was Pope from 440; during his life he greatly consolidated and increased the authority and prestige of the see of Rome, and he also played a leading role in the theological debate about the union of the divine and the human in the person of the incarnate Christ, which led up to the Council of Chalcedon in 451 (see 29). In this sermon he stresses that the full divinity and full humanity of Christ were needed to secure man's salvation. His conclusion: "Remember that, wrested from the powers of darkness, you are now translated into the light and the Kingdom of God", emphasises the important real consequences for the Christian of the fact of the incarnation.

28 Saint Leo the Great: The Passion

In this sermon Saint Leo sees the passion and death of Christ in the context of the incarnation: he stresses the insufficiency of human reason to grasp the whole mystery; indeed, contemplating God's omnipotence makes it all the more strange and wonderful. Saint Leo sets out what is sometimes known as the "classical" view of the atonement, that God Himself has reconciled man to Himself by taking human nature in Christ and dying on the cross, so that death itself was destroyed by the power of Christ's divinity. In this way he explains why Christians may see the events of Good Friday as a victory.

29 The Definition of Chalcedon

The Chalcedonian definition of the faith (451) marks the zenith of classical Christology. It was written as a result of and in an atmosphere of intense controversy, and after its formulation it continued for many years, and again in recent times, to be the subject of often heated debate. Its aim was to define the limits of orthodox speculation and to act as a protection against heresy. In its famous phrases it asserts that Christ was "perfect in manhood, perfect in Godhead, one and the same Christ . . . to be acknowledged in two natures". These phrases safeguard the meaning of the incarnation, ensuring that the humanity is not annihilated in Christ's divinity, but rather that the second person of the Trinity becomes incarnate, uniting a full human nature with Himself in one person. The Definition of Chalcedon sums up the work of the Church fathers on matters of belief. The form of creed it confirms, the Nicene Creed, is the one used in most liturgies today.

30 The Breastplate of Saint Patrick

Saint Patrick (*c.* 390–460) is known as the "apostle of the Irish". He went on a mission to Ireland in about 431 and spent the rest of his life there as evangelist and educator. This strongly rhythmical hymn, ascribed to him and known as his "Breastplate", is a powerful prayer invoking the protection of God, the Trinity and of all the powers of Heaven against the dominion of evil, and it ends with a famous stanza which sees the life of the Christian completely filled and supported by that of Christ.

31 Collects from the Sacramentary of Gelasius

Characteristically very short, a collect is a special form of prayer consisting of three distinct parts; an invocation to God mentioning His glorious attributes, a petition, and a pleading of the merits of Jesus Christ through whom the petition is made. These collects are taken from the Sacramentary of Gelasius, the earliest known Roman liturgical book, in which parts are arranged according to the Christian year. These collects have been used in various missals and prayer books, the translation here being that of the Prayer Book of the Church of England. These translations ("the jewels of the Prayer Book") have been greatly admired and are loved by many.

32 Dionysius the Areopagite: The Mystical Theology

During the sixth century, a number of important works were circulated under the name of Dionysius the Areopagite, Paul's convert at Athens. The real author of this treatise was probably a Syrian monk writing about 500 who is anonymous, but who acquired the pseudonym of Saint Paul's famous convert in Athens, as recorded in Acts 17:16–34. In this treatise on mystical theology, the author describes the ascent of the soul to union with God. Dionysius believed that the journey of the soul to God could only be by a way of "unknowing", since sense and intellect can never attain Him. In the unknowing, the soul will be illumined by what the author paradoxically calls a "ray of divine darkness" to bring him to the God who is above all our human categories.

33 The Spiritual Practices of Saint Benedict

Saint Benedict (*c.* 480–550) is the patriarch of western monasticism, and from him the Benedictine tradition is derived. His famous *Rules* provided a very human and wise directory for the spiritual and administrative life of a monastery, becoming one of the most influential texts of medieval Europe. There is a great emphasis on stability and obedience, and a moderate asceticism within the grasp of ordinary men is recommended.

34 Epistle of Saint Gregory the Great to John, Bishop of Constantinople, On Christian Leadership

The last of the four traditional doctors of the Western Church and the father of the medieval papacy, Gregory (540–604) was one of the most influential of popes. His impressive achievements as a leader must be seen in the context of his great personal humility; this gentle, edifying letter reveals that the servant of the servants of God should have an acute sense of responsibility to those under him coupled with strength of character.

35 Collects from the Sacramentary of Saint Gregory

Gregory the Great is credited with a substantial amount of liturgical work. A number of his prayers form the basis of the Gregorian Sacramentary which, together with the Gelasian Sacramentary, were the sources of the Roman missal, and were used extensively in the English Book of Common Prayer, the source of these translations. Eloquent and sublime, they exhibit a delicate musical cadence that commits them easily to the memory.

36 Agnus Dei

The *Agnus Dei* first appeared in the liturgy towards the end of the seventh century. It is based upon John 1:9 (itself drawn from Isaiah 53:7). The importance of this lovely petition lies in its recognition of the perpetual efficacy of Christ's atoning passion.

37 Saint Anselm: Praise and Thanksgiving to God and a Prayer to Christ for his Enemies

Saint Anselm (*c.* 1033–1109), a monk of Bec in Normandy and later archbishop of Canterbury, was the first of the great scholastic theologians of the medieval Western Church. He showed remarkable insight into the nature of God and man's need for atonement. The prayers to God and to Christ for his enemies are printed here. They convey an urgent longing for Christ and a sense of spiritual pain at being in the world, even as a believer, without Him.

38 Saint Bernard of Clairvaux: The Benefits of Loving God

Bernard (1090–1193), abbot of Clairvaux, was one of the most influential Christian figures in twelfth century Europe. In this mystical treatise, Saint Bernard gives expression to his profound insight that God must be loved for Himself alone, simply because He is God, and not for any personal reward that the believer can secure from Him. In fact, loving God for Himself alone, there is a fullness of reward beyond anything that could be attained by the measuring of our own expectations and desires.

39 Saint Bernard of Clairvaux: Annunciation Dialogue

Saint Bernard, through his deep personal devotion to the mother of God, gave impetus to the cult of the Virgin in the West. He presented Mary as being at the very heart of the mystery of the incarnation. Bernard inserts an imaginative meditation between the message of the angel in Luke 31:7 and the Blessed Virgin Mary's response of complete abandonment to the divine will. The tone of urgent beseeching draws out the great necessity of the incarnation for the salvation of humanity.

40 Aelred, Abbot of Rievaulx: The Pastoral Prayer

Abbot of Rievaulx, Aelred (1109–1167) is known as "the English Saint Bernard" and, though never formally canonised, he is venerated by many as a saint. His pastoral prayer has been described as "one of the most beautiful expressions of medieval devotion". Its charming and graceful style reveals an engaging, sympathetic personality and an overwhelming trust in God.

41 Saint Francis of Assisi: The Canticle of the Sun

Saint Francis (1181–1226), founder of the Franciscan order of friars, is one of the best known and best loved of saints: he has even been called the "second Christ". Breathing the spirit of the gospel, Saint Francis was conspicuous for his passionate love and zeal for God as well as for his deep love and commitment to his fellow men and women and indeed to the whole of God's creation. This brief canticle, full of charm and spontaneity, gives an impression of his love of the natural world.

42 Saint Bonaventure: The Goodness and Greatness of Saint Francis

Saint Bonaventure (*c.* 1217–1274), was the first notable theologian of the Franciscan order. He retells the story of how Saint Francis received the stigmata, the reproduction of the wounds of Christ, in his own body. He dramatically illustrates how far removed was Francis's ministry of compassion from any dreamy romanticism, but how the love of God which burned in him was the love which reached out from the cross in reconciliation.

43 Eucharistic Hymns of Thomas Aquinas

Saint Thomas Aquinas (1225–1274), a friar of the Dominican order, was the greatest of scholastic theologians and the greatest philosopher of the Middle Ages. His theology has been viewed as authoritative by the Roman Church. He aimed to create a synthesis between reason and faith (Aristotelian philosophy and Christian religion). This approach is evident in his famous teaching on the Eucharist, in which he expounded the doctrine of transubstantiation; that the substance of the bread and wine is changed into the substance of Christ's body and blood, but that their outward appearance ("accidents") remain the same. His eucharistic hymns contain insights of his sacramental theology. Note particularly the view that the real presence of Christ is of such a kind that the body is not affected by, for example, the breaking of the bread; he thus resists a grossly materialistic view, while stoutly defending the reality of the sacramental gift to be perceived and received in faith.

44 Jacobus de Voraigne: The Golden Legends of Saint Sebastian and Saint George

The *Golden Legends* were very popular medieval works, compiled by Jacobus de Voraigne between 1255 and 1266, comprising lives of the saints which were primarily designed to satisfy devotional needs. The accounts are written in a style evidently intended to entertain. The story of Saint George for example, is full of tales of heroism and of endurance through extraordinary tortures. The influence of these legends continued into the Renaissance, Saints Sebastian and George becoming the most often depicted church personages after Jesus and the Virgin.

45 Prayer of Saint Richard of Chichester: Day by Day

This short and well-known prayer by Saint Richard (*c.* 1197–1253), bishop of Chichester, was the product of his profound spirituality. It is cast in the form of a thanksgiving for the passion, and it is also a prayer for growth in the knowledge and love of the Lord and in true discipleship.

46 John Tauler: Mary Magdalene

John Tauler (*c.* 1300–1361), a German Dominican, was a mystical writer who had a great influence on, among others, the reformer Martin Luther. In this sermon on the feast of Saint Mary Magdalene he preaches from the text on Mary and Martha in Luke 10 (compare 13 above). He stresses the need for complete abandonment to the will of the Lord, and concludes with a section urging the Christian to be prepared to be crucified with Christ, for the Lord "in his great love and mercy towards his chosen ones, afflicts and crucifies them unceasingly in the world, in many secret, strange ways, often unknown to them". He writes in a straightforward, honest style, addressed to all Christians and not just to a spiritual elite.

47 Thomas à Kempis: How to Imitate Christ

The Imitation of Christ by Thomas à Kempis (*c.* 1380–1471), is perhaps the most popular devotional classic in modern literature, and has sometimes been described as the most influential Christian book after the Bible. It takes the form of a manual of Christian devotion which instructs the Christian on how to attain perfection by following Christ, setting out the advice in brief and pithy statements.

48 Martin Luther: Man is Free

Martin Luther (1483–1546) was the founder of the German Reformation and so is a key figure in the organisation of Protestantism. More books have been written about Martin Luther than any other historical figure except Jesus. What began for him as a personal revolt against a false doctrine of justification revealed deep theological, ecclesiastical, political and social tensions throughout western Christendom. This treatise on Christian liberty is a complete exposition of the principle of justification by faith alone, which created the cornerstone of his belief and the mainspring of the Reformation. The style is forcible, clear and idiomatic.

49 John Calvin: How to Endure Persecution

John Calvin (1509–1564) was the greatest systematic theologian of the Protestant Reformation. A relentless defender of the principles of the Reformation, he advocated a return to the spirit and teaching of the gospels, to the pure Christianity of the early Church. He placed particular emphasis on the omnipotence of God. This candid, forthright sermon is typical of Calvin's plain and outspoken style of address with its zealous appeal for a full and firm commitment to the faith.

50 The Ecstacies of Saint Teresa of Avila

Commonly known as Teresa of Avila (1515–1582), this Spanish Carmelite nun was one of the most famous mystics of the sixteenth century. Here she describes her most celebrated spiritual experiences, including that of the angel piercing her heart with a flaming spear which formed the subject of Bernini's sculptural masterpiece in St Peter's in Rome. An indefatigable reformer, she proved that mysticism could stimulate practical achievement. Teresa's strong and vivid personality shows itself in the highly colloquial and unaffected style of her writing.

51 Saint Ignatius Loyola: Prayers of Obedience

Saint Ignatius Loyola (*c.* 1491–1556) renounced a military career to become a soldier of Christ, devoting himself to a life of prayer, poverty and asceticism. He became the principle agent of the Catholic Counter-Reformation. He was the founder and first general of the Society of Jesus. In contrast to Luther and Calvin, he tried to reform the Church from within. These short prayers testify to his desire to conform the human will to the will of God in which is to be found true human salvation.

52 Saint John of the Cross: Poems of Love

Saint John of the Cross (1542–1591) was a writer on mystical theology of central importance, and joint founder with Saint Teresa of Avila of the order of Discalced (reformed)

Carmelites. He combined in his writings the abilities of theologian and poet, giving powerful expression to previous currents in western mystical theology. As evocations of human feelings arising out of the soul's changing relationship with God, these poems are unsurpassed.

53 Cranmer's Exhortation and Confession

Thomas Cranmer (1489–1556), archbishop of Canterbury from 1532, was the major influence on the liturgical developments of the English Reformation, being largely responsible for the shape and style of the Prayer Books of 1549 and 1552. The aim was to make public worship as meaningful as possible to as many as possible. His wording of the prayers have been much admired. His *Confession* puts a great emphasis on the sense of contrition with sonorous word pairs such as "erred and strayed" and "devices and desires". His *Exhortation* also gives an indication of the eucharistic theology of the time with the emphasis on the spiritual eating and drinking of the body and blood of Christ and the danger of unworthy reception.

54 Reynolds: General Thanksgiving

Edward Reynolds (1599–1676) was bishop of Norwich from 1661. He played a leading part in the reconciliation between Episcopalians and Puritans after the Civil War. He contributed this *General Thanksgiving* to the Prayer Book at the time of the revision of 1661. The prayer sees all the gifts of life for which thanks are due as culminating in the redemption wrought for us by Christ.

55 John Donne: Jesus Wept

John Donne (1571–1631), the greatest English metaphysical poet, and dean of St Paul's from 1621, was the most celebrated preacher of his day, preaching at the royal court during the reigns of James I and Charles I. His overriding theme was the power of God's mercy. His teaching achieved particular force from his standpoint as a reformed sinner who had experienced that mercy. Donne's great rhetorical skill and his profound religious sense are evident in this sermon.

56 The Sacred Maxims of Blaise Pascal

One of the greatest intellectuals of western history, a mathematical prodigy, inventor, physicist and religious thinker, Pascal's (1632–1662) greatest work is his *Pensées*. Although unfinished, it is a classic of apologetics and literature. Pascal believed that God is to be known through the person of Jesus Christ by an act of faith that is beyond the grasp of reason. No one has written more tellingly on the condition of man apart from God, nor dissected more incisively man's self-deluding attempts to evade God's call.

57 John Bunyan: The Pilgrim's Progress

John Bunyan (1628–1688) fought as a Roundhead in the English Civil War. Subsequently he was imprisoned for his preaching, and it was while in jail that he wrote his Puritan classic *The Pilgrim's Progress*.

58 Richard Baxter: Warning to the Born Again

Richard Baxter (1615–1691) was a Puritan divine and nonconformist of the time of Oliver Cromwell. In politics Baxter was a champion of moderation, but on matters of personal morality no man has preached more fiercely. He argued that reason should be used as a source of religious authority in addition to Scripture and church practice, and here his manner of address is forthright and sincere, showing great single-mindedness and a spirit of deep unaffected piety.

59 George Fox: Epistles to the New World and to Friends Everywhere

George Fox (1624–1691) was the founder of the Society of Friends (Quakers). He preached reliance on the "Inner Light", the Holy Spirit watching from within; in this he represented a development of the Puritan "spirit mystic" tradition. He believed that everyone has a divine spark within that can respond directly and personally to God. His plain, open style has a peculiar force in conveying his enthusiasm and moral earnestness.

60 John Wesley: The Almost Christian

John Wesley (1703–1791) was a clergyman of the Church of England who, partly in frustration with the Church at that time, became the founder of Methodism. Though pious in his early years, he nevertheless became aware of an essential lack and in 1738 (together with his brother Charles) he had an experience of conversion. He was zealous and tireless as a preacher of the word of God, advocating a return to the gospels. Frowned upon by authority, he was, however, greeted with enthusiasm as a popular preacher, and his practice of open-air preaching was instrumental in reviving Christianity in the working classes. This address illumines his personal pilgrimage and reveals his understanding of the difference between the appearance and the true being of a Christian.

61 Hymns by Wesley, Watts and Davies

Two of the most gifted and prolific of all English hymn-writers, Charles Wesley (1707–1788) and Isaac Watts (1674–1748) can be regarded as the founders of modern hymn-writing. They did much to make hymn-singing a powerful devotional force. Aiming for clarity and simplicity, their work achieves a precision of great majesty and force. Samuel Davies (1723-1761) was the leading Presbyterian of his day.

62 Jonathan Edwards: Sinners in the Hands of an Angry God

Jonathan Edwards (1792–1875) was a renowned American theologian and revivalist. It was largely as a result of Edwards's preaching that the Great Awakening occurred in Northampton, Massachusetts (a revival that was to exercise a profound influence in both America and Britain). Firmly in the tradition of New England Calvinism, he was fully committed to salvation by sovereign grace.

63 Charles Finney: How to Win Souls

Charles Finney (1792–1875) was the most famous American revivalist, whose preaching has greatly influenced the character of American evangelism today. Finney portrayed conversion as an act of will, emphasising man's responsibility for his own revival, and also the terrible risks he runs if he fails to take that responsibility immediately.

64 A Victorian Hymnody

The Oxford Movement, of which Cardinal Newman was a prominent representative, proved instrumental in breaking down prejudice against the rise of hymns in public worship. The nineteenth century ushered in an era of prodigious hymnody. Basic Christian beliefs were set out in popular and memorable form. These triumphant works, full of optimism, reflecting the boundless confidence and philanthropic energy of the Victorian period, remain some of our most enduring and best-loved works of Christian literature.

65 Søren Kierkegaard: Blessed Moments

Søren Kierkegaard (1813–1855), the Danish philosopher and theologian, fought against the nineteenth century's rationalistic concept of Christianity. His deeply introspective religion has been called "existentialist" because of its origin in personal experience of the conditions of human existence. Like Pascal, his view of the human condition is a very melancholy one, alleviated only occasionally by the mystical appearance of the divine in the everyday. Here Kierkegaard describes one such "blessed moment" and the feeling it inspired in him of being at home in the Universe.

66 The Way of the Pilgrim

This work comes from Russia between 1853 and 1861 and details the spiritual journey of an anonymous pilgrim. It provides an introduction to the use of the Jesus Prayer, a great treasure of the Orthodox Church. The use of the prayer is set out in the *Philokalia*, compiled at the end of the eighteenth century and containing works by the important spiritual writers of the Orthodox tradition. This extract from the *Way* concerns the desire of the pilgrim to learn how to pray without ceasing (I Thessalonians 15:17) and reveals the solution in the method of reciting the Jesus Prayer.

67 The Little Way of Saint Thérèse of Lisieux: Letter to Sister Maria

Saint Thérèse of Lisieux (1873–1897), known as the "little flower", was a Carmelite nun who has proved to be one of the most popular of modern saints. The publication of her autobiography led to her extensive cult. In this letter addressed to Sister Maria, also a Carmelite of Lisieux, and Thérèse's eldest sister, she outlines her "little way", the way of spiritual childhood whereby sanctity is to be attained through continual self-denial in small things, and small acts of charity towards animals, fellow nuns and strangers in trouble. Her artless style hides great depths of thought, and daringly she gives expression to her desire to respond to the call of an apostle, which she finds chiefly in St Paul's more excellent way (I Corinthians 12 and 13), the way of love which leads straight to God.

68 Karl Barth: Saved by Grace

Karl Barth (1886–1968) was one of the leading Protestant theologians of this century: indeed Pope Pius XII referred to him as the greatest theologian since Saint Thomas Aquinas. His position, a reaction against nineteenth century liberalism, having at its core an emphasis on the revelation of God as the ground of all theology, has sometimes been described as neo-orthodoxy, but he himself preferred the description kerygmatic, that is, a theology based on the preaching witness of the Church. In this sermon, originally preached to prisoners, Barth, with a touch which is light yet deep, shows how by grace we are released from our captivity.

69 C. S. Lewis: The Weight of Glory

C. S. Lewis (1898–1963) was a writer and Christian apologist of particular renown in the English-speaking world. His years as an atheist before his conversion to Christianity in 1929, related in *Surprised by Joy*, combined with his literary talents, peculiarly equipped him to speak to a fearful and doubting generation. In this sermon preached in the University Church of St Mary the Virgin in Oxford, he considers the often-hidden longing for God which is at the heart of human experience, and, aided by his literary appreciation, he explores the glory which is offered as the true goal of human existence. He shows why in his understanding nothing less than the reward of God in Heaven is our true end. His style is characterised by good humour and reasoning intelligence, and it has been said of him that he had "'the rare gift of making righteousness readable".

70 Martin Luther King: I've been to the Mountain Top

Martin Luther King (1929–1968) was an American Baptist minister and Civil Rights leader who played a central role in the non-violent mass demonstrations of the 1960s. His "social gospel" is a reminder that the Christian faith is not just about the individual soul's union with God, but that it is also concerned with securing God's true peace and justice, making His love incarnate in the world so that the full inheritance of eternal life may be gained. In this speech, which he delivered the day before his assassination, he shares his gospel of the promised land, which he, like Moses, had seen from the top of the mountain.

71 Mother Teresa of Calcutta: Poverty

Mother Teresa was born in 1910 in Skopje, Yugoslavia, of Albanian parents. At the age of fifteen, inspired by a missionary's letters, she volunteered to go to India as a missionary. In 1946 she secured permission to live outside the cloister and work in the slums of Calcutta, and in 1950 founded the Missionaries of Charity. Her "universal mission of love" (Pope Paul) has made this tiny Catholic nun admired and loved throughout the world. Her beautiful and moving prayer sums up a life's work and message: "to see Christ in the slums and in the broken bodies of the forgotten people."

72 Billy Graham: Open Your Heart Today

Billy Graham (b. 1918) is without doubt the most famous and successful evangelist of the twentieth century. Using modern techniques of mass communication, he preaches an effective biblical Christ-centred gospel of which this address is an example. The love of God shown in creation and redemption is a living witness reaching across the centuries and an invitation to turn to the Lord, and in the words of the *Teaching of the Apostles* to "remain steadfast in the faith", awaiting the day when "the whole world will see the Lord as He comes riding on the clouds of Heaven". Emphatic and impassioned, this sermon is typical of his charismatic style of preaching.